■ United States Holocaust Memorial Museum
Center for Advanced Holocaust Studies

Documenting Life and Destruction
Holocaust Sources in Context

SERIES EDITOR

Jürgen Matthäus

DOCUMENTING LIFE AND DESTRUCTION

HOLOCAUST SOURCES IN CONTEXT

This groundbreaking series provides a new perspective on history using first-hand accounts of the lives of those who suffered through the Holocaust, those who perpetrated it, and those who witnessed it as bystanders. The United States Holocaust Memorial Museum's Center for Advanced Holocaust Studies presents a wide range of documents from different archival holdings, expanding knowledge about the lives and fates of Holocaust victims and making these resources broadly available to the general public and scholarly communities for the first time.

BOOKS IN THE SERIES

This publication has been made possible by
support from

Claims Conference   ועידת התביעות
The Conference on Jewish Material Claims Against Germany

The William S. and Ina Levine Foundation

The Blum Family Foundation

and

Dr. Alfred Munzer and Mr. Joel Wind

Documenting Life and Destruction
Holocaust Sources in Context

JEWISH RESPONSES TO PERSECUTION

Volume III
1941–1942

Jürgen Matthäus

with Emil Kerenji, Jan Lambertz, and Leah Wolfson

Advisory Committee:

Christopher R. Browning
David Engel
Sara Horowitz
Steven T. Katz
Alvin H. Rosenfeld

AltaMira Press
in association with the United States Holocaust Memorial Museum
2013

For USHMM:

Project Manager: Mel Hecker

Translators: Norman Buder, Ania Drimer, Marcel Drimer, Ulrike Ecker, Gideon Frieder, Jolanta Kraemer, Hana Kubatova, Kathleen Luft, Margit Meissner, Alfred Munzer, Adam Peiperl, Lisa Peschel, Katrin Reichelt, Stephen Scala, Sam Schalkowsky, and Benjamin Thorne

Research Assistants: Kathryn Cornelius, Ryan Farrell, Holly Robertson, and Greg Wilkowski

Interns/Volunteers: Tomasz Frydel, Chris Henson, Abigail Miller, Romy Proschmann, and Jakub Smutny

Published by AltaMira Press

A division of Rowman & Littlefield Publishers, Inc.

A wholly owned subsidary of The Rowman & Littlefield Publishing Group, Inc.

4501 Forbes Boulevard, Suite 200, Lanham, Maryland 20706

www.rowman.com

10 Thornbury Road, Plymouth PL6 7PP, United Kingdom

British Library Cataloguing in Publication Information Available

Library of Congress Cataloging-in-Publication Data Available

ISBN 978-0-7591-2258-1 (cloth : alk. paper)
ISBN 978-0-7591-2259-8 (electronic)

♾™ The paper used in this publication meets the minimum requirements of American National Standard for Information Sciences—Permanence of Paper for Printed Library Materials, ANSI/NISO Z39.48-1992.

Printed in the United States of America

"[. . .] after seven months of war I have become an adult, in the full meaning of the word. And I have come to know grief, hardship, and terror. I have seen a great deal of blood and many tears with my own eyes. My hopes have collapsed like a house of cards. And although my faith in the future, in a better future, is alive and intact, like a sacred thing, will I live to see it? Will some percentage of the persecuted Jewish people live? I don't know."

— Nekhama Vaisman, unidentified ghetto in Transnistria, diary entry
for January 27, 1942 (see document 6-3)

Contents

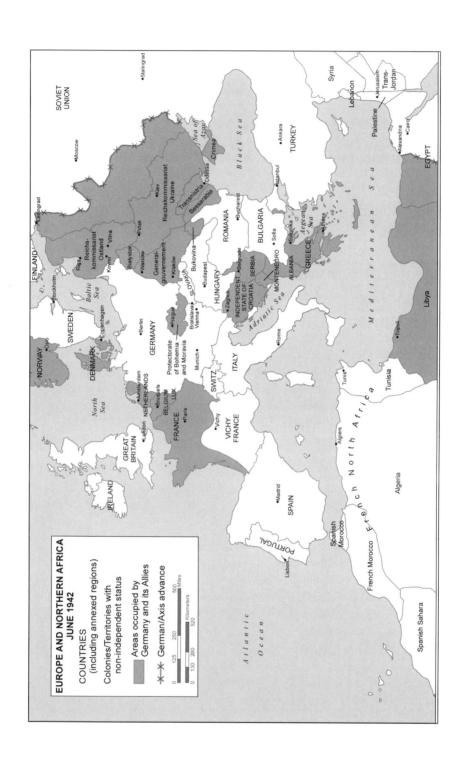

EUROPE AND NORTHERN AFRICA
JUNE 1942

COUNTRIES
(including annexed regions)

Colonies/Territories with
non-independent status

Areas occupied by
Germany and its Allies

German/Axis advance

0   125   250   500
Miles

0 130 260 520
Kilometers

SOVIET UNION

FINLAND

SWEDEN

NORWAY

DENMARK

GERMANY

NETHERLANDS

BELGIUM

LUX.

FRANCE

VICHY FRANCE

SWITZ.

ITALY

GREAT BRITAIN

IRELAND

SPAIN

PORTUGAL

Spanish Morocco

French Morocco

Algeria

Tunisia

French North Africa

Libya

EGYPT

TURKEY

Syria

Lebanon

Palestine

Trans-Jordan

ROMANIA

BULGARIA

HUNGARY

SLOVAKIA

GREECE

ALBANIA

SERBIA

MONTENEGRO

INDEPENDENT STATE OF CROATIA

Reichskommissariat Ostland

Reichskommissariat Ukraine

General-gouvernement

Protectorate of Bohemia and Moravia

Transnistria

Bessarabia

Bukovina

Crimea

Spanish Sahara

Stalingrad

Moscow

Leningrad

Stockholm

Oslo

Copenhagen

Berlin

Munich

Prague

Vienna

Bratislava

Budapest

Kraków

Warsaw

Białystok

Koyno

Vilna

Pinsk

Kiev

Riga

Odessa

Bucharest

Sofia

Belgrade

Zagreb

Salonika

Athens

Istanbul

Ankara

Rome

Madrid

Lisbon

Paris

Vichy

London

Amsterdam

Brussels

Tunis

Tunisia

Algiers

Tripoli

Alexandria

Cairo

Jerusalem

North Sea

Baltic Sea

Atlantic Ocean

Mediterranean Sea

Adriatic Sea

Aegean Sea

Black Sea

Sea of Azov

Reader's Guide

THE VOLUMES in this series embed original historical documents in an explanatory text by the authors. This text provides readers with clues about the context and distinctiveness of the documents presented and locates them in a narrative of communal and individual experiences. This volume moves for the most part chronologically and topically in an attempt to highlight certain developments, developments we find to be of particular relevance within the overall evolution of Jewish responses between the beginning of 1941 and the summer of 1942.

The documents in this volume have been printed in a distinct format to set them apart from our commentary. We have reproduced the form and content of the originals as faithfully as possible and worked to provide clear information about the provenance of each document. We have standardized emphases used by the authors of the documents by underlining them, and have corrected obvious orthographic mistakes made by the authors of English-language documents. In cases in which we could not print a document in its entirety, we have marked any omitted text with ellipses ([. . .]). For documents that are not clearly dated by those who produced them, we provide a date estimate (in parentheses) in the header that is based on indirect evidence drawn from the document itself or from additional extrinsic information.

Many foreign-language terms used by commentators during the war carry multiple, ambiguous, or complicated meanings difficult to capture in English. Sometimes they represent distinct religious concepts or the peculiar, new—often racialized—bureaucratic terms of the Nazi state or wartime occupation regimes. Sometimes, however, they simply constitute the distinctive vocabularies of sentiment, identity, mood, and so forth that pertain to every language. The nuances of particular terms can be important for understanding both the rhetoric of public appeals and the language of private reflection, and in some cases we have indicated the difficulty of translation by adding the original word or phrase in brackets after the English version.

Geographical names also vary from language to language and change to reflect the shifting power constellations of the war years. After the beginning of the war, Nazi planners and occupation officials renamed cities and entire regions to conform to their visions of a new order in Europe. We have worked to provide clear guideposts (and a map) that track this varying, often shifting, nomenclature. Furthermore, and different from the preceding volumes in this series, we have added place names and country designations to the document headers. Commonly known cities—Berlin, London, Moscow, New York, Paris, Prague, Vienna—are used without country or another qualification; for other cities or towns we added the names of (at the time) independent countries (e.g., Falmouth, United Kingdom; Nice, Vichy France; Split, Italian-occupied Yugoslav Dalmatia), or countries/regions occupied by Germany or its allies (Djurin, Transnistria; Opole, Lublin district, Generalgouvernement; Vilna, German-occupied Lithuania; Altfelden, Ostmark). Prewar and postwar variations in place names in the chapter texts can be found in the Index.

A number of names, events, and organizations appear in boldface throughout the volume when they are first mentioned in a chapter. This indicates that readers can find further information on the highlighted term in the Glossary at the end of the volume. Using the rich resources of the U.S. Holocaust Memorial Museum's library and archives, we have attempted to reveal the ultimate fate of each author of a document and persons mentioned in it by full name. Some of this information appears in the Glossary and some of it in footnotes to the original documents. Regrettably, we were unable to unearth information on every individual who makes an appearance in these pages.

Readers will find two other resources at the back of the volume to orient them in the complex events of this period. We have provided a basic chronology of important events that unfolded in the years covered by this volume. The Bibliography also offers the reader an opportunity to explore the topics and events touched on here in greater depth.

FORTHCOMING VOLUMES IN THE SERIES:

Volume IV: *Jewish Responses to Persecution 1942–1944*
Volume V: *Jewish Responses to Persecution 1944–1946*

ABBREVIATIONS

(Bold indicates a Glossary term.)

AJC	American Jewish Congress
AJDC, **AJJDC,** JDC, the Joint	**American Jewish Joint Distribution Committee**
AJYB	*American Jewish Year Book*
Aleynhilf	The "self-help" wartime Jewish relief movement in Poland
BAB	German National Archive (Bundesarchiv), Berlin
CAHJP	Central Archive for the History of the Jewish People, Jerusalem
CDJC	Center of Contemporary Jewish Documentation (Centre de documentation juive contemporaine), Paris
CZA	Central Zionist Archives
DÖW	Documentation Archive of Austrian Resistance (Dokumentationsarchiv des österreichischen Widerstands), Vienna
FZGH	Research Institute for Contemporary History (Forschungsstelle für Zeitgeschichte), Hamburg

Gestapo	Secret State Police (Geheime Staatspolizei)
GPU	State Political Directorate (Gosudarstvennoye Politiche-skoye Upravlenie), state security service of the Russian Federal Soviet Socialist Republic (1922–1934)
H&GS	*Holocaust and Genocide Studies*
HIAS	Hebrew Immigrant Aid Society
HICEM	Jewish aid organization, established in 1927 by a merger of HIAS, JCA, and the United Committee for Jewish Emigration
IKG	Vienna Israelite Community, Jewish Community of Vienna (Israelitische Kultusgemeinde Wien)
ISA	Israeli State Archive, Jerusalem
ITS	International Tracing Service, Bad Arolsen, Germany (copy of records at USHMM)
JA	**Jewish Agency**, **Jewish Agency for Palestine**
JCA, ICA	Jewish Colonization Association
JHM	Jewish Historical Museum, Belgrade
Joint	see AJDC above
JSS	**Jewish Social Self-Help** (Jüdische Soziale Selbsthilfe)
JTA	**Jewish Telegraphic Agency**
LBIYB	*Leo Baeck Institute Year Book*
LCSAV	Lithuanian Central State Archive, Vilnius
LHG	Ghetto Fighters' House Archives (Beit lohamei ha-getaot), Israel
NARA	U.S. National Archives and Records Administration
NKVD	People's Commissariat for Internal Affairs (Narodnyy komissariat vnutrennikh del)
ÖNB	Austrian National Library (Österreichische National-bibliothek), Vienna
ORT	Organization for Rehabilitation and Training
OSE	Children's Relief Association (Œuvre de secours aux enfants)

Pf	Penny, pennies in the German currency (Pfennig); see RM
POW	Prisoner of war
PSAŁ	Eldest of the Jews in the Łódz Ghetto (Przełożony Starszeństwa Żydów w Getcie Łódzkim), Polish State Archives, Łódź
Reichsvereinigung	Reich Association of Jews in Germany (**Reichsvereinigung der Juden in Deutschland**)
RELICO	Relief Committee for the War-Stricken Jewish Population
RGALI	Russian State Archive of Literature and Art (Rossiĭskiĭ gosudarstvennyĭ arkhiv literatury i iskusstva)
Ring.	Ringelblum Archive
RM	**Reichsmark,** German currency
RSHA	**Reich Security Main Office** (Reichssicherheitshauptamt), Berlin
SA	Nazi Storm Troopers (Sturmabteilung)
SD	"Intelligence service" of the Nazi Party (Sicherheitsdienst)
SS	Nazi Security Squad (Schutzstaffel)
UGIF	General Union of Jews of France (Union Générale des Israélites de France)
USHMM	United States Holocaust Memorial Museum, Washington, DC
USHMMA	USHMM Archives
USHMMPA	USHMM Photo Archives
WJC	**World Jewish Congress**
WL	Wiener Library, London
YIVO	Jewish Scientific Institute, Institute for Jewish Research (Yidisher Visnshaftlekher Institut), Vilna, later New York
YVA	Yad Vashem Archive, Jerusalem
YVS	*Yad Vashem Studies*
ŻIH	Jewish Historical Institute (Żydowski Instytut Historyczny), Warsaw
ŻIH Ring.	Ringelblum Archive, Jewish Historical Institute, Warsaw
ŻOB	Jewish Fighting Organization (Żydowska Organizacja Bojowa), Warsaw

Volume Introduction

From Persecution to Annihilation

"A NEW YEAR FOR SAVAGERY," wrote Warsaw ghetto chronicler Chaim Kaplan on January 2, 1941. "A year ago we expected salvation every day. We did not know our enemy's strength, just as we did not know our friends' weakness. Even those who still hope for ultimate victory see now that salvation will be long in coming."[1] Kaplan's diary entry reminds us that for Jews at the time, Hitler's demise was anything but certain. Indeed, Germany's victory in the war appeared ever more likely. From the beginning of the year 1941 until the summer of 1942, the Wehrmacht's reach expanded into the Balkans, the Mediterranean, North Africa, and the Soviet Union, as far as the outskirts of Leningrad in the north, and the roadways leading to Stalingrad in the south. And there was a new quality to the war: unlike the Reich's 1940 campaign in the West, its belligerent expansion to the southeast and east produced mass murder on a colossal scale, most notably committed by the SS and police, but also by other German agencies and their collaborators.

In the wake of Germany's "war of annihilation" against the Soviet Union beginning on June 22, 1941, what had been a seemingly random sequence of persecutory actions converged to form a highly destructive, complex, and increasingly coordinated pattern of persecution that, by the end of 1941, had

---

1. Chaim A. Kaplan, *Scroll of Agony: The Warsaw Diary of Chaim A. Kaplan*, ed. Abraham I. Katsh (Bloomington: Indiana University Press in association with the USHMM, 1999), 236.

claimed the lives of more than 1 million Jews. With the start of what would become "**Aktion Reinhard**" in mid-March 1942, the resumption of massive extermination of Jews in the occupied Soviet Union, increasing German pressure on its **Axis** partners to deliver their Jews, and the beginning of deportations from western Europe directly to death camps in eastern Europe in June 1942, what we now call the Holocaust had truly begun. It expanded from the German Reich and the countries lying to its east to cover what eminent Holocaust scholar Raul Hilberg has called "a vast semicircular arc, extending counterclockwise from Norway to Romania"[2] and into the Mediterranean, even threatening the existence of Jewish life in Palestine and northern Africa.

As this process gathered momentum through a combination of decisions made by German leaders in Berlin and their collaborators, Jews throughout Europe experienced the evolving "Final Solution" through diverse channels. Their awareness of the unfolding events depended on time and location, status and means, background and expectations. In the two previous volumes in this series we have seen examples of how Europe's Jews, Jewish groups, and communities responded to the myriad of local events in ways that reflected, refracted, or contradicted their traditions, interests, and perceptions.[3] In the time frame covered in this volume, however, Jewish responses to the Nazi onslaught became ever more fragmented. The all-encompassing scope of the war, combined with personal, often unpredictable reactions to the radical Nazi peril, elicited differing responses to the genocidal turn—differing among individuals as well as communities. In addition, a rapidly widening gulf had opened up between those subjected to extreme victimization on the one hand and those outside the reach of the Nazi empire on the other. Beyond this, Jews who lived near the borders of the Reich remained in an unstable, intermediate position, fearing that they, too, would be pulled into the vortex of destruction. Although

---

2. Raul Hilberg, *The Destruction of the European Jews*, 3rd ed. (1961; New Haven, CT: Yale University Press, 2003), 572. See also Peter Longerich, *Holocaust: The Nazi Persecution and Murder of the Jews* (New York: Oxford University Press, 2010); Saul Friedländer, *Nazi Germany and the Jews:* (vol. 2) *The Years of Extermination: 1939–1945* (New York: HarperCollins, 2007); Christopher R. Browning with contributions by Jürgen Matthäus, *The Origins of the Final Solution: The Evolution of Nazi Jewish Policy, September 1939–March 1942* (Lincoln and Jerusalem: University of Nebraska Press and Yad Vashem, 2004).

3. Jürgen Matthäus and Mark Roseman, *Jewish Responses to Persecution*, vol. 1: *1933–1938* (Lanham, MD: AltaMira Press in association with the USHMM, 2010), xxxvi–xxxvii; Alexandra Garbarini, with Emil Kerenji, Jan Lambertz, and Avinoam Patt, *Jewish Responses to Persecution*, vol. 2: *1938–1940* (Lanham, MD: AltaMira Press in association with the USHMM, 2011), xxvii–xxxviii. For the interwar period see Bernard Wasserstein, *On the Eve: The Jews of Europe Before the Second World War* (New York: Simon & Schuster, 2012).

sweeping transnational comparisons are tempting, especially since few historians have closely analyzed the course of events and fewer still the behavior of Jewish communities across different regions or countries in the first half of the war,[4] we must be cautious when drawing parallels or positing homogeneity. While the documentation presented here provides evidence for some similarities within and between countries, our sources also show that the ways in which Jews responded calls into question traditional and seemingly clear-cut categorization according to national affiliations, ideological orientations, gender, or age.

The years 1941 and 1942 were a kind of turning point in the history of the Holocaust, and indeed in the history of the world as well. Nowhere did the deadly trajectory of German genocidal policy become more obvious than in eastern Europe, first engulfing communities in the occupied parts of the Soviet Union and then in the **Generalgouvernement**, including large groups deported there from central and western Europe. For the commanders of German killing units, mass murder turned into an organizational problem to be solved by executions and gassings, be it in the proximity of ghettos or in death camps. In what Nazi officials vaguely referred to as "the East," mere weeks or months could bring drastic changes; what had seemed impossible earlier suddenly dominated the lives of most Jews without becoming any more comprehensible. Following the announcement of ghettoization in the Lithuanian city of Vilna, young **Yitskhok Rudashevski** wrote on June 24, 1941, that "our hearts are crushed witnessing the shameful scene where women and old people are beaten and kicked in the middle of the street [. . .] Tears come to my eyes: all our helplessness, all our loneliness lies in the streets. There is no one to take our part."[5] Four months later, Rudashevski's desperation had deepened as he witnessed **Ponar** undergo a transformation from a place of leisure into a killing field "soaked in Jewish blood."[6] For Rudashevski and the Jews in eastern Europe during this time, death stood on their doorstep, day and night, unyielding and ever-present.

Jews further west had not yet felt the lethal nature of Nazism's racial project directly. For French teenager Hélène Berr, life in German-occupied Paris continued in remarkably normal fashion until the second half of 1942. Nevertheless,

---

4. See Dan Michman, *Holocaust Historiography: A Jewish Perspective. Conceptualizations, Terminology, Approaches, and Fundamental Issues* (London: Vallentine Mitchell, 2003).

5. Yitskhok Rudashevski, *The Diary of the Vilna Ghetto* (Jerusalem: Hakibbutz Hameuchad Publishing House, 1973), 28–29; see also Alexandra Zapruder, ed., *Salvaged Pages: Young Writers' Diaries of the Holocaust* (New Haven, CT: Yale University Press, 2004), 198. For a short biography of Rudashevski, see the Glossary.

6. Rudashevski, *The Diary of the Vilna Ghetto*, 41; also Zapruder, *Salvaged Pages*, 204.

her diary still reflects the everyday persecution that she experienced, particularly the humiliation caused by having to wear the Jewish star. But she occasionally broke the law and did not wear it: the entry in her diary for June 10, 1942, states, "I went to the Trocadéro today. I didn't wear it [the star]."[7] Shortly thereafter, however, circumstances for Berr and thousands of other Jews in France changed for the worse, as the specter of "resettlement" drew near, and conditions rapidly deteriorated. In the spring of 1942, in the capital of Germany's Axis-partner Slovakia, Vojtech (Béla) Weichherz, a traveling salesman living with his wife, Estera, and their young teenage daughter, Katharina (Kitty), had to move into an attic room. "It is very small," Weichherz noted in a diary he kept for Kitty, "but I have the basics. We no longer have any great demands. Today we're happy if we still have four walls and a roof above us. The persecution of Jews proceeds: the star that we had to wear up until now 6 cm [2.4 inches] was not big enough, and so new ones were distributed, 10 cm [3.9 inches] in size and a garish yellow. That alone would be bearable, but deportation has begun." What that new threat meant was not clear to Weichherz, yet rumors pointed in a particularly ominous direction: "One thing is certain, that all transports have crossed the border in the direction of Poland. The official word is that all of the conscripted men and women are leaving as pioneers to prepare for the resettlement of the entire Jewish population of Slovakia. All Jews leaving Slovakia lose their citizenship."[8] As it turned out, Weichherz was wrong in his assumption that all Jews would be forced from Slovakia—deportations would stop in the fall of 1942—but his sense about his own fate was tragically on the mark. On June 6, 1942, the Weichherz family was deported to **Sobibór**

---

7. Hélène Berr, *The Journal of Hélène Berr* (New York: Weinstein Books, 2008), 58. Berr (1921–1945) was born in Paris to Raymond and Antoinette Berr (née Rodrigues-Ely), one of five children. At the beginning of the war she was a student at the Sorbonne, where she met her fiancé Jean Morawiecki. She and her family were sent to Drancy, and in March of 1944 they were deported to **Auschwitz II-Birkenau**, where her parents perished. Berr was transferred to Bergen-Belsen in November 1944, where she perished shortly before liberation. Several of her siblings and her fiancé survived the war.

8. Diary entries by Vojtech Weichherz, Bratislava, Slovakia, for early to mid-1942, USHMMA Acc. 2004.39.1 (Kitty Weichherz collection). Béla Weichherz (1892–1942), his wife Estera (1899–1942), and their daughter Katharina (1929–1942), lived in Bratislava before the war, where they spoke Hungarian, Slovak, and German. When Kitty was born, Béla began keeping a detailed diary of her childhood, which he continued until their deportation in 1942, a record of the increasing persecution of Jews in Slovakia. See Béla Weichherz, *In Her Father's Eyes: A Childhood Extinguished by the Holocaust*, ed. Daniel H. Magilow (New Brunswick, NJ: Rutgers University Press, 2008).

and probably killed on arrival; the diary written for Kitty by her father was recovered after the war.

In light of the unevenness of the process of persecution and the unpredictability of its future trajectory, it would be ahistorical to conclude that by 1941 to 1942 Jews across Europe, or indeed elsewhere, could have grasped the concrete meaning of the Nazi vision of a "Final Solution to the Jewish question." As the machinery of destruction was being assembled and tested, those who became its targets were forced to react based on partial information. As the war continued and what we now know as "the Holocaust" began to unfold, the range of options available to Jews marooned in various occupied and collaborationist countries narrowed. The existence of internationally active Jewish organizations notwithstanding, no uniform response could be expected in the face of the Nazi threat. There was instead, as the documents in this volume reveal, a vast spectrum of reactions by Jewish individuals, groups, and organizations to an equally varied range of situations—few benign, many life threatening. Our goal with this book is to help readers understand what Jews at the time thought and did, what prompted their responses, what aims they pursued, and what obstacles they faced. Thus, in keeping with previous volumes, we resist the temptation to impose ex post facto judgments as history unfolds; rather, we seek to gain a new understanding of these events from the perspective of those who did not yet know how the story would end.

In keeping with the structure of this series, we have organized this volume around two broad, partly overlapping themes that highlight both the evolution and the specific characteristics of Jewish responses through documentation produced by Jews at the time. Parts I and II follow the *trajectory of persecution* through the lens of Jews describing the course of events leading up to the summer of 1942. Parts III and IV focus on *specific patterns of Jewish action and reflection* after **Operation Barbarossa** began. The twelve chapters and their subsections are meant to provide chronological and topical orientation; headings are deliberately worded broadly to avoid the impression that one part of the book offers all that is required to know about an event or a country. We hope instead that readers will treat this volume—and the personal stories and specific episodes featured here—as a starting point for further investigation into the many facets of this crucial period.

By complementing accounts of everyday life written by individual Jewish men, women, adolescents, and children with protocols and other documents generated by Jewish organizations and press organs at the time, we continue the approach established in earlier volumes of this series. In particular, the records of the **American Jewish Joint Distribution Committee (AJJDC)** as well as the Geneva offices of the **World Jewish Congress (WJC)** and the **Jewish Agency** each open fascinating windows onto the time. While virtually all textual accounts, individual and organizational, share the fundamental lacuna at the heart of their production—namely, the more or less fragmentary knowledge of the genocide—they nevertheless work together to present a complex picture of contemporary Jewish understanding of persecution, as incomplete as that picture is, and as partial as that understanding was. Sources generated by many Jewish organizations transcend the immediate concerns of individuals condemned to death by the Nazis and convey—most often because of their distance from the killing sites—a broader image. So, too, do wartime publications, such as the New York–based American Jewish Committee's *Contemporary Jewish Record*, the German-Jewish émigré paper *Aufbau*; and even the tightly Nazi-controlled *Jüdisches Nachrichtenblatt* that was published by Jews in Berlin, Vienna, and Prague, offer a very small opportunity for writing between the lines under the radar of Nazi authorities. Personal papers from which we have drawn—such as letters by **Ruth Goldbarth** in the Warsaw ghetto and **Claartje van Aals** in Apeldoorn, the Netherlands, or the diaries of **Ruth Maier** in Lillestrøm, Norway, **Mirjam Korber** in Djurin, **Transnistria**, **Shlomo Frank** in Łódź, and **Hermann Hakel** in the southern Italian camp of Alberobello—reflect the realities of everyday life and show the many different ways in which Jews attempted to understand what was going on around them. Literary and artistic works as well as photographs present yet another medium to gauge wartime Jewish responses. We provide a handful of examples, many of them patently meager stand-ins for whole destroyed communities. Ultimately, no single source type that documents the Holocaust can convey the full range of its destructiveness and manifold meanings, past and present.

In Part I we follow the territorial expansion pursued by Germany and its allies up to the beginning of Operation Barbarossa, glimpsing the manifestations of "**Aktion T-4**," a systematic program of murder that targeted disabled children and mental patients in the Reich, among them a number of Jews. The push toward southeastern Europe and into the Mediterranean brought more people under Axis control and sped up the process of escalating anti-Jewish violence, even raising the terrifying specter of a Nazi invasion of Palestine. What happened to the Jews in the Balkans beginning in the spring of 1941, particularly in Yugoslavia, partly reflected German policy planning and military "pacification" strategies. But it also became entangled with conditions on the ground determined by long-standing conflicts among ethnic groups and political elites. As in other multiethnic situations in eastern Europe, radical German demographic policies spurred local genocidal activities in Yugoslavia—**ustaše** against

Serbs and Jews, Četniks against Bosnian Muslims.[9] In Poland and beyond, conditions worsened for Jews deported from other areas or herded into ghettos, calling into question the widely held belief that the German goal of economic exploitation implied setting and sustaining at least minimal standards of living for Jewish workers, their families, and their communities. As reports and letters written in the Łódź and Warsaw ghettos underline, Jews struggled to maintain any sense of normalcy in the face of starvation, forced labor, and eventually, deportations and mass death.

Historical writing, especially when it paints the course of events in broad brushstrokes, often obscures the critical importance of particular events and the complex nexus of factors that determined individual decisions and actions. Some episodes from the early stages of the war may have given Jews an idea of what lay in store for them; yet, as before, German anti-Jewish measures were shrouded in deceit and arbitrariness and seemed inconsistent with other occupation policies. No ordinary ghetto resident and few of its leaders had an inkling of what ends the Germans were so relentlessly pursuing with their anti-Jewish measures. They had no clear sense of whether ghetto labor would guarantee a reprieve from starvation; how much, or if any, bread would be on the table the next day; and whether escaping from a ghetto would lead to rescue or disaster. The presence of mass death—by starvation, by rampant disease, by systematic murder—became more and more common. That possibility by-and-by encompassed all the ghettos of eastern Europe, also throwing a shadow on areas within and beyond western Europe that had previously served as places of refuge.

The Wehrmacht's military successes increased the number of Jews living under Axis rule and closed many remaining escape routes; at the same time, the Nazis' unrelenting focus on pursuing their programmatic goal of "solving the Jewish question" previously expressed in the **Madagascar Plan** found new outlets. With Hitler's decision to invade the Soviet Union, an alternative "territorial solution" appeared on the antisemitic horizon that seemed, while still undefined in its concrete form, more realistic than shipping millions of Jews

---

9. Četniks were Serbian nationalist guerrillas led by General Dragoljub Mihailović (1893-1946) who initially resisted the German partition of Yugoslavia and occupation of Serbia. They fought the communist resistance movement, while seeking to secure a favorable political position for the postwar settlement in Yugoslavia, which, they thought, would be dictated by the Western Allies. This contradictory agenda brought them to coordinate their actions with both Allied and Axis powers, mercilessly fight Tito's partisans, and "cleanse" the allegedly "Serbian" territory in Bosnia in bouts of genocidal violence against Bosnian Muslims. See Jozo Tomasevich, *War and Revolution in Yugoslavia, 1941-1945: Occupation and Collaboration* (Stanford, CA: Stanford University Press, 2001).

across the ocean to an island blatantly unsuited for mass "resettlement." In Part II we will show how, after the onset of the German war of annihilation on June 22, 1941, this "territorial solution" began to gain momentum as a massive wave of killings—initiated by German SS, police, and Wehrmacht units and supported by aligned regimes and local collaborators—swept the region east of the German-Soviet border. Jews in areas rapidly overrun by Axis armies may have expected a continuation of the German discriminatory measures applied in the Reich and occupied Poland. They were unprepared for the escalating violence that within months would kill hundreds of thousands of Jewish men, women, and children, and, by the summer of 1942, would lead to the near complete destruction of Jewish communities in the occupied Soviet Union and the subsequent forcible enclosure of the surviving remnant in camps and ghettos. By that time, the lessons that German leaders had learned during the first months of the "war of annihilation" against the Soviet Union had been carried westward and coupled with local initiatives, stretching from Łódź in the German-annexed **Warthegau** to the Lublin and Galician districts of the Generalgouvernement. Deportations from the greater Reich to "the East" began in the fall of 1941, and many Jews were murdered on arrival. German planners constructed death camps for what in the spring of 1942 was to become "Aktion Reinhard." More deportations from central and for the first time also western Europe began, constituting the initial stages of a Europe-wide "Final Solution" discussed by high-ranking German bureaucrats in January 1942 during the **Wannsee Conference** on the outskirts of Berlin.[10]

With destruction now reaching unprecedented dimensions, but evolving in confusingly uneven patterns, Jews within and beyond Axis-controlled Europe scrambled to understand what was going on and what the next German move might be. As before, Jewish responses spanned a wide spectrum, ranging from "simply" surviving to open resistance. But as we will see, it was in German-controlled eastern Europe after June 1941 that oppositional behavior by Jews in the form of revolt, escape, and hiding emerged more prominently. The documentary legacy assembled through large-scale projects such as **Oyneg Shabes** in the Warsaw ghetto or individual efforts yields rich evidence of the everyday resilience of people from every walk of life, determined to attest to their plight in the midst of the most inhumane of conditions. The tone and tenor of these pieces range from the comic and satiric, to documentary reportage, to literary flourishes, to tragic acceptance. Nevertheless, we cannot forget that even this exhaustive archival legacy contains but a small sampling of what life was like under Nazi oppression

---

10. See Mark Roseman, *The Wannsee Conference and the Final Solution: A Reconsideration* (New York: Metropolitan Books, 2002).

and murder. How many other sources were lost, erased, or otherwise destroyed? Even the richest representation of Jewish responses to persecution remains incomplete, in itself a testimony to the scope of destruction.

From Jewish reactions to the perpetrator-driven course of events featured in Parts I and II of this volume, we move to post–Operation Barbarossa interactions and reflections in Parts III and IV. Despite the obvious overlap between these two angles, we feel a differentiation to be useful as it helps discern emerging patterns of persecution and Jewish responses at a time of massively escalating violence. This approach is also meant to provide deeper insights into the internal stratification of Jewish communities in Axis-controlled Europe, with their massive tensions between those in positions of power, as limited as this power was, and those living a life consumed by mounting destitution and despair. As we will see, Jewish documentation created at the time provides an irreplaceable tool for broadening our understanding of not only the consequences but also the driving forces of persecution. Where statements made by Jews reflect on persecutors' actions and motivations, they provide insights that we could not gain by only looking at records left by the Nazi regime and its allies.[11]

One of the key themes in Part III is how historical traditions and associations shaped Jewish responses to the new, threatening conditions of war and occupation. **Jewish councils**, for example, were rooted in earlier forms of Jewish self-governance and thus did not look altogether unfamiliar, although in reality they had little or no authority of their own. German officials used the illusion of "Jewish self-administration" against the councils as they were forced to make decisions about the allocation of resources and deportations without knowing their consequences. Similarly, when Jews in western Europe in their diaries or letters expressed the hope if not the expectation that they would be spared the terrible fate of Jews east of Germany's prewar border, they were acting on the basis of prewar assumptions and the available information about Nazi policy. In addition to the forces of the moment, more long-term factors affected how Jews thought and acted, be it past experiences, identification with political or religious ideas, personal bonds and loyalties, or societal norms linked to gender and age. The documents featured here indicate how Jews adapted to the new, constantly changing conditions, resulting in actions that were often highly specific to the situation in which they found themselves. The fact that leading Jews in Romania and Slovakia managed to influence, partly even to mitigate the course of anti-Jewish policy in their countries in 1941 and 1942 attests to small

---

11. See Mark Roseman, "Holocaust Perpetrators in Victims' Eyes," in *Years of Persecution, Years of Extermination: Saul Friedländer and the Future of Holocaust Studies*, ed. Christian Wiese and Paul Betts (London: Continuum, 2010), 81–100.

windows of opportunity that existed in specific locales and circumstances. In each and every setting, far beyond what we can feature in this volume, Jews had to weigh a dazzling array of factors to assess what challenges confronted them before they could decide how best to protect themselves and others.

Action implies choice, yet the closer Jews lived to the centers of destruction, the more limited their range of options and the more daunting the consequences of any form of noncompliant behavior became. With the crumbling of prewar social structures that accompanied German rule, the pressure on individuals to act purely out of self-interest and save their own lives grew exponentially. Some succumbed to this pressure, and many sources from the time attest to what their authors described as utter egotism surrounding them. However, the social, physical, and spiritual conditions within which Jews had to decide and act remain elusive as we evaluate these accounts many decades later. Moral categories derived from our twenty-first-century perspective are more problematic than adequate. What can we conclude, for example, about someone's decision to escape from a ghetto or camp or town under siege when he would leave kith and kin behind whose survival depended on his support? How can we judge militant resistance when it was clear that, no matter how successful or unsuccessful the individual act, any such demonstrations would be eagerly used by the occupiers to justify disproportionate "reprisals" and to unleash violence against innocent women, children, and men? If seen in its concrete context, Jewish agency almost invariably invokes dilemmas of the kind literary scholar Lawrence Langer has called "choiceless choices" and complicates our image of the already highly complex past.[12]

Action also involves reflection about present challenges, their antecedents and future implications, which forms the main subject of Part IV. Few Jews or anyone else living at the time had an understanding of the emerging "Final Solution" that comes close to how we in the present century see it. While today we understand the Holocaust as a pan-European genocide with massive, long-lasting repercussions, Jews across eastern and southern Europe experienced catastrophe up close without ever seeing the macro level of Nazi decision making and its evolution. The effect was overwhelming, often leaving nothing but devastation and despair. But some chroniclers of these times, even among those directly hit by disaster, saw connections between individual tragedy and similar, not always obviously related events, that added up to a wider pattern. It is in these documents that we can discern a perception of impending doom

---

12. See Lawrence L. Langer, *Versions of Survival: The Holocaust and the Human Spirit* (Albany: State University of New York Press, 1982); also idem, *Holocaust Testimonies: The Ruins of Memory* (New Haven, CT: Yale University Press, 1991).

significantly different from today's widespread image of a total, linear, if not predetermined, path to genocide; through these sources we can see the process of destruction evolve, with all its inconceivable, absurd, contradictory, and otherwise only partly comprehensible elements. Jews in eastern European towns and in rural communities knew full well that the Germans and their helpers were out to segregate, exploit, oppress, and brutalize them to a degree unprecedented in Jewish history. How that knowledge was processed—through what worldview, with what information, and under what circumstances—impacted how Jews assessed the situation and decided on future action.

As we will see, a few Jews remained uniquely positioned—in Geneva, in London, and even in less well-protected settings—to see the German path to genocide already in early to mid-1942. They did so by sifting through the available shreds of firsthand evidence collected close to the killing fields, in places of refuge, and in the centers of political decision making—a random, fragmentary, and constantly changing pool of information. Yet awareness of the unfolding genocide arguably mattered little, given the absence of any means to thwart German policy. Jewish observers on the outside felt the maddening frustration of half knowing what was going on inside German-held territories but not being able to send aid or to stop the juggernaut of anti-Jewish measures. And they saw, too, that in the broader context of total war, even these shocking measures may have lost their capacity to spark public outrage and empathy. **Emanuel Ringelblum**, the leader of the Oyneg Shabes archive in Warsaw, posed a rhetorical question in late June 1942, immediately after news of the annihilation of the Polish Jews had begun to resonate in the West (and less than a month before the start of mass deportations from the Warsaw ghetto to the **Treblinka** death camp): "Why should the world be shaken by our suffering when rivers of blood are spilled daily on every battlefield. In what respect is our Jewish blood more precious than that of the Russian, Chinese, English soldiers?"[13]

Perhaps more so than in previous volumes in this series, the authors of this book have faced the challenge of balancing the complexity of the documentation and events it is based on with our limited ability to tell the stories of the men, women, and children who lived in a different world and time. We have tried to cover as broad a spectrum of Jewish responses as possible, but are aware of vast gaps in the narrative. Drawing on a small selection of diaries, letters, reports, published articles, and visual documentation, including some artworks, we understand that the story told is fragmentary. We say little about crucial differences in the pre-Holocaust experiences and traditions of Jewish communities

---

13. Quoted from Jacob Sloan, ed., *Notes from the Warsaw Ghetto: The Journal of Emmanuel Ringelblum* (New York: McGraw-Hill, 1958), 296.

in different cultural spheres—**Ashkenazi** and **Sephardi**, observant and non-observant Jews, Jews in "the West" and those in "the East"—and in different countries, all of which played a role in determining these Jewish responses and call for further scrutiny and research. Neither the importance of gender nor that of age and social status is as fully explored in the following chapters as these subjects merit. Members of marginal groups, especially those forcibly labeled Jewish by their victimizers—converts or *"Mischlinge,"* for instance—play only a minor role in this book. Finally, the selection of sources and the contextualization we offer naturally reflects our primary areas of expertise to the detriment of other aspects of the topic. Still, we strive to provide an account that shows elements of the typical and the exceptional, the personal and the abstract, the awkward and the sophisticated, the "rational" and the "emotional."

Despite the book's limits, the documents featured display many of our topic's facets. These documents also provide entry points for further study as they pose a range of questions, including: What prompted the writer of a document to produce it at a given time? What do images—contemporary photographs, drawings, paintings—convey about events that might contradict or underwrite other contemporary and coterminous sources, or accounts written later by survivors and historians? To whom are the documents addressed, and what was their impact? What can we say about the use of language in view of the conditions under which diaries and other writings emerged and considering the fact that this series features mostly translated documentation? Each reader might answer these questions differently and pose others, equally relevant and difficult to answer. Beyond the contextual information we offer in these pages lies a world of knowledge yet to be explored.

This volume relies on the help of a greater number of people and institutions than we can acknowledge here. We are immensely grateful to the Conference on Jewish Material Claims Against Germany, the William S. and Ina Levine Foundation, and the Blum Family Foundation for their generous support, and to the Dorot Foundation for funding summer research fellows. Dr. Alfred Munzer was again a key supporter of our project in material terms as well as by helping us with Dutch sources. We could not have finished this book without the vital assistance by our brilliant and committed research assistants, Kathryn Cornelius, Ryan Farrell, Holly Robertson, and Gregory Wilkowski, and our wonderful summer fellows Tomasz Frydel, Abigail Miller, and Jakub Smutny. Equally invaluable were our volunteers Ilona Gerbakher and Hope McCaffrey; for their crucial help with translations and scholarly advice at different stages in the project we are indebted to Karen Auerbach, Ania Drimer, Marcel Drimer, Gideon Frieder, Kamil Galeev, Gershon Greenberg, Susanne

Heim, Jolanta Kraemer, Peter Landé, Kathleen Luft, Adam Peiperl, Vanda Rajcan, Katrin Reichelt, Steven Sage, Stephen Scala, and Sam Schalkowsky. Many USHMM colleagues have been involved in the project in one way or another. We thank the staff of the Center for Advanced Holocaust Studies (CAHS) as well as the Museum's Library, Archives, Photo Archives, and Art and Artifacts branch, particularly Judith Cohen, Ron Coleman, Rebecca Erbelding, Nancy Hartman, Radu Ioanid, Steven Kanaley, Ferenc Katona, Megan Lewis, Henry Mayer, Teresa Pollin, Vincent Slatt, Susan Snyder, Anatol Steck, Caroline Waddell, and Bret Werb. Paul Shapiro, director of the Museum's CAHS, remained a committed supporter of our series in more ways than one. Gwen Sherman and Wrenetta Richards provided vital administrative support. At AltaMira Press we would like to thank Marissa Parks and Elaine McGarraugh for their dedication to the project. We are grateful to the members of the USHMM's Academic Committee for their ongoing support. Special thanks go to Alexandra Garbarini (Williamstown) and Mark Roseman (Bloomington), coauthors of previous volumes in the series, for their extremely constructive comments and suggestions.

Jürgen Matthäus, Emil Kerenji, Jan Lambertz, and Leah Wolfson
February 2013

PART I
JEWS AND THE EXPANSION OF THE GERMAN EMPIRE
JANUARY TO JUNE 1941

I F WE LOOK at the political map of Europe in early 1941, we see that the German Reich had seized control over considerable parts of the continent. Great Britain remained the Reich's sole active enemy, with the Soviet Union acting as Germany's partner in ruling what had been Poland and the Baltic states. Hitler had reached the zenith of his power largely through the subjugation and exploitation of occupied peoples, but also by drawing on their affinity for certain elements of Nazi ideology, such as antisemitism and a desire to "homogenize" their respective nations by excluding groups deemed ethnic outsiders.[1] By the end of 1940, Hitler's ambition as well as the radical dynamic of the Nazi system had honed in on the Soviet Union, making it the next target of military aggression. However, he decided to help out his Italian ally in its expansionist drive first, in the spring of 1941, bringing southeastern Europe under German control. The start of **Operation Barbarossa** was thus delayed by several crucial weeks.[2]

---

1. See Ian Kershaw, *Hitler, 1936–1945: Nemesis* (New York: W. W. Norton & Co., 2000), 281–338. Saul Friedländer, *Nazi Germany and the Jews:* (vol. 2) *The Years of Extermination, 1939–1945* (New York: HarperCollins, 2007), 191, notes the "widespread acceptance of resegregation" in German-dominated Europe.

2. Gerhard Weinberg, *A World at Arms: A Global History of World War II* (Cambridge: Cambridge University Press, 1994), 205–25.

For German officials involved in solving the "Jewish question," this meant that an alternative to the **Madagascar Plan** beckoned on the eastern horizon: once Stalin's empire had succumbed to the Wehrmacht—a mere matter of weeks in the minds of German military planners—Europe's Jews, including those in German-occupied Poland, could be deported to some as yet undetermined destination beyond the "living space" claimed by the Reich. Such a "territorial solution" became all the more attractive in early 1941, since Hitler's underlings were eager to declare their areas of influence "free of Jews."[3] While systematic mass murder of Jews still seemed outside the realm of the possible, the Third Reich leadership's lack of inhibition about adopting extremely violent policies manifested itself in the secretly organized killing of disabled children and institutionalized patients, code-named **"Aktion T-4."** Designed to "cleanse" the German Volk of those deemed "useless eaters," the program claimed the lives of roughly seventy thousand people up to 1941. From its very beginning Jewish asylum patients, too, were among its victims.[4] However, a connection between those murders and the projected "Final Solution of the Jewish question" had not yet been established.

Nevertheless, that latter question had become ever more pressing in the minds of the Nazi leadership. As a result of the Reich's military successes, the number of Jews living under German rule had grown massively and nullified whatever achievements Nazi officials could claim in dealing with the "Jewish question." In late 1939, in addition to the roughly three hundred thousand Jews in the Reich, more than 1.7 million Jews lived in the newly Nazi-occupied parts of Poland, both the areas annexed to the Reich and the **Generalgouvernement**. The Wehrmacht's occupation of Belgium, Denmark, France, Luxembourg, the Netherlands, and Norway in the spring and early summer of 1940 added over a half-million Jews to this number. Not only had Jewish emigration dwindled due to the lack of countries willing to open their doors and a scarcity of passenger ship berths out of Europe, but the German army also caught up with many who had managed to flee before the outbreak of war. Moreover, Nazi leaders saw the unresolved "Jewish question" as part

---

3. See Friedländer, *Nazi Germany*, 2:187–91; Christopher R. Browning with contributions by Jürgen Matthäus, *The Origins of the Final Solution: The Evolution of Nazi Jewish Policy, September 1939–March 1942* (Lincoln and Jerusalem: University of Nebraska Press and Yad Vashem, 2004), 193–212.

4. Henry Friedlander, *The Origins of Nazi Genocide: From Euthanasia to the Final Solution* (Chapel Hill: University of North Carolina Press, 1995), 270–71, estimates that between four thousand and five thousand Jews were murdered during Aktion T-4.

of a broader crisis underlying the policy, adopted after the defeat of Poland, of securing "living space" for Germans in eastern Europe. While the resettlement of ethnic Germans stalled, the Reich stepped up its efforts to force Jews out of its territory, yet even in this instance fell short of its own sweeping goals. Up to April 1941, among a total of more than half a million people expelled from newly occupied areas, at least sixty-three thousand Jews had been forcibly moved from their homes, the vast majority in German-controlled Poland.[5] There, the Jewish deportees shared the harsh conditions of local Jews, whom German officials increasingly forced into ghettos and subjected to organized exploitation and mass starvation.

From our postwar perspective, the beginning of the German attack on the Soviet Union, with its massive eruption of violence, tends to overshadow what had happened a few months earlier in southeastern Europe. Yet the continuation of earlier measures directed against Jews under German rule combined with **Axis** military aggression in the Balkans, particularly the occupation of Yugoslavia, had terrible and wide-reaching consequences. This applied first and foremost to the people in the newly occupied areas. For Jews elsewhere in Europe, it further reduced the chance to escape from the continent. For Jews in the **Yishuv**, it brought German forces, now with a foothold in the Mediterranean, threateningly close to Palestine. Furthermore, the Balkan campaign in the spring of 1941 contributed significantly to the radicalization of German anti-Jewish policy as a whole: while in southeastern Europe deadly violence followed on the heels of the German army, those living in areas that had been under Nazi rule since before 1941 experienced new threats and greater challenges as the Germans moved from victory to victory.

In the following three chapters we pick up from the previous volume in the series and look at the process of persecution up to the summer of 1941, its consequences for the Jews of Europe, and how they responded. Chapters 1 and 2 focus on the effects of earlier discriminatory measures on the life of Jews in the Reich, in German-controlled Poland, and those en route to safety, while Chapter 3 explores the impact of the German conquest in southeastern Europe and the challenges facing those who sought to look ahead into their own future and the future of Jews in general. During this period, it became clear that the

---

5. For an overview chart of Nazi expulsions between September 1939 and April 1941, see Browning, *The Origins of the Final Solution*, 109. See also Götz Aly, *"Final Solution": Nazi Population Policy and the Murder of the European Jews* (London: Arnold, 1999), 124–25.

Nazi regime's resolve to apply anti-Jewish measures grew with the intensity of its military campaigns and that any hopes for Hitler's demise were premature if not illusionary. For Jews, the question was not whether the occupiers would continue to resort to violence, but in what form and to what degree they would do so. Despite vast changes brought about by the course of war, German policies directed against Jews seemed to have retained a strange predictability, with robbery, stigmatization, and abuse emerging as standard features, along with a powerful dynamic—particularly east and southeast of the Reich's prewar borders—toward greater and more deadly violence.

CHAPTER 1

FACING INCREASED PRESSURE

AS UNPRECEDENTED as Germany's expansion seemed, the state of affairs in early 1941 was widely viewed not as the war's culmination, but as a transitional stage. Nazi officials, functionaries, and supporters saw the Reich's recent gains as a phase during which the swastika would be hoisted over ever larger parts of Europe, if not of the world. And those suffering from German occupation or actively combating Hitler's armies wished for 1941 to become the turning point leading to the desperately desired Nazi demise, as the United States and other countries actively joined forces with Britain. In the months leading up to the German attack on the Soviet Union, expectations of Jews oscillated between hoping that things would improve—either as a result of the war coming to an end or by being able to escape to safety—and fearing that their situation would continue to deteriorate. Marking the beginning of the new calendar year, **Eva Mändl**, a twenty-year-old Jewish woman living in Prague, wrote in her diary about the anticipation triggered by President Roosevelt's speech, which underlined "that the war cannot end without the liberation of Europe. Optimism reigns everywhere. Hitler, too, gave a new year's speech to the effect that the year 1941 will be decisive, hopefully also for the Jews!"[1] At the same time in Vilna, eminent Jewish historian **Simon Dubnow** tried to collect "evidence for the last act of the 'Hitleriad' and especially for the

---

1. Eva Mändl Roubíčková, *Langsam gewöhnen wir uns an das Ghettoleben. Ein Tagebuch aus Theresienstadt*, ed. Veronika Springmann (Hamburg: Konkret Literatur Verlag, 2007), 13 (diary entry for January 1, 1941).

extermination of the centers in Poland containing 3 million Jews."[2] After the German occupation of the city and as part of the wave of killing actions sweeping through the Baltic states, Dubnow himself fell victim in early December 1941 to the extension of this "last act" foisted on vast tracts of Europe.

In the six months prior to Germany's attack on the Soviet Union, Jews living in the areas under Nazi rule experienced the escalation of earlier policies as well as a range of new threats. The following chapter sheds light on responses to those stepped-up measures across a broad sweep of regions, beginning with the effects of deportations from Vienna in early 1941 to the **Generalgouvernement**. The chapter turns to the growing predicament of Jews still in the Reich resulting from Nazi "euthanasia" programs and the now almost complete lack of opportunities for escaping from the Nazi grip. Finally, we will examine the situation of Jews—at home and as refugees—across western Europe before turning to the fate of those stranded in transit to what they hoped would be freedom. In diverse ways they, too, registered the fallout of ever more radical and ruthless Nazi policies in the Reich and eastern Europe.

IN THE "GREATER REICH"

Since the occupation of Poland in the fall of 1939, Nazi planners had treated the conquered territory, particularly annexed areas such as the **Warthegau**, as "living space" slated for "Germanization," while they intended to use the Generalgouvernement as a dumping ground for unwanted Slavs and Jews. For Polish Jews, this meant segregation into ghettos created by German officials as a stopgap measure until other more permanent solutions to the "Jewish question" could be found.[3] "We want to show the world," a German official in charge of resettlement in the Generalgouvernement stated in late January 1941, "that within the scope of our colonizing effort we are capable of managing the Jewish problem." The Warsaw ghetto in particular was seen as "a preliminary stage in the exploitation of Jewish labour in Madagascar, as planned by the Führer."[4]

---

2. Simon Dubnow, "The Martyrology of Our Time," (late 1940/early 1941), USHMMA RG 68.045M, reel 8, file 61. See also page 355–66.

3. See Christopher R. Browning with contributions by Jürgen Matthäus, *The Origins of the Final Solution: The Evolution of Nazi Jewish Policy, September 1939–March 1942* (Lincoln and Jerusalem: University of Nebraska Press and Yad Vashem, 2004), 137.

4. Quoted from Götz Aly, *"Final Solution": Nazi Population Policy and the Murder of the European Jews* (London: Arnold, 1999), 140. In the Generalgouvernement, compulsory labor for all Jews aged fourteen years and older had been introduced in late 1939. See Alexandra Garbarini, with Emil Kerenji, Jan Lambertz, and Avinoam Patt, *Jewish Responses to Persecution, vol. 2: 1938–1940* (Lanham, MD: AltaMira Press in association with the USHMM), 375–76.

The Lublin district of the Generalgouvernement had been the destination of deportation transports from the Reich since the fall of 1939. Most were small-scale, haphazardly organized "resettlements" to places that lacked any means to sustain a larger community. Left to their own devices, the newcomers barely managed to scrape together a living in the defunct **Nisko** settlement, or in towns such as Piaski and Bełżyce, supported by locals or by whatever reached them long distance from relatives and relief agencies.[5] In early 1941 more transports arrived in the area after the Nazi chief in Vienna, Baldur von Schirach, had managed to get Hitler's approval for deportation of the city's sixty thousand Jews before the end of the war. Rumors about the "dreadful situation" even reached Prague, where young Eva Mändl noted in her diary that "by spring all Jews have to be out [of Vienna]; transports are leaving from there to Poland, all old people."[6] Roughly five thousand Jews, hastily assembled in Vienna, reached the Lublin district in February and March. In mid-March the deportations were halted again due to train shortages, as the German military prepared its attack on the Soviet Union.[7]

Mändl learned that those who were deported sent families and friends in Vienna or elsewhere in the Reich "heart-wrenching letters. Great hunger, they are completely isolated, can't exchange anything with Aryans."[8] The deportees from the former Austrian capital had been transported to a rural environment that seemed as desolate as it was alien. In the second half of February 1941, 2,006 mostly elderly Viennese Jews arrived in the town of Opole, each with at most 50 kilograms, 110 pounds, of personal goods and next to no money, to share in the misery of roughly 4,500 local Jews and 2,500 Jewish deportees from other towns in the Lublin district.[9] Like those who preceded them and others who were to be deported later, the uprooted initially felt shell-shocked, a state of mind reflected in their correspondence. The unidentified author of the following letter was among those Viennese Jews who arrived in Opole in February 1941.

---

5. See Browning, *The Origins of the Final Solution*, 36–43.

6. Roubíčková, *"Langsam gewöhnen wir uns an das Ghettoleben,"* 18 (diary entry for February 15, 1941).

7. See Hans Safrian, *Eichmann's Men* (Cambridge: Cambridge University Press in association with the USHMM, 2010), 68–71; Aly, *"Final Solution,"* 168.

8. Roubíčková, *"Langsam gewöhnen wir uns an das Ghettoleben,"* 31 (diary entry for May 23, 1941).

9. See Laura Crago and Joseph Robert White, "Opole," in *The United States Holocaust Memorial Museum Encyclopedia of Camps and Ghettos, 1933–1945*, vol. 2: *Ghettos in German-Occupied Eastern Europe*, ed. Martin Dean (Bloomington: Indiana University Press in association with USHMM, 2012), 688–91.

DOCUMENT 1-1: **Letter from J. E. about the deportation of Viennese Jews to the Lublin district, February 18, 1941, in Else Behrendt-Rosenfeld and Gertrud Luckner, eds.,** *Lebenszeichen aus Piaski. Briefe Deportierter aus dem Distrikt Lublin 1940–1943* **(Munich: Biederstein Verlag, 1968), 167–69 (translated from German).**

Opole, February 18, 1941

If you all receive my letter today, then it is God's greatest miracle. I cannot describe to you what we've been through until now, since our departure from Vienna, and what we're suffering every minute.

On Friday at 5:30 a.m., we rode to the train [station] with our luggage, loaded on trucks. At night, there were 10 of us grouped together in a train compartment, terribly cramped and no toilet!

Sunday evening we arrived in a small town and were loaded onto open trains, in which we traveled among soldiers for two hours. Finally we reached our destination, Opole. I didn't know that such god-forsaken villages actually exist, and you can't even begin to picture such misery.

All of us, perhaps more than 100, were housed in a synagogue here, where beds of straw had been prepared, and here, dead tired, we threw ourselves down [to sleep]. The population is so poor that you can't even picture it: the rags hang from their bodies and they lead the most miserable life. You can hardly walk in the streets, you almost sink in the muck, and I can't even describe the houses, little bigger than doghouses. We have found accommodations for ourselves with a Jew, my mother and I sleep in one bed, but my father still hasn't found accommodations and must sleep on straw, on the floor of the temple; almost 80% of all the people are still sleeping there, they cannot find quarters. As for food, everything is available in abundance, but appallingly expensive, and each of us had only 40 złoty, from which we still had to pay 10 złoty per person as a "head tax," so only 30 złoty remained. A loaf of bread that looks like a brick costs 3 złoty, a liter of milk 1.10, sugar is exorbitant, flour is unobtainable. A kilogram of potatoes costs 0.30 złoty [30 Groschen].

You can imagine what our prospects are, absolutely no opportunities to earn money! I can only tell you, it would've been better if we had all been lined up against the wall in Vienna and shot. It would have been a fine death, but we must die in a more miserable manner. I can tell you one thing, though, as poor as these people are here, they've looked after us in such a touching way and are so obliging and good and helpful that all the Jews of Vienna are no match for these Polish Jews. The little that they have they want to share with us. For example, I want to tell you that the family with whom we're living consists of 6 family members and has three beds. Of these three beds, they gave us one, two girls have a makeshift bed on the ground, and the parents sleep in the remaining two beds with the other two children. What Viennese Jew would give up his bed for other people! Though poor and dirty, the people here are so beautiful in their genuineness. I can tell you that when I arrived, my mind almost failed me. Till this day, I still can't think straight. I do not know what all this will come to and how it will end. Everything is so incredibly expensive, and we have nothing.

With the money we have, we can live a week at most, and then we can flat out starve to death. We still have not received our suitcases; we'll get them only after the head tax of 1,000 złoty, which the Jews who've come here must pay, has been collected. You do not realize until you get here how well we fared before. Just now we're hearing that, starting tomorrow, we all have to wear armbands with the Star of David. We are in such a desperate state that we don't know at all what to do and profoundly regret that we didn't already put an end to this life at home. [. . .]

In this desolate environment, the newcomers could retain few elements of the lifestyle they had been used to in Vienna until impoverishment, disease, and desperation took their toll. The photograph that follows shows some of the arrivals from the Austrian metropolis once they had settled among local Jews in an area that in March 1941 became part of the newly created Opole ghetto. The armbands worn around the right arms of the adults are visible (the band on the man in the front row shows a Star of David). The elegant, almost festive attire of the elderly couple in the front clashes with the threadbare clothing of many others in the picture, as well as with the abject bleakness of their surroundings. As with most photographs that survived the war, we can only speculate about the reasons why someone—in all likelihood not a German, but a Jewish photographer or a friendly Pole—took the picture. Was it meant to be a memento, kept by its subjects for the time after the war, or a greeting to faraway friends, tucked into a letter? What survives is a portrait of Jews from vastly different backgrounds and pasts, forced to share a highly challenging present.

DOCUMENT 1-2: Group portrait of a family of Viennese Jews outside their living quarters in the ghetto of Opole, Lublin district, Generalgouvernement, no date (ca. mid-1941), USHMMPA WS# 18624.

Jews left behind in Vienna heard enough about the fate of those deported to "the East" to intensify their already frantic search for ways to escape the Reich. Once they had managed to overcome one of the many hurdles on the path to emigration, another one invariably lay in wait around the corner. One day before her deportation summons arrived, **Mignon Langnas**, who worked as a nurse in a Jewish hospital in Vienna, wrote to her husband Leon—"my most beloved!"—in

New York, desperately asking whether he had gone mad not to have arranged for boat tickets to the United States for her parents and herself when all other details seemed settled. A unique chance to get out, perhaps the last, appears to have been lost.[10] The next day, Mignon, signing with her Polish nickname, appealed to the Viennese Jewish community to forestall her imminent deportation so she could join Leon and their two children on American shores.

DOCUMENT 1-3: **Letter from Mignon Langnas to Josef Löwenherz,[11] Vienna, March 5, 1941, in Elisabeth Fraller and George Langnas, eds.,** *Mignon. Tagebücher und Briefe einer jüdischen Krankenschwester in Wien 1938–1949* **(Innsbruck: StudienVerlag, 2010), 139–40 (translated from German).**

Most Honorable Executive Director!

I just came from Mr. Breuer[12] and could not get any information, except that he regrets not to be able to help me further.

Herr Doctor, what will now happen?

Is there no possibility that I can be helped? I ask you this question with the hope that it will touch your conscience, honorable Executive Director, the highest authority to whom a human being can appeal. Believe me, Herr Doctor, it is not that I fear the discomfort of being evacuated [*Unbehaglichkeit einer Evakuierung*], but I am possessed by the pointless and incomprehensible thought that at this very moment, when I am at the threshold of the highest fulfillment of happiness, I will again

---

10. Letter from Mignon Langnas, Vienna, to Leon Langnas, New York City, March 4, 1941. Elisabeth Fraller and George Langnas, eds., *Mignon. Tagebücher und Briefe einer jüdischen Krankenschwester in Wien 1938–1949* (Innsbruck: StudienVerlag, 2010), 138.

11. Josef Löwenherz (1884–1960), a lawyer from Galicia, was elected leader of the Viennese Jewish community in 1937. He presided over the organization throughout Hitler's reign over Austria. Immediately after the liberation of Vienna, the Red Army arrested Löwenherz and deported him to Czechoslovakia on charges of Nazi collaboration. Löwenherz cleared his name before a special committee in London, after which he immigrated to the United States. Renate Evers, "Guide to the Papers of Joseph Löwenherz," Leo Baeck Institute, http://findingaids.cjh.org/?pID=121462#a18 (accessed March 16, 2012); "Lowenherz Cleared by Investigating Committee; Conduct Found 'Beyond Reproach,'" *Jewish Telegraphic Agency*, September 24, 1946.

12. Erich Breuer (1901–?), employee of the emigration department of the Jewish Community Vienna, he survived the war and in 1946 lived in Vienna. Israelitische Kultusgemeinde Wien, *Liste der in Wien Lebenden Glaubensjuden* (Vienna: Norbertus-Druck, 1946).

be torn apart from my husband and my little children, God knows for how long!

I wait every day to be summoned to Castellezgasse (I came by the Prinz-Eugenstr. most recently on February 19).[13] Once it [the summons] has reached me, all help will be too late: of what use will the tormenting thought of having missed a chance be then?

I implore you, Herr Doctor, I implore you desperately as only a mother who longs after her children can: help me if it is in your power!

Most respectfully,
Mamcze Langnas

Löwenherz did indeed ask his staff to grant Mignon Langnas a deferral. Although she and her father avoided deportation, they also failed to get another opportunity to escape abroad during the war.[14]

Mignon's employment at a Jewish hospital—a job she chose—did not resemble the typical regimen that now determined the daily life of Jews in the Reich. Since the aftermath of "***Kristallnacht***," Jewish adults in Germany had been subjected to forced labor. By the beginning of 1941, the number encompassed almost fifty thousand people out of a population of less than two hundred thousand.[15] But it was in German-dominated Poland that it became most starkly apparent what work organized by the regime in the context of "managing the Jewish problem" meant. Initially, as **Szmul Zygielbojm** put it in late 1939, "Jews were kidnapped from the streets the way dogcatchers catch dogs" and forced by Germans to perform backbreaking and humiliating tasks.[16] Over time, German bureaucrats established a system of less erratic, yet often equally brutal, exploitation in ghettos and camps. There, conditions for the Jewish laborers varied greatly according to region, place, the kind of work assigned, and the attitude of camp administrators and guards. In Łódź, in early 1941, seven thousand Polish Jews volunteered for labor in Germany in the hope of escaping

---

13. Prinz-Eugen-Strasse 20-22 was the address of the **Gestapo**-run "Zentralstelle für jüdische Auswanderung" ("Central Office for Jewish Emigration"), housed in the Palais Rothschild in Vienna.

14. Mignon took care of her mother, Charlotte Rottenberg (née Scheindel; 1872–1940), and her father, Moses Rottenberg (1866–1943); both of her parents died in Vienna.

15. Wolf Gruner, *Jewish Forced Labor under the Nazis: Economic Needs and Racial Aims, 1938–1944* (New York: Cambridge University Press in association with the USHMM, 2006), 128.

16. Szmul Zygielbojm, "Kidnapping for Labor," quoted from Garbarini et al., *Jewish Responses to Persecution*, 380.

the starvation raging in the ghetto. The letters they sent home did indeed, as seventeen-year-old Dawid Sierakowiak noted in his diary, "promise a degree of satisfaction no longer known in the ghetto: 'We can eat, eat, and eat again.'"[17] Those were exceptional cases. In one way or another, the following account by Moses Sufrin depicts the experiences shared by many Jewish forced laborers, primarily men.[18] After describing earlier abuse he suffered at the hands of the Germans and his experiences working on road construction projects, Sufrin told Swiss authorities the following.

DOCUMENT 1-4: **Account by Moses Sufrin, Switzerland, of his experiences in forced labor camps near Sanok, Kraków district, Generalgouvernement, written in early 1943, USHMMA RG 68.045M (WJC Geneva), reel 2, file 6014 (translated from French).**

I worked in the camps in 1939 and 1940. In 1941, I was able to obtain a medical certificate declaring me unfit for work and I was released from the camp. But a few days later an ordinance appeared declaring that all the medical certificates were no longer valid and that we had to return to the camp. The same night, the Polish police came looking for me at the house and I was once again taken to the camp.

The following night I consulted three comrades. Even at this time, there was already talk of extermination camps and we were afraid that that was what was in store for us. So we decided to flee. I was able to hide in the home of a Pole whom I knew. The next day, I learned that the Gestapo was looking for us and had demanded that the Jewish community give us up. They also approached our parents and said that the gravest dangers threatened all the Jews if we wouldn't give ourselves up. Two out of our four broke down and turned themselves in. A little later, I, fearing for my family, turned myself in too. My return went unnoticed. All of a sudden I saw my comrades, nearly lifeless, being carried on stretchers. They

17. Diary entry for April 16, 1941, quoted from Gruner, *Jewish Forced Labor*, 200–1. Dawid Sierakowiak (1924–1943) was born and attended school in Łódź. In the ghetto, he kept a detailed diary, of which five notebooks survived the war. He died on August 18, 1943, apparently of tuberculosis. See Alan Adelson, ed., *The Diary of Dawid Sierakowiak: Five Notebooks from the Łódź Ghetto* (New York: Oxford University Press, 1996).

18. Moses Sufrin (1918–1991), born in Bukowsko, Poland (near Sanok), managed to escape with his brother Hersch and two other Jews by train to Switzerland in early 1943, where he was interrogated by the Swiss police. In 1948 he immigrated to the United States, where he was known as Maurice Sufrin. See USHMMA RG 58.001M (Swiss Federal Archive), reel 185 (dossier 08364).

were horribly bruised and one could easily picture the blows they must have received. A Polish Aryan suggested I flee, but I took my chances and stayed.

I went back into the barracks where my two colleagues were lying, passed out.

At that moment, several Gestapo agents, accompanied by the technical head of the camp, entered.

The latter demanded from those who were present: do you know why they are sleeping? No one answered. He then said with unbelievable cynicism: they walked a great deal today and they're tired, that's why they're sleeping.

An agent demanded from someone: you believe him, right? The other answered with a voice choked with fear and rage: yes, I believe him.

But the agent did not find that he answered correctly enough and slapped him, commanding him to respond more correctly. He yelled: Yes, yes, it's true, I believe it! And I had the impression that he was about to die of fright. The Gestapo, satisfied, left. None of the officials up to this point had noticed my return.

The next day during the distribution of bread I was probably recognized because, as I was heading off to work, the technical head stopped me and led me into the barracks.

Why did you leave the camp?

I started to feel a chill run down my spine, but I kept my cool. I responded calmly:

I was cold at night and I was at my house looking for a blanket.

For the whole response I received two extremely violent slaps, and I was taken into a car to be brought to the Gestapo in Sanok.

There, it was again the same question followed by the same response.

I received a punch to the jaw that sent me tumbling to the ground. As I was getting up, the officer asked me whether I wanted to return to the camp and whether I could go there alone without being accompanied. Completely overjoyed to get off so lightly, I did not hesitate to answer in the affirmative. At that moment, the policemen who were present hurled themselves at me with their truncheons and the dance began.

I was manhandled so badly that it was absolutely impossible for me to sit or lie down.

The one who seemed to be the boss then asked whether I felt sick. I knew what that was supposed to mean and I hastened to tell him that I felt very good, despite the pain that was torturing me. Because it was evening and Jews do not have the right to go out without a permit, I was given one that I was supposed to hand in upon my arrival at the camp.

I walked all night and I arrived at 7 a.m. The director of the camp, a German, was very touched to see me again and was truly happy that I got out of it ok.

Death by abuse or as a consequence of disease and destitution were not the only threats to Jews in occupied Poland and in the Reich proper. Despite the veil of secrecy with which German officials had tried to camouflage the fatal effects of "Aktion T-4," in early 1941 rumors spread through the besieged Jewish communities in the Reich. Faithful diarists such as **Willy Cohn** in the Silesian city of Breslau recorded that mental patients in German asylums were being killed, thus indicating how accurate the rumor mills had become.[19] Concerned relatives of institutionalized patients desperately tried to obtain information about their loved ones.

Frieda Naumann, also of Breslau, had suffered from psychological problems for years before she was admitted to a mental hospital in the area. Her husband Kurt worked as the local representative for the **Reichsvereinigung** in that city, but was hoping to join his daughter, son-in-law, and two grandchildren in the United States. It remains unclear what, if anything, he knew about the T-4 murders. In his letters across the Atlantic, Naumann generally tried to steer clear of unsettling topics and sound upbeat, especially regarding the fate of his wife, Frieda ("Mutti"). Yet the news he was forced to convey in 1941 sorely tested this strategy.

DOCUMENT 1-5: **Letters from Kurt Naumann, Breslau, Germany, to Ilse and Marcel Sternberger in New York, December 24, 1940, and March 2, 1941, USHMMA Acc. 1999.A.0010 Naumann family papers (translated from German).**

[December 24, 1940]
My dear children!

I want to take advantage of the quiet holiday to write you once again.

I haven't done so for a long time, first, because in general I have little to

---

19. Willy Cohn, diary entries for January 28 and April 1, 1941, translated from Willy Cohn, *Kein Recht, Nirgends. Tagebuch vom Untergang des Breslauer Judentums, 1933–1941*, ed. Norbert Conrads (Cologne: Böhlau Verlag, 2006), 2:896, 921. See also references to the murder of mental patients in Victor Klemperer, *I Will Bear Witness: A Diary of the Nazi Years, 1933–1941* (New York: Random House, 1998), 1:427.

report, but mostly because I have no questions from you to answer, since I haven't received news from you. [. . .]

No word from Mutti. The other day I was informed that she has been moved to another institution [*Anstalt*], but from there she was supposedly transferred elsewhere though I don't know to where. Aunt Else could at least visit her on occasion in Branitz [asylum], but now that will be impossible, also of course for me. It is terribly sad that there is nothing at all I can do for her. She will also feel sad about no one visiting her, because sometimes she clearly perceives her situation, although this condition doesn't last long, which may be a blessing for her. [. . .]

This evening I will most likely spend with my fellow tenants. In this regard I'm really lucky as I always have company when I want it. And as we are keeping ourselves busy reading foreign languages the evenings are always stimulating. [. . .]

[March 2, 1941]

[After conveying thanks for a letter and photos, family trivia, and news of emigration plans by others.] And now to the most painful part of this letter. On February 27, I received the news that Mutti had died of influenza on January 15 in the mental asylum [*Irrenanstalt*] in Chelm [Chełm] near Lublin. The notification was delayed because my correct address could not be found in the files and the letter had been sent to Gross-Strehlitz [Naumann's previous place of residence], from where it was returned as undeliverable.

A sad life has come to its end, sad because Mutti spent so many years of her life in a condition which could not really be called life. Yet she had years of happiness and joy, too, rejoicing in her children, her son-in-law, and was even fortunate enough to meet her grandson. Still, what is all this compared to the long years she had to spend far from home in the care of others, even if this care in general might have been good. You know she was much attached to you and if on occasion she wasn't very nice, this resulted not from her will but from her disease. Now it's over for her and she has no pain, while we are left with the bitter feeling that she is no longer on this earth and that there is no hope left for her recovery or return, which we inwardly always maintained, even if we ourselves did not really believe in it. Although she had been separated from me for many years, her death still creates a void I cannot fill. Once you are old you feel this more strongly. You are young and still have hopes and dreams in life. Do not feel too sad. Retain a loving memory of her, remembering her as she once was. Back then she was still very approachable and nice.

With the most affectionate greetings and kisses to all of you

Your father

The truth about his wife's death may already have dawned on Naumann by that time; two weeks later, he wrote to his family again, informing them that no news had come about "Mutti's death, etc." and that he did not expect any further word.[20] Perhaps he had heard rumors similar to the ones recorded by Willy Cohn about this alleged asylum in Chełm in the Lublin district of the Generalgouvernement and that it served as a cover address for patients who had in fact been killed elsewhere.[21] Perhaps he hoped that his family, safely settled in New York, had learned to read between the lines, both of the officially worded notifications produced by cynical Nazi authorities and his own letters from a distant world and uncertain time. We can find clues about the welfare and fate of institutionalized Jewish patients buried even in the cryptic memos of German Jewish officials, written fully cognizant of the fact that the Gestapo could confiscate the records at any time and use them to terrorize those suspected of being critical of the regime or of oppositional behavior. Here, a file note by German Jews' central wartime organization, the Reichsvereinigung, hints at the financial aspects of these patients' treatment in the Generalgouvernement.

DOCUMENT 1-6: **File note by Reichsvereinigung, Welfare Department (Conrad Cohn),[22] Berlin, regarding costs for Jewish inmates of the Chełm mental institution, May 6, 1941, USHMMA RG 14.003M*1 (BAB R 8150), P75C Re1 (translated from German).**

Subject: Cost of care for Jewish mental patients in the Cholm [Chełm] asylum, Lublin (Generalgouvernement)

---

20. Letter from Kurt Naumann, Breslau, to Ilse and Marcel Sternberger in New York, March 16, 1941, USHMMA Acc. 1999.A.0010. Kurt Naumann was deported to his death on August 27, 1942.

21. Henry Friedlander, *The Origins of Nazi Genocide: From Euthanasia to the Final Solution* (Chapel Hill: University of North Carolina Press, 1995), 277–81; Susan Bachrach and Dieter Kuntz, eds., *Deadly Medicine: Creating the Master Race* (Washington, DC: USHMM, 2004), 171–76.

22. Conrad Cohn (1901–1942?) was a former lawyer who oversaw much of the Reichsvereinigung's relief program and vocational training for prospective émigrés. Arrested in the summer of 1942, he died in the Mauthausen concentration camp. See Ernst Lowenthal, ed., *Bewährung im Untergang. Ein Gedenkbuch* (Stuttgart: Deutsche Verlags-Anstalt, 1965), 36–37.

Last year, at the direction of central authorities, many Jewish mental patients were moved from public hospitals and nursing homes in Germany proper [*Altreich*] to institutions in the Generalgouvernement, the majority apparently to the mental institution Cholm. A considerable number of those patients have since died.

Initially we were not charged care and funeral costs from the time of the transfer. Only in recent weeks—since March 1941—have several district offices and [Jewish] communities received bills from the Cholm asylum. The mental institution Cholm demands care costs of 3 RM per day and funeral costs of 65 RM [per person]. To date, bills totaling approximately 110,000 RM have been submitted (see our circular dated March 27, 1941—41/101/150—zu II).

We request a decision about whether we are to pay for the costs of institutional care in the Generalgouvernement. One could argue against such payment that our jurisdiction is limited to the Altreich, including the Sudetenland,[23] and that individuals no longer residing or having their regular abode in our area of jurisdiction cease, upon their date of transfer, to be our members and thus are no longer in our care. Should it be decided that we have to bear these costs, this would mean a heavy financial burden, especially considering that the bills received represent only the smaller portion of the total number of cases.

Conrad Cohn was apparently not aware that since late March 1941 the Reichsvereinigung had been charged by the **RSHA** under **Reinhard Heydrich** for the costs of Jewish mental patients transferred to Chełm. A later memo documents that bills for 464 people amounting to almost 150,000 **Reichsmark** had accrued, including sixty-four persons of unknown, perhaps even non-Jewish, identity. Of the overall figure, 150 persons had already died.[24] In these cases, systematic robbery went hand in hand with organized murder, thus foreshadowing a new pattern that was to become a standard feature of German conduct after the beginning of the war against the Soviet Union.

Kurt Naumann's fleeting reference to his "luck" with his fellow tenants at his new Breslau address points to a development in German anti-Jewish policy that had gathered pace since the beginning of the war and in retrospect seems to be a prelude to deportation. By 1941, the displacement of Jews within

23. Western part of interwar Czechoslovakia annexed by Germany in September 1938.

24. Memo from Conrad Cohn to Dr. Eppstein, July 22, 1941, USHMMA RG 14.003M*1 (BAB R 8150).

Germany from their homes had led to conditions that vaguely resembled some of the features of east European ghettos, albeit without the same degree of visibility. In many German cities, Jews were relocated into specially designated "Jew houses" (*Judenhäuser*). The desire of local authorities to administer and control an unwanted minority lay behind these measures, as did the increasing scarcity of habitable urban living space caused by Allied bombing. Rather than being cordoned off with ghetto walls and fences, "Jew houses" in Germany were marked using signs tacked up next to the nameplates and doorbells in apartment buildings.[25] Despite the fact that conditions were much more tolerable in a *Judenhaus* in the Reich than in ghettos in "the East," the people uprooted from their old homes suffered from the effects of displacement and overcrowding, and were unable to bring more than a few fragments of their erstwhile belongings with them. Over the course of several weeks beginning in late November 1941, **Erich Langer**, a former judge and skilled musician with Zionist leanings from Essen, drafted a lengthy letter to his son abroad. In it he included an account of what he called, with some understatement, his long-standing "housing issue."

DOCUMENT 1-7: **Unsent letter from Erich Langer, Essen, Germany, to his son Klaus, Palestine, January 12, 1942, USHMMA Acc. 1994.A.322 Yakob Langer collection (translated from German).**

My dear, beloved boy! [. . .] Now I want to tell you about our housing issue [*Wohnungsangelegenheit*]. Since approximately July 1941, Gestapo and Order Police [Schutzpolizei] officers have come repeatedly to look at our apartment [Moorenstrasse 14 in Essen]. Because it apparently did not quite appeal to anyone, we were able to continue living there. Finally, in December, a Gestapo official told me that we [Langer and his mother-in-law] would have to vacate the apartment by January 1; at the same time, the prospect of a suitable replacement apartment was held out to me. We soon found quite a nice apartment in a Jewish building, Krawehlstrasse 4, 2nd floor. Here we have two nice rooms and quite a cozy kitchen. One room, the larger one, is furnished with our dining room furniture; Grandma sleeps

25. On "Jew houses" in Germany, see Marion A. Kaplan, *Between Dignity and Despair: Jewish Life in Nazi Germany* (New York: Oxford University Press, 1998), 154–56; "Judenhäuser in Germany," in *The Yad Vashem Encyclopedia of the Ghettos during the Holocaust*, ed. Guy Miron and Shlomit Shulhani (Jerusalem: Yad Vashem, 2009), 2:999–1001.

here. I have arranged a smaller room for myself as a study, and I will be sleeping here on our couch. But for now, because the study has no stove, I sleep in the eat-in kitchen, which is quite snug and comfortable. I sold our grand piano to our landlady on Moorenstrasse, Frau Willich, for 1,350 RM. I greatly regretted that I could not keep it for you, but because our entire existence is so uncertain now and there wouldn't have been any place for it here either, I thought this was the only right step. I have totally given up playing music. Although I had started practicing piano again after Mama's death, I lost all desire to do so once the transports began. Even though I'm not making music anymore, I'm still full of music inside, because all the music I heard and created myself for 50 years continues to live in me and fulfills me. We feel quite comfortable in the new apartment. The many Jewish residents in our building are friendly and helpful and really stick together. They get together in someone's apartment several times a week in the evening. Personally, I do not find these gatherings very pleasurable because the people have absolutely no intellectual interests and occupy their time with nothing but gossiping. To avoid secluding myself, I take part in the gatherings from time to time, but not too often. [. . .]

IN WESTERN EUROPE

After the beginning of the war, German expansion had caught up with many Jews who had managed to escape from Nazi rule in time and falsely believed themselves to be safe.[26] Their interactions with the outside world now atrophied further, often leaving only small circles of acquaintances from which to garner news and feed hope. In early April 1940 the Wehrmacht had invaded Norway, where Austrian-born **Ruth Maier** was among the 300 refugees in a country with a total Jewish population of only 1,800. They knew that the enemy had arrived on their doorstep, with as yet unknown consequences. Maier fell into a depression, and after a breakdown, she ended up in a mental clinic for some weeks in early 1941. There she met a woman who, though troubled herself, seemed much better equipped to confront the present circumstances than Ruth.

---

26. The number of Jews who had emigrated from Germany since 1933 and found themselves in countries occupied by Germany during the war is estimated at thirty thousand, roughly 10 percent of the total number of émigrés from the Reich. See Avraham Barkai and Paul Mendes-Flohr, *Deutsch-Jüdische Geschichte der Neuzeit, Bd. IV: Aufbruch und Zerstörung 1918–1945* (Munich: Verlag C. H. Beck, 1997), 226–27.

DOCUMENT 1-8: Ruth Maier, Oslo, German-occupied Norway, diary entry for March 3, 1941, in Ruth Maier, *"Das Leben könnte gut sein": Tagebücher 1933 bis 1942*, ed. Jan Erik Vold (Stuttgart: DVA, 2008), 369–70 (translated from German).

Monday, March 3, 1941, Ullevål Hospital

There's now a Jewish woman on the ward. She's forty-three, but looks much older. Her face is thin, emaciated, it's practically just bones. She is so strong and strident, with a protruding nose and shining, deep-set eyes. They remind me of the eyes of children who already know what "life" means. When she talks about her illness she looks as if she has suffered a great injustice.

Her eyes burn and she nods her head as if she were certain that all the rest of us feel the same way as her. All of a sudden a triumphant smile comes over her face.

We talk together. She speaks Yiddish. As her Norwegian is very poor, I ask her where she came from. She answers with a beaming smile, "But I'm Jewish!"

She holds my hand in hers, explores my features with her gaze, as if she were looking for Jewish signs in my face.

For her it's a matter of course that Jews can only feel comfortable in the company of other Jews, can only have Jewish friends.

"Do you have any friends?"

"Yes."

"Jews?"

"No."

"What do you mean 'No'? I don't understand."

When she learns that I live with "Christians" she shakes her head in astonishment.

"I don't understand. They're not Jews but they feed you, let you live with them. No! You have to go to the Jewish community. You must tell them that you don't have any parents, that you're alone in Oslo and ask them who you can live with who's Jewish. After all, it's better to live with Jews than Christians" [. . .]

Not only in Norway, but in all western countries directly or indirectly dominated by Nazi Germany, attitudes of non-Jews toward their Jewish neighbors mattered, since German authorities were much more sensitive to those countries' interests regarding the "Jewish question" than in eastern Europe.[27] The degree to which the elites and majority populations in these countries considered this question pressing differed greatly. In early 1941 in France with its altogether roughly 350,000 Jews, more than half of them foreign-born, the inclination to follow the German model was particularly strong. In the unoccupied south, **Vichy** authorities were preparing to tighten their anti-Jewish laws—resulting in the second *Statut des Juifs*, enacted in early June 1941—and specifically targeting foreign Jews, who formed the overwhelming majority of the internment camp population in the country.[28] Growing outside pressure and established traditions widened the gulf between French Jews—"*israélites*," some of whom traced their citizenship back to the birth of the French state in 1789—and immigrant or refugee Jews, or "*juives*," some of whom may have immigrated to France already before World War I, but who, along with their descendants, were widely considered "foreign," despite often holding French citizenship, by both non-Jews and "*israélites*."[29] In mid-March 1941, **Lucien Dreyfus**, who had escaped his home in the German-French border province Alsace and now lived in Nice with his wife Marthe, reflected in his diary on his own situation and the course of history.

DOCUMENT 1-9: **Lucien Dreyfus, Nice, Vichy France, diary entry for March 16, 1941, USHMMA RG 10.144 Lucien Dreyfus collection (translated from French).**

Glorious Sunday, glorious day. Marthe brings back a forest of mimosas from the market for one franc. What a country! The little one [his granddaughter Monique] is recovering so rapidly that what we called her operation can't be anything serious. She squeals and insists on playing ball with me from her bed. Why does this day, which makes me appear outwardly

---

27. As Mark Mazower, *Hitler's Empire: Nazi Rule in Occupied Europe* (London: Allen Lane, 2008), 111, puts it, "The sheer variety of [German] occupation regimes established in 1940 indicated Hitler's uncertainty about where they fit within his larger scheme, with its predominantly eastern orientation." For a brief description of the characteristics of German occupation rule in western Europe, see ibid., 103–11.

28. See Saul Friedländer, *Nazi Germany and the Jews:* (vol. 2) *The Years of Extermination, 1939–1945* (New York: HarperCollins, 2007), 169–78.

29. On the distinction between "*israélites*" and "*juives*," see Renée Poznanski, *Jews in France during World War II* (Hanover, NH: University Press of New England for Brandeis University Press in association with the USHMM, 2001).

a happy man, suggest to me precisely the idea of confiding to this journal my apprehensions, which are, rather, logical convictions coming from the depths of my Jewish soul?

Since 1880, when the era of pogroms began, the European bourgeoisie has tolerated antisemitism. Jews in western countries thought they were safe behind the rampart of laws, which, however, did not express the popular will but were instead measures of an ideological sort adopted by progressive governments. At first the idea was to remedy the ills that the Jews of eastern Europe were suffering, by providing material aid in a vast charitable undertaking. Herzl clearly perceived that this approach was inadequate and proposed instead emigration to an independent state, which had to be founded.[30] But he was misunderstood, and people scornfully declined to follow him. The inevitable had to happen. Nazi propaganda took advantage of the miseries of the postwar period to introduce itself into sectors that were previously closed to anti-Jewish hatred, and the success of the owner of Berchtesgaden[31] can be explained only by the complicity of all the European middle classes, which shared his dislikes or exploited them. The end of this movement will be the elimination of Jews from this continent. Is there a religious interpretation of the dethroning of the liberal Jew, who has played his role for one hundred years in de-Judaizing the traditional life of his ancestors?

These Jews, without always admitting it to themselves, wanted to disappear among the nations without considering those nations' inclinations, which were often opposed, very rarely identical, to the Jews' intimate wishes. They were no longer believers, and they hoped that the others would approve of their defection. Now they find no way to go back. The lesson of the war does not change their mentality. This generation, like that of the Desert,[32] is doomed to disappear. It persists in its obstinacy. Without being a prophet, I would not be surprised if the survivors find that we were unworthy to continue an existence that was inconsistent with the elements of Judaism and that Providence has shown, in the manner that pleases it, that the European Jews did not deserve to be the witnesses of divine redemption [*geula*].

---

30. Theodor Herzl (1860–1904), lawyer, journalist, and one of the founding fathers of Zionism.

31. Reference to Hitler's alpine retreat at Obersalzberg.

32. Dreyfus refers here to the biblical exodus of the Israelites from Egypt; led by Moses, they wandered for forty years in the desert in search of the promised land.

Dreyfus's conviction that French Jews were strangers in their non-Jewish environment did not represent prevailing opinion. Looking back, the majority of Jews felt a keen sense of belonging to the French nation, with its strong Enlightenment tradition. In fact, it was this traditional image of an inclusive "*grande nation*" that Jews could still tap when attempting to orient themselves in both the present and an unforetold future. From this perspective, the Vichy regime seemed like an aberration, a departure from the successful path of toleration and integration for Jews, even if recent events pointed to an ever more visible undercurrent of race hatred and segregation.[33] At a moment when the opportunities to articulate this position publicly had closed down in France itself, René Cassin—legal thinker, leader in the French World War I veterans' movement, and prominent in the French opposition in exile[34]—expressed support for a statement according to which "no laws concerning Jews were recognized by the Free French Movement and that with the victory of the Allies, equal rights for Jews will be reestablished."[35] In April 1941, his voice, directed to the "*israélites*," reached across the Channel from London to German-dominated France.

DOCUMENT 1-10: **BBC radio address by René Cassin to the "Israelites of France," April 1941, in René Cassin, Les hommes partis de rien. Le réveil de la France abattue (1940–41) (Paris: Plon, 1975), 480–81 (translated from French).**

Easter week is not complete without making a French voice heard and giving free public expression of feelings of loyalty to poor France, and also affording you some comfort.

That voice comes from neither a rabbi nor a chaplain in de Gaulle's army, nor even someone committed to upholding your rituals. [. . .]

French Israelites, you know that while the French people are not responsible for the enemy's and his collaborators' measures, they affront

33. See Poznanski, *Jews in France during World War II*, p. 1–29.

34. René Cassin (1887–1976) was an eminent French Jewish legal scholar, government administrator, and humanitarian activist who would in 1968 win the Nobel Peace Prize. During World War II Cassin served in different positions with the French government-in-exile; after the war he held a number of offices and from 1946 served on the United Nations Human Rights Commission, contributing to the drafting of the Universal Declaration of Human Rights approved by the General Assembly in December 1948. See Gérard Israël, *René Cassin: 1887–1976, la guerre hors-la-loi. Avec de Gaulle. Les droits de l'homme* (Paris: Desclée de Brouwer, 1990).

35. "Chronicles," *Contemporary Jewish Record* 4, no. 3 (June 1941): 299. See also Renée Poznanski, "Reflections on Jewish Resistance and Jewish Resistants in France," *Jewish Social Studies*, n.s. 2 (autumn 1995), 124–58.

your human dignity more than your interests. But in vain [is the enemy] bent on breaking the union between the spiritual families of France, the most precious of France's strengths. Through gestures of fraternal solidarity our citizens prove they resist this. Reciprocally, your natural loyalty to the *patrie* in these tragic times is a slap against Baudoin[36] and other traitors who dare to claim that "you have not accepted the spiritual and intellectual heritage of France." Jews in the Comtat Venaissin region, the South West, and Paris, Jews from the east who for ten centuries put down roots in France, have impregnated world Judaism with French liberalism and have, like other French people, sent its last five generations [of men] to fight for it, to defend it; you can scorn those accusations—but you also have the Jews of Algeria, Salonika, and from all over the world! The fallen zouaves[37] and Jewish volunteers in the Foreign Legion rise again and for centuries stand guard at Verdun and Carency around the Ile-de-France, which radiated the value of the currency of: liberty, equality, fraternity.

As for the living, they all too well recognize their eternal debt to the French nation and its thinkers. No sacrifice—none—will be too great to pay back a portion of that debt, to help France recover its liberty and its greatness.

At the moment when the German war machine has crushed other nations such as Yugoslavia and Greece, they [the Jews of France] remain faithful to their past and their love for France; evoke the ancient history of the Pharaohs with confidence! When others were also reduced to bondage, your ancestors saw the Red Sea swallow their pursuers, along with their chariots.

These days the same sea has witnessed the victory of British Empire forces, aided by the free French and the people of the Orient.[38] The final challenge of the modern barbarians will mark the resurrection of France and its freedoms.

In Mussolini's Italy, Jews had been stigmatized by the fascist state to a lesser degree and at a later date than in Nazi Germany. Though barred from many professions, attending public schools, or entering into "mixed marriages," most Italian Jewish civilians did not face mortal danger until late into the war, after

---

36. Paul Baudouin (1894–1964), banker, conservative politician with the nationalist Action française, and from June 1940 to January 1941 foreign minister in the Vichy government. After the war he was convicted of collaboration. See Bertram M. Gordon, ed., *Historical Dictionary of World War II France* (Westport, CT: Greenwood Press, 1998).

37. Light infantry regiments of the French army that served in French North Africa.

38. Reference to Italian military setbacks in North Africa and the Balkans.

the German occupation in September 1943.[39] As in Vichy France, the situation was different for those who found themselves in Italy as refugees or were treated as "enemies of the state" by Mussolini's regime; many ended up in a network of internment camps or were otherwise forced to restrict their movements. **Hermann Hakel**, a refugee writer who had fled from Austria in June 1939, was among those interned. His writing from the time reveals a longing to overcome the effects of confinement and boredom he shared with fifty other inmates, Jewish and non-Jewish, in an improvised camp on the grounds of an agricultural school in southern Italy. Rare visits from the outside world raised his hopes and those of his fellow internees, but also underlined the enormous gulf in understanding and expectations that existed between the inhabitants of two distinctly different worlds.

DOCUMENT 1-11: **Hermann Hakel, camp Alberobello near Bari, Italy, diary entry for May 20, 1941, ÖNB 221/04 (translated from German).**

Yesterday was a big day in camp. We were chased from our beds bright and early by the head of the Carabinieri [Italian police] force in full dress uniform. Top-to-bottom cleaning! Everything that was lying and hanging around had to be stowed away, and the floor, tables, and benches had to be washed. Hurry! Hurry! That could mean only a prominent visitor. Exactly the same thing happened in Oliveto [a camp where Hakel had been previously], and at that time Cardinal B. came and gave us splendid presents.

   In fact, as I predicted, toward midday and just as we were involved in a game of nine-pen bowling, a big limousine drives up, and the huge prince of the church and his secretary get out. We step up and wait for the gifts I had publicized. The cardinal says a few words in greeting (this time, far less solemn) and gives each of us a postcard with the photo of His Holiness Pope Pius XII; in addition, everyone gets a sweet treat worth 3 *lire*. The disappointed faces turn in my direction, and I assert for the nth time that in Oliveto, only five months ago, each of us got 30 *lire*, 50 cigarettes, 20 decagrams [7 ounces] of cookies, and 10 decagrams [3.5 ounces] of tea.

---

39. See Joshua D. Zimmerman, ed., *The Jews of Italy under Fascist and Nazi Rule, 1922–1945* (New York: Cambridge University Press, 2005); Renzo De Felice, *The Jews in Fascist Italy: A History* (New York: Enigma Books, 2001); Susan Zuccotti, *The Italians and the Holocaust: Persecution, Rescue, and Survival* (New York: Basic Books, 1987).

Then His Eminence asks to be shown the building. He disregards my room, the first one in the hallway, and enters the second, where the Orthodox Jews are housed. The rivalry interests him. There is also a Torah there. The people wear kippahs. His Eminence asks that he be shown the prayer books and then a passage from the Book of Daniel, which to everyone's amazement he reads aloud, translates, and interprets as proof of the birth of Jesus. It is a long-winded computation, but it adds up! Like a schoolmaster, the great man raises one finger of his heavily beringed hand and says that this, this little calculation, is the only difference between the two religions and that the Jews, as the guardians of the Bible, are owed the gratitude of all Catholics. (A feat of arithmetic as the only proof for the validity of the Catholic religion–!) The poor Orthodox Feintuch is utterly perplexed by this smooth calculation. And when David and his tribe are mentioned, Riebenfeld, a maliciously cunning Pole who also sleeps in the "temple room," pulls out his wallet and displays the photo of his son, who is also named David.

Later, back in the yard, many people cluster around His Eminence's little secretary. They want the Vatican to help their Catholic wives living in Vienna get permission to come here. Obligingly, the stout little monsignor accepts all the scraps of paper with addresses, and by now the gentlemen are at their car (which is being examined in detail by our people). Polite words are spoken once again, the two servants of the Church of Christ wave at us as if we were children, and then, after one hour, it's all over.

Far north of Hakel's confined world, eighteen-year-old **Claartje van Aals**, working as a nurse at a large Jewish mental hospital near the Dutch city of Apeldoorn, was equally struck by the contrast between the narrowness of her daily life and the vast universe outside. In her letters to a close non-Jewish girlfriend, the young woman shared what she was thinking and feeling in a down-to-earth style. Her account underlines the divergent experiences of Jews subjected to the same occupation regime. In January 1941, Jewish men and women in the city of Amsterdam, we learn here, faced tight restrictions on their movement at an earlier juncture than those living in other parts of the occupied country.[40]

---

40. See Friedländer, *Nazi Germany*, 2:178–84; Bob Moore, *Victims and Survivors: The Nazi Persecution of the Jews in the Netherlands, 1940–1945* (London: Arnold, 1997); Dan Michman, *The Emergence of Jewish Ghettos during the Holocaust* (New York: Cambridge University Press, 2011), 122–44.

DOCUMENT 1-12: **Letter from Klara (Claartje) van Aals, Apeldoorn, German-occupied Netherlands, to Aagje Kaagman, Utrecht, January 22, 1941, in** *Als ik wil kan ik duiken . . . : Brieven van Claartje van Aals, verpleegster in de joods psychiatrische inrichting Het Apeldoornsche Bosch, 1940–1943*, **ed. Suzette Wyers (Amsterdam: T. Rap, 1995), 39 (translated from Dutch).**

I just came home after a cultural [documentary] film evening about Bali.[41] In a word, beautiful! It was a movie with sound, nice, eh? If Head Nurse Terwiel knew that I was writing a letter, she'd have triplets from the shock.

Before the movie about Bali I had a serious conversation with the male nurse who is engaged: Jo de Vries. It was terrific. We both were as red as beets. That's how excited we were. That is to say, we talked about the future. How it looks to us at the moment. A whole hour. I believe that if we weren't forced to leave, we'd still be talking. Something like that does you a lot of good.

Things are very busy for me right now. There are nine sick patients. Most of them are very seriously ill. They have to be looked after constantly. [. . .] One patient has an infection in her leg and that is very contagious. I therefore smell of Lysol [a common disinfectant] for hours. I spend the whole day parading around with bedpans. Seems funny, but I am now learning the basics of nursing. I spent a half hour mopping the toilet because there was a leak. Finished the bathroom and scrubbed the bath with brown sand. That's how you get it to be white. With brown sand! Totally idiotic! [. . .]

We had an evening of dancing last week. I wrote to you that I danced with one male nurse almost the entire evening. They asked me if I went out with him. I thought that I'd die from laughing and said in all seriousness: Yes! They are raving mad around here. I don't see much difference between patients and personnel. [. . .]

It's now Friday evening. My sister wrote that in Amsterdam Jews aren't allowed in cafés. You should come to Apeldoorn quickly because then we'll still be able to enjoy going out. In a while that will of course no longer be possible. My sister also wrote that in Amsterdam there is hardly any underwear to be had anymore. *Mokum* isn't *Mokum* any longer.[42]

---

41. Indonesian island under Dutch colonial rule until 1949.

42. *Mokum* is the Dutch Jewish pronunciation of the Hebrew *makom*, literally, "place." Dutch Jews referred to Amsterdam as *Mokum*.

Early in 1941 in the context of upheaval in Amsterdam, German administrators in the Netherlands installed a **Jewish Council** (*Joodse Raad*) headed by Abraham Asscher and David Cohen, who had been active in Jewish relief work in the city before.[43] Created to help organize and implement occupation policies while struggling to meet the needs and expectations of their Jewish constituents, the Council would face a similar dilemma regarding how far to take their compliance and cooperation as the *Judenräte* in the ghettos of eastern Europe. As violent anti-Jewish actions by Dutch Nazis triggered expressions of public discontent, the Germans seized the opportunity to tighten the noose around the community. In The Hague, **Gabriel Italie**, a lyceum teacher, viewed these dramatic events of February 1941 as the manifestation of a long-held Nazi plan.

DOCUMENT 1-13: **Gabriel Italie, The Hague, German-occupied Netherlands, diary entries for February 1941, in** *Het oorlogsdagboek van dr. G. Italie. Den Haag, Barneveld, Westerbork, Theresienstadt, Den Haag 1940–1945*, **ed. Wally M. de Lang (Amsterdam: Contact, 2009), 128–32 (translated from Dutch).**

February 13, 1941
[. . .]
There have been riots in Amsterdam at the beginning of the week. According to an inane false newspaper account young Jewish elements bearing all sorts of weapons attacked NSB[44] members and destroyed the stores of such people in the Jewish neighborhood. Traffic in and out of the Jewish neighborhood was therefore first blocked and has now proceeded to allowing the departure of non-Jews from the Jewish neighborhood. Thus, the creation of a ghetto! Furthermore a "Jewish Council" has been formed under the leadership of Asscher and Prof. Cohen, who provided the municipal authorities with certain guarantees of the safety of

43. Abraham Asscher (1880–1950) was a Dutch businessman who, with David Cohen (1882–1967), cochaired the Amsterdam Jewish Council during World War II. Before the war, Cohen, a well-known academic and Zionist, had led the Committee for Jewish Refugees, which was carried over in substantive ways to the Jewish Council of Amsterdam, established in February 1941 at the behest of German occupation authorities in the Netherlands. See Dan Michman, "The Uniqueness of the Joodse Raad in the Western European Context," in *Dutch Jewish History*, ed. Jozeph Michman (Jerusalem: Hebrew University of Jerusalem, 1993), 3:371–80; Moore, *Victims and Survivors*, 62–73, on the creation of the Jewish Council. For a comparative analysis, see Pim Griffioen and Ron Zeller, *Jodenvervolging in Nederland, Frankrijk en België 1940–1945. Overeenkomsten, verschillen, oorzaken* (Amsterdam: Uitgeverij Boom, 2011).

44. Nationaal Socialistische Beweging (NSB), the Dutch Nazi party. See Philip Morgan, *Fascism in Europe, 1919–1945* (New York: Routledge, 2003), 97–101.

the Jewish neighborhood. The plan to create a ghetto certainly had been made a long time earlier, already before the invasion of The Netherlands, but without some, however flimsy and however nauseating and perfidious a pretext, they seemed reluctant to carry it out.

[. . .]

February 15, 1941

According to what I hear, Jews in Amsterdam really let loose during the uprising in Amsterdam. A "W.A. man"[45] succumbed to his wounds. I don't wish for Jewish responsibility in the case. But the entire story is a convenient excuse to declare that the Jewish question has become "acute" and will therefore require a radical solution. As far as Jewish students are concerned, it has now been determined that they can continue their current studies, but that they will have to apply for any further course of study. Anyway, Paul [his son] is safe until summer.[46]

[. . .]

February 19, 1941

[. . .] Last Shabbat attendance in the Wagenstraat synagogue was sparse; people are still too afraid. Among those present was Mr. Visser[47] (who otherwise is never there) all dressed up in a top hat!

February 25, 1941

[. . .] In Amsterdam on Shabbat there were again some disturbances in the Jewish neighborhood in which Germans participated as well; many Jews were picked up by Germans and taken to an undetermined location (it seems that something similar happened in The Hague as well). A sort of general strike has broken out in Amsterdam, probably in protest against such misdeeds. The Germans who have no concept of spontaneous actions, will certainly consider it an act of organized resistance (*"merkwür-dig: es gibt keine Organisation und immer klappt's"*[48] is a known expression)

---

45. Member of the NSB's military wing.

46. Paul Italie (1922–1942) was a student during the war. He was arrested in Belgium and sent from the Malines camp in Belgium to **Auschwitz** on August 25, 1942, where he was murdered. See *USHMM ITS Collection Data Base Central Name Index.*

47. Reference to Lodewijk Ernst Visser (1871–1942), a deposed member of the Netherlands High Council who was very active in Jewish causes, but not religious. Visser died shortly after the event described.

48. German, "strange: there is no organization and every time it works out."

and seek out leaders, meaning, I fear, that above all there will be a hunt for Jews.

A short time ago in Leiden a manifesto was glued to the wall by rebelling students, who demanded the opening of the university without restrictions (on Jews). It probably will not be of much help.

[. . .]

February 26, 1941

Received a letter today from Arthur Bondi[49] in America with information about possible immigration for us and the children.

The greatest sensation was and is the strike in Amsterdam, which is now over and which cannot be called general, but did include a number of enterprises (like the tram) and factories. It was a protest about treatment and mistreatment of Jews [note in the original: There is more to it; it also appears that the Germans wanted to compel many workers to go to Germany.], from whose ranks several hundred have been taken away in the meantime (according to some, to a camp near Schoorl, according to others, even to Germany). The newspaper only includes an announcement by von Christiansen, the military commander of The Netherlands: he has assumed executive power over North Holland and ordered the resumption of work in all enterprises. Marches, etc. are prohibited and all political parties in North Holland are to cease all their activities; the wearing of uniforms and insignia is also prohibited (the latter is very pleasant). Of course there is the threat of severe punishments. Let us hope that peace will indeed be restored and it is good that the military authorities have taken action.

I have now, like other Jews "relieved" of their duties, been <u>fired</u> and will receive 85% of my salary for 3 months, after that 70% for 5 years and thereafter 50%.

The German troops are now also engaged in North Africa. The British do not seem to be making more gains over there, but they are advancing in East Africa. According to the Germans, the submarine war has yielded huge results.

---

49. Arthur Bondi was a relative of Rose Italie-Hausdorff, Gabriel Italie's wife, who had managed to immigrate to the United States before the war. See Gabriel Italie, *Het oorlogsdagboek van dr. G. Italie: Den Haag, Barneveld, Westerbork, Theresienstadt, Den Haag, 1940–1945* (Amsterdam: Contact, 2009), 644n30.

Italie's hopes about the German military's restoration of peace and order in the Netherlands proved to be ill founded. Of the four hundred Jewish men arrested in the wake of the Amsterdam riots and deported to the Mauthausen concentration camp, none survived.[50]

HOSTILE SHELTERS ABROAD

The loss of a home, forced labor, and the threat if not actual physical violence added to the desperation of Jews to escape to distant safe havens. By 1941, however, the remaining options all entailed inordinate risks and sacrifices. In the Reich, despite many roadblocks created by the regime, German propaganda presented flight—euphemistically still termed emigration—as if it was a matter of personal choice, still available. "No Time to Lose" was the main message sent by the Nazi-controlled mouthpiece for channeling announcements to Jewish residents, the *Jüdisches Nachrichtenblatt*, with different editions issued in Berlin, Vienna, and Prague.[51] In early May 1941, the Prague edition of the paper sought to make its Jewish readers believe that individuals had been remiss in identifying opportunities to leave, while suggesting that the staff of the Jewish Central Emigration Organization (an agency imposed by the regime) had left no stone unturned in finding destinations for would-be immigrants. Yet a report on one of the few recent achievements of settlement planning that immediately followed—on the same page—offered little cause for optimism.

DOCUMENT I-14: **"One Year Sosua Settlement,"** *Jüdisches Nachrichtenblatt*, **Prague, May 2, 1941, 1 (translated from German).**

San Domingo, February 1941
    Though a year has now passed since the signing of the agreement for the settlement of 100,000 refugees in San Domingo [Dominican Republic], only 583 settlers have managed to make their way into the country thus far.[52]

---

50. Friedländer, *Nazi Germany*, 2:181.

51. "Keine Zeit zu verlieren," *Jüdisches Nachrichtenblatt* Berlin, May 16, 1941, 1.

52. For detailed studies on Jewish refugees in the Dominican Republic, see Marion A. Kaplan, *Dominican Haven: The Jewish Refugee Settlement in Sosúa, 1940–1945* (New York: Museum of Jewish Heritage, 2008); Hans-Ulrich Dillmann and Susanne Heim, *Fluchtpunkt Karibik. Jüdische Emigranten in der Dominikanischen Republik* (Berlin: Christoph Links Verlag, 2009). Between 1940 and 1945 the number of Jews in Sosúa did not exceed five hundred (Dillmann and Heim, *Fluchtpunkt Karibik*, 9).

The Sosúa colony covers a 26,000-acre stretch of land that extends from the coast to the fertile plain of the Yassica River, about 14 miles from Puerto Plata. [General Rafael] Trujillo, the president of the Dominican Republic, made this land available to James Rosenberg, the head of the settlement association [DORSA, Dominican Republic Settlement Association].[53]

The first group arrived in Sosúa on May 5, 1940. The great efforts and enormous sums expended to establish the settlement notwithstanding, only 583 emigrants came to San Domingo, and the number is unlikely to increase substantially over the course of this year.

Seventy percent of the Sosúa settlers are Jews from the various countries of Europe, while the rest are non-Jews.[54] The settlers are young, energetic people who were carefully selected. There are more men than women in the settlement, as well as many families with children. All have pledged to remain permanently in Sosúa and to do agricultural work there.

The settlement association allocated each family 20 acres of land, on which facilities for cattle breeding and poultry farming are located. The settlers raise grain, tobacco, and Dominican potatoes and plant lemon trees.

Three of the settlers are physicians. A school is in place, and language courses are offered on an ongoing basis.

The key reason why so few Jews made it to the Dominican Republic or any other "settlement" was that so many were unable to leave German-dominated Europe. Many more found themselves far from home, stuck in holding pens for people displaced by the war; thousands of Jews—men, women, and children—had been detained by Vichy authorities in southern France together with non-Jewish foreigners. The percentage of Jews in internment camps varied, but generally increased, while the overall number of detainees declined between March 1941 and July 1942.[55] In **Gurs**, one of these camps, Jews

---

53. James N. Rosenberg (1874–1970) was a New York City-based lawyer and **AJJDC** official who struck an agreement with Dominican dictator Rafael Trujillo Molina (1891–1961) for the Sosúa project. See Kaplan, *Dominican Haven*, 29–38; Allen Wells, *Tropical Zion: General Trujillo, FDR, and the Jews of Sosúa* (Durham, NC: Duke University Press, 2009), 44–54.

54. The actual figure is closer to 90 percent and the others were married to Jews.

55. For an overview of the camp system in France, see Poznanski, *Jews in France during World War II*, 173–201. Different estimates place the number of internees in these camps in early 1941 at between thirty-four thousand and forty-seven thousand Jews (ibid., 174); by July, the total had dropped to 11,577, among them almost eight thousand Jews (ibid., 176).

deported from southwestern Germany in late October 1940 were confined among men and women who had earlier been interned by French or Belgian authorities as "enemy aliens." Relief agencies assessed the situation, as in this unvarnished account of camp life.

DOCUMENT 1-15: **Anonymous account, "Report on the Situation in the Camp de Gurs," sent to AJJDC-Lisbon, January 8, 1941, AJJDC Archive AR 3344/618.**[56]

Origin and Composition of the Internees

13,000 persons, almost all Jews, are at present interned in the Camp de Gurs. Of these, 6,000 come from other French internment camps (St. Cyprien, Les Milles, Fremont, etc.) and 7,000 arrived on October 28th from Germany (Baden, Palatinate, Saar).

The internees recently transferred to the Camp de Gurs are all men (from 15 to 65 years old). These are political refugees who had lived in France or in Belgium for many years and who were arrested on May 10, 1940,[57] and sent to the camps where they were interned.

Those who recently arrived from Germany are, unfortunately, men, women and children. There are 400 children of all ages, some were born at the camp. There are numbers of old men, two of whom are over 100. The percentage of aged is very large, in fact, it is certainly more than half of the total. The groups arriving from Germany consisted also of sick, feeble minded, convalescents, pregnant women, people who had recently undergone serious operations; thus, the tragic situation at the camp.

[. . .]

Living Conditions and Food

The internees live in barracks without windows. For a surface of 150 square meters [1,615 square feet] there is only one stove; wood is very scarce. There are 50 to 60 persons in a barrack. When it rains, it is difficult to get about, the ilots [camp sections] are like marshes, the clay soil is slippery so that it is dangerous to go out. Even when the weather is good it is hard to get around for on a very limited surface there are 28

---

56. Facsimile printed in *Archives of the Holocaust: An International Collection of Selected Documents*, ed. Henry Friedlander and Sybil Milton (New York: Garland Publishing, 1995), 10/2:806–8.

57. On May 10, 1940, the German attack on the Netherlands, Belgium, Luxembourg, and France began.

barracks with 1,300 persons. These unfortunates are literally confined and penned up. Each ilot is surrounded by barbed wire and guarded by a sentinel. The families are separated, the men on one side, the women and children on the other.

The food is bad and insufficient; 1,100 to 1,300 [calories] instead of 2,400. For a week now there have [been] symptoms among many of the internees of a lack of vitamins (swelling of face, etc.).

The food consists of the following: in the morning, black coffee; at noon, soup without anything in it; evening, same soup and 300 grams [10.6 ounces] of bread per day. Only the children up to one year old receive a little milk. Many of the internees do not have warm clothing and the colds are increasing. There is a lack of medicaments; the doctors do not have the most primitive [instruments?]. In Ilot A there are 40 convalescing from typhoid fever who are in need of nourishing food; they only receive the same as is given the other internees. A few days ago, two new cases of typhoid were discovered. There is an epidemic of dysentery in the ilots occupied by the refugees from Germany. The women especially are affected. During two weeks 80 internees from Germany died, most of these were over 70 years old.

Conclusion

Winter has come and it will be very hard. These unfortunates must be saved. French and American Jews must do their duty. A special fund must be created for the camps.

The following is urgently needed:

1. More substantial food.
2. Warm clothing (underclothing, shoes, winter coats, blankets, stockings, shoes of a special kind made in the Basses Pyrenees). Many of these things can be procured in the department [region]. At Oloron St. Marie there is a shoe factory, a wool factory, a chocolate factory, so that much can be gotten in the vicinity.
3. Medicines, bandages, instruments, tonics and vitamins for the sick.
4. Milk for the children and aged.

Immediate intervention is necessary for in a month, if nothing has been done, it will be too late for many.

Organizations like the American Red Cross, the Quakers and the YMCA must be made cognizant of this situation. The interconfessional commission must draw the attention of the government to the sufferings which these unfortunate children and women are suffering.

On the other hand, I propose that the representatives of the OSE, HICEM, Joint, ORT and CAR[58] get together to examine the situation to see how they can bring aid to these people. The commandant at the camp asked me to intervene with all the Jewish institutions to collaborate quickly with him. He assured me that he would be happy to be able to ameliorate the conditions of the internees, but that he himself can undertake nothing alone. Let us reply to his appeal and organize at the camp:

For the children: a school and kindergarten (OSE)

For the aged: a home, by arranging the barracks for this.

For the sick: well equipped infirmaries

For adults: workshops (ORT)

Preparation of emigration of all these unfortunates (HICEM)

Distractions for all: study room, library, orchestra, radio, etc.

If we immediately apply ourselves to these tasks, we will save those who can be saved, and we will thus have accomplished our duty in restoring confidence and courage to our unfortunate brethren.

German-born painter **Felix Nussbaum** was among the internees in the **Saint-Cyprien** camp near the Mediterranean in Vichy France. He had lived in Belgium until his arrest as an "enemy alien" in May 1940 and his transfer to the camp. When a German commission visited Saint-Cyprien in August 1940 to ascertain the number of German inmates, Nussbaum was among those who applied for repatriation. Once in Bordeaux as part of the transfer procedure to the Reich, he escaped and returned to Brussels and his wife, Felka Platek. Both went into hiding when deportations of Jews from Belgium to the East started in the summer of 1942. Supported by friends in Brussels, Nussbaum produced a number of paintings and drawings in 1941 and 1942 that reflected back on his time in the camp in the eastern Pyrenees and conveyed a sense

---

58. The Comité d'assistance aux réfugiés (CAR) was a Jewish refugee organization established in 1936 in France. Led by Raymond-Raoul Lambert and Albert Lévy, CAR lobbied the government to expand refugee asylum and grant refugees the right to work, provided for the care of those in refugee internment camps, sought to establish refugee settlements in southern France, and campaigned to reverse or revise harsh anti-immigrant laws passed in 1938. After the Vichy government assumed power, CAR was largely confined to relief operations for refugees in internment camps. Among the organization's achievements was its role in petitioning the French government to allow passengers of the MS *St. Louis* asylum in France. See Raymond-Raoul Lambert, *Diary of a Witness, 1940–1943*, ed. Richard I. Cohen (Chicago, IL: Ivan R. Dee in association with the USHMM, 2007). On OSE, HICEM, the AJJDC, and ORT, see the Glossary.

of his desperation. Among them was a series of works depicting prisoners in Saint-Cyprien grouped around a globe in ways that resemble both Leonardo da Vinci's *Last Supper*, as well as traditional Jewish subjects.[59]

DOCUMENT 1-16: **Photograph by Felix Nussbaum of his painting** *Saint-Cyprien* **on the balcony of his apartment in Brussels, 1942, printed with permission by Felix-Nussbaum-Haus Osnabrück.**

In the course of 1941, Jews in hiding and Jewish refugees faced increasing difficulties in soliciting aid to meet their basic needs. Not only were the refugees in 1941 far poorer and more destitute than before; as a result of the course of the war it also became much harder for Jewish philanthropic initiatives to get help to those most in need. Jews living in neutral countries often endured the frustration of either being left with only abstract news about mass suffering or

59. See Eva Berger et al., *Felix Nussbaum: Art Defamed, Art in Exile, Art in Resistance* (Woodstock, NY: The Overlook Press, 1997), 325–74, with reproductions of Nussbaum's works during this period, including the Saint-Cyprien camp sequence. See also Dalia Hakker-Orion, "Felix Nussbaum—The Impact of Persecution on the Art of a German-Jewish Refugee in Belgium," in *Belgium and the Holocaust: Jews, Belgians, Germans*, ed. Dan Michman (Jerusalem: Yad Vashem, 1998), 453–73. In July 1944 the Germans discovered Nussbaum's hiding place in Brussels and deported him and his wife to Auschwitz via the Mechelen transit camp. They were both murdered. See Berger et al., *Felix Nussbaum*, 449.

with concrete details of a person's plight for which no effective remedy could be found in the German-controlled parts of Europe. The result would be somewhat random interventions made with good intentions, yet little success beyond sending a signal of moral support. The Jewish relief agency **RELICO** received the following letter that exemplifies just how sketchy the knowledge about how to offer assistance remained, even among well-meaning people in neutral Switzerland, which still enjoyed a free press and played host to a whole array of relief organizations.

DOCUMENT 1-17: **Letter from Marthe Nohèr, Zurich, to RELICO-Geneva, February 28, 1941, USHMMA RG 68.045M (WJC Geneva), reel 23, file 158 (translated from French).**

Sirs,

I do not know whether the address above is correct and whether a committee of this type exists, but I just received an awful letter from a family in Poland who asked me to contact you because they are literally <u>dying of hunger</u>. I would very much like to help them, if you could indicate what one must do to contact the Red Cross. They are two young women with children, whose husbands are in northern Africa, and I have been passing their correspondence back and forth since the war started.

I would be very grateful if you could advise me in this matter or, if needed, pass on the present message to the Red Cross directly in order to save time.

If it is possible to send foodstuffs through the Red Cross, I would be inclined to do so as quickly as possible as I fear that money will not be of much help to them.

In anticipation of your kind response and with gratitude in advance, I convey to you, sirs, my collegial greetings.

Private initiatives remained important, but more systematic efforts like the ones outlined in the report on Gurs became critical, ideally efforts that drew on the combined resources of more than one organization. Well into the second year of the war, the functions, goals, and parameters of Jewish aid work remained contentious, although many local initiatives such as the self-help groups operating in larger ghettos received vital support from the AJJDC and other outside institutions. The following letter from the **World Jewish Congress (WJC)** Geneva office (presumably written by **Gerhart Riegner**) is a response to what appears to have been a request by **Joseph Tenenbaum**, a top official with the AJJDC, for aid for one Miss Jafaite, a refugee in Switzerland.[60] After briefly assuring Tenenbaum that the WJC would do whatever it could to help Jafaite, the letter turned to a frank discussion of more general aspects of relief. The obstacles could seem insurmountable even to large Jewish organizations: the Reich's restrictions on imports and emigration, U.S. policies that made the transfer of funds to areas under **Axis** control very difficult, and skepticism even within aid organizations about the utility of large-scale assistance operations. Here a Jewish organization official in the Swiss "outpost" in the middle of Europe attempted to lay out what remained possible in early 1941.

DOCUMENT 1-18: **Letter from World Jewish Congress-Geneva to Joseph Tenenbaum, New York, March 24, 1941, USHMMA RG 68.045M (WJC Geneva), reel 59, file 449 (translated from German).**

Dear Dr. Tenenbaum,

I have just now received your letter of February 24, for which I thank you very much. I immediately got in touch with Miss Jafaite, and though I do not know in what way I can be helpful to her (actually, our aid work does not extend to Switzerland, but only to the countries affected by the war), we naturally will do everything within our power to improve Miss Jafaite's situation.

By and large, you will have been informed about our work by Dr. Tartakower and Dr. Goldmann.[61] Apart from the actual Congress [WJC] work, which for us consists nowadays of conveying important information and documentation to New York, we deal primarily with relief work here. Unfortunately, the resources at our disposal for this purpose are relatively small, but we attempt to substitute initiative for what we cannot provide in material terms. And in this sense, I believe that we can already lay claim to very considerable and major achievements. Not only by forwarding letters we have kept thousands of families in touch and brought thousands upon thousands of people news of missing persons, relatives, and friends. We have [also] successfully procured documents, passports, and other emigration papers for many poor refugees. Finally, through a campaign to generate parcels containing charitable donations, we have been able to provide some help to a number of our most valuable people and friends in their grim material situation. In addition, we managed to lend a hand to a great variety

---

60. The authors have been unable to locate further information about this woman.
61. For more information on Nahum Goldmann and Arieh Tartakower, see the Glossary.

of constructive aid programs, particularly in Poland and in France, where the fate of Jewish youth is especially near and dear to us, and where we are attempting, through constructive plans, to train these young people and to preserve our national Jewish lines of thought.[62]

I know that you are inherently rather skeptical with regard to relief work and are inclined to oppose it on general principles. You can rest assured that we share these general considerations of yours to a great extent and are trying in every possible way to do justice to the principles upheld by the great movement you have started. I can assure you that we have observed with the utmost strictness the principle that no foreign currency is to be sent into countries where we would not wish to send it. Also, with regard to the campaign to generate parcels with charitable donations, one thing must be kept in view: first, the campaign is absolutely not possible on a large scale; and second, it too is unable to relieve the local governments of their general worries. But we must not lose sight of one thing: Our Jewish friends in Warsaw and wherever else [they may be] are even worse off than the Polish and other established segments of the population. If they were to be sent nothing at all, they would simply starve and perish, and would not get anything more, for example, from the German authorities. Moreover, this small campaign is an extremely important connecting link and morale-booster for our friends there, and it is indeed mainly our friends that we are thinking about when we undertake this campaign. [. . .]

Of course, it is not the relief problems alone, however important they seem to us in a Europe overrun by war, which draw our attention. We believe that rarely has the hour called for an organization like that of the Congress as much as does the present hour. Unfortunately, we too regret the absence of a more focused and consistent Jewish policy, which—as is certainly clear in our mind—at the present moment can emanate only from America. This is why it is important that all our American friends, particularly at this moment, gather all their strength to make the concept of the Congress into a truly great organization. The decisions made known here only recently, regarding the start of the work of the institute for peace, imply—unless they merely express a propaganda requirement—that in our circles in New York, too, people seem to be coming closer to this point of view. For our part, we are extremely interested in this work and will certainly

---

62. German: *national-jüdische Gedankengänge*, reference to Zionist ideas.

be able to contribute our share to it as well. Here in Switzerland, thank God, we still have preserved a free view and, like an island in the sea of the European war, have been spared the travail of these times. We think of our position here as the vanguard, the most advanced outpost, of the Jewish position and as the only outpost that can retain a certain distance from things, by virtue of the fact that it is still in contact with all the Jewish communities, both those that have come under German control and the large neutral ones, as well as the English ones. We are determined to operate from this outpost as long as possible, and we hope that we will receive understanding and support for our work, precisely from great America.

I will be delighted to hear from you from time to time. With my best regards and those of Dr. Silberschein[63] as well,

[no signature]

As the letter indicates, many emigration programs had simply become casualties of the war. The Dominican Republic—where dictator Rafael Trujillo Molina sought to improve his international standing after having ordered the murder of thousands of black Haitians to "whiten up" his populace[64]—was as unlikely a place of refuge as Japan, Germany's Axis ally. Yet few alternatives remained. As the following report on the situation of Jewish refugees in Japan documents, those who had fled from Europe in early 1941 found themselves among other expatriates who had already been trying for years to eke out a living under precarious circumstances.[65] Competition for ever scarcer resources affected all émigrés, yet like everywhere else, access to the means of a livelihood depended on one's adaptability, skills, status, and happenstance. A Jewish organization official, himself a long way from home, wrote the following report from Kobe, Japan.

---

63. For information on Abraham Silberschein, see the Glossary.

64. Kaplan, *Dominican Haven*, 23–25.

65. See Pamela Rotner Sakamoto, *Japanese Diplomats and Jewish Refugees: A World War II Dilemma* (Westport, CT: Praeger, 1998). Sakamoto estimates that between July 1940 and August 1941, roughly 4,500 Jewish refugees came to Japan from Poland, Germany, and other countries via the Soviet Union, of whom 3,500 had left by the end of this period for other destinations, including the United States (ibid., 131). After the fall of 1941 only a few hundred Jews remained in Japan. Among the refugees were many with visas issued by the Japanese consul in Kaunas, Chiune Sugihara, and by other diplomats; see Susan Bachrach, *Flight and Rescue* (catalog for an exhibition at the United States Holocaust Memorial Museum) (Washington, DC: USHMM, 2001), 55–73.

DOCUMENT 1-19: **Report on the situation of Jewish refugees in Japan by Moise Moiseeff,[66] representative of the World Jewish Congress-Japan, June 7, 1941, USHMMA RG 68.045M (WJC Geneva), reel 3, file 20.**

SITUATION OF THE JEWISH REFUGEES IN JAPAN
[. . .]
REFUGEE RELIEF WORK

The Relief work for Jewish Refugees is done exclusively by the Refugee Committee of the Jewish Community of Kobe (Ashkenazic [*sic*] Jews), and falls into one of the following three categories:

1. Material assistance—the furnishing of food, shelter, medical care, clothing, transportation—costs in Japan proper, etc.
2. Aiding transients to change their status to that of immigrants.
3. Emigration work, which actually entails a certain amount of legal aid.

When the streams of refugees began to pour into Japan—this was in July, 1940—the local Jewry reacted with the sympathy and compassion which is characteristic of all Eastern-Jewish communities. Committees were immediately established in all the towns along the transit-routes. In the first days of this flight the refugees who came from Germany all had transit-visas through Manchukuo or Japan, and the centers for help were therefore Harbin, Dairen and Kobe.

In the actual sense of the word and in comparison with the element which came later, these early émigrés were not "refugees." We called them "tourists." They came fully armed with visas and with valises and trunks full to bursting with clothing and household goods. But, as victims of Hitler's regime, they were the objects of attention and sympathy to Japanese Jewry.

From the very first, Kobe was recognized as the center for émigrés and transients. But Yokohama, the port of departure for the Americas must

66. Moise Mendlevich Moiseeff (1905–1991) was born in Russia and obtained a doctorate in 1929 in Belgium, where he remained until 1940, working as a sales manager, editor of an economics journal, and contributor to the Brussels-based *Undzer Lebn*. In the summer of 1940, Moiseeff, his wife, Esther (née Ponevejsky), and their two children left Europe for Japan by way of Lisbon and New York. They remained in Japan until 1946. See Itzhak J. Carmin Karpman, ed., *Who's Who in World Jewry* (New York: Pitman, 1972), 630; ship passenger lists for August 19, 1940, and September 6, 1946, NARA.

not be overlooked. The German-Jewish residents of that city organized a "German Relief Committee" and their name is symbolic to this day.

• • •

The situation underwent a complete change from the moment that the Polish and Lithuanian emigrants began to avail themselves of Japanese transit visas. This element blazed its trail through Vladivostok. When the first few "pioneer"- émigrés appeared, their arrival was hailed as a miracle of endurance. It is only after the Jewish Community of Kobe intervened with the Japanese Government that hundreds and hundreds of refugees began to pour out of that living hell.

The following chart shows the migration of Jews for the months July, 1940 to May 30, 1941:

MONTH	FROM POLAND	FROM GERMANY	FROM OTHER COUNTRIES	TOTAL
July–Aug. 31, 1940	9	1085	25	1119
September	10	503	—	513
October	218	276	10	504
November	8	100	4	112
December	35	132	23	190
January 1941	208	95	25	328
February	762	51	8	821
March	624	154	27	805
April	80	66	12	158
May	8	36	70	114
TOTAL	1962	2498	204	4664

It was during the month of July, 1940 that the name "Tsuruga" [Japanese port] made its first appearance on the pages of the history of Jewish migration. Tsuruga became the haven for the Jewish wanderer, where first he came in contact with the "Jewcom."[67]

This preamble brings us directly to the chapter on Material Assistance. For the greater part, the refugees who arrive now are exhausted, despairing and hopeless. They arrive without any baggage, and many of

67. "Jewcom" was the cable address of the Kobe Jewish community, by which it became known. See Marvin Tokayer and Mary Swartz, *The Fugu Plan: The Untold Story of the Japanese and the Jews during World War II* (Jerusalem: Geffen, 2004), esp. 122–26.

them, on the verge of starvation. When they enter Kobe, they are quartered in Jewish homes. By the end of April, 21 such homes had opened their doors to:

837   men
151   women
 57   children
——
1045

This number, in terms of nationalities:

993   From Poland
 47   From Germany
  5   From elsewhere
——
1045

Each home is in the charge of a manager who is in constant touch with the Economics Director, a member of the Refugee Committee. The specific housing requirements for the European Jews made great demands on the local community and proved a severe problem for the refugees themselves. The situation was aggravated by the various social barriers and the professional groupings of the immigrants.

A study of the following chart will clarify the difficulties which had to be coped with:

PROFESSION OR VOCATION	POLISH REFUGEES (PROPORTIONATE %)	GERMAN REFUGEES (PROPORTIONATE %)
Merchants or Manufacturers	15.5	18.9
Rabbis and Yeshiva-students	9.9	.5
Lawyers	5.5	1.6
Engineers	2.5	4.0
Medical men	1.0	3.2
Other professions	4.2	5.8
Employees and workers	13.8	16.6
Evidently unemployed	43.3	46.0
Indefinite vocations	4.3	[3.4]

The majority of these people are orthodox in inclination.

It was the task of the Committee to group these people according to mutual interests and activities.

The material assistance was under the control of the "Women's Committee." The women were in charge of the sanitary conditions in the homes to which these refugees had been assigned, the distribution of daily maintenance and clothing, etc. Their devotion and sacrifice defy words. It is only thanks to their labor that the general situation is satisfactory. The work is by no means easy. It must not be forgotten that these <u>transients</u> have already been here almost two years and many of them have become destitute during that period—both financially and spiritually. Even the well-to-do among them have lost their sense of pride. [. . .]

Many stark differences separated Jews, those in the Reich proper, those in areas under direct or indirect German control in the first half of 1941, and those still in transit, hoping to elude capture and confinement, forced repatriation, or deportation. They shared much as well, documenting unrelenting pressure and its ever-increasing toll, be they refugees in Kobe, their sense of pride injured and on the brink of destitution or, like J. E. in Opole, feeling deep "regret that we didn't already put an end to this life" before their deportation to a most desolate place. As we will see in the next two chapters, the dual process of continued, intensified persecution in areas already under Nazi domination and the radicalization caused by Germany's military expansion into southeastern Europe had an impact on the lives of Jews that was as profound as it was wide reaching.

CHAPTER 2

STRUGGLING IN THE ŁÓDŹ
AND WARSAW GHETTOS

SINCE THE FALL of 1939, Nazi officials in German-controlled Poland had aggressively pushed for the "resettlement" and "concentration" of Jews in the context of their ambitious plans for a new German "living space." Eventually the annexed Polish territories, including the **Warthegau** and eastern Upper Silesia, were to be "cleansed of Jews" (made *judenrein*), while the **Generalgouvernement** was to receive them and the remaining Jews and other groups of unwanted people in the Reich. As a first step in this process, Polish Jews were to be concentrated in discrete locations so that their German overlords could control, segregate, and better exploit them. Many important elements of "Germanization," the grand design that Hitler had entrusted to **Heinrich Himmler** and his underlings in the occupied regions, never materialized, especially the large-scale transfer of ethnic German settlers into the annexed areas. The "Jewish question," however, remained high on the Nazi agenda.

By early 1941, despite considerable differences in German policies in the formerly Polish regions, Jewish communal life had largely become confined to ghettos, which German-appointed **Jewish councils (*Judenräte*)** administered internally.[1] Positioned between German authorities, with their restrictions, threats, and demands, on the one side and the desperate needs of Jews in ghettos on the other, the leaders and members of the Jewish Councils faced an insoluble dilemma: in view of the German administrators' "complete consensus on the need to exploit both the property and the labor of Polish Jewry,"[2] how could the Councils still provide for and protect the more vulnerable in their communities: children, the sick, and the elderly? German labor demands intensified the crisis of housing, sanitation, and subsistence in the ghettos, yet at the same time paradoxically guaranteed the communities' continued existence for as long as their perceived economic utility persisted. Not surprisingly, then, many *Judenräte* accepted the need for maintaining and increasing productivity, if need be with the help of Jewish policemen in the ghetto, viewing it as the key factor in securing a future for their people. But what was the impact on life in the ghetto, on ghetto residents braving the odds against survival on a daily basis?[3] The previous volume in this series has shown how Polish Jews were affected by ghettoization at the beginning of the German occupation.[4] This chapter will focus on subsequent events in Łódź in the Warthegau and Warsaw in the Generalgouvernement, with altogether more than half a million Jewish inhabitants. These two ghettos, the largest created during World War II, contained nearly one-third of all Polish Jews living under German control in early 1941.

The differences between the two communities are as significant as the features they had in common: Łódź had been the first major urban ghetto, with the gates closing on roughly 160,000 Jews on April 30, 1940. In Warsaw, the Germans sealed the ghetto, with its nearly four hundred thousand men, women, and children, on November 30, 1940. In both cases, ghettoization went hand in hand

---

1. See Dan Michman, *The Emergence of Jewish Ghettos during the Holocaust* (Cambridge: Cambridge University Press, 2010); Gustavo Corni, *Hitler's Ghettos: Voices from a Beleaguered Society, 1939–1944* (London: Arnold, 2002); Christopher R. Browning with contributions by Jürgen Matthäus, *The Origins of the Final Solution: The Evolution of Nazi Jewish Policy, September 1939–March 1942* (Lincoln and Jerusalem: University of Nebraska Press and Yad Vashem, 2004). *The United States Holocaust Memorial Museum Encyclopedia of Camps and Ghettos, 1933–1945*, vol. 2: *Ghettos in German-Occupied Eastern Europe*, ed. Martin Dean (Bloomington: Indiana University Press in association with the USHMM, 2012) consists of more than 1,100 entries on ghettos in German-controlled Poland and the later occupied parts of the Soviet Union.

2. Browning, *The Origins of the Final Solution*, 138.

3. See Isaiah Trunk, *Judenrat: The Jewish Councils in Eastern Europe under Nazi Occupation* (Lincoln: University of Nebraska Press, 1996); Corni, *Hitler's Ghettos*, 227–61.

4. Alexandra Garbarini, with Emil Kerenji, Jan Lambertz, and Avinoam Patt, *Jewish Responses to Persecution, 1938–1940*, vol. 2 (Lanham, MD: AltaMira Press in association with the USHMM, 2011), 349–86.

with forced relocation and overcrowding, but the situation was particularly bad in Warsaw, where 30 percent of the city's population was forced to squeeze into 2.4 percent of its territory. Furthermore, shortly after its closing in early 1941, the Warsaw ghetto had to accommodate about sixty-six thousand Jews from surrounding areas, bringing the total population figure up to 460,000 in April 1941, a third of them children.[5] And while both ghettos were internally administered by Jewish councils that oversaw a large staff—seven thousand in Łódź in June 1940 and six thousand in Warsaw in early 1941—and operated under a similar degree of unrelenting German pressure, the character and degree of control over their communities differed. In Łódź, Judenrat head **Mordechai Chaim Rumkowski** controlled affairs tightly, while in Warsaw **Adam Czerniaków** faced severe competition from a diverse range of groups, including communal welfare committees partly funded by the **AJJDC**, political activists with a variety of agendas, and professional smugglers primarily interested in serving their own needs.[6]

The Jewish councils in both cities were at the front line of intense battles fought within their communities in the first half of 1941. By that time, their German overlords seemed to have accepted the ghettos as an improvisation with longer-term potential by dint of their economic value. In Łódź, Rumkowski oversaw dozens of workshops with tens of thousands of employees (53,000 in March 1942) producing goods for the German war effort. In Warsaw, production lagged behind, but beginning in the spring of 1941, German companies established a range of factories with the expectation of sizeable profits, and Nazi officials thus considered providing increased food provisions to the ghetto.[7] Higher economic output came at the expense of workers and their families, not to mention those unable to work. Despite the creation of food kitchens and public health services, the Councils were unable to meet the most basic demands of the population due to deliberate neglect on the part of German administrators, raging corruption, and rapidly depleting resources for which smuggling could only partly compensate. Food riots broke out in Łódź in 1940. In Warsaw, Czerniaków noted in his

5. Browning, *The Origins of the Final Solution*, 114–31; Miri Freilich and Martin Dean, "Warsaw"; Laura Crago, "Łódź," *The USHMM Encyclopedia of Camps and Ghettos,* 2:76–82, 456–60.

6. From the vast and growing literature about both ghettos, see Isaiah Trunk, *Łódź Ghetto: A History*, ed. Robert Moses Shapiro (Bloomington: Indiana University Press in association with the USHMM, 2006); Lucjan Dobroszycki, *The Chronicle of the Łódź Ghetto: 1941–1944* (New Haven, CT: Yale University Press, 1984); Barbara Engelking and Jacek Leociak, *The Warsaw Ghetto: A Guide to the Perished City* (New Haven, CT: Yale University Press, 2009); Yisrael Gutman, *The Jews of Warsaw, 1939–1943: Ghetto, Underground, Revolt* (Bloomington: Indiana University Press, 1982).

7. Browning, *The Origins of the Final Solution*, 130–31, 154.

diary in May 1941, workers received neither the salaries they have been promised nor their rations.[8] Many struggled to avoid backbreaking labor for the Reich's war effort and to supplement the starvation rations and the irregular relief packages sent from the outside with purchases on the black market. However, forces beyond their control both inside and outside the ghetto ultimately worked against them. The documents in this chapter show that despite the differences between the two cities, what united them was the growing destitution of their residents and their desperate attempts to improvise and carry on, physically and psychologically, in these exceptional circumstances.

CONFLICTS OVER BREAD

Thrust into a situation of chronic scarcity, food and how to obtain it became the most important subject of conversations and worries. Meals were the focus of everyone's attention, from the Jewish Council members to relief and self-help groups to ghetto archivists determined to record the trials of these times. In the Warsaw ghetto, soup kitchens handed out 100,000 to 120,000 meals every day during June 1941. In Łódź, Rumkowski's ration plan for the same month listed a range of items including carrots, peas, oil, and sugar.[9] But the many hungry ghetto residents knew from past experience that rations might appear on paper only, and what the soup kitchens offered today could be terminated tomorrow. Bread was the most widely sought-after item in the ghetto diet, yet also remained in short supply. The following poem by Władysław Szlengel, a Polish-Jewish poet of some note prior to the war, explores the struggle for food and its impact on the psyche.[10] "Bread" forms part of ten poems that Szlengel contributed to the

---

8. Raul Hilberg, Stanislaw Staron, and Josef Kermisz, eds., *The Warsaw Diary of Adam Czerniakow: Prelude to Doom* (Chicago, IL: Ivan R. Dee in association with the USHMM, 1999), 233 (diary entry for May 10, 1941).

9. Hilberg et al., *The Warsaw Diary of Adam Czerniakow,* 250 (diary entry for June 20, 1941); Corni, *Hitler's Ghettos,* 129.

10. Born in Warsaw, Władysław Szlengel (1914–1943) was active in literary circles before the war, serving as a theater director in Białystok. He fought with the Polish army against the German invasion and later became part of the literary and cabaret scene in the Warsaw ghetto. Szlengel served with the ghetto's Jewish police until the mass deportations of July 1942. He died in the Ghetto Uprising in April of 1943. See Rafael F. Scharf, "Literature in the Ghetto in the Polish Language: Z otchlani—From the Abyss," in *Holocaust Chronicles: Individualizing the Holocaust through Diaries and Other Contemporaneous Accounts,* ed. Robert Moses Shapiro (Hoboken, NJ: Ktav, 1999), 35; Frieda Aaron, *Bearing the Unbearable: Yiddish and Polish Poetry in the Ghettos and Concentration Camps* (Albany: State University Press of New York, 1990), 41; Samuel O. Kassow, *Who Will Write Our History? Emanuel Ringelblum, the Warsaw Ghetto, and the Oyneg Shabes Archive* (Bloomington: Indiana University Press, 2007), 316, 321.

Oyneg Shabes archive. Unfortunately, most of his poems written in the Warsaw ghetto suffered from extreme water damage as a result of being buried beneath the streets of the ghetto and are virtually illegible today.[11]

DOCUMENT 2-1: **Poem "Bread" by Władysław Szlengel, Warsaw, July 1941, USHMMA RG 15.079M (ŻIH Ring. I/526) (translated from Polish).**

Three quarters of a loaf of bread lie on the table,
it is coupon bread, given out for ration cards.
As I devour the white-rye bread with my eyes,
these thoughts run through my head:

A street . . . in the midst of the traffic and noise,
in the gutter, on the pavement, or on the sidewalk,
Bread sellers stand.
Excuse me, sir?—No need.
They praise their white bread, they praise their rye bread,
the deluxe or black, "two-tone" bread.
A young vendor presses a loaf
against his dirty black shirt.
He holds it tight, like a valuable treasure,
A large, white, fragrant loaf of wheat bread.
Basket by basket, like troops in formation,
How much bread is at the market today!
Haggling and shouting, curses, oaths,
Around the sellers, circles of buyers,
extended arms, feverish faces,
the street sells bread, the street buys bread . . .
The street . . . a man lies stretched out
across the sidewalk like a crumpled rag.

[. . . ; part here illegible]

[. . .] nimbly avoids streetcars,
a man runs, pursued by a policeman's truncheon.

---

11. A collection of his 1943 poems is anthologized in Polish with an introduction by the literary critic Irena Maciejewska, *Władysław Szlengel: Co czytałem umarłym* (Warsaw: PIW, 1977), and was later translated into Hebrew by Halina Birenbaum (Tel Aviv, 1987) and German by Ulrike Herbst-Rosocha (Leipzig, 1990).

To this he pays no mind and voraciously devours
chunks of bread, eager for once to eat his fill.
The indifferent street, dumbfounded, has stopped,
blows rain down upon the man's bones,
never mind that he is hungry, beat him mercilessly,
never mind that the policeman abuses him so,
this is how it should be, the street says so: . . .

The street . . . beneath the separation wall,
beneath a barrier to protect against typhus,
a quiet whisper, an agreed-upon sign, and over the barrier
a sack full of bread is tossed.
Quickly the bread is seized, wrapped in old rags,
the faster to escape the nearby watch.
Yet smuggled bread without ration cards is expensive
and a poor man can only dream about it.
Only for some, those chosen by fate,
does the Community or the ŻYTOS[12] offices distribute bread.
So for a change, another picture—an office,
behind a small table, a clerk armed with a pen;
shouting, hubbub, tumult, raised voices,
it's stuffy, crowded, hot, there's smoke, cigarettes,
and at the door, there's a line that stretches far.
They jostle, hunger won't wait, it has no patience.
A policeman or janitor, deaf to entreaties,
lets the next ones through, slowly, and drives away the screaming ones,
So one, another one, a tenth one stands and waits
for bread, the bread they have dreamt of, tallied in decagrams.
For the bread tallied in decagrams, almost in grams,
bread which, alas, so often we do not have,
bread which has become a dream, has become a poem,
its prices are the main subject of conversations today.
I . . . do not listen to these conversations, they cannot fill one's stomach,
what's the use of talking . . . it's better for hunger to be hidden.
Why upset both others and oneself?

---

12. Żydowskie Towarzystwo Opieki Społecznej, the Jewish Organization for Public Welfare. This organization was later absorbed into the JSS, the major organization for Jewish welfare in Warsaw.

It's best to say nothing today, and that's what I do.
Never mind that there's constant pressure in your stomach,
pain for oneself, but a smiling face for strangers,
and though sometimes with difficulty because it's almost through tears,
laugh, brother, laugh, because people like you
must endure, and mustn't cry.
A time will come when there will be
plenty of bread for everybody, for everybody! You hear?
A time when life will start anew.

The deep longing expressed in Szlengel's poem was especially pertinent to those at the bottom of the social hierarchy, those abused by the police and others in the ghetto who held positions of power. The have-nots, like the boys in the following photograph, may have been useful for transporting bread into the Łódź ghetto, but they had very little hope of ending up with more than a meager share of their valuable cargo.

DOCUMENT 2-2: **Jewish teenage boys move a wagon loaded with bread for distribution in the Łódź ghetto, Warthegau, no date (1941), USHMMPA WS# 24415.**

As pressure from the outside grew, social disparities widened and produced conflicts within ghetto communities. Only rare accounts have survived that reflect the discordant perceptions of different groups in the ghetto about needs, space, priorities, and vital issues. One such case relates to Łódź, where in late 1940 the German administration had decided to increase food provisions for working Jews to the level of non-Jewish prison inmates. At the same time, conditions deteriorated massively for those ghetto residents who—as a result of age, illness, or other factors—were unable to perform labor. The Jewish Council had to act, but saw few options, given the scarcity of resources. In January 1941, *Judenrat* head Rumkowski introduced new ration levels that left workers with a reduction in the most essential element of their already meager staple, bread; simultaneously, he increased bread rations for the population as a whole. Protests ensued among organized, largely left-leaning laborers, and Rumkowski ordered the ghetto police to help quash the unrest.[13] These events constituted the most intense labor dispute in the ghetto's history, and accounts told from different angles survived the war. One originated with long-time Łódź resident **Shlomo Frank**, a Zionist journalist, who was born in 1902 and had reported for the city's Yiddish press in the 1920s and 1930s. After the ghetto was created, he served as a member of the ghetto police in Rumkowski's administration. The entries in his wartime diary signal his prewar profession, for many passages were written with a fluid, engaging journalist's hand, with all the virtues and limitations that entails. One of two known Łódź diarists who survived the war, Frank edited his wartime writings for publication in 1958, eliminating all references to potentially incriminating parts of his own personal history. His terse depiction of the strike's background lays out the extreme situation reigning in the ghetto.[14]

---

13. See Trunk, *Łódź Ghetto*, 325–28.

14. The original transcript of Frank's diary, available at the Jewish Historical Institute in Warsaw (ŻIH 302/03) and in copied form at USHMMA RG 02.208M, only begins with entries from June 1941, while the published version begins earlier. Historian Lucjan Dobroszycki, who in 1959 compared the original transcript of the diary in the holdings of the Jewish Historical Institute in Warsaw with the published version, found many inconsistencies and changes. For a brief history of the provenance of Frank's diary and later revisions, see Shapiro, ed., *Holocaust Chronicles*, 101–2. Frank, who died in 1966 in Israel, made these revisions in all likelihood to avoid being drawn into an investigation of his wartime service in the ghetto police and charges of having "collaborated." On postwar charges of Jewish "collaboration," see chapter 9; Leah Wolfson, *Jewish Responses to Persecution, 1944–1946*, vol. 5 (Lanham, MD: AltaMira Press in association with the USHMM, forthcoming).

DOCUMENT 2-3: **Shlomo Frank, Łódź, Warthegau, diary entries for January 1941, in Shlomo Frank, *Togbukh fun lodzher ghetto*, ed. Nakhman Blumental (Buenos Aires: Tsentral-farband fun poylishe yidn in Argentine, 1958), 17–27 (translated from Yiddish).**

January 1, 1941

Today it has been 16 months since the war broke out. How many victims have the 16 months already cost the Jewish population of Łódź! How many have died from hunger and cold! And how many holy souls have taken leave of their exhausted and starving bodies! And who knows how long until it is over, and who knows how much misfortune we will still face.

January 2

A group of 60 workers was sent out this morning to the cemetery in order to increase the tempo of digging graves because, no matter how much they dig, it is still not enough. Tens of the dead lie about, unable to be buried on the same day [as they died].

Today the Jewish ghetto police found the woman Roza Merina [or Merino], 36 years old, lying not far from her apartment—frozen.[15]

[. . .]

January 5

Today was a very difficult day: four people froze to death. Unfortunately, it has not been determined who the people are. It is believed that they are people who recently arrived from the small towns around Łódź. The people fall without screaming, like quiet pigeons.

January 6

Again this morning two young people who had frozen to death were found: Leybl Stoler and Volkan Mardyan. Both were found in their dark little homes. Both left behind emaciated, half-dead wives and children. The tragedy did not make any impression whatsoever on the wives because they too are standing at the edge of the grave.

---

15. The authors were unable to find further information about the people mentioned in this document unless otherwise noted.

January 7

The "fast help" [emergency medical transport service] today brought 110 people to the hospitals. Among them were 22 children who were barely alive. All were so weakened and so frozen that they did not know where they were and what was being done with them. [. . .]

January 10

The woman Hannah Birentsvayg was found dead today. She died from hunger and cold. A letter to Rumkowski was found on the unfortunate woman's table. She writes: "I would never in my life believe that Jews could be so bad. The neighbors stole from me, they took my bread ration from me. I have not eaten a single piece of bread for several days. I am dying from hunger and cold." In the same letter she asks the president to punish the bad neighbors.

January 11

Today a large demonstration of women and children took place. The demonstrators demanded bread. They screamed: "Give us bread, we are starving! We are dying from want! Our husbands are becoming swollen from hunger and cold. Our children are dying before their time. Death to the president! Death to all who stand with him!" As the demonstrators were being dispersed [by the Jewish police], three women were badly wounded. The women were taken away to the hospital. One of the women, Rivke Birkel, died in the hospital.

[. . .]

January 14

Today was a terrible day. People are dropping like flies. There is not one house where someone has not died. Laments, cries, screams can be heard everywhere. Wringing their hands, those who are still living run about and beg for someone to take away the dead that have been lying in their homes for several days already. One must have a lot of pull to get someone buried nowadays. If not, the dead must lie [unburied] until their turn comes. The majority of people are dying today of hunger and cold. Their weak hearts cannot withstand the difficult winter together with the great frost. Unfortunately there is nothing with which to save oneself. It is impossible to revive so many weakened hearts, the cold and hunger are our greatest enemies. They have joined hands and sworn to destroy the Jewish community [*kibuts*] of the city of Łódź.

[. . .]

January 20

The frost let up today. May God grant that the hunger also lets up as the frost has, then it would certainly be better for us. Today 160 dead were brought to be buried. This is the largest number since the ghetto has existed.

It is worth noting that not only Jews have been buried at the Jewish cemetery but various Christians too who were secretly brought by the Gestapo, shot, and buried at the Jewish cemetery. In recent months such executions have taken place almost every day.

January 21

The 27-year-old Freyde Unger took her life this morning. As the neighbors told it, she had decided long ago to commit suicide. She was the only one remaining from her entire family. She had declared to the neighbors: ["]Why should I wait until the angel of death comes to me? It will be much easier for me if I go to him["].

The chairman [Rumkowski] announced today that from Friday on all ghetto residents will receive rations of 40 decagrams [14 ounces] of bread. The news greatly delighted the starving. [. . .]

January 22

The carpenters went on strike today. They selected a commission of five men to negotiate their demands with the chairman. As soon of the chairman learned of this, he summoned their leader, Mr. Bernard Froynd [Freund],[16] and ordered him not to yield to the demands of the workers "even at the expense of casualties." After Froynd conveyed the chairman's words to the workers, they all left the factory. At mid-day, the assault team of the police [*Iberfal-Komando*] occupied the factory and arrested every worker who came to take care of something for a few hours. If a worker protested, he was brutally beaten.

January 23

Today, the tailors informed their commissars that they too will go on strike if they are not given the half-kilo [1.1 pounds] of bread they were promised as a bonus for heavy labor. The tailors posted a written appeal

16. An accountant by profession, Bernard Froynd (Freund) (1896–1944) was born in Łódź and was married with one child. He became head of the carpentry (or furniture) and carpet divisions in the ghetto. See Sascha Feuchert, Erwin Leibfried, and Jörg Riecke, eds., *Die Chronik des Gettos Lodz/Litzmannstadt. Supplemente und Anhang* (Göttingen: Wallstein, 2007), 354.

and called upon all residents of the ghetto to show solidarity and stop working and simultaneously to eliminate the disguised fratricide, starting with the chairman. Police are standing guard and awaiting orders.

January 24

Today, workers from all the tailor shops stopped working. The chairman declared: ["]I won't yield, I won't receive a single delegation you send. Whoever might want to intervene on behalf of the workers will get a good beating from me, and if it becomes necessary, I'll call on the Gestapo and they'll certainly put things in order.["]

January 25

At 60 Franciszkańska Street, the young Miss Blume Likhtenshteyn jumped from the fourth floor and died on the spot. Hunger was the cause of the suicide.

The strike intensified today. The chairman won't yield. He threatens that there will be serious consequences. The striking workers put up several posters written in two languages, German and Yiddish, with the following content: "We do not seek a monetary award. Our children are starving. As we work, we drop like flies. We want to work and eat until we are full. Down with the police. Death to the chairman. Death to all his accomplices." Things are extremely tense because of the strikes. The chairman is trying to ensure that the German authorities don't learn of this.

Today at Bałuty Market,[17] the Germans had themselves a bit of fun. When the Jewish porters came to do their normal work, they were beaten terribly, some with clubs, some with switches. The game went on for two hours until Bibov [Biebow][18] came and supposedly shouted and asked what was going on.

[No January 26 entry]

January 27

The frost grew even more severe today, it's a sad situation. People are dying on a mass scale. Hunger has reached its highest level. The entire

---

17. The market on "Baluter Ring" served as the main exchange for goods between the city and the ghetto.

18. Hans Biebow (1902–1947), coffee trader from Bremen, was the German city administration's top official in charge of the Łódź ghetto's food supply and economic production.

population of the ghetto is staging massive protests against the rulers and the police. In the afternoon, the chairman summoned the heads of the tailor and carpenter shops, Mr. Froynd, Mr. Shvartsovski, Mr. Terkeltoyb, Mr. Rozner, Mr. Zbar, Mr. Vishinski, Mr. Radzheyevski, Mr. Nakhtshtern, and Mr. Pshebishevitch.[19] The chairman appealed to them and asked them to induce the workers to get back to work; if they didn't, they too would be called to account. When Froynd and Shvartsovski heard what the chairman demanded of them, they declared on the spot that they were resigning from their positions. The workers want a bit more to eat—they said—the best solution is to yield. Fine—the chairman declared—tell them that I will yield a bit. If the leaders of the workers come to see me today, I'll talk to them. Thus ended the meeting.

Extraordinary rumors are circulating today in the ghetto. People are saying that the chairman is negotiating with Bibov on opening the ghetto two hours a day so that the Christians can bring in goods to ghetto residents. Would that this were true . . .

People are also talking a lot about how supplying the ghetto in its entirety will be removed from Jewish responsibility. The head office of the Bałuty Market itself will supposedly distribute goods among the population.

January 28

The strike broke. Several carpenters could no longer bear the extreme hunger and broke off the strike today. They came into the shops with tears in their eyes and asked that they be permitted to work since they can no longer watch as their children starve. The workers were soon accepted and the work began. [. . .]

---

19. Szolem Shvartsovski (Szwarcowski) (1903–?) lived in the city before the war and served as manager of a ghetto furniture workshop. Szoel or Schoel Terkeltoyb (Terkeltaub) (1910–?), was a Łódź native who had owned a cabinetmaking business and became manager of a ghetto carpentry workshop. Rozner may have been Pinkus Rozner (b. 1901–?), who had previously worked in sales and came to manage a ghetto furniture workshop. Zbar, possibly Wolf Zbar (1881–?), had lived in the city before the war and owned a cabinetmaking business. In the ghetto he became manager of a knitwear factory and other carpentry workshops. Vishinski may have been Izydor Wiśniewski (1900–1944?), who lived in Łódź before the war and became manager of a ghetto knitwear workshop; in August 1944 he was deported to **Auschwitz**. Dawid Lajb Nakhtshtern (Nachsztern) (1896–?) managed the hat workshop and had likewise lived in the city before the war. See Feuchert et al., *Die Chronik des Gettos Lodz/Litzmannstadt*, 379, 388, 398, 399, 508.

Josef Zelkowicz, born in 1897, shared a background in journalism with Frank and like him, worked for Rumkowski's *Judenrat*. His position proved less controversial. As one of the ghetto's archivists—a group including other journalists, scholars, authors, and activists—he devoted his energies to creating a massive trove of documentation on the German occupation similar to the clandestine Oyneg Shabes archive in Warsaw. Unlike Frank, Zelkowicz did not live to see the liberation of his home city Łódź, and his private diary has only been partly preserved.[20] His depiction of the January 1941 strike, written as an exposé for a more refined journalistic piece he might have been planning, juxtaposes different accounts and was based on interviews with managers, workers, and policemen taken immediately after the events.

DOCUMENT 2-4: **Interviews collected by Josef Zelkowicz on the carpenters' strike in Łódź, January 1941, in Josef Zelkowicz, *In Those Terrible Days: Writings from the Lodz Ghetto*, ed. Michal Unger (Jerusalem: Yad Vashem, 2002), 205, 209–14.**[21]

[January 23, 1941]

Today, after [Rumkowski] had the ghetto population's bread rations increased and simultaneously abolished the extra bread ration for those who did physical labor, riots broke out at the carpentry workshop at 3 Urzednicza Street, with the carpenters walking off the job and occupying the factory building. In the resulting clash between police and workers, several on both sides were wounded and first aid was summoned in a few cases.

[January 24, 1941]

[. . .] The manager of the carpentry workshop, Mr. Freund,[22] describes yesterday's events and their background:

["]The carpenters are paid 14 marks per week on average. Nutrition is poor, so the workers demanded a wage increase and the special food rations that persons who do hard physical labor receive.

---

20. For a brief biography of Zelkowicz, see Josef Zelkowicz, *In Those Terrible Days: Writings from the Lodz Ghetto*, ed. Michal Unger (Jerusalem: Yad Vashem, 2002), 11–18. The remaining parts of his diary are available at the Jewish Historical Institute in Warsaw (ŻIH 302/111), and in reproduction at USHMMA RG 02.208.

21. Partly printed, with slight differences in the translation from Yiddish, in Trunk, *Łódź Ghetto*, 372–74.

22. See note 16 above, p. 57. The authors have not been able to locate information on many of the people mentioned in this document.

When I contacted the President [Rumkowski] and presented these demands to him, he agreed in principle to give the wage increase and authorized special food supplements such as meat, sausage, and other commodities for those who do hard labor. However, he categorically rejected the [demand for] bread and soup beyond [the quantities stipulated on] the ration cards, explaining that when the entire population's bread rations have been increased, family members receive—irrespective of the special increment for those who do physical labor—the same quantity of bread that the family of a worker who gets a special bread increase would receive.

Yesterday morning, the workers reported at roughly 8:30 a.m. in their usual manner and went to work. At around 9:00, they stopped working. Instead of responding to my suggestion that they continue to work, they gathered up their tools and moved to the Second Department, where they assembled with the workers there and occupied the workshop building. I consequently contacted the President, who instructed the police to remove all people from the premises. When the policemen came, I dissuaded them from entering the plant and attempted again to persuade the workers to leave the area voluntarily. My request was not heeded.

While the policemen were on the first floor (the first floor was not obstructed), their commander, Inspector Frenkel, accepted my proposal and gave the workers five minutes to disperse on their own volition. Instead of a response, pieces of wood were hurled at the policemen. After a brief ten-minute-struggle, the first floor was cleared.

The entrance to the second floor was blocked inside and out. The policemen removed the outer barrier and threw pieces of old furniture, from which the inner barrier had been made, through the window. Then, after a twenty-minute struggle, they purged the second floor, too.

Several workers and several policemen were lightly injured in this operation. One worker sustained light injuries and was taken home by the first-aid people, who said he could return to work within a few days.["]

In respect to these events, the following notice in German appeared this morning at the entrances of the factories and workshops:

Irresponsible provocateurs have been attempting to disrupt the sound conduct of work in the factories, and yesterday I was forced to oust the workers from one enterprise.

According to information in my possession, similar riots were being planned in other enterprises as well. On several occasions I have warned about such disruptions and explained that the workers must bear in mind that <u>most work in these factories is performed for the Wehrmacht</u>. I am responsible for all occurrences and mishaps in the enterprises, and such disturbances by workers are absolutely intolerable. For this reason, I have decided to <u>impose a lockout in all factories</u>.

The wage that is payable today will be sent to workers at their homes on Friday, January 24, 1941, Saturday, January 25, 1941, and Sunday, January 26, 1941, by mail.

Only those who worked are personally entitled to the money. If the worker is not at home, the mailman will <u>not</u> hand over the money. The employee must confirm its receipt <u>personally</u>.

I must note again that, concerned about assuring work for many people and allowing them to support themselves in peace, I have spared no effort in organizing the enterprises. I will continue to do everything within my power to provide the population with food in the most regular and plentiful manner possible. However, it should be understood and taken into account that various factors, including disruptions caused by weather and transport difficulties, often prevent the honoring of all promises with respect to food supply.

Vile and irresponsible people have been exploiting this progression of events. Individual disrupters of order have been arrested and further arrests will be made until full <u>quiet</u> is restored to the ghetto, this being my duty, for which I bear responsibility.

[signed] Ch. Rumkowski
Chairman of the Judenrat in Litzmannstadt
January 24, 1941

The notice is typed (not mimeographed) in German, without a heading, and carries a handwritten signature.[23]

---

23. A similarly worded version of Rumkowski's announcement is included in the official ghetto chronicle; see Feuchert et al., *Die Chronik des Gettos Lodz/Litzmannstadt 1941*, 39–40.

• • •

The chief of the police, Commander Rosenblatt,[24] describes the events:

["]Yesterday at approximately 1 p.m., the President ordered police officer Frenkel, by telephone, to purge the area of the factory at 3 Urzednicza Street of the workers who had occupied it. When the officer informed me about the order, I went to the location, where more than three hundred workers had congregated.

After Inspector Frenkel gave the assembled workers five minutes to leave the area, the workers presented him with active resistance and attacked the policemen with work tools and pieces of wood.

This happened on the first floor. Obviously the police could not tolerate such aggression, and a clash between them and the workers was inevitable.

Twenty minutes later, the first floor was cleared and the workers were forced out of the factory entrance gates.

On the second floor, the policemen encountered a blocked door. The outer obstruction, made of miscellaneous pieces of furniture, was removed. The objects were thrown out of the window and the door was forced open.

Here, too, the workers were extremely aggressive but their resistance was weaker and fell short of serious clashes. After ten minutes, the second floor was also purged.

Slightly more than sixty policemen took part in the operation and the entire area took thirty to forty minutes to clear. One of the most serious incidents during the clash involved a worker named Mitzmacher, for whom, at my insistence, the first aid was summoned. It is my impression, however, that this Mitzmacher was not injured but, rather, fainted from the strain. Several people, policemen and workers, were lightly injured in the clash. One worker was arrested there. I do not know the reason for the arrest since I have not yet received the report.["]

[Question by Zelkowicz:] ["]Is it true, Mr. Inspector, that you instructed the policemen to lay down their rubber truncheons?["]

---

24. Leon Rosenblatt (Rozenblat) (1894?–1944), lived in Łódź before the war and had been a bank director and officer in the reserves. He headed the Jewish police—the Order Service or Order Guard—in the ghetto until he was deported to Auschwitz when the ghetto was liquidated in the summer of 1944. See Lucjan Dobroszycki, ed., *The Chronicle of the Łódź Ghetto, 1941–1944* (New Haven, CT: Yale University Press, 1984), 3n3; Feuchert et al., *Die Chronik des Gettos Lodz/Litzmannstadt*, 387.

[Answer by Rosenblatt:] ["]No, I could not have given such an order because that would have left the policemen totally defenseless amid workers who presumably were not altogether passive . . . However, as an opponent of all violence, I told the policemen that they should not be the aggressors.["]

• • •

Rumors are circulating in town about serious injury to a worker, who is dying.

[January 26, 1941]

In the workers' circles, the following version of events is being told: When the President called Inspector Frenkel and ordered him to assemble a large police contingent to clear out the occupied area, Inspector Frenkel told him that he could accomplish this with his own people only (the "raid squad")[25] and demanded that the President excuse his unit from the dismissals that are currently being carried out among the police. The President gave him a promise to this effect, which is why the police treated the workers so aggressively.

Later on—according to the same sources—when the policemen broke into the factory hall and the workers retreated, they looked through the factory windows that open onto the even-numbered side of Urzednicza Street (the side not included in the ghetto) and saw that German policemen with automatic weapons had arrived. The sources of this account do not know whether the arrival of the German police had to do with the event or whether it was a coincidence.

On Friday, [January] 24, posters were found at the factory entrances, next to the aforementioned notice from the President, with the following message:

> Shame and disgrace on Rumkowski and his raid squad. We report the following fact to the ghetto public:
>
> For several months, the workers at the ghetto carpentry, 600 in number, have been attempting to attain a whole series of demands that will allow them to do their work:

---

25. A special unit (Iberfal-Komando) of the Jewish ghetto police, or Order Service (Ordnungsdienst); see Trunk, *Łódź Ghetto*, 64–68, 327.

1. A wage increase
2. Receipt of part of the wage in the form of food, not money
3. Larger portions of bread and soup, apart from those in the ration cards.

In response to these just demands, the President called out his thugs, who subjected dozens of laborers to cruel beatings.

This adds another crime to Rumkowski's collection of felonies and shameful actions.

Workers! Express your protest and your embitterment.

Carpenters' Group

I [Zelkowicz] did not personally see this poster in the original. It was shown to me as a handwritten copy, which I present here. Rozensztain (a worker at the Archives) claims that he personally read the poster when it was pasted up at the entrance to the factory at 10 Dworska Street. Since he had no paper at hand to copy it, he entered his nearby apartment at Number 14 to bring paper. When he came back, the poster was gone. [. . .]

With more pressure emanating from Rumkowski and despite solidarity displayed by workers of other professions, the strike collapsed without direct German intervention. By the beginning of February, hunger had forced the striking carpenters to return to their workshop. Frank's and Zelkowicz's depictions of the January strike signal the presence of a vast range of competing perceptions, expectations, and interests residing with Jewish men and women as they struggled to eke out an existence and hold their officials accountable in the ghettos of German-occupied Poland.

Within the confines of the ghetto, Jews had to rely on very limited, at times contradictory information to gauge what was going on around them. In their attempts to strategize about organizing material aid, Jews in the west or in unoccupied lands had even fewer firsthand accounts to draw upon. The number of those escaping from eastern Europe to bear witness about new and tragic developments dwindled, while the German grip on information channels tightened. Soon after arriving in the United States from Europe, the Polish journalist Leib Spiesman offered a commentary in the *Contemporary Jewish Record* about the contents of a German-controlled Jewish newspaper that had been published in the Generalgouvernement since the summer of 1940.[26] Studying the newspaper against the background of his own recent experiences, Spiesman attempted to puzzle out what had happened to living conditions in Warsaw at a time when the number of deaths in the ghetto had increased beyond four thousand people per month.[27] Like Frank and Zelkowicz, he sought to tap what actually lay behind the German-built façade, offering a collection of diverse Jewish voices, albeit at a great remove.

DOCUMENT 2-5: **Leib Spiesman, "In the Warsaw Ghetto,"** *Contemporary Jewish Record* **4 (August 1941): 357–66.**

With the arrival in the United States of the sole Jewish newspaper published in the Generalgouvernement, more exact information has been made available about the life of Jews in Nazi-occupied Poland. The *Gazeta Żydowska* is a Polish-language newspaper published in Kraków every Tuesday and Friday since July 1940. It is issued by a private corporation and sells for 30 groszy (15 German pfennigs). In addition to the Polish title, the masthead also carries the Star of David and the words *Jüdische Zeitung* [Jewish newspaper] in small Hebrew characters.

While war news is limited to the official German and Italian communiqués, there seems to be little if any censorship of news about internal Jewish affairs, which fills most of the paper. These items are treated from a strongly religious and Zionist point of view. The rebuilding of Palestine and the problems connected with it are frequently discussed, while weekly language lessons in Hebrew, as well as a serialized novel

---

26. The journalist Leib Spiesman (1903–1963), known in various transliterations as Spizman, Szpizman, and Shpizman, was active in the Labor Zionist movement in the 1930s in his home city of Warsaw before seeking wartime refuge, first in Vilna and then late in 1940 in the United States. After settling in New York, Spiesman conducted Yiddish radio broadcasts and wrote extensively in Yiddish, including books on Jewish life during the Holocaust: *Di Yidn in Natsi-Poyln* (New York: Farlag "Yidisher kemfer," 1942), and *Di getos in oyfshtand* (New York: Tsentral-komitet fun Poyle Tsion-Tsire Tsien, 1944). See "Directories, Lists, Necrology," *American Jewish Yearbook* 65 (1964): 437–38; obituary, *New York Times* (June 22, 1963).

27. Freilich and Dean, "Warsaw," in *The USHMM Encyclopedia of Camps and Ghettos,* 2:456–60.

by J. Burla[28] dealing with Palestinian life, serve to emphasize its Zionist character. Appeals for faith in Divine Providence and for a return to the traditions of Judaism testify to its religious character. The *Gazeta*'s question and answer department, with its replies to legal and emigration problems, reflects the life of Polish Jews and also helps to bolster their courage. In addition all decrees and ordinances affecting Jews are printed in full and carefully explained. Advertisements of all kinds fill one or two pages, although commercial notices predominate, the most striking of which are those advertising Jewish armbands made of celluloid. Yet, despite all these evidences of oppression and persecution, there is room from time to time for a children's section to which boys and girls contribute some surprisingly good poems. [. . .]

German, Yiddish, Hebrew and Polish are the four official languages of the ghetto, and a knowledge of Yiddish is required of all community employees. An ordinance issued by the head of the Warsaw Council on January 20, 1941, fixes the Jewish Sabbath as the official day of rest. All business establishments must be closed on Saturday, Rosh Hashanah, Yom Kippur, and the first and last two days of Sukkoth and Shabuoth.[29] While Sundays and minor Christian holidays are ordinary work days in the ghetto, important Christian festivals are also legal days of rest. Exempted from the compulsory Sabbath holiday are hotels, restaurants, pharmacies, the public utilities, and Jews of the "non-Mosaic" religion, i.e., converts to Christianity.[30] That this strict observance of the Sabbath is not considered an unmixed blessing by all can be seen from the petition presented to

---

28. Judah (Yehuda) Burla (Bourla) (1886–1969), descendent of rabbis and scholars from Izmir, Turkey, was a novelist in Jerusalem famous for his portrayals of Middle Eastern Jews. See Ann Kahn, "Burla, Yehuda," in *Encyclopedia of the Modern Middle East & North Africa*, 2nd ed., Philip Mattar, ed. (Detroit: Macmillan Reference USA, 2004), 1, 547; Zachary Lockman, *Comrades and Enemies: Arab and Jewish Workers in Palestine, 1906–1948* (Berkeley: University of California Press, 1996).

29. In 1941, Rosh Hashanah fell on September 22, Yom Kippur on October 1; both are high holidays in the Jewish liturgical calendar, marking the beginning and the end of the Ten Days of Repentance. Sukkot, commemorating the biblical exile of the Israelites, fell on October 6–12, and Shavuot, celebrating the giving of the Torah on Mount Sinai, on June 1, 1941.

30. There were around two thousand Jews of Christian denomination in the Warsaw ghetto, roughly 0.5 percent of the ghetto population. See Havi Ben-Sasson, "Christians in the Ghetto: All Saints' Church, Birth of the Holy Virgin Mary Church, and the Jews of the Warsaw Ghetto," *YVS* 31 (2003): 153–73.

the [Jewish] Council by the photographers and barbers (*Gazeta Żydowska,* May 9, 1941), in which they asked to be exempted on the ground that it seriously harmed their business.[31] [. . .]

Provisioning the ghetto is one of the Council's most serious problems. While food in all countries under German rule is rationed, Jews receive considerably less than either Poles or Germans. They are allotted only 60 grams of bread per day (approximately 0.13 pounds), half the amount which Poles may buy and less than one-third available to members of the German "master race."[32] Similar gradations are the rule in the distribution of all other products, according to the regulations published in the *Gazeta Żydowska.* The issue of February 3, 1941, for instance, notified Jews that henceforth they would not receive any soap, eggs, or fruit juices. Meat has been entirely unobtainable by religiously observant Jews since the prohibition of *shehitah* [ritual slaughter] on October 26, 1939. One year in jail or concentration camp is the penalty for those found guilty of kosher slaughter. [. . .]

Compulsory labor, introduced by the Nazi authorities immediately upon the establishment of the Generalgouvernement, provides a number of Jews with a scant livelihood. In many cities and towns labor battalions are formed and sent out to work in various parts of the country. Failure to register is punishable by imprisonment at hard labor up to ten years. These battalions drain swamps, dredge lakes, and build roads. Much of the work was done in connection with military projects on the Russian frontiers. The number of Jews employed in forced labor can be judged by the fact that in Warsaw and its environs alone, over 25,000 were sent out, according to the *Gazeta Żydowska* of April 24, 1941. [. . .]

Relatively little is known about the health situation in the ghettos. It is certain, however, that the typhoid epidemics which followed the war affected Jews more than other elements of the population. [. . .] Since then, improved sanitary conditions have practically eliminated epidemics

---

31. See Hilberg et al., *The Warsaw Diary of Adam Czerniakow,* 228 (diary entry for May 1, 1941).

32. The difference in the official allocation of bread in Warsaw can be measured in the ratio 4:2:1 for Germans, Poles, and Jews; see Leonard Tushnet, *The Uses of Adversity: Studies of Starvation in the Warsaw Ghetto* (New York: Thomas Yoseloff, 1966), 22–23. Tushnet conducted studies in the Warsaw ghetto himself. Yet this ratio does not take into account the vast disparity between these groups in their access to unofficial sources or the internal differences among the comparatively privileged and the destitute sections of the ghetto population. See Engelking and Leociak, *The Warsaw Ghetto,* 416–17; Hilberg et al., *The Warsaw Diary of Adam Czerniakow,* 59–60.

of this kind, as stray references in the *Gazeta Żydowska* testify. There is no doubt, however, that overcrowding, lack of parks, absence of recreational facilities, and particularly inadequate diets are exacting a serious toll of health and lives. Statistics gathered by the Lublin Council show that of 28,806 Jews over the age of fourteen registered in that community for compulsory labor, 10,330 or about 35% were disqualified for physical labor because of the precarious state of their health. [. . .]

Examples of Jewish self-reliance and communal cohesiveness found in the pages of the *Gazeta Żydowska* do not at all dispel the horrors of the Nazi terror. A full picture of the situation of Jews in Nazi Poland would include the ghastly chapter of Lublin,[33] the concentration camps, mass starvation and misery. It would also include a description of a different kind of torture, the petty annoyances by which Nazis seek to break the unyielding spirit of the Polish Jews. [. . .]

All the more amazing, therefore, is the stamina and courage of these men and women as seen in the *Gazeta Żydowska*. Despite terrible conditions, the inhabitants in this largest ghetto in Jewish history show an indomitable determination to outlast their enemies. Articles in the *Gazeta Żydowska* encourage them to endure their hardships even as their ancestors did in other critical periods of Jewish history. The tone of the paper is a proud one. There are no traces of groveling before the Nazis. Instead, national pride is emphasized, and faith in humanity and the brotherhood of mankind is kept alive.

The religious spirit, too, is much in evidence. A touching example of the sinking of the interest of the individual in the collective sufferings of the community is provided by a letter from a ten-year-old Jewish boy of Maków, published in the children's section of the *Gazeta Żydowska*. "O Lord, Thou who art omnipotent, show me how I may help my people," wrote the child. Also characteristic of the present attitude of the Jews of Poland is the old adage, published in the newspaper, about the rabbinical students whose ship was wrecked in a storm. They managed to cling to the debris until the waves cast them back on the shore. When they were asked how they had managed to save themselves, they explained that they had bowed their heads before each towering wave instead of resisting it.

To bow their heads before the engulfing waves of oppression is the present way of life of Polish Jewry.

---

33. This was a reference to the horrific conditions of life for Jews deported to the Lublin district in the Generalgouvernement; see document 1-1.

LETTERS AS A LIFELINE

Spiesman's depiction of stamina and endurance in the Warsaw ghetto attests to perseverance in the face of a massive crisis. Despite their concentration of human misery and widespread suffering, the ghettos also offered a modicum of normalcy and the illusion of stability to those few residents not completely consumed by worries about basic survival. In the first half of 1941, Jews—individuals, families, and groups—struggled on and tried to find new ways to earn a living and sustain body and soul in some fashion. They used official as well as clandestine channels to improve conditions for themselves and for those who remained worse off.

Volume II of this series introduced the correspondence running between three Jewish youths: **Ruth Goldbarth** in Warsaw, **Edith Blau** in Minden, Germany, and **Lutek Orenbach** in Tomaszów Mazowiecki, Radom district, Generalgouvernement. They had met in Poland before the war began, and their three-way wartime exchanges became a source of support for one another, despite the distance between them and the ever greater obstacles crowding into their respective lives. The following excerpts, taken from the letters written by Ruth to Edith, give a sense of the enduring strength of friendships and the vital function of letters in daily ghetto life. They became a lifeline cast between two worlds.[34] Lutek retained a more feeble line of communication with his two female friends, but the exchange between Warsaw and Minden was remarkably intense, in large part due to the young women's ingenuity and commitment. Hundreds of miles away from Edith, Ruth lived with her father, who was a dentist, and her mother and younger sister in the Warsaw ghetto. Despite their lack of direct connections to the Jewish Council, the family occupied a relatively privileged position in the ghetto that initially allowed Ruth to send frequent missives through the mail or through non-Jewish friends.

By 1941, the exchanges between the two young women—of which only Ruth's letters to Edith ("Dita," "Ditlein") survive—acquired a distinct style that combined lively descriptions of daily events with ironic, tongue-in-cheek remarks, and with cryptic references to more contentious, even dangerous issues. Ruth and Edith could not spell out everything they felt or experienced, for their letters remained subject to German surveillance. Similar to Leib Spiesman in his attempt to decipher the articles written by Jews in the Nazi-controlled *Gazeta Żydowska*, Edith had to read between the lines of Ruth's letters. Her descriptions of apparently benign events often became coded shorthand for something altogether more perilous: "Adi [short form

---

34. Garbarini et al., *Jewish Responses to Persecution*, 2:457–76.

for Adolf] turned up too, with four friends, and turned the entire apartment upside down. The parents weren't even at home—it was great. Best of
all he liked our little electric stove—he couldn't bear to part with it at all!"[35]
Edith would have had no problem making sense of Ruth's veiled references
to a German raid on her Warsaw apartment.[36] Other phrases in the letters
also gave away their hidden meaning easily, such as "Mogen," camouflaged
as the name of a child, but in reality part of the Yiddish term *mogen Dovid*,
meaning the shield of David, the traditional source of the Jewish symbol of
the hexagram, which the Nazis used to mark Jews ("Star of David"). Because
Ruth's use of code was inconsistent, it is possible that, despite the crucial
explanations provided by Edith Brandon (née Blau) after the war, we have
misread or failed to identify some of the phrases used in the young women's
correspondence.

The following selection of letters by Ruth, dating from January to June
1941, shows starkly what communication could mean for Jews living in dire
circumstances. The mere fact of being able to write to a friend and to read what
she wrote back mattered, irrespective of how important the events depicted
were. "[W]henever I get another letter from you and see you so vividly before
me," Ruth writes in early January 1941, "and when I know that I can tell you
everything, every little thing, and that you understand me, often without words,
then it's not as bad as all that anymore. Then one believes and hopes again!"[37]
The positive memories of a past spent happily together—in Ruth's case, with
Edith and their mutual friend Lutek—helped them to see the present in a more
positive light, even when circumstances grew drastically worse and more fraught
from one day to the next.

DOCUMENT 2-6: Letter from Ruth Goldbarth, Warsaw, to Edith Blau, Minden, Germany, January 19, 1941, USHMMA RG 10.250*03 #47 Edith Brandon collection (translated from German).

My dearest little factory girl,

Are you already worrying because I haven't gotten in touch for so long?
Yes, just imagine, on the afternoon of the 14th as I was going to the

---

35. Ruth Goldbarth, Warsaw, to Edith Blau, Minden, Germany, January 10, 1941,
USHMMA RG 10.250*03 #46.

36. See Edith Brandon, *Letters from Tomaszow* (London: self-published, 1994), 280.

37. Ruth Goldbarth, Warsaw, to Edith Blau, Minden, Germany, January 10, 1941,
USHMMA RG 10.250*03 #46.

mailbox with some letters and cards, suddenly the mailbox was gone; so I went to the next one—it was gone too, as were the third and fourth ones. I ran around like an idiot through our entire part of town—in vain. Finally I came to "our" post office—I go up, open the door, and it's closed!! The Polish Post Office had moved out, you see, and taken everything along, even the furnishings inside the post office building and all the mailboxes. And "our" [ghetto] post office wasn't set up yet and didn't have any mailboxes yet. [. . .]

What does Lutek write, and what do you hear apart from that? What's going on with you? Write soon and in detail. Has Aunt Gertrud learned anything in the meantime? Then you'll write me at once, won't you?

When will I get the pictures you promised?—

Yours, with a kiss,

Ruth

At any time Edith's status could have deteriorated from a "factory girl" doing compulsory labor in Minden to that of deportee. Yet she still asked Ruth faithfully what she could send her from Germany. We see this in Ruth's expressions of gratitude and her somewhat reluctant addition of lists of sought-after items for her own use or for other more destitute neighbors in the ghetto. Between January and June 1941 the officially recorded monthly figure of deaths in the Warsaw ghetto rose from less than 900 to 4,290, and this massive toll shadowed the friends' exchange.[38] Ruth writes about the clash between the mass abject poverty and the lavish life of the few wealthy individuals who attended balls, concerts, parties, and dinners in the ghetto that were billed as "charity events." To Ruth's mind, they become foremost an expression of the urge to live life as fully as possible under the circumstances and escape grim everyday reality. The arrival of more deportees strained the collective level of deprivation even further, and Ruth stops to reflect on the hard fate of some of the individuals around her.

---

38. Corni, *Hitler's Ghettos*, 206.

DOCUMENT 2-7: **Letter from Ruth Goldbarth, Warsaw, to Edith Blau, Minden, Germany, February 26, 1941, USHMMA RG 10.250*03 #51 Edith Brandon collection (translated from German).**

[. . .] A few days ago, Renia Nest[39] was at my place. I feel terribly sorry for the poor girl. I've probably already written you that her sister, Mrs. Schmid, registered back then to return [to the Warsaw ghetto], in order to get the child, who is here. As a result, she was deported, and her husband had a heart attack and died within 24 hours. Now she is also somewhere in the interior, working in the forest like all the others, and is completely crushed. Her husband dead, the child so infinitely far away, and no hope of seeing the child again. One of Schmid's sisters lives here with Renia and her family (of course, all of them in one room) and to this day still knows nothing of her brother's death. It's an unbelievable tragedy. . . . Oh, just don't think about it [. . .]

Imagine, every day 5 to 8 złoty go for bread alone.[40] Our monthly bread consumption (besides the bread we get with ration cards) totals 220 to 240 złoty. Where is this headed, anyway?! Really, Dita, the time is no longer so far off when we'll have to think about where we'll get food for the next day. Every day, hundreds of people arrive here, all of them destitute, with no possibility of earning anything here, with no prospect of getting even the bare necessities of life. Allegedly the Viennese also are already on the way here.[41] What will that be like?? There are rumors that

---

39. The authors were unable to identify this woman and the members of the Schmid family or ascertain their later fate.

40. In his Warsaw ghetto diary, Hersh Wasser noted already in early January 1941 that "[b]read is becoming a dream"; on February 10, he has the price for two kilos [4.4 pounds] of coarse bread in the ghetto at 6.10 złoty, compared to 5.50 to 5.70 złoty outside the ghetto. Joseph Kermish, "Diary Entries of Hersh Wasser," *YVS* 15 (1983): 239, 262.

41. While there were no direct transports of Viennese Jews to the Warsaw ghetto at any point during the war, the rumors recorded by Ruth Goldbarth point to information regarding the deportations from Vienna that followed discussions at the **RSHA** on January 8, 1941. The plan was to deport sixty thousand Viennese Jews as part of the overall goal of roughly 890,000 deportees into the Generalgouvernement. Transports starting in mid-February brought five thousand Viennese Jews to Opole, Kielce, and other cities and towns in Frank's fiefdom, but on March 15 the RSHA stopped these transports. See Hans Safrian, *Eichmann's Men* (Cambridge: Cambridge University Press in association with the USHMM, 2010), 69–70; Götz Aly, *"Final Solution": Nazi Population Policy and the Murder of the European Jews* (London: Arnold, 1999), 144; and Alfred Gottwaldt and Diana Schulle, *Die Judendeportationen aus dem Deutschen Reich 1941–1945. Eine kommentierte Chronologie* (Wiesbaden: Marix Verlag, 2005), 46–51.

starting on March 1, everything here will be even more tightly sealed, and every kind of communication with the outside is to be broken off; what then? The telephone, too, will supposedly be only for internal use. You can go mad if you think about it all. And yet we mustn't fall into despair now, we mustn't give up, we young ones. We have to live to see different times someday; after all, we have a right to that! [. . .]

While German policy planners in occupied Poland were arguing about whether to use the ghetto to quickly starve the Jewish population or exploit ghetto workers on a more long-term basis,[42] the Jews of Warsaw were already experiencing the profound distress caused by deliberately created shortages. They faced skyrocketing prices, fast-spreading, unstoppable disease, and a growing number of dead. On top of this, the Germans—"uncle" or "Adi"—could at any time invade even those places Jews considered relatively safe.

DOCUMENT 2-8: Letter from Ruth Goldbarth, Warsaw, to Edith Blau, Minden, Germany, April 10, 1941, USHMMA RG 10.250*03 #57 Edith Brandon collection (translated from German).

[. . .] The prices climb from one hour to the next, there has been no delivery for the past few days, and groceries are becoming scarcer and costlier minute by minute. Today bread already costs 9.50 zł. per kilo, white bread even 11 zł., and potatoes 3.50. How can that be endured? We still don't have the potatoes that we were due to get through our ration cards since early March, and bread, too, is very rarely available, in small quantities and irregularly. It's unspeakable! When you go out on the street, every 100 paces you see someone lying on the ground, unable to go any farther because of hunger. Our doorbell never stops ringing anymore, one beggar after another comes to the door. Shops are said to have been looted today! And there's no hope that it will be better in the foreseeable future. It's not much better at Jurek's either. We're already quite frantic. Whatever should we do!! And the many thousands of poor people who have nothing!!—If it continues this way, it's really just a matter of weeks for us! [. . .]

---

42. For different plans by German administrators in Poland regarding the ghettos, see Browning, *The Origins of the Final Solution*, 111–68, esp. 127–31, on the debate between the "productionists" and "attritionists."

[After a description of quarantine and disinfection procedures for typhus in the building:]

Now I have to tell you about another adventure. Last Sunday I had gone out with Dorli and various acquaintances to a concert café with performances. A very nice little presentation was scheduled to take place there. And it was really quite fine, a caricature of our life here, quite witty and very true to life. The café is really large and has a balcony in addition to the main room. And now imagine this: suddenly a chair sails from the balcony into the middle of the crowd below. The music stops short, dishes clink, there's a great uproar, which settles down at once, however. Everything goes on as before, until five minutes later a second chair flies down, followed immediately by a third, a fourth, one sailing down after another, each time in a different direction. The commotion was indescribable. Everybody was running and shouting in great confusion, tables and chairs were knocked over, dishes fell to the floor—in short, a dreadful shambles, as always, an immediate panic. And the cause of all the fuss? Two friends of Adi's—drunk out of their minds. Suddenly they appeared in the room; all at once—God only knows how it was possible—not a sound was to be heard. They walked through the café, everybody exhaled, thinking they were about to leave, but suddenly one of them started quarreling with somebody and starting bashing people right and left like a madman; the second one, to add some variety, starting throwing chairs around again. Nobody else could get out, because they were standing at the exit—anyway, the affair got really dangerous at this point, so we retreated to the kitchen, to wait there and see how things turned out. Luckily, the Gendarmerie[43] turned up at last and took the two men away. But it was quite exciting indeed. [. . .]

If Ruth's letters provided a spellbinding and dramatic account of events unfolding in the ghetto, they could not ultimately mask her fear that the situation was growing worse. What she writes also shows that Spiesman's assumption, based on German-controlled newspaper reportage that "improved sanitary conditions" had "practically eliminated epidemics," was wrong.[44]

---

43. It is not clear to what German unit "Gendarmerie" refers; it could be German Order Policemen guarding the ghetto.

44. See document 2-5. For an overview on disease and mortality in ghettos, see also Corni, *Hitler's Ghettos*, 195–210.

DOCUMENT 2-9: **Letter from Ruth Goldbarth, Warsaw, to Edith Blau, Minden, Germany, April 15, 1941, USHMMA RG 10.250*03 #58 Edith Brandon collection (translated from German).**

[. . .] Dear, I can't possibly describe what joy your package has produced here. The people from the Point view it virtually as a miracle. Many of them don't know you at all and simply can't grasp the idea that a totally unknown person is helping them in this way. I'm convinced that a collection of clothes for charity all over the city would not have yielded so many things, and above all such decent things. Not everything has been distributed yet, but the people are deliriously happy that they have a change of clothes, that they don't have to wear the same thing day after day, and that they have an opportunity to wash out some things occasionally. In some cases, we also swapped things; for example, Adas Dobrin got 2 pairs of stockings in exchange for 2 pairs that are too small for him and just fit a boy from the Point. In any event, the people are as happy as children. In the name of the people, the Committee, and the *Landsmannschaft*,[45] I've been asked to wholeheartedly thank you and all those who contributed something. And I myself would like to give you a very warm kiss, my dear. At last, through you, I've been able to help again. Edith, the misery is so dreadful! Sometimes I'd like to close my ears and shut my eyes and run far, far away so that I don't have to see and hear any more. Such pitiful creatures, of the kind found here on the street at every turn; wound only in a few rags, barefoot, half-naked, and freezing, they slog along, and more and more people, often well-dressed, simply collapse and lie there without moving—and the others walk past heedlessly, as if nothing had happened. Seeing it is enough to make you crazy—but you yourself are condemned to the same inaction. Because what can you do? Buy a kilo of bread (for 10 zł.) and give it to the poor man? Then he'll collapse again from hunger tomorrow. And who's able to feed the many who are in need!! You'd have to be a millionaire! Theft is routine nowadays. A few days ago, someone tore a loaf of bread from my hand in the street and wouldn't give it back, although several people were chasing him. A man from our building had his hand bitten so badly by a thief that you can still see the wound today.

---

45. For the work of house committees in the Warsaw ghetto, see Garbarini et al., *Jewish Responses to Persecution*, 2:372–74. "Landsmannschaft" in this context presumably refers to the Warsaw ghetto association of Jews from the city of Bromberg (German name for Bydgoszcz in Poland, annexed to Reichsgau Wartheland from 1939 to 1945), which Ruth Goldbarth was involved in by helping at a charity referred to as the "Point."

Recently I was at the hospital; it was about 12:30 p.m.; the patients still hadn't been given any breakfast. The conditions are so terrible that they can't even be described. So is it any wonder that the number of typhus cases is growing at an alarming rate? The day before yesterday I had an errand fairly far from here, in the downright poor area—entire streets are shut off because of the threat of typhus. Can the people take care of themselves when bread and potatoes are unaffordable treasures for them? (Using our cards, we've received 750 grams [1.7 pounds] of bread per person this month.) It's simply enough to make you crazy!! Despite all that, Uncle continues to take his pick of the people he wants to hire (I wrote you about it last year); a great many have already started work and have determined that once again he's absolutely not keeping his promises regarding food, housing, and pay, and that they have to put up with quite a lot of incivility and roughness besides. And Adi is also swaggering around like a savage. His old friends who were here until now have left, and the ones who have come are decidedly disagreeable.[46]—But enough of that for now! I've really moaned and groaned to you enough for the moment! Don't be cross, dear, but from time to time I simply can't stand it anymore, and you're my closest friend and the only one to whom I can tell everything. [. . .]

This evening is another holiday;[47] the dentist's office is closing earlier than usual, and I'll have free time tomorrow and the day after tomorrow in the afternoon. Terrific! At the moment it's fairly quiet in general. The lockdown of the building [due to typhus], the holidays, the rising prices, and the overall despondency have played a big role there. Anyway, there's not enough work: in March, there was really a lot to do [in the dental practice of Ruth's father], and something came of it: 60% of the expenses were covered. And that was an exceptionally good month.—But in the end: let's be glad that it's still like this! I have to tell myself repeatedly that I must not complain. Only 25% of the population—when things go well—are doing as well as we are. However: the lack of gas is slowly driving us crazy. For breakfast, at lunch, and in the evening, a fire has to be made in the hearth; we have no coal, the wood is always damp, the fire won't burn, and one after another we try our luck & the meals are never ready at the right time. And all that with the *nervus vagus*[48] of my boss! [. . .]

---

46. This is a reference to a change of the German police units guarding the ghetto.
47. April 15, 1941, fell in the middle of Passover week.
48. *Nervus vagus*, or "wandering nerve," is a nexus of nerves located in the throat; here Ruth makes reference to her father's mood swings.

This young woman's flights of fantasy could pull in different directions: some fed into depression, a future too bleak and challenges of daily life too demanding to bear. Still others nurtured dreams of life without war and of being reunited with long-lost friends.

DOCUMENT 2-10: **Letter from Ruth Goldbarth, Warsaw, to Edith Blau, Minden, Germany, May 6, 1941, USHMMA RG 10.250*03 #62 Edith Brandon collection (translated from German).**

My dearest,

Last night, after a long while, I finally got some mail from you again, and it was such a lovely, detailed letter. How good it is that we're not limited to 25 words.[49] Just imagine that! My family always wonders what we have to tell each other at such great length. After all, one day goes by pretty much like the next, nothing happens, and still we write each other letters at least once a week: letters that often cost double the usual postage. To understand this properly, I think that one probably has to be 20 years old and as close as the two of us are. My God, if only we could see each other sometime and tell each other everything! Maybe in Madagascar?[50] Or . . .? Who knows? One would have to be able to look into the future, and then one would at least know whether all the energy and all the strength one has to muster are even worth it, or whether one would do better just to turn on the gas right now. Actually, even that wouldn't be of much use here in our building. Apparently we've been shortchanged again with this business. It would indeed be inconceivable for us to pass up any opportunity to be robbed.—[. . .]

Things are really terrible for Lutek [in Tomaszów Mazowiecki]. He writes me the same thing: that he's drinking and ruining himself with a vengeance. How can he be helped? Can't you appeal to his conscience? For God's sake, we mustn't let each other fall apart. If we give up on each other, everything really is lost. [. . .]

The chance of retaining a degree of stability in one's private world became ever more remote, given the rapid deterioration of living conditions in the

---

49. Reference to the official Red Cross cards with their tight word limit.

50. A reference to serious debates in the upper echelons of the Nazi leadership, still going on at the time the letter was written, about one possible "territorial solution" of the "Jewish question" in the form of the Madagascar Plan. See the introduction to Part I of this volume, and the Glossary entry for the Madagascar Plan.

ghetto. Even hospitals no longer provided protection, and where successful efforts had been made to create sheltered spaces, such as playgrounds for children or cafés for adults, the dramatic clash between the pleasure of a few and the hard lot of the many undercut a sense of real contentment.

DOCUMENT 2-11: **Letter from Ruth Goldbarth, Warsaw, to Edith Blau, Minden, Germany, May 29, 1941, USHMMA RG 10.250*03 #67 Edith Brandon collection (translated from German).**

My good little Edith,

Yesterday evening your letter and your parcel from the 19th and 21st respectively arrived here by the same post. As always, my sincere thanks for all the love and care with which you picked out the many fine things for us. Everything arrived in perfect condition, and once again, we're all quite delighted about the parcel. I won't even tell you anything at all about the fantastic prices here; the circumstances here are such that you simply <u>cannot</u> believe them without experiencing them yourself. Is it really humanly possible that a kilo of bread increased from 20 to 30 zł. in the course of a single day? Everything else, of course, rises along with it to an equal extent. And nevertheless, people buy everything they can get and at any price. A real state of panic! And add to this the large numbers of corpses, the famished children, etc., it's quite something! Actually, you don't even dare to go out into the street carrying a package, without having it ripped from your hands within the space of two minutes. It is all indescribable, and unfortunately it will get even worse; but we can't be grateful enough for the fact that we needn't go hungry yet. It's really a miracle to be able to eat one's fill these days. But enough of this! I also try to think about it as little as possible, and since luckily I am busy from morning till night and usually sit together with our folks here well into the night (just to have some diversion), I generally succeed in my attempt, too.

[. . .] Ditlein, how I envy you the outings to enjoy the springtime! I don't even know anymore what a green tree looks like. In the narrow streets here, there's nothing but dust and dirt and "stinkis" [*sztynki*] (little fish that are sold on the street here in large quantities and have this beautiful name because of their strong odor. In the past few days, when it was so hot, you could pass out in some streets), flowers in only two shops, at insanely high prices. Do you know how much I would like to get out sometime, into the countryside, into the fresh air, hear birds singing, and see water! Viktor wants to take me along one day; just recently he has been allowed to go to Jurek again, but it's not worth the risk—he can allow himself to go without Mogen more easily than I can.[51]

But we're happy indeed about our balcony. From the street side we have sun until 11:30 a.m., and on the courtyard side until 3:30, and on all the floors a "beach life" is developing. Using an extension cord, we brought a light onto the rear balcony, and bridge is played there; in front, the young people get together (those who aren't playing bridge) and chat. And in addition, "our" café is now open. The passageway from our building hasn't been created yet, of course, but our residents are among the most grateful patrons. Admittedly, I haven't yet managed to go over there, although I had three invitations for Saturday and Sunday; I was just recently in the kindergarten next door, which has a swing, seesaw, sandbox, etc., with Marcyś and Henryś Kuschner. It's really nice there, even quite lovely for our circumstances, but I always think that in these times one shouldn't spend money on such things, money that can be used to help others. At any rate, I always have pangs of conscience whenever I think of going to such a café. And somehow I have a sense that I wouldn't feel comfortable there, either. [. . .]

Goldbarth and her friends were not the only young people in the Warsaw ghetto trying to enjoy the warmer weather and create the semblance of a normal life. Photographic depictions by Jews of recreational scenes in the Warsaw ghetto are rare compared to the frequent Nazi propaganda images staged or otherwise artificially created to exaggerate the gulf between rich and poor Jews. The following photograph, taken in the summer of 1942, on the day of graduation from the illegal Jewish gymnasium, attests to the harsh realities of ghetto life. A photograph of high school graduates—a memento, in normal circumstances, of the end of carefree school years—is framed by barbed wire and bombed-out buildings.

---

51. "Going without Mogen" refers to taking off the yellow badge before leaving the ghetto part of the city.

DOCUMENT 2-12: **Group portrait of six young Jewish women**[52] **sunbathing in the Warsaw ghetto, July 6, 1942, USHMMPA WS# 23282.**

The effects of the constant strain on residents of the ghetto became more and more discernible, even in the lines of letters written by the relatively well-off, ever-helpful and optimistic Ruth Goldbarth. After a long sequence about things to send and the suffering of her sick grandmother, she wrote her friend in Germany the following.

DOCUMENT 2-13: **Letter from Ruth Goldbarth, Warsaw, to Edith Blau, Minden, Germany, June 5, 1941, USHMMA RG 10.250*03 #68 Edith Brandon collection (translated from German).**

[. . .] Dearest, I only wish there would come a time when I can thank you with something besides mere words for all your love & friendship, for all your letters, for every one of your warm and understanding words. As everyone knows, people can withstand a lot, but I think I would already have collapsed on various occasions if I hadn't had such firm support from

---

52. In the front row, left to right: Gina Szczecińska, Gina Tabaczyńska, Dziunia Uczeń, and Hanka Ginsburg. In the upper right, Zosia Perec. We have no information about the sixth woman. Only Gina Tabaczyńska and Dziunia Uczeń survived the war.

you; merely the awareness that you, a brave little person, are there and demand of me the same strength and energy that you have to muster has given me new heart time and again. Lutek is right when he writes: in this mass catastrophe, mass misery, and mass depravity, one feels so small and insignificant, so trampled on and beaten down to the ground, that one often has to summon up a lot of courage to keep from collapsing oneself. Anyone who hasn't been to the cemetery here, where 250–300 people are buried every day, anyone who hasn't seen the "Maska" movie theater, where the police bring all the starved, ragged beggars who sit and lie in hallways, on the sidewalk, and on the causeway, can't understand it at all. And you'd have to go insane if you could really still empathize and share the pain of all that. But, thank God, we are completely apathetic by now. [...]

In June 1941 listlessness described the mind-set and physical state of large numbers if not the majority of Jews in the Warsaw ghetto. We can assume that the same applied to most other Jewish communities across German-controlled Poland. Despite the absence of a coherent, systematic plan, Nazi officials had managed to improve the effectiveness of the ghettos as mechanisms for draining Jewish resources. While economic production in Warsaw and particularly in Łódź increased, the health of workers and their families plummeted and mortality rates grew; the Germans were withholding vital staples, and Jews were exhausting their remaining supplies. If in the spring of 1941 German officials in Warsaw had decided that, as historian Christopher Browning puts it, "[t]he ghetto was not to be starved to death but made into a productive entity,"[53] the onset of war in the East made these decisions obsolete and prompted Nazi planners to favor more radical measures in dealing with the "Jewish question." With the beginning of **Operation Barbarossa**, Germans not only carried the concept of the ghetto further east but also redefined the key parameters of their anti-Jewish policies by embarking on mass violence unprecedented in world history. Even in the months before the attack on the Soviet Union on June 22, 1941, some major elements of this progression toward genocide became visible in close conjunction with the German campaign in the Balkans.

---

53. Browning, *The Origins of the Final Solution*, 131.

CHAPTER 3

Confronting New Challenges

I N THE MONTHS before the German attack on the Soviet Union, Jews around the world were affected by the Reich's unbroken string of military successes in direct and indirect ways, but few escaped the pessimistic conclusion that the war would stretch on and on without any foreseeable conclusion. As will be shown in this chapter, anti-Jewish violence was not only propagated and practiced by Nazi Germany but also by its allies and other groups far from the Reich's power base. Even in relatively safe places outside of Europe, the specter of ever greater, ever more violent **Axis** victories added to the challenges and fears already burdening refugees. Those who had fled their homes were invariably forced to adjust to new, often strange environments and scrape together aid for this transition. But, as news of Nazi incursions into the furthest reaches of Europe filtered across the globe, imagining the contours of a Jewish future after the war became impossible for many of these individuals and families. The months leading up to Germany's attack on the Soviet Union in mid-1941 revealed a prevailing sense among far-flung refugees and Jewish communities that Nazi domination would find no end, not even a severe setback. This was to become a mind-set afflicting Jews, but one shared by their non-Jewish neighbors as well.

VIOLENCE IN SOUTHEASTERN EUROPE AND BEYOND

As unique as conditions in the ghettos in German-controlled Poland were, many of the threats and challenges of daily life described by **Ruth Goldbarth** and others in the previous chapter also applied to Jews in areas that the Reich incorporated into its realm of influence in the spring of 1941: southeastern Europe, including Romania, with its just under 1 million Jews. At the time the Third Reich attacked Yugoslavia and Greece, the region had seen more than half a century of turmoil marked by a massive redrawing of borders and violent attempts at the "unmixing" of peoples.[1] At the Congress of Berlin in 1878, European powers recognized the independence of Romania, Serbia, and Montenegro, and the autonomy of Bulgaria, bringing the Ottoman Empire's claims in the Balkans to a symbolic end. The second decade of the twentieth century (1912–1922) saw a sequence of interrelated, extreme outbreaks of mass violence, which historians have subsequently separated into four distinct wars: the two Balkan wars (1912–1913), World War I (1914–1918), and the so-called Greco-Turkish War (1919–1922). Geographically scattered and influenced by a wider European conflict in distinct ways, all of these wars nevertheless were inevitably a piecemeal answer to the practical problem emerging from nationalist thought: how could homogenous nation states be created on the ruins of what had been a cosmopolitan imperial order?[2]

Groups of people construed as "ethnic minorities" were already at the heart of the issue in 1878. European powers had mandated the granting of citizenship to ethnic and religious minorities in Romania, Serbia, and Montenegro as a condition for the political recognition of independence.[3] During the Balkan wars, armies routinely practiced what is now often labeled "ethnic cleansing."[4]

---

1. For a brief overview of this process and its unfolding in the Balkans in this period, see Rogers Brubaker, "Aftermaths of Empire and the Unmixing of Peoples," in idem, *Nationalism Reframed: Nationhood and the National Question in New Europe* (New York: Cambridge University Press, 2004), 148–78.

2. See Mark Biondich, *The Balkans: Revolution, War, and Political Violence since 1878* (New York: Oxford University Press, 2011), 45–94.

3. See paragraph 44 in the Congress Treaty with Romania, in Paul Mendes-Flohr and Jehuda Reinharz, eds., *The Jew in the Modern World: A Documentary History* (New York: Oxford University Press, 1995), 406–7. Despite large numbers of Muslims in Serbia, the clauses relating to "ethnic and religious minorities" were widely understood to pertain to Jews. While Serbia's foot-dragging with respect to the recognition of Jewish citizenship lasted until the passing of a new constitution in 1888, hundreds of thousands of Jews in Romania had to wait until 1923 to become full citizens of the country.

4. See Richard C. Hall, *The Balkan Wars, 1912–1913: Prelude to the First World War* (New York: Routledge, 2000).

Further east, more than a million Ottoman Armenians were killed during World War I in bursts of genocidal violence, or otherwise perished through ill treatment at the hands of the Ottoman state.[5] And that same war not only spelled the formal end of the Ottoman Empire and saw the emergence of the Turkish republic but also prompted the victorious powers to sanction the "exchange" of populations through expulsion, en masse, of Orthodox Christians ("the Greeks") from Turkey and Muslims ("the Turks") from Greece.[6] Yet in the early 1920s, the Balkan Peninsula was still a multiethnic region, crisscrossed by political boundaries that did not correspond to ethnic divisions. The nation states that had emerged from the wars did not resemble the pristine ethnic homogeneity promised by nationalist ideologues who viewed minorities with deep distrust. In the words of historian Mark Mazower, "The tensions created by the dream of national purification lay at the heart of inter-war European politics."[7]

Although Nazism and its promise of ethnic homogeneity ambivalently fascinated many Balkan elites, biological determinism was largely absent from radical Balkan nationalisms. Changing one's name, converting to the "correct" religion, and learning an official language usually made good (or at least good enough) Albanians out of ethnic Greeks, Greeks out of Vlachs and Slavic Macedonian speakers, Serbs out of **Sephardi** Jews, and even Serbs or Bulgarians out of Muslims.[8] The situation of Jews in Romania was an exception. There, government corruption coalesced with antisemitic sentiment in bouts of physical aggression against the Jews and state-sponsored theft of their property. Since the Paris peace treaties after World War I, minority rights advocates had attempted to achieve a means of preventing discrimination against minorities, but the effort fell victim to the demise of the **League of Nations**, lack of democratic structures in Romania, and the rise of nationalist dictatorships elsewhere in the region.[9] By the summer of 1940, the loss of Bessarabia and

---

5. See Donald Bloxham, *The Great Game of Genocide: Imperialism, Nationalism, and the Destruction of the Ottoman Armenians* (Oxford: Oxford University Press, 2005).

6. Ibid., 134–69.

7. Mark Mazower, *Dark Continent: Europe's Twentieth Century* (New York: Vintage, 2000), 42, and 41–75 for a succinct overview of the minorities question in interwar Europe. See also Donald Bloxham, *Genocide, the World Wars and the Unweaving of Europe* (London: Vallentine Mitchell, 2008), 1–19.

8. Mark Mazower, *The Balkans: A Short History* (New York: Random House, 2002), 122.

9. See Carole Fink, *Defending the Rights of Others: The Great Powers, the Jews, and International Minority Protection, 1878–1938* (Cambridge: Cambridge University Press, 2004); Donald Bloxham, *The Final Solution: A Genocide* (Oxford: Oxford University Press, 2009), 78–91.

northern Bukovina inflicted on Romania by Germany and the Soviet Union had triggered a sharp move to the right and pogroms that claimed the lives of hundreds of Jews, whom Romanian nationalists regarded as Soviet agents disloyal to Romania.[10] The short-lived coalition between General **Ion Antonescu** and the ultranationalistic and murderously antisemitic **Iron Guard** movement of "Legionnaires" further radicalized Romanian politics. In January 1941, the Legionnaires murdered more than a hundred Jews in Bucharest during the failed Iron Guard coup in a pogromlike outburst of anti-Jewish violence. Antonescu quashed the rebellion with the help of the Romanian army and the acquiescence of the German regime, not out of any love for the Jews but for the political threat it posed for his position. Hitler regarded Antonescu as a reliable ally, much more so than the unstable Legionnaires, who were driven by revolutionary zeal.[11] An unknown correspondent, possibly an eyewitness, sent a summary of the pogrom to the **World Jewish Congress** offices in Switzerland.

DOCUMENT 3-1: **Account of the pogrom in Bucharest, Romania, January 21–23, 1941, USHMMA RG 68.045M (WJC Geneva), reel 2 (translated from French).**

[. . .] On the morning of January 21, after all the Legionnaire prefects had been summoned to the presidential offices of the counsel, and after the military heads of garrisons were provisionally named in their place in order to prevent any surprises, the army was ordered to occupy all state institutions, ministries, courts of law, post offices, and the posts of the T.S.F.[12] The order was given to lay siege to all the rebels' points of resistance, and when the soldiers were set on fire alive after being doused with gasoline, the response of the army was severe and resolute. Although the Legionnaires had tried to intimidate the army by pushing girls and children who were not even 14 into the front ranks, the army fired without

10. Alexandra Garbarini, with Emil Kerenji, Jan Lambertz, and Avinoam Patt, *Jewish Responses to Persecution,* vol. 2: *1938–1940* (Lanham, MD: AltaMira Press in association with the USHMM, 2011), 260–64.

11. See Radu Ioanid, *The Holocaust in Romania: The Destruction of Jews and Gypsies under the Antonescu Regime, 1940–1944* (Chicago, IL: Ivan R. Dee in association with the USHMM, 2000), 52–61, on the Iron Guard's attempted coup and the pogrom in Bucharest in January 1941. See also idem, "The Sacralised Politics of the Romanian Iron Guard," *Totalitarian Movements and Political Religions* 5 (Winter 2004): 419–53; Mihail Sebastian, *Journal, 1935–1944* (Chicago, IL: Ivan R. Dee in association with the USHMM, 2000), 310, 314–16.

12. French, *télégraphie sans fil,* literally "wireless telegraphy," the original French term for radio.

taking account of anything and the sound of machine guns and cannons fired continuously from January 21 to January 23, when this revolution was pitifully aborted.

Hundreds of Legionnaires, young girls, and children fell in this fratricidal struggle alongside workers and students who believed that they were fighting for a better cause.

Their superiors, however, cowards without a conscience, succeeded in hiding or in getting passports that enabled them to leave the country in a hurry.

Hundreds of soldiers also fell in this carnage for the defense of the country because they hesitated to fire upon the hordes of savage rebels that had formed and were armed in military fashion. In the course of all this fighting, a pogrom was unleashed, claiming the lives of hundreds of innocents who had never sought power and who were not armed to defend themselves. The flower of the Jewish population was decimated with the bestiality and the cruelty of the darkest times in history.

Hordes of Legionnaires, organized into massive groups and well-armed, invaded Jewish neighborhoods Tuesday evening and night, setting fire to synagogues, looting and carrying away in trucks all the merchandise from shops, setting fire to houses and the furniture left in the streets, and stealing everything in their path in a frenzy, like the worst barbarians.

The pitiable look of these houses struck even the Germans, who were mere passive witnesses and specialized in this trade of inhuman handiwork. In the course of Tuesday night, dozens of Jews were forcibly taken from their houses to be subjected to "inquiries." Those who had not managed to slip away to the house of some Christian who did not denounce them, the "social police" also took away some of those [in hiding]—massed in corridors and synagogues, and they were transported by truck in groups of 30–40 to Yilova [Jilava] [13] into the forests in the area around Bucharest, to the slaughterhouse, and to different Legionnaire centers. They were executed during the night by torture and shooting. In some houses 10–15 men are missing and have not been found. Of course, after the kidnapping of the men, teams of thieves arrived who carried away all the furniture and all the belongings, and threw everything out the window that did not interest them, for later burning in the street. With one exception, none of those who were taken away have come back. The

---

13. Beginning in late 1940 the Iron Guard used Jilava, a prison located near Bucharest, as an execution site.

massacre began with the men found in the synagogues Tuesday evening. Entire families, father and son who were praying to God, were taken away. Rabbi Guttman [Gutman], denounced by the parish priest, had to watch with his own eyes how his two sons were killed in his arms because they opposed the kidnapping of their father.[14] He alone escaped without mortal wounds, lying all night long stretched out on the bodies of his sons. The trucks with these living transports to the other world did not manage to carry away their merchandise, though they worked the entire night, to the sound of cannon fire and the crackling of machine guns.

The executions were generally carried out by specialists, at Yilova, at Serban Voda,[15] and in all the Legionnaires' "nests," even by women; all the corpses remained at the mercy of bandits and professional thieves, enrolled in the Legion. While the Jewish population as a whole enjoyed no protection at all, not even one soldier having been ordered to defend the lives of tens of thousands of men in the Jewish neighborhoods, organized bands, following lists drawn up in advance, everywhere in town took away those Jews who enjoyed a certain wealth or social situation, put them into buses requisitioned beforehand, and took them to previously designated places that had been prepared for the tortures that would follow.

Thus were the members of the Committee of the Jewish Community kidnapped and invited to place at the disposition of the assailing invaders the contents of their safes at the time, and after that was done, they were executed. Rich people were tortured in order to force them to give up any claim to their fortunes as well as reveal their location, and after their millions had been found and seized, they were simply defiled and murdered.

Carried off by this "social service" were innocent young people, taken from their families and tortured so that they would confess to holding communist beliefs; others were tortured to extort the addresses of rich persons in their families; afterward they were struck and beaten until their blood flowed and finally they were shot, indiscriminately. This is the great work of the Legion.

All these political crimes, which are without precedent in the entire history of pogroms, are striking for the cruelty and bestiality of the criminals and the great number of persons killed, but above all for the sadism

---

14. Rabbi Zvi Gutman's sons, Iacob and Iosif, were murdered in the pogrom. The rabbi survived the war and subsequently settled in Tel Aviv. See Ion C. Butnaru, *Waiting for Jerusalem: Surviving the Holocaust in Romania* (Westport, CT: Greenwood Press, 1993), 40, 46.

15. Serban Voda is a southern suburb of Bucharest, some two miles south of the city center.

and barbarism of the odious acts committed. Those who examined the corpses that were gathered at the Medico-Legal Institute found traces of the most abominable savageries that can be imagined and that the human consciousness cannot even conceive of. Wild animals bite and kill, but never think of defiling dead bodies, as was the case for all these innocent beings. Tongues cut out, eyes plucked out, fingers and hands chopped off, skin torn from still-living bodies, bodies mistreated, hacked, and wounded hung on slaughterhouse hooks with a label attached marked "kosher," heads cut off, and organs torn out—this is the balance sheet of the Legionnaires' heroism. And if criminal instincts on the one hand and Christian vengeance on the other have not provided all the satisfaction desired, I should complete this tableau full of horrors with the image of hundreds of bodies murdered in the forest of Yilova, stripped bare, from which even the teeth in their mouths had been removed, from which the nails had been torn, and some of which even presented the abominable image of corpses that had been violated! It has been impossible thus far even to compile exact statistics to determine the number of dead Jews, for only some of them could be found and identified. It is believed that the number of Jews killed and murdered must be around 1,000–1,500 men, women, and children. The hundreds of millions found in the houses of the Legionnaire commanders represents what could be inventoried, in the form of silver, merchandise stolen, carried to, and loaded into hundreds of trucks, furniture taken and stolen from Jewish households, money stolen from strong-boxes of the state—and to all these thefts at the same time one must add acts of espionage and treason against the country. Who planned and organized such unequalled murders and housebreakings, and who was able to launch with so much cruelty and bestiality a pogrom like the one that just took place, which will remain in the history of antisemitism as an example of bestiality, horror, and human baseness, who could thus drag in the mud the reputation of this country? I do not know. In any case, it is certain that the Legion and its Christian commanders have succeeded in demeaning the name of the Romanian nation to an unprecedented degree!

With the onset of the campaign in the Balkans, the German use of superior force quickly overcame the military problems encountered by its Italian ally and dealt a severe blow to its opponents' earlier hopes for the year 1941.[16] Yugoslavia

---

16. See Eva Mändl Roubíčková, *"Langsam gewöhnen wir uns an das Ghettoleben." Ein Tagebuch aus Theresienstadt*, ed. Veronika Springmann (Hamburg: Konkret Literatur Verlag, 2007), 24–25 (diary entries for April 6 and 15).

and Greece were defeated in rapid succession in April 1941. Yugoslavia was partitioned, with parts occupied or annexed by Germany, Italy, Hungary, and Bulgaria.[17] The most important political entity emerging from the ruins of Yugoslavia was the Independent State of Croatia, encompassing the former Yugoslav territories of Croatia, Slavonia, Dalmatia, and Bosnia-Herzegovina. Under German protection and divided into German and Italian zones of interest, the new state was run by a previously politically marginalized small group of exiles called **ustaše**. Their single-minded goal was to "purge" Croatia of non-Croats, primarily Serbs, but also Jews and Roma. The ustaše's treatment of Bosnian Muslims proved ambivalent: On the rhetorical level they accepted the Muslims as part of the new Croatian order, but in practice they viewed them with deep distrust.[18] The Wehrmacht had occupied Serbia, while a collaborationist Serbian government ruled with limited authority from the late summer of 1941 until the liberation in October 1944 through a communist-led movement and the Red Army.[19] The government of Bulgaria had already officially joined the Tripartite Pact in March 1941 and was happy to annex the territories of Yugoslav Macedonia, eastern Serbia, and Thrace, following the defeat of Yugoslavia and Greece. By early June, after the Wehrmacht had taken control of the Greek Aegean Islands and zones of occupation had been negotiated with Italy, Hitler turned his attention back to the Soviet Union and decided upon June 22, 1941, as the day of the attack.[20]

Despite the quick victory in Yugoslavia and Greece, the conquered parts of southeastern Europe presented an immense challenge to the Germans, who were intent on "securing" and "pacifying" their newly acquired areas of

---

17. The Independent State of Croatia (NDH) was proclaimed on April 10, 1941, encompassing most of what today are the countries of Croatia and Bosnia-Herzegovina, as well as Srem/Srijem (today in Serbia). Serbia came under direct military occupation by Germany, with a collaborationist Serbian government under Milan Nedić (1877–1946) established in Belgrade. The Yugoslav Banat was under German occupation, effectively run by ethnic Germans. Hungary annexed Bačka, Baranja, and Prekmurje, today in Serbia, Croatia, and Slovenia respectively. Germany occupied northern Slovenia, while Italy annexed southern Slovenia, including Ljubljana. Italy also annexed parts of Dalmatia and the Montenegrin coast, while occupying most of Montenegro. Northern Kosovo remained in German-occupied Serbia, while Italian-occupied greater Albania annexed southern Kosovo as well as western Yugoslav Macedonia. See Jozo Tomasevich, *War and Revolution in Yugoslavia, 1941–1945: Occupation and Collaboration* (Stanford, CA: Stanford University Press, 2001), 47–174.

18. See Ibid., 488–510.

19. For a history of World War II in Yugoslavia, see Ibid. On Greece, see Mark Mazower, *Inside Hitler's Greece: The Experience of Occupation, 1941–44* (New Haven, CT: Yale University Press, 1995).

20. See Gerhard Weinberg, *A World at Arms: A Global History of World War II* (New York: Cambridge University Press, 1994), 187–205, 215–24, 264–70.

influence as soon as possible and shifting their focus on the upcoming invasion of the Soviet Union. The task at hand was daunting, especially in Serbia. There, a spontaneous and decentralized uprising, fueled by traditional Serbian anti-German sentiment and harnessed by the Communist Party of Yugoslavia, proved particularly challenging. Among the Wehrmacht, SS, and police officers were many Austrians, who had already served in the region during World War I; they tended to view the Serbs as Balkan troublemakers perennially blocking Austro-German interests in the region, and they did not shy away from using radical violence as a means of "pacification."[21] Over the summer and autumn of 1941, a radical reprisal policy in Serbia—the Germans shot one hundred hostages for each dead German—took the lives of thousands of Serbian civilians.

Over time, however, "reprisals" evolved into a wholesale murder of Jewish males, whom the Germans had registered and kept as hostages since the summer, rather than ethnically Serb civilians. The reasons for this transition are complex, but they include German officials' ambitions to "solve the Jewish question" in Serbia, coupled with the understanding that shooting ethnic Serbs indiscriminately would fuel the uprising.[22] In the Independent State of Croatia, radically exclusivist Croatian nationalism drove ustaša gangs to bursts of genocidal murder of Serbian peasants in the late spring and summer of 1941, and the arrest and murders of well-known Jews.[23] Many factors fed into the escalation of violence in the former Yugoslavia in the late spring and summer of 1941.[24] By the autumn of 1941, the wanton but unorganized persecution perpetrated against Jews in the early days following Yugoslavia's fall gave way to more systematic violence. In Serbia, the Germans shot Serbian Jewish males en masse, retaliating for acts of violence and sabotage that, in reality, were not of their doing. Jewish women and children who had survived their murdered husbands,

---

21. For a slightly different reading of the Austrian officers' experience of occupation of Serbia during World War I, see Jonathan Gumz, *The Resurrection and Collapse of Empire in Habsburg Serbia, 1914–1918* (New York: Cambridge University Press, 2009). See also Andrej Mitrović, *Serbia's Great War, 1914–1918* (West Lafayette, IN: Purdue University Press, 2007).

22. See Christopher R. Browning, "Wehrmacht Reprisal Policy and the Murder of the Male Jews in Serbia," in idem, ed., *Fateful Months: Essays on the Emergence of the Final Solution* (New York: Holmes and Meier, 1985), 39–56.

23. For an introduction to the various aspects of history of the Independent State of Croatia, see Sabrina P. Ramet, ed., *The Independent State of Croatia, 1941–45* (New York: Routledge, 2007). See also Slavko Goldstein, *1941: Godina koja se vraća* (Zagreb: Novi liber, 2007), and Tomislav Dulić, *Utopias of Nation: Local Mass Killing in Bosnia and Herzegovina, 1941–42* (Uppsala: Uppsala University Press, 2005).

24. For Nazi plans to expel Slovenians from the occupied areas, see Tomasevich, *War and Revolution in Yugoslavia*, 83–129.

brothers, and fathers were deported in early December 1941 to the German Judenlager Semlin (or, as it was known in Serbian, Sajmište) across the Sava River from Belgrade.[25] In the Independent State of Croatia, ustaše deported large numbers of Serbs, Jews, and Roma to the newly created camps at Stara Gradiška, Loborgrad, and most infamously, **Jasenovac**. Jews in the Italian-occupied zones of the former Yugoslavia considered themselves lucky compared to community members terrorized by the Germans and local fascists elsewhere.[26]

Unlike in Serbia, where organized Jewish life had already been extinguished by the end of 1941, formal Jewish communities existed in Croatia at least until mid-1943. This was due to ustaše's preoccupation with Serbs, as well as the relatively large number of Jews with "honorary Aryan" status in the country, a consequence of the inconvenient fact that many high ustaša officials were married to Jews. This, of course, does not mean that lives of Jews under the ustaše were truly protected and that the latter did not consider Jews as a foreign body that should ultimately disappear. The Croatian Jewish communities were thus left with the insoluble dilemma already familiar to the **Jewish councils** in German-occupied Poland, trying to secure their community's survival at the cost of obeying problematic orders from above. The following report, written immediately after the war for the Geneva office of the World Jewish Congress, looks back at Jewish life in Croatia during the war. We see here that the Zagreb Jewish community prided itself on radiating "great initiative and brisk activity in all areas of Jewish life" at a time when the number of people under its wing far surpassed the prewar membership figure of eleven thousand.[27] Everything

---

25. See Jovan Byford, *Staro sajmište: Mesto sećanja, zaborava i sporenja* (Belgrade: Beogradski centar za ljudska prava, 2011).

26. In the Italian occupation zone of the Independent State of Croatia, authorities set up concentration camps for Jews in Kraljevica, on the island of Brač (Sumartin, Postira, Milna, Nerežišće), in the town of Hvar, as well as in Gruž, Kupari, and Lopud, all near Dubrovnik. The conditions in these camps, while harsh, were much better than in ustaša camps, and no systematic murder occurred there. The camps contained about 3,200 Jewish inmates, who were all transferred in June 1943 to a camp on the island of Rab in the northern Adriatic. After the fall of Italy in September 1943, most of the Jewish inmates joined the Communist-led Yugoslav partisan movement. See Nataša Mataušić, *Jasenovac, 1941–1945: logor smrti i radni logor* (Jasenovac-Zagreb: Javna ustanova Spomen-područje Jasenovac, 2003), 23; also, Tomasevich, *War and Revolution in Yugoslavia*, 130–37.

27. It is difficult to list the number of Jews in different parts of wartime Yugoslavia with certainty because of the artificial divisions and the unreliable and varying methods of counting Jews on censuses. However, we can estimate that about thirty thousand Jews resided in the Independent State of Croatia (Croatia, Dalmatia, Slavonia, Bosnia-Herzegovina) in 1941 and about fifteen thousand in German-occupied Serbia (Serbia proper and Serbian Banat). See the table in Tomasevich, *War and Revolution in Yugoslavia*, 583.

changed with the German attack on Yugoslavia and the creation, under German tutelage, of the Independent State of Croatia.

DOCUMENT 3-2: Report on the activities of the Jewish community of Zagreb, Independent State of Croatia, after April 1941, July 8, 1945, USHMMA RG 68.045M (WJC Geneva), reel 3, file 17 (translated from German).

[. . .] The laws issued in the very first days of the ustaša terror were aimed at the complete material and moral destruction of Jewry. Even before people could be informed regarding the directives of this antisemitic policy, the deportation of the Jews to extermination camps began, along with the rapacious plundering of their possessions. First came the banning of Jews from public restaurants and parks; then came the order for their resettlement out of the northern part of [Zagreb]. There followed a decree requiring the wearing of a Jewish badge. The yellow patch, to be worn on the chest and on the back, was intended to subject its wearer to mockery and assaults.

It must be acknowledged, however, that despite the hostility of part of the non-Jewish population, this intention of the ustaše and their German instructors was largely ineffective. Other measures then followed soon thereafter. "Trustees" were installed in Jewish firms and shops; the Jews had to leave their homes; all of their property, first the movable goods and then the real property, was confiscated; the deportation of the Jews to the camps began. Jews were hunted down on the streets in broad daylight. Numerous Jews were shot in Maksimir Park, in the eastern part of town. The only possible means of escape was leaving the country immediately or fleeing to one of the Italian-occupied areas of Yugoslavia. Robbed of all their possessions, even these refugees were usually unable to escape with anything but the clothes on their backs.[28]

Things were the same, in some places even worse, for the Jews in the provinces. In some localities (for example, in Brtschko [Brčko]), the ustaše slaughtered them in large numbers; in other places it was [ethnic German] members of the "German Culture Association" who rendered themselves conspicuous [in the abuse] (Osijek, Vinkovci), physically attacking the Jews, marching them away for forced labor, and crowding them together in warehouses.

The Community, of course, sought to do whatever it could to allay the disaster. First and foremost, it set up a communal kitchen, distributed

---

28. For the history and timeline of early anti-Jewish ustaša measures, see Ivo Goldstein, *Holokaust u Zagrebu* (Zagreb: Novi liber, 2001), 103–246.

financial assistance, created additional homes for the elderly, and organized campaigns to collect clothing and money. While the Community
thus far had been sustained on the basis of its regular budget by contributions from its members, this source of income now diminished gradually;
indeed, the Community now had to support its members. It must be
acknowledged that the Community leaders of that time succeeded, despite
endless difficulties, in raising relatively substantial sums to relieve the most
pressing needs.

[. . . ; a description of various local relief institutions, including the
Camps Welfare Office follows]

The activity of this agency [the Camps Welfare Office] began shortly
after the first concentration camps [in the Independent State of Croatia] had
been established.[29] At first, when the number of Jews in Zagreb and in the
province was still rather large, this welfare work consisted predominantly
of collecting money and goods, from which parcels were made up and sent
to the camps. The first shipments were received by the Jasenovac camp.
Then, in the fall of 1941, when the Community succeeded in taking on the
provisioning of the Loborgrad camp, the camp welfare office sent the food
there directly from Zagreb in regular truck transports. It also supplied this
camp with other things it required. The parcels provided by relatives and
friends of the camp inmates were included in the transports as well. Over
time, this institution became so popular that even non-Jews liked to make
use of it. [. . .] With the exception of isolated instances in which the parcels
were sent by individuals to camp inmates, the vast majority came from the
Community's Camps Welfare Office. These parcels—this can be said without boasting—were expertly assembled and replete with useful items; exact
records were kept of their dispatch. In turn and in the same order, parcels
were sent to every internee who was assumed with even the slightest degree
of probability to still be alive. Special parcels were assembled for children
and adolescents, which, along with the usual items, also contained some
sweets, jam, and vitamins.

---

29. On November 26, 1941, the ustaše decreed the "Legal provision for the sending of
suspicious and dangerous individuals to forced sojourn in concentration and work camps
[*u sabirne i radne logore*]." This law in effect "legalized" what had already been going on for
months: round-ups and deportations of "suspicious and dangerous individuals"—primarily
Serbs, many Jews (already almost half of the Jewish population of the Independent State of
Croatia), but also communists and other antifascists and political opponents—to ustaša camps.
Inmates were systematically ill-treated and wantonly murdered in the camps. For the activities
of the Camps Welfare Office-Zagreb, see Goldstein, *Holokaust u Zagrebu*, 385–402.

Although for the most part uniform parcels had to be assembled, their contents still had to be adjusted to the conditions or in accordance with the reports that we received from people "living freely" in the camps[30] or from people who had been released from the camps. Thus we learned that all food that required cooking had been taken away from the camp inmates in Stara Gradiška, and they were left with only the dry, ready-made items. On another occasion we learned that everything except baked goods had been taken away from the female inmates. Then a report came on Jasenovac, to the effect that everything except items that had to be cooked was being taken away; later, it was the complete reverse. In accordance with these messages, we changed the contents of the parcels. It is known with certainty that despite our regular deliveries, the distribution of the parcels was quite sporadic, and that some parcels were stolen, while others were robbed of their more valuable contents.

The Community also supplied some articles of clothing. We had suits and men's undergarments made, and the International Red Cross delegate allowed us to send the parcels with clothing in his name and with his official badge, on the assumption that this would better protect the parcels against plundering. But then we saw that only a few of the internees confirmed the receipt of clothing and undergarments; later we learned that the ustaše appropriated 90% of the clothing and undergarments and handed over almost nothing to our internees. Consequently we ceased these shipments almost entirely; only from time to time did we send a few articles of clothing, and it appears that these individual items mostly arrived all right, as was true of late for parcels in general. How important the parcels were, we learned from the personal accounts of those who, in extremely small numbers, came back from the camps. The contents of these parcels were the only thing that kept these unfortunates alive; without them, they would have starved to death much earlier. Moreover, the sending of these parcels had a favorable effect on the morale of the internees, for the parcels were, after all, the only sign that someone outside was thinking of them and looking after them. Sometimes the internees received permission to write postcards up to three times a month, each with a 20-word maximum. Because they had no one else, they wrote most of these cards to the Community. It was not always possible, however, to answer these cards. Nevertheless, the internees understood us correctly;

30. The document does not explain to what "living freely" (German: "*sogenannte 'Freilebende'*") refers; it may have been persons with a special status allowed to move in and out of the camp.

they knew that we were keeping a record of the people who wrote, and these messages were thus the only sign that they were still alive. Anyone who did not write for three or four months in a row was eliminated from our card index, on the assumption that the writer was no longer alive, which unfortunately proved to be true almost without exception. [. . .]

Among the Jews uprooted by the German occupation was the family of eleven-year-old Đura Rajs in the city of Petrovgrad (today Zrenjanin in Serbia) in the German-occupied Yugoslav Banat. Forced to move into a camp for Jews, the boy decided to write down what he was experiencing in the "*lager*," leaving us with a unique account from the hand of a child. Following radical anti-Jewish measures, ill-treatment and murder of Jews, and their confinement in ad hoc camps—like the one in Petrovgrad, in which Đura Rajs started his never-to-be-finished writings about the lager—the remaining Jews from the region were deported to Belgrade in late August.[31] Men were immediately transferred to the Topovske Šupe camp, where they joined the ranks of Jewish hostages. Left to their own devices, women and children were either taken in by Belgrade Jewish families or stayed in the Jewish community building.

DOCUMENT 3-3: **Text fragment, "Lager," by eleven-year-old Đura Rajs, Petrovgrad, German-occupied Yugoslav Banat, August 11, 1941, USHMMA Acc.2012.35.1, Đorđe (Đura) Rajs collection (translated from Serbian).**

Introduction

I have dedicated this book to the "lager." Readers will be surprised and will wonder what a "lager" is, and what kind of word that is. It's a German word, which, translated into Serbo-Croatian,[32] means camp. All

31. Tomasevich, *War and Revolution in Yugoslavia*, 585–88. See also Thomas Casagrande, *Die Volksdeutsche SS-Division "Prinz Eugen." Die Banater Schwaben und die nationalsozialistischen Kriegsverbrechen* (Frankfurt am Main: Campus Verlag, 2003).

32. "Serbo-Croatian" was the official name of the common literary language and the vernacular spoken to this day in most of the former Yugoslavia. In socialist Yugoslavia (1945–1991), the official name of the language was "Serbo-Croatian, that is, Croato-Serbian." For political reasons, the languages of Yugoslav successor states became new "national" languages, called "Serbian," "Croatian," "Bosnian," etc. The accepted international term is "Bosnian/Croatian/Serbian." In actuality, it remains one literary and spoken language, with differences in dialect, stresses, spelling, and cognate words not greater than those between British, American, Canadian, Australian, and South African English. In order to avoid the political minefield and be as precise as possible, the authors have decided to denote the language by geographical origin of the writer. Note that this document was written in Roman script.

Jews of Petrovgrad were resettled into that camp. Earlier the camp was an army barracks, which had been totally neglected and thus full of lice and bedbugs. Before the Jews were moved into the barracks, it was a breeding place for infectious diseases. The courtyard was full of various military things which the retreating Yugoslav army left in great disorder. In the rooms, soldiers unloaded their things from suitcases, trunks, etc. Bedbugs promenaded among those things just as people take an evening stroll in town. In a word, there was a big mess in this building, and the only inhabitants were lice and bedbugs. We, the children, still lived relatively well because we were together and we were able to play to our hearts' content all day long. But the adults could not boast anything like that. They worked and sweated very hard, and when they returned, the commissar [*komesar*] would harass them. And so it went. This book cannot be written in the form of a novel, because it wouldn't have any content, and therefore I am writing in the form of short stories. The stories in this book are not fabrications but rather the plain truth which I lived through. Readers will see how a young boy of 11 feels and imagines the "lager." Because I am writing this book when I am only 11 years old.

So, let's begin . . .

Petrovgrad, August 11, 1941   Đura Rajs
Moving to the "Lager"

After the entry of German troops into Petrovgrad all Jewish males between the ages of 18–60 were taken to a former elementary school and locked up there. They were escorted by guards every day to work at various places. My father was also among them. So it went for about a month. On May 2, 1941, a fateful day for the Jews, an order was issued that all Jews must resettle to the former Hungarian army barracks [*u bivšu Honvedsku kasarnu*].[33] The resettlement began. . . . Just to be safe we moved to the house of my grandmother who was also alone because grandpa was also in the school, to await the day when we, too, would have to be resettled. That day soon arrived. On May 8 a police vehicle [*štrafkola*] pulled over with two auxiliary policemen [*hilfspolicista*] armed to the teeth.[34] They

---

33. This region belonged to Hungarian crown lands and was part of Austria-Hungary until 1918.

34. In this sentence, the author coins two words by combining German with Serbo-Croatian: first, the bastardized German štraf (from *Strafe*, punishment) and the Serbo-Croatian word for *kola* (vehicle); second, a Serbo-Croatian declension of the German word *Hilfspolizist* ("auxiliary policeman").

showed us an announcement that said that we must immediately resettle
to the barracks. Dad and grandpa then came to help with the move. My
uncle Franja, a medical student in Zagreb, who, immediately upon arriving in Petrovgrad, went to the school and voluntarily signed up for labor,
came along with them.

The policemen allowed us to bring along two beds, a sofa, and an
armoire. Also, a table with four chairs, a wash basin, some food stuffs, and
so on and so on. Then we loaded all of that on a cart, bid farewell to our
acquaintances, friends, and relatives, and we took off in a carriage to our
future apartment, actually to our future jail.

The Germans executed Đura's father in a mass reprisal shooting in early
October. When the remaining Jewish women and children were ordered to
report for deportation to Sajmište in early December, Đura and his mother duly
reported, while Đura's younger brother, Jovan, eight at the time, was sent to stay
with his aunt, who was married to a Serb; it saved his life.[35] Like so many others in the region, the author did not survive. Đura and his mother were killed
between March and May 1942 in a gas van sent from Berlin used to murder
some seven thousand remaining Serbian Jewish women and children.[36]

Compared to those countries in the region under direct German rule, the
situation in Bulgaria changed less radically for its roughly fifty thousand Jews of
predominantly Sephardic background, half of whom lived in Sofia, the capital.
The country joined the Axis in its war against Greece and Yugoslavia, in return
for which it received the province of Thrace from Greece and Macedonia, as
well as parts of eastern Serbia from Yugoslavia.[37] Seen from within, Bulgaria had
appeared since early 1941 set to join the German bandwagon in its pursuit of
the "Jewish question" through discriminatory measures of its own.

---

35. See Jovan Rajs, *Opunomoćenik ućutkanih* (Belgrade: Partenon, 2004). The author
of the memoir is the only one from his family who survived; after the war and completing
medical school at Belgrade University, he settled in Sweden.

36. See Christopher R. Browning with contributions by Jürgen Matthäus, *The Origins of
the Final Solution: The Evolution of Nazi Jewish Policy, September 1939–March 1942* (Lincoln
and Jerusalem: University of Nebraska Press and Yad Vashem, 2004), 421–23.

37. See Frederick B. Chary, *The Bulgarian Jews and the Final Solution 1940–1944*
(Pittsburgh, PA: University of Pittsburgh Press, 1972); Marshall Lee Miller, *Bulgaria During
the Second World War* (Stanford, CA: Stanford University Press, 1975).

DOCUMENT 3-4: Report on the situation of the Jews in Bulgaria, no date (early 1942), USHMMA RG 68.045M (WJC Geneva), reel 4, file 32 (translated from French).

[. . .] It was at the end of 1940 that draft legislation aimed directly at Jews appeared. Most well-informed people continued, however, to believe that this bill would not be received favorably by the public and would never become law. But gradually the situation changed; youth organizations such as the Legion and Ratnik published anti-Jewish pamphlets.[38] Thousands of tracts were distributed. Anti-Jewish posters covered the walls of the town [most likely Sofia], and, finally, anti-Jewish talks began to be broadcast over the radio. All this propaganda found—as everywhere else in Europe for that matter—adherents, and soon the number of antisemites grew very large in the bigger towns.

The steps taken with certain important persons by representatives of the Consistory [the representative body of the Jewish community] produced a specific result at first. The situation seemed to ease for a brief period, only to become still worse later. Finally, on January 21, 1941, the draft bill was submitted to the [parliament] Chamber. After a long discussion, during which some elder statesmen spoke up in our defense, a large majority approved the draft bill.[39]

Since then, the situation of Jews as Bulgarian citizens has been clear. The Jew is the "ballast" of the nation; he has no rights; every possibility for economic prosperity has been taken from him. Several decrees have been published that aim at impoverishing the Jewish population. A very small group of Jews, war volunteers, war orphans, holders of the order of valor, and finally those baptized before the law came into force, are privileged— up to a certain point.

[. . .] As soon as this law became effective, certain Jews attempted to get around it to save part of their property, and others attempted to send

---

38. The Union of Bulgarian National Legions (known simply as the Legion, or Legionnaires) and Warriors for the Advancement of the Bulgarian National Spirit (known as *ratnitsi*—warriors—or, in singular, *ratnik*) were two major Bulgarian far right-wing organizations with ties to Nazi German associations, including the SS. See Chary, *The Bulgarian Jews and the Final Solution*, 8.

39. The "Law for the Defence of the Nation" enacted in January 1941 provided the platform for a range of discriminatory measures, had since the summer of 1941 expanded to include compulsory labor in units comprised of Jews only. See Chary, *The Bulgarian Jews and the Final Solution*, 36–66.

part of their capital abroad. The police got wind of several of these transactions, and the guilty were severely punished.

The guilty were locked up like real criminals and treated as such. The interrogations dragged out for entire days. The prisoners were ill-treated and given little food in tiny cells without light. It is obvious that after being treated this way for a time, the prisoner confesses everything. Then his fate is among the most miserable; his property is seized and he is imprisoned for years on end. In similar cases, money can also take care of everything. The fate of the prisoner can be improved by the distribution of money among the guards who surround him. After the tribunal issues its decision, money can also modify the verdict. In the same way, the periods of imprisonment imposed on Jews can be shortened. Put another way, thanks to the prevailing corruption, the fate of Jews is eased, but at the cost of considerable impoverishment of the entire Jewish population. It is obvious that in such cases, the Jews often fall victim to being swindled, against which they can do nothing. A civil servant promises to ease the fate of a Jew in return for a sum payable in advance. The money is spent, but the fate of the Jew is unchanged. The Jews cannot complain in response because they would be punished still more. [. . .]

The cultural life of Jews in Bulgaria is reminiscent of that of Jews in the ghetto of the Middle Ages. Several factors contribute to this. The curfew, the lack of Jewish cultural organizations, the elimination of Jews from Christian cultural centers, the impossibility of Jews attending lectures and concerts, and the absence of radio make the Jew a being who is withdrawn into himself and leads his life only among family members. Cases are not rare where a father begins to study or read at home with his son or even to learn music, etc.

Owing to the prevailing atmosphere in the population, Jews do not dare frequent cafes and restaurants, given that incidents between Jews and Bulgarians have occurred on several occasions.

In general, morale is low in the Jewish population, which, assaulted from all sides, wonders how it will all end. [. . .]

Axis expansion into the Balkans led to an extensive redrawing of borders. In addition to Yugoslavia being dismembered, Germany and Italy divided up occupied Greece between themselves, cutting off its northern area (parts of Greek Macedonia and Thrace), which Bulgaria annexed. Italy administered the bulk of the Greek mainland and islands, while the city of Salonika in the north, with its roughly fifty thousand Jewish inhabitants, fell under German occupation.

Since the early twentieth century, tens of thousands of refugees had come to Salonika as a result of war and turmoil in the region, culminating with the 1923 "exchange of populations" mentioned earlier. In 1941, however, comparatively few Jewish refugees had found their way into the city before the Wehrmacht arrived.[40] Among the city's residents was Yomtov Yacoel, a lawyer who worked as counsel for the Jewish Community and in 1943 began writing a memoir on the wartime fate of the Jews in his city.[41] Both his position in the community and the point at which he chose to begin writing—after the war had reached the Balkans—flavor his observations. Anti-Jewish measures that might have shocked him early on, soon after the German occupation began, appear in a less stark light from the distance of 1943, with its more dramatic events. Here we find Yacoel also commenting on the behavior of his fellow Jewish functionaries, highlighting some of the fissures and conflicts seen in other communities under Nazi rule.

DOCUMENT 3-5: **Yomtov Yacoel, "In the Anteroom to Hell: Memoir," 1943, in** *The Holocaust in Salonika: Eyewitness Accounts*, **ed. Steven Bowman (New York: Sephardic House, 2002), 30–34.**

[. . .] From the entrance of the Germans in Salonika in April 1941 until July 1942, that is to say, during 15 months of Occupation there was no Jewish racial problem in Salonika. The arrest and imprisonment of a few Jewish notables for a couple of months at the beginning of the Occupation and the confiscation of the archives of the Jewish Community as well as the Jewish libraries were not measures forming part of a systematic anti-Jewish persecution, because Christian notables were also arrested preventively and confiscations of Christian properties also took place. The attitude of the German authorities toward the Jewish element was, during

---

40. See Bea Lewkowicz, *The Jewish Community of Salonika: History, Memory, Identity* (London: Vallentine Mitchell, 2006); Steven Bowman, ed., *The Holocaust in Salonika: Eyewitness Accounts* (New York: Sephardic House, 2002). There were some forty-eight thousand refugees from the Bulgarian zone in Salonika in 1941; it is difficult to estimate the number of Jews among them, but it was not high. See Mark Mazower, *Salonica, City of Ghosts: Christians, Muslims, and Jews, 1430–1950* (New York: Alfred A. Knopf, 2005), 392.

41. Yacoel was born in Trikala, Greece, in 1899 or 1902, studied in Athens, and subsequently set up a law practice in Salonika. As legal counsel to Salonika's Jewish community, he helped negotiate with the German occupation authorities. He fled to Athens in 1943, but was subsequently arrested and sent to **Birkenau** in March 1944, where he was murdered. See Bowman, *The Holocaust in Salonika*, 23.

this 15-month period, one of indifference. From time to time various anti-Jewish leaflets were printed and circulated under the Germans' tolerance. Also the radio emitted anti-Semitic propaganda programs; and confiscations of business assets of certain Jewish companies used to take place, and certain Jews suffered arbitrary expulsions from their own stores; and certain blackmailing financial transactions against Jews were noted. But all these had the character of isolated acts perpetrated by certain agencies (such as the billeting services of the Occupation authorities or the German Military Supplies Office), or by certain German military personnel, or finally at the instigation of local Christians. No programmatically defined anti-Semitic policies were revealed by the German authorities during the first 15 months of Occupation.

As mentioned before, the Jewish Community was immediately placed under the jurisdiction of the Gestapo. Jewish clubs and organizations were closed. The community's Hebrew schools stopped functioning. The activities of philanthropic foundations slackened and all Jewish communal activity stopped. The Community existed as a local organization for registering births and deaths, for overseeing the exclusively religious operation of synagogues and for paying the employees. Chief Rabbi Dr. Koretz[42] was arrested in Athens in May 1941 and was transported to Vienna where he was kept in prison for several months. After his release and return to Salonika he was restricted to the duties of overseeing the religious functions and services of the community. The President of the [Jewish] Community, Saltiel,[43] was in almost daily contact with the Gestapo, where he received orders and executed them with no discussion. From the moment of his appointment he had an assistant J. Albala

---

42. Dr. Zvi (also Tsevi, Tzevi, or Sevy) Koretz (1894–1945) was born in Rzeszów, Poland, and served as the Chief Rabbi of Salonika. Educated at the Berlin Rabbinical Seminary, he was appointed to the post in 1933 after the local Salonika Jewish community decided to look outside of Greece to fill the position. Following his arrest shortly after the German invasion, Koretz was sent to Vienna, but he returned to Salonika less than a year later and resumed his post. In August 1943, Koretz, his family, and a number of other Jewish community leaders were deported to the Bergen-Belsen camp. He was liberated at the end of the war, but died in early June 1945. See Minna Rozen, "Jews and Greeks Remember Their Past: The Political Career of Tzevi Koretz (1933–43)," *Jewish Social Studies* 12 (2005): 111–66.

43. Saby (Sabbetai) Saltiel (1915–?) was appointed head of the Jewish Community of Salonika after the German invasion of Greece in April 1941 (Saltiel was judged ineffectual and replaced in December 1942 by Koretz).

[Alballa],[44] a refugee from Vienna, who knew German well and served as interpreter and liaison with the German authorities. [. . .], besides Albala, the Gestapo imposed on the community to maintain some 30–40 Jewish refugees from Germany, Czechoslovakia and Poland, who happened to be in Salonika at the start of the Occupation. This strange protection of Jewish refugees by the Gestapo—to which the refugees turned whenever the community denied their unreasonable and excessive demands—caused mistrust among Salonika's Jews concerning the role of those refugees. And many times suspicions were voiced among Jewish circles concerning the extent of those persons' Jewishness. Their later behavior proved those suspicions right. [. . .]

But what was the attitude of the Jews as individuals and as a racial group toward the Germans from the beginning of the Occupation in Salonika? Did they give any signs of insubordination toward the orders of the Occupation authorities? Were there any cases of sabotage or clandestine activities aimed at the Germans in which Jews participated? The answer to these questions is negative. The Jews of Salonika, having been informed of the fate of the other organized coreligionist communities of Central Europe, Poland and Serbia, and of the brutal punishment imposed on thousands of their fellow Jews for the acts or omissions of one person, were seized by real terror from the first day of the Occupation. Lacking any guide or any signal, as if by instinct, every Jew placed restrictions on himself for the whole of his behavior, so that the invader would not find the least grounds to justify the imposition of an anti-Semitic policy. [. . .]

With the expansion of Axis control into the Balkans, most of the continent had fallen under totalitarian rule. While the fate of Jews living under the swastika seemed particularly grim, Jewish observers reserved judgment about whether refugees escaping from Hitler's grasp into the Soviet sphere of influence

---

44. Jacques Alballa (1901–?) was born in Belgrade and worked as a travel agent in Vienna before he moved to Salonika, where he held multiple positions in the Jewish community under the German occupation. The Jewish community came to revile Alballa for his abuse of power and corrupt practices as Jewish community president Saltiel's interpreter (Alballa knew German, Saltiel did not), as head of the Jewish Police in the Baron Hirsch ghetto, and as Jewish community president after Chief Rabbi Koretz was removed in April 1943. In the summer of 1943, Alballa was deported to Bergen-Belsen and liberated at the end of the war. See Rozen, "Jews and Greeks Remember Their Past"; Rena Molho and Joseph Robert White, "Thessalonikē," in *The United States Holocaust Memorial Museum Encyclopedia of Camps and Ghettos, 1933–1945, Ghettos in German-Occupied Eastern Europe*, vol. 2, ed. Martin Dean (Bloomington: Indiana University Press in association with the USHMM, 2012), 1844–48.

were indeed better off. That concern applied particularly to those Jews caught in the dragnet of Soviet arrest and deportation campaigns designed to root out "enemies of the state." A standard feature of Stalin's rule, the scope and intensity of the purges had increased to genocidal proportions in the 1930s in Ukraine. In the spring and early summer of 1941, the geographical focus of the GPU/NKVD's[45] terror shifted to areas incorporated into the Soviet Union since the beginning of World War II, particularly the formerly independent Baltic states and the Ukrainian-Romanian border regions in the south.[46]

The city of Chernivtsi (also Czernowitz, Cernăuți) had come under Soviet domination after Germany had forced Romania to cede the provinces of Northern Bukovina and Bessarabia to Stalin. Chernivtsi and its large Jewish community had a colorful history, with the era of Habsburg rule before 1918 popularly regarded as a "golden epoch."[47] Once the Soviets had taken over in the city, arrests and deportations—often to the Gulags in the Arctic Circle—affected a disproportionate number of Jews. The issue of how to evaluate Soviet oppression presented a further problem after Stalin had joined the anti-Hitler coalition. Starting in late June 1941 the Red Army had clearly begun to bear the brunt of the military campaign against Germany, with Jewish organizations waging public appeals for supporting the Soviet war effort. It also became clear by and by that those deported to the Gulags had involuntarily escaped from almost certain death at the hand of Germany and its Romanian ally. Still, the issue of "Soviet crimes" weighed on those contemplating eastward flight and became an unsettling propaganda tool deployed by the Axis. The following letter was sent in late 1942 from Chernivtsi, then again under Romanian rule, to the Swiss-based **RELICO** organization by a prominent Jewish functionary with good connections to the Romanian regime and reflects some of the concerns for those deported earlier by Soviet authorities.

---

45. GPU (Gosudarstvennoye Politicheskoye Upravlenie, or State Political Directorate) was the state security service of the Russian Federal Soviet Socialist Republic from 1922 to 1934. Emerging from the Bolshevik revolutionary secret police, it was reorganized and renamed several times but is often used interchangeably with the NKVD (Narodnyy komissariat vnutrennikh del, or People's Commissariat for Internal Affairs) and the KGB, two of the most famous names for the Soviet secret service. See Paul R. Gregory, *Terror by Quota: State Security from Lenin to Stalin* (New Haven, CT: Yale University Press, 2009); Paul Hagenloh, *Stalin's Police: Public Order and Mass Repression in the USSR, 1926–1941* (Washington, DC: Woodrow Wilson Center Press, 2009).

46. See Timothy Snyder, *Bloodlands: Europe between Hitler and Stalin* (New York: Basic Books, 2010).

47. See Marianne Hirsch and Leo Spitzer, *Ghosts of Home: The Afterlife of Czernowitz in Jewish Memory* (Berkeley: University of California Press, 2010).

DOCUMENT 3-6: Letter from Manfred Reifer,[48] Cernăuți, Romania, to RELICO–Geneva, on Soviet deportations of Jews in June 1941, November 15, 1942, USHMMA RG 68.045M (WJC Geneva), reel 12, file 109 (translated from German).

Dr. Manfred Reifer

Cernăuți [Chernivtsi], Masarykgasse 9

Cernăuți, November 15, 1942

To the Relief Committee

for the Warstricken Jewish Population,

Geneva

As a result of inquiries made of various friends here by your Committee, I learned of the Committee's existence and am hastening to submit the following request to you:

In June 1941, the Bolsheviks, who at that time occupied the Northern Bukovina and Bessarabia, forcibly deported the leading Jewish figures— landowners, factory owners, lawyers, physicians, merchants, representatives of the Jewish people, as well as legislators, community presidents, and judicial and police officials, etc., etc.—and confiscated their assets. Those most severely affected were the Zionists, who were rightly viewed as the greatest enemies of Bolshevism. Labeled "political criminals," they were deported, separated from their families, and placed in areas where contact with the outside world is forbidden to them. The majority of these unfortunates are located in the Novosibirsk region. Only from the so-called "non-politicals" has a limited amount of news gotten through to us, by way of the Geneva Red Cross. They are asking for money, clothing, and food. But they are not the only ones who must be taken care of; the "politicals," who are not allowed to write letters, are also first and foremost in need of care. In America, everything must be done to help these unfortunates as quickly as

---

48. Manfred Reifer (1888–1952) was a prominent member of the Jewish community in Bukovina and heavily involved in the Zionist movement in Chernivtsi. A World War I veteran, Reifer served in the Romanian Parliament from 1930 to 1932 as a member of the Jewish Party of Romania. Due to a heart condition, Reifer was spared being sent eastward during the Soviet occupation of 1940–1941, or being deported to **Transnistria** during the German occupation. In 1943 he and his wife fled to Bucharest around the time their son Theodor Gideon died while serving as a soldier in the Romanian military. The couple and their daughter Ditha succeeded in immigrating to Palestine via Turkey in 1945. See Wilhelm Filderman, *Memoirs and Diaries: 1900–1940*, vol 1 (Tel Aviv: Goldstein-Goren Diaspora Research Center, 2004), 549; Claims Resolution Tribunal Award: www.crt-ii .org/_awards/_apdfs/Reifer_Manfred.pdf (accessed December 6, 2011).

possible. I believe that the world has no inkling of the sufferings of these people who are under the heel of the Bolshevik "emancipators of man." I myself escaped deportation only through a miracle, particularly because the infamous GPU had specially targeted me as a former Jewish legislator.

I assume that your office is headed by Mr. Lichtheim,[49] and I expect him to act swiftly and effectively.

The last and only news that reached me from the deportee Dr. Theodor Weitzelberger—the former acting president of the Zionist organization in Bukovina—is dismal.[50] The message does not come directly from him, but was passed on to me through a "Comité de secours" [relief committee] via the Red Cross.

In general, the whole wide world will sit up and take notice once it hears the truth about the brutal deportations carried out by the Bolsheviks.

I have written to Wise[51] about this matter but received no information. I await your answer by return post.

Respectfully yours,
[Signed] Manfred Reifer

It is not clear whether Reifer received an answer to this carefully worded letter designed to pass the Romanian censors. The much more imminent threat to Jews elsewhere probably meant that his pleas never became a priority for Jewish officials observing the war from their offices in neutral Geneva. Jews were facing hostile environments and lethal attacks even beyond the borders of Europe—beyond the major centers of western racist thinking and Christian antisemitism—as political crises fostered anti-Jewish violence during the first half of 1941. As far away from Hitler's Berlin as Iraq, with its roughly ninety thousand Jews mostly concentrated in Baghdad and other major cities, the onslaught of Nazi propaganda provided cover for anti-Jewish interests. These had grown with the mounting frustration over British rule. Several months after more than 150 Iraqi Jews, including several dozen women, had been killed and

---

49. On Richard Lichtheim, see the Glossary.

50. Theodor Weitzelberger (Weisselberger) (b. 1888 in Stanisławów, Poland), lawyer and leader of the Zionist movement in Bukovina. He was arrested along with many other prominent Zionists when the Red Army invaded. In the fall of 1941 the **JTA** issued a plea for his release and that of other Jewish leaders held in the Soviet Union. See Yad Vashem, Central Database of Shoah Victims Names, www.yadvashem.org; "Seek Release of Rumanian Jewish Leaders in Russia," *Jewish Telegraphic Agency*, October 16, 1941.

51. On Rabbi Stephen S. Wise, see the Glossary.

many more injured and raped in the aftermath of a failed coup in Baghdad, the **Board of Deputies of British Jews** received the following report.[52]

DOCUMENT 3-7: **Anonymous report submitted to the Jewish Agency for Palestine on "The Position of the Jewish Population in Iraq," March 24, 1942, USHMMA RG 59.023M (Board of Deputies of British Jews), reel 24, frame 280.**

THE POSITION OF THE JEWISH POPULATION IN IRAQ

The following account on the position of the Jewish population in Iraq was given to the Jewish Agency for Palestine by two very trustworthy persons—an Army Chaplain and a high Intelligence Officer, who have recently come from Baghdad.

The horrors perpetrated by the Arabs in Baghdad and in several provincial towns on June 1st & 2nd [1941] before the entry of the British troops still haunt the memories of the Iraqi Jews. A high British Officer who was at Baghdad at the time gave most shocking details of the way women were treated. Jewish families whose members had fallen victims to the outrages are doing their utmost to hide the "disgrace," but it is known that many girls had committed suicide after what they had gone through.

Nor are the massacres forgotten and none of the Arabs guilty of taking part in the pogrom have yet been prosecuted. Of the compensation that was to be paid to the victims and the surviving members of these families of those who had been murdered, not a penny has been paid and the Jews are so terrorised that they dare not ask.

To these memories and dejection a new mortal fear has now been added to what may happen to the Jewish population if, for reasons of military tactics, the British troops may have to withdraw or in the event of a German invasion of Turkey, or in a panic during bombardment from the air. The Arabs are making it clear to their Jewish neighbours that at

---

52. On April 1, 1941, a nationalist group sympathetic to Nazi Germany led by Rashid 'Ali al-Kailani overthrew the British-backed Iraqi government. A battle between German-supported Iraqi forces and the British military for control of Iraq ensued, which ended on May 31 in a victory for Britain. In the brief, one-day period after the coup's leader, al-Kailani, had fled Iraq and before the old government could reassert its power, anger caused by the success of the British forces was directed at the local Jewish population in the infamous Farhud pogrom. See Esther Meir-Glitzenstein, *Zionism in an Arab Country: Jews in Iraq in the 1940s* (New York: Routledge, 2004), 13–14; Klaus-Michael Mallmann and Martin Cüppers, *Nazi Palestine: The Plans for the Extermination of the Jews in Palestine* (New York: Enigma Books, 2010), 66–68; Jeffrey Herf, *Nazi Propaganda for the Arab World* (New Haven, CT: Yale University Press, 2009), 60–62, 237–38, 264.

the first opportunity a wholesale massacre will be organised. The Arabs are openly discussing among themselves how they will divide the spoils and especially the Jewish women. Two young Arabs recently appeared before a judge in connection with a brawl over the allocation of a Jewish girl whom each wanted to have for himself.

Jewish women now feel compelled to dress in Arab garb hoping in this way to escape violence.

The whole population is utterly dejected and helpless. The air is full of rumours of a coming German attack on Turkey and the position fills everybody with alarm and anxiety.

STALLED HOPES ON THE EVE OF OPERATION BARBAROSSA

In mid-1941, rumors abounded among Jewish communities everywhere, but the much-longed-for end of the war was nowhere in sight. Worse still, the advancing Wehrmacht raised the prospects for realization of Hitler's assurances—as he had expressed them in his notorious and subsequently oft-repeated "prophecy" of January 1939—that should there be a world war, "the annihilation of the Jewish race in Europe" would be the outcome.[53] At the same time, the growing strains of war reduced Jewish organizations' ability to function, not only in the warring but also in neutral countries. In the United States, with antisemitic attitudes a force to reckon with and the struggle between isolationist and intervention-ist forces growing sharper, World Jewish Congress president **Stephen S. Wise** was eager to turn more of his organization's work to domestic priorities and to curtail funding relief work in the ghettos of German-controlled Poland. In the spring of 1941, Wise cabled to the organization's offices in London and Geneva that—in light of the U.S. embargo of Germany and despite the fact that the United States had not entered the war—all relief activities "with and through Poland must cease at once, and at once in English means AT ONCE, not in the future." Yet not all WJC officials agreed that reacting to outside pressure by turning inward was the right strategy, and continued providing aid for Jews in the Reich's realm of control as best as they could.[54]

---

53. Garbarini et al., *Jewish Responses to Persecution*, 2:103–4.

54. Cf. Saul Friedländer, *Nazi Germany and the Jews:* (vol. 2) *The Years of Extermination, 1939–1945* (New York: HarperCollins, 2007), 304–5 (emphasis in the original). See also Raya Cohen, "The Lost Honor of Bystanders? The Case of Jewish Emissaries in Switzerland," in *"Bystanders" to the Holocaust: A Re-Evaluation*, ed. David Cesarani and Paul A. Levine (London: Frank Cass, 2002), 162–65.

Jews who followed the world news needed no reminder from Hitler about the growing global dimensions of the "Jewish question." Yet what could be done in the near and more distant future? In the following article, philosopher and peace scholar Morris Cohen took a broad look at possible postwar constellations.[55] Focusing on problems regarding immediate relief, migration, and the fight for human rights, Cohen took Germany's status in early 1941 as the dominant European continental power as his point of departure and discussed possible, equally catastrophic, scenarios for the Jewish future. They included the **Madagascar Plan**—one of the "territorial solutions" discussed by the German Foreign Office, **Heydrich's Security Police** and **SD** apparatus, and other agencies since the summer of 1940—which was designed to ship Jews en masse from the continent to a French colony off the coast of East Africa. Cohen's piece—reflecting, inevitably, the contours of mid-century western colonial imagination—also considered a hypothetical extension of the Wehrmacht's aggressive drive toward the **Yishuv** in Palestine with its half a million Jews, as well as the likelihood of Nazi aggression targeting the Soviet Union.

DOCUMENT 3-8: Morris R. Cohen, "Jewish Studies of Peace and Post-War Problems," *Contemporary Jewish Record* **4 (April 1941): 110–25.**

[. . .] We must also consider the contingency of a German-dominated Europe, in which case some measures will have to be taken by us to counteract the well-known Nazi plans for the expulsion of Jews to uncivilized territories, without regard as to habitability. We must have a knowledge of these territories in order to expose the possible attempts of the Nazis to disguise their hideous plans under the form of a totalitarian "solution" of the Jewish question.

Thus, we are reliably informed that Hitler plans to dump the 5,000,000 Jews of Europe into Madagascar, to promise them local autonomy, and to demand that the rest of the Jews of the world support his

---

55. Morris Raphael Cohen (1880–1947) was born in Minsk to an Orthodox Jewish family that later immigrated to New York City. After training as a philosopher, Cohen spent his career teaching at CUNY and the University of Chicago. Increasingly active in Jewish organizational work, Cohen promoted vocational training programs, helped establish the Conference on Jewish Relations, and became a founder and editor of *Jewish Social Studies*. In 1941, he took over as chair of the AJC's "Committee on Peace Studies." See "Contributors to this Issue," *Contemporary Jewish Record* 4, no. 2 (April 1941): 197; *New York Times*, January 30, 1947, 25; Milton R. Konvitz, "Morris Raphael Cohen," *The Antioch Review* 7 (winter 1947): 487–501.

plan or else see it carried out in a more brutal way. We have made a careful study of the opportunities of Madagascar and are prepared to show what horrors are involved in the plan.

The transplanting of human beings to radically different climatic and social conditions is always a grave and perilous undertaking. The record of many failures at colonization, e.g., by the British in the West Indies, shows the necessity of taking all factors into account, the economic and ethnographic as well as the geographic. On the other hand, the record of Jewish colonization in Palestine, in Argentina and in Southeastern Europe shows that with proper selection and training Jews can make excellent colonizers. It is important that American Jews, as well as men of goodwill everywhere, should get rid of the myth that Jews have always been traders or in the professions and entirely unfit for pioneer labor. [. . .]

There are those who think that if Hitler is victorious all the Jews that he can reach will either be killed outright or at once dumped into some pesthole in Africa. But reflection shows that while the amount of harm that he can thus effect is unfortunately enormous, large numbers of human beings cannot be so easily wiped out or readily disposed of. And if the history of the Jews since the Hadrianic persecutions[56] be any guide, it is reasonable to assume that there will be Jews in Europe after Hitler's days are over.

It is thus, in any case, necessary to study the precise position of the Jews in the Nazi plans for the new economic order. This is not as difficult to do as it might at first appear. For a thorough examination of Hitler's general policies shows that they have little originality, that they are all but a brutal intensification of plans and measures previously discussed or even in part carried out in Germany since the reaction that followed the Napoleonic wars. We must know these plans and measures if we are to do anything about them before it is too late.

If I say little about the problems of Palestine it is not because I do not think they are important but because they have already received a relatively great deal of attention from the Jewish Agency, the various Zionist organizations, the Palestine Economic Corporation and various Jewish scholars in all

---

56. Hadrian (76–138 CE), Roman Emperor from 117–138 CE, attempted to "Romanize" the city of Jerusalem and sparked the Bar-Kokhba Revolt of the years 132–135 CE. Harsh reprisals and laws severely curtailing Jewish religious life followed the Roman victory. See Samuel Abramsky and Shimon Gibson, "Bar Kokhba," in *Encyclopaedia Judaica*, eds. Fred Skolnik and Michael Berenbaum, 2nd ed. (Detroit, MI: Macmillan Reference USA, 2007), 3:156–64.

lands. There is, however, one aspect of the situation which has not been as yet duly considered because it seems too horrible to contemplate, and that is the possibility that the Axis powers may capture Palestine. No matter how remote that may seem today, we must not fail to consider it.

We must therefore investigate the Nazi and Fascist attitude on the problem of Palestine and also the attitude of the Catholic Church, which has always regarded itself as the proper guardian of the Holy Places. In any case, the future of Palestine and the problem of Arab-Jewish relations must be viewed from a long range point of view if we are to be prepared for the various situations which may develop.

Nor must we forget that the problem of five million Jews in Soviet Russia may become a burning one in the very near future. It will certainly be so if war breaks out between Germany and the Soviet Union; and it may also develop into an acute form if German influence in Russia should increase, as it may do in certain contingencies. At present we have inadequate knowledge of Jewish conditions in Russia not only because of the general attitude of its government in discouraging the sending out of news but also because we have not established sufficient means of contact to enable us to gather available information. [. . .]

While political grand designs for the postwar era remained academic as long as there were no prospects for peace, Jews fleeing from crisis regions had no choice but to adapt their personal lives to their new environments. For most refugees, adjustment proved to be a gradual process involving a myriad of large and small steps. Severe culture shock often awaited Central European Jews who landed in South America, Asia, and other far-flung locales they once considered "exotic." Shanghai, for instance, remained one of the few ports of refuge in early 1941, but it demanded much adjustment from the newcomers.[57] Arriving in May, writer Yehoshua Rapoport[58] noted his confusion about a place that seemed strange and familiar at the same time.

---

57. See David Kranzler, *Japanese, Nazis & Jews: The Jewish Refugee Community of Shanghai, 1938–1945* (New York: Yeshiva University Press, 1988).

58. Born in Białystok, Yehoshua Rapoport (1895–1971) was a respected writer and translator in multiple languages, but primarily Yiddish. Rapoport had lived in Warsaw before the war, fleeing to Shanghai in 1941 via Lithuania and the Japanese port of Kobe with his wife Mala and a group of Polish Jews. In Shanghai, Rapoport continued his publishing work and made refugee issues much of his focus. He moved to Australia with his wife and son shortly after the end of the war. See Irene Eber, ed., *Voices from Shanghai: Jewish Exiles in Wartime China* (Chicago: University of Chicago Press, 2008), 65.

DOCUMENT 3-9: **Yehoshua Rapoport, Shanghai, diary entries for May 12, 28, and June 2, 1941, in** *Voices from Shanghai: Jewish Exiles in Wartime China*, **ed. Irene Eber (Chicago: University of Chicago Press, 2008), 91–92 (ellipses and brackets in the original).**

[May 12, 1941]

I remember now my first meeting with Jewish Shanghai. Such a disappointment, such a blow to my hopes. . . . I had longed for even a small Jewish community where I can work again. When fate brought us to Shanghai, which was to be a solution to my spiritual imprisonment, I rejoiced: a city with a Jewish population! But the reception . . . was not what I expected. We arrived in the middle of the night after five hours at sea without warm food. The Jewish community in Shanghai did not receive the fifty refugees in their homes, but sent us to the Jewish Club, where we were to sit for the rest of the night. The rabbi did prepare a home for the rabbis and the rabbinic students, but for the writers and the simple Jews there was no place and we . . . were tossed into the Pingling shelter, into the pigsty, without a table, without a chair. . . . It was so hard to receive a few dollars for a flat—the local Jews regarded this with misgivings: why are we better than the German Jews [they asked]? They can live in the "Heime" [homes], and you cannot?

[May 28, 1941]

HICEM[59] gave us the first month's rent. This was not that easy. But the second month's rent we had to receive from EastJewCom. . . . But that too is not that easily obtained. For this task a special person was selected . . . H. B.-R., a Jew, a rich man, who accumulated enormous wealth in dark deals, and owns whole streets in Hongkou. To him one must go and undergo an examination in order to receive fifteen dollars, or twenty Shanghai dollars per head. My conversation with him was brief but typical.

First, he does not speak Yiddish, Russian, or Polish. . . .

"How much do you pay?" he asks me.

"Eighty dollars."

---

59. On HICEM, see the Glossary.

"You have two rooms?" he asks and looks at me, quickly raising his eyes from the paper . . . like the investigating judge in a cheap criminal novel. I am thinking, he is well informed. And he is satisfied that he has caught a refugee at a crime—two rooms. I don't hesitate to tell him exactly how the rooms look so he should know how the Shanghai Jews have provided a Jewish writer and his family with a roof over his head.

[June 2, 1941]

　　I stood . . . and didn't know how to go to Albert Avenue and, as always this month, when I have to ask directions, I cannot stop wondering at how few Europeans one sees in the Settlement. To ask directions of a Chinese is useless, as I know from previous experience. First, they don't understand my question; second, I don't understand their answer. With my English it is difficult for me to communicate with a Jewish Englishman. . . . Finally I saw a face that was similar to a Jewish face. I approached him and asked in English. It turned out that he was going in the same direction. . . . After a few minutes, aware of my poor English, he asked if I speak Russian. I felt more at ease. One less torture. Now conversation was a little easier. But when he heard I am from Poland, he asked if I speak Yiddish. What a question! I grabbed it with both hands. Now my tongue became untied. My young man [he was only twenty-odd years old] spoke Yiddish quite well, considering the place and his age.

In every place of refuge, those who had already managed to make it through the ever tighter encirclement created by the Axis power were assailed by newcomers, desperate for advice and assistance. But to help them often required considerable material and psychological resources, a reserve rarely available to more established Jewish residents. Even someone as prominent as Austrian writer **Stefan Zweig**, who found refuge in Brazil, could do little more than explain to his ex-wife why his desire to help did not match his ability to deliver.

DOCUMENT 3-10: **Letter from Stefan Zweig, New Haven (CT), to Friderike Zweig,**[60] **New York, no date (stamped March 20, 1941), in Stefan and Friderike Zweig, *"Wenn einen Augenblick die Wolken weichen." Briefwechsel 1912–1942*, ed. Jeffrey B. Berlin and Gert Kerschbaumer (Frankfurt am Main: S. Fischer, 2006), 363–65 (translated from German).**

[. . .]

1) I had written you <u>imploringly</u> from Rio, saying that my head and my work require a respite of several weeks from visas, permits, etc. For three years I have done nothing but help others—I <u>must</u> have a rest, as others do throughout their lives.

2) An affidavit long ago stopped being a "favor," as you put it. For the person writing the affidavit, it means guaranteeing ca. $7,000 for two persons and backing it up with income tax forms and bank returns, which people aren't keen on doing, as I see it. One can ask that <u>once</u> of a <u>friend,</u> as I did with Schalom [Sholem] Asch on your behalf and where I could give a guarantee, because you were covered, but one can no longer ask "acquaintances" for such a thing.

3) I don't even have "acquaintances" here, however. I haven't seen a single American in my two months here, or visited anybody, with the exception of Huebsch and Asch, and van Loon on one occasion. Whom should I suddenly drop in on now and say, I need an affidavit, give me the bank return! Whom?

4) I can't take on a counterguarantee either for two people who can't support themselves. Of course, I'll still help, but in increasingly small proportions, in keeping with my situation. This throwing around of a "mere"

---

60. Friderike Maria Zweig (née Burger; 1882–1971) was an accomplished Austrian author, educator, journalist, and translator. Born into a Viennese-Jewish family, she converted to Roman Catholicism in 1905 and attended the University of Vienna. She married Stefan Zweig in 1920, and the two cohabitated until his immigration to Great Britain in 1933. Friderike remained in Salzburg to manage their estate until 1938, and their divorce was finalized the following year. Following the ***Anschluss***, she immigrated, along with her two daughters from a previous marriage, to France and Portugal before reaching the United States in 1940. In exile she was involved with numerous cultural and relief agencies—including the Central Organization for Austrian Emigres in Paris, the American-European Friendship Association, and the Writers' Service Center—and assisted persecuted intellectuals to immigrate to France, Mexico, and the United States, in addition to pursuing her literary career. See Herbert A. Strauss and Werner Röder, eds., *International Biographical Dictionary of Central European Émigrés, 1933–1945: The Arts, Sciences, and Literature*, vol. 2 (Munich: K. G. Saur, 1982), 1287; obituary, *New York Times*, January 20, 1971.

six hundred or twelve hundred dollars for a ship ticket, as is customary now, does not apply to me. Everybody sees that I manage my household so simply and frugally here—we do not budget every penny, but every half dollar we do. Having been a man of propriety all my life, I can't assume responsibility for any guarantee in dollars, because I don't know whether I'll ever earn any more of them. I also can't jump up every time a telegram or a letter comes—and that has been happening <u>week after week</u> for years—drop everything, drive to New York, and make the rounds. I simply <u>can't</u> do it anymore. I can't. As it is, I'm barely able to keep my head together. And I know that the affidavit is just the beginning, you see with your own sister that one then is still morally and financially tied to these helpless people. I know it all—but it's too much. I can't think continuously about visas and affidavits, it's been going on incessantly for years (ever since England). Thomas Mann, [Franz] Werfel,[61] they all have taken flight now, because they, too, are emotionally at the end of their rope and have already exploited all their acquaintances to the utmost. I myself, as you know, am here only by grace, have no contacts—as the Hölderlin poem goes, *"Ich bin nichts mehr, ich lebe nicht mehr gerne."* [I am nothing now, I have no pleasure in life any more.][62] [. . .]

Preemigration networks that continued to function abroad reduced feelings of isolation and loss. Among those who maintained close ties after they had managed to get out of Nazi-dominated Europe were the former residents of **Gross-Breesen**, a Jewish agricultural training school in Germany near Berlin. In the first volume of this series, we saw how the school was established and how its organizers, most notably its director Curt Bondy, tried to create a safe haven abroad that replicated the original Gross-Breesen communal

---

61. Thomas Mann (1875–1955), was an esteemed German novelist, Nobel Prize laureate, and social critic. His most important works include *Buddenbrooks* (1901), *Death in Venice* (1912), and *The Magic Mountain* (1924). After Hitler's seizure of power, he immigrated to Switzerland and then to the United States, where he lived during the war. See Hermann Kurzke, *Thomas Mann: Life as a Work of Art. A Biography* (Princeton, NJ: Princeton University Press, 2002). Franz Werfel (1890–1945) was a Prague-born, German-speaking Jewish writer. One of his most important works, *The Forty Days of Musa Dagh* (1933), was based on historical events of the Armenian genocide in the Ottoman Empire during World War I. Werfel fled Austria after the German takeover, settling in Paris, but had to flee again after the Nazi occupation of France in 1940. He settled in Los Angeles, where he lived until his death. See Hans Wagener, *Understanding Franz Werfel* (Columbia: University of South Carolina Press, 1993).

62. The German poet Friedrich Hölderlin (1770–1843).

experience. (Hyde Farmlands in the state of Virginia became the centerpiece of that attempt.)[63] In 1939 the **Reichsvereinigung** had taken over administration of Gross-Breesen, with its reduced number of students. Beginning in late 1940, however, the **Gestapo** conducted raids and arrests at the school, bringing its activities to a virtual standstill by mid-1941. With a new year beginning and against the backdrop of a raging war, Curt Bondy reflected on the ideas that had brought the group together in a circular sent to Gross-Breesen alumni dispersed throughout the world. He broached the question, too, of what had motivated its supporters to turn down opportunities for escape so that they could continue to help others.

DOCUMENT 3-11: **Circular letter from Curt Bondy, Richmond (VA), September 20, 1941, USHMMA Acc. 2000.227 Herbert Cohn collection (translated from German).[64]**

[. . .] What has the past year brought us, and what has come of all our great plans? Only disappointment and grief, only trouble? It almost looks that way. Gross-Breesen is really closed now. Only a few boys are still there as workers.[65] We know almost nothing about the fate of the others. The *Werkdorf* [Werkdorp Wieringen/Nieuwesluis in Holland][66] has been closed down. A letter I received from Holland a few days ago says, "Wieringen had to be closed. To some extent, the boys are in individual jobs.—But 60 are no longer here; many of them surely won't return, and there's great concern about the others." A letter that arrived later from Holland makes it more explicit that many are dead.—Hyde Farmlands is

---

63. See Jürgen Matthäus and Mark Roseman, *Jewish Responses to Persecution,* vol. 1: *1933–1938* (Lanham, MD: AltaMira Press in association with the USHMM, 2010), 224–28, 306–13.

64. Curt Bondy (1894–1972) had taught social pedagogy at Göttingen University until his dismissal in 1933. He then dedicated himself to adult education initiatives for German Jews, and in 1936 he became director of the training farm for prospective emigrants located at Gross-Breesen. Bondy ran the project until "*Kristallnacht,*" when he and many of his colleagues were arrested and sent to the Buchenwald concentration camp. Released in early 1939, Bondy fled to the United States, but briefly returned the following year in order to aid fellow Jewish refugees in their efforts to leave. See Werner T. Angress, *Between Fear and Hope: Jewish Youth in the Third Reich* (New York: Columbia University Press, 1988).

65. See Gross-Breesen Letter 11, October 1941, USHMMA Acc. 2000.227 Herbert Cohn collection, 210–12.

66. See Gertrude van Tijn, "Werkdorp Nieuwesluis," *LBIYB* 14 (1969): 182–99; Gross-Breesen Letter 12, November 1942, USHMMA Acc. 2000.227 Herbert Cohn collection, 231–32.

disbanded, and the boys and girls are scattered all over America. Some of them probably will not stay in agricultural work.

This was a bad year, and we still do not know in the least what the new year will bring us. But it would surely be wrong to conclude from all these sad events that everything we wanted to build up in G.B. [Gross-Breesen] was futile and wrong, that we aimed at the wrong goals, and that the past year brought the collapse of everything.—That is certainly not so. Above all, let's not forget that our people in other countries have made progress as farmers. Hyde Farmlands was not the only "New Gross-Breesen." [. . .]

So many letters are arriving now in which people complain about the meaninglessness of their present lives and repeatedly raise the issue of a fulfilling task. It is no surprise that more of these letters come from the girls than from the boys. Yes, this question of prospective tasks is posed so keenly and urgently in some cases that I began to wonder whether this searching for a task in the future is not sometimes a little (or big?) self-deception and only a pretext. One is not satisfied with the way life is now or cannot quite cope with it. Some of us will still have to learn—and it's surely not easy—to make every stage of life—present-day life—as meaningful as is at all possible. That can be done, whether one is a concentration camp prisoner or a domestic worker.

We will still have to make some sacrifices until <u>we are at that point.</u> The number of our dead, too, will surely continue to increase.

You know that Otto Hirsch[67] died in the concentration camp. He was one of us. Perhaps you are not aware how great a part he played in the development of Gross-Breesen and how interested he was in our people's fate. He was in G.B. only rarely, but he really felt he belonged there. Now I recall our visit to Martin Buber[68] in Heppenheim in late 1935; Otto Hirsch, Kantor,[69] and I; and how passionately Hirsch talked over

---

67. On Otto Hirsch, see the Glossary.

68. Martin Buber (1878–1965), eminent German Jewish philosopher who taught at the university in Frankfurt am Main until 1933. In 1938, he immigrated to Palestine and settled in Jerusalem, where he taught at the Hebrew University. See Laurence J. Silberstein, *Martin Buber's Social and Religious Thought: Alienation and the Quest for Meaning* (New York: New York University Press, 1989).

69. "Kantor" was possibly Dr. jur. Ernst Kantorowicz (1892–1942), who served as special advisor to the board of trustees of the Gross-Breesen project. He had been a jurist, sociologist, and professor in Frankfurt am Main (as distinct from Ernst H. Kantorowicz, the renowned Frankfurt medieval historian who survived the war in the United States). Deported from the Netherlands to **Auschwitz**, he perished in 1944. See *Gedenkbuch*, www.bundesarchiv.de/gedenkbuch; "Gross-Breesen-Silesia," http://grossbreesensilesia.com/pdfs (accessed December 8, 2011).

with us at that time the plan for an agricultural training farm for people who were not Zionists, especially members of the B.d.J.J.[70] Do you know that he could have emigrated long ago and that only his incredibly strong sense of duty kept him in Germany? As head of the Reichsvertretung der deutschen Juden,[71] he accomplished an enormous amount. He died for his calling, in the truest sense. And this is more than the heroic death of a soldier in the field! In the past, we repeatedly said in all earnestness that our dead comrades must live on through us and through our work, but today I say this to you even more urgently, beseechingly and indeed imploringly with regard to Otto Hirsch. We must carry on his mission and continue to live with his attitude and according to his principles. I say this with the greatest solemnity and urgency.

I note how difficult it is to write something like this and how much more compellingly I could say it to you if you were here. I had almost forgotten just now that you are not here, that I'm not speaking to you at all, and that I can only write to you. Get started on a good new year, prepare yourselves for bigger tasks, stay "Gross-Breeseners." That is my sincere wish for you all this evening.

Mastering a new language and fostering new friendships played a crucial role for refugees in moving forward and thinking about the future. This was especially the case for youth coming of age in an environment that initially seemed alien or inhospitable. For many, such as the thirteen-year-old author of the following diary entry, their place of refuge was a long way from what they could call home. The parents of Elisabeth Orenstein (Orsten) sent her to Frankfurt from her native Vienna in the summer of 1938, following the radical anti-Jewish measures in former Austria in the wake of the *Anschluss*. She began keeping her diary in German in January 1939 at age eleven. Shortly afterward, she found refuge in England as part of a **Kindertransport**, later in the United States. In the summer of 1941, six months after her arrival in America, she

---

70. The Bund Deutsch-Jüdischer Jugend (League of German Jewish Youth) formed in Germany in 1925 and was disbanded by the Gestapo in late 1936; see Matthäus and Roseman, *Jewish Responses to Persecution*, 1:225.

71. The Reichsvertretung der deutschen Juden was formed in September 1933 by German Jewish leaders around **Leo Baeck** and was the precursor to the Reichsvereinigung, created by the Gestapo.

switched to English to describe the burden of childhood experiences she still carried with her.[72]

DOCUMENT 3-12: Elisabeth Orenstein, Buffalo (NY), diary entry for July 3, 1941, USHMMA Acc. 2000.417 Elisabeth Orsten collection.

[. . .] I had learned a great deal in England, first and foremost I had learned English, but I had also learned some Latin and had developed my French. I had been taught more graceful movements, better manners and several other subjects. But I had also been ridiculed and hated and that has left a strong impression on my mind. To this day, six months later and I believe it will be for always, I have been afraid of humans, I don't want to admit it, but it is true. In my mind I always feel "they don't like me, there's something wrong with me." At the most difficult stage of our growth I was being constantly critizised and I still feel constantly that everyone "weighes" [*sic*] me, and I am afraid. At school, in the street, in church, at home, even when I play with children of only five or six I have that feeling and I cannot conquer it. That was one of the defects of my education, others I will mention later. Nevertheless

Here the diary breaks off and was not continued, apparently no longer needed as a bridge between the past and the future.

Despite its personal nature, Orenstein's diary fragment reflects how many Jews regarded the first six months of the year 1941: as a transitional period, ominous as a string of German victories brought increasingly violent Nazi anti-Jewish policies all across Europe, with deep incursions into the southeastern continent. Europe's Jews began to measure success ever more in terms of escaping Axis rule to a place of relative safety, and they clung to a fading hope that the Nazi war machine would sooner or later run out of steam. Many Jews expected the German attack on its Soviet ally to turn the tide against Hitler, and in the long run, they were right. **Operation Barbarossa** prompted the Nazi demise. Yet what happened after June 22, 1941, led to an escalation of violence unprecedented not only in the history of the Jews but also in world history.

---

72. See Elisabeth M. Orsten, *From Anschluss to Albion: Memoirs of a Refugee Girl, 1938–1940* (Cambridge: Acorn, 1998).

PART II

ESCALATING VIOLENCE
JUNE 1941 TO JULY 1942

B Y THE TIME the Wehrmacht crossed the border into the Soviet Union in the early hours of June 22, 1941, the image of "Jewish Bolshevism" as Germany's most formidable enemy was firmly lodged in the mind of the Reich's elites. Conversely, Jews in the region had a sense of foreboding about German rule without knowing exactly how it would affect their lives. Wartime German anti-Jewish policy had established a particularly violent precedent during the invasion of Poland, far more harsh than in occupied western and northern Europe after the defeat of France. With the German war machine pushing further eastward, a repetition of the atrocities perpetrated in Poland seemed likely. Still, no one was prepared for the situation that developed almost immediately after Germany broke with the USSR. In a deliberately planned war of annihilation, Germans and their allies embarked on a path that within one year led to the death of the majority of the 2.5 million Jews in the occupied parts of the Soviet Union.

The parameters for the German campaign against the Soviet Union had been set in early 1941 by military and policy planners, who minced no words about the harshness of measures designed to ensure the systematic "pacification" and economic exploitation of the occupied area's population. One memo speculated matter-of-factly that "umpteen million" (*zig Millionen*) civilians would not be able to survive for lack of food and that occupied areas would be stripped of resources used to support the German war effort.[1] Hitler's criminal orders call-ing on the Wehrmacht to show no mercy and ignore established rules of warfare fell on fertile ground among Germany's officer corps. Fierce fighting on the eastern front led to a rapid escalation of violence directed not only against Red Army soldiers and POWs, 2 million of whom would die in German captivity in the first year of the war, but also against "Slavs" and other groups the Germans perceived as undesirable.

From the outset, the Wehrmacht's 3 million soldiers were supported by comparatively small yet highly mobile SS and police units. Roughly three thou-sand men made up the four units of the **Einsatzgruppen** of the **Security Police** and **SD**, and several thousand men filled the ranks of German Order Police and the **Waffen-SS**. Directives by **Heinrich Himmler** and **Reinhard Heydrich** to the Einsatzgruppen called for the execution of a range of "enemy" groups, including "Jews in state and party functions." Even more importantly, given the vague wording of these directives and the eagerness of SS and police officers deployed along the vast front to excel, these directives provided a stimulus as well as a cover for mass murder after the start of the campaign. Allied to the Reich, the Romanian regime under Marshal **Ion Antonescu** initiated its own violent, deadly anti-Jewish campaign, primarily targeting Jews in the newly occupied territories in the southern parts of the front and adding fuel to the German drive toward genocide. To the planners of **Operation Barbarossa**, the war in the East formed the basis for what historian Peter Longerich has called the "genesis of the Final Solution on a European scale."[2]

After June 22, 1941, in the context of waging war against the Soviet enemy, German anti-Jewish policy moved swiftly from persecution to mass murder, as the occupiers first executed Jewish men of military age, followed within weeks by the murder of Jewish women and children. By the end of the year, the death toll recorded by Himmler's officers in the occupied parts of the Soviet Union had reached half a million. This escalation proceeded unevenly and in stages owing to a range of factors, many emanating from decisions made by unit com-manders with the approval or backing of their superiors in Berlin. As before in occupied Poland, the Germans established **Jewish councils** and ghettos to enforce their rules. But in the occupied part of the Soviet Union, ghettoization resembled the radicalized dynamic of anti-Jewish policy from the start: more often than not, mass killings preceded segregation of the Jewish population.

---

1. Geoffrey P. Megargee, *War of Annihilation: Combat and Genocide on the Eastern Front, 1941* (Lanham, MD: Rowman & Littlefield, 2006), 19–41.

2. Peter Longerich, *Holocaust: The Nazi Persecution and Murder of the Jews* (Oxford: Oxford University Press, 2010), 258–310.

Many, especially smaller ghettos, served as a brief and temporary expedient before their residents, women and children included, were murdered. Yet within a few months, the experiences gained in the newly conquered East triggered more radical action further west as well. With Hitler's approval, regional potentates in the Greater Reich and **Adolf Eichmann**'s men began deporting Jewish men, women, and children to the Polish city of Łódź and to several cities in the occupied Soviet Union, and many of these deportees were murdered immediately after their arrival. By June 1942, the **Reichssicherheitshauptamt (RSHA)** had reached its goal of deporting fifty-five thousand people from the Reich.

The Nazi leadership was eager to make use of the new possibilities emanating from the war in the East for more radical ways of "solving the Jewish question." Ultimately, many factors and strands of thought—some purely German, others flowing from old and new sources of diverse nationalist sentiments and interests—fed into and accelerated the complex process leading to genocide. Murderous initiatives taken by local officials in occupied Poland with the approval of Berlin played a key role. Beginning in early December 1941, Jews were killed en masse in gas vans in **Chełmno** near Łódź in the German-annexed **Warthegau**. At the same time, in Galicia—which had been incorporated into the **Generalgouvernement** as a result of Operation Barbarossa—and in the Lublin district of **Hans Frank**'s fiefdom, German SS and policemen under the command of Heinrich Himmler's henchman Odilo Globocnik and assisted by staff from the **Aktion T-4** "euthanasia" program, also embarked on the path of industrialized mass murder. In March 1942, the **Bełżec** death camp became operational, its first victims roughly forty-four thousand Jews deported from Lublin and more than fifteen thousand Jews from neighboring Galicia, leaving behind few men and women in the ghettos of both districts to work (at least temporarily) as forced laborers.[3]

At the **Wannsee Conference** on January 20, 1942, RSHA chief Heydrich could point to the "successes" of his Einsatzgruppen to assert himself and his office as the key authority for the ensuing "Europeanization" of anti-Jewish policy. Beginning in March 1942, trains with Jewish deportees were running from Slovakia and France to **Majdanek** and **Auschwitz**. In the latter camp, improvised gas chambers claimed the first victims from among former Jewish

---

3. See Saul Friedländer, *Nazi Germany and the Jews:* (vol. 2) *The Years of Extermination, 1939–1945* (New York: HarperCollins, 2007), 336–47; Laura Crago, "Lublin Region (Distrikt Lublin)," and Martin Dean, "Eastern Galicia Region (Distrikt Galizien)," in *The United States Holocaust Memorial Museum Encyclopedia of Camps and Ghettos, 1933–1945, Ghettos in German-Occupied Eastern Europe*, vol. 2, ed. Martin Dean (Bloomington: Indiana University Press in association with the USHMM, 2012), 604–9, 744–48.

forced laborers from eastern Upper Silesia on March 20. In the occupied
Soviet Union, the Wehrmacht's military setbacks and harsh winter of 1941 to
1942 slowed down the momentum of mass murder. But with the beginning
of spring, the regions behind the eastern front were hit by what Holocaust
scholar Raul Hilberg has called a "second sweep" of mass killings that claimed
the lives of tens of thousands of Jewish men, women, and children, and eradicated entire communities.[4] Among the victims were newly deported Jews from
the Reich, murdered on arrival in mass shootings or gas vans. In late April and
early March, Hitler, Himmler, and Heydrich seem to have agreed on a massive
European expansion of deportations to death camps in the East, building on
the expertise of German officials on the ground and starting with the roughly
1.7 million Jews still living in the **Generalgouvernement**. There, two new
death camps—**Sobibór** and **Treblinka**—had been established. The wounding
of Heydrich by Czech partisans and his subsequent death in June 1941—in
combination with an unrelated, unsuccessful arson attack in Berlin conducted
in mid-May by a small group of communist resisters (including German
Jews)—boosted the regime leaders' determination to hasten the elimination of
"enemy number one" and triggered a new phase in the history of the Holocaust.
German officials would annihilate the vast majority of Polish Jews in "**Aktion
Reinhard**" during the second half of 1942. In **Auschwitz II-Birkenau**, with
construction beginning in September 1941 for the purpose of housing fifty
thousand Soviet POWs, gassings of Jews deemed "unfit for work" started on
July 4, 1942.[5]

How did Jews perceive the gradual confluence of different strands of persecution into what from our postwar perspective appears to be a flood of measures, overwhelming and inexorable? At the time, the information available to
most Jews was too fragmented, contradictory, and unreliable, the assumption
of systematic annihilation too fantastic, and the pattern of events too incoherent for more than uneasy speculation about what lay ahead. Rumors abounded.
Victor Klemperer, a linguist writing in Dresden, Germany, noted on March 16,
1942, in his now famous diary, "In the last few days I heard Auschwitz (or
something like it) near Königshütte in Upper Silesia, mentioned as the most

---

4. Raul Hilberg, *The Destruction of the European Jews*, 3rd ed. (1961; New Haven, CT:
Yale University Press, 2003), 1:382–408.

5. Mark Roseman, *The Wannsee Conference and the Final Solution: A Reconsideration* (New
York: Metropolitan Books, 2002); Peter Longerich, *Heinrich Himmler* (New York: Oxford
University Press, 2012), 554–74. For the course of events after the summer of 1942, see
volumes 4 and 5 in this series (forthcoming).

dreadful concentration camp. Work in a mine, death within days."[6] Parts III and IV will explore in greater detail how Jews tried to make sense of the events they experienced directly and those they learned about through a variety of channels. In the three chapters that follow here, we focus on more immediate Jewish reactions to the crushing intensity of violence during and after what historian Christopher Browning has called the crucial months in the emergence of the "Final Solution."[7]

A word of warning about the historian's ability to tell the stories of the victims of Operation Barbarossa, "Aktion Reinhard," or any of the numerous other murder crimes perpetrated in this time. As Saul Friedländer writes, "There is something at once profoundly disturbing yet rapidly numbing in the narration of the anti-Jewish campaign that developed in the territories newly occupied by the Germans or their allies. History seems to turn into a succession of mass killing operations and, on the face of it, little else."[8] With hindsight we see the whole gruesome picture, with its descent into mass killings, but we need to reflect on the insights available to those who had no inkling of what was to come, or what deportation, "resettlement," and ghettoization ultimately meant, even as late as the summer of 1942. The following chapters offer a series of distinctive Jewish voices from this new, more lethal phase of the war. They speak not only to the perceptions of Jewish men and women along the eastern front but also of conditions and fears experienced further afield—in southeastern Europe, Hungary, and Palestine, and in all the distant reaches of the globe where Jews had sought a haven.

---

6. Victor Klemperer, *I Will Bear Witness: A Diary of the Nazi Years, 1942–1945* (New York: Random House, 1999), 28–29.

7. Christopher R. Browning with contributions by Jürgen Matthäus, *The Origins of the Final Solution: The Evolution of Nazi Jewish Policy, September 1939–March 1942* (Lincoln and Jerusalem: University of Nebraska Press and Yad Vashem, 2004), 244–423.

8. Friedländer, *Nazi Germany*, 2:240.

CHAPTER 4

MASS MURDER IN THE OCCUPIED SOVIET UNION AND DEPORTATIONS TO "THE EAST"

"**S**UNDAY, JUNE 22, 1941: Russia at war with Germany!" **Eva Mändl** in Prague wrote in her diary. "It was completely unexpected, we had no clue. Just the other day great friendship all over the newspapers. [. . .] We are upbeat, this is a blow to the Germans. Now they scold the Bolsheviks together with the Jews."[1] Like Mändl, many Jews were conflicted about the prospects raised by the German surprise attack on the Soviet Union. On the one hand, Hitler's gamble of opening a second front against a formidable enemy increased the chances for German defeat even at a time when the United States had not yet joined the war; on the other, while the Nazi machine was raging forward, Jews within its reach faced an immediate life threat. "We do not know what is in store for us," mused fourteen-year-old **Yitskhok Rudashevski** at the beginning of German occupation in the Lithuanian capital, Vilna.[2] And how could he or anyone else? True, Germany had defeated France within just a few weeks the previous year, continued its belligerent push across Europe, and established a foothold in North Africa. But surely the Wehrmacht would

---

1. Eva Mändl Roubíčková, *"Langsam gewöhnen wir uns an das Ghettoleben." Ein Tagebuch aus Theresienstadt*, ed. Veronika Springmann (Hamburg: Konkret Literatur Verlag, 2007), 34–35.
2. Yitskhok Rudashevski, *The Diary of the Vilna Ghetto: June 1941–April 1943* (Tel Aviv: Ghetto Fighters' House, 1973), 30.

not be able to accomplish what Napoleon's armies had failed to achieve, surely Britain's immense resources and international backing, particularly from the United States, would prevail. As it turned out, no one could have foreseen what happened after German troops and police units had started to cross the Soviet border. Nothing contributed as decisively to the emergence of the Holocaust defined as the systematic mass murder of Jewish men, women, and children than Hitler's attack on the Soviet Union, not only in the areas occupied by Germany and its allies but also by triggering mass deportations of Jews from the Reich to destinations where many of the deportees would share the fate of local Jews murdered since the beginning of the campaign.

CAUGHT UP IN DEADLY AGGRESSION

It is impossible to convey the intensity of the German assault and magnitude of destruction facing Jews, along with others in the areas under attack. Cities were particularly hard hit, first by fighting that often left few buildings standing—as in the Belorussian cities of Minsk and Vitebsk—and subsequently by German attempts to impose control over the population, to "pacify" captured areas as thoroughly as possible. Among the millions evacuated by Soviet authorities up to the end of 1941 were, according to recent estimates, roughly 1.5 million Jews,[3] but in the chaos of the war, many were left behind. Iakov Borisovich Gertsovich, a Jewish man working for a Soviet newspaper in Minsk at the beginning of the German attack, witnessed German bombing of his city on the second day of **Operation Barbarossa** and the pervasive confusion that followed.

DOCUMENT 4-1: **"Conversation of the writer A. A. Bek with Comrade Iakov Borisovich Gertsovich,"[4] November 18, 1941, USHMMA RG 22.006 (RGALI 2863-1-1), folder 4 (translated from Russian).**

[. . .] The war started in this way.

On the morning of the 22nd [of June], we were intending to have a group outing with the editorial staff. [. . .] I wanted to be at home on

---

3. Vadim Dubson, "Toward a Central Database of Evacuated Soviet Jews' Names, for the Study of the Holocaust in the Occupied Soviet Territories," *H&GS* 26, no. 1 (2012), 102.

4. The interview is in the first-person voice of Gertsovich, recorded by Bek. Aleksandr Alfredovich Bek (1902 or 1903–1972) was a writer and novelist. Born in Saratov, Bek fought for the Bolsheviks in the Russian Civil War and during World War II served as a war correspondent. His novel *Volokolamsk Highway* was acclaimed in the Soviet Union for its depiction of the defense of Moscow against the German attack in 1941. See Victor Terras, ed., *Handbook of Russian Literature* (New Haven, CT: Yale University Press, 1985), 43. The authors were unable to uncover further information on Gertsovich.

Sunday, because our son turned 2 on Saturday, the 21st, but we postponed the celebration of his name-day to Sunday.

In the morning I was intending to go to the editorial office. There was a phone call from the *Voenkomat*.[5]—I was told to bring my documents and report there. I went and produced my documents, and was told to go to "Krasnoarmeiskaia Pravda" [a Soviet army newspaper]. I requested permission to go home. They granted it. While I was going home, Molotov gave his radio address.[6] Then I understood what was going on. I listened to the speech and went to the editorial office of "Krasnoarmeiskaia Pravda," and have been there since the first day of the war.

This is how things turned out for me.

We were living on the edge of town, in Liakhi. This is Minsk's industrial area.

On the 23rd they [the Germans] bombed the Voroshilov, Kirov, and "Bolshevik" factories. The fragments flew all the way to our courtyard, to our apartment. Then I sent our son to my wife's parents on another street. I checked on them several times. There was very heavy bombing on the 23rd and they sat in the cellar the whole time. At 4 o'clock I went to check on them and calm them down, because my presence alone, my visit, calmed them down. They all were very frightened, especially my wife's elderly mother. They thought I could help in some way, even if it was only to tell them what was going on all around.

I sent my wife to the Komsomol Central Committee and the Party Central Committee, to find out what they thought there about evacuation. They told her that without instructions from the Party and Komsomol Central Committees, no one was to leave the town. Toward evening very large fires started in the area where they were living. I got permission from the editors to leave the office, and I went there to see them. I came to the building. The building of the Stalin School was burning. They were at home in the cellar. The house was burning, the building was burning, the town

---

5. *Voenkomat* is an abbreviation of *voennyi komissariat*, meaning "military commissariat," the local military administration in charge of enlisting troops for the Red Army and mobilizing forces. For a history of the Soviet Union during World War II, see Richard Overy, *Russia's War: A History of the Soviet War Effort, 1941–1945* (New York: Penguin, 1998); Catherine Merridale, *Ivan's War: Life and Death in the Red Army, 1939–1945* (New York: Picador, 2006).

6. Vyacheslav Molotov (1890–1986) was the Soviet minister of foreign affairs from 1939 to 1949 and again from 1953 to 1956. On June 22, 1941, authorized by Stalin, he announced the "predatory attack" on the Soviet Union by the "bloodthirsty Fascist rulers of Germany." See "Molotov Charges Nazi Perfidy; Full Text of His Broadcast," *Washington Post*, June 23, 1941, 4.

was burning. I went there, but they were not there. I went through all the hiding places looking for them, looking, looking, I went everywhere but didn't find them. Since then, I don't know where they are. And at night we were led out of the town. In the morning my wife may even have gone to the editorial office to find out where I was, but we were no longer there.

Then I went on trips, encountered people I knew from Minsk, encountered Party workers from Belorussia, we exchanged opinions, but I learned nothing concrete. I gave them my address and they gave me theirs, so that if somebody heard about my family, they would inform me, and in turn, if I learned anything about their families, I would inform them properly. One *politruk* [political officer] said that they questioned all the people from Minsk and were told that my little son was killed in the bombing when they were leaving Minsk. The inhabitants were basically walking along the Mogilev highway at that time. Some people got mixed up. There was no organized evacuation. They were all fleeing in any direction they wished. Some people headed in the direction of the front. I myself came across people who were going to Bobruisk, but Bobruisk was captured before Minsk; however, people did not fully realize what they were doing. My wife was with the army, and now I don't know whether she fell into the Germans' hands or was evacuated somewhere with a hospital. I appealed to the Resettlement Administration. There she was registered as being alive. They said she had proceeded to Cheliabinsk, but in the past couple of days I got an express telegram saying that she's not in Cheliabinsk.

The war started on the 22nd. We, like many others as well, were educated by the newspaper. Therein lies a great tragedy and a great misfortune. We read that we would reply to the attack with an attack three times as big, that dealing with the enemy would be a piece of cake, that we would go all the way to Berlin, that the war meant a world revolution. This was the popular formula at the start of the war, and that is why we thought that any day now we would head westward on the offensive. And we firmly believed it, because this formula gave rise to various rumors. Rumors that we were taking Warsaw, and there was fighting on the streets of Warsaw, and then a rumor that we were headed to Bulgaria, and then that we were going to Finland. These were not rumors meant to incite the public; people were just saying what they thought, and others took it at face value. In our sector, we knew that the Germans were on the offensive, but we firmly believed that any day we would drive the enemy out and our own offensive would begin. [. . .]

I cursed Stalin's *Voenkomat* for my being sent to the editorial office rather than to the front line. I cursed both myself and my immediate superiors, because we were quite disorganized. You go out to the front and you see that people are doing their jobs, but they had gathered a huge crowd of us (now there are fewer of us) and there was no work to be done at all, the situation was completely unknown. You don't know what to undertake. We loafed about that way from town to town, from one locality to the next. Then things gradually began to take shape for us. [. . .]

By the end of June, roughly a week after crossing the border, German troops had occupied vast areas of Soviet territory, from the Baltic States in the north down through Belarus to Ukraine, exacerbating deep divisions already present in the local population. In those regions incorporated into Stalin's empire only a year before through the **Molotov-Ribbentrop Pact**, the arrival of German troops met with ambivalent expectations, including feelings of relief held by those who had experienced Soviet repression or had seen friends and relatives, Jews and non-Jews, deported by Soviet authorities as alleged "class enemies." Among these deportees were many Jews; still, against the background of Nazi propaganda, nationalist right-wing groups in these regions perceived the measures taken by the Soviets between October 1939 and June 1941 as part of a Jewish plot to thwart their respective nations' striving for national autonomy.[7] Scapegoating of Jews appealed particularly to nationalists in formerly independent Lithuania and in Galicia in the Polish-Ukrainian borders areas; it would play an important role in triggering violence against Jews in the early phase of Operation Barbarossa. In Shavli (Yiddish; Lithuanian: Šiauliai; German: Schaulen), the third-largest city in Lithuania, rising nationalism and the populist appeal of antisemitic slogans deeply impacted Jewish life prior to World War II. Here physician Aron Pik[8] recalled

---

7. For Soviet deportations from eastern Poland and the Baltic States prior to June 22, 1941, estimated in the range of over 150,000, see Timothy Snyder, *Bloodlands: Europe between Hitler and Stalin* (New York: Basic Books, 2010), 126, 141–43. According to Christoph Dieckmann, *Deutsche Besatzungspolitik in Litauen 1941–1944* (Göttingen: Wallstein, 2011), 153, more than 1,600 Jews were among the roughly 17,000 Lithuanians deported by Soviet agencies in June 1941.

8. Aron Pik (1872–1944) was a physician living in Shavli with his wife Dvora and their son Tedik David Pik. In September 1941 the Pik family was forced to move to the ghetto in Shavli, where Dr. Pik worked in the ghetto hospital and continued writing his diary, apparently in two versions, one in Yiddish, the other in Hebrew. After Pik died in June 1944, his son David buried his father's writings, which consisted of three notebooks. David then escaped the ghetto and joined a partisan unit. His mother Dvora was deported to Stutthof and died there. After Soviet forces liberated Shavli, David Pik dug up the notebooks and later immigrated to Israel. See Aharon Pik, *Reshimot mi-ge ha-haregah: Zikhronot ketuvim be-Geto ha-Shulai (Lita) bi-shenot 702, 703, 704* (Tel Aviv: Igud yots'e Lita, 1998), 13; Arūnas Bubnys and Avinoam Patt, "Šiauliai," in *The United States Holocaust Memorial Museum Encyclopedia of Camps and Ghettos, 1933–1945,* vol. 2: *Ghettos in German-Occupied Eastern Europe*, ed. Martin Dean (Bloomington: Indiana University Press in association with the USHMM, 2012), 1118–21.

the Soviet presence with a certain fondness and witnessed the onset of German occupation with deep apprehension.[9]

DOCUMENT 4-2: Aron Pik, Shavli, German-occupied Lithuania, diary entry for June 27, 1941, USHMMA RG 26.014 (LCSAV R-1390), reel 58, file 170 (translated from Yiddish).[10]

June 27, 1941

Yesterday (Thursday), in the evening, I suddenly saw from the window that Germans were walking about on the sidewalk opposite—my heart sank! Does this mean that four days after the start of the war the dogged Jew-haters [*yidnfresers*], the beastly [*zoologishe*] murderers, were already able to penetrate into Lithuania? If so, then the fate of the Lithuanian Jews has been sealed, too, like that of our unfortunate brothers in the other countries occupied by the Germans. The bitter experiences of Czechoslovakia, Austria, Germany itself, and so on reveal that very sad days await us and that boundless calamities and pain are in store for us. And all the evil afflictions gather over our heads after we have already suffered such a great deal. How much humiliation and persecution have we endured in recent years in our own blessed fatherland, Lithuania! In all areas, decrees and restrictions have rained down upon us like hail. [. . . ; a catalogue of discriminatory measures enacted in prewar Lithuania follows.] Government antisemitism went hand-in-hand with societal antisemitism and they, together with the agitation of the antisemitic press, formed a nice "threefold chord,"[11] a triumvirate which, in time, created for us in Lithuania a complete pogrom mood. [. . .]

From that day on [in the summer of 1940] the Bolshevik regime was established in our territory and an immense change in our way of life and

9. See Yitzhak Arad, *The Holocaust in the Soviet Union* (Lincoln: University of Nebraska Press, 2009), 65–121; Christoph Dieckmann and Saulius Sužiedėis, *Lietuvos žydų persekiojimas ir masinės žukynės 1941 m. vasarą ir rudenį: Šaltiniai ir analizė* (Vilnius: Margi raštai, 2006).

10. The two versions of Aron Pik's diary are similar, though not identical: the Yiddish text starts only with the German occupation while the Hebrew version (buried in the ghetto in 1944) also deals with the Soviet occupation. The Hebrew version is more polished and flowing than the Yiddish (which Pik might have written earlier). The Yiddish diary version from the Lithuanian State Archive in Vilna is catalogued at the USHMMA as RG 26.014 (Acc. 1998.A.0073), the Hebrew version as Acc. 2000.132.

11. He used the Hebrew expression here (*hut hameshulash*), quoting a passage from Ecclesiastes 4:12: "Also, if one attacks, two can stand up to him. A threefold chord is not readily broken."

our psychology came about. And the hooligans and the pogromists disappeared. For the time being, many of them, so to speak, withdrew into themselves and "took on a second skin." And many became turncoats and, as it were, loyal communists, [and remain so] even today. In any event, we breathed more easily and felt equal to [other] people: from second-rate, inferior citizens up to that point, we became fully entitled, bold and active members of society, and many of us received very respectable positions and became materially well-established. The workers and a large segment of society came to life! One cannot deny that the Jewish community [*kolektiv*] on the whole [*in corpore*] paid dearly for all the freedoms since the majority consisted of merchants, industrialists, shopkeepers, and other so-called bourgeois exploiters, most of whose wealth was nationalized and expropriated; but the workers and the more conscious, who properly assessed the rights of the proletariat on the one hand and the unjust basis of the capitalist order on the other—they all felt that the sun of a new, free life shone with the Bolshevik regime. How great, therefore, was our desperation and heartache when, after one year of rule, the Bolsheviks suddenly abandoned us at the beginning of the war and we were left defenseless in the teeth and claws of the wild, bloodthirsty German beasts!

Now, after the troubles with the Lithuanian regime and the unpleasantness of the Bolshevik upheaval for a large part of the Jewish community, the [illegible] begins; the German regime comes, with its unbounded hatred of Jews and its beastly wickedness which hold a bleak future in store for us. *Gevalt!* Where will we find the strength and endurance to bear this all after all these experiences?

[. . .] The arrival in Shavli of large masses of soldiers immediately affected my situation as administrator of the polyclinic. A surgical unit of the Germans unceremoniously broke into the polyclinic and their chief doctor immediately began to "boss [us] around," as though he was at home. His first accomplishment was to make the polyclinic free of Jews. At that time Dr. B . . . n, dentist W. and nurse L . . . n were in the polyclinic, all with typical Jewish appearances—brunettes with true "Jewish faces."[12] He went to each of them and ordered them to leave as soon as possible: "You are a Jew, you must disappear immediately. I should never see you again." [. . .]

---

12. Here Pik uses the Hebrew term *tseylem elohim*, which literally means "image of God," but in Yiddish can also have the meaning of a "Jewish face," that is, "Jewish looks."

Now I sit at home idle, without work, and have ample time to write my recollections, more or less in detail. To go out into the street, to refresh oneself somewhat, one is in any event afraid to do (unless there is an important reason for doing so), so as not to run into the hatred of our brainwashed masters [*farpropagandirte balebosim*], the Lithuanians. They were furious about the deportation of their families to Soviet Russia, which they considered to be the work of the Jews, disregarding the fact that more than a few Jewish families were also deported, suspected of being "counter-revolutionaries." They blamed all the deeds of the Bolsheviks on the Jews, whom they held responsible for everything that has taken place and that is presently taking place, including the war, according to the formula of the modern Haman and the clique of his followers. And in return, they have broken into the homes of those who ran from Shavli and robbed whatever their heart desired. A new beginning was initiated! Afraid of going out into the street, we sit already without milk, without meat and without butter. What is going to happen next? Certainly, there will be no improvement, more likely it will get worse. [. . .]

Pik rightly sensed the mutually reinforcing effects of the prevailing pogrom mood and German anti-Jewish policy as it emerged in the first days of the campaign. **Reinhard Heydrich** had ordered the **Einsatzgruppen** to foster "self-cleansing measures" against communists and Jews, and it was particularly in those regions taken over by the Soviet Union since late 1939—eastern Poland in October 1939 and the Baltic states of Lithuania, Latvia, and Estonia in the summer of 1941—where parts of the local populations staged murderous attacks against their Jewish neighbors, sometimes in direct cooperation with the occupiers, sometimes independently from them.[13] In Pik's home town of Shavli, locals killed roughly one thousand of the city's eight thousand Jews in the first week of German occupation; in Kovno, also in Lithuania, pogroms claimed the lives of almost five thousand people, mostly men, of the thirty-six-thousand-strong Jewish community.[14] Overall, it is

13. See Arad, *The Holocaust in the Soviet Union*, 88–95; Christopher R. Browning with contributions by Jürgen Matthäus, *The Origins of the Final Solution: The Evolution of Nazi Jewish Policy, September 1939–March 1942* (Lincoln and Jerusalem: University of Nebraska Press and Yad Vashem, 2004), 268–77; Jan T. Gross, *Neighbors: The Destruction of the Jewish Community in Jedwabne, Poland* (New York: Penguin, 2002); Snyder, *Bloodlands*, 187–223.

14. Yitzhak Arad, *Ghetto in Flames: The Struggle and Destruction of the Jews in Vilna in the Holocaust* (Jerusalem: Yad Vashem, 1981), 46.

estimated that around ten thousand Jews were murdered during pogroms in Lithuania alone.[15]

In the eyes of local activists with nationalistic agendas, the more violently they displayed their hatred of Jews, the higher the likelihood that the Germans would support their cause. Some of the pogroms—most notably in Kovno (Lithuania) and Lwów (Galicia)—even became public events. German onlookers widely documented them and milked them for their propaganda value, along with the uncovering of NKVD killings of prisoners prior to the withdrawal of the Red Army.[16] These episodes could be exploited to attest to the strong antisemitic and anti-Bolshevik impulse of a local population now "liberated" from the Soviet yoke.[17]

The following article published in Warsaw by a **Hashomer Hatzair** group gives an account of the early fate of those Jews who tried to escape the Germans by going eastward and others who became targets of aggression in Vilna. The city had been part of Poland until the beginning of World War II but was claimed by independent Lithuania, which acquired it and the surrounding territory as a result of the partitioning of defeated Poland by Germany and the Soviet Union in the autumn of 1939. Because Lithuanians were a minority in Vilna, with its mostly Polish and Jewish population, the city's Jews were spared from pogroms of the extent occurring in Kovno, Shavli, and other Lithuanian towns during the German occupation in late June 1941. Yet Lithuanians collaborating with the Germans contributed to an escalation of violence beyond what the document's author regarded as "normal" based on Nazi occupation policies in Poland after the autumn of 1939. By the time the Vilna refugee told the story featured in the following document, German authorities had forced the Jews of Vilna into two ghettos formed in early September 1941 as part of organized mass murder in the city that Jews regarded as the "Jerusalem of Lithuania" due to its rich cultural tradition. Of the roughly nine thousand Jews crowded into

---

15. According to Dov Levin, *The Litvaks: A Short History of the Jews in Lithuania* (New York: Berghahn Books, 2001), 218, at the onset of the Wehrmacht's attack on the Soviet Union, Lithuanians staged roughly forty pogroms without direct German instigation; see also Dieckmann, *Deutsche Besatzungspolitik in Litauen*, 300.

16. The NKVD was the People's Commissariat for Internal Affairs (*Narodnyy komissariat vnutrennikh del*), the Soviet secret police.

17. See Alexander V. Prusin, *The Lands Between: Conflict in the East European Borderlands, 1870–1992* (Oxford: Oxford University Press, 2010), 150–60; Dieter Pohl, *Nationalsozialistische Judenverfolgung in Ostgalizien 1941–1944* (Munich: Oldenbourg Verlag, 1997), 54–65. For firsthand accounts of the pogroms that swept Lithuania, see Ernst Klee, Willi Dressen, and Volker Riess, eds., *"The Good Old Days": The Holocaust as Seen by its Perpetrators and Bystanders* (New York: The Free Press, 1991), 23–45.

the smaller ghetto (north of Niemiecka Street), six thousand to seven thousand were ultimately taken to the killing site of **Ponar** 12.9 kilometers (eight miles) south of the city and murdered in multiple "*Aktionen*" (actions) before Germans and their Lithuanian collaborators finally liquidated the small ghetto entirely on October 24, 1941.[18]

DOCUMENT 4-3: **"Bloody Days of Vilna,"** *Neged Hazerem*[19] **Warsaw, no. 7–8 (late 1941), USHMMA RG 15.079M (ŻIH Ring. I/698), 39–40 (translated from Polish).**

One of our comrades from Vilna arrived on October 16 [1941] and brought news of the terrible events that have taken place there. We present his account word for word.—The editors

It was only the third day of the war, a Tuesday, when the Germans entered Vilna. On the first night of the war the Germans carried out a heavy air attack on the Porubanek airport, during which numerous Soviet planes were destroyed. The city was bombed the next day, but not too heavily. The Russians began to retreat on Monday. That day several evacuation trains, all of which were available for use, left Vilna for the east. Those who did not make it in time or for whom there was not enough room set out on foot after the army. Some of these people were later caught by the Germans and some who were able to reach the old Soviet border had to turn back because the Russians were not letting anyone cross the border except for a small group of party members, and that only with great difficulty.

In Vilna, in the meantime, German rule was established, and Lithuanians in particular took the lead. From the very start of the war, they had carried out an anti-Soviet partisan war. Their army, which had been joined with the Red Army, largely defected to the Germans, so they enjoyed privileges and took over full executive authority. And their vengeance against the Jews exceeded even the Germans' cruelty.

At the beginning, everything was "normal." People were seized, some for work, sometimes they were beaten at work, but that was it. A Judenrat comprised of prominent members of society was organized and handled the delivery of laborers itself. Sometimes people were even paid for working. But then they suddenly began seizing people and sending them to the

---

18. See Arad, *Ghetto in Flames*, 101–42; Herman Kruk, *The Last Days of the Jerusalem of Lithuania: Chronicles from the Vilna Ghetto and the Camps, 1939–1944* (New Haven, CT: Yale University Press, 2002), 124–27; Rudashevski, *The Diary of the Vilna Ghetto*, 39–46.

19. Underground newspaper of Hashomer Hatzair–Warsaw.

prison in Łukiszki, where they were segregated into those who were fit and unfit for work. The fit were reportedly sent to the front to work (which was equivalent to a death sentence) and the unfit were simply killed. The executions took place in Ponary [Ponar], where the Russians had dug large, deep pits to store fuel. The executioners, exclusively Lithuanians, stripped their victims down to their underwear, killed them with salvos from their rifles, and then covered them with a thin layer of earth, onto which the next group of condemned came. The fate of those sent to the front is unknown, but it is a fact that none of them returned.

The dispatches of people to Łukiszki were not an extraordinary phenomenon. They were systematically repeated every day and were handled by special units of Lithuanian "snatchers" that circled about the city all day to that end. There were raids day and night. On average, 100–300 persons were captured each day, and none of them ever returned. The Lithuanians didn't even honor the *Scheine* [certificates] issued by the Germans. They snatched up not only men, but also women, children younger than 14, and elderly persons no longer able to walk, and all were sent to their death in Ponary. The Jews of Vilna hid in cellars and tunnels. In all [Jewish] homes, people stood on guard through the night. There was tremendous panic.

Independently of this, every now and then provocations and pogroms were carried out again. In the Sznipiszki neighborhood, Germans, mainly airforce men, burned down the synagogue and hounded the rabbi naked through the streets. A contribution in the amount of 5 million rubles was imposed upon the Jews, but it was not collected, even with the help of Poles. Then finally, in the middle of September, the general provocation that delivered the coup de grâce to the Jews of Vilna took place.[20] In the city, posters appeared announcing that a German had been shot dead by Jews on Niemecka Street. Although the killers had been killed on the spot, the entire Jewish community was said to bear responsibility. That very night, the entire Jewish quarter was surrounded by German and Lithuanian assassins who took several thousand persons from their homes to their death in Ponary and sealed their homes. The next day, without any preparations, all the Jews of Vilna were herded into the sealed homes, out of which two closed ghettos, divided by Niemecka Street, were immediately created.

---

20. The so-called Great Provocation, a murder action conducted by German security policemen and Lithuanian collaborators in Vilna during the first days of September 1941, marked the expansion of mass killings from men to women and children in the region. For September 2 alone, the Germans reported 3,700 Jews executed, among them 2,019 women and 817 children; see Arad, *Ghetto in Flames*, 103–7.

The situation of the Jews locked up in the ghettos was terrible. The larger of the two was designated for skilled workers so it was assumed that it would enjoy privileges. For precisely this reason, considerably more people became concentrated there than in the other ghetto and the population density was extremely high. There were 20–25 persons per room and thus up to 1,500 per building. The Germans named two new Judenräte [*Judenrathy*], one for each ghetto. Within the ghettos, a Jewish police was created comprised in one of Revisionists,[21] and in the other of generally dubious elements. Most importantly, the creation of ghettos did not impede the mass executions. One day the order was issued that, in light of overpopulation in the larger ghetto, 5,000 Jews needed to move to the smaller one. When only a small number of individuals complied with the demand, the Lithuanian assassins forcibly captured 5,000 people, but they were sent to Ponary instead of the smaller ghetto. Since these people were almost exclusively skilled workers who possessed passes, the Germans hurried to save them, but they were able to save only a few hundred persons, who subsequently returned to the ghetto.

In the course of three months, the Jewish population of Vilna, which had numbered 70,000 under the Soviets, fell to 35,000. Of those, only a small number has been able to get out of the city. Through mass executions, the smaller ghetto has been nearly completely liquidated. Terrible panic and depression prevail among the Jewish population. All are convinced that they will soon die, and they simply wait for their turn. Whoever can, fights through to Belarus, where the situation is not as terrible. Whoever knows where they are, fights through to the partisan units operating in the Vilna region.

Only scant news comes from within Lithuania, but we know with certainty that terrible massacres of Jews have taken place there as well. Jews have been killed literally down to the last man in a number of small towns in Vilna District. For example, all the Jews from Landwarów and other small towns were rounded up and taken to Troki. There, on an island, they were stripped down to their underwear and shot. Their clothing was subsequently distributed among the local peasants. In the small town Ejszyszki, which contained several thousand Jews, not a single Jew remains alive. Only several dozen were able to flee to Bastuny, in the territory of Belarus.

---

21. For Revisionist Zionists, see the Glossary.

The Wehrmacht's rapid advance left pockets behind the front line with few or no German forces present. The last sentence in the Hashomer Hatzair article refers to one such zone of relative and temporary safety. With the establishment of a stable German occupation regime, however, these areas became the targets of "actions" similar in deadly destructiveness to the mass executions conducted in the cities. Until the beginning of the winter, German military and police units, supported by local collaborators, swept the countryside. The small town of Ejszyszki mentioned in the article and located in the border region of Lithuania and Belarus was just one of countless settings in which Germans and their agents annihilated the Jewish population, leaving few if any survivors who could bear witness to the crimes.[22]

While the occupiers depicted the brutality of the war and their own actions in letters and photographs sent from the front to their families back home, Jews documented their experiences during this period first and foremost by keeping diaries, many of which—even when they were meant to preserve the memory of events for posterity—would remain private long after the war. Sitting down to reflect on the impact of German occupation required pen, paper, and focus, as well as a sense of relative tranquility, prerequisites in very short supply. Not surprisingly, many accounts of the war's early phase were written weeks or months later, when conditions seemed sufficiently settled and events clear enough to permit reflection.[23]

In March 1942, a young Jewish woman in the Galician city of Stanisławów reminisced in the context of recent violence and imminent change, prompting her to reflect on the purpose of her life as well as the suffering brought about by war. She had survived the city's so-called bloody Sunday of October 12, 1941, the mass murder of between ten thousand to twelve thousand Stanisławów Jews committed by German units on the Jewish holiday of Hoshana Rabbah. The situation seemed eerily tranquil for the time being.[24]

---

22. See Yaffa Eliach, *There Once Was a World: A 900-Year Chronicle of the Shtetl of Eishyshok* (Boston, MA: Little, Brown & Co., 1998).

23. See, e.g., Rudashevski, *The Diary of the Vilna Ghetto*, 10–11; for the broader context, see Alexandra Garbarini, *Numbered Days: Diaries and the Holocaust* (New Haven, CT: Yale University Press, 2006), 89–90.

24. See Dieter Pohl, "Hans Krüger and the Murder of the Jews in the Stanisławów Region (Galicia)," in *Yad Vashem Studies* 26 (1997): 239–64; Andrea Löw, "Stanisławów," in *The USHMM Encyclopedia of Camps and Ghettos*, 2:831–34. Hoshana Rabbah falls on the seventh day of Sukkot (or Feast of the Tabernacle), and is marked by an eponymous synagogue service, with a procession with lulavim (closed fronds of the date palm tree) and etrogim/esrogim (citrons).

DOCUMENT 4-4: **Unidentified woman, Stanisławów, Galicia district, General-gouvernement, diary entry for March 13, 1942, regarding "bloody Sunday" (October 12, 1941), USHMMA RG 02.208M (ŻIH 302/267) (translated from Polish).**[25]

[. . .] I am currently 22 years old. This ought to be the time of the most beautiful days of my life. When I ponder my life today, I see how joyless it has been, full of sad experiences and trials. [. . .] Today, I live in constant fear of losing my life. When we get up in the morning, we do not know whether we will lie down in our own beds at night and, when we go to bed at night, we do not know whether we will peacefully and safely live to see the next day. On that famous Sunday of October 12, 1941, I was at the cemetery together with my sister Bronka. I stayed calm to the end. I could not come to terms with the thought of my impending death; I did everything I could to save myself. Death reigned all around me. In front of me is an open grave, and hundreds of people fall into the grave at the shot of a revolver. Behind me, people are clustered, beaten into a cramped mass, bloodied, beaten, suffocating in horrible agony. Next to me lie several people who wanted to feign death. They were, in fact, killed when a Ukrainian policeman, beating and mocking them, stands on their stomachs and stomps with his boots until their insides come out. But I had grown hardened, I did not cry and I did not lose my head. I blushed heavily as my coat and sweater were removed, I moved smoothly and lightly, continually making my way to the back. Hoping to gain some time, I begged the Germans to spare our lives and asked that they rather take us to some labor camp, so we could live.

My young life up to that point, without sun, without happiness, flashed before my eyes and a powerless anger toward the injustice of life arose within me. Now, when I find myself in the full bloom of youth, which occurs only briefly and once in everyone's life, I am to die, having experienced nothing good? Why? Did I commit some sin by being born to a Jewish mother? Did I cause someone irreparable harm? Why is a human

---

25. Diary entries for March 13 and March 18, 1942, including the passage published above, were written by an unnamed woman in the diary that was otherwise kept by Elsa Binder, in her teens when the Germans occupied Stanisławów. Elsa Binder was murdered in early 1943, when the ghetto was liquidated. Because there is no indication who the author of the March 13, 1942, entry was, no information could be found about her and her sister Bronka's fate—or, crucially, how she survived to write about "bloody Sunday." See also Alexandra Zapruder, *Salvaged Pages: Young Writers' Diaries of the Holocaust* (New Haven, CT: Yale University Press, 2002), 301–28 (with a different translation of the document's text). The verb tense shifts occur in the original source.

being—who is equal to me, whom I am seeing for the very first time—my mortal enemy and why does he have the right to deprive hundreds of thousands of innocent people of their lives? Those who believe in God and expect mercy or a response from him are naïve. Unfortunately, I see the culture and barbarism of the twentieth century, which reveals itself precisely in such deeds.

Every article in the newspaper, every poster in the city contains a vow to exterminate the Jews. We have been shut inside the ghetto like lepers, without any prospect of making a living. The only way to survive here is by selling clothes.

[. . .]

Our powers are at their end, our bodies are exhausted and malnourished. We constantly delude ourselves with the hope that change will come, a hope that keeps us alive. But how long can one live on spiritual strength alone, which is already starting to weaken? [. . .] This is a horrible feeling. You feel that the noose is already around your neck and you are surrounded by guards so you cannot escape. But on the other hand, you are aware that you could still live, that you are healthy, strong, but deprived of all human rights [*ludzkic prawo*[26]].

More than once, when I have felt bad, I have wished for death. I do not know whether I am sinning by uttering such a wish, but I feel that I should and must come to terms with this thought. [. . .]

Extreme experiences produced extreme accounts from those who lived through them. The vast majority of Jews caught in the round-ups and ghetto "actions" did not survive. By the end of 1941, Germans, Romanians, and their collaborators had murdered more than half a million Jews in the occupied Soviet Union—among the victims, increasing numbers of women and children. **Heinrich Himmler**'s SS and police apparatus was the first to aim at the "de-Jewification" of entire areas, his unit commanders competing to outdo one another as the most radical executioners of Nazi policy. Among the many sites of carnage during the waning days of the summer of 1941, some Ukrainian cities stand out due to the combination of the speed and scope of the mass murder committed there. In the ravine of Babi Yar near Kiev, more than thirty-three thousand Jews of all ages and without regard to gender were killed in the last days of September. And in Kamyanets-Podilsky German SS and police units, acting in accord with regional Wehrmacht commanders, murdered 26,500 Jews between August 26 and 29, 1941, among them many expellees

---

26. The term is distinct from the later concept of human rights, in Polish: *prawa człowieka*.

from Hungarian-controlled Carpatho-Ukraine, including many women and children.[27] A few photographs secretly taken by Gyula Spitz, one of the more than two thousand Jews drafted into the Hungarian army due to their special skills, documented the murderous action; one follows.

DOCUMENT 4-5: **Photograph secretly taken by Gyula Spitz of Jews led to their execution in Kamyanets-Podilsky, German-occupied Ukraine, August 27, 1941, USHMMPA WS# 28216.**

The feeble protection afforded Spitz by serving with the Hungarian army did not last. Eventually arrested by the Germans and deported to the Mauthausen concentration camp, he did not survive the war.[28]

In order to delude the prospective victims and to avoid protests from foreign governments, the Nazi regime tried to keep the ensuing genocide a secret

27. Browning, *The Origins of the Final Solution*, 268–94; Klaus-Michael Mallmann, Andrej Angrick, Jürgen Matthäus, and Martin Cüppers, eds., *Die "Ereignismeldungen UdSSR" 1941: Dokumente der Einsatzgruppen in der Sowjetunion* (Darmstadt: Wissenschaftliche Buchgesellschaft, 2011), 444–46.

28. A Jewish cab driver from Budapest, Spitz was drafted into regular army service rather than the labor service, probably because of his driving skills. From 1940 to 1942 he transported valuables plundered from occupied territories by Hungarian officers. See Zoltán Vági, László Csősz, and, Gábor Kádár, *The Holocaust in Hungary: Evolution of a Genocide* (Lanham, MD: AltaMira Press in association with the USHMM, 2013), chapter 2. The USHMMPA also holds copies of three other photographs taken by Spitz in Kamyanets-Podilsky.

while its propaganda continued to beat the anti-Jewish drum. Yet increasing references to the necessity of "solving the Jewish question" along the lines of Hitler's speech of January 30, 1939, cropped up among the standard slogans. The speech had "warned" that a world war would result in the "annihilation of the Jewish race in Europe."[29] Accounts from the East reaching Germans in the Reich and Germany's partners' less tight control over published opinion, especially in Hungary and Romania, created cracks in the wall of deception. By the fall of 1941, Allied intelligence agencies such as British decryption specialists were intercepting classified German radio transmissions that mentioned staggering execution figures. Soviet officers interrogating eyewitnesses of mass executions had also gathered enough evidence to ascertain that the Germans were systematically using deadly violence against civilians in the Soviet Union.[30]

Deemed highly sensitive, information that would have confirmed fears about the existence of a systematic persecution pattern was not publicized at the time (and in the case of the British intercepts, remained hidden away in archives for almost half a decade after the end of World War II). Through various channels some news of mass murders nonetheless found its way into the western press. Already in late 1941, several newspapers in the United States carried stories about the carnage in Kamyanets-Podilsky and Babi Yar.[31] Jewish organizations with extensive networks such as the **World Jewish Congress** also received, sometimes many months after the fact, reports based on eyewitness accounts or hearsay indicating the breadth and depth of the German rampage. Similar to accounts of mass killings in Vilna and other Lithuanian ghettos, the following document—introduced by the WJC's commentator as a "report on the extermination [*Ausrottung*] of the Latvian Jews from an eyewitness"—describes the murder of roughly twenty-six thousand Jews from Riga on November 30 and December 7–8, 1941, in the nearby forest of **Rumbula**.[32]

---

29. "Extract from the Speech by Hitler, January 30, 1939," in Yitzhak Arad, Israel Gutman, and Abraham Margaliot, eds., *Documents on the Holocaust: Selected Sources on the Destruction of the Jews of Germany and Austria, Poland, and the Soviet Union* (Lincoln: University of Nebraska Press, 1999), 134–35.

30. See Richard Breitman, *Official Secrets: What the Nazis Planned, What the British and Americans Knew* (New York: Hill and Wang, 1998).

31. "Chronicles," *Contemporary Jewish Record* 5, no. 5 (October 1942): 533. In Babi Yar in October 1941, foreign press correspondents from ten countries brought in from Berlin were given a tour by German officials in which they claimed that the number of Jews in Kiev had been brought down from roughly 350,000 to zero. See Karel C. Berkhoff, *Babi Yar: Site of Mass Murder, Ravine of Oblivion* (Washington, DC: USHMM Occasional Paper, 2012), 8.

32. See Andrej Angrick and Peter Klein, *The "Final Solution" in Riga: Exploitation and Annihilation, 1941–1944* (New York: Berghahn, 2009), 146.

DOCUMENT 4-6: **Report on the fate of Jews in Riga, German-occupied Latvia, in November/December 1941, written June 1942, USHMMA RG 68.045M (WJC Geneva), reel 3 (translated from German).**

[. . .]

Thus the situation remained steady until November 28 [1941]. On that day a decree was issued calling for one area of the ghetto to be vacated. All the Jews who had been living in this area of the ghetto were transferred into the other part of the ghetto. The part of the ghetto that was cleared as a result was fenced off in turn and set up to serve as the "Little Ghetto." All the men who worked for German entities outside the ghetto had to move into this new ghetto. The wives and families of these men remained in the old "big" ghetto, now reduced in size.

On November 29 a new decree was enacted, requiring all men between 18 and 60 who were fit for work to line up in columns on a street by the new ghetto area on November 30 and directing the rest of the population to be sent to camps. Each person had the right to take along 20 kilograms [44 pounds] of baggage. The assembly took place on November 30. All invalids and all persons over the age of 60 were sent home, and all physicians were released to provide treatment in the ghetto hospitals. Thus 4,000 persons were placed in the Little Ghetto. Conditions in this small, newly created ghetto were appalling. There was even less room than in the old ghetto. One small room had to accommodate 16 people, with 5 sleeping together in one bed.

On the night of November 30 and early morning of December 1, 8,000 people from one area of the big ghetto were assembled. Each one had 20 kilos of baggage. The people stood outdoors all night long and were led away on December 1, heavily guarded by the Latvian auxiliary police under German direction. In an act of particular cruelty, the people were made to file past the fence of the small ghetto, so that the transport took place before the very eyes of the deportees' male relatives. The treatment of the people was brutal; anyone who could not keep pace was shot without further ado. As it was later learned, these people were taken to two forests in the vicinity of Riga, known as the forest of Bickern [Biķernieki] and the forest of Zarnikau [Carnikava], where they were summarily shot. After this mass execution, around 16,000 people remained in the big ghetto.

The next week was somewhat calmer. Only 800 women were led away one day, with 400 of them taken to prison and 400 others later returned to the ghetto. On December 7 all women were ordered to be at home at 7 p.m.

On the night of December 7 and early morning of December 8, all the people still in the big ghetto—around 16,000 in total—were led away in the same manner as the 8,000 one week before. As was later learned from a report of the commandant of the Latvian ghetto guard, who made these statements in a somewhat intoxicated state, the 16,000 were led into the woods that very night. Russian prisoners of war had to dig three or four deep graves; then men and women were lined up separately in columns. All valuables had to be tossed onto a pile. The people were forced to undress: the men had to strip bare, while the women were allowed to keep a chemise on. All clothing had to be tossed onto a second pile. Then the order was given for the men, stark naked, to lie down in the graves. Then three or four German machine gunners opened fire on the men lying in the graves. The next group had to lie on top of the still warm corpses, and these men were murdered in the same manner. The women and children met the same fate.

In this way the entire remaining population of the large ghetto in Riga perished on the night of December 7–8.

This report, which originated with the ghetto commandant, was confirmed later by a number of members of the Latvian police who had witnessed the scene. In Riga itself, one could be convinced of the truth of this report inasmuch as shortly thereafter, the clothing and underclothing of the murdered Jews were carried publicly through the streets of Riga, and one could see the Jewish badges that had been sewn onto the garments. Then these clothes were sent to Germany. The *Aktion* took place under German direction. It was German gunners who carried out the murderous activities. But the *Aktion* could take place only with strong participation by hundreds of Latvian policemen, who were responsible for guarding and cordoning off the area. Most of the Latvian auxiliary policemen involved in this *Aktion* were subsequently sent to the Russian front to prevent them from speaking out. Two of the Latvians involved in the *Aktion* are said to have gone insane.[33]

On December 9, all the Jews remaining in the small ghetto were ordered to assemble so that they could be taken to work. The physicians and members of the Jewish Committee were assembled at another site and taken away in a bus. Two physicians, Dr. Kretzer and Dr. Guttmann, took

---

33. Most of the Latvian auxiliaries involved in the Riga massacre formed part of a unit (12th Schutzmannschaft Battalion) subsequently deployed in many other mass murder actions throughout the occupied Soviet Union. No evidence exists for mental breakdowns among the perpetrators triggered by participation in the late 1941 executions. See Angrick and Klein, *The "Final Solution" in Riga*, 161.

poison. Dr. Guttman died as a result. Suddenly the *Aktion* was called off again, and the Committee members and doctors were taken back. Thus Dr. Kretzer's life could be saved. Some time later, however, several members of the Committee, including Blumenau and Eliaschoff, were likewise shot. Dr. Blumenfeld had withdrawn from the Committee and resumed his medical work in the hospital.

Thus 4,000 Jews still remained in Riga in mid-December. In addition, there were a few hundred women who had been arrested in early December and imprisoned, and then suddenly taken back to the ghetto one day.

In December the old ghetto was empty, and now there were new arrivals from Germany: the Jews deported from Düsseldorf, Cologne, Mannheim, and elsewhere. Some trains reached Riga with freight cars in which all the deportees had frozen to death. The people arrived completely destitute, with no baggage. Most of them carried small bags with a few belongings with them. Their treatment was even worse than that of the Riga Jews. For example, they received only 50 grams [1.8 ounces] of bread per day, whereas the Riga Jews had been given 100 grams. For many, however, the ghetto was only a way station. Part of them stayed in the ghetto, and part were housed in camps, where some froze to death and others starved. The barracks were not heated.[34]

Our reporter cannot say much about the time period from late December 1941 to June 1942 because he was living then in hiding in the countryside. [. . .]

Only 4,700 survivors remained in the Riga ghetto after the murder of early December 1941. The information clearly pointed to a crucial new stage in the process of destruction: "the East" had become not only the site of mass murder for local Jews, but for Jewish men, women, and children deported from the Reich as well.

DEPORTATIONS FROM THE REICH AND THE PROTECTORATE

While the momentum for mass murder had been generated after June 22, 1941, in the occupied parts of the Soviet Union, the anti-Jewish dynamic reached back into the heart of the Nazi empire in the fall of 1941. Within two months

---

34. The one thousand German Jews arriving in Riga on the first transport on November 30, 1941, were also murdered in the Rumbula forest.

of the war against the Soviet Union, the range of execution targets had widened from men of military age to women and children, leading to the annihilation of entire communities in some regions. In October, German authorities started to deport Jews from the Greater Reich, from Germany, Austria, and the **Protectorate**, on an unprecedented scale.[35] Hitler appears to have set the course toward systematic deportation in the first days of September 1941. On September 24, 1941, Propaganda Minister **Joseph Goebbels** noted in his diary: "The Führer believes that the Jews must be gradually removed from Germany. The first cities to be made free of Jews [*judenfrei*] will be Berlin, Vienna, and Prague."[36] Hitler decided on Minsk, Riga, and Łódź as the destination of the first transports: Each city was to receive twenty-five thousand deportees (the Łódź contingent would include five thousand "gypsies" in addition to twenty thousand Jews) and left to determine how the uprooted would be treated at their destination. In retrospect, the new phase of deportations can be grouped into two waves, the first comprised of twenty and the second of thirty-four transports of roughly one thousand Jews each. The first wave of Jews from Vienna were sent to the Łódź ghetto starting on October 15 and continued until November 3. Transports from Prague, Luxembourg, Berlin, and a range of other German cities followed. The second wave began on November 8, with deportees headed for Minsk (seven transports), Kovno (five transports), and Riga (twenty-two transports), and continued until early February 1942.[37] As the unknown author of the previous document put it, these destinations indeed turned out to be "way stations" to immediate or eventual death.

Continuing its crucial role from the first steps taken toward Nazi anti-Jewish policy in 1933, Germany's bureaucracy cleared the path to "the East." A supplementary decree to the 1935 **Nuremberg Law** on citizenship stripped the deportees of all property rights once they had crossed the border; already on September

---

35. See Saul Friedländer, *Nazi Germany and the Jews:* (vol. 2) *The Years of Extermination, 1939–1945* (New York: HarperCollins, 2007), 262–67; Browning, *The Origins of the Final Solution*, 374–88; Peter Longerich, *Holocaust: The Nazi Persecution and Murder of the Jews* (Oxford: Oxford University Press, 2010), 259–76.

36. Elke Fröhlich, ed., *Die Tagebücher von Joseph Goebbels, Teil II Diktate 1941–1945*, vol. 1: *July–September 1941* (Munich: K. G. Saur, 1996), 85.

37. For different variations on how historians have grouped these deportations from the Reich in "waves," "phases," or "segments," see Browning, *The Origins of the Final Solution*, 375–77; Friedländer, *Nazi Germany*, 2:266; and Longerich, *Holocaust*, 286. No transports occurred between December 16, 1941, and January 8, 1942. See also Alfred Gottwaldt and Diana Schulle, who offer a meticulous breakdown of the deportations in *Die "Judendeportationen" aus dem Deutschen Reich 1941–1945. Eine kommentierte Chronologie* (Wiesbaden: Marix Verlag, 2005), 62–136.

1, 1941, a police regulation ordered German Jews over the age of six to wear a yellow "Star of David" in a visible place at all times starting later that month.[38] **Willy Cohn** heard about the new directive at the barber shop on September 8, and although he remained determined to keep calm—if only for the sake of his two small daughters—he felt, like most other German Jews, deeply denigrated.[39] Initially, regulations for wearing these signs created as much confusion as concern. In Hamburg, where British bombs were wreaking increasing havoc, **Luise Solmitz**, the Christian wife of decorated World War I veteran Fredy Solmitz, went to city hall to find out whether the measure applied to her husband (it did not because the decree exempted Jewish spouses living in "privileged mixed marriages").[40] Many wondered how non-Jews would react in the streets to what its creators intended as a badge of dishonor. Informed observers abroad understood the danger signaled by the transfer of the Star of David from the East to the West, even though the announcement reached them in the obligatory guarded language of the remaining Jewish periodical in the Reich. In the Swiss city of Geneva, **Jewish Agency for Palestine** official **Richard Lichtheim** was well-positioned to put the measure into a broader perspective.

DOCUMENT 4-7: Richard Lichtheim, Jewish Agency-Geneva, to Joseph Linton, Jewish Agency-London, September 16, 1941, CZA RG L22, and page from the *Jüdisches Nachrichtenblatt*, Berlin, September 12, 1941.[41]

Dear Linton,

I am sending you herewith enclosed an original copy of "Jüdisches Nachrichten-Blatt," the only Jewish paper now appearing in Germany. You will see from this miserable little sheet that this paper is not allowed to say anything of real interest or importance. The number I am sending you is characteristic for all the others. There is always some sort of leader containing general remarks about moral duties to help each other and the rest of the paper contains information about emigration-possibilities or

---

38. Friedländer, *Nazi Germany*, 2:251–56.

39. Willy Cohn, *Kein Recht, Nirgends: Tagebuch vom Untergang des Breslauer Judentums, 1933–1941*, ed. Norbert Conrads (Cologne: Böhlau, 2007), 954–55, 957, 963 (diary entries for July 13, 14, 15, 19, and August 3, 1941).

40. Diary entries, Luise Solmitz for September 9–20, 1941, FZGH 11 S 11.

41. Lichtheim's letter is also printed in *Archives of the Holocaust: An International Collection of Selected Documents*, ed. Henry Friedlander and Sybil Milton (New York: Garland Publishing, 1990), 4:31.

Jüdisches NACHRICHTENBLATT

Verlag: Jüdischer Kulturbund in Deutschland e. V., Abt. „Jüdisches Nachrichtenblatt", Berlin N 4, Oranienburger Str. 40/41 / Redaktion: Berlin N 4, Oranienburger Str. 40/41 (Tel.: 42 59 21)
Bezugsgeld einschließlich Bestellgeld je Monat RM 0,76, je Vierteljahr RM 2,28 / Anzeigenschluß jeweils Montag 17 Uhr / Postscheck-Konto: Berlin Nr. 173 605 Jüdischer Kulturbund

Nr. 61 | Freitag, den 12. September 1941 | Jahrgang 1941

Kinder haben Pflichten

L. I. K. Was können, so fragen uns zahlreiche betagte Eltern, unsere schon früher nach Uebersee ausgewanderten Kinder für unsere Nachwanderung tun? An diese Fragen werden dann noch die verschiedensten Bemerkungen geknüpft, es wird hervorgehoben, wie häufig man sich bereits an die Kinder gewandt habe, ohne daß es gelungen wäre, einen abschließenden Erfolg zu erzielen. In den meisten Fällen werden von den ausgewanderten Kindern die überseeischen Einwanderungsbestimmungen und ihre Handhabung zur Entschuldigung für einen verzögernden oder gar negativen Bescheid angeführt, und manchmal ist der Einwand richtig, vielfach aber trifft er nicht den Nagel auf den Kopf. So viele Lobeshymnen über zahlreiche Söhne und Töchter angestimmt werden können, die rastlos um die Nachwanderung ihrer bejahrten Eltern bemüht sind und so ergiebige Resultate bereits bisher durch viele dieser Anstrengungen erzielt werden konnten, zuweilen lassen es selbst die engsten Angehörigen an dem notwendigen Eifer fehlen, man vermißt bei ihnen Energie und Hingabe, schon die ersten Hindernisse genügen, um sich mit einer unzureichenden Erledigung abzufinden. Die Einwanderungsbestimmungen der Ueberseeländer bilden gewiß schwer zu überwindende Hindernisse, aber wer wollte behaupten, daß sie überhaupt nicht überstiegen werden können. Besonders dann, wenn in einem Ueberseelande das Einwanderungsreglement sich geändert hat, pflegen die Absagebriefe von drüben nur so zu regnen, man weist auf die verschärfte Praxis hin und glaubt damit getan zu haben, was von einem erwartet werden konnte. Wenn fremde Menschen, an die sich die älteren Leute wenden, so antworten, wird man das bedauern, aber es nur selten zu ändern vermögen; schreiben jedoch die eigenen Kinder in dem gleichen Tone, dann wird man für eine solche Resignation keinerlei Verständnis aufbringen können. Daß die Beschaffung von Einwanderungsvisen schwer ist, läßt sich keineswegs leugnen, aber dem unentwegten Eifer gelingt, was der lauen Pflichterfüllung mißraten muß.

Um die Nachwanderung der Eltern

Wir sind noch nicht lange genug im Lande, so begründen manchmal Söhne und Töchter ihre verschleierten Ablehnungen, wir können deshalb keine Bürgschaft ausstellen oder ein Recht zur Anforderung geltend machen. Wir vermögen das Geld nicht aufzutreiben, so antworten andere nach Uebersee ausgewanderte Kinder, um eine Zwischenwanderung zu finanzieren, und sie denken, daß das für die alten Eltern eine überaus einleuchtende und leicht zu verstehende Begründung ist. Daß dem keineswegs so ist, zeigen ja die an uns gerichteten Anfragen der Eltern, die solche Briefe erhalten haben, wobei schon deren oberflächlichste Prüfung ergibt, daß die Kinder in Uebersee keineswegs alle in Betracht kommenden Möglichkeiten genugend geprüft haben. Weshalb unterlassen es diese Kinder, wenn die eigene Bürgschaft nicht ausreicht, befreundete Personen, die schon länger in dem bezüglichen Lande leben, zur Unterstützung heranzuziehen, sie könnten auch auf den Gedanken kommen, das für eine Zwischenwanderung benötigte Kapital darlehnsweise aufzunehmen, um es später in kleinen Beträgen zurückzuzahlen. Es mag schwer sein, alle diese Wege zu gehen, sie dürften jedoch allen den Kindern leicht fallen, die daran denken, welche Opfer die Eltern für sie gebracht haben und deren Erinnerung mit den Jahren nicht verblaßt ist. Es hat zahlreiche Eltern gegeben, die jahrzehntelang außerordentliche Aufwendungen gemacht haben, um ihren Kindern eine gute Erziehung angedeihen zu lassen; diese Eltern haben ihren eigenen Lebensunterhalt eingeschränkt, um den Kindern den Zugang zu einem Beruf zu eröffnen. Das war gewiß auch nicht leicht, es hat viele Entbehrungen gekostet, um das Ziel endlich erreichen zu können. Die Kinder haben alle diese Anstrengungen als eine Selbstverständlichkeit hingenommen, sie haben wohl immer das Gefühl gehabt, die Eltern erfüllten eine Pflicht, die naturgegeben sei. Dieses Gefühl war durchaus richtig, aber auch von den Kindern, die in den vergangenen Jahren ausgewandert sind, darf man die Betätigung einer solchen natürlichen Pflicht erwarten, und sie sollten sich deshalb nicht mit konventionellen Entschuldigungen begnügen, die nur allzu deutlich den mangelnden Eifer erkennen lassen.

Gelockerte Bindungen

Liest man die Absagebriefe von Kindern aus Uebersee an ihre noch hier weilenden alten Eltern, dann muß man manchmal mit Bedauern konstatieren, wie locker die Bindungen geworden sind, durch die sich Söhne und Töchter mit ihren Eltern noch verknüpft fühlen. Das geht freilich nicht nur manchen Eltern mit ihren Kindern so, auch andere ausgewanderte Personen fühlen sich ihrer moralischen Pflichten gegen die noch nicht ausgewanderten Verwandten und Freunde enthoben, wenn sie einige Monate in den Ländern der Einwanderung leben. Wie schnell wird da alles vergessen, was vorher bekräftigt worden ist, man staunt über die Leichtigkeit, mit der manche Ausgewanderte über förmliche Versprechungen hinweggehen, noch mehr verblüfft die Verständnislosigkeit gegenüber den einfachsten Wünschen um Unterstützung und Förderung der Nachwanderung. Diese Bemängelungen sollen keineswegs das beispielhafte Verhalten der großen Mehrheit der ausgewanderten Juden aus unserem Kreise in bezug auf die Nachwanderung ihrer Verwandten und Freunde in den Hintergrund rücken, wir wissen nur allzugut, daß die individuelle Wanderung ihren großen Umfang nicht angenommen hätte, wenn ihr das beseelte Verständnis der in den früheren Jahren Ausgewanderten gefehlt hätte. Wir möchten aber, daß der Eifer sich auf alle diejenigen erstreckt, die ihn bekunden können, vor allem aber erwarten wir von den nächsten Angehörigen, daß sie sich auch weiter um die Auswanderung ihrer älteren Verwandten bemühen und daß sie es dabei nicht bei bloßen Gesten bewenden lassen, sondern daß sie Opfer bringen, Opfer an Bequemlichkeit und am eigenen Lebensstandard. Es gibt noch Länder, in die eine vorläufige Zwischenwanderung möglich ist, wenn auch die Einwanderung in diese Ueberseestaaten mehr oder minder erhebliche Kapitalien beansprucht. Darin aber sollte sich gerade die Opferfähigkeit der ausgewanderten Kinder zeigen, ihre Geschicklichkeit kann sich an der Aufbringung der Geldmittel erproben, die zur Finanzierung einer vorübergehenden Einwanderungsmöglichkeit benötigt werden.

Auswanderung geht weiter

Ist auch die Erlangung von Einwanderungserlaubnissen und Visen schwieriger geworden, so sehen wir doch, daß die Auswanderung unvermindert weiter geht, es werden Transporte nach Uebersee abgefertigt, deren Organisation sowohl bezüglich des Land- und Seeweges als auch in jeder anderen Hinsicht ausgezeichnet ist; zahlreiche und gerade ältere Personen gelangen in den Besitz von Affidavits und Anforderungen und andere, die sie noch nicht haben, setzen ihre Anstrengungen unbeirrbar fort, um alsbald in den Besitz der erforderlichen Papiere zu kommen. Tun alle Kinder in Uebersee ihre Pflicht in dem Sinne, wie wir es hier erörtert haben, dann kann der Umfang der Auswanderung betagter Eltern sich weiter vergrößern, und wir haben ja bereits vor kurzer Zeit dargelegt, wie vorteilhaft in mannigfacher Beziehung gerade die Auswanderung älterer Menschen für uns ist. Die sozialen Lasten werden dadurch vermindert, die spätere Auswanderungsfähigkeit jüngerer Menschen kann gesteigert und die altersmäßige Struktur der noch nicht ausgewanderten jüdischen Bevölkerung in günstigster Weise beeinflußt werden. Das sind wesentliche Vorteile, die sich erwarten lassen, die aber schon heute mit jedem Auswanderertransport, der abgefertigt wird, eintreten, die jedoch noch ausgeweitet werden können, wenn sich vor allem die Kinder und sonstigen engsten Verwandten, die in früheren Jahren den Weg nach Uebersee angetreten haben, um die Steigerung und Vervollkommnung der Nachwanderung ihrer alten Eltern und Verwandten so hingebungsvoll bemühen, wie man es von ihnen verständigerweise erwarten darf. In den Bemühungen um die Schaffung von überseeischen Einwanderungsmöglichkeiten für ältere Menschen kann es keinen Stillstand geben, mit Eifer und Verständnis muß jeder einzelne Fall behandelt werden, denn die Fülle der Einzelfälle ergibt dann jenen Erfolg, der in den Sammeltransporten in die neutralen Häfen seinen sichtbaren Ausdruck findet.

Transporte unterwegs

DER DAMPFER „NAVE MAR" AUS LISSABON ABGEFAHREN

Der Ueberseedampfer „Nave Mar" hat am 16. August den Hafen von Lissabon verlassen und hat seine Ueberseereise angetreten. Die auf dem Schiff untergebrachten jüdischen Auswanderer waren alle bei bestem Wohlsein. Das Schiff dürfte inzwischen das Ziel seiner Reise erreicht haben.

„CABO DE HORNOS"

In Buenos Aires ist der spanische Ueberseedampfer „Cabo de Hornos" mit zahlreichen jüdischen Einwanderern an Bord eingetroffen.

Die nächste Abfahrt ab Bilbao ist für den 19. September vorgesehen. Das Schiff nimmt Auswanderer nach Venezuela, Curacao, Brasilien und Argentinien auf.

NACH MITTEL-AMERIKA

Der Ueberseedampfer „Magellanes" mit jüdischen Passagieren an Bord verläßt am 22. September Bilbao, um seine Fahrt nach Kuba und USA anzutreten.

VON SPANIEN NACH UEBERSEE

Eine größere Anzahl jüdischer Auswanderer ist im Sondertransport nach Spanien befördert worden. Unter den Auswanderern befinden sich in erster Reihe ältere Personen, die nach Nord- und Südamerika gehen.

„NYASSA"

Am 8. September ist die „Nyassa" aus dem Hafen von Lissabon mit Einwanderern nach Kuba und den Vereinigten Staaten ausgelaufen. (Fortsetzung Seite 2.)

Polizeiverordnung über die Kennzeichnung der Juden

Vom 1. September 1941

Auf Grund der Verordnung über die Polizeiverordnungen der Reichsminister vom 14. November 1938 (Reichsgesetzbl. I S. 1582) und der Verordnung über das Rechtsetzungsrecht im Protektorat Böhmen und Mähren vom 7. Juni 1939 (Reichsgesetzbl. I S. 1039) wird im Einvernehmen mit dem Reichsprotektor in Böhmen und Mähren verordnet:

§ 1

(1) Juden (§ 5 der Ersten Verordnung zum Reichsbürgergesetz vom 14. November 1935 — Reichsgesetzbl. I S. 1333), die das sechste Lebensjahr vollendet haben, ist es verboten, sich in der Oeffentlichkeit ohne einen Judenstern zu zeigen.

(2) Der Judenstern besteht aus einem handtellergroßen, schwarz ausgezogenen Sechsstern aus gelbem Stoff mit der Aufschrift „Jude". Er ist sichtbar auf der linken Brustseite des Kleidungsstücks fest aufgenäht zu tragen.

§ 2

Juden ist es verboten,

a) den Bereich ihrer Wohngemeinde zu verlassen, ohne eine schriftliche Erlaubnis der Ortspolizeibehörde bei sich zu führen;

b) Orden, Ehrenzeichen und sonstige Abzeichen zu tragen.

§ 3

Die §§ 1 und 2 finden keine Anwendung

a) auf den in einer Mischehe lebenden jüdischen Ehegatten, sofern Abkömmlinge aus der Ehe vorhanden sind und diese nicht als Juden gelten, und zwar auch dann, wenn die Ehe nicht mehr besteht oder der einzige Sohn im gegenwärtigen Kriege gefallen ist;

b) auf die jüdische Ehefrau bei kinderloser Mischehe während der Dauer der Ehe.

§ 4

(1) Wer dem Verbot der §§ 1 und 2 vorsätzlich oder fahrlässig zuwiderhandelt, wird mit Geldstrafe bis zu 150 Reichsmark oder mit Haft bis zu sechs Wochen bestraft.

(2) Weitergehende polizeiliche Sicherungsmaßnahmen sowie Strafvorschriften, nach denen eine höhere Strafe verwirkt ist, bleiben unberührt.

§ 5

Die Polizeiverordnung gilt auch im Protektorat Böhmen und Mähren mit der Maßgabe, daß der Reichsprotektor in Böhmen und Mähren die Vorschrift des § 2 Buchst. a den örtlichen Verhältnissen im Protektorat Böhmen und Mähren anpassen kann.

§ 6

Die Polizeiverordnung tritt 14 Tage nach ihrer Verkündung in Kraft.

*

Die Verordnung ist durch Ausgabe der Nr. 100 des Reichsgesetzblatts 1941 Teil I am 5. September 1941 verkündet worden, tritt also am 19. September 1941 in Kraft. (Red.)

Ausgabe der Kennzeichen an die Juden in Berlin

Die Verteilung der Judensterne an die in Berlin ansässigen Juden erfolgt durch die Jüdische Kultusvereinigung zu Berlin e. V. Dies gilt auch für diejenigen Juden im Sinne des § 5 der Ersten Verordnung zum Reichsbürgergesetz, die nicht der jüdischen Religionsgemeinschaft angehören.

Jeder kann zunächst nur **einen** Stern erhalten. Eine weitere Verteilung soll im Oktober stattfinden.

Die Ausgabe erfolgt am Mittwoch, dem 17. September, für die Buchstaben A—K und am Donnerstag, dem 18. September, für die Buchstaben L—Z durchgehend von 8 bis 20 Uhr in den nachstehend angegebenen Verteilungsstellen:

für die Bewohner der Verwaltungsbezirke	in den Verteilungsstellen
Charlottenburg, Tiergarten	Synagoge Levetzowstr. 8; Schule Joachimsthaler Str. 13 (Turnhalle und Aula)
Horst Wessel, Lichtenberg, Weißensee	Schule Kaiserstr. 29/30 (Turnhalle)
Köpenick, Mitte	Alte Synagoge, Eingang Rosenstraße 2/4
Neukölln, Treptow, Tempelhof, Kreuzberg	Synagoge Thielschufer 10—16
Pankow, Prenzlauer Berg, Reinickendorf, Wedding	Schule Choriner Str. 74 (Turnhalle)
Schöneberg, Steglitz	Synagoge Münchener Str. 37
Wilmersdorf, Zehlendorf, Spandau	Schule Joachimsthaler Str. 13 (Turnhalle und Aula)

Die Ausgabe erfolgt nur gegen **Vorlegung** des lila Bezugsausweises der Reichshauptstadt Berlin. Wer für andere mitbesorgt, muß deren lila Ausweise **mitbringen** und ihre genaue Kennkartennummer mit Kennort, bei Staatenlosen und Ausländern die ausstellende Paßbehörde und die Paßnummer **angeben**.

Die Ausgabe des Kennzeichens erfolgt gegen Zahlung von 0,10 RM.

Jüdische Kultusvereinigung zu Berlin e. V.

Der Vorstand.

the situation in some overseas-countries. The rest are official communi-qués and advertisements showing the death or marriage of the unfortunate Israels and Saras still living in Germany.[42]

But the copy I am sending you contains something of greater inter-est, i.e. the official text of the latest Order prescribing the wearing of the famous yellow badge by Jews.

According to their established practice, the police has ordered the Jewish communities to inform their members about this newest move of the Gestapo. I think it would be a good idea to have this Order photocopied as it appears in the paper and to send photocopies to all the big papers.

Of course there have been so many brutalities committed against the Jews that this latest measure may seem to be of minor importance. But it is my experience that this sort of thing makes a greater impression on many minds than the other well-known brutalities. People who don't care any longer about news telling them how the Jews have been robbed or imprisoned or beaten up may be shocked when reading that all male and female Jews from six years upward cannot appear in public without the yellow star showing the word "Jude" and it adds to the appreciation of the Nazi methods when reading the elaborate instructions regarding the issu-ing of these yellow badges in the various Synagogues or schools in Berlin. Therefore I think you should use this material for the press or in any other way which you may think advisable.

To-day it has been announced that this Order applies not only to Germany and the Protectorate but also to the Netherlands.[43]

The reason why this Order has been issued just now may be the desire to find some new way of humiliating the Jews and at the same time of diverting public opinion which is certainly preoccupied with more impor-tant issues. It may also be the preparation for a general Pogrom in case the events of war become more and more unfavourable to the Nazis as no doubt they will become in the course of the next months.

---

42. "Israels and Saras" refers to the middle names German Jews were forced to add to their names as of January 1, 1939.

43. Wearing of the "Star of David" became compulsory in the Protectorate on Septem-ber 15, 1941, but in the Netherlands only in May 1942 in conjunction with the start of deportations. See Jacob Presser, *Ashes in the Wind: The Destruction of Dutch Jewry* (London: Souvenir Press, 2010), 118–27; Bob Moore, *Victims and Survivors: The Nazi Persecution of the Jews in the Netherlands 1940–1945* (London: Arnold, 1997), 89–90.

According to the latest private information received from Germany, dissatisfaction and unrest among the population are growing. The enormous losses in Russia are beginning to have their effect on the Germans who until now have been accustomed to comparatively easy victories. There are even people here and in Germany who believe that German morale is much nearer [a] breaking-point than public opinion in Great-Britain and America believes it to be. Three or four more heavy bombardements of Berlin would have a great effect, much greater than such bombardements have ever had on the British population. These views may seem somewhat optimistic but there can be no doubt that German morale is a very different thing as compared with British morale and that the hysterical belief in Hitler can quickly be transformed into fear and despair the moment the masses begin to feel that the time of easy victories is over. [. . .]

While Lichtheim interpreted the introduction of the Jewish star as a possible "preparation for a general Pogrom" within Germany proper, it in fact preceded even more destructive, more systematic measures for moving the "solution of the Jewish question" to the East. Building on earlier functions of Jewish organizations in the Third Reich, the **Gestapo** charged them with preparing deportations, often referred to in regime parlance as "resettlement," "evacuation," or some other benign-sounding term. Throughout German-dominated Europe, the level of involvement of Jewish organizations varied at this juncture. Those Jewish leaders and functionaries willing to assist with the deportations acted on the assumption that they could somehow still aid those being sent away, as well as protect the remainder of the larger community. As historian Beate Meyer points out, when the board of the **Reichsvereinigung** met in October 1941 to discuss the **RSHA**'s demands, its members assumed that "resettlement—not extermination—would take place" and that not all German Jews would be affected. Consequently, "[t]hey believed their efforts could alleviate the severity of the [deportation] campaign" and "hoped to be able to prevent anything bad from happening."[44]

44. Beate Meyer, "The Fine Line between Responsible Action and Collaboration: The Reichsvereinigung der Juden in Deutschland and the Jewish Community in Berlin, 1938–45," in *Jews in Nazi Berlin: From Kristallnacht to Liberation*, ed. Beate Meyer, Hermann Simon, and Chana Schütz (Chicago: University of Chicago Press, 2009), 318; Beate Meyer, *Tödliche Gratwanderung: Die Reichsvereinigung der Juden in Deutschland zwischen Hoffnung, Zwang, Selbstbehauptung und Verstrickung (1939–1945)* (Göttingen: Wallstein, 2011), 123ff.

Developments in "the East" remained largely hidden from Jewish functionaries and activists, clouded in Nazi propaganda phrases, with alarming
yet nebulous rumors kept in check. Restrictions imposed by the regime had
clogged up all channels for gathering and disseminating reliable information.
The *Jüdisches Nachrichtenblatt*—what Lichtheim had dubbed a "miserable
little sheet"—functioned as one of the few permissible channels of communication, with authors cautious not to overstep boundaries drawn by the Gestapo
and their readers playing a guessing game over what was truth and what was
fiction. The following article from the *Nachrichtenblatt*'s Vienna edition, published six days after the first transport of roughly one thousand Jews had left the
city for Łódź, attempted to invoke Jewish history and convey a shred of hope,
all while the Jewish community was grappling with Nazi pressure to organize
further transports as swiftly as possible.[45] The author plays on the resemblance
of the term "*migration*" (*Wanderung*) to "*emigration*" (*Auswanderung*), thus stirring up connotations of escape from the ever sharper persecution measures at a
time when the regime was moving toward prohibiting emigration and the desire
among Jews to flee abroad was never higher.[46]

DOCUMENT 4-8: **E. R., "The obligation to be prepared,"** *Jüdisches Nachrichtenblatt*,
Vienna, October 31, 1941 (translated from German).

A sense of history—which cannot be denied the Jewish people, always
concerned about the continuity of its historical existence—tells us Jews
that nowadays we are yet again on the path of migration [*Wanderstrasse*]

---

45. See Doron Rabinovici, *Eichmann's Jews: The Jewish Administration of Holocaust Vienna,
1938–1945* (Malden, MA: Polity, 2011), 99–104.

46. On October 23, 1941, the RSHA issued a secret ban ordered by Himmler on the
emigration of Jews from Germany for the duration of the war, with the exception of "special
individual cases." While the top-level functionaries of the Reichsvereinigung were informed
about this ban immediately, the majority of German Jews were deliberately left in the dark.
Beate Meyer, "Between Self-Assertion and Forced Collaboration: The Reich Association of
Jews in Germany, 1939–1945," in *Jewish Life in Nazi Germany: Dilemmas and Responses*,
ed. Francis R. Nicosia and David Scrase (New York: Berghahn Books, 2010), 157; Clemens
Maier, "The Jüdisches Nachrichtenblatt, 1938–1943," in *Jews in Nazi Berlin*, Meyer, Simon,
and Schütz, 104. Still, the Reichsvereinigung's emigration department continued to operate
until January 1, 1942, and the emigration advice bureaus of the Hilfsverein der Juden
in Deutschland were not shuttered until February 14, 1942. See Browning, *The Origins
of the Final Solution*, 368; Joseph Walk, ed., *Das Sonderrecht für die Juden im NS-Staat.
Eine Sammlung der gesetzlichen Maßnahmen und Richtlinien–Inhalt und Bedeutung*, 2nd ed.
(Heidelberg: C. F. Müller, 1996), 353–56, 361, 363–64.

and still have quite a way to go on it. Yes, all of us must set out on this path, each one of us must leave his dwelling and journey to other regions. There is not one among us who can tell himself that he will be spared this fate. Therefore it is the moral obligation of every Jew in our community—to himself, to his next of kin, to his fellows in the broadest sense—not only to take in this idea and get used to it, but also to live up to it by making preparations to begin migration [*Wanderung*], once the call to him is issued, and to stand ready, prepared in both emotional and material terms.

We do not escape historical necessity by playing blind and deaf to the challenges of the age in which we live. Head-in-the-sand policy has never profited anyone. Anyone who is willing to see and hear realizes plainly today that everyone around him is on the move, and that sooner or later it will be his turn, too, to bundle up his belongings. Anyone who is being realistic and does not want to be unprepared when the command is issued will see to his possessions in good time, will sort and sift and gather together all the things that will be useful and necessary to him in the new and unfamiliar environment, where he can only gradually make himself feel at home. In particular, he will put in warm clothing and undergarments, as well as appropriate footwear, and he also will not forget his tools, with which he can pursue his profession and make a living.

If many of us are not—or no longer are—fortunate enough to possess warm clothes and good shoes, their bundles nonetheless should not fail to contain these items. Anyone who has clothing, undergarments, and shoes that can be spared, anyone whose baggage would be too heavy if he took along all his possessions, should therefore give some of his excess to his poorer companions on the journey. In times of cataclysmic changes in the lives of Jewish communities, the old Jewish expression has always remained valid and stood the test thus far: do not isolate yourself from the community! And so it will be this time as well. It is something that is self-evident. It is inherent in human nature that we seek each other out at such moments and find one another, for everyone senses it unconsciously: through mutual support, we gain the self-confidence and strength to accomplish something positive again. Thus optimism is born, revived by new confidence to become individual destiny, and thus it becomes our exhilarating duty to continue to build for the future, as we Jews always have done—preserving the continuity of our history, to continue to build for future Jewish generations.

If Jewish readers at the time drew spiritual comfort from this article or similar ones, their trust was betrayed. The fate of those engulfed in the deportation waves that swept through the Reich between the fall of 1941 and early 1942 varied on a spectrum ranging never short of inhumane.[47] Most of the deportees found themselves in already overcrowded ghettos (Łódź) or in places stripped of their original inhabitants to "make room" for the new arrivals (Minsk and Riga), while others being sent to "the East" fell victim to immediate and total annihilation: Germans and their auxiliaries murdered all of the roughly five thousand Jews destined for Kovno from the Reich in November 1941 and the Jews on three of the transports to Riga (November 30, 1941, from Berlin; January 15, 1942, from **Theresienstadt**; and February 10, 1942, from Vienna) were taken directly to execution sites near the city.

Deception and uncertainty left those about to be deported or en route to "the East" with no clear idea about what would happen to them at their destination. On November 15, 1941, when he received notice for his family to vacate their home in Breslau, Willy Cohn speculated in his diary "where to and so forth one does not know yet," and added: "But now all this must be dealt with, and one must try to bear up, on behalf of the children, and the words I've called out to other people—chazak ve'ematz [Hebrew: be strong and have courage]—now apply to me as well." Trudi and Willy Cohn and their young daughters Susanne and Tamara were deported from Breslau on November 25, 1941, to be shot in Kovno on November 29. The report by the German police officer in charge of the execution for that day merely noted "693 male Jews, 1155 female Jews, 152 Jewish children. 2000 [total] (Resettled from Vienna and Breslau)."[48]

Few accounts exist from the hands of those being carried away to mass murder sites in the occupied Soviet Union. An excerpt from one such source follows, the last entries in an only partly legible diary fragment found among the remains of tens of thousands of victims killed near Fort IX in Kovno, the last testimony to a life cut short. The author was a young woman not yet twenty years old at the time of her deportation in late November 1941 together with 997 Jews from Vienna. All were murdered upon arrival. The fragments of her diary found after the war near the killing site tell us little more about her life: she loved to read books, among them Margaret Mitchell's *Gone with the Wind.*

---

47. See Browning, *The Origins of the Final Solution*, 375–77.

48. From the report by the leader of the Einsatzgruppen unit for Lithuania, quoted in Browning, *The Origins of the Final Solution*, 395.

Her brother Paul had already made it to Palestine in 1938, and she had hoped until the end to be able to escape, too.[49]

DOCUMENT 4-9: **Unidentified woman deported from Vienna, diary entries for November 19–28, 1941, USHMMA RG 26.014 (LCSAV R-1390), reel 65, folder 68 (translated from German).**

[. . . November 19, 1941]

The transport leaves tomorrow. Yesterday in the evening rumor had it that we would not travel until Sunday but it is all in vain [Yiddish word used here: *Bonkes*]. [. . .] Yesterday in the afternoon our visa number [for immigration to the United States] came, but it is no longer of use to us.

November 20, 1941

Today we are supposed to travel. Thank god no order has come yet for departure. Perhaps the dear lord loves us and will not let us travel to Poland. We only have hope left. [. . .] [largely illegible page]

[no date, most likely November 28, 1941:]

On the train to the unknown.

"I have no homeland, I have nothing in this world, my destination is unknown, the grey [deleted: blue] sky is the roof over my head [literally, the grey sky is my tent]. . . ."[50]

It is indescribable how we are sitting here. Pressed together. Properly there should be only 6 people in the compartment, and we are 9. We have no inkling where we are going to and what awaits us there. We are not traveling to Poland. They say to Riga. For the time being we are in Eydtkau,[51] this is supposed to be the border station between Germany and Latvia. Sadly no one here has an atlas so that we [are] without any orienta-

49. Wolfgang Scheffler and Diana Schulle, eds., *Book of Remembrance: The German, Austrian and Czechoslovakian Jews Deported to the Baltic States* (Munich: K. G. Saur, 2003), 1: 153–69, lists one woman among the 998 deportees who was born in 1921: Ilse Weiss of Vienna, born December 15, 1921, deported with her father Erwin (born 1891) and mother Margarete Weiss (born 1895), and three women born in 1922 (Edith Stern, Anni Ormianer, and Erna Altbach). We could not establish the identity of the diary author with certainty from among the names on this list.

50. Lines from a popular song penned in 1933 by Austrian composer and lyricist Friedrich Schwarz while in exile in France and popularized by the orchestra of Marek Weber, entitled "I Have No Homeland," with the subtitle "Jewish tango." See Rainer Lotz, *Deutsche National-Discographie. Serie 6, Discographie der Judaica-Aufnahmen* (Bonn, 2006).

51. Eydtkuhnen, renamed Eydtkau in 1938, was the border town between Germany and Lithuania (not Latvia).

tion. Sunday at 6 a.m. we left Vienna. (Trucks took us to the train. Like cattle!) During the night we passed through Brünn [Brno] then we went on through Upper Silesia toward Poland. In Poland it is hopeless [trostlos]. In general the entire region is monotonous like this.—Just now we traveled across the border. It is recognizable by wire barriers and bunkers. The houses are shot up. However they are already being built again. Just now passed a military cemetery [soldiers' graveyard]. Here we are directly in the war zone.—From Poland we are traveling to East Prussia and we just now traveled across the Latvian [in reality: Lithuanian] border.

Rather than proceeding to Riga in Latvia, the transport was heading for Kovno in Lithuania. From Kovno we get a rare glimpse of the reactions of local Jews to the arriving transports from the pages of a ghetto history compiled by anonymous members of the Jewish police over the course of 1943.[52] The Jewish community in the city had experienced massive loss of life in the previous months. After the pogroms during the first days of German rule and the closing of the ghetto in mid-August 1941, major "actions" had decimated the ghetto, reducing the population from more than thirty thousand to roughly fifteen thousand.[53] The fleeting image of German Jews passing by on the way to their death in late 1941 formed a brief, yet important, chapter in the ghetto's history.

DOCUMENT 4-10: **Account by the Kovno ghetto police on "The 'Episode' of the German Jews," no date (early 1943), USHMMA RG 26.014 (LCSAV R-973), reel 31 (translated from Yiddish).**[54]

On the [55] _____ the ghetto was again shaken by a tragic event—a continuation of the "action" that had just taken place behind the barbed wire that fences us in.

---

52. Samuel Schalkowsky and Samuel D. Kassow, eds., *The Clandestine History of the Kovno Ghetto Jewish Police* (Bloomington: Indiana University Press in association with the USHMM, forthcoming).

53. Avraham Tory, *Surviving the Holocaust: The Kovno Ghetto Diary* (Cambridge, MA: Harvard University Press, 1990), 31–61; United States Holocaust Memorial Museum, *Hidden History of the Kovno Ghetto* (Boston, MA: Bulfinch Press, 1997), 32, 35.

54. Schalkowsky and Kassow, *The Clandestine History of the Kovno Ghetto Jewish Police*, forthcoming.

55. Space left blank by the document's authors for entering the date at a future time. From the context it seems certain that the passage relates to the arrival of close to five thousand Jews from Munich, Berlin, Breslau, Frankfurt am Main, and Vienna in late November, all of whom were murdered on arrival in Fort IX on the outskirts of Kovno. Further transports of German Jews were expected in the ghetto in early 1942, but did not arrive. See Tory, *Surviving the Holocaust*, 66.

A rumor spread that a large transport of German Jews had been brought from Germany to the Kovno railroad station. It was also said that a part of the transport had been led past the ghetto during the night in the direction of the 9th Fort.

Regrettably, this information was confirmed the next morning. We saw with our own eyes several thousand Jews—men, women, and children—trudging through Paneriai Street, close by the fence, in the direction of the 9th Fort. Again, we all camped by the fence, but were afraid to come near because the S.A. men[56] and G. [Gestapo] who were leading them threatened to shoot. We stood around the fences with congealed tears, dry eyes—because all our tears had already been shed[57]—with clenched fists and bloodied hearts, and once more we had to experience what had happened to us only a few days earlier.

The episode with the German Jews is the most shocking chapter in the series of persecutions and oppressions of German Jewry. We later learned the precise details of the circumstances under which our unfortunate brothers-in-suffering from Germany and Austria perished. It was impossible to believe that people could sink so low, impossible to imagine such a sophisticated deception. Such cruel, sadistic, contemptuous dealing with people's lives has no precedent in the history of the Jews. [. . .]

They arrived here (we heard that all together about 15,000 Jews were brought here)[58] and were told to leave their luggage on the train, that it would be sent on to the ghetto later. Everyone was lined up in groups and led past the Slobodka ghetto . . . to the 9th Fort. A few of the Jews being led along the ghetto, seeing that this was the Slobodka ghetto, asked the Jews standing behind the fence how much farther it was to the ghetto.

About ten or fifteen minutes later, they became aware of their dreadful, bloody mistake. They saw and felt the ugly deception that was perpetrated upon them, the slaughter that was to take place there. But, naturally, it was too late. Apparently, some did have an idea of what was going to be done to them, because a few, passing by, shouted to our Jews standing near the fence, "We know already, we are being led to the slaughter."

---

56. Several German functionaries in the Kovno city administration held ranks in and wore the uniforms of the SA (Nazi party storm troopers). See Tory, *Surviving the Holocaust*, 30–38.

57. Reference to the mass murder actions of the fall of 1941 targeting Jews in the Kovno ghetto.

58. Here and elsewhere in the text, the authors gave incorrect numbers for the German and Austrian Jews deported to Kovno in late 1941.

This is how, by disgusting deception, about 15,000 Jews were brought to the valley of slaughter, all taken to the Fort and all murdered.

Later their belongings were brought from the station to the G. [Gestapo]. For months they were sorted there by Jews working in this brigade. The finest possessions that the eye can see were found in these suitcases: the nicest of foods, all prepared with a generous hand to last a long time, the best clothing, the rarest medicines, and various professional instruments. An endless number of books—scientific, professional, Jewish books, prayer books, prayer shawls—all kinds of equipment, everything a cultured person can imagine could be found amongst the belongings of the German Jews; all packed with care, prepared with so much hope for their new life in the Kovno ghetto—yet they were so shockingly deceived. Their first step toward their new life was also their last—to the pits of the 9th Fort.

From the letters, papers, notices, etc., found amongst their belongings we saw the entire picture, the complete shocking truth of the tragedy, the conclusion of which played itself out before our eyes.

In the first few days after the large "action," many of us believed that not all who had been taken in the "action" had been killed. We wanted to believe that some of them, at least the young and able-bodied, were separated and sent somewhere to work. The episode with the German Jews destroyed even this little hope. If Jews could be brought here from such great distances to be slaughtered, what hope could we have for our own dear loved ones who had been taken along the same route? The Jews in Germany who had accompanied their loved ones to the train and watched as they boarded the cars with their luggage were certain that their close ones were being resettled; to this day they are awaiting letters from them. But we have seen what they meant by resettlement; we have seen the tragic, heartrending end.

Woe, what has become of us, what have they made of us.

The mood that descended upon the ghetto after this was clear. One could not think about anything at all, could not concentrate on anything—every hour of every day one was expecting something. The situation brought to mind the famous curse of the Tokhakhah[59]: "Ba-boker tomar mee yiten lailah u-ba-erev tomar mee yiten boker v-lo-ta-amin bekhayekha," in the morning you will wish that it were night, and in

---

59. Chapters of the Old Testament listing the punishments awaiting Jews who do not follow God's teachings.

the evening that it were day, and you will not believe that you will live.[60] People looked upon themselves as the next candidates for the Fort; they sat dejected in the houses, waiting for the next "action," when the remainder of the Kovno Jewish community would be annihilated.

But life goes on, regardless of our terrible experiences; those who remained, those who survived, had to live and eat. The instinct, the drive, the need to secure a source of livelihood, of a way to exist, drove everyone on, for himself and for his family.

The survivor, in spite of his grief over the loved ones who are gone, still wants to live, clings to life with all his might. With all one's soul, with all one's will, one wants to survive, to be freed from the ghetto and perhaps to experience something good in life.

In Kovno, the German deportees never encountered the Jews already there, standing on the other side of the ghetto fence. In Łódź, Jews from the Reich were squeezed into the ghetto, thus aggravating the already catastrophic conditions described in chapter 2. In addition to goods, customs, and attitudes unfamiliar to Łódź Jews, the newcomers brought varied impressions from outside the ghetto walls that contained a degree of hope. That spirit was reflected in **Shlomo Frank**'s chronicle, written with an eye to please **Mordechai Chaim Rumkowski** and the **Jewish Council**.

DOCUMENT 4-11: Shlomo Frank, Łódź, Warthegau, diary entries for October 19–28, 1941, in Shlomo Frank, *Togbukh fun lodzher ghetto*, ed. Nakhman Blumental (Buenos Aires: Tsentral-farband fun poylishe yidn in Argentine, 1958), 179–84 (translated from Yiddish).

October 19 [1941]

Today a thousand refugees from Vienna arrived in the ghetto. Among the new-arrivals are doctors, engineers, professors, famous chemists, dentists, former big merchants, several priests whose parents had converted, as well as twenty Christian women who came with their husbands and children. The Viennese Jews brought a lot of provisions and things, they said they traveled from Vienna to the Polish border in second-class train

---

60. This quotation combines parts of verses 66 and 67 of *Deuteronomy 28*: "The life you face shall be precarious; you shall be in terror, night and day, with no assurance of survival. In the morning you shall say, 'If only it were evening!' and in the evening you shall say, 'If only it were morning!'—because of what your heart shall dread and your eyes shall see," *Deuteronomy 28*:66–67, Jewish Publication Society edition, 2003.

cars, they were treated well. The greater part of the Viennese population—
they said—["]pitied us. Some Viennese women cried out loud and begged
the beloved God that we would see each other again soon. As soon as we
crossed the Polish border, however, the guards bid farewell and the good
conditions soon came to an end. The farther we traveled on Polish land,
the worse we were treated.["]

By the barbed wire, between Zgierska and Drukarska Streets, a young
woman was found shot to death today. The police were not able to determine who the woman is or where she is from. She was apparently not a
ghetto resident.

October 21

One thousand fifty Jews from Prague arrived in the ghetto this morning. All the new-arrivals were lively. When the ghetto police welcomed them
in Moravian, the Prague Jews greeted them with a hearty "Shalom." Some
comforted us with verses from the prophets that the end of the war is near.

October 22

Today another 1,200 Jews arrived from Vienna and from the smaller
towns around Vienna. The majority of the new arrivals were elderly,
including many who were ill; it appeared that all the new arrivals had just
yesterday been taken out of hospitals or old-age homes. The people arrived
in the evening. It was dark outside. In darkness, the old, broken Viennese
Jews, with their heavy rucksacks on their backs, walked step by step, with
lowered heads, bleary-eyed and extremely dejected. One Viennese Jew by
the name of Morris Kelerbakh declared that in one group of the expelled
Viennese Jews he saw the Viennese Jewish baron.[61] It's possible that he is
already here with us, but is hiding his name.

October 23

Frankfurt Jews arrived in the ghetto today. 4 men were missing when
they were taken down from the train cars. The transport list showed 1,200
souls, and 1,196 souls arrived. Almost all the new arrivals held up well.
They greeted [us] with a hearty "Shalom, Yehudim" [greetings, Jews]. They

---

61. Baron was a hereditary aristocratic title in the pre–World War I Austro-Hungarian
Empire, typically awarded for service to the country and commonly used in daily parlance to
address a man of high social standing. It is unclear to which baron Shlomo Frank is referring,
if in fact the rumor in the Łódź ghetto was true.

joked around and one slapped another on the back and asked him to hold up, not to break, not despair. "To lose one's courage is to lose everything." The Frankfurters say that dramatic scenes took place as they were leaving the city. The German population brought them cake and various other provisions. Some of the women cried. While bidding farewell they expressed great sympathy. Some of the women loudly begged the beloved god to protect the Jews and return them to their old home.

October 24

Today another 1,000 souls from Prague arrived. All the new arrivals were doing well. Among the newly arrived Prague Jews there are 300 lawyers, 26 doctors, 30 engineers and [individuals] from many other free professions. Almost all carried themselves well and courageously.

October 25

560 Jews from Luxembourg arrived today via the Moravian train station. The new arrivals were beside themselves. Bitterness, sorrow and pain could be seen on each of their faces. They relate that they had a very difficult journey. All the train cars were strictly guarded and locked. If someone wanted to leave the car, he was quickly punished on the spot.

The punishments varied. Some had to run around the train 25 times. Others had to scream out loud "Heil Hitler" [and] "Juda verrecke" ["Jews croak," a Nazi slogan]. A few were beaten bloody.

In Luxembourg itself the Jews were not treated badly. The local population deplored the expulsion of the Jews. The population brought apples, prunes, biscuits and various other provisions to the Jewish homes. A part of the population accompanied the expellees with tears in their eyes to the train station.

October 26

Today another 1,200 Jews arrived from Vienna. Almost all held up well. Some yelled down while still in the train cars: "Łódź Jews, know that the 'Sh'ma Yisroel' will hold longer than the 'Heil Hitler.'" Those who arrived today were housed in very poor conditions, no beds or straw sacks were allocated to them. They were sent to broken down little houses with straw on the floor. The president was asked why the people were treated in this way. Why were they treated worse than those who had been incorporated earlier? His answer: "I still have 1,000 straw sacks lying in reserve that I'm keeping for the Berlin Jews."

October 27

Today 1,000 Jews from Berlin arrived in the ghetto. Nearly 90% of the new arrivals were elderly, hunched, broken, barely able to hold themselves on their feet. Many lugged heavy rucksacks with various items on their backs. They were allowed to take with everything they could carry. They all rode first and second class up to the Polish border. As soon as they crossed the border, they were hastily moved into simple train cars.

October 28

25 weddings took place simultaneously in the ghetto today. 25 couples from various cities, including Prague, Vienna, Berlin and Łódź, took their wedding vows before Rumkowski. The president delivered a celebratory speech at the ceremony. The president declared: "We find ourselves in a ghetto, pressed in like herring in a barrel. We have no right to appeal or to advance [*avansim*, to improve conditions]. When various nominations are made in the ghetto, it is simply a local disciplinary affair. It is not possible for your Jews or my Jews to rule in the ghetto.[62] We are all marked (even including myself) with a yellow star. If one of us makes a mistake or commits a crime, we all are guilty. [. . .] I for my part do everything in my power to ensure that work in the ghetto goes smoothly, that you have something to eat and heating materials for winter. I want complete calm to prevail in the ghetto. That is my main concern—that there is calm, that there is food and work. I will be strict toward those who disregard my orders. I won't look to see whether it's a doctor, or a lawyer from Berlin, or whichever other person it might be. You should keep your intelligence and your culture to yourselves. A war is on, and war has other demands. Work and obedience. I won't speak only of bad things at your shared celebration today, but I will take advantage of your get-together so you can get to know me better. My name is Mordechai Chaim Rumkowski. I have a strong hand that can hit hard and hit hard indeed. If you are docile and obedient and if you work, I will be gentle and kind. But if, God forbid, you don't, then woe be to you." Thusly ended the president his celebratory warning speech.

After the speech, the famished crowd sat down around the five set tables. Each guest received two slices of bread, a full bowl of soup, a helping of horsemeat "gulash," together with sweet black coffee. The crowd

---

62. With this phrase, Rumkowski alluded to local Jews on the one hand and deportees from the Reich and the Protectorate ("your Jews") on the other.

laughed and entertained themselves with various jokes. Some people took up a little tune, singing "And Purify Our Hearts to Serve You in Truth," and others sang national songs. After the wedding ceremony and the banquet, the couples bid farewell to the president and wished him a long life. [. . .]

The eighteenth-century fortress town of Theresienstadt in the German-controlled Protectorate assumed a special role among the "resettlement" destinations of late 1941 and early 1942. First, its Jewish population only consisted of newcomers; many among those who arrived early on acquired elite status compared to later transports. Second, Theresienstadt was to become a site that, according to its function, organization, and the fate of its inmates, could alternately be called a ghetto, a transit station, or a concentration camp.[63] And third, whatever the designation, Theresienstadt served as the key destination for Jews "resettled" from other parts of the Protectorate, as well as for so-called privileged German Jews, mostly decorated World War I veterans, the elderly, and Jewish partners of "mixed marriages." Adding to the illusion of Theresienstadt as a "privileged" deportation destination, the RSHA charged German Jews through the Reichsvereinigung with funding the site and ordered deportees to use their remaining assets to purchase shares in Theresienstadt residences (so-called *Heimeinkaufsverträge*), as if they were buying into some kind of retirement community; ultimately, however, most of the inmates were to be transported further east to their death.[64]

At the time when deportations to the fortress town began, none of the deportees faced the threat of immediate and direct annihilation like those Jews taken to Minsk, Riga, or Kovno. However, conditions in Theresienstadt declined steeply, and, indeed, became lethal for many older and sick deportees.

---

63. For the greater structural similarities of Theresienstadt with ghettos than with concentration camps see Peter Klein, "Theresienstadt: Ghetto oder Konzentrationslager?" in *Theresienstädter Studien und Dokumente* (2005): 111–23; for a synopsis of Terezín's history during the war see Vojtěc Blodig and Joseph Robert White, "Terezín," in *The USHMM Encyclopedia of Camps and Ghettos*, 2:180–84.

64. See Hans Günther Adler, *Theresienstadt, 1941–1945: Das Antlitz einer Zwangsgemeinschaft; Geschichte, Soziologie, Psychologie* (Tübingen: Mohr, 1960); an English translation of Adler's still unsurpassed work is forthcoming from Cambridge University Press in association with the USHMM in 2013. See also Egon Redlich, *The Terezin Diary of Gonda Redlich*, ed. Saul S. Friedman (Lexington: University Press of Kentucky, 1992); Livia Rothkirchen, *The Jews of Bohemia and Moravia: Facing the Holocaust* (Lincoln: University of Nebraska Press, 2005), esp. 233–83; Zdenek Lederer, *Ghetto Theresienstadt* (New York: Fertig, 1983).

In Prague, the capital of the Protectorate where the segregation of the Jewish population had so far been partial and pockets of relative freedom existed, rumors and fears about deportations from the Czech metropolis began to materialize as grim reality from mid-October 1941, shortly after RSHA chief Heydrich was appointed as the de facto German chief administrator of the region (*Reichsprotektor*). According to the diary of twenty-year-old Eva Mändl, who was at that time still working in an "Aryan" hat workshop,[65] events unfolded in rapid succession. Her entries show that especially for young Jews, involvement in organized and improvised self-help could soften the blow of deportations dealt by the Germans.

DOCUMENT 4-12: **Eva Mändl, Prague, diary entries for October 10 to December 14, 1941, in Eva Mändl Roubíčková, ed. Veronika Springmann, *"Langsam gewöhnen wir uns an das Ghettoleben." Ein Tagebuch aus Theresienstadt* (Hamburg: Konkret Literatur Verlag, 2007), 52–54, 57, 62, 64–66 (translated from German).**

[October 10, 1941]
Quiet in the workshop. Afterwards at Mama's [her fiancé's mother, Marie Roubíčková]. A transport of Jews is leaving Prague, nobody knows where it is headed, some say to Poland. It's unimaginable. The first 1,000 people have to be ready as soon as Monday. One just must not lose one's head! It is terrible, we have to hope that we'll survive this too, one can endure a lot. A state of panic prevails everywhere. [. . .]

[October 13, 1941]
Political situation rather bad for the Russians. Several divisions have been trapped by the Germans. But what is important for us now is what they're going to do with us. The poor people in the first transport [summoned that day for deportation to Łódź] couldn't prepare at all, could not buy anything, and today they have to report to the Messepalais,[66] where they will be interned for several days before being taken away. They'll be examined, their hair will be cut off, and their bags will be searched. At work again, afterwards everybody at Benny's [Benny Grünberger, a friend] listened to the phonograph. Zwi [Zwi Holzmann, a friend] quite

---

65. For another diarist's account of deportations from Prague, see Chava Pressburger, ed., *The Diary of Petr Ginz 1941–1942* (New York: Atlantic Monthly Press, 2007), 35–55.
66. Collecting place at Prague-Holešovice.

depressed, he was assigned to assist with the transport and had to lug suitcases around all day. He saw terrible scenes. [. . .]

[November 5, 1941]

Somebody came to take a look at the apartment, claiming that we're supposed to go on the next transport and no longer have an interest in the apartment. We were perplexed, because we are not registered yet. [. . .] It is all very implausible and strange, but we have to be prepared in any event. Gi [her uncle Ernst Wolf, her mother's brother] is very agitated. We thought we were almost ready, but there's still an awful lot to do. All the Jews in the building are extremely agitated. Met Zwi in the afternoon, went to the workshop, took a few things to the girls. I feel totally hollow, I make conversation but it's all just superficial, as if there were a different person inside me. I still cannot grasp that a week from now, I won't be here anymore. In the evening, all the Jewish tenants [in her apartment house] at our place, like a family, everybody lent a hand.[67] [. . .]

[November 30, 1941]

With Eva at Zwi's, he is already completely ready, then at Benny's, helped out some more. Zwi went to see the top people in the Community, all sorts of things were discussed. The situation doesn't look good, many people probably will not survive it, one should not despair, the young surely will survive it. One should say nothing to parents. These two good ones [most likely, Zwi and Benny, who were about to be deported] are really very brave and courageous. Also packed up food, Frau Grünberger is incapable of getting anything ready. Eva very unhappy, she's never showed it but probably she does like Zwi best. It's all so sad. [. . .]

[December 13, 1941]

[. . .] Learned early today from the Jewish Community [*Kultusgemeinde*] that our request [for exemption from deportation] was turned down, we have to go. Gi immediately volunteered. In the morning, all the bags were picked up. In the afternoon, the entire pantry was cleaned out, that was the biggest job. In the evening, a lot of other things were carried away, all the carpets, furniture swapped. All day long it was as if I was paralyzed. Thank God, there was no time for thinking about things, I

---

67. The person checking out the apartment and announcing Eva's and her mother's imminent departure was an impostor. They stayed in Prague until they got the deportation notice in mid-December 1941.

feel as if I had been given an injection, I know that it must hurt, but I'm completely devoid of feeling. [. . .]

[December 14, 1941]

[. . .] Farewell to Prague. Just don't think about it. Have to join the others at 1 p.m. Saying goodbye to everyone [living in the apartment house] went very quickly. The gate was closed behind us, and from now on we're prisoners, not free human beings any longer. The Messepalais is a terribly large exhibition hall with various sections. The first impression is appalling. On account of Mutti [her mother, Antonia Mändl née Ernst], I couldn't show my feelings and appeared to be as cheerful as a lark.

The ground is covered everywhere with mattresses, only little pathways between them. One stays on the mattresses day and night. Some people are quite good-tempered, others are terribly agitated, withdrawn into themselves in misery. We're in the former group, and set out on a journey of discovery right away. I've run across lots of acquaintances. [. . .] At 4 p.m. a fatally ill man with a sobbing wife and a screaming child was suddenly brought in, we took a closer look, and it was Paul Mändl [a relative of her mother]. After a short time we managed to find out that he was only putting on an act, so that he'd possibly be sent home. Next to me on the other side, a girl [Fanny[68]] of my age, apparently very nice, I immediately made friends with her. She's been married for six weeks and is going voluntarily in order to follow her husband. In front of the exhibition hall on one side are big pipes with water faucets for washing, on the other side, open to the air, is the kitchen, just covered with a roof. A little wooden shed with a wash basin for women to wash. The best is the toilet, a long wooden shed with pails that have to be carried out every day. Everybody is quite aghast and terribly unhappy about it, but I make little of it. My new friend is with me constantly, I'm glad that I have her. Very athletic, very jolly, everything is much easier when there are two. [. . .]

From our vantage point today, we can discern patterns in these deportations, be it in their time of departure, place of origin and destination, or the fate of the transport participants. For those living through this period, deportation was often a protracted threat; it was not only wholly unclear what would happen to them after having been transported off but also whether and when they would be summoned by a deportation order. Among Jews waiting for such an order, a few shared their apprehensions, expectations, or reflections with family and friends

---

68. The authors have been unable to find any information about her identity and fate.

despite the distance lying between them. In the German city of Essen, **Erich Langer** reflected in a long letter to his son Klaus in Palestine on a life dominated by the striving for normalcy and by emigration attempts, all of which failed. Erich Langer, from whose letter we have quoted earlier in this volume,[69] continued writing in the months prior to his deportation in the hope that Klaus would some day be able to read what had happened to his parents back in Germany.

DOCUMENT 4-13: Unsent letter from Erich Langer, Essen, Germany, to his son Klaus, Palestine, late 1941/early 1942, USHMMA Acc. 1994.A.322 Yakob Langer collection (translated from German).

[November 23, 1941]

My dear beloved boy! Today I begin a letter to you that is not likely to reach your hands in the near future. But being transported off [*Abtransport*] to Poland remains a ghost in the shadows that threaten all of us unable to emigrate, and whether I will return from there and still have the chance to write to you is very uncertain. Therefore I want to inform you in these lines about the events and our life in the last years, especially about the all too early passing of your beloved mother, and want to entrust this letter to an acquaintance who promised me that he will pass it on to you after there is peace. [. . .]

[January 12, 1942]

Since the death of your good mother [in September 1941], our fate here has rapidly deteriorated. Today is January 12, 1942—I'm writing this letter in stages—and I must sadly say that in the last four months nothing positive has occurred. On the day of your mother's death a provision was issued that we would have to wear a yellow-colored star of David with the inscription "Jew" on our clothing, and that we could only leave our place of residence with a police permit. And then, about six weeks later, the terrible evacuations of Jews to the East in hunger and cold started. The first transport from the Rhineland, in which approximately 130 Essener were taken, left at the end of October, the second, with about 250 Essener, 14 days later. These poor people were only allowed to take 50 pounds of luggage with them, along with provisions for the three-day trip and food for three weeks. The entire wealth of the deported was forfeited to the state. The first transport went to Łódź; there is still no concrete news from the

---

69. See document 1–7.

second here. It apparently went to Minsk.[70] Poor Aunt Käthe was also transported away. I have still not received news from her. I do not need to tell you how much we all have been shaken by the fate of these unfortunate people. And furthermore, the sword of Damocles hangs over us, too, and we always have to ask ourselves: when is it your turn. In case I have to go along, I have decided that if it is in any way possible, I will hold out by thinking of you and keeping the hope that I will see you again. But as soon as I see out there that life is unbearable and amounts to a slow withering-away, then I will end it. You will understand this step and will not, as I want to hope, berate me for it. The decision will surely not be easy and will be dictated by the most pressing necessity. I probably do not need to tell you that many have already chosen this path. [. . .]

When I reflect on all these sad occurrences, I often say to myself that fate might have meant it well with mother, in that it spared her from all this, the grave sorrow and worry about our fellow human beings. How much her compassionate soul would have suffered from this! Many of my acquaintances said that they envy her of her fate. For me this is indeed a weak consolation. I feel like a tree whose crown has been cut off, and whose trunk continues to vegetate and ekes out a beggarly life. [. . .]

[April 15, 1942]

The die have been cast. The long awaited has occurred: last Saturday I received the news that I must be at the ready for transport to the occupied Eastern territories. I received the information with great calm. As more than 400 people from our Community are leaving, especially many youths, the composition is quite fortunate. It is also pleasant that we are getting closer to summer. It is believed that we will be sent to the former province of Posen and will work there in agriculture. So not bad prospects. The mood of the people is good. Yesterday, unfortunately, the message came that all the remaining fellow believers must vacate their apartments and will be housed in barracks.[71] That really makes me feel sorry for grandma [Langer's mother-in-law]. But she is quite composed and has several nice acquaintances.

---

70. Deportation transports from Düsseldorf and Cologne left for Łódź on October 26 and 30, 1941, respectively, and from Düsseldorf to Minsk on November 11, 1941. Browning, *The Origins of the Final Solution*, 375–76; Gottwaldt and Schulle, *Die Judendeportationen aus dem Deutschen Reich*, 62–83.

71. This refers to the Holbeckshof in Essen-Steele, a barrack camp fenced in with barbed wire where the remaining Jews were concentrated prior to their deportation. Hermann Schröter, *Geschichte und Schicksal der Essener Juden. Gedenkbuch für die jüdischen Mitbürger der Stadt Essen* (Essen: Stadt Essen, 1980), 432.

Now I want to share some addresses with you that you must turn to soon after the end of the war; it will be of great benefit to you: Dr. Carl Jung, Rüdesheim on the Rhine Bahnhofstrasse; [. . .].[72]

Now I will close, my beloved boy, and part from you with a heavy heart. Live quite well and stay healthy! Hopefully there will be a reunion. God bless you! I kiss you with devoted fatherly love.

Your papa.

I have written this letter twice myself and given it to two different acquaintances with the hope that one will definitely reach you. On your birthday [April 12] I was with grandma at mother's grave and laid down some tulips on your behalf.

On April 22, 1942, together with 941 fellow Jews from the Rhine area, Erich Langer was deported to Izbica in the **Generalgouvernement**'s Lublin district, where he arrived two days later. He did not survive the war.[73]

Months after Hitler and the Wehrmacht had initiated the war against the Soviet Union, Jews all over Europe were feeling the fallout, most intensely in the newly occupied areas, where Germans and their collaborators annihilated entire communities, including women and children. The unrelenting brutality with which the Einsatzgruppen and other units on the ground addressed the "Jewish question" appealed to their superiors in Berlin in their search for a radical answer. They found their answer by deporting Jews from the Reich to "the East," where they were supposed to share the fate of local Jews. But this major step toward genocide did not mark the end of the process. As Raul Hilberg put it in his magnum opus on the history of the Holocaust, the killings in the German-controlled parts of the Soviet Union "were a prelude to a greater undertaking in the remainder of **Axis** Europe. A 'final solution' was going to be launched in every region under German control."[74] In the following two chapters we will look at some of the ramifications of this broadening scope for the Jews and Jewish communities it affected.

---

72. Dr. Carl Jung received Erich Langer's letter for safekeeping. According to Yakob Langer, Jung was arrested in 1943 and his house searched, but the Gestapo did not find the letter. After the war, Jung gave it to Yakob Langer (letter by Yakob Langer, October 28, 1992, USHMMA Acc.1994.A.322).

73. On Izbica, see Robert Kuwałek and Martin Dean, "Izbica (nad Wieprzem)," in *The USHMM Encyclopedia of Camps and Ghettos*, 2:639–43.

74. Raul Hilberg, *The Destruction of the European Jews*, 3rd ed. (New Haven, CT: Yale University Press, 2003), 2:409.

CHAPTER 5

WIDENING CIRCLES
OF PERSECUTION

BY LATE 1941, the Nazi regime clearly understood what it regarded as the lessons of **Operation Barbarossa** in relation to advancing the "Final Solution of the Jewish question." Mass murder of Jews had become a fixture of German anti-Jewish policy, and the start of mass deportations to the East marked a further step in the escalating process. One experience shared by all European Jews living in the area of **Axis** rule was that of loss: loss of one's home, belongings, and familiar surroundings; of a sense of security, one's bearings, and any real choices about how to respond to persecution; of social status and ties and, above all, of family and friends and community. As certain as it seemed that Germany and its partners in the anti-Jewish project would continue on the path of violence, the scope of this progression toward annihilation was anything but certain. Just as it was hard to predict whether the Axis could eventually be stopped, it was difficult to judge how long those in relatively safe areas would remain out of harm's way. Jews living just beyond the reach of the Wehrmacht watched developments in Axis-controlled Europe with a close eye and mounting anxiety. Their safety seemed fragile indeed, as the first half of 1942 found the Germans advancing, most notably in the southern reaches of the eastern front and in North Africa, where the **Yishuv** by and by came under threat.

DEATH AND DEFIANCE IN "THE EAST"

With persecution intensifying, the fates of individuals seem to disappear in an ocean of suffering. Most accounts attesting to the scope of murder that survived the war come from the hand of the perpetrators. **Heinrich Himmler**'s officers were reporting staggering execution figures from the occupied Soviet territories in the second half of 1941. Already in mid-October 1941, the leader of **Einsatzgruppe** A stated that his men had killed 125,000 Jews, of those, more than eighty thousand were murdered in Lithuania.[1] Jewish sources of the time tell the stories behind the statistics—stories of death and despair, but also of endurance, defiance, and solidarity. The following letter was sent from within the Riga ghetto to Carolina Knoch, who had managed to escape the ghetto with the assistance of a local Latvian. By the time the letter was written, the family had experienced the full scope of German brutality toward Jews in Latvia. Carolina, her mother, and sister Berta were the only surviving family members of the initial massacre in the **Rumbula** forest, near Riga, in late November 1941. During that event, Germans and their Latvian helpers had murdered more than twenty-seven thousand Jews from the ghetto as well as the first transport bringing one thousand deportees from Berlin.[2] In early December—just days prior to the second phase of the Rumbula *Aktion*— Carolina had gotten out but contemplated returning so that her mother could be safe.[3] Sending the letter through clandestine channels and using plain, unambiguous language, Carolina's sister warned her against both useless sacrifice and undue optimism.

---

1. Christopher R. Browning, with contributions by Jürgen Matthäus, *The Origins of the Final Solution: The Evolution of Nazi Jewish Policy, September 1939–March 1942* (Lincoln and Jerusalem: University of Nebraska Press and Yad Vashem, 2004), 277–308.

2. See Andrej Angrick and Peter Klein, *The "Final Solution" in Riga: Exploitation and Annihilation, 1941–1944* (New York: Berghahn Books, 2009), 130–74.

3. Carolina Taitz (née Knoch; 1929–2011) was born in Riga, Latvia, and raised in the nearby Zemgale region. After her escape from the Riga ghetto in December 1941, Carolina found shelter in the house of Vladimir Micko, a local stoker, and his family until Riga's liberation in October 1944. During this time, Micko frequently ventured into the ghetto to provide Carolina's mother and sister (and others) with supplies and to exchange correspondence. Carolina resided with the Micko family until her marriage in 1946 and immigrated to the United States in 1967. See donor files, USHMMA RG 05.004*01; USHMMA RG 50.030*0231, interview with Carolina Knoch Taitz, November 13, 1990; Mordecai Paldiel, *The Path of the Righteous: Gentile Rescuers of Jews during the Holocaust* (Hoboken, NJ: Ktav, 1992), 262–64.

DOCUMENT 5-1: **Letter from Berta Knoch in the Riga ghetto to Carolina Knoch in hiding, February 10, 1942; USHMMA RG 05.004*01 Carolina Taitz collection (translated from Latvian).**

My darling little girl. I want so much to call you by your name or nickname, as I called you when we were a happy family, but I cannot, I am afraid. I will not answer your letter now. I think that you are not normal or are absolutely crazy that you want to come back in the ghetto and die with us. You ran away, so stay where you are and don't make me and Mama suffer more than we do already. I know that my last letter hurt you terribly, but what should I do, who else can I tell of all the tragedy that has happened here. You are the only one. I [illegible word] was dreadfully upset about what happened here and was scared to death about Mama. You know that she is all that I have. I love her more than anything in this world. I can very well understand that you would like to sacrifice yourself for Mama. You want Mama to go to your place and you will come here to replace Mama. Are you crazy or something? When I told her what you want to do, she was hysterical and almost fainted. She begs you to stay put wherever you are. She will never, you hear me, never change places with you. Never. If we must die, we will die together. You cannot help a thing if you were to be here or not. Right now is the most dangerous time for us. We are happy that you do not see or hear what is going on here. Intrigues between women. All are scared for their lives. Scared to go to work in the morning and to come back into the ghetto in the evening. But this is not everything. As you remember, we, four women in our room, don't have it so bad. Our room is warm because every other day Mrs. N. sends us wood for the stove. We can make tea on the hot stove and when we are lucky, black coffee. Like tonight, Monday, we had hot soup, kasha, and a tiny piece of meat that a good person gave us. Mama is a very good cook. She can make a delicious meal from a stove. Then we drank tea with zwieback. Sunday Mama and Mrs. Sh. stayed in the barrack, but I and M. worked. I came home at about 3 p.m. and what did I see? In the yard of our house was a big crowd of women from Lithuania. My God, how they looked. 138 women and about 200 men were sent here from Kaunas [Kovno]. They said they were supposed to work in a lumber yard.[4] [. . .]

---

4. The Jewish laborers from the Kovno ghetto had been rounded up by German and Jewish policemen and arrived in Riga on February 9, 1942; see Avraham Tory, *Surviving the Holocaust: The Kovno Ghetto Diary*, ed. Martin Gilbert and Dina Porat (Cambridge, MA: Harvard University Press, 1990), 69–70 (diary entries for February 5, 6, 8, and 10, 1942).

10,000 Jews were killed in Kovno on December 28.[5] They [the women from Kaunas] told us that these kinds of actions must be happening all over Europe. In Kaunas there is still a ghetto with 17,000 Jews. All the families stay together. Also in Shavli there is still a ghetto with 60,000 Jews.[6] Some women of this group, when they were travelling through Shavli, threw little scraps of paper out of the cattle cars so that maybe somebody would find the paper scraps and notify the families in Kaunas what happened to them. These women were all crying. I am surprised that they still have tears to cry. Their men who are now here were placed together with our men, and tomorrow they will go to work. Some women had their husbands there, and they were happy about this because the women will be able to see their husbands through the iron fence.

My darling, you tell me that I am hysterical and that I see everything in black colors. You are right, but when I see the tragedies here, I want to scream. I want to run. I want to beg the whole world to help. Why is the world not doing something? Please forgive me, do not be mad that I tell you all this. You asked me in your letter to tell you absolutely everything that is going on here, whether they shoot or they hit or they torture or they kill. So I am telling you, all this is going on here. If all my letters disturb you too much, then I will not tell you what is going on. I want you to understand and stay calm. Who in the big world can I tell everything that is going on here, if not you. Who will believe me that this is the truth? Nobody! Therefore, sis, be strong, grit your teeth and wait. Revenge [*atmaksa*] must come for this. But it is so difficult to live in constant fear about what is going to happen tomorrow. [. . .]

Carolina in fact survived the war through the kindness of the family that hid her. She learned, however, that both Berta and their mother had been killed at an unknown point toward the end of the war.

With the threat of death intensifying, rumors about less severe conditions elsewhere traveled over circuitous paths, often getting distorted in the process,

---

5. This date should be October 28, 1941.

6. At the time of the creation of the ghetto in Shavli in August 1941, it had between four thousand and five thousand residents; mass killings in September 1941 further reduced this number. See Arūnas Bubnys and Avinoam Patt, "Šiauliai," in *The United States Holocaust Memorial Museum Encyclopedia of Camps and Ghettos, 1933–1945*, vol. 2: *Ghettos in German-Occupied Eastern Europe*, ed. Martin Dean (Bloomington: Indiana University Press in association with the USHMM, 2012), 1118–21.

and many individuals and families continued sowing plans to disobey German orders and relocate based on information received from more or less distant relatives or friends. The decision to leave or to stay depended as much on conscious decision making—the weighing of family responsibilities, calculating risks—as on serendipitous opportunities and connections to those who could facilitate a getaway. Rampant corruption among Germans and the greed or the good heart of a non-Jewish neighbor played their part in these decisions, just as destitution, bad luck, and erroneous or outdated information could spell disaster at every turn. In the following account written in hiding, **Paula Stein** describes her family's high-risk escape from Vilna in the "**Reichskommissariat Ostland**" to Białystok in the German-annexed part of Belorussia. They hoped to reach their home city of Warsaw in the **Generalgouvernement**, and while we cannot know why this young woman and her husband decided that conditions back home—a distance of roughly 250 miles across a war-torn land—would be better, we know they were not. In fact, just at the point when the Steins undertook this perilous journey, the remaining Jewish communities in Vilna and the Baltic region, heavily decimated by the mass executions of the summer and the fall of 1941, were experiencing a time of relative quiet devoid of major killing actions.[7]

DOCUMENT 5-2: **Memoir by Paula Stein, Białystok, Białystok-Grodno district, East Prussia, about her escape from Vilna in December 1941, written 1943/1944, USHMMA Acc. 2008.345 notebook #3 (translated from Polish).[8]**

[. . .] Several times a car from Białystok came to the ghetto [in Vilna] but they wouldn't talk to anyone. They came for pre-arranged people who had relatives in Białystok. These people had special passes and were rescuing their relatives from our hell. We followed the car with our envious eyes but it was out of reach for us. We had no one there who could bring us a miraculous rescue. Our real goal was Warsaw; therefore we tried for some opportunity in that direction. After a number of fruitless negotiations we decided, with a group of 15 people, to take the offer of a German who proposed to take us to Warsaw in a car leaving the front. Everything was set to take place on Tuesday, December 9 [1941]. On Sunday at 3 p.m.

---

7. Yitzhak Arad, *The Holocaust in the Soviet Union* (Lincoln: University of Nebraska Press, 2009), 158–61; Yitzhak Arad, *Ghetto in Flames: The Struggle and Destruction of the Jews in Vilna in the Holocaust* (New York: Holocaust Library, 1982), 164–71.

8. The authors have been unable to identify persons whom the diary mentions by first name only.

Marta came with the news that there was a car from Białystok willing to take two people. Two empty spots were left because the people who were supposed to go have been taken away earlier. We immediately decided to give priority to Marta. But she didn't want to be separated from us and started to plead tearfully with the organizer of the car to take pity on us and take two more people with the child. After talking to the German who was driving the car, he agreed and demanded an exorbitant price. We offered him what we deemed to be indispensable till now, i.e. two new coats and 200 rubles and finally came to an agreement. This way we were totally deprived of clothing and cash. At the time we didn't even think how we would pay for a slice of bread. Our dream was to get out of Vilna, of that damned hell. At 3:30 p.m. Marek [Paula's husband] decided again to leave immediately. We filled our backpack; we could take only that much, because there was room to rescue people but not luggage. It didn't bother us because the backpack was our only possession. Artur could not join us and decided to wait for another chance. Ready to leave, we went to 9 Szpitalna Street where the car had been parked. The yard was full of spectators. Some come to get information, others in pursuit of sensation. There were also some who tried to force their way into the car, taking advantage of the last-minute commotion. The reason was that the news of a red car from Białystok being in Vilna again, spread like lightning. There were 13 actual passengers. When dusk fell we were told to get into the vehicle. But it is easier said than done since the doors are blocked by the spectators. Marek held Izio [his and Paula's son] by his hand and I had the backpack. In an instant, I felt a dreadful crowd around me and shortly afterwards two shots. It was the driver who shot into the air to scare and disperse the unwelcome people. Yet we didn't know what it meant. Terrified, Izio slipped out of his father's hand and was pushed away together with the crowd. We were able to find the child with great difficulty and after a lot of effort we landed in the vehicle. It was a postal van that carried letters. Ten people were let in and the doors were slammed shut. The organizer together with two women sat by the driver. We set off. We left the ghetto gate behind us with relief and, at the same time, the Vilna ghetto, a place of such misery inflicted on us during that short period of time. We were not allowed to talk and exchange impressions during the trip. We had to keep quiet until we reached the city limits.

We were lying motionless, in the position we were loaded in and tried not to utter a sound. We grew numb, when the vehicle suddenly stopped. The German got out, opened the door and said: "Finally we are outside the city. Now you can breathe, please, get out."[9] We were surrounded by snow, with a thick forest on the horizon. Our hearts were full of dread. We thought we were ambushed. We knew of instances when Jews were cheated this way. Fortunately for us, this wasn't the case. We truly took a deep breath. After a short break, the expedition moved forward. [. . .]

In Sokółka we were met by the chairman of the local Judenrat, Dr. Sonnabend,[10] who had dispatched the vehicle. To our great astonishment we learned that we had reached our destination. We started pleading with Dr. Sonnabend to instruct the driver to take us to Białystok. Though Białystok was as unfamiliar as Sokółka, yet we believed that it would be easier to get to Warsaw from Białystok, which was our aim. Negotiations with the organizer started, when he declared that in fact we can continue on our way if each passenger contributed another 100 rubles. We were helpless because we had no cash whatsoever. Dr. Sonnabend, a truly respectable man, took our situation into account and offered to drive us to Białystok for free. We had a short stop. We entered the first hut in order to warm up. The owner of the hut, an extremely poor woman, but rich in offspring, offered us potatoes boiled in their skin, which we swallowed with great satisfaction as if it were a refined delicacy. Her youngest child was one, the oldest—nine years old. The Germans took away her husband and she was left alone with the children. She didn't have to tell us of her misery. It was evident that utter poverty reigned in that hut. Nonetheless, that poor woman refused any payment for the hospitality she displayed. We parted with the words "May heaven reward you," when the vehicle, ready for the drive, arrived.

The distance to Białystok was 40 kilometers [almost 25 miles]; it went by quickly while we chatted with Dr. Sonnabend. It turned out that he lived in Warsaw close to our acquaintances. He told us about his tragic life when he lost his beloved wife and was left with a small child. He even promised to facilitate our next leg of the trip from Białystok to Warsaw in

---

9. Quote written in German in the original.

10. Little information survives about the fate of Dr. Sonnabend, a local physician in Sokółka. He might have been the chairman of the **Judenrat**; other sources name a certain Friedburg, an attorney, holding this position. In early November 1942, the Germans liquidated the Sokółka ghetto, and sent all Jews—save for four hundred laborers—to Kiełbasin, a regional transit camp, from which they were deported to **Treblinka** in December and gassed on arrival. Sonnabend was deported to Kiełbasin, but managed to get himself transferred to the Białystok ghetto, where he headed the labor department of the *Judenrat*. It is unclear whether he managed to survive the war. See Laura Crago, "Sokółka," in *The USHMM Encyclopedia of Camps and Ghettos,* 2:955–57.

the same vehicle. He stipulated that we could pay for it when we arrive in Warsaw since we have nothing but our backpack, while our whole family and belongings have been left behind in Warsaw when we escaped on the memorable day of September 5, 1939.

Finally we reached Białystok. Another stop at the gate of the ghetto at Sienkiewicza Street. A question emerged: how to get into the ghetto? The most convenient way would be to drive in by car but in order to do that one had to have a special permit. The resourceful Dr. Sonnabend rescued us again in this difficult situation. He approached the guards and after striking a bargain for 800 rubles which he collected among the passengers he drove our van into the ghetto. [. . .]

Paula Stein's account confirms that defying German orders required not only determination, courage, and initiative but also involved resorting to bribery or other forms of exchange of goods or valuables. Many people without money and connections felt doomed. On October 23, 1941, as part of the ninth transport in the so-called first wave of deportations from Vienna, forty-year-old Irene Hauser, her husband Leopold (Leo) and their five-year old son Erich (Bubi) were deported to Łódź.[11] Irene Hauser brought along a notebook in which she documented her family's deprivation, disintegration (she accused her husband of stealing from their rations), and utter despair. One of her first entries appears to have been a list of "hunger days" (*Hungertage*). By June 1942, the reality in the ghetto and rumors about German mass murder of those "resettled" left no hope for the future.

DOCUMENT 5-3: **Irene Hauser, Łódź, Warthegau, diary entries for June/July 1942; USHMMA RG 02.208M (ŻIH 302/299), reel 42 (translated from German).**

[. . .] On January 21 [1942], Leo got his job putting the markings on watch and clock faces. From late January to June, difficult days of hunger and cold. In that span of time, Leo lost 20 kilos [44 pounds] and Irene, 10. Ghetto diseases, rashes, attacks of dysentery, itchy scalps, etc. Flies a nuisance at 4 a.m. Weakness in feet, falling asleep from weakness, Bubi has temperature of 39°C [102.2°F], lots of vomiting, heartburn, dizziness.

---

11. Irene Hauser (née Hacker; 1901–1942), from Waidhofen an der Ybbs in Lower Austria, was deported with her husband Leopold (b. 1898) and son Erich (1936–1942) from Vienna to Łódź in October 1941. Leo Hauser was deported from Łódź to Skarżysko-Kamienna in 1944, survived a death march to Buchenwald, and was liberated at the end of the war. See Sascha Feuchert, Erwin Leibfried, and Jörg Riecke, eds., *Die Chronik des Gettos Lodz/Litzmannstadt: Supplemente und Anhang* (Göttingen: Wallstein, 2007), 361.

Lungs affected. No sex since January 30, 1942. Today, June 15, Father's birthday, we're very hungry and have nothing to eat. Bubi and I have had diarrhea and fever for three days, had been at the baths beforehand. [. . .] Late June, menstrual periods have stopped [. . .] July 5, gold crown broke off. Leo annoyed because of Bubi's diarrhea. [. . .]

July 19, 1942.

Delivery of vegetables between 12 and 2 p.m. I come downstairs; it's changed to between 7 and 8 o'clock, so you run up and down the stairs for nothing, and every day this state of affairs. Standing in line for sausage for 5 hours. Bread, 5 a.m., in vain. Windows get ruined, that's how they carry on, it's a matter of life and death, the clerks are worthless, you can't get any information. Allegedly the people who were taken away from here between May 5 and 15 were gassed, that is, exterminated [German "*vergast*, also *vertilgt*"].

July 23. [Leo] goes and sells the child's clothes. He wants to take everything, if only the end would come now, I lie here as if paralyzed, he's not willing to get a doctor because he doesn't want to pay, I feel sorry for the poor child. [. . .]

July 24. As of today we've been here 9 months, also a Friday. Two executions for stealing half a loaf of bread and 60 RM. 18-year-old young men are collapsing. My neighbors below me, woman of 40 and daughter of 17, 2-year-old child, starved to death, etc. We must be rescued soon or we'll all be dead, God help us. Mr. and Mrs. Fuchs [neighbors] help me in every way to lighten our dreadful lot, and Bubi gets many a bite to eat, he's so hungry. These people are my saviors. Leo is going today about the apartment, didn't go, decided we'll stay alone.

July 26. Sold summer dress for a little fat. All three of us completely exhausted, medicine and yeast have to keep us going one more week, have nothing left to sell.

On September 11, 1942, Irene and her son Erich were sent on to **Chełmno**, where they were murdered. Three days earlier she had written the last entry into her diary.[12]

---

12. See Emil Kerenji, *Jewish Responses to Persecution,* vol. 4: *1942–1944* (Lanham, MD: AltaMira Press in association with the USHMM, forthcoming).

Very few in the ghetto could have observed the deteriorating conditions with any degree of detachment. For a handful of Jewish physicians, the
ghetto presented a horrendous yet unique laboratory to study the effects of
long-term undersupply and food shortages, acute epidemics, especially typhus,
and chronic deprivation on a large group of individuals, including themselves.
Accumulating data, sampling case studies, and drawing up charts satisfied their
intellectual interest and offered an alternative reality in which personal misery could be rationalized as a scientific challenge. In a report on the effects of
hunger conducted by twenty-eight physicians in the Warsaw ghetto between
February and July 1942, the authors noted: "[. . .] Passage from life to death
is slow and gradual, like death from physiological old age. There is nothing
violent, no dyspnea [breathing problems], no pain, no obvious changes in
breathing or circulation. Vital functions subside simultaneously. Pulse rate and
respiratory rate get slower and it becomes more and more difficult to reach the
patient's awareness, until life is gone. People fall asleep in bed or on the street
and are dead in the morning. They die during physical effort, such as searching for food, and sometimes even with a piece of bread in their hands."[13] In
addition to these deaths, many committed suicide, while the will to survive
prompted extreme behavior in others. In Warsaw, one of the most horrible cases
was reported by ghetto officials and members of **Oyneg Shabes**, creating a stir
within a community already too familiar with boundless suffering and loss.[14]

In the Kovno ghetto, the head of the Jewish Council's health department
in the spring of 1943 created a graphic depiction of the long-term health effects
of malnourishment, exploitation, and mental stress on women.

13. Quoted from Myron Winick, ed., *Hunger Disease: Studies by the Jewish Physicians in
the Warsaw Ghetto* (New York: John Wiley & Sons, 1979), 36.

14. See report on a case of cannibalism in the Warsaw ghetto, February 19, 1942,
USHMMA RG 15.079M (ŻIH Ring. I/241).

DOCUMENT 5-4: **Diagram by Dr. Jacob Nochimovski, Kovno, German-occupied Lithuania, May 1943, indicating the illnesses affecting women in the Kovno ghetto, USHMMPA WS# N03334.01.**[15]

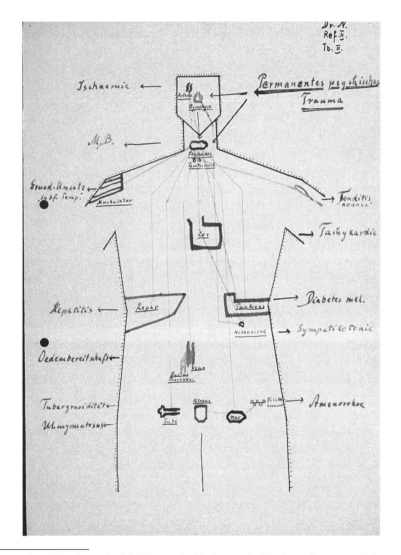

15. Jacob Nochimovski (Nochumowski, Nachimowski, Nochimovksy; 1907–?), born in Russia and a Lithuanian national, was chief physician of the Labor Department in the ghetto and issued medical exemptions from labor. The report was presented at a medical symposium in the ghetto at which he described conditions resulting from the labor of the residents. He was subsequently transferred to the Dachau concentration camp in July 1944 when the ghetto was dissolved and was liberated from the camp at the end of the war. USHMMPA WS# N03334.00; *USHMM ITS Collection Data Base Central Name Index.*

Among the medical terms displayed on the diagram are "permanent psychic trauma," increased heart rate ("tachycardia"), "diabetes mellitus," stimulated condition of the sympathic nervous system ("sympathicotonia"), absence of a menstrual period in a woman of reproductive age ("amenorrhea"), "tubal pregnancy," "susceptibility to edema," and a decrease in the blood supply to tissues ("ischemia").

Throughout the region, Jews at the bottom of the ghettos' social ladder suffered greatly, such as the Hausers in Łódź, to the point where they could only document their physical decline, despair, and outrage. In June 1942 in Stanisławów in Galicia, Elsa Binder confided to her diary that "all of this scribbling is useless. It is a fact that we will not survive this. And history will know of everything without my enlightened information. The *Judenrat* is still standing. May those thieves be damned, but what does it matter to us."[16] But others insisted that "all this scribbling" was useful nonetheless. Organized documentation efforts such as Oyneg Shabes were key in attempting to preserve a record of what happened in the German-dominated parts of eastern Europe in the attempt, as Samuel Kassow puts it, to "arm the struggle for a better world."[17] The result was a clandestinely assembled collection of narratives that attests to what many Jewish men and women knew at the time and how they recorded this knowledge.

More and more eyewitness accounts from different regions gave evidence about the Germans' systematic mass murder policies across its administrative borders in German-controlled eastern Europe, allowing terrifying glimpses of what converged to become the overall process of annihilation. Historians have stressed the importance of the Lublin district as a breeding ground for a mass murder campaign that would spread across the entire Generalgouvernement and culminate in "**Aktion Reinhard**."[18] The following report—based on Jewish firsthand observers or hearsay and compiled randomly in what appears to have been less than an hour—confirms this interpretation. At the same time, it points to very similar events going on simultaneously outside the Lublin district, even outside

---

16. Diary entry by Elsa Binder, Stanisławów, June 9, 1942, USHMMA RG 02.208M (ŻIH 302/267), reel 39.

17. Samuel D. Kassow, *Who Will Write Our History? Emanuel Ringelblum, the Warsaw Ghetto, and the Oyneg Shabes Archive* (Bloomington: Indiana University Press, 2007), 8.

18. See Yitzhak Arad, *Belzec, Sobibor, Treblinka: Operation Reinhard Death Camps* (Bloomington: Indiana University Press, 1987); Dieter Pohl, *Von der "Judenpolitik" zum Judenmord: Der Distrikt Lublin des Generalgouvernements, 1934–1944* (Frankfurt am Main: P. Lang, 1993); and Bogdan Musial, ed., *"Aktion Reinhardt." Der Völkermord an den Juden im Generalgouvernement 1941–1944* (Osnabrück: Fibre Verlag, 2004).

the Generalgouvernement: in Belarus—the areas of Słonim and Nowogródek, on the territory of the "Reichskommissariat Ostland," as well as in the annexed **Warthegau**. Scholars have only fairly recently begun to place such events in context, particularly after the opening of archives in eastern Europe and following in-depth studies of regional developments in the German-occupied East.[19] Pulling together his short text, naturally without any recourse to German sources and in defiance of German orders, Abraham Lewin reached unnerving conclusions from his confined, yet centrally located, vantage point in the Warsaw ghetto.[20]

DOCUMENT 5-5: **"In One Half Hour," Abraham Lewin, Warsaw, March 26, 1942, USHMMA RG 15.079M (ŻIH Ring. I/1052) (translated from Yiddish).**

The "news" that I heard in just a half hour of walking through the ghetto can serve as an example and illustration of how deep the sea of troubles in which we are drowning currently is. Today I left my home at one o'clock in the afternoon and went to visit a sick person on the former Kupiecka [Street], later Majzel [Street], and today, in the times of German occupation, "Piner Street." In that home I met a girl of 19 to 20 who arrived today from the small town of Wąwolnica in the Lublin region. The girl relayed to me the terrible news about the slaughter the Germans carried out there this past Sunday, March 22, 1942. In that small town, a newly arrived ethnic German [*Volksdeutsche*] had been killed several days earlier; it was probably Poles who killed him as some sort of act of revenge. For the Germans, however, this was a sufficient pretext to attack and murder an entire community of Jews. This past Sunday three automobiles with Germans came down and brought all the Jews who had been seized, including the Judenrat, to the market square and shot them there. Because many Jews had hidden in the houses of Christians, the Germans went around to all the Polish homes, and wherever they found a Jew, they led him outside and shot him on the doorstep. As many as 90 Jews were murdered in Wąwolnica. I did not receive a clear response to my question of how many Jews lived in the town [before the massacre]. The girl only stated that "all, all the Jews in Wąwolnica were killed." I walked back by way of Nowolipki Street and encountered a Jew I knew from before the

---

19. See most recently Peter Longerich, *Holocaust: The Nazi Persecution and Murder of the Jews* (New York: Oxford University Press, 2010), 330–35, 356–60.

20. On Abraham Lewin and his work for Oyneg Shabes, see Abraham Lewin, *A Cup of Tears: A Diary of the Warsaw Ghetto*, ed. Anthony Polonsky (Oxford: Blackwell, 1988), with a slightly different translation of the document printed here (61-62).

war who had just come from Słonim two weeks prior. In the short conversation I had with him, he again revealed to me the terrible wound of "the story of Słonim."[21]

"Right before me, right before my eyes," he says, "mothers with children were seized and slaughtered. I myself miraculously survived. In my house, where four families lived, I and an older Jew remained. Come to my home, he'll tell you, too. Nowogródek[22] was completely slaughtered, too." I arrange with the acquaintance to visit him several days later, and I continue on.

Coming to my street, on Nowolipie, I meet another Jewish acquaintance, who tells me several sad pieces of news which he had read from a letter. Here they are:

1. In Zduńska Wola this past Purim, 10 Jews were seized and Jews were forced to hang them in the market square on 10 gallows.
2. The same thing happened in Łęczyca, too, which is also located in that region (the same is supposed to have happened in Brzeziny, too).[23]
3. All the local Jews, numbering 500, were deported from Izbica, in the Lublin region. 1,000 Czech Jews were brought in their place. The latter brought with them trunks with their belongings.

As Yehuda Ha-Levi says, "The cup of sorrows, long ago drained of its beauty, souls filled up with bitterness . . . "[24]

Truly a little too much for one half hour . . .

As the Oyneg Shabes activists around **Emanuel Ringelblum** expanded their unique archive, they documented a process that was growing in scope and intensity, coming ever closer, to threaten their own lives in Warsaw. The following account is from a woman who, before escaping to Warsaw with her husband, had spent nine months in Hrubieszów in the Lublin district of the Generalgouvernement. It attests to a sequence of dramatic events between the beginning of the first deportations to the **Sobibór** death camp on June 1, 1942, and a follow-up "action" one week later that left only

---

21. Słonim (Polish spelling); today Slonim in Belarus.

22. Nowogródek (Polish spelling), today Navahrudak in Belarus.

23. Zduńska Wola, Łęczyca, and Brzeziny were at the time located in the Warthegau region.

24. This last section was written in Hebrew. Yehuda Ha-Levi was one of the best-known Jewish poets in Spain in the eleventh and twelfth centuries.

2,600 Jews in the ghetto. At the same time, Mrs. Dychterman's meticulously detailed, lengthy testimony—recorded by Hersh Wasser, a close collaborator of Emanuel Ringelblum's[25]—gives voice to the unique perspective of an eyewitness who at any moment could have fallen victim to the violence she described.[26]

DOCUMENT 5-6: **Testimony by Mrs. Dychterman,[27] recorded for the Oyneg Shabes archive by Hersh Wasser, on an "Aktion" in Hrubieszów, Lublin district, Generalgouvernement, in early June 1942, June 30, 1942, USHMMA RG 15.079M (ŻIH Ring. I/814), 4–7 (translated from Polish).**

[. . .] On Saturday, May 30 of last year [1942], it became known that five sealed letters for the following cities reached the Jewish Council: Hrubieszów, Dubienka, Grabowiec, Uhanie, and Bełz. The letters came, as people said, from Kraków, from the central authorities, and they pertained to "resettlement actions" for the cities mentioned above. In a roundabout way, we learned that the ordinances in the letters concerned, among other things, a prohibition on the Jewish population moving from place to place in the period from June 1 to 7. A panic erupted in the city. On that day the last group of Jews, primarily mothers with children, left Hrubieszów legally. Everywhere people were talking about the registration of those fit for work and about resettlement—where and in what way, no one knew. The most fantastic conjectures and rumors found a hearing among the frightened, helpless, and disoriented masses. Even distant Bessarabia as a resettlement point provided a certain reassurance for people's strained nerves. The Jewish Council immediately began a process of issuing labor cards. Everyone believed that possession of a labor card would be a sufficient guarantee to remain in the city. Yet it was unsettling that on Saturday

---

25. Hersh Wasser (1912–1980) was the secretary of Oyneg Shabes and one of the very few activists who survived the war. See Kassow, *Who Will Write Our History*, 149–51.

26. On the eve of World War II, around 7,500 Jews lived in Hrubieszów, the majority of the town's population. By May 1943, after several murderous sweeps and deportations, only about 450 Jews were left in the town, the majority of whom were then taken to the labor camp in Budzyń. See Alexander Kruglov and Martin Dean, "Hrubieszów," in *The USHMM Encyclopedia of Camps and Ghettos*, 2:634–36.

27. The authors have been unable to find further information about the fate of Mrs. Dychterman. German and Yiddish phrases were used in the original; the transliteration of the Yiddish follows Polish phonology.

the *"pyziacy"*[28] went from house to house offering Poles and Ukrainians work laying cable on the stretch between Werbkowice and Uhanie, where, after all, some 600 Jews had been working. There was a terrible feeling in the air, but it was impossible to define it in greater detail. The next day, Sunday, May 31, was probably the most terrible with respect to the general mood. A certain nervous bustle had seized everyone. People were preparing bundles of luggage. Women were baking bread. No one was cooking. A crowd gathered in front of the Jewish Council building. Everyone wanted to know where things stood. People took consolation in the fact that it might be possible to ward off the danger at the last minute. A disorderly commotion without a goal or purpose. Some checked up on the hiding spots they had built earlier (they were built, wherever possible, in the period from mid-April until the "action"; I know, for example, that walls were built and secret passages and underground "dungeons" were made. We, in our turn, living in the attic at 5 Stazica Street, made a hiding spot by cutting out a board from the floor of the attic, and putting ourselves in the ceiling (i.e., the space between the floor of the attic and the ceiling of the apartment located beneath it). Small groups of women and men could be seen everywhere. People nervously discussed the "action," but no one grasped the meaning of this terrible word. It is strange how words that say little simply took on macabre meaning in Hitlerite practice. Under the cover of some permissible (of course, within Hitlerite practice) acts, a massacre of the civilian population was carried out unprecedented in human history. Everyone was worried. I cannot, in fact, find the most fitting definition for this psychological state. I feel as though everyone was in a state of partial insanity. No one was capable of reflecting on the situation that had been brought about, of identifying with it. People's mental faculties were "chloroformed." Parcels and bundles were everywhere. Some are on the verge of insanity. From their eyes emanates a mad, wild fear. One hears everywhere: *"m'myz hubn rahmin, m'myz hubn hylef, m'myz raasn kwurem, zolt eltern zych far yndz aaszelteln"* [We need God's mercy, we need help, we must run to the cemetery and ask our parents to intercede on our behalf]. After lunch, there was a momentary relaxation of tensions. Chairman Brand[29] is supposed to have said: *"Der az hot gepłact"* [the

---

28. Apparent slang, literally "fat-faced," referring to members of the Polish police (Sonderdienst) working for the Germans.

29. Szmul Brand served as chairman of Hrubieszów's *Judenrat*, established in November 1939; his subsequent fate is not known. The authors were unable to find information on the fate of individuals subsequently mentioned in this document.

ice has cracked]. Someone saw the members of the Judenrat leaving the city. It was presumed that they would still try to do something at the last minute, to intervene, to help, to bribe. I would also like to mention that I heard (I cannot guarantee accuracy) that Chairman Brand initially did not want to agree to supply the quota of Jews and was supposed to have said: "*Mir ale weln arosgajn of plac. Mir zenen ale glach*" [We will all go out to the square. We are all equal]. This was an absolutely human response. On the other hand, I don't know if it was logical. On that day after lunch, I coincidentally found myself at the house of Poles on Piłsudskiego Street. One of the Poles brought news that the "resettlement" had allegedly been postponed for an entire week for the price of 4 kilos [8.8 pounds] of gold and he spoke caustically of Jews, saying that they were the only ones who had gold. When I returned to Szewska Street at 5 o'clock, I found a completely different picture. I saw small groups of women lamenting and crying. Women were tearing the hair from their heads. Families were bidding farewell to each other. Apologies were given and forgiveness was sought. A true Day of Judgment. The still-living were mourned. Tension and fear grew as the curfew approached. Mothers spasmodically embraced their children. Men [illegible] in pious concentration. Their actions were carried out, rather, subconsciously. Starting at 6 in the evening, members of the Order Service [Jewish Police] started to go around to all the Jewish houses. They ordered everyone to be ready at 2 o'clock in the morning and to have 15 kilos [33 pounds] of luggage and food for 7 days. On that day, Jews moved about after 7 o'clock as well. Lights burned everywhere. No one went to sleep. I was overtaken by a boundless sadness and sorrow for past happiness and for the freedom that we were all seeking. Our neighbors came to our apartment. We sat together until 3 o'clock in the morning. At 3 o'clock, we heard shouts of "*raus*" and "come out" coming from the street as well as some general screaming.

Our brother-in-law, Josel Feld, a baker from Warsaw, knocked on our door. A terrible fear was visible in his eyes. He yelled: "*Hałct ofn dy tyjo, wy m'gefynt dy tyrn cy szyst men ofn oret*" [Leave the door open, wherever they find the doors closed, they shoot [people] on the spot]. In the event that they took us, we were prepared to go (although today I see the sheer nonsense of our decision. Is it at all conceivable that I, with a one-and-a-half-year-old child and a 15-kilo bundle as well as food, could embark on any sort of journey, even if it did not take place according to the German "interpretation"?). At 3:30, a Jewish policeman came to us upstairs and ordered us to leave. We got up, put on our bundles, woke the child, and went downstairs. On Szewska Street, we saw a long line, divided into fours, of Hrubieszów's poor. It was growing dusky. The severe cold paralyzed us. The "*pyziacy*" darted in all directions like rabid dogs (the Sonderdienst, composed of Volksdeutsche, was renowned in the region for its cruelty). We still had not seen any people who had been killed. At 4 o'clock, we marched out to the [Market?] Square. Jews from Wodna Street and others were already there. In contrast to the staging areas on Szewska and Wodna Streets, where one could hear the lamenting and wailing of women and the crying of children, a strange, uncanny silence reigned at the gathering point on the square. This silence was the most oppressive for us and depressed us [more] than the crying of Jews and the screams of the "*pyziacy*." The Jewish Order Service and the Sanitary Service stood arrayed along the sides, and Germans bustled through the square. The crowd of people gave off the impression of a resigned mass, reconciled to its fate. The comparison to a herd of sheep driven to the slaughter, as banal as it is, nevertheless is the most appropriate. One could hear: "*Geb mo ynto s'pekl*" [Give me my bundle], "*Halt mo s'pekl*" [Hold my bundle]. Szyfra Waldman with her seven children (the oldest was 17) only checks whether they are nearby: "*Kyndo, gajt nyszt awek fyn myjo*" [Children, don't leave my side]. Froim "Cziusz" Feler, who came to our house the day before together with Lejzor Mangl because he had heard that we had some sort of hiding place and who asserted that, although the hiding place might be suitable for him, he nevertheless cannot settle for it since he must afterall care for his wife and two small children, the younger of whom was 7 months, now sat on his bundle, holding the infant in his arms. Next to him stood his wife with the older son. I read in his face that he could have saved himself, but his duty was driving him into the terrible unknown. All attempts at escape ended in death. "*Pyziacy*" fired dum-dum bullets. The Polish Police were also at the square. The Germans counted all those present, threatening that for one missing person 20 would be killed. At the last minute, I was able to escape unhurt together with my child and husband with the help of a "fainting" trick. As I found out, the Landrat had demanded a quota of 2,500 people, but approximately 3,000 reported. This fact allowed the members of the Jewish Council to remove persons holding patents (certificates) from the lines. In the hospital, where we, the sick ones, were taken, only a woman who was nine months pregnant was admitted. We, declaring that the "action" had already taken place, were not admitted (aside from the pregnant woman, I, and another "fainting" woman with four children in the hackney cab). We went to the home of my husband's brother, Berysz Dychterman (a second brother-in-law, Josel Feld, was massacred in cruel fashion during an escape attempt). Berysz D. had suffered a nervous shock. He, too, had been at the market even though he had a craftsman's card. Joel Rabinowicz saved him. This is what caused the shock. He yelled continuously: "*Uuuu, m'szyst*" [ohhh, they're shooting], "*ch'hob gefynen a brydo yn a szwesto*" [I found brother and sister], "*dus yz nyszt daan kind*" [This is not your child]. The shock lasted a few hours. The first "action" claimed 2,500 victims. On Monday, June 1, a transport of victims from Dubienka arrived at Hrubieszów—3,000 "resettlers" (as I was informed, only persons possessing craftsman cards and without families remained in Dubienka, 100 Jews total). The destination of the transport is not known. At the station in Hrubieszów, 15 Jews from Dubienka were killed. On Tuesday, June 2, a "transport" of victims arrived from Bełz, 3,500 people total. In Hrubieszów, 500 of those from Bełz were released. Those who were released were given red residency cards.

Throughout the entire week after the first "action," the Jews "sold off" everything they owned. Polish merchants exploited the favorable situation by paying pennies for Jewish property. Everyone wanted to have a little bit of cash since, it was generally believed, money would be needed in every situation. No one doubted that the matter was not yet over and that the extreme point of the tragedies had not been reached. Everyone is trying to make themselves useful, of course, with the aim of saving their lives. All sorts of swindlers are making a fortune off the misfortune of their fellow human beings.

Vox populi [Latin: voice of the people]: We won't go the square any more. Better death than going through the nightmare of the first "action" again. An intensified wave of religiosity could be noticed.

On Saturday, June 6, Jukiel Brand declared that all Jews were to report to the square for the purpose of obtaining a residency card. On that day, the German commission (the Landrat was also among them) registered the members of the Jewish Council, the Order Service, the hospital personnel, and six nurses. On that day, many marriages took place between members of the Order Service and local ladies (in order to save Jewish women—the marriages were fictitious).

On that day, it became apparent that something was in the works. After 7 p.m., we hid in our hiding place in the attic together with the sister-in-law of my husband and two neighbors (we left our child in the hospital). We had two pillows and blankets in the hiding place. We could barely lie on our backs. Spiders, centipedes, and other bugs crawled on us. Due to the lack of space, air, and darkness, we didn't have a moment of peace. Our food consisted of bread and water. Around 10 o'clock at night, we heard the Jewish Police calling for people to report to the square on Sunday, announcing, "*der jidnratz nyszt farantloch far kaj szym korbunes*" [The Jewish Council is not responsible for any victims]. At 5 in the morning, we heard "*raus.*" At 6 o'clock, the *pyziaki* conducted the first search. They concluded: "*hier sind keine Juden*" [there are no Jews here]. We observed what was happening on the street through cracks in the walls (they were wooden buildings). Polish and Ukrainian youths went from house to house, helping to uncover hidden Jews. Beyond that, they pillaged (Franek, look at how nice this bag is, Stasiek, what a hat). The city was emptied of life. We did not see a single Jew. Jewish homes were open. Some movement could be seen in the square. The stalls were open. We observed how a cart full of linen (probably from Jews) moved in the direction of the square. The plundering went on.

After lunch we saw German soldiers going with girls to see the deserted post-Jewish [pożidowski] district.[30] There was a thunderstorm with lightning on Monday at 2 o'clock. We lay covered in water. Through the cracks, we saw the following scene: during the storm, an older Jew, Matys Blas, was on Szewska Street (and this was in the period of the second "action," when any Jew who was happened upon or discovered in a hiding place was killed). He walked at a slow pace, paying no mind to the rain and the lightning. He raised the window of his house and calmly went inside, with his bundle on his back. After a certain amount of time, he came out of the window, without rushing, and calmly walked away. Set against the background of the storm, the deserted street, and the lifeless city, this made an uncanny impression on us.

On Monday evening, we noticed the first Jews holding the red residency cards. Early on Tuesday, we learned that the Germans had carried out a great massacre in Hrubieszów the previous day. Some 500 men, women, and children (180 children) were assembled at the local cemetery; they were divided into three groups and all were killed. A driver from the Gestapo distinguished himself (I don't know his last name—people say that, for lack of another activity (shooting at Jews), he shot at the birds). The issuing of residency cards was one great tragedy for the Jews.

---

30. On the peculiar history of this neologism, see Jan T. Gross (with Irena Grudzinska Gross), *Golden Harvest: Events at the Periphery of the Holocaust* (New York: Oxford University Press, 2012), 29.

Entire families were separated. Thus from the family of Matys Kirszner, a gaiter worker, consisting of the parents and seven children, three children remained—Szulim (20), Basia (21), and Frajda (16). The rest were sent away. The commission consisted of the Landrat, Akerman, the trustee of Jewish property, and Meyer (or a major). We decided against going to the square because, as we had been informed, everyone who did not themselves report to the square was killed. In the evening, we—my husband and I—left for Warsaw as Poles from Hrubieszów. The topic of conversion on the train was the slaughter in Hrubieszów. No one knew the exact number of victims; some claimed that 800 Jews had been deported, others that it was 1,500. Polish women, smugglers (the local element) held typical opinions: "They (the Jews) have to be poisoned starting from infancy," "I would poison them immediately after birth," "They have such poisoned blood." I did not hear any other opinions. I have the impression that people were afraid (it is well-known that these areas teem with the most varied spies).

In Werbkowice, we waited for a long-distance train from [illegible] to 11:30 p.m. We experienced an unpleasant identification process. Indeed, it was a miracle that we made it out of the hands of the controllers: a gendarme, a *pyziak*, and a Polish policeman. I used a bankbook to identify myself and justified our departure for Warsaw with the wish of buying clothing for my fiancée, Franek. After the transfer in Rejowiec, at one of the smaller stations (we stopped for a few minutes), we noticed a train with about a dozen freight cars parallel to ours and full of Jews. A small, maybe 4-year-old Jewish boy stuck his little hand through the door, which was not fully closed, and asked: "*get myjo a sztykele brojt*" [give me a piece of bread]. I saw the little faces of Jewish children pressed up against the small windows of the cars.

After various wanderings, we reached Warsaw on Thursday, June 11. At Savior Square, we were uncovered by a Polish policeman. The policeman took us to the police station on Poznańska Street, where, after lengthy haggling, in which the commissioner himself took part, a deal was struck that we would be released into the ghetto for 200 złoty. My husband first had to make it to the Jewish District and try to come up with such an incredible amount of money, while I sat in prison as a hostage until 5 o'clock. Only after paying the said amount to a special envoy, a Polish policeman, at the "Centralniak" building (the central prison of the Jewish Council in Warsaw), I, too, was released into the ghetto through the entrance at Leszno and Żelazna.

On Friday, June 19, a Polish acquaintance brought my child. She informed me that 1,000 Jewish souls remained in Hrubieszów and that a Jewish District was to be established. She also intimated that only 600 Jews would have the right of residency (there would thus be a further "action").

Miserable and impoverished, lacking the most basic clothing, with no money, we seek support.

And what now, unfortunate Jewish wanderer?

UNSAFE IN "SAFE HAVENS"

We know now that the Holocaust did not reach certain areas that the Nazi regime intended to include in the "Final Solution." Given the uncertainty about how the war would evolve and end, Jews could attain at best a feeling of relative security, even in those places that seemed to offer the best of prospects for refuge. With the expansion of Axis rule, this sense of security diminished. In Palestine, the bombing of Haifa by the Italian air force in September 1940 provided a shocking yet isolated reminder that the war had spread beyond Europe. As the Germans drew ever closer, Jews in Palestine became increasingly aware of the vulnerability of the Zionist experiment and the complexity of their relationship with the British and their Arab neighbors. In the spring of 1941, like many others looking at the military map of North Africa, Leo Kohn, a key functionary of the **Jewish Agency** in Jerusalem, dreaded the "terrible prospects [. . .] that might await the virile and constructive Jewish community in Palestine if it fell under the heels of the Nazi hordes" and was convinced that a German invasion of Palestine would have catastrophic consequences.[31]

The growing danger facing the Yishuv fed internal dissent over key policy issues, the paramount question being the primacy of the long-term goal of establishing and maintaining a Jewish national home versus the immediate

---

31. Memorandum by Leo Kohn, May 7, 1941; ISA Leo Kohn Papers P575; quoted in *Archives of the Holocaust: An International Collection of Selected Documents*, ed. Henry Friedlander and Sybil Milton (New York: Garland, 1991), 13:238–40. Leo Kohn (1894–1961) had left Germany for Palestine in 1921 and became a scholar and later a diplomat. After acting as political secretary for the Jewish Agency in the 1930s and 1940s, Kohn (a.k.a. Yehudah Pinhas) served as an advisor to Chaim Weizmann and Israel's Ministry of Foreign Affairs from 1948 to 1952. See Shmuel Bendor, "Kohn, Leo," *Encyclopaedia Judaica*, ed. Fred Skolnik and Michael Berenbaum, 2nd ed. (Detroit: Macmillan Reference USA, 2007), 12:263.

needs created by the military situation. Zionist leaders complained—as did **Nahum Goldmann**, head of the Jewish Agency's New York office in May 1942—about the "rivalry and personal competition" and the "lack of real cooperation" impeding the ability of the Jews in Palestine to meet the demands of the present.[32] In addition, British censorship and other measures restricted the Yishuv's ability to grasp the full impact of what was happening to Jews elsewhere. Well into 1942, despite incoming reports from Nazi-controlled Europe, historian Dina Porat has concluded, "Leaders in the Yishuv still believed that the sufferings of the Jews were incidental to the German occupation." As late as October 1942, Jewish Agency executive board member David Ben-Gurion was, according to his biographer Tuvia Friling, "still not aware of the full meaning of what the Nazis were doing to the Jews."[33]

The following report, created from diary notes by Ludwig Foerder,[34] an émigré lawyer from Germany and written in June 1941, criticized the Yishuv leadership's preoccupation with state building and its oblivious attitude toward the real nature of the German threat. Jews who had been forced out of Nazi Germany long felt they could attest most authoritatively to that threat, despite the fact that the anti-Jewish policy of the Third Reich had become far more destructive since their departure. As Foerder wrote after the war, he sent the report to a group of "members of the German **Aliyah**" and received mostly positive responses that confirmed his interpretation.[35]

---

32. Nahum Goldmann, New York City, May 25, 1942, to Richard Lichtheim, Geneva; quoted in Friedlander and Milton, *Archives of the Holocaust*, 4:377.

33. Dina Porat, *The Blue and the Yellow Stars of David: The Zionist Leadership in Palestine and the Holocaust, 1939–1945* (Cambridge, MA: Harvard University Press, 1990), 22; Tuvia Friling, *Arrows in the Dark: David Ben-Gurion, the Yishuv Leadership, and Rescue Attempts during the Holocaust* (Madison: University of Wisconsin Press, 2005), 1:64. For perceptions of the Yishuv leadership, see also Tom Segev, *The Seventh Million: The Israelis and the Holocaust* (New York: Hill and Wang, 1993), 67ff.; idem, *One Palestine, Complete: Jews and Arabs under the British Mandate* (New York: Metropolitan Books, 2000), 452ff.

34. Ludwig Foerder (1885–1954) was an attorney from Breslau active in combatting antisemitism in Germany while also involved in Zionist causes. He immigrated to Palestine in 1933 via Czechoslovakia and died in Jerusalem. See "In Memory of Ludwig Foerder" in *AJR Information* 9, issued by the Association of Jewish Refugees in Great Britain (August 1954): 4; Joseph Walk, *Kurzbiographien zur Geschichte der Juden 1918–1945* (Munich: K. G. Saur, 1988), 94.

35. Letter from Ludwig Foerder, Jerusalem, to Friedrich Brodnitz, New York, July 4, 1946, USHMMA Acc. 2008.189 Brodnitz family collection.

DOCUMENT 5-7: **Report by Ludwig Foerder, Jerusalem, on the attitude of Zionists and non-Zionists toward rescue measures in case of a German occupation of Palestine, June 1941, USHMMA Acc. 2008.189 Brodnitz collection (translated from German).**

When the Germans in the course of April 1941 conquered Yugoslavia and Greece in a rapid advance, in late May seizing Crete as well, the Jewish population of Palestine was struck by panic. The Germans' objective seemed clear: conquering Cyprus, Syria, and Palestine in order to bring the Suez Canal and the entire Middle East under their control. [. . .] Naturally, the mood of panic was especially intense among the members of the Central European Aliyah. After all, they had personal experience of the Nazis' brutality and cherished the hope that they would be protected here, once and for all, from their violent bullying. Therefore, members of these circles made a special effort to learn whether and what kinds of rescue operations were planned in the event of an occupation of the country by the enemy. [. . .]

On May 28, 1941, a general meeting of Hitachdut Olei Germania[36] took place in Jerusalem. The president of the HOG, Mr. F. Rosenblüth[37] of Tel Aviv, gave a speech in which he stated the following about the topic under discussion here:

> I can imagine that Palestine soon will be occupied by the enemy. How must we conduct ourselves then? Exactly as all other peoples do; that is, our government will take itself out of harm's way at the right time. As for the rest, not a single woman or child may leave the country. Not even a few hundred may leave. Palestine is our last stop, there is no train traveling any farther on this line. And if 50,000 perish in the process, there will still be 450,000 Jews left.

---

36. Literally, in Hebrew, Union of German [Jewish] Immigrants [in Palestine]; an organization of German Jewish immigrants in Palestine.

37. Pinhas Rosen (1887–1978) was born Felix Rosenblüth in Berlin and early in his life became active in Zionist causes. He studied law in Berlin and Freiburg and fought in the German army during World War I as an officer. Rosen headed the Zionist Organization of Germany from 1920 to 1923 before settling in Palestine in 1926. There he represented immigrants from Central Europe on Tel Aviv's City Council (1935–1950) and founded the Hitachdut Olei Germania for German and Austrian immigrants. After 1948, he was elected to the Israeli Parliament, and played a prominent role in the development of Israel's legal system, both as a member of parliament and during several tenures as minister of justice. See profile at the website of the Israeli Parliament: www.knesset.gov.il/mk/eng/mk_eng .asp?mk_individual_id_t=615 (accessed April 25, 2012).

Only in that way can we justify our claims to the land at the upcoming peace conference.

These remarks, which encountered open resistance in some cases and awkward silence in others while the meeting was still under way, aroused lively criticism in numerous conversations connected with them. In opposition, the following assertions were made:

The comparison with "other peoples" is just as false as it is un-Jewish. In every place the Germans have reached in their expeditions of conquest, the Jews have had to endure a <u>special fate</u> that placed them in a far worse position than the non-Jewish population of the occupied territories. Anyone who reads the newspaper knows that. But anyone who is familiar with the National Socialist mindset knows that it is precisely <u>the Jews of Palestine</u> who in addition would experience special treatment in the worst sense, for it would give the Nazis a special thrill to massacre the Jews right here, in their own country. [. . .] But the fate of Palestine's Jews is still a special one, to the extent that they would also be threatened from the Arab side and above all by famine, as well as by the Nazis. Should the Germans invade the Middle East, it is not difficult to foresee that the Jews in Palestine, especially in the vacuum between the withdrawal of the British troops and the entry of the German ones, would be threatened by a fate far worse than that of the Baghdad Jews not long ago under Rashid Ali and comrades.[38] [. . .]

If someone sees another person in a life-threatening situation, he is morally obligated to come to his aid and do everything possible to save him. Does this principle not apply to Jewish policy? Everyone who succeeded in evading the grasp of the Nazi murderers in Germany has been congratulated for having done so. Yet here it is suddenly supposed to be a moral obligation to allow ourselves to be beaten to death by the same murderers?

Entitlement to the land is not bought through senseless sacrifices of that kind. When murderers and robbers break into a house and the owner evades them by fleeing, no reasonable person will conclude that the owner is thereby giving up his claim to his home. Such a conclusion certainly will not be drawn by a peace conference over which a Churchill and a Roosevelt preside. Moreover, each person must be free to exercise control over his own life. But to deny all help to someone who wishes to be rescued, and to set oneself up as master over the life and death of others, amounts to the apotheosis of a state-sponsored fiction that has its basis solely in the intellectual

---

38. Reference to the Baghdad pogrom; see above, document 3–7.

attitudes of fascism and has not the slightest thing to do with the Jewish vision or with a properly understood Zionism.

Throughout the war, the Yishuv remained a longed-for destination, yet few could make their way there. Up to January 1942, almost eight thousand boys and girls had reached the shores of Palestine as part of the Youth Aliyah. By that time, however, the number of certificates granted by the British had dwindled to a trickle.[39] That illegal immigration to Palestine (Aliyah Bet) was difficult and dangerous was highlighted by the case of the **Struma**, a poorly equipped transport ship chartered by **Revisionist Zionists** and embarking in December 1941 from the Romanian port of Constanța with 769 Jewish passengers. Despite extended negotiations, British authorities refused to grant the émigrés certificates to enter Palestine, and Turkish officials would not allow the group to land. On February 23, 1942, Istanbul port authorities towed the vessel out into the Mediterranean. Shortly thereafter it was torpedoed; only one passenger survived. The incident captured headlines, triggered a protest resolution by American Jewish organizations against Britain for "creating unparalleled tragedy and suffering for Jewish refugees from Nazi terror,"[40] and prompted Churchill's government to adopt a more lenient policy toward illegal immigrants.[41] The tragedy long remained a potent symbol for Jews, underlining the detached and indifferent attitude of the authorities governing Palestine; some argued that their policies were hard to distinguish from those promulgated by their adversaries in the European war.

---

39. Henrietta Szold, foreword (February 19, 1942), in Walter Gross, *Youth Aliyah in Wartime 1939 to 1941* (Youth Immigration Bureau, Jerusalem, 1942), 1, 6.

40. Letter by **Stephen S. Wise** and other representatives of the American Jewish Committee, American Jewish Congress, B'nai B'rith, and the American Emergency Committee for Zionist Affairs to Acting U.S. Secretary of State Sumner Wells, March 19, 1942; quoted from *Contemporary Jewish Record* 5, no. 3 (June 1942): 315.

41. See Porat, *The Blue and Yellow Stars of David*, 160–63; Bernard Wasserstein, *Britain and the Jews of Europe*, ed. 2 (London: Leicester University Press, 1999), 129–38; Ronald W. Zweig, *Britain and Palestine during the Second World War* (Woodbridge, Suffolk: The Boydell Press, 1986), 118–35; Louise London, *Whitehall and the Jews, 1933–1948. British Immigration Policy, Jewish Refugees and the Holocaust* (Cambridge: Cambridge University Press, 2000), 187–90.

DOCUMENT 5-8: Letter from Richard Lichtheim, Jewish Agency for Palestine-Geneva, to Joseph Linton, Jewish Agency-London, on the aftermath of the "Struma" disaster, March 25, 1942, CZA RG L22, file 134.[42]

Dear Linton,

The news of the "Struma" tragedy has created a very painful impression here as everywhere else. I have also received letters from our friends in Sweden asking for more details and an explanation.

The Swiss papers have also reported on the incident.

It is really very difficult for us to explain the attitude of the British Government with regard to these unfortunate refugees. There are also Englishmen here who simply refuse to believe that such a thing could have happened. The British military attaché in Berne, when asked about it in a private conversation, said that he did not believe it and that it was apparently German propaganda. This is only to the credit of this gentleman but he had to be told that he was mistaken.

[...]

From my observations here I must say—I regret to say so but it is the truth—that the only country behaving decently to Jewish refugees is Italy. But then of course they are bloody Fascists and not fighting for freedom and liberty. Many Italian officers have brought Jewish refugees from Jugoslavia to Italy and hundreds of such refugees have crossed the frontier from Croatia to Italy. Part of them have been placed in camps but quite decent camps in southern Italy where the families can live together in some house or barrack and are not separated from each other as in the [British-run internment] camps of Atlit or Mauritius. Many other refugees have simply been told to go to small towns or villages in Italy where they can move about without being in any way molested and where they are treated with great friendliness by the population and also by the officials. Of course these officials have not had the privilege of an education in Eton and Oxford, so the poor blighters don't know how to behave, otherwise they would know that Jewish refugees must be put in prison-camps behind barbed wire or sent back to their persecutors. [...]

---

42. Printed in Friedlander and Milton, *Archives of the Holocaust*, 4:152–53.

Neither **Lichtheim** nor anyone else could have known that the situation of Jews in Italy or under Italian control would change dramatically for the worse with the German occupation in September 1943, while refugees held in British detention would be safe from Nazi persecution for the remainder of the war.[43] At the time, Jewish detainees in British camps mentioned by Lichtheim struggled to get rid of their stigma as "enemy aliens," the label conferred on them when the war broke out. In late October 1941, after having spent eleven months in the Atlit camp in Palestine, Egon Weiss received the good news that he was about to be released. A young Jew born in Czechoslovakia who had escaped Europe on board the *Milos* and the ill-fated **Patria**,[44] Weiss found it incredible "to be able to move around freely, to think of white bed linen, a good meal, city life and what we have longed for in the past almost eighteen months."[45]

Aharon Zwergbaum, a young lawyer with Zionist leanings originally from Prague, had been one of the passengers on the *Helios* and the **Atlantic** bound for Palestine in 1940, but was intercepted by the British. In December 1940 he was shipped on to Mauritius together with more than 1,500 people, including survivors of the *Patria*, to the camp of Beau Bassin for civilians from enemy nations.[46] In his summary of events written in early 1943 primarily for his fellow detainees, Zwergbaum compared conditions in the British camp in 1942 with the preceding year, during which ten camp inmates had died, many had been sick, and all had struggled with adapting to the tropical climate of the island.[47] Despite an overall positive balance, worries over the fate of fellow Jews in Europe and the Yishuv cast a pall over the life of the internees, which to some obscured the huge differences between Nazi and Allied camps. The excerpt reproduced here followed

43. See Susan Zuccotti, *The Italians and the Holocaust: Persecution, Rescue, and Survival* (Lincoln: University of Nebraska Press, 1996).

44. See Alexandra Garbarini, with Emil Kerenji, Jan Lambertz, and Avinoam Patt, *Jewish Responses to Persecution*, vol. 2: *1938–1940* (Lanham, MD: AltaMira Press in association with the USHMM, 2011), 257–60.

45. Diary entry by Egon Weiss for October 20, 1941, USHMMA Acc. 2011.128.1.

46. For a fascinating account based on a diary by an eleven-year-old boy from Vienna on board the *Atlantic* and *Patria* published in late 1941, see "Von Wien nach Haifa. Das Tagebuch eines Elfjährigen," *Yediot hayom*, November 21, 1941, 8.

47. The author, Aharon (also Aaron) Zwergbaum (1913–2010), served as a leader among the detainees in Maurititus and liaison with outside Jewish organizations. He had trained as a lawyer in Brno before the war and briefly served in the Czech army. In September 1942 he married Regina Kroj, a fellow internee, and their son was born in Mauritius. When the war ended, they moved to Palestine, where Zwergbaum again practiced law and eventually became legal adviser to the World Zionist Organization in Jerusalem. See Itzhak J. Carmin Karpman, ed., *Who's Who in World Jewry: A Biographical Dictionary of Outstanding Jews* (Tel Aviv: Olive Books of Israel, 1972), 998.

Zwergbaum's descriptions of day-to-day living conditions and cultural activities organized in the camp.

DOCUMENT 5-9: Aharon Zwergbaum, account and drawing on his second year in Mauritius, January 1943, USHMMA RG 17.008M (DÖW 51123-2) (translated from German).

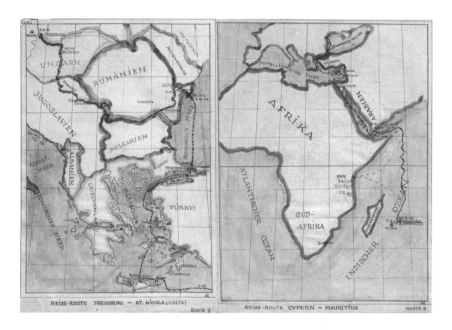

[. . .] The front in the Middle East was definitely the most important for us. After all, this is where Palestine was being defended, many of our relatives fought there, our volunteer recruits[48] were sent there, and, finally, we also knew that the fate of war in the Middle East had a direct influence on our chances of returning.

[. . .] The banners carried during the demonstrations in Tel Aviv demanded our repatriation. Moshe Shertok,[49] the director of the Jewish

48. Camp prisoners who had successfully applied for military service with the British, Czech, or Polish armies.

49. Moshe Shertok (1894–1965), a.k.a. Moshe Sharett, was born in Ukraine and immigrated to Palestine at the age of twelve. Fluent in Arabic and Turkish, he fought in the Ottoman army in World War I. After studies in Istanbul and London, he joined the Jewish Agency in 1933 and headed its political department until 1948. After the independence of Israel that year he became a prominent politician, holding the posts of minister for foreign affairs and prime minister. See Gabriel Sheffer, *Moshe Sharett: Biography of a Political Moderate* (Oxford: Clarendon Press, 1996).

Agency's political department, said in his opening speech in Assefath Hanivcharim:[50] ["]For us Mauritius is politically the same as Dachau, humanly the difference is like light and darkness.["] We gladly recognized the correctness of the second half of this sentence, but were also pleased that the first half was spoken by such an authoritative voice. Shertok also wrote us a very heartening letter which, among other things, stated: "We never forgot you all, not even for one day. The efforts for you have never stopped and continue. One day, until we come together again—and we will come together—we will surely listen to a moving story. But we will also have something to tell you."

[. . .] In the year 1942, very many things, large and small, have improved considerably, from family life to other outside activities. And in the same year the situation of the European Jews, our brothers and sisters, continually became more intolerable and escalated from disfranchisement and theft to organized German mass murder. One thanked God every day that one was spared this fate and with every bite, with every small enjoyment one had to think of those relatives who lived in this hell. The comparison between Mauritius and Europe imposed itself often on us and we had the right and duty to draw it; but others should not have imposed it on us, because that implied that ghetto and disenfranchisement were our normal fate [*Normallos*] and that we should be thankful for everything better, not only to fate, but also to its instruments. [. . .]

With great trepidation, Jews looked to the few remaining gateways to freedom or safety that could close any time and entrap those who had been unable to leave early enough. In December 1941, seventeen-year-old Sophie Freud from Vienna, a granddaughter of Sigmund Freud, got stuck with her mother in the Moroccan city of Casablanca after a long odyssey that had first taken them to Paris and Nice. Although they had managed to obtain visas for immigration to the United States, the country's entry into the war greatly reduced the number of passenger ships across the Atlantic. What had started as an adventure for the young woman quickly turned into a frightening situation of entrapment in which former social status did not seem to offer any advantage.

---

50. An elected Jewish assembly in Palestine, precursor to the Israeli parliament after 1948.

DOCUMENT 5-10: Sophie Freud,[51] Casablanca, Morocco, diary entry for January 24, 1942, USHMMA Acc. 2010.401.1 Sophie Freud collection (translated from German).[52]

Today our visa expires.

[looking back on the last days after disembarking in Casablanca harbor in December 1941:] At last we arrived, 8 km [almost 5 miles] from Casablanca. We stopped before a pleasant garden, at the front of which there stood a large glass pavilion. It was a greenhouse of some sort. Straw mattresses were lying there, one next to the other, with no space in between, and that was our dwelling place, bedroom-dining room and parlor. I enjoyed it all immensely. All my life, I wanted to give sleeping on straw mattresses a try. For washing, there were three or four washstands in the middle of the garden, where everybody could look at us. The toilet was unimaginable. That really was unpleasant. Nothing had been prepared for us to eat, either, and like hungry rats we rushed to the nearby inn and to the market. At the inn, with great grace, for two days we were given food, but then the landlord threw us out and we ate "at home," which was all right, too. We each got a *bol* [French; bowl] handed out to us by HICEM,[53] and then Arabs with carts came and doled out food to us, and we stood in line. It was always heavy stuff like beans and mushy peas, I liked the taste at first, but now I can hardly get such things down anymore.

[. . . ; a description of life in the makeshift camp and tours through the city follows.] And now I come to my tale of woe.[54] One morning recently, we suddenly got the news that the *Serpapinto* [ocean liner that was supposed to bring them to the United States] isn't arriving until the

---

51. In May 1938, Sophie Freud (born 1924), the daughter of Sigmund Freud's oldest son Jean-Martin and his wife Ernestine fled with her mother to Paris, where Sophie attended high school and her mother opened a speech clinic. Two days before the German army entered Paris, Sophie and Ernestine Freud fled to Nice, where they obtained visas for the United States and left for Casablanca in December 1941. In the autumn of 1942 they finally sailed to Baltimore via Lisbon. See Sophie Freud, *Living in the Shadow of the Freud Family* (Westport, CT: Praeger, 2007).

52. Published, in a different translation, in Freud, *Living in the Shadow*, 259–65.

53. For HICEM, see the Glossary.

54. Freud, *Living in the Shadow*, 261, makes this the first sentence of the January 25, 1942, diary entry. In the original document in USHMMA Acc. 2010.401.1, however, it is a continuation of the January 24 entry.

25th [of January 1942]. Mother immediately got terribly upset, but I wasn't upset at all, [because] I didn't think they would simply leave us here. Then Spaniel came, the big boss of all of HICEM in France, a Russian Jew, big, fat, with a mustache, and as obnoxious as all get-out. [follows small drawing of a man's face with mustache].[55] Mother started to cry dreadfully, he yelled at her like fury, saying that he'd straighten it out and we shouldn't talk about it, and all his shouting made us trust him again [most likely meant ironically]. Spaniel is a terrible shouter in general, as arrogant as anyone could possibly be, except that he just barely keeps from spitting on us. He thinks he's really something, the big boss. Maybe he thinks he's the Lord God himself, but we're finer than he is by a long shot. Everybody hates him because he's already done something to everyone, and he doesn't care about anybody, as has certainly been demonstrated. He'll get a bullet in his belly someday, too, like the HICEM man in Marseilles,[56] and he will honestly deserve it.

[. . . ; a description of their relocation to more confined quarters (Maternelle) in Casablanca and the first day spent there follows.] The day before, we had gone to see the [US] consul, an ice-cold Russian Jewish woman who couldn't care less about us if we were flies. She explained to us coldly and firmly that we have to be on board on the 24th [of January], and if the ship still hasn't arrived by then (we knew that it wasn't sailing [from Lisbon] until the 24th), we have to send a telegram to the State Department in Washington, and go to Nice first to have it [the visa] extended. Since [the entry of the United States into] the war, there's been a new law prohibiting extension of the visas of all hostile nationals. And she added that America is a democratic country that makes no exceptions

55. Freud may have been confusing Raphaël Spanien with another **HICEM** official, Russian-born Vladimir (Wladimir) Schah. On Spanien, a French national and prominent HICEM official who worked on behalf of Jewish refugees in France, Morocco, and Portugal during the war, see obituary, *Jewish Telegraphic Agency*, October 16, 1974; *American Jewish Year Book* 76 (1976): 312; and Raymond-Raoul Lambert, *Diary of a Witness, 1940–1943*, ed. Richard I. Cohen (Chicago, IL: Ivan R. Dee in association with the USHMM, 1985), 129n7. On Schah, see Lambert, *Diary of a Witness*, 94n5; obituary, *New York Times*, July 12, 1949.

56. The authors have been unable to identify this official. On HICEM's rescue work in Marseille during the early war years, see Donna F. Ryan, *The Holocaust & the Jews of Marseille: The Enforcement of Anti-Semitic Policies in Vichy France* (Urbana: University of Illinois Press, 1996), 137f. The organization employed a large staff in the city until November 1942, and a number of its foreign employees were eventually deported to the East.

even for the name of "Freud." (That was immensely consoling, of course.) And she said that we could just as well wait in Nice for the new permit and then return here. Once back in Nice, I'm not undertaking all the Alps again! And [Thomas] Cook took his customers through all of Spain in sealed railroad cars. On account of 24 hours. We're really especially unlucky devils! But I think the indifference of HICEM and of the consulate is to blame for many things. HICEM, which has leased the entire *Serpapinto*, could certainly wangle things with a little good will, after all. I'm good and angry at Spaniel. And now here we sit in Casablanca and wait for the permit from Washington, and meanwhile all the ships are leaving without us. Everybody says that we'll probably be put in a camp in the meantime, because we don't have permission to stay in Morocco, of course. A sad situation. [. . .]

Spain, ruled since the end of the civil war by a fascist dictatorship, and Portugal, also under an authoritarian regime, were among the very few European countries still at least theoretically accessible for Jewish refugees in transit. With the Soviet Union fighting off the Wehrmacht and the Balkans firmly in the grip of Germany and its allies, the Iberian pensinsula had become the sole hope for many "transemigrants" in their attempts to reach a safe destination across the ocean.[57] Once there, they confronted the extremely limited shipping capacities for transatlantic travel and the stringent rules and regulations imposed by the Spanish and Portugese governments on aliens. Certain groups experienced unique difficulties, both in negotiating with foreign bureaucracies and tapping relief and aid. In the following letter, internees held in a Spanish camp tried to raise awareness about their borderline status, which had been compounded for several of them when their countries of origin had declared them stateless.[58]

---

57. On Portugal, see Ronald Weber, *The Lisbon Route: Entry and Escape in Nazi Europe* (Lanham, MD: Ivan R. Dee, 2011), and Avraham Milgram, *Portugal, Salazar, and the Jews* (Jerusalem: Yad Vashem, 2011); for Spain, see Haim Avni, *Spain, the Jews, and Franco* (Philadelphia, PA: Jewish Publication Society of America, 1982), and Bernd Rother, *Spanien und der Holocaust* (Tübingen: Niemeyer, 2001).

58. On the history of the Miranda de Ebro camp, see José Angel Fernández López, *Historia del campo de concentración de Miranda de Ebro, 1937–1947* (Miranda de Ebro: J. A. Fernández López, 2004).

DOCUMENT 5-11: **Petition by Jewish internees at Miranda de Ebro camp, Spain, to AJJDC-representative Samuel Sequerra,[59] March 24, 1942, USHMMA RG 68.066M (AJJDC Archives, Jerusalem), reel 29, frames 835-36 (translated from French and Spanish).**

Hans Maison   March 24, 1942
Miranda de Ebro Concentration Camp [*Campo de Concentración*]

[in stamped box, in Spanish:]
Received: March 28, 1942
Answered: May 19, 1942

Dr. S. Saquerra [Sequerra]
Barcelona

Dear Sir,

The Jews interned at Miranda whose names we send you on the attached list hereby take the liberty of asking you to put them on the same footing as the other Jews in the camp, concerning your kind efforts with a view to liberation for emigration to a country overseas.

The internee who asked that the questionnaire concerning emigration be filled out some time ago did not address himself to the Jews who are no longer part of the Jewish community, as he did not address half-Jews and baptized Jews. Nonetheless, all of them are subject to the anti-Jewish laws in the same way as the others. Some of them have been interned in the camp for more than 18 months. Almost all have lost their citizenship and are thus without consular protection of any kind.

59. Samuel Sequerra (1913–1992) was the secretary of the Jewish community in Lisbon, one of the points in Europe through which the **AJJDC** ran its relief operations until the United States' entry into the war. In the late summer and early fall of 1941, Sequerra, a Portuguese national, moved to Barcelona as an official representative of the Red Cross, enjoying quasi-diplomatic support provided by the Portuguese consulate. He embarked on running a de facto JDC office in Barcelona, which was, despite frequent raids and other kinds of pressure, tolerated by the Franco regime. In this capacity, he worked on behalf of inmates at Miranda de Ebro. See Yehuda Bauer, *American Jewry and the Holocaust: The American Jewish Joint Distribution Committee, 1939–1945* (Detroit, MI: Wayne State University Press, 1981), 46, 49–50, 209–10, 255–56; Avni, *Spain, the Jews, and Franco*, 79, 99–100, 106, 113–14. See also the article by Nelson Menda on the Sequerra brothers in the Lisbon Jewish Community publication, *Tikvá* 8 (September–October 2007): 18–19: www.cilisboa.org/documents/tikva_08/bu_8_65.pdf (accessed June 19, 2012).

If inclusion on your list for liberation with a view to emigration, whether for individual internees or for internees with families living in Spain, depends on forms, we ask you to kindly have your questionnaire sent to us.

We thank you in advance.

Respectfully yours,

H. J. Naar

H. Fuchs

H. Maison

Read and approved: Hochwald[60]

A list with the names of ten stateless persons followed, as well as five of "various nationalities."

One of the largest groups of displaced Jews whose status seemed most precarious were the more than 250,000 Polish Jews living on Soviet territory not occupied by the Germans. The majority of them had escaped from the advancing Wehrmacht or had been deported by Soviet authorities, together with roughly 1 million non-Jewish Poles, after September 1939 in Stalin's attempt to "cleanse" the USSR's newly acquired Polish territory of potential enemies.[61] After the Soviet regime had become an ally of the West, an agreement was reached with the London-based Polish government-in-exile in August 1941 that Polish army units would be created using men drawn from the roughly two hundred thousand Polish citizens held by the Soviets as POWs since the end of the Polish campaign in October 1939. The units were later referred to as "Anders's Army," after its commander. Supply problems and an arrangement with the British led to the transfer of these units in March 1942 into

---

60. Henry or by then José Henry Naar may have been a Turkish national; the authors have been unable to locate further information about his background or fate. Hermann Fuchs was a Viennese-born Jew (b. 1887) who was sent to Miranda de Ebro in November 1941, a month after his arrest. Freed in April 1943, he continued on to Barcelona, and in November of that year to Lisbon. From there he sailed to Philadelphia. Hans Maison (b. 1893) was a German Jewish architect, possibly declared stateless by this point. A World War I veteran, he had edited an architectural journal in Berlin in the 1920s and early 1930s. Initially interned at Miranda de Ebro on October 31, 1941, Maison left Spain in August 1944. *USHMM ITS Collection Data Base Central Name Index*; USHMMA RG 36.003M; Myra Warhaftig, *Deutsche jüdische Architekten vor und nach 1933* (Berlin: Reimer, 2005), 340. Hochwald was most likely an official of the camp.

61. See Yosef Litvak, "Jewish Refugees from Poland in the USSR, 1939–1946," in *Bitter Legacy: Confronting the Holocaust in the USSR*, ed. Zvi Gitelman (Bloomington: Indiana University Press, 1997), 123–50.

Iran. En route they blended with the refugee population already lodged in the southern part of the Soviet Union. Relief efforts for Jews in the area had to take into account the mistrust between Soviet and Polish authorities, barely glossed over by propaganda images of a joint anti-German campaign, as well as the prejudices held by the Polish and Russian population against Jews.[62] The following document, written in late 1942 by an AJJDC administrator, looks back on events in 1941 and provides a glimpse of how national stereotypes and rivalries worked against Jewish refugees living far beyond the corridors of central Europe. He begins by recounting a conversation with a man he deemed "a well-known Zionist."

DOCUMENT 5-12: Harry Viteles,[63] "Report on visit to Bagdad (2.XI to 9.XI 1942) and to Tehran (11.XI to 2.XII 1942)," Jerusalem, to AJJDC-New York on the situation of Jewish refugees in the southeast of the Soviet Union and across the border into Iran, December 31, 1942, USHMMA RG 68.066M (AJJDC Archives Jerusalem IS/1/6), reel 10, 31–34.

[. . .] Like nearly all the other Jews he lived by selling his clothes and other belongings; they were inspired with the hope by the radio announcement by the Polish Government [in Exile] leaders that the Jews too would be treated justly and the same as non-Jews. But they soon lost hope; discrimination against the Jews was the practice from the outset. He cites [the] following examples:

(1) There was only one Senior Jewish official and he was kept only two months among the 21 [Polish] Delegateurs; 40 District Officers and 25 travelling controllers. There were few Jews among the 200 Distributors, and only in districts where there were no non-Jewish Refugees. (2) Though Jews were in the majority, they received a maximum of 15–20% of the general supplies and cash. He recalled the following two [sic] incidents

---

62. See Keith Sword, "The Welfare of Polish-Jewish Refugees in the USSR, 1941–1943: Relief Supplies and their Distribution," in *Jews in Eastern Poland and the USSR, 1939–1946*, ed. Norman Davies and Antony Polonsky (New York: St. Martin's Press, 1991), 145–60.

63. Harry Viteles (1894–1971), an American "banking manager and general troubleshooter," as Yehuda Bauer describes him, was living in Palestine at this time. He was asked by the New York office of the AJJDC to make the trip to Baghdad and Tehran and explore the condition of Jewish refugees there and the possibilities of bringing them to Palestine. See Bauer, *American Jewry and the Holocaust*, 299; Jay Levinson, *Jewish Community of Cuba: The Golden Age, 1906–1958* (Nashville, TN: Westview, 2006), 58; obituary, *New York Times*, March 3, 1971.

and made a note of the date: (a) 22.4.41 [April 22, 1941]—A Jewish refugee arrived and applied for clothes and assistance. He was given some winter underwear though it was hot and 54 Roubles. A few minutes later a non-Jewish refugee was clothed from head to foot. (3) According to Regulations, every family was to receive 30 Roubles monthly for a child. None of the 20 families in his vicinity received anything, on the excuse that they did not work. (4) Jewish refugees were not given employment in the offices, etc.—even of the most minor character—if non-Jews were available. [. . .] When he left Russia on 25.8.41 [August 25, 1941]— 80% of Jews were without any visible means of support. Many of them had spent their last Rouble to cable to their relatives for assistance. Prices had gone up so much since he left (100 R.[oubles] a kilo [2.2 pounds] bread) so that it will be impossible for 80% of the Jewish refugees to survive the winter unless packages with contents varied according to district were sent.

[. . .] The following extracts from two Polish official sources explain why there were so few Jewish refugees evacuated [to Iran]. In the first extract quoted below, the number of Jews included in the first evacuation is given as 1,500; actually the number of Jews was less than 500.

First quotation

"In April of this year (1942) over 14,000 Polish citizens, together with part of the Polish Army, left Soviet Russia for Iran. Among the emigrants are 1,500 Jews, care of whom has been taken by the local Jewish community in addition to protection by the Polish authorities. Evacuation was not carried out according to any plan; it was rather a disorderly emigration. After the conclusion of the Polish Soviet agreement and after the organization of the Polish Army having been commenced in Southern Russia, masses of Polish citizens travelled from the North to the South. Most of the evacuated population arrived in rags, without shoes and underclothes, dirty, covered with lice, undernourished and exhausted.["]

Second quotation

" . . . that so few Jews among the refugees who were given the opportunity of leaving Russia. He said that this was due to the attitude of the Soviet Government who regarded as Russian citizens all persons coming from those parts of Poland that had been occupied by the Soviet troops after the [1939] agreement with Germany. Almost all the Jewish refugees were from those regions, and when they presented themselves for enlistment in the Polish Army or for passage across the frontier they were told that they were Russian citizens. He said that the Russian authorities seemed to be more anxious to get rid of the Poles, whom they regarded as fascists, then they were to get rid of the Jews." [. . .]

While officially opposed to antisemitic ideology, the Soviet regime was anything but tolerant of the religious traditions and cultural orientation of the Jews within its borders. It criminalized many, sending them to labor camps and subjecting them to terrible living conditions. The Jews living east of the front with Germany would form the largest component of Holocaust survivors in Eurasia after the war ended.[64] During the war they shared the precarious position with a variety of Jewish groups living outside the Reich's direct sphere of influence, yet they resided close enough to have reason to fear being drawn into the vortex of Nazi rule. We now turn to central and southeastern Europe, where since the summer of 1941 more intense persecution and anti-Jewish violence also loomed on the horizon.

---

64. See, e.g., Albert Kaganovitch, "Stalin's Great Power Politics, the Return of Jewish Refugees to Poland, and Continued Migration to Palestine, 1944–1946," *H&GS* 26, no. 1 (2012): 59–94.

CHAPTER 6

In the Grip of
Germany's Allies

I N CENTRAL AND southeastern European countries aligned with the Reich, a mixture of German pressure, domestic interests, and rivalries with their neighbors determined how politicians and elites perceived the "Jewish question" and how they proceeded to answer it. Nazi military successes and the radicalization of the war gave a massive boost to the realization of utopian visions, some deeply rooted in a nineteenth-century history of national aggrandizement at the expense of ethnic minorities. In Romania, Hungary, and Slovakia in particular, Jews were to become, as historian Holly Case put it, "casualties of the war between allies," as the regimes in these countries pursued anti-Jewish policies in close conjunction with their territorial claims.[1] Jewish refugees and other foreign Jews stood out among those who were "unwanted" in these visions, and **Axis** regimes, with the notable exception of Italy, eyed long-disputed or recently acquired areas as particularly desirable places for dumping deportees. As mentioned earlier, a large percentage of the 23,600 Jewish men, women, and children murdered in the city of Kamyanets-Podilsky by German police and SS units in late August 1941 had been deported just weeks before from Transcarpathia (formerly a part of Slovakia), which had come under Hungarian rule in March 1939. Depending on the interests of their ruling elites, other countries in the German camp soon adopted their own anti-Jewish measures as the Reich's policy around a "Final Solution" emerged.

---

1. Holly Case, *Between States: The Transylvanian Question and the European Idea during World War II* (Stanford, CA: Stanford University Press, 2009), 182–86.

ROMANIA AND TRANSNISTRIA

Against the backdrop of the long tradition of antisemitic policies in the country and the determination of its leaders to expand its boundaries, Germany's ally Romania entered the military campaign against the Soviet Union with a similar anti-Jewish agenda that aggravated the violence described in the previous chapters.[2] Already in the first days of the war, before the country's reannexation of Soviet territory and before the beginning of deportations, this radicalization became visible in the city of Iași, which was located in Romania proper (the so-called Regat). The following testimony, recorded a few weeks after the end of the war in Europe, provides both a dramatic account of the murderous events in Iași in late June 1941 and some background on the atmosphere in Romania in the summer of 1941. Immediately following the pogrom in the city, more than four thousand survivors were forced into two trains without water or food, causing the death of at least half of them.[3]

DOCUMENT 6-1: **Testimony and drawing by Amita Grimberg on massacres of Jews in Iași, Romania, June 24, 1945, USHMMA RG 25.051 (WJC Bucharest), Locality Iași, file 3b (translated from Romanian).**

Ana Grimberg[4]

On June 29, 1941, Romanians together with the Germans removed us from our house. They took us to the police station. My fiancé and a brother, age 29,[5] were recruited for forced labor at the firefighters station. They had been told on Saturday to be ready the next day, Sunday, June 29,

---

2. See Radu Ioanid, *The Holocaust in Romania: The Destruction of Jews and Gypsies under the Antonescu Regime, 1940–1944* (Chicago: Ivan R. Dee in association with the USHMM, 2000); Dalia Ofer, "The Holocaust in Transnistria: A Special Case of Genocide," in *The Holocaust in the Soviet Union: Studies and Sources on the Destruction of the Jews in Nazi-Occupied Territories of the USSR, 1941–1945*, ed. Lucjan Dobroszycki and Jeffrey S. Gurock (Armonk, NY: M. E. Sharpe, 1993), 133–54. Jean Ancel published a massive body of documentation in his twelve-volume book *Documents Concerning the Fate of Romanian Jewry during the Holocaust* (New York: Beate Klarsfeld Foundation, 1986).

3. Ioanid, *The Holocaust in Romania*, 63–90.

4. Ana was presumably her nickname. According to a form preceding the document, Amita Grimberg was born in Iași in 1920, to a family of five children. At the time the declaration was written (1945), she was single and working as a seamstress. The authors have been unable to ascertain her later fate.

5. The name of Amita's older brother was Leon Grimberg. The authors were unable to ascertain her fiancé's name and further details on other persons mentioned in the document, unless otherwise noted.

at 5 a.m. in the morning, or they would be in trouble. These criminals, including the Romanians, had known all along what they intended to do to them, but we did not know. So my brother and my fiancé got up to go to the firefighters station. I offered them a cup of tea in the morning, but they refused to have it for fear of arriving late.

I had a younger brother, age 21,[6] who was taken with us to the police station. When we arrived there, the guards and commissars were sitting around, laughing at our pain. Some of them were shouting, "Look, the Kikes" [*Jidani*].[7] They took a gold ring from me. At 11 p.m. in the evening, a command was given that all women with small children should go home. We went home after obtaining free passes. Not everybody received a free pass, but my 21-year-old brother bought one, so he came home. I was waiting for the other brother and my fiancé to return home as well, but I waited in vain.

At 3 o'clock in the afternoon the [air raid] alarm rang; it was a false alarm, but we didn't know that, so we ran to the cellar. There were four Romanians hiding with us there: one bartender with his wife and another one with his sister. At some point, this bartender and the other man began shouting for somebody to call the Germans to kill us. So the Germans came with these Romanian hooligans. They fired guns into the cellar to make us come out from hiding. We were about 50 tenants hiding there. But when my 21-year-old brother got up the stairs to come out, he turned to help mother[8] because she climbed with difficulty. They shot him. He fell near the cellar door. I had no idea what happened to him, because the situation was chaotic. I thought he fell to the ground intentionally, because of the alarm that was still sounding or at the sight of the Germans. But eventually I realized what had happened to him. I lifted him up from there and moved him next to a nearby house. He begged me for water and to bring him a doctor, but from where? They didn't even let me bring him a bit of water, so they pushed me away from him. Mother, sister, and nephew went ahead, but I stayed a little longer near him. These Romanian hooligans, however, came again and shouted for me to move away faster. I left my dying brother there. His blood needs to be avenged.

---

6. Amita's younger brother, David Grimberg.

7. The Romanian term "*Jidan*" ("Kike" in English) has a strong pejorative flavor and is used to denigrate those named in this way.

8. Amita's mother, Frida Grimberg (1885–?), survived the war.

Drawing by Amita Grimberg of the killing of her brother David during the June 1941 massacre.

They put us in the street, hands up in the air, to shoot us. Then they changed their minds. Instead, they took us to the police station to prevent us from seeing what we had been seeing: dead and dying people, transported in garbage carts. We [Amita Grimberg and her remaining family] fell to the ground, just like everybody else there. Automatic guns were brought to our heads. We waited to die and see the end of our lives. We were lying one on top of the other because there was no space left. We heard loud screams of children and mothers. A command was given again, allowing women and children to go home. By the time we arrived home, [my] brother had died. My fiancé and the other brother remained at the police station and I do not know what has happened to them.[9] These two brothers were our support, because we were fatherless from the previous war [World War I].

Two policemen came Monday morning to pick up the body of the brother who had been shot. They put him in the garbage truck and I do not know where they took him. They prohibited us from mourning him, threatening we would have the same fate if we cried for him. I wanted to remove from my brother's pocket a silver watch that he used to carry on him, but they wouldn't let me.

Not only should the Germans be blamed for this, but the Romanians, too. If they had not showed them where the Jews were hiding, they would have not known. Stars had been pinned on to the front of our clothes to distinguish us from the rest of the population, and when Romanians would meet us, they would spit on us and call us "Bolshevik Jews, shop only after 10 a.m.," but even at 10 a.m. we were not allowed to shop many times.[10] [. . .]

Word got around quickly. As one observer reported to the **World Jewish Congress**, the Romanian pogroms stemmed from the regime's desire, given the favorable conditions created by the invasion of the Soviet Union, both to indulge the antisemitic sentiments of parts of the population and make a positive impression upon the Germans, "particularly in light of the antisemitic hate fostered for a number of years."[11]

Once **Operation Barbarossa** had gained ground, Romanian leader Marshal **Ion Antonescu** was determined to lay permanent claim to the provinces of Bessarabia and northern Bukovina, which had been under Soviet

---

9. According to Amita Grimberg's postwar deposition, they died at Podul Iloaiei (a town in Iași county), in circumstances not stated. However, it is known from other sources that the second "death train" left Iași on June 30, 1941, at 6 a.m. with 1,902 Jews on board. Eight hours later, it arrived at Podul Iloaiei, its final destination, where the corpses of 1,194 Jews were unloaded off the train. Anita's brother and fiancé most likely met their end on that train.

10. According to Grimberg's statements elsewhere in the questionnaire, she wore the "Star of David" from August to September 1941. The statement is plausible as the Antonescu regime introduced forced wearing of the star in August 1941 to the Jews throughout Moldova. The application of the law in the Romanian core territory (Regat) was abrogated on September 8, 1941, at the intervention of Nicolae Lupu, one of the leaders of the National Peasants Party, and **Wilhelm Filderman**, leader of the Romanian Federation of Jewish Communities. See Ioanid, *The Holocaust in Romania*, 31–34.

11. Account of the massacre of Iași in June 1941, no date, USHMMA RG 68.045M (WJC Geneva), reel 2.

rule since the summer of 1940. Survivors of the large-scale executions conducted by Romanian and German units during their advance into these two provinces, especially in the major cities of Chişinău (Kishinev) and Cernăuţi (Czernowitz or Chernivtsi), were subsequently rounded up and pushed over the Dniester River into the province of **Transnistria**, which the Germans formally transferred to Romanian control in late August 1941. Between October 1941 and August 1942, Antonescu's regime deported between 125,000 and 145,000 Jews from Bessarabia and Bukovina to ghettos and forced labor camps in Transnistria.[12] Only about one-third of them were still alive in 1943. Up to the summer of 1942, Romanian units had murdered an estimated 280,000 Jews.[13]

Based on hearsay evidence from a German soldier, **Willy Cohn** in distant Breslau described the "fate of the Romanian Jews," remarking "a true butchering [was] taking place there. Gruesome!"[14] In late October 1941, triggered by bomb explosions after the occupation of Odessa, the Black Sea city with the largest Jewish population in the Soviet Union, Romanian units with little German assistance killed nineteen thousand Jews in the city's harbor area. Even in light of the country's history as a stronghold of antisemitic persecution, displayed vividly during the **Iron Guard** pogrom in early 1941 in Bucharest, the Antonescu regime's policy seemed extreme. "In no other country," a World Jewish Congress memo stated in early 1942, "has the persecution and the savage slaughter of Jews reached such an extent as in Romania."[15]

Compared to the situation in the Reich, the ability and willingness of Romanian Jewish leaders to directly appeal to the country's top government officials stood out. In early October 1941, Wilhelm Filderman, head of the

---

12. For a discussion of the number of Jews deported from Bessarabia and Bukovina to Transnistria, see Ioanid, *The Holocaust in Romania*, 170–75.

13. See Dennis Deletant, *Hitler's Forgotten Ally: Ion Antonescu and His Regime, Romania 1940–1944* (New York: Palgrave Macmillan, 2006). Radu Ioanid estimates that "at least 250,000 Jews under Romanian jurisdiction died, either on the explicit orders of Romanian officials or as a result of their criminal barbarity." See Ioanid, *The Holocaust in Romania*, 289. Jean Ancel gives a figure of 310,000; see Jean Ancel, *Transnistria 1941–1942: The Romanian Mass Murder Campaigns* (Tel Aviv: Goldstein-Goren Diaspora Research Center, Tel Aviv University, 2003), 1:531.

14. Willy Cohn, *Kein Recht, Nirgends: Tagebuch vom Untergang des Breslauer Judentums, 1933–1941*, ed. Norbert Conrads (Cologne: Böhlau Verlag, 2006), 2:958 (diary entry for July 22, 1941).

15. Report on the situation of the Jews of Romania, 1942, USHMMA RG 68.045M (WJC Geneva), reel 2, file 9; see also "Chronicles," *Contemporary Jewish Record* 5, no. 1 (February 1942): 93.

Romanian Federation of Jewish Communities, publicly implored Marshal
Antonescu on behalf of the deportees from Bukovina and Bessarabia to stop
this "exodus" because it "would be equal to death, under the circumstances."[16]
The following letter to Antonescu—a copy transmitted by Filderman to the
U.S. Embassy[17]—forms part of a more extensive correspondence between the
key representative of the Romanian Jews and the head of the Romanian regime.
(The two men had in fact been schoolmates as boys.) Filderman's plea attests to
the unusual political constellation in the country, which allowed for a kind of
public, high-level intervention that would have been impossible in Germany,
even before the beginning of the war.[18]

DOCUMENT 6-2: **Letter from Wilhelm Filderman, head of the Romanian Federation of
Jewish Communities, Bucharest, to the Romanian head of state Marshal Ion Antonescu,
no date (late October 1941), in Paul A. Shapiro with contributions by Brewster
Chamberlin and Radu Ioanid,** *The Kishinev Ghetto, 1941–1942: A Documentary
History* **(Tuscaloosa: University of Alabama Press in association with the USHMM,
forthcoming).**

To
Mr. Marshal Ion Antonescu, Leader of the State and
President of the Council of Ministers.
    Translation of Third Letter of Head of
    Jewish Communities to Marshal Antonescu

Federation of the Union of
    Jewish Communities of the
    Country.
    No. 1387.

---

16. Letter of Wilhelm Filderman to Ion Antonescu, October 9, 1941, in Paul A. Shapiro
with contributions by Brewster Chamberlin and Radu Ioanid, *The Kishinev Ghetto, 1941–
1942: A Documentary History*, document translations by Angela Jianu (Tuscaloosa: University
of Alabama Press in association with the USHMM, forthcoming). See also Garbarini et al.,
Jewish Responses to Persecution, 275–81.

17. See USHMMA RG 84 (U.S. Embassy Ankara), File 840.1, Confidential report (no.
2108) by U.S. Embassy Bucharest (Franklin M. Gunther) on "Recent Developments in the
Situation of the Jews in Rumania," November 4, 1941.

18. In general, Jews in the Regat—Romania proper—were less persecuted than those
living in the occupied territories. See Ioanid, *The Holocaust in Romania*, 31–34, 110–15,
128–38.

Mr. Marshal,

CONCERNING:

I. Deportation of Jewish Rumanian citizens
    from Bucovina and Bessarabia.
II. Expulsion from the Old Kingdom of Jewish
    Rumanian citizens, originally of Bucovina
    and Bessarabia.
    A cry of despair, as never before, is heard through the length and
breadth of the land. In the face of the terrible responsibilities I have
assumed, this fact makes me shudder and forces me, in these days of joy
for the country and glory for you, to convey my concerns to you.

I. Deportation of Jewish Rumanian Citizens
    from Bucovina and Bessarabia.
    A few days after the Governor of Bessarabia appealed to us to bring
help to our brothers of that province, an order was issued for the deportation of all Jews from Bessarabia and Bucovina.

The Vice President of the Council, in an audience which I had
on October 14, was kind enough to give his approval that intellectuals, tradesmen, merchants, industrialists, and landlords should not be
deported. At that time he said that he would consider my plea to postpone
the deportation of all Jews until the spring and return the deportees to
their homes with a view of making the selection promised above.

This order was put immediately into execution in Bucovina. In
Bessarabia, however, the order, although apparently sent, was not executed. The Military Command, having no knowledge of this order, sent
off from Chisinau [Kishinev] several transports of deportees, and my
informants say that all those who left with the first transport are strewn
between Orhei and Rezina, and that no information could be obtained
regarding the transports that left on October 14, 16, and 18, except that
at Orhei all the possessions of the deportees were taken away.[19]

Where are they now? Are they still alive or have they suffered the fate
of those who are lying dead between Orhei and Rezina?

What fate awaits those who are due to leave the morning of October
20, 1941, and thereafter? [. . .]

---

19. On the fate of Jews in Czernowitz under German occupation, see Florence Heymann,
Le Crépuscule des Lieux: Identités juives de Czernowitz (Paris: Stock, 2003), 298–356. For
letters from Jews deported to Transnistria to their relatives in Bukovina, mostly Czernowitz,
see USHMMA, RG 31.006M (Chernivtsi State Oblast Archive 1061-1-1 and 2), reel 21.

I trust, Mr. Marshal, that you will understand that what I have stated above has been done with the best intentions and, please believe me, with a pure Rumanian conscience deserving of your special attention.

Please accept the assurance of my respectful consideration.

President,
Dr. W. Filderman

In an earlier response in the form of an open letter, Antonescu assured Filderman of his sensitivity toward "the suffering of humble and defenseless creatures." Yet at the same time—as a rebuke to Filderman's declaration of unflagging allegiance—he unleashed accusations that "the Jews" had communist leanings and engaged in "acts of hatred, of madness" against Romanians. Filderman refuted the accusations of communism and protested against "all the Jews of Rumania [being] held responsible for the deeds of the Jews of Russia."[20]

The widely publicized exchange between the two leaders left Romanian Jews deeply troubled about the future; writer Mihail Sebastian felt "petrified with fear and anxiety."[21] In light of Antonescu's response, he thought anything was possible, recording in his journal, "Tomorrow morning we could be taken from our homes and thrown into ghettos—without this seeming excessive to anyone."[22] Government actions, ranging from the beginning of the deportations in October 1941 to the replacement of Filderman's Federation with a "Jewish Central Office" imposed by the regime in December, to the proclamations by its highest leader, left little doubt that Romanian leaders were eager to follow the German example of using any sign of Jewish opposition as a justification for intensifying anti-Jewish measures. Yet in Romania proper and despite German pressure, Romanian Jews would remain unaffected by deportations until Antonescu's regime decided in October 1942 to back away from the Reich's policy toward the "Jewish question."[23]

Uncertain of what lay ahead, the beleaguered and expropriated Jewish community in Romania proper tried to help the deportees in Transnistria whose

---

20. Shapiro, *The Kishinev Ghetto.*

21. Mihail Sebastian (1907–1945), Romanian author born Iosif Hechter, was a member of a circle of prominent intellectuals that in the 1930s adopted far-right Romanian nationalism. As a Jew, Sebastian became increasingly marginalized from the intellectual scene and bitter about his former friends' fascist allegiances. His diary, covering the years 1935 to 1944, chronicles the worsening plight of the Romanian Jewish population under successively more extremist antisemitic regimes. For biographical details, see Radu Ioanid's introduction in Mihail Sebastian, *Journal, 1935–1944* (Chicago, IL: Ivan R. Dee in association with the USHMM, 2000), vii–xx.

22. Sebastian, *Journal 1935–1944*, 434 (diary entry for October 26, 1941).

23. See Ioanid, *The Holocaust in Romania*, 239–48; Deletant, *Hitler's Forgotten Ally*, 207–10.

condition quickly deteriorated. Funding for community kitchens and shipments of clothing and tools provided some relief but were far from sufficient to prevent, as a report by the Romanian Jewish Aid Committee to the WJC put it, that in the winter of 1941–1942 "people perished in frightening numbers from hunger and cold."[24] In April 1942, the *Contemporary Jewish Record*, a journal published in New York, noted "the unverified and almost incredible claim by the Minister of Jewish Affairs, reported Jan. 11 [1942], that Bessarabia is now completely cleared of its Jewish population of 200,000."[25] In Vapniarka, a camp for Jewish prisoners from Odessa, Bukovina, and Bessarabia, many of those arriving in late 1941 died of malnutrition and typhus by early 1942.[26] In March 1942, before the site was enclosed with barbed wire, three of the roughly 1,200 prisoners escaped. They were later recaptured, and Romanian interrogators recorded all three men as saying that they had fled so as not to die from hunger.[27]

Forced labor added to the misery of the deportees. Yet, not unlike the situation in German-controlled ghettos of occupied Poland and the Soviet Union, in some instances the expectation of economic gain on the part of the regime helped to improve conditions and ensured a level of temporary security. In the Transnistrian city of Mohyliv-Podilskyi, the head of the local Jewish community, Siegfried Jägendorf, who himself had been expelled from Bukovina, managed to convince Romanian authorities of the advantage of using Jewish labor and to establish kitchens and hospitals that helped many thousands of Jews to survive; still, even there, almost one-third of the twelve thousand ghetto residents died in the winter of 1941–1942.[28] In late January 1942 somewhere in Transnistria,

---

24. Report on relief actions for the Romanian Jews deported to Transnistria in 1941 and 1942, no date, USHMMA RG 68.045M, reel 2. On Transnistria, see also Wolfgang Benz and Brigitte Mihok, eds., *Holocaust an der Peripherie. Judenpolitik und Judenmord in Rumänien und Transnistrien 1940–1944* (Berlin: Metropol, 2009).

25. "Chronicles," *Contemporary Jewish Record* 5, no. 2 (April 1942): 197.

26. See Ioanid, *The Holocaust in Romania*, 195–224; Jean Ancel, *The History of the Holocaust in Romania* (Lincoln and Jerusalem: University of Nebraska Press and Yad Vashem, 2011), 315–26. For an in-depth look at the typhus epidemic, see Ancel, *Transnistria*, 1:339–428.

27. USHMMA RG 25.003M, reel 20, folder 1128, quoted from Paul A. Shapiro, "Vapniarka: ITS and the Holocaust in the East," *H&GS* 27 (2013, forthcoming).

28. Siegfried Jägendorf, *Jagendorf's Foundry: Memoir of the Romanian Holocaust* (New York: HarperCollins, 1991). Jägendorf (1885–1970), born in northern Bukovina, had studied engineering in Austria and Germany and served in World War I. Jägendorf, his wife, and their two daughters were deported to Mohyliv-Podilskyi in Transnistria in October 1941, where he directed an operation to fix the city's damaged electrical works. He also established a foundry, which enlisted a large Jewish labor force that would otherwise have faced an uncertain fate. In December 1946 Siegfried and Hilda immigrated to the United States, where he worked for an electrical company in southern California.

young **Nekhama Vaisman** reflected in dramatic terms on the meaning of her fate and that of her parents since their deportation from Bessarabia.

DOCUMENT 6-3: **Nekhama Vaisman, unidentified ghetto in Transnistria, diary entry for January 27, 1942, USHMMA Acc. 2010.264 Nekhama Vaisman diary (translated from Russian).**

January 27, 1942

Tomorrow, the 28th, I'll turn 18. The 17 years I've lived are behind me, full of fire and life, seething and joyful. I was expecting to celebrate my 18th birthday after coming for summer vacation from the institute [i.e., university]. . . . But life has turned around and cruelly lashed out at me. Fate is mocking me, like an old jester. Now I'm sitting at the table, in the faint light of an oil lamp, in a damp room in which water drips from the walls, and snow lies on the ground. This room seems like a palace in comparison with the hovels where the Jews who have been deported from Bukovina and Bessarabia by the flower of contemporary civilization now huddle. Filth, cold, hunger, epidemics. Every day in this small town, we have at least 30–40 and as many as 80 corpses, which, because of the impossibility of digging graves (it's –20 to –30°C. [-4°F to -22°F]), are thrown into the cemetery and freeze on the ground. [. . .] what will happen in the spring! [They] will be food for the dogs. I'm afraid to look at my relatives and acquaintances: they're unrecognizable. My mother and father are emaciated, have grown old.[29] They always called me a child. The only daughter in the family, I lightheartedly had faith in life, and it always tossed the flowers of success to me. I passionately loved my homeland, the embodiment of the ideas of the great son of my people K. M. [Karl Marx], completely failing to notice the injustices and difficulties of the life of the proletariat and peasantry. I completed 10 grades of school and earned respect and honor. With my outstanding abilities, I comprehended everything quickly and with excellent grades, and got a gold medal with my high school diploma. I literally devoured the volumes of our Russian and western classics. Books were my best friends, but I also had many friends. But now I feel that after seven months of war I have become an adult, in the full meaning of the word. And I have come to know grief, hardship, and terror. I have seen a great deal of blood and many tears with

---

29. Vaisman uses several diminutives to refer to her parents: Mama/Mamka/Mamusia; Papa/Papka/Papusia. This translation uses "Mama" and "Papa" throughout.

my own eyes. My hopes have collapsed like a house of cards. And although my faith in the future, in a better future, is alive and intact, like a sacred thing, will I live to see it? Will some fraction of the persecuted Jewish people live? I do not know. It is not without reason that my dear mama says that I've aged five years. I still want so much to live and survive! But along the streets walk living corpses, covered with lice, miserable, unfortunate people. And alongside them are robbers, oppressors, people who have plundered, who have destroyed people and burned their corpses before my eyes. People who are animals that buried small children alive. Papa is groaning. In the damp, his rheumatism has flared up again and made all his bones ache. He is suffering, there are no earnings, and he has become nervous and irritable. Mama is calling me. I have to help, I'm stopping now.

The fact that in the spring of 1942 conditions in the Transnistrian towns and villages had hardly improved can be taken from the diary of eighteen-year-old **Mirjam Korber**. Born in Bukovina, she and her family were deported on October 20, 1941, to the town of Djurin in Transnistria. The Korbers had been comparatively well off and thus were able to bring some money along. This gave them a massive advantage over those who reached Transnistria already in a state of destitution, yet the family's descent into poverty was just a question of time. Looking back on the months since her arrival in Djurin, Mirjam described the changes she and her family had experienced and wondered what the future would hold.

DOCUMENT 6-4: **Mirjam Korber, Djurin, Transnistria, diary entries for February to May 1942, USHMMA Acc. 2010.93.1 Mirjam Korber Bercovici collection (translated from Romanian).**

[Monday, February 16, 1942]

My grandparents have died. They died one after the other in Mogilev [today Mohyliv-Podilskyi in Ukraine], my grandfather on January 3, my grandmother four weeks later. On Saturday we received the sad news of their death. My mother read the letter first, I watched her, and I could already tell everything from her face. Father, poor man, bore the blow of fate more bravely than I expected. He wept inwardly, and mourns in his heart. He, the only son, does his duty by saying kaddish every day. A few tears ran down my cheeks as well, and my heart shrank when I thought about their sad death. I weep for them not because they have died, for death is everyone's fate, and they lived full lives for 80 years. I weep for them only because they died in Mogilev, far from their home, from their nice, clean bed, from the fruits of their long years of work, which they had to leave behind. [. . .] I remember my grandparents with love and sadness. What became of their lives? What did they work for? For what sins did they have to die so alone? For what sins, whose sins, did they have to atone? Their sins were not so great as to require such a harsh atonement. Working all the time, thinking and honoring God ceaselessly, and yet, like other people who were better or worse than them, they died, and who knows when and how their children will visit them and honor them as they deserve. I weep for you, dear grandparents. You no longer have any sins, you atoned for them in the last weeks of your lives, you more than atoned for them. Perhaps, if there is a life after death, we'll meet each other sooner or later, and then I'll continue to be what I was for you until now, your Mimi, your dear granddaughter. Sleep easy and pray for us, if the prayers of the dead are of value where our fate is concerned. [. . .]

[Thursday, March 19, 1942]

It's 7 in the morning. Father gets up early to look for a place where he can say Kaddish, because that, too, has become difficult. It has been pro-hibited in the synagogue because of diseases, and they don't want people to gather there now on that account. That's why we're awake early, too, not because we sleep soundly at night, but it's so pleasant to lie there with one's eyes closed. Millions of thoughts, beloved landscapes, and moments from the past follow automatically in quick succession, and so time passes faster and more comfortably than with open eyes. [. . .] The days pass, one like the other, no change. What are we waiting for? What can save us? We lie to ourselves, saying that spring may bring us the long-desired turn-ing point. But who knows what spring will bring us? Oh, you wandering Jew, continue on your way! You're not a human being, you're a Jew. This mark is deeper than the mark of Cain. Like him, you can find no rest in this world. Everyone knows your destiny and drives you onward.

[. . .]

[Saturday, May 2, 1942]

[. . .] Yesterday I read a good book, good for home, too, not only for Djurin; it was "Amok" by Stefan Zweig.[30] How fine it would have been

---

30. *Amok* is a novella by **Stefan Zweig**, first serialized in 1922 in the Viennese newspaper *Neue Freie Presse*. The novella recounts an obsession of a German physician with a white English woman in Indonesia, and his confessions to the narrator on board an ocean liner en route to Europe from Australia. It may be more than a coincidence that Mirjam Korber refers to a "colony" several sentences down in her diary entry.

to read it at home, lying on the sofa, by the light of an incandescent bulb rather than a kerosene lamp, and not on this hard bed with the straw mattress. But I ought to be quiet, because it's a billion times worse for other people, people who have nowhere to sleep, who are dying without anybody's learning of their death. If we go back home someday, there won't even be 40 percent of the people who were evacuated, because typhus and starvation are devastating the ranks of the deportees. We were named the "Jewish colony in Transnistria." Yes, we're colonists with no land and no house. We colonize the air, falling prey to illness and hunger. I'd like to have a boyfriend, too (or rather, headaches like Lida, who has Mr. Kiwa or Iboy);[31] it would be much better and much easier. But since I left home, I haven't been able to think of a boy as anything other than a companion who is supposed to carry the baggage. On the other hand, nobody is thinking about me and nobody is interested in me, because it seems as if my sex appeal was forfeited on the day we crossed the Dniester.

HUNGARY, SLOVAKIA, AND FORMER YUGOSLAVIA

Like Romania, Hungary pursued its own discriminatory policy. It targeted not only Jews in annexed Carpatho-Ukraine, but also Jewish men of military age living in Hungary proper. The latter group was drafted into special units of the Hungarian army deployed along the Eastern front for construction work and other hard labor. Lack of food and medical care in combination with deliberate abuse by Hungarian officers resulted in many deaths.[32] The following **Jewish Telegraphic Agency** press release points to the conditions of Jews forced into the Hungarian labor battalions as reported at the time. Seen from our vantage point, the news item—reported from the Soviet Union—vastly overstates these units' destructive character, both in terms of numbers (the overall casualties before 1944 are now estimated at forty-two thousand)[33] and with regard to later, even more deadly persecution: after the German occupation of Hungary

---

31. The authors have been unable to identify these people (they are not characters from Zweig's novel).

32. On Hungarian Jewish labor battalions, see Randolph Braham, *The Hungarian Labor Service System, 1939–1945* (Boulder, CO: East European Quarterly, 1977). See also Zoltán Vági, László Csősz, and Gábor Kádár, *The Holocaust in Hungary: Evolution of a Genocide* (Lanham, MD: AltaMira Press in association with the USHMM, forthcoming 2013).

33. László Varga, "The Losses of Hungarian Jewry: A Contribution to the Statistical Overview," in *Studies on the Holocaust in Hungary: Evolution of a Genocide*, ed. Randolph Braham (Boulder, CO: Social Science Monographs, 1990), 260.

in March 1944, many Jewish members of labor battalions in fact escaped deportation to **Auschwitz**. But within the distorted overall picture painted by the article we can discern the fate of individuals who would otherwise have remained anonymous.

DOCUMENT 6-5: "240,000 Hungarian Jews Driven to Death at Forced Labor for Nazis on Russian Front," *Jewish Telegraphic Agency*, November 11, 1942.

MOSCOW, Nov. 10 (JTA)—

About a quarter of a million Hungarian Jews have been driven to the Ukraine for forced labor with the Hungarian and Nazi armies since the outbreak of the Russo-German war, it was revealed today by Soviet military authorities on the basis of information reaching them from captured prisoners and intelligence reports.

The majority of the Jews who were pressed into service at various sectors of the front were killed by the Hungarians and the Germans as soon as they had completed the tasks assigned to them, in accordance with orders from Heinrich Himmler, chief of the Gestapo, the prisoners disclosed. The Hungarian Jews were used to build roads, construct fortifications, lay mines and clear out Russian mines, the Soviet military authorities state. Frequently they were compelled to work at the most advanced sectors of the front directly under fire from Russian artillery. Last summer, during the Nazi advance to the Don, thousands of these Jewish prisoners were used to construct the German fortifications along the river bank.

In appearance the Jewish laborers look like anything but soldiers, the Russian military officials assert. They are unarmed and dressed in rags. One of the Jews, Laslo Gutman, who recently fled to the Russian lines, reported that he was drafted for forced labor in March, 1942 and assigned to a labor battalion. About a month ago his unit was attached to a Hungarian infantry regiment. The entire Jewish battalion, comprising about 330 men, was doomed to be executed as soon as its work on the roads and fortifications was finished, but Gutman escaped before the construction was completed.

Another Jew who escaped to Russian-held territory, Ferenc Hedvigi, a young electrical engineer, told the Russians that the laborers were governed not by military regulations but by prison rules. When his group arrived at Kursk[,] military police searched all the Jews and confiscated all their money, food, soap, cigarettes and any articles of clothing they wanted, Hedvigi said. "We were not surprised at such treatment," he added, "since we were accustomed to that sort of thing. The commander of the company, Lieut. Tot Szandor, instructed guards to 'beat the Jews and make them work until they are dead. The fewer of them that return home the better.'"[34]

High up on the list of the "unwanted" in central and southeastern European dictatorships were Jews "acquired" when these countries expanded their territory. Few sources from the time provide a record of what happened to Jews from Transcarpathia, whom Hungarians forced over the border with Ukraine. The following account describes an episode in a part of Galicia administered by the Germans as part of the **Generalgouvernement**. There, a large group of these deportees became the object of a macabre joke. It may have led to wholesale murder had it not been for the courageous intervention of the local Jewish doctor, Baruch Milch.[35]

DOCUMENT 6-6: Baruch Milch, Tłuste, Galicia district, Generalgouvernement, diary entries written July/August 1943 on the persecution of Hungarian deportees in the second half of 1941, USHMMA RG 02.208M (ŻIH 302/98) (translated from Polish).[36]

[. . .] These condemned persons [Jewish deportees from Hungarian-occupied Transcarpathia] were torn from their homes with harsh ruthlessness and guile and driven to Ukraine on trucks along the path of Hungarian forces advancing along the eastern front. Some were taken

---

34. The authors have been unable to find further information on the fate of Laslo Gutman and Ferenc Hedvigi.

35. Baruch Milch (1907–1989) grew up in the Galician town of Podhajce and studied medicine in Prague. He was involved with the Zionist youth movement and worked as a doctor in his hometown, since late 1940 in nearby Tłuste, then occupied by the Soviet Union. Following the German invasion of Galicia, he became a member of the local *Judenrat* until the end of 1941. His son was killed in a German "Aktion" in May 1943, and Ukrainians murdered his wife shortly thereafter. Milch wrote his memoir account in July and August 1943 while in hiding; in 1946 he submitted it to the Jewish Historical Commission in Poland before he left for Israel, where he settled in 1948. Parts of his memoir account have been published in Polish in Baruch Milch, with Archiwum Żydowskiego Instytutu Historycznego, *Testament* (Warsaw: Ośrodek Karta, 2001). The Hebrew edition is Barukh Milkh, *Ve-ulai ha-shamayim rekim*, ed. Shosh Milch-Avigal (Tel Aviv: Yediot Aharonot, 1999), which was translated into English as Baruch Milch, *Can Heaven Be Void?*, ed. Shosh Milch-Avigal (Jerusalem: Yad Vashem, 2003).

36. The changes in tense here appear in the original.

from their jobs during the day, others were awoken from their sleep during the night and immediately loaded into cars. Some were allowed to take with [them] the most important [items], and others were not. Some were told that they were only being taken to be registered; a second group was told that they were being interned in *lagers* for a short time; a third group that they were being resettled to other areas of Hungary; and a fourth group that they were being taken to Ukraine, where housing and farmsteads had been prepared for them, as cities and villages had been deserted and emptied due to the Soviets' removal of the population.

Thus were they lied to and mystified, and in the end they were completely destroyed. It was a terrible sight how for two weeks in a row, groups of trucks, 5 to 10 cars together, loaded full of Jews, the elderly, cripples, women, and small children, were driven day and night under escort from the military or the Hungarian police in white gloves and comical outfits, in hats with long feathers tucked in. They were left to their fate in little towns and villages on the other side of the Dniester starting all the way from Kamieniec Podolski [Polish spelling for Kamyanets-Podilsky]. Sometimes they were dumped from the trucks in some woods or in a field, from where they made their way in entire waves to the nearest small towns. Often the Hungarian soldiers themselves robbed them of everything they had, but they were tormented the worst by Ukrainian peasants, who lurked everywhere, on roads and in fields, in entire bands, mercilessly attacking, robbing, and killing them.

Many of them, immediately after being let out of the trucks, realized what was happening and tried to cross back to the other side of the Dniester in order somehow to be able to return home, but a notorious Hungarian officer with the last name of Simon stood on the bridge, a young snot, supposedly the son of some count or prince, who often arranged with these people that for a certain sum of money he would let them through, but when they arrived at the bridge, he robbed them of everything they had, threw them naked into the river, and shot at them. Far from the bridge, all along the banks of the river, bands of Ukrainians wandered doing the same thing, but in a still crueler way so that for a rather lengthy period of time the water of the Dniester was pink from blood and Jewish corpses floated on it like dead fish.

One time, a wagon came for me from the neighboring village [Sicz], four kilometers [2.4 miles] away, and requested that I go see a sick peasant woman there. Although the times were very uncertain, I left immediately, as God forbid I might deny medical help to a Ukrainian. Prior to entering the village, I noticed from far away a mass of people gathered on one square and I heard loud screaming and, from time to time, shots. It was already too late to go back, and when I entered, a boy from the village runs up to the wagon, to the man who had driven me there, a very dangerous man, and tells him that the Hungarian Jews have attacked the village and want to murder them. He answers that he'll show them right away, as he has a machine gun and hand grenades at home. I said to him that there must be some misunderstanding and, appealing also to his reason and conscience as well, that he should abstain from spilling blood, and I set out, after examining the sick woman, to clarify the situation.

[. . .]

On one side of the open square stood about 300 Hungarian Jews—women, the elderly, and children with bundles. A corpse, over which a young woman—the wife of the murdered man, as I later learned, was mourning, already lay in front of them, and the wounds of others—men and a woman—were being treated in primitive fashion next to them. On the other side, a little behind a fence, there stood a considerably smaller number of village peasants—since thirty-some people lived in the entire village—with scythes, rakes, axes, and other bandit's tools, and a few had rifles and hand grenades. Suddenly, a few Ukrainian residents of Sicz also arrived from the city with arms and wanted to do formal battle with these unarmed, unfortunate people.

I, feeling somewhat safe, since I had a sick woman next to me and, as the doctor of Sicz and an acquaintance of these villagers, I expected some respect, drove my wagon between the one group and the other, I stood on my wagon and, speaking to one group in German and the other in Ukrainian, I got them to agree and I forbade any further shedding of blood. I worked for almost 3 hours, addressing and trying to convince the one group like the other, sweat was streaming down my face, and I didn't leave that spot until I separated them.

The issue was that the Magyars had dumped a dozen Jews from the trucks in this village, telling them that "this village has been designated for them and these fields and homes will be theirs," and left, laughing into their fists. These Jews entered some homes, realized that people were already living there, and understood immediately that they had been deceived. Because it was harvest time, the houses were mostly full of women and children. They asked for water and a piece of bread, but since they didn't know the local language, they could not make themselves understood, so they perhaps allowed themselves to take some things. Thus arose the misunderstanding that the Jews attacked them.

Later they wanted to go to our little town, i.e., the nearest one, yet Sicz did not want to let them in and a misunderstanding arose once again, but what was worst was that the ignorant mob immediately wanted to exploit the situation for plunder and murder. I was at great risk then, but I was able to steer them to the nearest estate, and this under the escort of a few acquaintances from Sicz, who were paid. They [the Jews] spent the night there and later scattered in all directions. I took two wagons of things that they could not carry and gave them to the *Judenrat*; later some of them claimed ownership of them. [. . .]

In our little town [Tłuste], which numbered about 4,000 residents, there were more than 5,000 Hungarian Jews. That is why there was nowhere to place them, so they lived in basements, attics, synagogues, stables, chambers, and outdoors. More and more new waves of Jews arrived by foot because they had typically been released from the trucks outside the city, so the Ukrainian authorities ordered that they be driven farther. It was a terrible sight, the passing trucks carrying these crying, decrepit, unfortunate people, but even worse were the images of people driven on foot through Ukrainian Sicz who were not given the slightest moment in the city to stop and refresh their bodies. They were beaten and robbed of everything they had, and they were hounded from place to place in such a way that the Germans got involved and made of them a Caesarian section [meaning a mass execution].

Milch's account shows that the determination to help others who were worse off—despite the high risks—was not restricted to Jewish leaders at the top, such as Wilhelm Filderman. Motivated by a range of reasons, across the region Jews from all walks of life counteracted the atomizing effects of persecution on communal life by lending support to one another in word or in deed. Doing so also provided a powerful counterforce against despair, even if the measures amounted to little. In German-occupied Serbia, after the execution of almost all male Jews in the country during the second half of 1941 as part of the German "reprisal" campaign, roughly five thousand Jewish women, children, and elderly remained behind. In early December 1941, the survivors from Belgrade were deported along with the city's remaining "gypsies" to the newly established *Judenlager Semlin* (German, literally, "Jew camp Zemun"; Sajmište in Serbian) on the ill-equipped former fair grounds near Zemun, across the Sava River.[37] Here, beginning in March 1942, the **Security Police** and **SD** murdered most of them using a gas van imported for that purpose from Germany. About a thousand more fell victim to the inhumane conditions at the camp, while the "gypsies" were released.[38]

Hilda Dajč was born in 1922 in Belgrade, the daughter of a well-to-do father who after the German occupation of Serbia became vice president of the German-controlled "Vertretung der Jüdischen Gemeinschaft," the representative body of the Jewish Community in Belgrade. The family thus felt protected from the arrests and killing of Jewish men that marked German policy in the area. While exempt from deportation due to her father's position, at the end of 1941 Hilda defied her parents' wish to stay with them and volunteered to go to the *Judenlager Semlin* to help nurse the sick. As she explained to a friend, "there are so many people in need of help that my conscience dictates to me that I should ignore any sentimental reasons connected with my home and family for not going and put myself wholly at the service of others." The detailed letters printed here convey her first impressions of camp life after her arrival in "Pavilion no. 3" at the Sajmište camp.

---

37. The camp was built specifically to house the Jews of Belgrade and Serbia remaining after the shooting of thousands of male Jews as hostages in the fall of 1941. It was located on the left bank of the Sava River, across from Belgrade's central Terazije Square, from which it was fully visible. The name *Semlin* derives from the German name for the town of Zemun, a former frontier town in Austria-Hungary. During World War II, Zemun was technically incorporated into the Independent State of Croatia, but jurisdiction over the camp remained German, and collaborationist authorities in Belgrade provisioned the camp. Today Zemun is one of Belgrade's municipal counties and fully integrated into the city. For the history of the German murder of Serbian Jews, see Christopher R. Browning, "Wehrmacht Reprisal Policy and the Murder of the Male Jews in Serbia" and "The Semlin Gas Van and the Final Solution in Serbia," in *Fateful Months: Essays on the Emergence of the Final Solution*, ed. Christopher R. Browning (New York: Holmes & Meier, 1985), 39–56, 68–85.

38. For a full history of the camp and the trajectories of postwar memory, see Jovan Bajford (Jovan Byford), *Staro sajmište: Mesto sećanja, zaborava i sporenja* (Belgrade: Beogradski centar za ljudska prava and Heinrich Böll Stiftung, 2012); Dalia Ofer and Hannah Weiner, *Dead-end Journey: The Tragic Story of the Kladovo-Šabac Group* (Lanham, MD: University Press of America, 1996), 164–68; Christopher R. Browning with contributions by Jürgen Matthäus, *The Origins of the Final Solution: The Evolution of Nazi Jewish Policy, September 1939–March 1942* (Lincoln and Jerusalem: University of Nebraska Press and Yad Vashem, 2004), 421–23.

DOCUMENT 6-7: **Letters from Hilda Dajč, Judenlager Semlin near Belgrade, Serbia, to Mirjana Petrović in Belgrade, December 9, 1941 and early 1942, USHMMA RG 49.007, reel 5, file 2, and Historical Archives of Belgrade, IAB, 1883, 3126/ II-XXIX-1122 (translated from Serbian).**[39]

[December 9, 1941]

My dear Mirjana,

I'm writing to you from the idyllic surroundings of a cowshed, lying on straw, while above me, instead of the starry sky, stretches the wooden roof construction of Pavilion No. 3 [a barrack in the Semlin camp]. From my gallery (the third), which consists of a layer of planks and holds three of us, and on which we each have an 80 cm. [31.5 inches] wide living space, I am gazing down on this labyrinth, or rather this ant heap of wretched people whose tragedies are as widespread as those who live, not because they think that one day things will be better but because they haven't got the strength to end it all. If indeed that is the case. [. . .]

Dear Mirjana, there are now 2,000 women and children here, including nearly a hundred babies for whom we can't boil any milk because there's no fuel and you can imagine what the temperature is towards the top of the pavilion with the *košava* [a cold southeasternly wind in Serbia and the eastern Balkans] blowing as hard as it does. I'm reading Heine and that does me good, even though the latrine is half a kilometer [0.3 miles] away and fifteen of us go at the same time, and even though by four o'clock we've only been given a bit of cabbage which has obviously been boiled in water, and even though I have only a little straw to lie on, and there are children everywhere and the light is on all night, and even though they shout "*idiotische Saubande*" [German; "stupid bunch of pigs"] and so on all the time, and even though they keep on having roll calls and anyone missing these is "severely punished." There are walls everywhere. Today I started to work in the surgery, which consists of a table with a few bottles and some gauze, behind which there is just one doctor, one pharmacist, and me. There's a lot to do, believe me—with women fainting and goodness knows what else. But in most cases they put up with it all more than heroically. There are very rarely any tears. Especially among the young people. The only thing I really miss is the possibility of washing myself adequately. Another 2,500 people are due to

---

39. This document was written in Cyrillic script.

arrive and we only have two washbasins, meaning two taps. Things will gradually sort themselves out—I have no doubt about that. The hospital will be in another pavilion. They frequently count us, and for the same reason the pavilions are surrounded by barbed wire. I don't regret coming here at all—in fact I'm very satisfied with my decision. If every couple of days I can do as much as I've done these first two, then the whole thing will begin to have some point. I know, in fact, I'm absolutely convinced that all this will pass (which doesn't exclude the possibility that it will last several months) and that it will all end well, and I feel good about this in advance. Every day I meet lots of new people and gain new experience—I get to know people as they really are (there are very few here who put on an act). Many of them are taken in as some sort of "commanding officers" [most likely to mean prisoners with supervisory authority]. Even though I would be up to this, it isn't for me—my ambitions don't point in that direction. My dear Mirjana, you'll still be able to recognize me—I won't change—it is only now that I realize from my presence of mind that I am strong enough not to let external things affect me. All I want is for my parents to be spared all this. [. . .]

[Signed] your Hilda

[not dated (probably early February 1942)]
My dear,

I could never have imagined that our meeting, even though I was expecting it, would arouse in me such a flurry of emotion and create even more unrest in my already frenzied soul which simply won't calm down. All philosophizing ends at the barbed-wire fence, and reality, which, far away on the other side you can't even imagine or else you would howl with pain, faces one in its totality. That reality is unsurpassable, our immense misery; every phrase describing the strength of the soul is dispersed by tears of hunger and cold; all hope of leaving here soon disappears before the monotonous perspective of passive existence, which, whatever you compare it with, bears no resemblance to life. It is not even life's irony. It is its profoundest tragedy. We are able to keep going, not because we're strong, but because we are simply not conscious all the time of the eternal misery that surrounds us—everything that makes up our life.

We have been here for almost nine weeks and I am still quite literate—I can still think a little. Every evening, without exception, I read your and Nada's letters and this is the only moment when I am something else, not just a *Lagerinsasse* [German for camp inmate]. Hard labor is golden compared with this; we don't know why—on what charge—we've been convicted, nor how long we'll be here. Everything in the world is wonderful, even the most miserable existence outside the camp, while this is the incarnation of every evil that exists. We are all becoming evil because we're starving—we're all becoming cynical and count everyone else's mouthfuls—everyone is desperate—but in spite of this, no one kills anyone because we're all just a bunch of animals that I despise. I hate every single one of us because we've all fallen as low as we can go.

We are so near the outside world, yet so far from everyone. We have no contact with anyone; the life of every individual out there carries on as usual, as if half a kilometer away [from Belgrade] a slaughterhouse containing six thousand innocent people doesn't exist. Both you and we are equal in our cowardice. Enough of everything!

Even so, I'm not the anti-hero you might think I am from what I'm saying. I put up with everything that's happening to me calmly and painlessly. But the people around me. That's what upsets me. It's the people that get on my nerves. Not the hunger that makes you weep, not the cold that freezes the water in your glass and the blood in your veins, nor the stench of the latrines, nor the *košava* wind—nothing is so repulsive as the crowd of people who deserve to be pitied, but who you are unable to help and can do nothing else but put yourself above them and despise them. Why do all these people talk about nothing else other than what is offending their bellies [*sic*, meaning they only think of food] and all the other organs of their so highly esteemed cadavers. A propos, a couple of days ago we were laying out the dead bodies—there were 27 of them—in the Turkish pavilion, right at the front. I don't find anything repulsive anymore, not even my filthy work. Everything would be possible if only we could know what can never be known—when the gates of compassion will be opened. What do they intend to do with us? We are in a continual state of tension: are they going to shoot us, blow us up, transport us to Poland . . . ? All that is of secondary importance! We just have to get through the present, which is not pleasant in the least—not in the least. [. . .]

You don't know, just as I didn't know, what it's like to be here. I hope you will never find out. Way back when I was a child I was afraid they would bury me alive. And now this is some sort of vision of death. Will there be some sort of resurrection? I've never thought so much about the two of you as I do now. I continually talk with you and yearn to see you, because to me you are that "paradise lost."

Love from your camp inmate

Hilda Dajč was murdered less than half a year later in a gas van brought to Zemun for the purpose of killing close to seven thousand Jewish women, children, and elderly in the camp.

For Jews in Slovakia, a country that had become independent in 1939 following the dismemberment of Czechoslovakia by the Nazis, conditions had deteriorated massively in early 1942. Since August 1940, SS-Captain Dieter Wisliceny, a close associate of **Adolf Eichmann** within the **RSHA**, acted as "Adviser for Jewish Affairs" at the German diplomatic legation in the Slovak capital, Bratislava.[40] In October 1941, **Himmler** had offered the Slovak head of state, Catholic priest Dr. Jozef Tiso, to help deport the country's roughly ninety thousand Jews to the Generalgouvernement. Shortly thereafter, Tiso's regime began a new discriminatory push, "dislocating" six thousand people, or roughly half of Bratislava's Jewish population, from the capital to smaller cities and the newly created labor camps in Nováky, Sereď, and Vyhne. When in February 1942 the German Foreign Office asked Tiso's government on behalf of the RSHA to deport twenty thousand "young, healthy Slovak Jews," the Slovak authorities, according to German sources, "eagerly took up this suggestion" and even agreed to pay RM 500 for the "accommodation, provisioning, clothing and retraining" of each deportee.[41]

Slovak Jews witnessed the tightening of measures after the turn of 1941 to 1942 firsthand, but even their leaders had little idea of what lay ahead. Rabbi **Abraham Frieder** noted in his diary that the new year brought "a whole range of laws, regulations, and announcements" restricting Jewish life in the country; the capital Bratislava was turning into "a very gloomy city with frequent anti-Jewish demonstrations, all of which ending in brawls or destructions and defilements of synagogues."[42] In late February, the specter of deportation haunting other communities across Europe began to take on a real form here, too. Frieder learned from Sala Gross—a leading functionary in the Nazi-inspired umbrella organization created by the regime, the "Jewish Center" (Ústredňa Židov, ÚŽ)—about far-reaching, yet unspecified, plans developed in the Slovak Interior Ministry. Gross might have known more but refused to share his insights, since he opposed Frieder's pro-Zionist stance. What followed were desperate attempts by Frieder and his associates, the core of what would emerge

---

40. Hans Safrian, *Eichmann's Men* (New York: Cambridge University Press in association with the USHMM, 2010), 142–44.

41. Raul Hilberg, *The Destruction of the European Jews*, 3rd ed. (New Haven, CT: Yale University Press, 2003), 2:766–86.

42. Rabbi Abraham Frieder, Nové Mesto (Slovakia), diary entries for January to March, 1942, YVA RG M5.193, 1, 7.

as the Slovak Jewish "Working Group,"[43] to fathom the depths of the regime's commitment to anti-Jewish measures.

DOCUMENT 6-8: Rabbi Abraham Frieder, Nové Mesto, Slovakia, diary entries for February 1942, USHMMA Acc. 2008.286.1 Frieder collection (translated from German).

[. . .] Meanwhile, several anxious days elapsed. Then, on the night of February 25, 1942, that is, around 2 a.m. Wednesday morning, there was loud knocking at the front door of our apartment building. We heard nothing, but my housekeeper, Mrs. Elze [Else?] Herzog, went to open the big door. Ludewit Tauber and Heinz Tauber had come to call on me;[44] the latter was sent with instructions to see me and inform me that I should come to Bratislava immediately, for there was very serious talk of a plan to deport Jews to Poland. Thus: an expulsion of the Jews in the twentieth century, analogous to the forced displacements of Jews in the Middle Ages and modern era. Heinz Tauber had nothing to add, as he was only delivering the message and traveling on to Trenčin, on the same mission. I took the first train to Bratislava. In the meantime there was also a telephone call for me, but I was already on my way. I went to the UŽ [Ústredňa Židov, the regime-appointed "Jewish Center"], where a room was made available for a meeting. When I arrived, I found the following already assembled there: from the Orthodox Jews, that is, representing the Orthodox Bureau, Rafael Levi from Bardejov,[45] Arnold Kämpfner from Bratislava, Salomon

---

43. Gila Fatran, "The 'Working Group,'" *H&GS* 8, no. 2 (1994): 164–201.

44. The authors have been unable to find information about these individuals.

45. Rafael Levi (also Löwi/Lowy; 1886–1944) was a merchant and president of the Orthodox Jewish Community in Bardejov, Slovakia. Levi intervened with the Bardejov public health department to have a typhus epidemic (falsely) declared, which allowed many Jews marked for deportation to flee to Hungary or otherwise go into hiding. In conjunction with the Slovak uprising in 1944, Levi was captured by the **Hlinka Guard** and deported to Auschwitz, where he was murdered. For further information on Levi and the other people mentioned in this document see Fatran, "The 'Working Group'"; Emanuel Frieder, *To Deliver Their Souls: The Struggle of a Young Rabbi during the Holocaust* (New York: Holocaust Library, 1991); Joan Campion, *In the Lion's Mouth: Gisi Fleischmann and the Jewish Fight for Survival* (Lanham, MD: University Press of America, 1987); Abraham Fuchs, *The Unheeded Cry* (New York: Mesorah Publications, 1984).

Gross and Geley from Topolčany, and Weiss from Nitra;[46] representing the Neolog congregations [liberal Yeshurun group], Dr. V. Winterstein, Dr. Kondor, and Dr. O. Neumann;[47] and non-affiliated persons such as Dr. Fleischhacker, Dr. Tibor Kováč, and the architect Ondrej Steiner.[48]

Dr. Winterstein was the actual chairman; that is, it was he who kept the discussion moving. He reported that there was a plan in existence requiring all Jews to leave the territory of Slovakia. The 14th Department had been established in the Ministry of the Interior for that purpose. It is supposed to collect statistics on all Jews and then proceed according to a certain schedule. First the young people, that is, our children, are to go, and then the adults, that is, the families, until all the Jews have been deported. No exceptions will be made; everyone must go.

---

46. Arnold Kämpfner from Bratislava headed the Social Department of the Jewish Center in 1940–1941. Salomon (Shlomo) Gross (1884–1944) of Trnava headed the Work and Construction Department of the Jewish Center. He entered into negotiations with SS Captain Wisliceny to find Slovak Jews a route to Spain for a large sum of money. When the negotiations failed, Gross feared retribution and fled with his family to Budapest. He was caught in Budapest and deported to Auschwitz, where he was killed.

47. Vojtech (Adalbert) Winterstein (1903–1970) was a Zionist and general secretary of the Jewish Center. He was arrested and deported from Sereď to **Theresienstadt**, later to Auschwitz, where he was liberated in January 1945. He immigrated to Brazil and served as the director of the Brazilian section of the WJC. Arpad Kondor (1885–1944) was Deputy Jewish Elder of the Yeshurun congregation and a member of the Jewish Center in Bratislava. He fled to Budapest when the deportations began, but was killed during the German occupation of Hungary in 1944. Oskar (Jirmiyahu) Neumann (1894–1981), the prewar chairman of the Zionist Organization of Slovakia, was appointed head of the Jewish Center from late 1943 to September 1944, after which the Center was dissolved. His efforts were crucial for the Working Group for he aligned the interests of the organizations involved and mobilized the Jewish Center's resources.

48. Tibor Kováč (also Kovács; 1905–1952) was a member of both the Jewish Center and the Working Group. In 1942, during the height of the deportations, Kováč worked in the Jewish Council's Appeals Department, set up to handle appeals of Jews who received deportation summons but had paperwork stating they were exempt. Kováč was tipped off before his planned arrest in October 1944 and went into hiding. He remained in Czechoslovakia after the war and was the main witness for the prosecution during Anton Vašek's trial for crimes committed as director of the Slovak government's Jewish Affairs Bureau. Ondrej Steiner (also Andrej, later Andrew) (1908–2009), an architect who headed the Labor and Construction Department of the Jewish Center, was instrumental in establishing a work training camp for Jews in Sereď, which helped many to avoid deportation. After the German suppression of the Slovak revolt in late 1944, Steiner fled to the Tatra Mountains with his wife and son. He survived the war and headed a rehabilitation center for Jewish children. In 1948 Steiner traveled to Cuba, and in 1950 he and his family immigrated to the United States.

We were speechless, and dread and bewilderment were evident on every face. GERUSH GZERA [Hebrew, "deportation decree"], those were the words, the specters. We were aware of what it must mean to be sent to this enemy country. We could not determine, however, what dimensions it will assume. We expected various technical and organizational difficulties. After all, expelling 90,000 human beings and dealing with all the complexities of this undertaking is no small thing. We did not believe that it would be possible; nevertheless, we agreed that it was necessary to take action and to intercede [with various bodies] in order to do our job well and avert the great catastrophe. A very small committee was chosen—actually, not even chosen, as a group of six simply emerged, consisting of three men from the Orthodox Bureau and three from the Neolog Federation. The former were Raphael Levi, Salomon Gross, and Arnold Kämpfner; the latter were Dr. Winterstein, Dr. Kondor, and I. Of course, a great many people were arranged around this *šestka*, or group of six, as it was called, who had connections and contacts, and who were then supposed to lobby on our behalf according to uniform guidelines. The following guidelines were set:

1) To begin with, the community associations and the union of rabbis would submit a memorandum to the President of the Republic [Jozef Tiso].

2) An appeal would be made to all economic institutions, pointing out what this would mean for the Slovak economy and what damage the abrupt depletion [of manpower] would inflict.

3) An appeal would be made to the clerical leadership and regular clergy and to the Christian side, stressing what the disintegration of families and mass destruction in general would mean from a religious standpoint.

[. . .] The danger mounts with each passing day. On February 27, an Erev Shabbat [Shabbat eve] before Parshat Zachor [the Shabbat before Purim], I was granted an opportunity to express my views privately to Education Minister Jozef Sivák. In a meeting that lasted two hours, I talked over the entire situation and discussed all the details, and I saw that the situation was more serious than I ever believed. In particular, I was unwilling to believe that God wants to destroy us, and that it is precisely the Slovak people, which after all has a Christian tradition, that is to be the Scourge of God, plunging us into the greatest distress.

But now I learned that the matter has already been decided. Prime Minister Dr. Vojtech Tuka has decided the entire matter with the German Embassy and with Advisor to the Slovak Government on Jewish Affairs SS Hauptsturmführer Dieter Wisliceny, and the deportation must take place. There was no way for us to monitor the situation on the German side, because only one Jew has had access here: the engineer Karl [Karel] Hochberg, whom we have regarded as a grumbler [*Moserer*] and to whom we have had no access.[49] He was with the Advisor [Wisliceny] daily and formed a separate department at the UŽ, the so-called Department for Special Missions, ZU (*zvláštne ukony*). He also carried out special missions conscientiously, by making statistically accurate material available like clockwork, in an unbelievably short time. Now the Minister's well-meaning words more than answered my questions, and I was forced to realize that the Jews of Slovakia were utterly lost. I burst into tears during this meeting. The Minister himself was very moved and wished he could help, but unfortunately the matter was under the jurisdiction of the Minister of the Interior, who completely shared the opinion of Prime Minister Tuka: Slovakia must be cleansed of Jews. We did not succeed in finding a direct contact to these two leading proponents of deportation, and all indirect contacts, too, broke down completely. So I saw both the imminent peril and the lack of any recourse.

[. . .]

After two hours, I left the Minister and went to my group, where the six men plus Oscar Horvát from Nové Mesto were waiting for me.

I reported everything truthfully and in forthright terms, and we all burst into tears. For the first time I saw Dr. Winterstein, a strong man, crying as well. I could not help sobbing as I made my report; I finished it, and I will never forget Winterstein's words after I had finished my report: "I had been fearful before the Rav's [Frieder's] report, because I believed that he would give his report an undertone of his characteristic optimism, but now he has done the opposite. Therefore the situation is very grave, and we must try everything possible from now on!" [. . .]

---

49. On Karel Hochberg (1911–1944), see Hilberg, *The Destruction of the European Jews*, 2:780. Yehuda Bauer, *Jews for Sale? Nazi-Jewish Negotiations, 1933–1945* (New Haven, CT: Yale University Press, 1994), 70, describes Hochberg as being "in the mold of Jewish traitors during the Holocaust."

Deportations from Slovakia began on March 25, 1942, starting with a transport of 999 young women from near Bratislava to Auschwitz. Nineteen more transports followed up to October 1942. Initially planned to include only able-bodied Jews suitable for forced labor, the scope of the transports was quickly expanded to include entire families. From early April onward almost forty thousand deportees were shipped to the Lublin district in the Generalgouvernement, where they met the fate of earlier arrivals from the Reich and local Jews, most murdered in the **Sobibór** and **Bełżec** death camps. By July 1942, roughly fifty-two thousand Slovak Jews had been deported. Nearly eight thousand probably escaped over the border to Hungary, but roughly twenty-four thousand Jews remained in Slovakia in October 1942 when the deportations stopped.[50] Transit camps that served as way stations for the deportation transports were set up in Patronka, Nováky, and Žilina, and the latter featured in photographs and sparse annotation in Frieder's diary.

DOCUMENT 6-9: **Photographs from Rabbi Abraham Frieder's diary from the Žilina deportation camp, no date (spring of 1942), USHMMA Acc. 2008.286.1 Frieder collection (annotations/captions translated from German).**

At Žilina, in the camp. People cluster around their fellow Jews who are destined for transport.

50. See Hilberg, *The Destruction of the European Jews*, 2:784–85.

Under heavy guard, they leave the camp and, wearing numbers over their hearts and carrying parcels in their hands, walk to the train station, and they are beaten every time they fail to march quickly enough. The place is crawling with men on duty, providing supervision (including Hlinka guard members in uniform), although these (the deportees) are honest, upright folks, who, true to their people, are bearing their fate heroically. They all are on the move.

Regardless of whether someone has collapsed from illness and is unfit for transport, or whether someone has valid credentials in his pocket. No exceptions are possible; anyone who is not in favor with his commandants must go.

Frieder and the "Working Group" members continued to pursue their goal of stopping the deportations and providing protection for the remaining Jews: pressuring Slovak authorities for exemptions and an end of the transports; urging the Vatican, Catholic dignitaries, and foreign representatives to intervene; and bribing Wisliceny. When deportations from Slovakia stopped after October 1942, they were not resumed until the Germans invaded Slovakia in August 1944.[51] Clearly, the high-risk maneuvering of Jewish leaders that had started in the spring of 1942 played a direct and indirect role in the Slovak regime's decision to halt deportations. Yet there were other factors involved. These arose from conflicts between the Slovak elites, the German course of action, as well as from the delicate interplay between Slovakia and its neighboring rivals.[52] Nevertheless, it is clear from the small selection of sources in this chapter that the spectrum of Jewish reactions in central and southeastern Europe in this phase of the war was broad, ranging from escapes across borders via organized help and relief efforts to interventions with state leaders like in Romania and Slovakia.

From his office in Geneva, **Jewish Agency** official **Richard Lichtheim** observed the drama unfolding in Slovakia and in other parts of Axis-controlled Europe. In mid-May 1942 he reported to London that twenty thousand Jews had been deported from Slovakia. Attempts by the Vatican to intervene proved futile: "[C]ontrary to the declaration made by the Minister of the Interior, Mr. Mach, the Jews are not sent to labor camps in Slovakia [. . .] but are sent to Poland. [. . .] What is happening in Poland when the transports are arriving there is not yet known."[53] According to Lichtheim, a proper response would have involved widespread reporting in the British and American press in combination with Allied warnings—particularly to peripheral Axis countries such as Slovakia and Romania—sending a clear message that the world was watching and war crimes would be punished. But if the world was watching the mass violence taking place in eastern Europe in the spring of 1942, very few observers were seeing as coherent a picture as Lichtheim. Before we explore the limits of understanding inherent in the events unfolding across Europe, we will focus in Part III on the interactions within and between Jewish groups, as well as their dealings with non-Jews in response to the unfolding genocide.

---

51. Longerich, *Holocaust*, 324–26.

52. See Bauer, *Jews for Sale*, 66–101.

53. Letter from Richard Lichtheim, Jewish Agency Geneva Office, to Dr. Leo Lauterbach, Zionist Federation of Great Britain, London, May 13, 1942, USHMMA RG 59.023M, reel 24, frame 279.

PART III

BEYOND COMPLIANCE AND RESISTANCE

INTERACTIONS AFTER JUNE 1941

I N RETROSPECT, it is evident that **Operation Barbarossa** marked a watershed in the overall process of German anti-Jewish policy: in the crucial months of the second half of 1941, genocide became a reality. Fueled by the decisions of those involved in executing the "Final Solution" and a range of other factors, the process would end in the destruction of European Jewry, making 1942 the most lethal year in Jewish history.[1] Yet outside the areas overrun by the Wehrmacht in its push toward Moscow, the epic importance of the summer and fall of 1941 for the planning and perpetration of the Holocaust finds no clear-cut corollary in the experience of Jews, be it for individuals or groups. At the time, Jewish communities in eastern and southeastern Europe had already been subjected to extreme forms of violence, with many Jews losing family and friends. Contemporaries' time line of catastrophic events only partially resembled what have today become the key fixtures in a chronology of the Holocaust: the beginning of World War II, the **Wannsee Conference**, and the establishment of **Auschwitz II-Birkenau** and other camps as mass murder sites. Instead,

---

1. Christopher R. Browning with Jürgen Matthäus, *The Origins of the Final Solution: The Evolution of Nazi Jewish Policy, September 1939–March 1942* (Lincoln and Jerusalem: University of Nebraska Press and Yad Vashem, 2004), 244–45; Raul Hilberg, *The Destruction of the European Jews*, 3rd ed. (1961; New Haven, CT: Yale University Press, 2003), 3:1321, estimates the number of Holocaust-related Jewish deaths for the year 1942 at 2.6 million.

for each community we see a complex nexus of contributing factors, with each also marked by crucial local events: the arrival of the Germans, the beginning of mass deportations, and the dates of killing "actions." For individuals, it was the destruction of their closest relationships, their dignity and integrity, and their means of earning a livelihood that left the deepest marks.

Jewish reactions to these developments not only call into question perpetrator-centered definitions of key events; they also confound the usefulness of clearcut, stable geopolitical categories. Flight and deportation, defiance and despair moved across national borders, indeed also continents. At the same time, not all Jews were equally affected, even within one region. While the Holocaust was raging in large parts of Hitler's empire, whole segments of the Jewish population elsewhere in Europe, but also in the areas facing the direct threat of "de-Jewification," managed for a time to retain some sense of normalcy in their daily lives. And they dared to hope that they would survive the war, that the Reich and its allies would be defeated, and they dared to plan for a postwar life.

Many scholars focusing on understanding the process of persecution continue to situate "the center" of action at the seat of power, most notably in Berlin, and regard the events unfolding in eastern Europe as "the periphery." Yet if we look at Jewish reactions instead and give them primacy, "the East" becomes the center, the central story: it was here that Jews first and most directly confronted the genocidal turn of German policy and began to grasp the true meaning of the phrase "Final Solution to the Jewish question." Conversely, Jewish communities in Berlin and other central or west European cities formed the periphery, along with the United States and other countries, all more removed from what could be called the "genocidal core": the ghettos, camps and killing sites in the East. Distance from this core not only shaped the perception of German anti-Jewish policy, but also gave rise to a greater degree of hope about surviving the war, in many instances with the help of the surrounding Gentile communities. The **Yishuv**—Palestine—was situated in a precarious position on this wartime map of Jewish experience, lying close enough to the East European center of suffering that, depending on the course of war, it could easily have been sucked into the vortex of war and annihilation.

Most armed opposition, Jewish and non-Jewish, in the period featured in this volume took place in eastern and southeastern Europe. It was there that Jews desperately trying to escape a murderous foe could still find remote hiding places or a refuge. Because the "Final Solution" was closely tied to the Third Reich's broader policies around race, empire, war, society, and the economy, Jews were persecuted not only as Jews, but also as members of vanquished and occupied states or of other victimized groups. Consequently, they shared many experiences with others who suffered under the Germans and reacted in similar ways, according to the setting and situation. Where distinctly Jewish responses can be discerned, it is unclear in many cases whether these distinctions resulted from personal preferences, a specific local setting, or more general and widely shared circumstances. Furthermore, it remains very difficult to ascertain from the historical record to what degree people did what they did due to their identities as Jews, as a result of other subjective considerations, or in response to outside forces. In fact, given the complexity of modern, twentieth-century life in Europe and the intricate factors weighing on personal decision making, rigid categorizations of Jewish behavior create too narrow and ahistorical depictions of the past.

Similarly, one rarely finds clear-cut answers to many of the pressing questions relevant to our understanding of this past. What correlation existed between the immediate experience of an existential threat that confronted Jews in eastern Europe and their willingness to become agents of their own fate in these changed circumstances, most visibly by violently resisting German measures? To what extent were Jews able to surmount the huge hurdles impeding the path to active resistance, and how is one to gauge the many acts of noncompliance that remained unsuccessful, went unrecorded at the time, or that have become overshadowed today by a preoccupation with violent, military-style opposition to the Nazis? What measure of success can one reasonably apply to Jewish resistance when the persecutors controlled all elements in the destruction process? And finally, how do we read escalating tensions and restratification *within* Jewish communities and *between* different Jewish groups?

Parts III and IV attempt less to reflect the quality and scope of persecution (which figured more prominently in Parts I and II). Instead, it highlights the effects of persecution on the Jewish social fabric, on group relations, and individual mechanisms for coping. The chapters in Part III are organized around varying forms of interaction and behavior that created part of the broad spectrum of Jewish responses in the period from the beginning of Operation Barbarossa until the summer of 1942. From the beginning of Nazi rule, the power to define what "Jewish" meant had shifted away from the individual to state agencies that ranked and treated Jews within its borders as public enemies. As we have already seen in Volume I of this series, not all who were persecuted as Jews saw themselves as such; the spectrum of Jewishness contained renegades, converts, apostates, "***Mischlinge***," and varied according to time and place. The result made for an extremely heterogenous group that only from the outside appeared to be a cohesive collective. The experience of persecution and loss shared by all Jews under German domination did not cancel out the historically rooted diversity lodged within and between communities. It remains a matter of contention whether living under the Nazi threat enhanced or degraded a collective sense of belonging. If one includes those living beyond the German reach, the notion of Jewish identity and interaction becomes even more difficult to fathom.

"One of the striking aspects of the dramatically changing Jewish condition," historian Saul Friedländer writes about this phase in the war, "appears to be the ongoing disintegration of overall Jewish solidarity—insofar as it ever existed."[2] If there was a Jewish collective in the period covered in this volume, it existed only notionally; it took a positive form in the aspirations of those Jews conscious of the powers of tradition and invested in a common course—and it assumed a negative form in the hateful images projected by Nazi propaganda. In truth, fragmention along many long-standing social divisions prevailed. While this trend did not always start with the war, nothing contributed to it as massively and violently as the measures taken by Germany and its allies in Europe. Yet, as we will see, Jewish identity, solidarity, and opposition to persecution continued to be expressed in word and deed, especially among members of close-knit groups, despite mounting outside pressure. Surviving Jewish voices from the time provide a stark means of counteracting the dehumanizing picture of "the Jew" that antisemites painted in order to legitimize the looming "Final Solution."

---

2. Saul Friedländer, *Nazi Germany and the Jews:* (vol. 2) *The Years of Extermination, 1939– 1945* (New York: HarperCollins, 2007), 192.

CHAPTER 7

ELITES AND ORDINARY JEWS

THE NAZI MONOPOLY on power in the Reich and the unbending nature of German anti-Jewish policy meant that a whole range of tensions and struggles surfaced in what was left of Jewish communal structures. An intense and acrimonious struggle for subsistence played out in the ghettos in particular, with a destitute majority on the bottom and the *Judenrat* (**Jewish council**) and an assortment of German cronies and other "war profiteers" on the top. By the summer of 1941, the incoherent system of German-controlled ghettos in "the East" had become even more complex, with hundreds of sites emerging in the newly occupied Soviet Union that existed for brief periods of time only and functioned as staging areas for mass murder.[1] Caught between the claims of armed occupiers and those of the diverse community members they served, the Jewish councils in most ghettos faced opposition from below, while exerting no leverage with their overlords. The *Judenräte* also confronted challenges from rivals who either invoked or actually enjoyed the support of German officials, as well as from clandestine opposition groups attempting to organize dissent and disrupt orderly compliance. These groups became especially popular among

---

1. See Martin Dean, ed., *The United States Holocaust Memorial Museum Encyclopedia of Camps and Ghettos, 1933–1945*, vol. 2: *Ghettos in German-Occupied Eastern Europe* (Bloomington: Indiana University Press in association with the USHMM, 2012), xliv–xlvi.

ghetto youth, who still had the energy and flexibility to devise new ways of confronting the unprecedented crisis. Beyond this, people who had once enjoyed communal authority—rabbis, teachers, organizers—often continued to act as informal leaders and attracted a fluid assortment of followers, but rarely adjudicated over limited, scarce goods and resources.

Under the circumstances, assurances of good intentions and stopgap measures were all the Jewish councils could offer those who demanded assistance. In Warsaw and, as seen in chapter 2, in Łódź, demonstrations were organized to protest the councils' food distribution system.[2] But in the absence of sufficient means for everyone, what was given to one person had to be withheld from another; access to authority and assets often became the critical factor in the chain of distribution, not justice or level of need. At the same time, occupation administrators expected many Jewish councils to establish "productivity" and "order" by force, through courts and prisons and, above all, by Jewish policemen, a stratum of men often described as "shady elements."[3] Over time the councils' claim to be providing basic subsistence and communal cohesion became ever more suspect in the eyes of those at the bottom of a brittle food chain: what use were community leaders who did more to placate and satisfy the Germans than ensure the physical survival of all those in need? Was invoking the rules of social justice and fair play still possible when a community's power structures had slipped into pervasive corruption and cronyism? Many of those who answered these questions in the negative withdrew into passivity

---

2. See Joseph Kermish, "Diary Entries of Hersh Wasser," *YVS* 15 (1983): 241 (dairy entry for January 6, 1941); Lucjan Dobroszycki, ed., *The Chronicle of the Łódź Ghetto, 1941–1944* (New Haven, CT: Yale University Press, 1984), 5.

3. See document 2-4. See also Alexandra Garbarini, with Emil Kerenji, Jan Lambertz, and Avinoam Patt, *Jewish Responses to Persecution*, vol. 2: *1938–1940* (Lanham, MD: AltaMira Press in association with the USHMM), 415–20. Herman Kruk writes under the date of January 29, 1942: "The Jewish Police are more German than the Germans." Herman Kruk, *The Last Days of the Jerusalem of Lithuania: Chronicles from the Vilna Ghetto and the Camps, 1939–1944* (New Haven, CT: Yale University Press, 2002), 187.

or opted for what historian Konrad Kwiet has called "the ultimate refuge" by committing suicide.[4]

Jews who had not succumbed to the draining effects of deprivation or to lethargy used any means at their disposal to intercede with ghetto authorities. To some extent they marshaled familiar tools such as old-style bureaucratic appeals; where these had no effect and resources had dwindled to a frightening degree, they also explored new avenues of appeal, some directed at those invested with the power by the Germans, others at individuals or groups working outside the system imposed by the occupiers. As we will see later in this chapter, Jewish men and women also approached non-Jewish authorities, including heads of state, police agencies, and other figures of apparent influence to improve their lot, irrespective of the massive imbalance between the minimal changes of success and the high risks that such appeals invited.

EXPECTATIONS AND DEMANDS

Publicly posted proclamations became one feature of ghetto life that underlined the skewed communal structure typical for all ghettos. Posters mounted by the Jewish council alerted residents to new regulations and other changes. Clandestine groups in fact used similar means to voice discontent. In early 1942 in Vilna, chronicler Herman Kruk saw a subversive poster insisting, "There must be no hungry person in the ghetto." It "made a colossal impression" and prompted police action.[5] Far more typical, however, were the official announcements—grave and sober, though sometimes designed with artistic skill—such as one released by Council head **Mordechai Chaim Rumkowski** that greatly alarmed many men and women living in the Łódź ghetto.[6]

---

4. Konrad Kwiet, "The Ultimate Refuge—Suicide in the Jewish Community under the Nazis," *LBIYB* (1984): 135–67. On the increase in the number of suicides by Jews in all areas facing deportations "to the East," see Saul Friedländer, *Nazi Germany and the Jews: (vol. 2) The Years of Extermination, 1939–1945* (New York: HarperCollins, 2007), 308, 320, 426, 428.

5. Kruk, *The Last Days of the Jerusalem of Lithuania*, 176 (entry for January 19, 1942).

6. See document 7-5.

DOCUMENT 7-1: **"Public notice no. 372" by the Eldest of the Jews in the Łódź ghetto (in German and Yiddish), March 25, 1942, USHMMPA WS# N13853 (translated from German).**

Public Notice No. 372.

Regarding:
Resettlement

As I have learned, rumors were spread that resettlement has stopped. This is at odds with the truth. The resettlement is continuing. Therefore, persons destined for resettlement absolutely must, as before, report to the gathering point in question at the designated time, on schedule, or they will be resettled without their baggage.

(-) Ch. Rumkowski
Elder of the Jews in Litzmannstadt [Łódź]

Litzmannstadt Ghetto,
March 25, 1942

Beyond such public edicts, the councils also issued communications more personal in nature and similar in style to prewar, "normal" administrative procedures, even where they bore substantial threats. Bureaucratic form conveyed a sense of order and normalcy, of common rules and procedure. Yet here, that familiar discourse stood in marked contrast to the missives' content and the chaos and tyranny raging in the ghettos, especially in the occupied parts of the Soviet Union. In Pińsk, then part of **Reichskommissariat Ukraine** (today Pinsk in Belarus), **Waffen-SS** units had murdered roughly half of the Jewish population, with its formerly more than twenty thousand members, in early August 1941 as part of a gigantic "sweep" through the Pripet and Polesie region.[7] The Germans only established a ghetto for the remaining Jews in Pińsk in early May 1942. This followed the creation of a *Judenrat* nearly a year earlier, in July 1941.[8] Faced with the occupiers' demand for a "contribution" in many towns and cities, the Jewish Council compiled the following letters as part of its attempt to raise the necessary funds from community members. We do not know the reason for the difference in the amounts charged (fifty versus one hundred rubles) to both recipients of the letters. In all likelihood, it was caused by the two men's different economic status, which impacted their ability to pay the forced "contribution."

DOCUMENT 7-2: **Letters from the Pińsk Judenrat to two Jews, levying money for a "contribution" imposed by the Germans, Pińsk, German-occupied Ukraine, October 19, 1941, USHMMA Acc. 1996.A.0169 (YVA M-41/942, from Brest State Archives 2135-2-124), reel 28 (translated from Russian).**

[Letter to Abram Ber Vaynshteyn, Domikanskaia Street 29]

In connection with the authorities' imposition of a contribution on the Jewish population of the city of Pińsk, the "Judenrat"[9] of the city of Pińsk asks that by 5 o'clock today you tender 50 (fifty) rubles to the treasury of the "Judenrat," at Albrekhtovskaia no. 24. In the case of non-payment of the indicated sum within the [designated] time frame, you

---

7. Christopher R. Browning with Jürgen Matthäus, *The Origins of the Final Solution: The Evolution of Nazi Jewish Policy, September 1939–March 1942* (Lincoln and Jerusalem: University of Nebraska Press and Yad Vashem, 2004), 279–82; Yitzhak Arad, *The Holocaust in the Soviet Union* (Lincoln: University of Nebraska Press, 2009), 163.

8. Katharina von Kellenbach, Nahum Boneh, and Ellen Stepak, "Pińsk," *The USHMM Encyclopedia of Camps and Ghettos*, 2:1442–44.

9. German term used here in Cyrillic orthography and with quote marks (similar usage, but no quote marks in letter dated October 19, 1941).

will be entered onto the list of those who have declined to participate in the contribution, which will be passed on to the *Gebietskommissar*.[10]

Chairman of the Judenrat of the City of Pińsk
[signed, probably Minski][11]

[Letter from the Pińsk Judenrat to Yakov (middle name illegible) Ashkis, Domikanskaia Street 84, October 19, 1941:]

In connection with the authorities' imposition of a contribution on the Jewish population of the city of Pińsk, the Judenrat of the city of Pińsk ask that by 5 o'clock today you tender 100 (one hundred) rubles to the treasury of the Judenrat, at Albrekhtovskaia no. 24. In the case of non-payment of the indicated sum within the [designated] time frame, you will be entered onto the list of those who have declined to participate in the contribution, which will be passed on to the *Gebietskommissar*.

Chairman of the Judenrat of the City of Pińsk
[signed; probably Minski]

To most Jews living in ghettos, the greatest daily threat next to a confrontation with the German intruders was becoming the target of the Jewish police or *Judenrat* officials. In 1941 to 1942, Jewish policemen rarely received direct orders from the Germans; rather, they followed directives issued by the Jewish councils, which in turn answered to German functionaries. Unusually visible with their armbands, badges, uniforms, and sometimes even such symbols of executive power as sticks or clubs, they were ultimately viewed as upholders of the extremely oppressive and unjust system under which they had to live. Those who were members of the Jewish police or had relatives or friends among them benefitted by having access to resources that remained for the most part out of reach for the majority. Yet they had no power outside the ghetto or

---

10. German term used here in Cyrillic orthography denoting the regional leader of the German civil administration as part of the "Reichskommissariat Ukraine."

11. Mordekhai Minski (1880–1942) served as deputy to Benjamin Buksztanski, the Pińsk *Judenrat* chairman. In practice Minski was the acting chairman. As a former resident of Danzig, Minski knew German and therefore served as a liaison with German authorities. He was murdered in the liquidation of the ghetto in October 1942. See Tikva Fatal Knaani, "The Jews of Pinsk, 1939–1943, Through the Prism of New Documentation," *YVS* 29 (2001): 161; von Kellenbach et al., "Pińsk," in *The USHMM Encyclopedia of Camps and Ghettos*, 2:1442–44; and Yad Vashem's Central Database of Shoah Victims' Names, www.yadvashem. org. The authors have been unable to uncover the fate of the addressees of these letters.

when it came to non-Jews. Many policemen must have felt the absurdity if not the immorality of their positions. In Warsaw in July 1941, *Judenrat* chairman **Adam Czerniaków** observed how a member of his "Order Service" dealt with beggars—"the plague of the street," as Czerniaków put it—and the many children among them: "In a matter-of-fact fashion he wards them off, away from my window, with handouts. No policeman of any other nationality would act in this way."[12] By contrast, most ordinary ghetto residents harbored a less benign opinion toward this agency, documented by members of the Kovno ghetto police.

DOCUMENT 7-3: **Account by the Kovno ghetto police on the establishment of the Jewish police, no date (early 1943), USHMMA RG 26.014 (LCSAV R-973), reel 31 (translated from Yiddish).[13]**

[. . .]

On August 10 [1941] it became known through the committee— already referred to as the Council of Elders [*Ältestenrat*; or Jewish Council]—that men were being accepted into the police force, priority being given to those who had served in the military. Twenty-six applications had been received, of which 10 were accepted.

The rank and file of the young people did not, in general, wish to join the police. It is also of interest that some in this group who participated in the almost daily meetings and consultations concerning the organization of the police were willing to help organize and structure the police force, but were not willing to join it themselves.

The reasons for this attitude were as follows:

First, as noted, our future was clouded and veiled. We had no contacts with the [German] authorities, except for those instances when demands were received for workers, or if we happened to hear instructions concerning a new evil decree. We were completely in the dark as to the intentions of the authorities concerning us, not only with regard to general questions affecting the entire community, but also as to their preferences concerning the establishment of the administrative life of the ghetto

12. Raul Hilberg, Stanislaw Staron, and Josef Kermisz, eds., *The Warsaw Diary of Adam Czerniakow: Prelude to Doom* (Chicago: Ivan R. Dee in association with the USHMM, 1999), 262 (diary entry for July 25, 1941).

13. Samuel Schalkowsky and Samuel D. Kassow, eds., *The Clandestine History of the Kovno Ghetto Jewish Police* (Bloomington: Indiana University Press in association with the USHMM, forthcoming).

and the shape and duties of the offices. It was therefore feared that, outside the direct duties of the police to maintain peace and order in the ghetto, the force would be given other work and become a tool of the Gestapo, and that all of our police officials would have to serve as their [i.e., the Gestapo's] functionaries.

Second, there was fear of the external administrative aspects, which could make each policeman individually responsible for any misunderstanding, any trivial matter.

Third, the very creation of a Jewish police was big news in the life of our community; we know from experience that Jews have difficulty getting along with Jews; that a Jew hates to obey a Jewish functionary [*tshinovnik*]. The members of the organizing group figured—with all due respect, but rightly so—that Jews would not obey, that there would be quarrels with everyone, such that the task would be difficult—indeed, thankless.

[. . .] Since there were very few applications [for leadership positions], it was decided to mobilize men with previous military service, sportsmen, members of the Maccabea [Jewish sports club] and war veterans. The mobilization was planned so as to recruit men from all classes and quarters of the population, without consideration of party affiliation, position, or social standing, so that neither this nor that tendency or group would have a monopoly in the police, so that it would be the protector and advocate of the entire ghetto.

And indeed, the attitude of those who either volunteered or were mobilized into the police during those first days was idealistic—to work for the good of the people, in contrast to the later times, beginning with the gold "action" [requisitioning of valuable items by Germans in early September 1941], when everything became so cheap and gray and very far from any kind of idealism. Initially, people worked day and night unselfishly for the well-being of the ghetto. These first weeks were the cleanest period for the police. Whether these good intentions had any practical significance is a separate question.

The ghettos with their "Jewish self-administration," as German propaganda called it, were not the only places where Jews tried to "work for the good of the people" within a structure established by the oppressor. In many camps in eastern and southeastern Europe, a large part of Jewish organizational work consisted of shoring up and maintaining some semblance of orderly communal life, even if those participating had little hope of succeeding. In these endeavors, too, we find the authors of regulations and other decrees resorting to bureaucratic formalism as a means of establishing stability in the chaos of life under persecution. The following circular by the Jewish camp administration of the Đakovo women's camp in Croatia exemplifies this attempt to create normalcy and order through written rules, here with a special emphasis on increasing the inmates' "productivity" in the administration and use of scarce resources. The camp regulations were meant to be temporary, until the county police in nearby Osijek provided the final rules, but it is not clear whether this ever happened. The camp in Đakovo was established in December 1941, when the first transport, consisting of 1,830 Jewish women and children as well as fifty Serbian women, all from Sarajevo, was deported there. The Jewish Community of Osijek had to supply provisions for the camp. Sanitary conditions were appalling, resulting in a typhoid fever outbreak in May 1942. No systematic murder in the camp took place, but those inside were routinely ill treated and humiliated, and individual murders occurred as well.[14]

DOCUMENT 7-4: **Circular letter no. 1 from the Jewish administration of the women's camp in Đakovo, Independent State of Croatia, December 8, 1941, USHMMA RG 49.007M (JHM 4159 k.21-7-1/11), reel 1 (translated from Croatian).**[15]

ADMINISTRATION OF THE CONCENTRATION CAMP [*sabirnog logora*] ĐAKOVO

Circular letter no. 1

Đakovo, December 8, 1941

For the purposes of information and unconditional obedience, the following regulations are being announced to all [female] prisoners. The regulations are of temporary character, and the final "house rules" and "disciplinary rules" will be composed later, in agreement with the county police in Osijek.

---

14. In February 1942, a further 1,200 Jewish and Serbian women were deported to Đakovo from the camp in Stara Gradiška. The camp was liquidated in June and July 1942, when the remaining inmates were deported to **Jasenovac**, where most were murdered. See Zoran Vasiljević, *Sabirni logor Đakovo* (Slavonski Brod: Centar za povijest Slavonije i Baranje and Spomen-područje Jasenovac, 1988); Jozo Tomasevich, *War and Revolution in Yugoslavia: Occupation and Collaboration* (Stanford, CA: Stanford University Press, 2001), 246–48, 592–97.

15. The document was written in Roman script.

Command of the camp:

    The camp is under command of the county police in Osijek, and the commander of the order guard [*zapovjednik redarstvene straže*] Dragutin Majer is named commander.[16]

Administration of the camp:

    The camp is <u>for now</u> under administration of the Jewish Community in Osijek (until a special camp committee is formed). The Jewish Community in Osijek has named Mr. Vlado Grünbaum[17] director of the camp with full powers. He is given the task of undertaking a full organization of the camp within 14 days starting today, with help being provided by the Jewish communities of Osijek, Zagreb, and Sarajevo, as well as all prisoners. Within those two weeks, Mr. Grünbaum will propose to the Osijek county police the Administrative Committee of the camp consisting of 11 members. Certain members of the Administrative Committee will also head the following sub-committees:

Supplies sub-committee:

    [illegible] Mr. Julio Sternberg[18] from Osijek, without the members of the committee, to conduct business as required in Đakovo and Osijek, and his work is for now limited to procurement and transport of food to Đakovo. In the end, this sub-committee will consist of 5 members.

Kitchen sub-committee:

    FOR THE TIME BEING, ALL BUSINESS OF THIS COMMITTEE IS PERFORMED by Mr. Scheiber[19] from Osijek, and the

---

16. The "order guard" was the regular police in the Independent State of Croatia.

17. Vlado Grünbaum was a civil servant from Osijek and one of the leaders of the Jewish community in Osijek. He survived the war. See Zlata Živaković-Kerže, *Stradanja i pamćenja: Holokaust u Osijeku i život koji se nastavlja* (Osijek: Hrvatski institut za povijest, 2006), 187.

18. Julije Sternberg (1892–1942) was the manager of a flour mill in Osijek and one of the wartime leaders of the Jewish Community in Osijek. He was deported to **Auschwitz** in late August 1942, where he was murdered. See Živaković-Kerže, *Stradanja i pamćenja*, 297.

19. The list of the Jews from Osijek deported and murdered during the war in Živaković-Kerže's book lists three male Scheibers, all deported to Auschwitz and murdered in August 1942: the first man listed without his first name, born in 1887; Dragutin, born in 1885; and Tibor, born in 1880. It is possible that the "Mr. Scheiber" listed in the document was one of those three individuals (Živaković-Kerže, *Stradanja i pamćenja*, 168). The authors were unable to find information on Margita Izrael.

cook Margita Izrael, also from Osijek. This committee is to be extended to 5 members by adding prisoners.

Health committee:

This committee is comprised of Dr. Jurković,[20] Dr. Atijas [both female],[21] and Miss Reder, as well as Mr. Lederer[22] and Mr. Weiss.[23] The final shape of this committee is 5 members, in addition to Mr. ph. Hecht,[24] who will send medications from Osijek.

Disciplinary committee:

The Director of the camp will name 5 members of this committee, with a task of drafting the final version of the house rules and rules of discipline. This committee will oversee the implementation of the former, and will simultaneously be appointing the prisoners for individual duties. It will [illegible] administer the camp card file and will keep the up-to-date work list as well as daily reports. It will collaborate with the productivization committee.

---

20. Nada Jurković, most likely the person marked as "N. Jurković" (born in 1918) in the list of Jews from Osijek deported and murdered during the war. She was deported to Jasenovac in August 1942, where she was murdered a month later. See Živaković-Kerže, *Stradanja i pamćenja*, 120, 156.

21. Regina Atijas, born in 1903, was a physician from Bihać. She joined the communist-led Army of National Liberation and became a physician in the military hospital in the Tuzla district in 1945. Jaša Romano, *Jevreji Jugoslavije 1941–1945: Žrtve genocida i učesnici Narodnooslobodilačkog rata* (Belgrade: Savez Jevrejskih opština Jugoslavije, 1980), 326. The authors were unable to find information on the fate of Miss Reder.

22. Ladislav Lederer (1915–1953) was a physician from Osijek. In late 1942, the **ustaša** regime sent him and at least eighty other Jewish physicians to Bosnia on a mission to suppress an outbreak of endemic syphilis. This was part of a cynical ploy to remove the "protected" Jewish physicians from Zagreb, loot their property, and make them more vulnerable to eventual deportation. In April 1943, Lederer joined a partisan unit and was promoted to the rank of major by the end of the war. (See Živaković-Kerže, *Stradanja i pamćenja*, 286). On the rescue of physicians in the Independent State of Croatia, see Ivo Goldstein, *Holokaust u Zagrebu* (Zagreb: Novi liber, 2001), 215–22.

23. Most likely this is a reference to Franja Weiss (1909–1942), one of the leaders of the Osijek Jewish Community since the outbreak of the war in 1941. He was deported to Auschwitz in August 1942, where he was murdered. See Živaković-Kerže, *Stradanja i pamćenja*, 119, 172.

24. Adolf Hecht (1890–1943) was a pharmacist from Osijek and a member of the Osijek Jewish community leadership during the war. He was killed in Jasenovac in 1943. See Živaković-Kerže, *Stradanja i pamćenja*, 97, 155.

Internal administration:

This sub-committee will consist of all employees of the administrative offices, which will be taken exclusively from the ranks of the prisoners. The administrative offices should be formed within 14 days. Materials are supplied by the Jewish Community of Osijek. The scope of this committee includes: correspondence with suppliers, maintaining the card file, the distribution of children [to Jewish families in Osijek and other places in the vicinity], performing all administrative duties, etc. The functioning of the entire camp is predicated upon good work in administrative offices.

Productivization committee:

This sub-committee will be founded by younger prisoners, with the task of suggesting to the Command and Administration of the camp ways to fulfill the plan. The plan is to make the prisoners more productive, and thus ease the upkeep of the camp.

Other sub-committees will be founded as needed.

As is already known to the prisoners, the Administration of the camp wishes to cut costs by placing the children between the ages of 2 and 10 with Jewish families in Osijek and other towns. Considering that the number of families who wish to receive children is sufficient, all children will be able to find shelter in those families. We ask all parents to prepare these children for transportation, and the distribution will take place from Friday through Sunday,[25] that is, from the 12th to the 15th of this month. Envoys from individual communities will come to the camp, where they will take the children allocated to them. A list of children turned over will be compiled, and the data from this list will be later entered into the card file.

Correspondence of prisoners with members [words missing] is allowed through the Jewish Community of Osijek. Prisoners will receive cards from the camp Administration. Mail to prisoners is addressed to the

25. It remains unclear whether this particular intervention on behalf of children took place; however, a similar "distribution" did occur in late February and early March 1942, when the ustaša authorities in Osijek approved the housing of thirty-seven Jewish children in the homes of local Jewish families. According to a survivor of the camp, the Osijek Jewish community managed to put up as many as fifty-seven children. Contemporary correspondence between the Jewish communities of Sarajevo, Brod na Savi, and Osijek indicates that some mothers refused to surrender their children to Jewish families outside the camp. It is unclear how many of the "saved" children survived. Most were eventually deported to Jasenovac, together with their host families. See Vasiljević, *Sabirni logor Đakovo*, 28–34.

Jewish Community of Osijek, and will be delivered daily. Censorship of mail will be performed by the commander of the concentration camp. We ask that correspondence is limited to strictly family matters and it is, at least for now, limited to only the most necessary. Letters are not allowed at all, only unsealed camp postcards.

Appeal to all prisoners: we call on you to unconditionally obey and follow all rules, orders, and advice from the Command and Administration, as well as subcommittees. As long as we appear disciplined and obedient, the camp administration is able to fulfill its already difficult task. If, however, there are instances of disobedience, there may be direst consequences for ALL prisoners. That is why we call on the old and the young and the old [*sic*] to watch their behavior as well as that of their fellows. Only thus are we able to secure all needs of prisoners.

DISCIPLINE AND ORDER ABOVE ALL.

Whether negotiating over mundane matters or those of vital importance, appeals to those Jews whom the Germans had placed in positions of power remained a last critical gamble, the only official channel still open for many. Letters to Jewish authorities implied the persistence of a proper process in which decision makers would consider, just as in normal times, the merits of the case according to fair and lawful rules. Accordingly, most supplicants consciously crafted the content, style, and appearance of their letters, for these factors could easily impact on the success of their appeals vis-à-vis the recipients who were swamped with requests, appeals, and pleas. Ultimately, however, many of these letters read like SOS messages, desperate signals for desperate times.

The start of deportations from the ghettos to unknown destinations prompted anxious attempts to obtain exemptions. In January 1942, almost two months after local German officials had initiated mass murder by gassing as a routine feature at the **Chełmno** death camp,[26] a flood of petitions reached the office of the Eldest of the Jews in Łódź, Mordechai Chaim Rumkowski. His office had sent out the "departure orders" to meet the Germans' deportation quotas. Showing signs of haste and fear, the appeals used a range of arguments—from health reasons and blamelessness to the hardship entailed by the deportation order—in the hope they could help avert what some understood to be certain death. The surviving documentation conveys very little about the process in which

---

26. Browning, *The Origins of the Final Solution*, 418f.; Lucjan Dobroszycki, ed., *The Chronicle of the Łódź Ghetto*, 124–25, 128.

ghetto officials made decisions. It is fair to assume, however, that the Council worker who processed an appeal faced the daunting choice between rejecting it and thus ensuring the deportation plan's smooth implementation (while knowing or at least guessing the consequences for those affected) or granting the exemption and having to find someone else to fill the quota. The following letters are a small sample from a massive number of pleas, the likes of which must have been received by all Jewish councils issuing deportation notices.

DOCUMENT 7-5: **Letters of appeal to the Deportation Commission of the Eldest of the Jews in Łódź, January 11/12, 1942, USHMMA RG 15.083 (PSAŁ, file 1238, 62–63, 164–65; file 1280, 581–82) (translated from German).**

[letter by Hinda Bendkowska,[27] January 11, 1942]

I, a sick 60-year-old woman, have just received the departure order for myself, my daughter, and son. My son works in the stocking workshop and benefits the ghetto. Last year, he unfortunately got onto the wrong path. Now he earns a living by the work of his hands and supports me and my daughter. I swear to you that my son will keep on supporting us and himself in an honest way.

I beg you to exempt the three of us from resettlement out of the ghetto. Have mercy on us, and don't make us homeless and even poorer than we already are! Keep in mind that you will be killing three people if you resettle us.

In expectation of your confident reply,
Respectfully yours,
[signature; on the first page a margin note (presumably by the processing officer; in Polish): rejected (*odmowa*)]

[letter by Estera Berkowicz,[28] January 11, 1942]

In an indescribably desperate situation, I am strongly appealing to you to give my plea your fullest attention. It has to do with a great

---

27. The authors have been unable to find details on the further fate of Hinda Bendkowska and her family.

28. The authors have been unable to uncover the fate of Estera Berkowicz, her family, and Rozia Goldsztajn. Their appeal was rejected and they were probably murdered in Chełmno.

error on your part, and as a result I have been struck by a huge calamity. Therefore, I ask for your consideration in every regard.

Today, quite unexpectedly and for reasons completely unknown to me, I received a departure order for me and my child, 1½ years old. There is no reason for it, because I have no criminal record, am not aware of the slightest offense, and have never been guilty of any misconduct.

I live in an attic room, and because my child had a lung catarrh, Dr. Mandelson recognized that the room was unhealthy and advised me to move out of there. Because a neighbor, Rozia Goldsztajn, had a big, roomy apartment, I planned to move in with her and registered for her place on April 24, 1941. In fact, as all the residents of the building can also testify, I did not sleep a single night in her apartment, but immediately asked the building custodian the next day to cancel my registration. Through the fault of the custodian, who kept refusing to surrender the registration book, the cancellation was delayed. I myself worked the whole time as a cook in Community Kitchen 444, Rybna 10, and therefore had no time to attend to it. Thus the registration cancellation took place on October 15, 1941. Now this woman, Rozia Goldsztajn, Königsbergerstr. 4/48, has received a departure order, as have I, who am innocent, and my helpless 1½-year-old child. Should we who are blameless suffer and perish? I beg you, have mercy on the child, in winter, in this cold weather it would inevitably freeze to death. In addition, I myself am a sick woman and can provide you with a doctor's certificate. My husband suffers from epilepsy, there would be nobody to take care of him and I would not know where to leave him behind alone.

I ask for your sympathy and help, after all, we are victims of a mistake, we have nothing in common with Mrs. Rosia Goldsztajn. For this reason, please show consideration for me, especially for my child, deportation would be certain death for him.

Therefore, I request that you withdraw the departure order.

I am confidently hopeful that you will show me the fullest understanding and will fulfill my wish. Thank you very much in advance.

Respectfully,
[signature; on the first page a margin note (presumably by the processing officer; in Polish): rejected]

[letter by Sara Meschenberg,[29] January 12, 1942]

A cry of woe to you, Mr. President! [*Ein Wehgeschrei zum Herrn Präses!*]

Today I received an order for departure. I and my five children

1. Perla Dwojra[?]
2. Chazkiel Dawid
3. Majer
4. Mirla
5. Abram Pinkus

yet I also have another child, a newborn
Efraim Fajgenbaum-Meschenberg
born on [month illegible] 24, 1941 and for whom
<u>Mr. President himself was the sole sandek [godfather]</u>.

How should I now go out into the world with six children? My husband was the building custodian at Lwowska No. 13, and he registered voluntarily for work [detail outside of L.], and now I'm the custodian of this same building. I've done my duty and performed it honorably, I've never had to pay a fine, I watch the building day and night, and as far as I know no complaint has ever been received. For what reason must I now leave the ghetto, for what sin must I and my
<u>6 small children</u>

go out into the world! Have mercy on me, Mr. President; leave me just where I am, so that I and my
<u>6 children</u>

are not destroyed! Just as I as a mother want to stay with my children, I also want to keep on taking care of the building and looking after it—after all, I'm the
<u>custodian [*Hauswächter*]</u>.

Why am I being sent away? I have a child three months old, why am I being sent away? Have mercy on me! Perhaps there's been a mistake here? Because it just can't be that Mr. President wants to destroy a whole family.

Sara Meschenberg
Departure No. 3250/3255
[margin note on the first page (presumably by the processing offer; in Polish): approved (*uwzglednione*)]

---

29. The authors have been unable to uncover what happened to Sara Meschenberg and her family.

Among the chorus of desperate Jews pleading to the *Judenrat* for exemption from deportation, some asked for even less. In early May 1942, Anna Brandeis, a Jewish woman who had been deported with her husband, Leopold, from Vienna in the first transport to Łódź, wrote to Rumkowski's officials asking "to give us permission that I and my husband can depart on the same day, together with all the other Catholics," so that they would not be separated.[30]

In Germany, shrinking opportunities to evade the Nazi dragnet of racial policy prompted the more than 160,000 Jews remaining in the Reich in October 1941 to make use of every small loophole. After the deportations to "the East" had begun, the question of "*Mischlinge*" also remained unresolved, for the Nazi leadership was careful to avoid measures that could endanger quiet on the home front. They were not eager to face a public outcry like the one brought on by revelations about the "**Aktion T-4**" killings of hospital patients; protests led to the measure's "official" end in August 1941.[31] German officials could not agree whether and to what extent "*Mischlinge*" were to be treated like Jews; however, for those affected, it was clear that being labeled as a "*Mischling* of the 1st degree" offered better future chances than being marked as a Jew, while the status of "*Mischling* of the 2nd degree" seemed even less susceptible to deportation. For many, the inconsistencies built into the **Nuremberg Laws**' definition of who was a Jew seemed worth exploring, despite the risks involved. Ever more men and women attempted to evade membership in the **Reichsvereinigung**—which was tightly regulated by the regime—as the threat of deportation increased.[32]

Jewish representatives who answered to German officials had to process these claims and rejected most of them. As the surviving files of one German Jewish community show, many of those driven by despair or unrealistic expectations into relinquishing their ties to Judaism reacted with indignation when informed about the futility of their attempt. One even threatened "to bring

---

30. Letter by Anna and Leopold Brandeis, Łódź ghetto, to the Jewish Council, May 3, 1942, USHMMA RG 15.083M reel 299, folder 1288:4. The appeal was rejected. On the various issues facing Christian converts in the ghettos, see Peter Dembowski, *Christians in the Warsaw Ghetto: An Epitaph for the Unremembered* (Notre Dame, IN: University of Notre Dame Press, 2005).

31. See Henry Friedlander, *The Origins of Nazi Genocide: From Euthanasia to the Final Solution* (Chapel Hill: University of North Carolina Press, 1995), 111–34.

32. The 10th supplementary decree to the Reich Citizenship Law enacted July 4, 1939, made membership in the Reichsvereinigung mandatory for all Jews. It also stipulated: "In the case of a mixed marriage only the Jewish partner is a member a) if the Jewish partner is the man and the marriage has produced no children, or b) if the children are legally Jewish." Jewish partners in "mixed marriages" to whom this clause did not apply, as well as foreign citizens, were "free to join the Reichsvereinigung." See Karl Schleunes, *Legislating the Holocaust: The Bernhard Loesener Memoirs and Supporting Documents* (Boulder, CO: Westview, 2001), 167f.

the matter to the attention of the Reich Interior Minister," ignoring the fact that it was that very ministry and its executive branch, Heinrich **Himmler**'s police, that left no leeway for German Jewish organizations to be more accommodating.[33] In this as in other settings, the underlying responsibility of German institutions and individuals became hidden behind the smokescreen of "Jewish self-administration." On the other side of the spectrum stood those women and men who embraced their Jewish identity and chose to express solidarity with friends and family at a time when deportation and probable death loomed large.

DOCUMENT 7-6: **File note by the Jewish community Leipzig, Germany, January 18, 1942, regarding a request by Martha Weinhold to join, USHMMA RG 14.035M (Leipzig Jewish Community records), reel 2 (translated from German).**

Miss Martha Marianne Weinhold,[34] resident at [blank], appears today without a summons, identified by passport no. 438 W

She makes the following declaration for the aforesaid record:

I am a *Mischling* of the 1st degree, and do not adhere to Judaism. But I would like to join the Jewish community, and am aware that by filing this declaration of enrollment [in the Jewish community] I lose my status as a *Mischling* of the 1st degree and am regarded as a Jewish woman for the purposes of §5 Paragraph 2 Clause A [of the 1st Supplementary Decree to the Reich Citizenship Law enacted November 14, 1935].

I am declaring this enrollment [in the Jewish community] for the following reason. I would like to move away [*abwandern*] together with Mrs. Frankenstein, whom I have known for a long time and hold in high esteem.

Read aloud, approved, and signed Martha Marianne Weinhold

[certified:] Felix Israel Salomon, Clerk

---

33. Letter by Charlotte Elise Krebs, Barby, to Reichsvereinigung regional office (Bezirksstelle) Sachsen-Thüringen, November 6, 1942, USHMM RG 14.035M, reel 11.

34. She and Mrs. Frankenstein may have been relatives. Martha Marianne Weinhold, born in Leipzig in 1911, ended up on a transport to Riga with Elisabeth Frankenstein (née Urbach; b. 1880); in the summer of 1944 both were sent to the Stutthof camp and appear to have survived the war. A former salesman, Felix Salomon, born in Breslau in 1887, was deported to Auschwitz in 1943 and killed, as were his wife Alma (née Schlapp) and daughter Margot. Wolfgang Scheffler and Diana Schulle, eds., *Buch der Erinnerung: Die ins Baltikum deportierten deutschen, österreichischen und tschechoslowakischen Juden* (Munich: K. G. Saur, 2003), 829–30; Ellen Bertram, *Menschen ohne Grabstein. Die aus Leipzig deportierten und ermordeten Juden* (Leipzig: Passage-Verlag, 2001), 95, 206–7; German "Minority Census," 1938–1939, USHMM RG 14 013M.

APPEALS TO NON-JEWISH AUTHORITIES

While facing the possibility of abuse at every turn, Jews outside ghettos and camps could and did still access public space in many places under German control. Yet they were increasingly forced to inhabit housing designated for Jews only and to wear the Star of David and other visible markers designed to reduce their contacts with non-Jews. Despite isolated displays of solidarity revealed in some of the documents featured earlier in this volume, stigmatization by and large achieved the regime's desired goal, contributing to the further numbing of non-Jews toward the fate of Jews and to what some observers have called their "social death."[35]

Still, Jewish "social death" was never ubiquitous, and Jews continued to interact with non-Jewish agencies of power. Where they could, they used personal appeals to universal standards of moral behavior and pointed to the incompatibility between official regulations, with their vestiges of administrative normalcy and the reality of discriminatory practices. In Germany, any chance of successfully approaching the very top of the regime had long been restricted to cases in which the Jewish identity of a prominent person or family was in question. Based on ancestral proof, political considerations, or acknowledgment of the applicant's extraordinary services to the Third Reich, Hitler could grant "honorary Aryan" status to individuals and did so in a few cases, most involving distinguished "*Mischling*" soldiers or civil servants.[36] Individuals could pursue a similar outcome with only slightly higher chances of success—but higher risks—through the German court system based on a law enacted in 1938 to clarify cases of contested ancestry.[37]

With the specter of deportation to "the East" growing after October 1941, the number of German Jews seeking to escape the trap set by the Nuremberg Laws by appealing to the German courts grew significantly. Few could ultimately provide sufficient proof for their claim that official birth records did not

35. For Germany, see Marion A. Kaplan, *Between Dignity and Despair: Jewish Life in Nazi Germany* (New York: Oxford University Press, 1998), 198–200.

36. See Bryan Mark Rigg, *Hitler's Jewish Soldiers: The Untold Story of Nazi Racial Laws and Men of Jewish Descent in the German Military* (Lawrence: University Press of Kansas, 2002). The soldiers he describes were mostly "*Mischlinge*," with no connections to or personal identification with their Jewish ancestral roots.

37. See Jürgen Matthäus and Mark Roseman, *Jewish Responses to Persecution*, vol. 1: *1933–1938* (Lanham, MD: AltaMira Press in association with the USHMM, 2010), 296–99.

match their real ancestry.[38] In the case reflected in the following short document, Hermann Marschner, who—like many of the roughly seventy thousand Jews left in Berlin—worked as a forced laborer, and his wife, Charlotte, both "full Jews" according to the Nuremberg Laws, had filed an application in June 1941 for a racial recategorization of their son Karlheinz, born in October 1926. The parents asserted that Karlheinz's real father was an "Aryan" with the very common name of Alfred Schulz, which would have upgraded their son to the status of "*Mischling* of the 1st degree." The racial examination of the family at a Berlin clinic was scheduled for November 6, 1941, but the **Gestapo** was faster: Karlheinz and his mother were deported on the fourth transport leaving Berlin for Łódź on November 1 (not, as Hermann Marschner claims in the letter below, on November 4).[39] Hermann Marschner—presumably at that time no longer living with Charlotte and Karlheinz—only found out days later about his family's deportation, officially referred to as "voluntary evacuation," and contacted the Berlin prosecutor's office asking whether he would have to come to the clinic and thus miss work.[40]

DOCUMENT 7-7: **Letter from Hermann Marschner, Berlin, to Berlin Public Prosecutor's Office, November 6, 1941, USHMMA RG 14.070M (LAB A Rep. 358-02, #56385), reel 1534 (translated from German).**

On November 6 [1941] I was supposed to report to the Kaiserin-Auguste-Victoria-House [Berlin hospital] regarding a case of disputed paternity [*Ehelichkeits-Anfechtungssache*]. Due to the fact, however, that on November 4 young Karlheinz Israel Marschner evacuated voluntarily together with his mother, I assume I do not have to be absent from work. I only heard about the move [*Verzug*] today, November 6.

---

38. Based on the records of the prosecutor's office at the Berlin district court (Staatsanwaltschaft bei dem Landgericht Berlin), the most comprehensive collection of German prosecutorial files and the place of residence of the largest remaining part of German Jewry during the Nazi era, it appears that roughly half of the applications filed by Jews for racial reclassification dated from the years 1941 and 1942. See Jürgen Matthäus, "Evading Persecution: German-Jewish Behavior Patterns after 1933," in *Jewish Life in Nazi Germany: Dilemmas and Responses*, ed. Francis R. Nicosia and David Scrase (New York: Berghahn Books, 2010), 47–70.

39. Browning, *The Origins of the Final Solution*, 356.

40. Hermann Marschner was deported to Kovno on November 17, 1941, and was killed on arrival (Scheffler and Schulle, *Buch der Erinnerung*, 107).

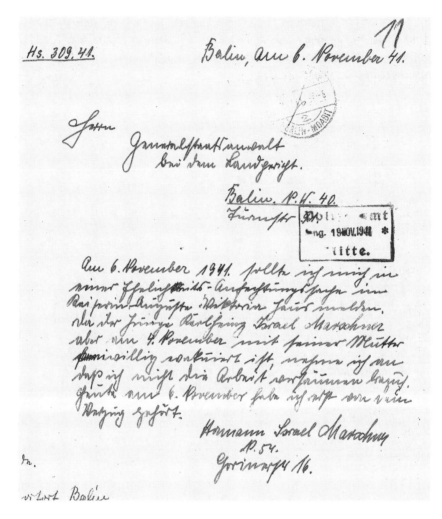

Of those in Germany who had approached a court to claim "Aryan" ancestry, an unknown percentage was in fact deported by the Gestapo without the knowledge or consent of the courts, while the racial reclassification case was still pending. Such was the case for Charlotte and her fifteen-year-old son, Karlheinz Marschner; both were murdered, either in Łódź or Chełmno.

In the Independent State of Croatia, closely associated with Nazi Germany, similar regulations were put in place that allowed for exemptions from racial laws, yet few were granted. As elsewhere, the more prominent the claimant and the better his or her connections to the ruling elite, the higher the chances of at least partial success.

DOCUMENT 7-8: **Letter from August Nović, Zagreb, Independent State of Croatia, to the Minister of Internal Affairs of the Independent State of Croatia, May 7, 1941, USHMMA 1998.A.0018 (Croatian State Archive, box 277, inv. no. 27167), reel 1 (translated from Croatian).**[41]

The case:
　　August Nović, municipal veterinary adviser
　　Zagreb, Boškovićeva 10, appeals that rights
　　accorded to persons of Aryan descent be recognized
　　to him and his descendants

　　To the Minister of Internal Affairs of the
　　Independent State of Croatia
　　Zagreb

1. Before I make an argument about my case, I take the liberty of noting that my late father Albert Neuman, born in Križevac in 1844,[42] was during the anti-Croatian regime and especially during the presidency of the late Dragutin Grdenić,[43] one of the most esteemed advocates of the ideas of Dr. Ante Starčević,[44] and that as an outspoken member of the opposition he was subject to chicanery and persecution, and that he was, in that stronghold of Croatdom, elected the opposition representative in the city council several times. This can be proven easily by the minutes of the municipal council meetings in Križevac, and this fact will

---

41. The document was written in Roman script.

42. It is interesting that Nović refers to the town as Križevac; it was actually (and is still today) called Križevci (plural, instead of singular). His consistent incorrect use of the name of the town, as well as numerous odd turns of phrase in the letter, indicate that Croatian was not his first language.

43. "Anti-Croat regime" could either refer to the Hungarian rule in Croatia after 1867, or the period of the Yugoslav kingdom (1918–1941). Dragutin Grdenić was a minor intellectual and politician in Križevci at the turn of the twentieth century.

44. Ante Starčević (1823–1896) was a Croatian writer and politician and the founder with Eugen Kvaternik (1825–1871) of the Croatian Party of Right (1861), which advocated the establishment of an independent Croatian state for a Croat nation, which, although his ideology was contradictory, he usually defined along racial lines, excluding Serbs and Jews. His ideas are often seen as precursors of the radical ustaša ideology, although there is no straight line that connects the two movements intellectually, and although Starčević's political program in the nineteenth century attracted a wide range of nationalists, not all of whom were antisemitic and racist.

be confirmed readily by Marchesi,[45] a Zagreb-based barber and a maker of wigs, who was born in Križevac.

It is therefore no coincidence that I was brought up in the spirit of science of Dr. Ante Starčević, and that I always worked in the interest of the Croats. I was born in Križevac in 1876, and, feeling myself a Croat, I changed my last name Neuman in 1896, so 45 years ago, into a Croatian name Nović.

2. I especially have to emphasize that neither I nor my son have ever voted for any anti-Croatian regime and, in accordance with this, I have along with my son always found myself in Croat ranks, and each of us in his own area have worked for the benefit of our Croatian homeland.

3. Wherever I found an active advocate of the Croat cause, and [wherever I found] an ustaša, I tried to help. The case of *bojnik* [low military rank] Ćiril Ćudina,[46] whose leanings and quiet work I was familiar with, confirms this. Because precisely when, during the dictatorship,[47] he got in trouble at the Zagreb Fair because of his patriotism and work, I stood for him energetically in every respect. The facts mentioned above will be confirmed by Mr. Ćiril Ćudina, *bojnik* and director of the Zagreb Fair.

4. I think that I have contributed to Croatia, and especially to our city of Zagreb, where I have conscientiously fulfilled all duties concerning my profession.

Draft plans were made for a new slaughterhouse and fairgrounds in accordance with my ideas and directions, and under my supervision. That my tremendous and responsible work has been successful is proven by the fact that many foreign and domestic experts recognize that today's slaughterhouse, and especially the cattle exposition grounds, is the most

---

45. The authors could find no information on Marchesi.

46. Ćiril Ćudina (1894–1972), long-time director of the Zagreb Fair, joined the ustaša movement during the war. Among other duties, he headed the national State Directorate for Renewal, in effect the state agency for "aryanization." See Ivo Goldstein, *Holokaust u Zagrebu* (Zagreb: Novi liber, 2001), 176.

47. This refers to Yugoslav King Alexander's abolition of political parties and the introduction of personal dictatorship on January 6, 1929, in an attempt to curb the escalating Serbo-Croatian political struggles. Limited and controlled liberal democratic order was reintroduced in 1931. In 1934, ustaša-trained Macedonian irredentists assassinated the king. The Serbo-Croatian tensions in Yugoslavia were alleviated in 1939, when Croatia (mostly in today's borders, and including a part of today's Bosnia-Herzegovina) was recognized as an autonomous principality with confederal status with the rest of the country.

beautiful and most functional in Europe, and that it can serve as an example to anybody concerned with the problem of how to build such institutions. I note, in passing, that I was one of the most important initiators of this building project.

The current mayor [of Zagreb] Mr. Ivan Werner[48] praised my successful work on many occasions and in front of many witnesses, saying that in that city institution my name should be prominently displayed in recognition [of my work]. This will surely be confirmed by Mr. Mayor [g. gradski načelnik] before the most competent forum.

My family consists of my wife Cecilija, born Weiser in Zagreb in 1885, and my unmarried son Feodor, a certified civil engineer, born in Zagreb in 1907. We were all baptized in the parish of St. Mark in Zagreb, on February 7, 1939.

Taking into consideration the above facts, I plead that this appeal be forwarded, with a recommendation, to the Leader [poglavnik][49] of the Independent State of Croatia, so that he can kindly approve that all rights pertaining to persons of Aryan descent, in accordance with paragraph 6 of the [Croatian] Law Regarding Racial Belonging, no. XLV/68-Z.p.-41, be recognized for me and my descendants.

In Zagreb, May 7, 1941

Signed: August Nović

Testimonies about the truthfulness of claims made in my appeal:
For point 1, handwritten testimony by Mr. Marchesi
For point 3, handwritten testimony by Mr. Ćudina
For point 4, handwritten testimony by Mr. Werner

According to a note by Croat officials, Nović's appeal was granted in late May insofar as he was exempted from wearing a badge. Unfortunately, this

---

48. Ivan Werner (1877–1944), a butcher, member of the ustaša movement, and the ustaša mayor of Zagreb (1941–1944). He is infamous for having signed the order to tear down the centrally located Zagreb synagogue, allegedly for zoning violations. Goldstein, however, claims that the decision had been made in the upper echelons of the ustaša movement. See Goldstein, *Holokaust u Zagrebu*, 385.

49. The official title of Ante Pavelić (1889–1959), the head of the ustaša movement and the leader of the fascist ustaša state.

temporary exemption did not help: August Nović, his wife, Cecilija, and their son, Fedor, were murdered in Jasenovac in 1942.[50]

Attempts to claim non-Jewish ancestry in the East had an even smaller chance of success. Edwin Geist, a German-born "*Mischling*" refugee living with his wife Lyda in Kovno, Lithuania, in the **Reichskommissariat Ostland**, tried desperately to get his wife out of the ghetto.[51] Helene Holzman, herself a "*Mischling*" living outside the Kovno ghetto after the murder of her Jewish husband and daughter early on in the German occupation, was a good friend of the Geists; her diary describes how helpless Edwin and Lyda were and how the Germans took pleasure in making fun of the gullible couple.[52] Geist's diary, dedicated to Lyda, recorded his efforts to rescue her by having her "upgraded" to "*Mischling*" status, and it includes the account of a bizarre meeting with Helmut Rauca, the Gestapo officer responsible for the murder of thousands of Jews in the Lithuanian city.[53] In light of the story told by their good friend, Holzman, the risks involved in the meeting for Geist, and the couple's later fate, his description of the encounter could be read as a testimony to his own recollections or as an expression of wishful thinking. The diary excerpt quoted here begins when Geist switches over to writing dialogue.

50. See Jelka Smreka and Đorđe Mihovilović, eds., *List of Names of the Victims of Jasenovac Concentration Camp, 1941–1945* (Jasenovac: Spomen-područje Jasenovac, 2007).

51. Edwin Geist (1902–1942), Berlin-born composer and musicologist, left Germany in 1938 and settled in Kovno, where he married Lyda (née Bagrianskytė), a pianist, and continued his career. After the arrival of the Germans he followed his wife into the Kovno ghetto until his release in the spring of 1942 based on his "*Mischling*" status. He managed to get his wife reclassified as a "*Mischling*" so that she was allowed to leave the ghetto in late August 1942. After failing to divorce his wife as demanded by the Gestapo, he was arrested and murdered in early December 1942. Geist's wife was murdered in 1943. See Reinhard Kaiser and Margarete Holzman, eds., *"Dies Kind soll leben." Die Aufzeichnungen der Helene Holzman 1941–1944* (Munich: List Taschenbuch, 2001), 246–47, 356, 364. According to Jokūbas Skliutauskas and Dina Porat, Lyda committed suicide upon hearing of the death of her husband. See Edwin Geist, *Für Lyda. Tagebuch 1942*, ed. Jokūbas Skliutauskas (Vilnius: Baltos Lankos, 2002), 12; Avraham Tory, *Surviving the Holocaust: The Kovno Ghetto Diary*, ed. Martin Gilbert and Dina Porat (Cambridge, MA: Harvard University Press, 1990), 158–59 (the edition lists them as Ernest and Lydia Geist).

52. Kaiser and Holzman, *"Dies Kind soll leben,"* 12, 35–37, 162. Holzman wrote her account after the liberation of Lithuania in the summer of 1944.

53. Albert Helmut Rauca (1908–1983), Gestapo officer in Kovno, fled Germany after the end of the war and in 1950 became a citizen of Canada. He was extradited to Germany in 1982 on the charge of aiding and abetting in the deaths of more than ten thousand people in Kaunas between the summer of 1941 and in 1943. He died while awaiting trial. See Sol Littman, *War Criminal on Trial: Rauca of Kaunas* (Toronto: Key Porter Books, 1998).

DOCUMENT 7-9: **Edwin Geist, Kovno, German-occupied Lithuania, diary entry for June 10, 1942, in Edwin Geist, ed. Jokūbas Skliutauskas,** *Für Lyda. Tagebuch 1942* **(Vilna: Baltos Lankos, 2002), 54–59 (translated from German).**

R. [Rauca] . . . First you wanted out [of the ghetto], and now your wife. I can understand your great distress, to be sure, because I'm not a monster, but inconsistent characters are repugnant to me. You should have thought about all this beforehand. Am I right?

I [Geist]: You're completely right, Herr R.

R.: So you're not happy?

I: How could I be?

R.: What do you actually want, Herr Geist? I just can't get rid of you here!

I: What I want? I want to have my wife back. She is innocent, but suffering in the gh[etto]! And I will come to you again.

R.: All J[ews] are guilty.

I: No, Herr R., no. If we're talking about guilt now, all J[ews] are certainly not guilty.

R.: Perhaps, but you understand nothing about it [because you are not an Aryan].

I: (silent)

R.: I don't want to see you here again! And if you have even the slightest contact with your wife, I'll send you back or have you locked up! Do you understand me?

I: I wrote my wife back then solely to clear up a few points that I need for the divorce you want me to get.

R.: So that's how matters stand; you're still not divorced?

I: No! because my wife is not a J[ew]!

R.: Can you bring me proof of that? Your wife's parents (pointing to the window) are no longer alive. I would at least have to question her mother.

I: What is one supposed to do? I can't bring the dead back to life, you know!

R.: (abruptly) Do you know that I had the J[ew] who delivered this letter to your wife arrested and put in prison? That's the reward you have for it!

I: For God's sake, Herr R., the man is certainly innocent! Let him go; it was a <u>Lithuanian</u> who took care of that.

R.: Naturally <u>you</u> asked him to do it.

I: Not at all. The suggestion was made <u>to me</u>, and I even assume that the man in question must have informed you beforehand, otherwise the whole thing would never have come out in the first place.

R.: We know everything, Herr Geist.

I: (sobbing) Herr R., release my wife. I'm an artist, and you know what a wife can mean, especially for someone who is creative. Be merciful, even if I don't succeed in clarifying the case fully.

[. . .]

R.: If you can't live without your wife, then go back into the gh[etto].

I: No!

R.: And why not?

I: As I've already said—to save my art. A talent comes with obligations; it doesn't belong exclusively to itself. But above all: my wife is not a J[ew]. She has no place in there!

R.: Let's assume that your wife has a Christian father, she's a half-J[ew] nonetheless, by blood, and I won't release half-J[ews].

I: In the Reich, half-Jews are even liable for military service.

R.: The [Reichskommissariat] Ostland is indeed part of the Reich, but the regulations here are different. A woman can be taken out of the ghetto, provided that she has herself sterilized at her own expense. In the case of women older than 45, of course, that is no longer a possibility, and I abide by my regulations!

I: But my wife is three-fourths Aryan, as I emphasized on my first visit, <u>inasmuch</u> as my mother-in-law was a half-J[ew] by blood.

R.: That's a different matter, of course. In <u>this</u> case, there should no longer be any obstacle present. But for the time being, as far as I'm concerned, your wife is a Jew, and the decisions are not made by me alone. Bring me written confirmation, at once, that you have filed for divorce. I'll give you a week from today to do so. If you don't obey my order this time, I'll have you arrested immediately and taken back to the gh[etto].

I: Fine, Herr R., I think I've understood you correctly; pending clarification of the case, I file suit for divorce through a lawyer with the "German Court" in Kovno.

R.: So, off with you now; I have much more to do than keep messing around with this blasted J[ewish] stuff!

I: (<u>loudly</u>) Heil Hitler!

R.: Heil Hitler!

I: (<u>already at the door</u>) May I venture to ask one more little question?

R.: What is it? What is it?

I: You may not give me any information, but I'd like to know, maybe you'll tell me after all: will any more A[ktions] take place?

R.: Good grief, of course I wouldn't tell you! But don't be concerned, there won't be any more; at most, there'll be deportations. Not

that I'm not sorry for this rabble—but we need workers; especially in
wartime.

    I: Thank you, Herr R. Good day.

    R.: Enjoy your lunch.

As we have seen earlier in our series and previously in this volume, in other
countries aligned with Germany, the upper echelons of the regime were often perceived as more accessible to appeals by Jews.[54] In Romania, **Wilhelm Filderman**,
the head of the Romanian Federation of Jewish Communities whose letter to his
old schoolmate **Ion Antonescu** is featured in Part II, intervened with the country's highest authority, despite the fact that the regime's leader had ordered or
sanctioned abuse, deportations, and mass murder. But Jews without personal connections turned to Antonescu as well. Shortly after the beginning of **Operation
Barbarossa** in the southernmost part of the Eastern front and in conjunction
with Romanian forces, **Einsatzgruppe** D and its subunits began to wreak havoc
among local Jewish communities, following the modus operandi established further north.[55] The following letter by the desperate wife of a man arrested by the
German **Security Police** is similar to appeals written by Jews in the Baltics to
German authorities in the first stage of the occupation.[56]

DOCUMENT 7-10: **Letter from Luţa Kaufman,[57] Piatra Neamţ, Romania, to Marshall
Antonescu, August 6, 1941, in Jean Ancel, ed.,** *Documents Concerning the Fate of
Romanian Jewry during the Holocaust***, vol. 2 (New York: Beate Klarsfeld Foundation,
1986), 507 (translated from Romanian).**

Dear Marshall,

    Permit me, the undersigned Luţa Kaufman, residing in Piatra Neamţ,
str. Petru Rareş Nr. 19, to bring to your attention with the most profound
respect the following:

---

    54. See Garbarini et al., *Jewish Responses to Persecution*, 2:262–63, 266–83.

    55. See Dieter Pohl, "The Murder of Ukraine's Jews under German Military Administration
and in the Reich Commissariat Ukraine," in *The Shoah in Ukraine: History, Testimony,
Memorialization*, ed. Ray Brandon and Wendy Lower (Bloomington: Indiana University
Press in association with the USHMM, 2008), 23–76; Andrej Angrick, *Besatzungspolitik
und Massenmord: Die Einsatzgruppe D in der südlichen Sowjetunion 1941–1943* (Hamburg:
Hamburger Edition, 2003).

    56. See the examples in Wolfgang Benz, Konrad Kwiet, and Jürgen Matthäus, eds.,
*Einsatz im "Reichskommissariat Ostland": Dokumente zum Völkermord im Baltikum und in
Weissrussland, 1941–1944* (Berlin: Metropol, 1998), 177–79.

    57. The authors have been unable to ascertain the fate of this woman.

On the day of July 30, 1941, two German NCOs from E. K. 1258 presented themselves at our domicile and arrested my husband Bernard Kaufman, age 37, and from that date I have heard absolutely nothing further about my husband.

Marshall, permit me, with the most profound respect, to make an appeal to your sovereign benevolence, to make an intervention in order to establish what happened to my husband.

Permit me to bring to your attention that my husband [was] an advance scout from the War of 1916,[59] is the son of the veterinarian Iosef Kaufman (b. 1877) and the brother of the university lecturer, Dr. O. Kaufman-Cosla.

This family of Moldavians has always been known to sacrifice anything for the fatherland and has never gone against the interests of the country in the slightest way.

Based on these facts, I had to resort to your sovereign protection.

With the most profound respect,
[Signature]

It is not clear whether this letter triggered any action on the part of Romanian authorities. We know, however, that Antonescu received other such appeals by Jewish individuals and groups and did on occasion take an interest in remedying their plight.[60]

Clearly, pleas to dictators and other **Axis** authorities cannot be compared with citizens' appeals to governments or leaders in democracies with an established rule of law. Yet among the Allies, too, administrative procedures facilitated and at the same time regulated the interaction between citizens and state; furthermore, politicians had to heed public opinion. Prior to the entry of the United States into the war in December 1941, long-standing concerns about emigration in times of economic crisis, a groundswell of antisemitic sentiments in small, yet influential parts of society, and widespread fears of the country being dragged into the affairs of European powers dominated American domestic discourse. Jewish organizations in the country were hypersensitive about these underlying issues and adapted their relief policies accordingly, to

---

58. Einsatzkommando 12 was a subunit of Einsatzgruppe D. See Angrick, *Besatzungspolitik und Massenmord*, 319–21.

59. "The War of 1916" refers to World War I, which Romania entered on the side of the Entente (Britain, France, and Russia) in August 1916.

60. See Jean Ancel, ed., *Documents Concerning the Fate of Romanian Jewry during the Holocaust* (New York: Beate Klarsfeld Foundation, 1986), 7, 5–6 (Clara Şufăr to Marshall Antonescu, Moghilev, March 14, 1942).

the point where—as Saul Friedländer puts it—"[o]fficial American Jewry was paralyzed."[61] Approaching U.S. government agencies lacked any of the risks that Jews ran when approaching the powerful in the Axis' realm. But, for the most part, these overtures did not have dramatically higher chances of success where government policy writ large and bureaucratic practice stood in the way. The following letter by Irma Czerner, a refugee from Prague, to the First Lady represents the efforts of many Jewish émigrés on American shores. Prompted by the frustrations built into the existing emigration regulations, they attempted to sidestep the official apparatus and approach a prominent and sympathetic figure.[62]

DOCUMENT 7-11: **Letter from Irma Czerner, Chicago (IL), to Eleanor Roosevelt, October 31, 1941, in Raya Czerner Schapiro and Helga Czerner Weinberg, eds.,** *Letters from Prague, 1939–1941* **(Chicago: Academy Chicago Publishers, 1996): 187–88.**

Dear Lady:

The pictures of you and your family in the newspapers gave me the idea and the courage to do the unusual thing and approach you— although a stranger. I always liked and enjoyed the nice and happy expression of your face and always felt strongly attracted. I am sure you get many letters asking for some favor. Therefore, I shall be brief.

Who am I? A refugee from Prague, Czechoslovakia, here with my husband and 3 children, two girls, seven and nine, and a boy two and a half years old.

What do I want? An affidavit for my mother [Paula Czerner] and brother [Erwin Froehlich]. We are earning enough to take care of them, but not so much that our affidavits alone would be sufficient. It is my anxious desire to give them quick and effective help that makes me turn to you. I am sure an affidavit from you as an outstanding personality would be one hundred per cent effective if only you would be willing to help me.

Who is my brother? Erwin Froehlich, Prague physician, 38 years old, single, lives with my mother. He is a specialist for gastroenterology and had made himself known already as an excellent young doctor by his medical ability, his good character and a number of works published in medical journals.

---

61. Friedländer, *Nazi Germany*, 2:304–5.

62. On Eleanor Roosevelt's position on émigrés and relief efforts, see Richard Breitman and Alan M. Kraut, *American Refugee Policy and European Jewry, 1933–1945* (Bloomington: Indiana University Press, 1987), 129–32.

Since the Occupation more than a year ago,[63] he is no longer allowed to work in his profession. He and our mother were forced to move three times during one year and to share their four-room apartment with two other families. He is now working in a social institution without pay. Some of his publications are known in this country and I feel sure that some of the specialists in the USA would be glad to give references for him if required, including Professor Dr. Schindler at the University of Chicago, the inventor of the gastroscope.

Since I have no right to take much of your time with a long story, I will let these lines be enough, hoping that you will understand that behind the few facts and words given to you lies a world of anxiety and hope.

My husband and I can give you every possible assurance that my people would never be in any sense a burden to anybody should your kind help make my dreams come true and decide to sign the papers for them. They will of course live with us in our six-room apartment at the above address.

Should you decide to kindly help my dreams come true I would take the liberty of sending you the necessary forms for signature.

Very respectfully yours,
[signature]

Irma Czerner may have built up her hopes that her appeal would resonate with the president's wife, since the First Lady had helped another family member stay in the country during a visit in late 1938.[64] Nevertheless, Czerner's plea was transferred to the State Department in Washington, DC, where the chief of the visa division informed her in November 1941 that "since there are no American consular offices operating in German-occupied territories, no action may be taken on the cases of your relatives who are residing in Prague."[65]

Not all powers fighting the Axis subscribed to western democratic ideals, yet their joining the anti-Hitler coalition offered new chances for interventions by Jewish organizations. The beginning of "Operation Barbarossa" brought the Soviet Union—until June 22, 1941, a loyal partner in the **Molotov-Ribbentrop**

---

63. German troops occupied Prague beginning in March 1939, thus much earlier than Czerner states in her letter.

64. Raya Czerner Schapiro and Helga Czerner Weinberg, *One Family's Letters from Prague, 1939–1941* (Chicago, IL: Academy Chicago Publishers, 1996), 204–6.

65. Letter by A. M. Warren, U.S. Department of State, November 18, 1941, to Mrs. Max Czerner; facsimile copy in Schapiro and Weinberg, Ibid., 189. Paula and Erwin Czerner were deported in 1942, via **Theresienstadt**, to their deaths in **Treblinka** and Auschwitz respectively. See Schapiro and Weinberg, Ibid., xvii.

Pact, which had led to the dismemberment of the Polish state—into the Allied fold. With Soviet leaders eager to raise awareness among Jewish audiences in the West about the battles being waged on the eastern front and to solicit arms and aid for the Red Army, a newly formed **Jewish Anti-Fascist Committee (JAFC)** painted the plight of those living under German rule in graphic terms. Furthermore, Jewish relief agencies suddenly experienced better access to Soviet officials and greater chances of working on behalf of Jews living in the unoccupied parts of the Soviet Union, many refugees from areas newly under German rule. As we have seen in a prior document,[66] they also faced the legacy of the recent past and uncertain prospects for the future. The following report describes a meeting by representatives of the Joint Foreign Committee of British Jews with the Soviet ambassador in London, Ivan Maisky.

DOCUMENT 7-12: **Notes on a meeting between Selig Brodetsky, Adolph Brotman, and Leonard Stein[67] with Soviet ambassador Ivan Maisky, London, September 29, 1941, USHMMA RG 59.023M (Board of Deputies of British Jews), reel 22, frames 224–25.**

Professor Brodetsky, Mr. Leonard Stein and Mr. A. G. Brotman called by appointment on M[r]. Maisky at the Soviet Embassy at 3.30 p.m. on Monday, 29th September, 1941.

Professor Brodetsky expressed the thanks of his colleagues and himself for the opportunity to meet M[r]. Maisky. He said that the

---

66. See document 5-12.

67. Ukrainian-born Selig Brodetsky (1888–1954) had been a mathematics professor at the universities of Bristol and Leeds before he became president of the **Board of Deputies of British Jews** in 1940. In 1948 he served as president of the Zionist Federation of Great Britain and Ireland and in 1949 became president of the Hebrew University in Jerusalem. See Edgar Williams and Helen Palmer, eds., *The Dictionary of National Biography, 1951–1960* (Oxford: Oxford University Press, 1971), 143–44. Leonard Stein (1887–1973) was a tax lawyer, Zionist leader, and president of the Anglo-Jewish Association from 1939 to 1949. Until 1943, the Anglo-Jewish Association (AJA)—considered the non-Zionist counterpart to the Board of Deputies of British Jews (even though Stein had Zionist leanings)—cooperated with the Board of Deputies to form the Joint Foreign Committee, which documented the persecution of Europe's Jewish population and demanded action from the British government on its behalf. See S. I. Levenberg, "Stein, Leonard Jacques," in *The Dictionary of National Biography, 1971–1980*, ed. Robert Blake and Christine S. Nicholls (Oxford: Oxford University Press, 1986), 804–5. Adolph G. Brotman (1896–1970) was General Secretary of the Board of Deputies of British Jews from 1933 to 1966. In 1948 he assumed the position of vice chairman of the United Restitution Organization until his death. See tribute in *AJR Information* 25, no. 4 (April 1970), 11 (issued by the Association of Jewish Refugees in Great Britain).

Jewish Community were, of course, very much concerned about the fate of the various Jewish groups from the Baltic States, from Hungary and Bessarabia, and from Rumania, who had fled before the German onslaught. The position of the Soviet Jews was identical to that of their fellow-citizens, and the position of Polish Jewish subjects was being regulated through the agreement between the Soviet Union and the Polish Government. The nationals of the other states mentioned and also a very large number who were stateless were in a different position, and Professor Brodetsky said that the Jewish Community would be glad to have information concerning them.

M[r]. Maisky, in saying that he would make enquiries, said that the majority of the Jews of the Baltic States had become Soviet citizens soon after the union of these States with Soviet Russia [i.e., the Soviet annexation in the summer of 1940], and their position, therefore, in Russia was one that was in line with the general position of Soviet citizens. The Soviet Union was doing all that could be done for the refugees of other nationalities and stateless persons, without distinction of race, religion, or nationality, but of course conditions in Soviet Russia were extremely serious at the moment, and he had no definite information as to what was being done. Whatever help could be given by outside groups would be welcome.

Professor Brodetsky referred to the Federation of Jewish Relief organisations, which was anxious to help in co-operation with the Joint Distribution Committee [AJJDC], and they wished to know in what way they could best give assistance.

M[r]. Maisky said that the Red Cross in this country and other voluntary organisations doing the same kind of work, or created ad hoc for the purpose, were active, but it was necessary—in order to avoid confusion—that their activities should be co-ordinated. He therefore suggested that the Federation of Jewish Relief Organisations might, in the first place, get into touch with the Soviet Embassy in order that such assistance as they could render might be organised and co-ordinated.

Professor Brodetsky added that a suggestion had been made by the Relief Federation that a small delegation, representing that Federation and the Joint Distribution Committee, might go to Moscow in order to see what could be done at first hand.

Mr. Maisky said that there was no objection to such a delegation in principle, but there were very great practical difficulties from the transport point of view, which were increasing owing to the advent of winter. He thought, however, that a necessary preliminary step would be for the Federation to discuss with the Embassy what help was available and could be provided, before proceeding with the suggested delegation.

Professor Brodetsky then raised a matter on which he had communicated with the Embassy regarding the possibility of somebody from Palestine proceeding to Moscow in order to supervise the emigration to Palestine of one hundred Polish Jewish nationals now in Russia for whom certificates for immigration into Palestine had been allocated. He pointed out that the tracing of the individuals, as well as the possible replacing of such as could not be traced by others entitled to, and suitable for, such immigration, could best be done by a Palestinian Jew thoroughly familiar with the whole matter and possibly knowing many of the people personally.

M[r]. Maisky said that he had already made telegraphic enquiries in Moscow on the subject, and agreed that the question of transport of such a person would be much simpler from Palestine to Russia than from this country or America to Russia. M[r]. Maisky said that he had had enquiries and requests for release from the Chief Rabbi of Palestine and the Chief Rabbi of this country, of Rabbis interned in the Soviet [Union]. M[r]. Maisky said that in most cases these requests had been made without giving sufficient details of the persons concerned to enable the authorities to identify them.

Mr. Leonard Stein asked whether it would not be possible for the Soviet War News to publish the text of the reply sent by the Board of Deputies to the Message from the Jewish Rally at Moscow on 24th August.[68] M[r]. Maisky said he would see what could be done on this.

With this the interview terminated.

A.G.B.

The Soviet response to the British Jewish leaders indicated Moscow's sensitivity to issues that would become important at the end of the war, such as claiming Jews from annexed areas as "Soviet citizens." In a similar manner, the Polish government-in-exile tried to preempt particular demands by presenting the entire Polish population as victims of German occupation policies. In

---

68. For a summary of the rally and list of speakers, see Nora Levin, *The Jews in the Soviet Union since 1917: Paradox of Survival* (New York: New York University Press, 1988), 2:380–81.

conjunction with an inter-Allied conference held in January 1942 to discuss German atrocities and matters of potential postwar relevance, the leaders of a joint Anglo-Jewish committee approached Polish exile politicians to ensure the special plight of the Polish Jews would be appropriately acknowledged.

DOCUMENT 7-13: **Letter from Selig Brodetsky and Leonard Stein, Joint Foreign Committee, to Władysław Sikorski, Prime Minister of the Polish Government-in-Exile, London, January 12, 1942, USHMMA RG 59.023M (Board of Deputies of British Jews), reel 24, frame 801.**

To the President of the Meeting of Allied Governments,
St. James's Palace, S.W.

Your Excellency,

In view of the Meeting of the Allied Governments on the subject of Nazi atrocities against the populations of occupied territories,[69] the Joint Foreign Committee of the Board of Deputies of British Jews and the Anglo-Jewish Association[70] desire to bring to the notice of the Allied Governments, some considerations relating to the atrocities committed by the Nazis and the German Army against the Jewish section of these populations.

The interval between the announcement of the Meeting and the Meeting itself has been too short for a full and detailed statement of all the evidence in our possession, but this will be prepared and sent to the Allied Governments in due course.

The Joint Foreign Committee had no desire to differentiate between the sufferings and brutalities inflicted by the Nazis on Jews and non-Jews,

---

69. Conference held on January 13, 1942, in London with delegates representing governments-in-exile of the Netherlands, Belgium, Luxembourg, Norway, Poland, Czechoslovakia, Yugoslavia, Greece, and Norway. The delegates passed a resolution declaring punishment of German war crimes as one of their major goals. See Arieh J. Kochavi, *Prelude to Nuremberg: Allied War Crimes Policy and the Question of Punishment* (Chapel Hill: University of North Carolina Press, 1998), 19–20.

70. The AJA was established in 1871 to provide Jewish communities in foreign countries with material aid. During the war it cooperated with the Board of Deputies of British Jews via the Joint Foreign Committee until the latter's dissolution in 1943. See Meier Sompolinsky, *Britain and the Holocaust: The Failure of Anglo-Jewish Leadership?* (Brighton: Sussex Academic Press, 1999), 15.

but as is well known, the Jews have as Mr. Winston Churchill recently stated borne "the brunt of the Nazis first onslaught upon the citadels of freedom and human dignity . . . and continued to bear a burden that might have seemed to be [be]yond endurance."[71]

In the course of the advance of the German Armies across Europe they have occupied territories, the Jewish population of which numbered over eight million souls, and particularly in Polish and Russian areas wanton and merciless destruction was wrought and calculated atrocities perpetrated in cities in which the Jewish population formed a considerable proportion.

Following mass executions and innumerable murders of individuals the Jewish population was either driven out or forcibly segregated in walled ghettos under conditions of physical starvation resulting in epidemics and an appalling rate of mortality. Any attempt at escape from the ghettos is punished by torture and death. There is evidence that in order to incite the non-Jewish population against the Jews, the latter have in many cases been compelled to destroy Churches and historic and national monuments.

The Joint Foreign Committee trusts that in the condemnation by the Allied Governments of the barbaric behaviour of the German Army in the occupied countries and in any measures which may be concerted in counteracting Nazi brutalities, due consideration will be given to the sufferings of Jews and to the part played by them in the common struggle.

We have the honour to be,
Your Excellency's obedient servants,
(signed) S. BRODETSKY.
L. J. STEIN,
Joint Chairmen.

The letter did not reach the Polish prime minister's office in time for the conference in London, which ended in "great disappointment over the fact that a statement on Nazi atrocities against Jews was completely ignored."[72] Sikorski, in his capacity as its president, did not reply until four months later. He reassured committee officials that "the governments represented are unanimous in

---

71. The quote is from a letter Churchill wrote to the *Jewish Chronicle*. The letter appeared on the front page of the November 14, 1941, issue of the *Jewish Chronicle* commemorating the journal's one-hundredth anniversary.

72. *Contemporary Jewish Record* 5, no. 2 (April 1942), 191.

deploring and in condemning all the crimes committed against the Jews in occupied territory, in the same manner as those committed against those of other origin." This notwithstanding, he asserted that "[t]here was no reason explicitly to recall the suffering endured by the Jews, all the more so as such a reference might be tantamount to an implicit recognition of the racial theories which we all reject."[73]

German censorship in combination with Allied reluctance to acknowledge the "special treatment" facing the Jews under the Nazi regime helped to keep the deadly reality of the "Final Solution" from the public eye everywhere. A few astute observers in the West picked up on the many, often subtle signs of increasing persecution and struggled with the impossible dual task of trying to prevent greater catastrophe and alerting the public. When in mid-March 1942 **Richard Lichtheim** wrote to the Board of Deputies of British Jews from Geneva about the "new wave [of] persecution sweeping Europe," including the concentration of the eighty-nine thousand Slovak Jews and further discriminatory measures planned by the Slovak regime,[74] he was referring to a set of events that Rabbi **Abraham Frieder** had not only witnessed but was also involved in documenting and subverting.

An extract from Frieder's diary featured in an earlier chapter depicts the dramatic two-hour meeting that took place between Frieder and a Slovak cabinet minister in late February 1942.[75] Once the deportations had begun—affecting more than fifty thousand Slovak Jews until they were halted in the second half of 1942—Frieder and a group of other Jewish leaders tried to do what they could to mollify, derail, and obstruct the workings of the Slovak state's apparatus of persecution, including using their direct access to key Slovak officials and informing representatives of neutral countries. As part of these efforts, Frieder met with the new department head of the interior ministry responsible for the plans, Anton Vašek, who had risen through the ranks of the Slovak fascist party and had good connections to the regime's leadership. Vašek was eager, as Frieder put it, "to prove his scholarly talents" with the help of an "appropriate person"

---

73. Sikorski to the Joint Foreign Committee, May 16, 1942, USHMMA RG 59.023M (Board of Deputies of British Jews), reel 24, frame 809. See also David Engel, *In the Shadow of Auschwitz: The Polish Government-in-Exile and the Jews, 1939–1942* (Chapel Hill: University of North Carolina Press, 1987), 178.

74. Telegram from Richard Lichtheim, Jewish Agency for Palestine, Geneva office, to Joseph Linton, London, March 16, 1942, USHMMA RG 59.023M (British Board of Deputies), reel 24, frame 245.

75. See document 6-8.

who would do the actual research and writing of a work, and Frieder was ready to use this opportunity.

DOCUMENT 7-14: Rabbi Abraham Frieder, Nové Mesto, Slovakia, diary entries for early March 1942, USHMMA Acc. 2008.286.1 Frieder collection (translated from German).[76]

He [Vašek] summoned me to his office and started talking with me about the Jewish problem. In a long talk, I set forth the history of the Jews for him and referred to potential problems of the Jews. As it later turned out, he was quite enthusiastic about me as an individual, and thus began our "so-called friendship." On every occasion, he emphasized how intelligent and decent the "hlavný rabín" [chief rabbi] was, and thus began our work together. I pursued two objectives in this work. First, to deal with his topics in such a way that the Jews would emerge from this work fairly unscathed and unencumbered; second, I had to keep his position in mind, of course, as well as the prevailing anti-Jewish times and conditions, and therefore had to write things against the Jews now and then; and third, I didn't want to stay in the role of a historian who wrote speeches, papers, and books for him, to which he merely added his name. Rather, I wanted above all to make the most of this connection to help Jews, to influence him, and ask him to relieve the great distress wherever possible.

Our meetings took place twice a week, and each time I handed him the material first, and then presented my request.

I very often got various and sundry requests approved and had a good influence on him in a great many matters, so that I got the anti-semitism of the bloodthirsty [Nazi German journal] *Stürmer* out of his head altogether. Not to mention the achievement I regarded as the most positive one: that I was left alone in his room on innumerable occasions and simply tore up or threw into the stove various anonymous notices, anti-Jewish letters, letters that were dangerous to us, and thus helped countless people who did not and could not know that people

---

76. For a different, more edited translation of the diary section see Abraham Frieder, *To Deliver Their Souls: The Struggle of a Young Rabbi during the Holocaust*, ed. Emanuel Frieder (New York: Holocaust Library, 1990), 86–87.

were trying to attack them behind their backs. He himself never had a head for the job, never knew what file was on his desk, could never get the idea, and his assistants didn't bother much about it, because they were usually unaware that he had received such things. For me, however, it was always emotionally gratifying to come home from there with my pockets full of torn-up letters and files, each of which signified that another Jewish victim had been saved.

Such access to authorities remained unusual. A few Jewish men could also exert some leverage when they found themselves grouped with fellow nationals, even as prisoners of war. David Alkalaj, a prominent official from Belgrade, was among several hundred Jewish POWs in German camps for Yugoslav officers. Although they were marked as Jews, separated from non-Jewish prisoners, and discriminated against in the camps, their treatment differed markedly from the murderous practices used by the German army against Soviet POWs that led to the death of roughly 3.5 million of them, including at least fifty thousand Jews, by the end of the war.[77] In the letter below, Alkalaj approached a Serbian general, a fellow camp inmate, about intervening on behalf of Jewish prisoners so that they could contact their families in the *Judenlager Semlin*. Yet by May 1942, when the letter was written and unbeknownst to Alkalaj and his fellow POWs, almost all women and children at Sajmište had already been murdered in a gas van sent from Berlin.

---

77. On the Wehrmacht treatment of Soviet POWs, see Christian Streit, *Keine Kameraden. Die Wehrmacht und die sowjetischen Kriegsgefangenen, 1941–1945* (Bonn: J. H. W. Dietz, 1997), 128–90. After the invasion and collapse of Yugoslavia, the Germans took about two hundred thousand POWs—predominantly Serbs, Jews from Serbia among them—and deported them to Germany; most of them survived the war. See Jozo Tomasevich, *War and Revolution in Yugoslavia, 1941–1945: Occupation and Collaboration* (Stanford, CA: Stanford University Press, 2001), 656. David Alkalaj (1897–1981) was a lawyer from Belgrade and a prominent Zionist. He served as deputy chairman and then president of the Jewish Community of Belgrade until April 1941, when he was taken as a prisoner of war after the Axis invasion of Yugoslavia. Alkalaj directed postwar reconstruction efforts in Yugoslavia as president of the Autonomous Relief Committee in Belgrade, which headed the relief work for Yugoslav Jews, until he immigrated to Israel in 1950. See Jennie Lebel, *Until "The Final Solution": The Jews in Belgrade 1521–1942* (Bergenfield, NJ: Avotaynu, 2007), 199; Emil Kerenji, *Jewish Citizens of Socialist Yugoslavia: Politics of Jewish Identity in a Socialist State, 1944–1974* (PhD thesis, University of Michigan, 2008).

DOCUMENT 7-15: **Letter from David Alkalaj, POW in the German-run Eversheide camp to General Miloje Popadić, May 26, 1942, USHMMA RG 49.007M (JHM 5499 k.20-1-2/22), reel 4 (translated from Serbian).[78]**

Non-commissioned [rank] David A. Alkalaj
Prisoner no. 2189/34

To the superintendent of the prisoner [of war] camp Oflag VIc
Division General Miloje Popadić

As an elder of the 34th barrack, I take the liberty of addressing you in the name of my comrades, Yugoslav officers, prisoners of Mosaic faith, who are inmates in this camp, with the following appeal:

In accordance with the order of the German police in Belgrade, on December 12, 1941, all Jews without exception, regardless of age, sex, and medical condition were interned in the camp at Sajmište, by the Zemun bridge.[79] This terrible measure affected many of us—prisoners in this camp, who left their wives and children, brothers and sisters, old parents in Belgrade, because this severed any connection between them and us. Since December 12 of last year, only in two instances did we receive sporadic news, while the overwhelming majority of us have not heard from their loved ones in Sajmište in almost six months, even though we send our mail regularly to that camp.

Desperate because of uncertainty about the fate of our loved ones in the said camp, after a difficult winter without firewood and protection by anyone, I have on two occasions—as an elder of the barrack and in the name of my comrades—addressed the Serbian Red Cross, and once the Department for Prisoners of War, asking them to 1) allow for reestablishment of postal connection between us and our loved ones at Sajmište, and 2) that aid that we get as officers be delivered to our families, that is, be given as food by the Red Cross because they are certainly hungry at the camp. Unfortunately, neither of these two institutions had any sympathy for us officers who, like other Serbian comrades, remained faithful to the

---

78. The document was written in Cyrillic script.

79. The first deportation of Belgrade's Jews to Sajmište commenced on December 8, 1941. See Christopher R. Browning, "Wehrmacht Reprisal Policy and the Murder of the Male Jews in Serbia," and "The Semlin Gas Van and the Final Solution in Serbia," in *Fateful Months: Essays on the Emergence of the Final Solution*, ed. Christopher R. Browning (New York: Holmes & Meier, 1985), 39–56, 68–85; also, document 5-3.

King and the Fatherland,[80] and they did not reply to my appeals, leaving us in despair and uncertainty.

For these reasons, Mr. General, I kindly ask you to please intervene on our behalf with the Serbian Red Cross in Belgrade: to make sure that our letters and postcards are delivered to our families at the camp, as well as allow them to reply to [our correspondence]; that the Red Cross delivers our officer aid, which we haven't received since December of last year, aid in goods—food, to the extent possible.

Certainly the Red Cross should inform us whether our loved ones in the camp are alive and well.

In the event, however, that the camp at Sajmište should be relocated, we ask that the above be applied in that case as well, so that we can reestablish contact with our families, unhappy and forgotten by everyone—which is an elementary right of prisoners of war, according to the [Geneva] Convention.

Reminding you of your verbal promise that you would help us in this matter, I beg you, Mr. General, to have sympathy for us, whose souls suffer indescribably for our families, and convey to you, in the name of my comrades, our deepest gratitude.

Eversheide, May 26, 1942 David A. Alkalaj
    NCO
    Prisoner no. 2189/34

The documents in this chapter only show parts of a wide spectrum of relations between different strata within Jewish communities, and between these communities and non-Jewish authorities. Many of the actions taken by Jews in Axis-controlled regions remained undocumented, especially those outside the narrow margins of what was permissible. Obviously, smuggling food into the ghetto or bribing members of the Jewish police was nothing that one could or would proclaim publicly; only in diaries and personal letters did these kinds of illicit and "illegal" behavior surface at the time. What the documents exemplify, however, is the remarkable degree of activism and risk taking that arose for the purpose of improving not only one's own lot and that of loved ones, but also that of fellow sufferers who were even worse off. Individuals and groups tried to fill the massive and growing gaps in the German-controlled communal systems, even if conflicts arose continuously over the best path forward, the most auspicious times and ways to approach authority structures and leaders. The following chapter looks at more variations on the theme of help and solidarity within and beyond Jewish groups.

---

80. King Peter II of Yugoslavia fled Yugoslavia in April 1941 for London, along with the Yugoslav government-in-exile.

CHAPTER 8

Support Networks

S INCE THE BEGINNING of the war, mounting pressures and deteriorating infrastructures undermined long-established bastions of Jewish aid work and community cohesion. Everywhere the staff of relief organizations felt the strain of inadequate resources and unprecedented demands, which spelled disaster for short-term activities as well as long-term planning. The results of their work were nonetheless impressive. Looking back on the first three years of the war, the **American Jewish Joint Distribution Committee** reported that it had "aided nearly 1,000,000 persons each year, made possible the emigration of 93,000 Jewish refugees from Europe, sent medical help to 600,000 Polish Jewish refugees, and gave relief to 60,000 Jewish refugees in unoccupied France. Through the UPA [United Palestine Appeal] more than 30,000 homeless Jews were sent to Palestine, 20 new agricultural colonies, and 400 new factories were established, and 165,000 dunams of land were bought."[1] What these figures do not convey is a sense of the huge organizational efforts involved and the personal sacrifices made by staff, be it in danger zones where the chances for escape were dwindling, or at a long remove, with aid workers often unable to gauge either the extent of need or the impact of their interventions. If maintaining day-to-day aid required immense efforts and constant adaptation, planning for Jewish life in a postwar world—a discussion that many considered a luxury—presented even larger problems. The following

---

1. "Chronicles," *Contemporary Jewish Record* 5, no. 6 (December 1942): 627. The United Israel Appeal (formerly United Palestine Appeal, UPA) was founded in 1925 as a fund-raising organization to encourage Jewish immigration to Palestine. A dunam is a unit of land measurement equivalent to about one-quarter of an acre of land. The measurement is used in the Ottoman successor states, including Israel today.

chapter explores the structures in which Jewish solidarity carried on in the war and the tensions that arose between communal goals and the fate of individuals, between immediate demands and future prospects.

PRIVATE AND PUBLIC INTERESTS

To be effective in reaching more than a few recipients, aid work requires structured and sustained efforts carried out by devoted and competent individuals. As we have seen in previous chapters, the foundations for effective relief in Nazi-dominated Europe were under perpetual assault, affecting the operation of both the large-scale, often AJJDC-funded programs, as well as grassroots initiatives offered by Jewish organizations and "house" committees in German-occupied Poland. In Britain and the United States, Jewish organizations found their access routes to the disaster areas largely blocked and channels of communications into war zones severely curtailed. At home, where preexisting antisemitic prejudice combined with the effects of Nazi propaganda to heighten anxieties, these efforts met with skepticism and even hostility. In a situation in which only further bloodletting on the battlefields and more radical German anti-Jewish measures seemed certain, activists struggled to align their relief efforts with what remained possible. In addition to the fortunes of military warfare and international politics, a vast and changing range of factors defined the forms and outcomes of these struggles.

In the Reich, most of the Jewish youth and youth support groups still in existence in 1941 to 1942 were rooted in pre–Nazi-era structures and ideas, but they had been adapted under the leadership of highly devoted, sometimes charismatic activists to the changed circumstances of war. In Vienna, twenty-four-year-old Aron Menczer, who had a strong Zionist and altruistic orientation and was until May 1941 leader of the local Youth **Aliyah** (Jugendalijah or JUAL),[2] saw the needs of the city's young people in what was arguably a clearer light than the heads of the **Gestapo**-controlled Jewish community

---

2. Aron Menczer (1917–1943) was a Zionist youth leader involved since 1939 in Vienna's Youth Aliyah School. Menczer devoted his efforts to helping Jews immigrate to Palestine, refusing multiple opportunities to escape there himself. When the Youth Aliyah School and other Jewish organizations in Vienna were shut down by German authorities in May 1941, Menczer was sent to the Doppl labor camp, where he strove to nurture a positive outlook among young Jews. Menczer was deported to **Theresienstadt** on September 24, 1942, and on November 7, 1943, to **Auschwitz II-Birkenau**, where he was murdered on arrival. See Doron Rabinovici, *Eichmann's Jews: The Jewish Administration of Holocaust Vienna, 1938–1945* (Malden, MA: Polity Press, 2011), 164–67.

(Israelitische Kultusgemeinde, IKG). Sent to a "retraining camp" (in Doppl near Altenfelden),[3] he nurtured high hopes for his youth work, despite the dire conditions in the camp and the narrow confines of what the IKG community head Josef Löwenherz could do for hundreds of Jewish youth.[4] Menczer also struggled with the strong lure of his fiancé living in Berlin on the one hand and his parents and brothers in Palestine on the other.

DOCUMENT 8-1: **Correspondence between Aron Menczer, Altenfelden (near Linz), Ostmark, and the head of the Jewish Community in Vienna, Josef Löwenherz, July 1941, USHMMA RG 17.017M (CAHJP A/W 180 I), reel 289 (translated from German).**

[July 23, 1941]

Dear Doctor,

I hope you will not take it amiss if I write to you again after a fairly long silence. You will understand that I feel a certain sense of disquiet that is not due to personal things alone. In the countless letters coming to me from Vienna, I find confirmation of the pressing need for a youth center. Fall is already approaching, and the young people must not degenerate for lack of a home. Clearly this is a danger, given the present housing shortage.

As things stand, I feel an extremely close bond with these youths and am aware that the feeling is reciprocated. Moreover, I also know that in the past years, I have done everything within my power. Clearly, I made

---

3. Initially the camp in Doppl was run by the IKG before it was taken over by the Gestapo's Vienna-based Central Office for Jewish Emigration to provide labor for construction projects. See Wolf Gruner, *Zwangsarbeit und Verfolgung: Österreichische Juden im NS-Staat 1938–1945* (Innsbruck: Studien Verlag, 2000), 180–87.

4. Josef Löwenherz (1884–1960), Zionist activist in Vienna and lawyer by profession, throughout the 1920s and 1930s occupied multiple high-level posts in the Jewish Community in Vienna (IKG). After the **Anschluss**, Löwenherz dealt with Nazi and Gestapo authorities in the IKG and regime-imposed Central Office for Jewish Emigration, and made multiple trips abroad to open new routes for fleeing Jews. After the war, Soviet authorities arrested Löwenherz on allegations of collaboration with the Nazi occupiers, but he was cleared of charges based on testimonies by many survivors in the Viennese Jewish community before he immigrated to New York City with his wife, Sofie, in 1945. See the biographical note at the Center for Jewish History, at http://findingaids.cjh.org/?pID=121462#a2 (accessed on May 3, 2012); also Rabinovici, *Eichmann's Jews*; George E. Berkley, *Vienna and Its Jews: The Tragedy of Success, 1880s–1980s* (Cambridge, MA: Abt Books, 1988).

mistakes. What person, and what young person, never makes a mistake? But my intention was always pure, I did not do this for personal gain. The cause was the main thing. Probably everyone who watched me at work was aware of that. I was also proud to enjoy your trust, and I hope I still possess it, in spite of everything. Therefore I am requesting that you give me the chance to establish the youth center.

In the ten weeks that I've been here, I've had ample opportunity for thinking and planning. I can say without exaggeration that my thoughts were with my children day and night.

Therefore allow me to suggest: Please make rooms, heating, and lighting available to me, and I will present a model home [*Musterheim*] to you within three or four weeks. All staff, [illegible word], teachers, [illegible word], helpers—all will work for free and voluntarily. And this home shall offer:

a) For employed youths: evening and Sunday courses (foreign language instruction, technical training, etc.). Roughly 250 to 300 youth up to age 20.

b) For those who have finished school, but are not or only partly employed: vocational training with theoretical and practical elements. Roughly 150 to 200 [youth].

c) Added to this are this year's school-leavers. Special supplements to elementary education and practical training. Roughly 80 to 100 y. [youth].

d) For older pupils (ages 13 to 14): help for pupils with tutoring, assignments, supplements for Jewish classes. Takes the children off the streets and alleviates the domestic situation (see [illegible] home, which <u>cannot</u> take everyone).

e) Leisure activities and observance of religious and traditional holidays. For youth of all [social] classes.

And all this—I guarantee and promise—will be done at no cost to the community. Of course the plan can be subdivided, [but here] this would go too far.

For this purpose, I ask that you bring me to Vienna! (Or [illeg.], you want to use me in a different way) I hear of a plan for me to go to Berlin. Doctor, perhaps you know that I have friends in Berlin, but I don't want to go to Berlin. I'd rather wait here in Doppl for the various dates being offered. Why? In April 1939, when I went from Palestine to

Europe (leaving my dear parents and 5 brothers there), I was drawn to the youth of Vienna. Our bonds have only grown stronger since then. And if I have postponed my aliyah several times since the war started, then it was because I saw and still see that the young people here need me. Anyone who knows me knows that these are not mere conventional phrases.

I ask you to tell me where I stand at this time. Regardless, if there is no prospect of my return—I will bear it. But please understand that I am immersed here in ideas and plans—and at the same time I assume, of course, that this center will be under the close supervision of the Youth Welfare Office and the Board of Education [of the IKG-Vienna]—and I do not know where I stand. I hope very much indeed that I will continue to enjoy your confidence, and I intend to prove myself worthy of it once again.

I ask for your indulgence and apologize for the long letter. As my mother used to say: it's straight talking.

Respectfully yours, and with Zion's greeting,

[signed] Aron Menczer

[July 28, 1941:]
Dear Mr. Menczer,

I received your letter dated the 23rd of this month and am informing you that I myself am already thinking about how I could employ you. The difficulty is that I am now faced with a cutback and do not know whether I can get approval for hiring you.

The young people are now busy with the project for using small lots of marginal land for gardening. We set up a wading pool for the children there and gave them an opportunity to play outdoors while the work is going on. I am planning courses for the fall and have had several rooms in Castellezgasse [a building owned by the IKG in Vienna] set up for this purpose. In addition, I want to assign the young people to individual skilled craftsmen and have them trained as paperhangers, carpenters, painters, metal workers, and electricians.

We will resume normal school operations in Castellezgasse on August 1; the teaching has never stopped at the other establishments.

At the next available opportunity, possibly even in the course of this week, I will speak with Obersturmführer Brunner[5] on your account, campaign hard for your return to Vienna, and let you know the outcome of my intervention.

Kind regards,

[Josef Löwenherz]

Those like Menczer who deliberately decided to stay so they could help people made a personal sacrifice, with enormous, potentially fatal consequences. Sometimes the sense of duty to one's community overlapped with private desires, most notably in situations in which individuals decided to forego opportunities to leave in order to stay with loved ones. However, the choice was rarely clear-cut, as we have seen in the case of **Mignon Langnas**, who drew comfort from caring for her ailing parents in Vienna while longing to be reunited with her husband and children in distant America.[6] For **Claartje van Aals** in the Netherlands, working as a nurse in a clinic not only satisfied her urge to assist others and provided a sense of identity; it also led to her falling in love with one of her colleagues.[7] While those working in familiar surroundings could quickly acquire a sense of the most urgent needs, uncertainty reigned among Jews further afield about what should or could be done for those trapped by the occupation. Small incidents like the ones featured in the next two documents could trigger more profound questions about how to bridge the divide. In the following letter, still in draft form, an official at the Geneva office of the **World Jewish Congress** (presumably the head of the organization's Polish Relief committee,

---

5. Alois Brunner (1912–?) was one of the Nazi Party's early supporters in Austria. He joined the SS in 1938 and was assigned to **Adolf Eichmann**'s Central Office for Jewish Emigration in Vienna. Eichmann sent Brunner, who had gained expertise as a "deportation specialist" during the war and a reputation for brutality, to multiple European cities—in October 1942 to Berlin, in February 1943 to Salonika, later that year to Paris and Nice, and in September 1944 to Bratislava, to organize mass deportation of Jews to death camps and other destinations. He evaded capture at the end of the war and fled to Damascus, Syria, in 1954, where he allegedly died a few years ago. See Hans Safrian, *Eichmann's Men* (New York: Cambridge University Press in association with the USHMM, 2010), esp. 120–23, 223–24; Rabinovici, *Eichmann's Jews*, 101–2, 120, 129–30.

6. See document 1-3.

7. See document 1-12; also Suzette Wyers, ed., *Als ik wil kan ik duiken . . .: Brieven van Claartje van Aals, verpleegster in de joods psychiatrische inrichting Het Apeldoornsche Bosch, 1940–1943* (Amsterdam: T. Rap, 1995), 74, 76, 79–81 (letters dated August 26–27, September 3–4, October 9–10, 13–14, and 31, 1941).

Abraham Silberschein), voiced passionate objections to a request by the city's Jewish Youth Committee to hold a festive fund-raising event.

DOCUMENT 8-2: Draft letter from the WJC-Geneva to the Jewish Youth Committee-Geneva, expressing disapproval of the committee's plans to hold a charity ball, December 18, 1941, USHMMA RG 68.045M (WJC Geneva), reel 63, file 458 (translated from French).

Monsieur,

I thank you for your kind invitation to assist in your charity gala. I am deeply disturbed by the fact that the Jewish youth of Geneva, at just this moment and even after having consulted various persons, are organizing a ball to aid the victims of a catastrophe that has struck the Jewish people and that is rendered unique in the history of our people by the suffering and the death it has unleashed among our brothers in Europe, with the exception of your small country. I would like to think that even the persons whom you consulted are ignorant of what is currently taking place. In Romania, thousands of Jews, particularly among the youth, have been shot, others have been hounded and hauled into the forest, where they suffer hunger and cold. No one knows what will become of them. In Croatia, all the Jews have been deported—women, the elderly, children— mainly to the uninhabited salt isles.[8] They live there, without shelter, and

---

8. This is a reference, obviously based on incomplete and partly inaccurate information, to the **ustaša** camp for Serbs and Jews in Slana, on the island of Pag. Slana (the name of the camp in Croatian contains the root for "salt" or "salty") operated between May and August 1941; it was situated on an uninhabitable barren rock plateau in the middle of the Adriatic, buffeted by the elements—the scorching sun and sea winds—with no running water or other minimal conditions for human habitation. The estimates for the number of people killed at Slana range from ten thousand to fifteen thousand, about one thousand of whom were Jews (the rest were overwhelmingly Serbs, with some Croat enemies of the ustaša regime). Once the spontaneous Serb uprising spread in the Independent State of Croatia in the summer of 1941, following the ustaša massacres against Serb civilians, Italian forces occupied their zone of the Independent State of Croatia on the pretext of curbing chaos in these areas. Ustaše then dismantled the camps in this zone and built new ones in the fall of 1941, in the German zone—Stara Gradiška, Loborgrad, Đakovo, and, the most infamous one, **Jasenovac**. On Slana, see Ivo Goldstein, *Holokaust u Zagrebu* (Zagreb: Novi liber, 2001), 276–93. See also Joseph White, ed., *The United States Holocaust Memorial Museum Encyclopedia of Camps and Ghettos, 1933–1945*, vol. 3: *Camps and Ghettos under European Regimes Aligned with Nazi Germany* (Bloomington: Indiana University Press in association with USHMM, forthcoming).

bringing them any aid is forbidden, all contact with family members is prohibited, and the salty air erodes the lungs in less than three months.

In Hungary, hundreds of Jews have been deported to Poland. But what is happening in Poland is indescribable. It is nothing but one massive concentration camp where hunger and epidemics reign supreme. Those who write envy those who are no more because their fate is certainly better than that of those who remain. Approximately 300 to 400 persons die each day in Warsaw. There is no work, and thus no earnings to be had. Behind the walls of the ghetto, the Jews are condemned to a slow death, and yet their situation is not at all comparable to that [of the Jews] in Romania and Croatia. And what is this in comparison with the camps in France, such as Gurs, for example. And now in non-occupied France the martyrdom is already beginning. In recent days, our brothers have once again been arrested in broad daylight and locked away in camps. And in Germany, the clean-up has speeded up and the Jews, irrespective of age, are locked up in provisional camps before being deported. According to the most recent news from Paris, hundreds of Jews have likewise been deported to Poland. One can only comprehend what this means if one understands the situation of the Jews who are already in Poland.

And what is our youth doing in the large Jewish centers? In Poland and Romania, they are closing ranks, providing aid to one another, they are searching for and finding work, they are striving to organize professional re-education and adapt, they are seeking by all means—sometimes very dangerous ones—to provide material and moral aid to those who lack energy and are without hope. Neither hunger nor poverty prevents this youth from working courageously. But this same youth is dying because they cannot get the fresh air of the countryside—there are not even gardens in the ghetto. The majority has contracted tuberculosis. And those whom typhus and tuberculosis spare die of hunger.

I ask the Jewish youth of Geneva whether they truly have the heart to dance in order to alleviate this misery. Should a ball be organized to provide aid to our brothers? Will their conscience [i.e., of the Jewish youth in Geneva] be soothed even if this ball is a financial success? Do you believe that balls are an appropriate expression of solidarity in light of this unspeakable suffering? Do you not think it would be preferable and that the results might be superior if the youth were to do their duty calmly and with an earnestness appropriate to the situation? And in full appreciation of the fact that they can continue to live in one corner of the globe that fate has spared and that they carry out their charitable action from individual to individual, from house to house, continually and without pause?

I beg you to excuse me if I have believed it necessary to express my opinion on this question. But it would have been difficult for me to remain silent and not express at least in part the feelings that trouble me.

Opinions about what was "appropriate to the situation," as Silberschein put it, differed among individuals and within communities, and the level of external threat was never the only determining factor. In Vilna, Herman Kruk regarded the notification about the first ghetto concert in January 1942 as "[a]n offense to all our feelings," prompting calls by the local **Bund** for a boycott and the distribution of leaflets reading, "You don't make theater in a graveyard."[9] In her diary, sixteen-year-old Esther van Vriesland depicts a scene during an event at the Jewish community in the Dutch town of Gorkum that attests to tensions between Jews of different generations and political orientations.

DOCUMENT 8-3: **Esther van Vriesland,**[10] **Gorkum, German-occupied Netherlands, diary entries for May 15 and 31, 1942, in** *Esther: Een Dagboek, 1942* **(Utrecht: Stichting Matrijs, 1990), 110–11, 116–17 (translated from Dutch).**

[May 15, 1942]

Let me first say something about Wednesday evening.[11] It was very special. I was supposed to sit with Ies Kalker but did not want to. I find him such a creep. I stuck with Toedie. Then I switched with Simon, who sat between Philip and Phlip van Dam. We sang and made quite a racket. Mr. Seijffers gave a speech, so dull, not at all appropriate. He talked about

9. Herman Kruk, *The Last Days of the Jerusalem of Lithuania: Chronicles from the Vilna Ghetto and the Camps, 1939–1944* (New Haven, CT: Yale University Press, 2002),174 (entry for January 17, 1942).

10. Esther van Vriesland (1926–1942), from Gorinchem in the Netherlands, was sent to Auschwitz via Westerbork. See Esther van Vriesland, *Esther: Een Dagboek 1942* (Utrecht: Stichting Matrijs, 1990), 7–14, 158; www.geheugenvannederland.nl/?/nl/collecties/oorlogsdagboeken (accessed May 22, 2012). The Amsterdam Jewish Historical Museum holds the original in its "Collectie Joods Historisch Museum." The authors have been unable to find information about the people mentioned in this diary unless otherwise noted.

11. Most likely a reference to a special meeting for the youth of the Jewish community, in advance of the centennial celebration of the opening of the local synagogue (May 30, 1942). Mr. Seijffers (or Seyffers) was the local rabbi and Uncle Flip (Vos) was the chairman of the board of the Jewish community of Gorinchem (personal communication, Bert Stamkot, May 20, 2012).

Uncle Flip as chairman as if he were dead. Such as, "He was always good for the community." At the end big Ies wanted us to sing the *Wilhelmus* [national anthem], but we young people began to sing the *Hatikvah*.[12] No one else stood up, just us. It was so sincere, diary. You felt how "together" you were. I want to go to Palestine, in the future there has to be a new Jewish state, and we will work the land. That powerful feeling that took possession of me could not be described. It sounded so proud. Now I suddenly remember what the Chief Rabbi said during a Chanukah *midrash* [lesson]: "our future rests on you, our youth." With as much fire and passion as I have never heard from him. And now I had the same feeling. Later they all stood up. [. . .]

[May 31, 1942]

Friday we had another Jewish lesson, which was again tremendously interesting. And when I walked home last evening I thought about his words. He [Mr. Vorst] spoke about the feeling of inferiority that all of us Jews have, that we tell ourselves we are only Jews. He said also that our youth had been poisoned. But then what are we living for? To be taunted? I am well aware of the answer: "to found a Jewish state." If only it had already come to pass. And when you walk along the street, it feels as if everyone is looking at you or as if they are talking about you. You try to keep your head proudly up high, but that feeling! Why on earth do I study? What does it matter to me? What does it matter to a rotten world? I suddenly remember a sentence from a story, "wretched world, good night." That is how I fell asleep last night. I cannot begin to tell you how low I felt yesterday. [. . .]

Support between Jews typically went from those living in relative safety to those in utter distress. Paradoxically, however, at times a kind of support was also channeled in the other direction. Among those deported in the spring of 1942 from the Reich to towns in the Lublin district of the **Generalgouvernment** was the Krombach family from Essen, consisting of Dr. David Krombach, one of the Essen Jewish community's remaining leading figures, his wife, Minna, and their son, Ernst, born in 1921. Ernst had been secretly engaged to Marianne Strauss, born in 1923, the daughter of another established Jewish family in Essen that was expecting to immigrate to Cuba.[13] Witnessing the train with the

---

12. The Zionist anthem, later the national anthem of Israel.

13. For information on the Krombach family and Marianne Strauss, see Mark Roseman, *A Past in Hiding: Memory and Survival in Nazi Germany* (New York: Metropolitan Books, 2000).

Krombachs and roughly 940 other deportees—among them **Erich Langer**[14]—leave the Essen train station on April 21, 1942, Marianne was thrown into deep despair and wanted to join her great love en route to what turned out to be Izbica, a "resettlement" center for Jews some fifty-eight kilometers (thirty-six miles) southeast of Lublin and way station to the death camps in the district.[15]

What historian Mark Roseman calls "the stange mixture of information and ignorance" emanating from Ernst's letters to Marianne (whom he calls Jeanne) no doubt resulted from not wishing to upset his fiancée or cause censors to withhold the mail altogether.[16] At the same time Ernst's notes reflect the shock many deportees experienced when they discovered what "evacuation to the East" really meant. In his first letter from Izbica, Ernst tried to come to grips with the situation, as well as the problem of how to communicate it to his beloved back home. He also did what he could to dissuade Marianne from joining him (as she had announced), while assuring her of his devotion.

DOCUMENT 8-4: **Letter from Ernst Krombach, Izbica, Lublin district, Generalgouvernement, to Marianne Strauss, Essen, Germany, April 28, 1942, in Mark Roseman,** *A Past in Hiding: Memory and Survival in Nazi Germany* **(New York: Metropolitan Books, 2000), 175–76 (translated from German).**

Dearest,

Sadly I have not yet had any mail from you. So I am waiting for something nice. What shall I write about? In terms of food and cleanliness the conditions here are more extreme than anything we imagined; it's simply impossible to put them into words. Words could never convey the reality of life here. The Wild West is nothing compared to this. The attitudes and approaches to life here are so incomprehensible. Anyone not firmly grounded will find himself spiritually derailed forever. There is neither culture nor morality, two things we once thought we could manage

---

14. See document 4-13.

15. On Izbica, see Robert Kuwałek and Martin Dean, "Izbica (nad Wieprzem)," in *The United States Holocaust Memorial Museum Encyclopedia of Camps and Ghettos, 1933–1945*, vol. 2: *Ghettos in German-Occupied Eastern Europe*, ed. Martin Dean (Bloomington: Indiana University Press in association with the USHMM, 2012), 639–43; Robert Kuwałek, "Das Durchgangsghetto in Izbica," *Theresienstädter Studien und Dokumente* (2003), 321–52. While the exact fate of the Krombachs has never been established, it is known that Izbica was cleared in April 1943 and all remaining Jews at that time were deported to **Sobibór**.

16. Roseman, *A Past in Hiding*, 170.

without. Once you experience the extremity of this place, you're cured of that particular view. It is terrible not to be able to help people. One is simply powerless in the face of it all!

[. . .] Postal orders are not always accepted. But we are allowed to receive money via letters and letter-parcels do get here. It's probably better not to send proper parcels. It is possible to put old clothes in letter-parcels. It is possible to receive food.

You must be terribly curious about the appearance of this place. There are 7,000 Jews ruled by a Council of Elders, and the council is ruled by the Gestapo. That might sound fine, but the reality is different. You might be able to sketch a rough picture of the place, but I doubt it would bear much resemblance to the reality.

Now the page is used up, Jeanne!

The unsettling effects of relocation for the deportees did not end at their arrival in far-flung ghettos and camps. Once they had arrived, their makeshift arrangements could tip at any time into something even more precarious and life threatening. Still, hope occupied a small, critical corner here, especially if "resettled" Jews brought with them the energy to stretch the limits of what was possible and work together to alleviate their plight. In late December 1941, **Eva Mändl** was sent with her mother from their home in Prague to Theresienstadt, where she tried hard to make the best of the strange, new situation in which she found herself.

DOCUMENT 8-5: Eva Mändl, Theresienstadt, Protectorate, diary entries for December 27, 1941, to April 19, 1942, in Eva Mändl Roubíčková, *"Langsam gewöhnen wir uns an das Ghettoleben." Ein Tagebuch aus Theresienstadt*, ed. Veronika Springmann (Hamburg: Konkret Literatur Verlag, 2007), 75–76, 78–79, 82, 85, 90–92 (translated from German).[17]

[December 27, 1941]

Finally we got a room, but still without a stove. A few old ladies have moved into our room, but we're still sleeping in the old room. Have lost my watch. Not much food, but one can deal with that. We still have some from home. I don't wear dresses at all, just trousers, unfortunately I brought only some of poor quality. A man made us an offer: we can write

---

17. For a different translation of parts of the diary, see Eva Roubíčková, *We're Alive and Life Goes On: A Theresienstadt Diary* (New York: Henry Holt, 1998), 13–33.

a letter, and he'll send it. Wrote to Mama [the mother of her fiancé]. True, the punishment for that is always death, but everybody writes nonetheless. Actually I imagined everything as much worse, along the lines of dying, because it was something you couldn't form any idea of at all, and when we met the people who have already spent considerable time here, I also thought they were like strangers from another world. But we live here, too, our mood is not all that bad, we even laugh fairly often, which I never would have thought possible in Prague. In a nutshell: life goes on. You just mustn't think about things. You're busy all day, in the evening you lie down on a mattress and sleep. Just don't think about it. Just don't do that. You even chat with boys.

[. . .]

[January 1, 1942]

Everything that is supposed to be turned in has been collected, but we haven't decided yet where we'll hide it. In the afternoon there was a concert in the office. One accordion player, one singer. People felt carried back to normal times again, a strange feeling, many cried. German and Czech songs were sung. Fredy Hirsch[18] made a speech and had the courage to say all kinds of things, that we've touched bottom now and that it will be better again soon and that no rulers are in power forever. It had to be interrupted about halfway through and all the men had to leave. The gendarmes didn't let it continue.

[. . .]

[January 13, 1942]

In the morning another 50 women were ordered to report [for transports leaving Theresienstadt for Poland], because many "pets" [those with connections to people of influence] were kept back. Letter from Zwi [friend from her Prague circle]. To keep us from going to Poland, he wants

---

18. Fredy Hirsch (1916–1944), from Germany, worked in the orphanage in Theresienstadt. Deported in September 1942 to the "Theresienstadt family camp" in Birkenau, he continued to work with children. He eventually committed suicide in the spring of 1944 as the Germans were liquidating the "family camp" and sending its inmates to the gas chambers. See Lucie Ondrichová, *Fredy Hirsch. Von Aachen über Düsseldorf nach Frankfurt am Main durch Theresienstadt nach Auschwitz-Birkenau. Eine jüdische Biographie 1916–1944* (Konstanz: Hartung Gorre Verlag, 2000). On the "family camp" in Birkenau, see Saul Friedländer, *Nazi Germany and the Jews:* (vol. 2) *The Years of Extermination, 1939–1945* (New York: HarperCollins, 2007), 579–80.

to sign me up with the gardeners, possibly as his fiancée, only formally, of course. That's really tremendously decent.

[. . .]

[February 5, 1942]
Three-fourths of all the women don't get their periods here, my last one was on the journey to Theresienstadt.[19]

[. . .]

[February 26, 1942]
Once again, ten people executed. Some for smuggling letters, some for resisting when Seidl[20] thrashed them. The mood was horrible again.

[. . .]

[April 9, 1942]
People ordered to report for the transport to Poland.[21] This affects mainly the new transports [arrivals] from Brünn [Brno]. They don't have many people and will also have to take some from the old transports. The transport to Pürglitz [Křivoklát, a small town some 56.3 kilometers (35 miles) west of Prague] left on the tenth. In the evening, an 18-year-old German, a rascally type, went through all the rooms, we had just moved out. I don't know how it happens, but most people here can wangle something for themselves after all. It's terribly sad that you can achieve everything here only by trickery, lies, or theft. Will people be able to fit into normal life again, will they ever be normal, decent human beings again? Won't we all be criminals when we get out of here?

[. . .]

[April 19, 1942]
There's such a terrible amount of wickedness, and only those who are bad can get anywhere. Anybody who steals or is brutal or flirts can get

19. This was largely due to the effects of malnutrition.

20. SS Captain Siegfried Seidl (1911–1947) commanded the Theresienstadt ghetto from 1941 until 1943. After the war he was sentenced to death in Vienna and executed. See Tomáš Fedorovič, "Der Theresienstädter Lagerkommandant Siegried Seidl," in *Theresienstädter Studien und Dokumente 2003* (Prague: Theresienstädter Initiative, 2003), 163–200.

21. This transport left on April 18 with one thousand Jews from Theresienstadt for Rejowiec. See Eva Mändl Roubíčková, *"Langsam gewöhnen wir uns an das Ghettoleben." Ein Tagebuch aus Theresienstadt*, ed. Veronika Springmann (Hamburg: Konkret Literatur Verlag, 2007), 230n129.

somewhere. Anybody who can't be that way can absolutely starve to death. I can't, just can't, exploit people and be calculating, and it's something I'll never learn, either. I work hard and let myself be exploited.

Symbolic action often remained the only bond between deportees and those left behind in ever more precarious situations. Invoking solidarity could take the form of proclamations and commemorative gatherings, some featured later in this chapter. These gestures cultivated a sense of belonging and positive identity under oppressive conditions, while also courting very real danger, particularly when they were staged by groups. Operating increasingly outside the borders of legality as defined by the regime, but with an enduring sense of commitment to a common cause, was the youth group in Berlin led by Jizchak (Hans-Joachim) Schwersenz.[22] Schwersenz directed the Youth Aliyah school under the **Reichsvereinigung**'s youth department and led Zionist boy scout groups (Makabi-Hatzair/Brit Hatzofim) that met regularly for training and religious sessions away from the Gestapo's watchful eye. Like other clandestine youth groups in German-controlled Europe, Schwersenz's group circumvented a vast array of prohibitions for Jews, such as those against holding meetings, use of public transport, or wearing of group insignia, and it maintained an active program structured around Zionist and religious holidays. These young people's infractions gave their meetings a cultlike aura and alleviated at least to a degree the massive psychological effects of the deportations around them and other vital threats to their group or family members.[23] The following report, written by Günter (Arje) Dawidowicz[24] on a ceremony conducted clandestinely in Berlin on the Day of the Jewish Boy Scout (Yom Hatzofim), sought to reach and resonate with a wide Zionist audience in Germany and abroad, sharing news about the amazing feat of bringing together fifty young Jewish activists right in the heart of the Reich. Ambitions notwithstanding, it probably reached no more than a few people at the time.

---

22. See Beate Meyer, Hermann Simon, and Chana Schütz, eds., *Jews in Nazi Berlin: From Kristallnacht to Liberation* (Chicago: University of Chicago Press, 2009), 134–36.

23. On Schwersenz and his clandestine activities, see David Engel, Yitzchak Mais, and Eva Fogelman, eds., *Daring to Resist: Jewish Defiance in the Holocaust* (New York: Museum of Jewish Heritage, 2007); Jizchak Schwersenz and Edith Wolff, *Jüdische Jugend im Untergrund. Eine zionistische Gruppe in Deutschland während des Zweiten Weltkrieges* (Tel Aviv: Verlag Bitaon, 1969); Jizchak Schwersenz, *Die versteckte Gruppe. Ein jüdischer Lehrer erinnert sich an Deutschland* (Berlin: Wichern-Verlag, 1988).

24. Günter Dawidowicz (born in 1925) survived the war and immigrated to Israel in 1948. Leon Brandt, *Menschen ohne Schatten: Juden zwischen Untergang und Untergrund 1938 bis 1945* (Berlin: Oberbaum, 1984), 149.

DOCUMENT 8-6: **Report by Brith Hazofim-Berlin on a clandestine meeting held in March 1942, in Jizchak Schwersenz and Edith Wolff,** *Jüdische Jugend im Untergrund. Eine zionistische Gruppe in Deutschland während des Zweiten Weltkrieges* **(Tel Aviv: Verlag Bitaon, 1969), 33–34 (translated from German).**[25]

Brith Hazofim
Emunah Company

Berlin, March 1942

To our Chawerim [*haverim*] and Chaweroth [*haverot*] in
the Galuth [*galut*] countries and in Erez Israel [Eretz Israel]

Although we do not know whether this letter will reach you, we want to write it nonetheless—in the hope that one of us will survive and can hand this letter to you then.

Weeks ago, we were already talking in our groups about the celebration of this year's "Jom Hazofim" [*Yom Hatzofim*, Day of the Jewish Scouts]. Will it still be possible? We live in extremely hard times. Many of us have already been taken away to face an uncertain fate in Poland. But a Zofeh [*tzofeh*], a Jewish Scout, will never fall down on the job, and thus it was clear to us—we'll meet again, this time, too—for this special day.

On Wilsnacker Strasse, in a classroom of the school located there [a Jewish "Haushaltungsschule" or "housekeeping school"], we met on that Wednesday afternoon. Regardless of the danger, almost all appeared in their white shirts, or the girls, in white blouses {under their coats}. An atmosphere of exhilaration filled the room in which those who were left, about 50, had gathered. Herbert Growald and Fanny Bergas from the Neuendorf Chewrah [*hevra*] had come as our special guests, and to our great delight, Alfred Selbiger, the Chawer [*haver*, in Zionist vocabulary,

---

25. Stray ellipses appear in the original publication; { . . . } indicates annotation used in Schwersenz and Wolff, *Jüdische Jugend im Untergrund*, 33–34. The authors have been unable to find information about all of the people mentioned in this report.

comrade] from our association leadership,[26] was there as well. We were sitting in a big circle when the first songs were raised, {such as} our "Hejèh muchàn" [*heyeh muchan*] {be prepared}. The candles flickered merrily, and all eyes were on the flames. Then our Chawerah [*havera*, in Zionist vocabulary, female comrade] Mary Simon read a story aloud, telling about the planting of the trees in our Jewish homeland, a story that made us forget our suffering and distress. Then we sang some more. Some poems were read aloud, and then the shrill whistle was heard, with the command "Lamifkàd histadèr!" [*lamifkad histader*] {fall in for roll-call}—In an instant, we were standing in a square and striking up the association's anthem. Then, when the flag, which was still with us despite all the danger, made its appearance, we saluted it with the scout salute and sang the flag song, "S'u zijona" [*su tziona*] {carry the banner to Zion}. The individual groups were called out, and the group leaders made their report to Jizchak [Schwersenz], who then could inform Alfred [Selbiger] that the Berlin chevra had reported for Jom Hazofim.—Now Chawer Erwin Tichauer[27] stepped up and called out to his group the

---

26. Herbert Growald (1914–?) studied law in Berlin, and under the Nazis became a teacher in Jewish schools and a prominent Zionist youth leader. In 1942 and 1943, Growald led the Neuendorf agricultural farm and was among the last deported to Auschwitz, in April 1943. After forced labor in the Dora Mittelbau camp and Bergen-Belsen, Growald was liberated in April 1945. He was reunited with his girlfriend, whom he married; they immigrated to Palestine at the end of 1946. See Herbert Fiedler, *Träume und Geschichte,* vol. 3: *Ein Lebensweg* (Nuthe-Urstromtal/Luckenwalde: Förderverein für eine Internationale Begegnungsstätte Hachschara-Landwerk Ahrensdorf, 2001). Fanny Bergas (1900–1943) was from Berlin and a member of the Neuendorf training camp. In 1943 she was deported to Auschwitz, where she was murdered. Margit Naarmann, *Die Paderborner Juden 1802–1945* (Paderborn: Verein für Geschichte an der Universität GH-Paderborn, 1988), 469; *Gedenkbuch,* www.bundesarchiv.de/gedenkbuch (accessed July 9, 2012). Alfred Selbiger (1911 or 1914–1942) served as head of the Makabi-Hatzair/Brit Hatzofim and since early 1940 head of the Youth Aliyah of the Reichsvereinigung until his arrest and murder in December 1942. See Meyer, Simon, and Schütz, eds., *Jews in Nazi Berlin,* 355.

27. Erwin R. Tichauer (1920–1996) was a Berlin-born member of Schwersenz's group until his arrest by the Gestapo in February 1943. Deported to Auschwitz, he worked in the Jawiszowice coal mine, went on death marches in January 1945, and was liberated in the Ampfing concentration subcamp. After the war, Tichauer headed the police in the Feldafing displaced persons camp, where he met his wife, Helen, née Spitzer, also an Auschwitz survivor. In 1967 both settled in New York City, where he became professor of biomechanics. See Erwin R. Tichauer, "Ich ergebe mich. Das Ende einer KZ-Haft in Ampfing," *Dachauer Hefte* 13 (1997): 92–98.

names of all those who had been taken away in the past few months—
since the beginning of the deportations. Upon hearing each name, they
all answered as one: "Hinnèni" [*hineni*] {here I am}. They all are with
us, of course, because we think about them, as they surely think about
us, too . . . Then Jizchak spoke about the significance of this day . . .
and said that the chain of our fellowship would never break . . . He
recalled the great Jom Hazofim in 1939, when he read out the watchword from the beautiful Bible verse: "Lo b'chajil w'lo b'choach, ki im
b'ruchi . . ." [*lo b'hayil v'lo b'koah*] {Not by might, nor by power, but by
My Spirit, saith the Lord of hosts.—Zechariah 4:6}. The watchword, he
said, {applies} for us today more than ever. Because however different
it may look out there in the non-Jewish environment, we Jews believe
that the spirit alone, the human factor, will prevail. . . . Then Jizchak
awarded the silver and gold braid to some chaverim who had . . . proven
themselves, appointing them to be "Mezapim" or "Zofim" [*metzapim,
tzofim*] {"Pathfinders" or "Scouts"}.

Now our dear Alfred [Selbiger] took the floor: He was happy
to be in our midst, he said, after the difficult hours of work in the
"Reichsvereinigung," after the dreadful news and things he experienced
daily. That alone gave strength and purpose to our life as well as to his!
He was happy, he added, to see how our Chewrah had progressed . . .
Above all, however, {he said}, "Let us turn our eyes and our thoughts to
Erez Israel, where our people can lead a free and happy life. There may
be fighting there as well, but there it has a meaning!—Soon we all will
be doing our part in the work there and be able to live as free men again.
But today we want to express our gratitude to those who have given their
all to ensure that our association can continue to operate and, despite all
the difficulties, has remained our home, and—though this usually is not
the way of our association, which regards the performance of one's duty
as a matter of course—we want to confer on them a distinction that we
hope will be a lasting reminder of this time for them. In the name of
Hans Wendel,[28] who stayed to the very last at his post as a chaver of our

---

28. Hans Wendel (1911–1940), born in Chemnitz, Germany, was aboard the **Patria**
and among the passengers who drowned in the Haifa harbor. See Ulrich Schwemer and
Hans-Georg Vorndran, *Wer hätte das geglaubt: Erinnerungen an die Hachschara und die
Konzentrationslager* (Heppenheim: Evangelischer Arbeitskreis Kirche und Israel in Hessen
und Nassau, 1998); Jürgen Nitsche and Ruth Röcher, eds., *Juden in Chemnitz. Die Geschichte
der Gemeinde und ihrer Mitglieder, mit einer Dokumentation des jüdischen Friedhofs* (Dresden:
Sandstein, 2002), 234n1.

Hanhalah {association leadership} and now is no longer among us, I award you, Jizchak Schwersenz, and you, Herbert Growald, the Golden Pin of our association, with the certificate . . . Chasàk w'emaz [*hazak v'ematz*] {be strong and steady}!"

Now the command rang out: "Hakschèw—dom- kawod tèn!" [*hakh-shev-dom-kavod ten*] {Stand to attention—eyes right, salute!} The flag was lowered. We thought about our dear, loyal Chawerim and Chaweroth [*haverim, haverot*, plural forms for male and female comrades] who no longer stood with us in the circle, thought about our parents and about friends who had been torn from us. But then we heard the sounds of "Hatikwah,"[29] which gave us courage . . . to look ahead to the future and assuredly even more difficult times.

Therefore, we greet all of you out there in this difficult hour. Do not forget us, just as we also will not forget you who are already living in the land [of Palestine] and building our future, and we greet all of you in other countries as well who are living in freedom. Let us all stick together until the day comes when we all can be together again. We greet you— Schalom! Chasàk w'emaz!" [*Shalom! Hazak v'ematz!*]

POSTWAR PLANS FROM ABROAD

At a time when Nazi officials were working with passionate intensity to coordinate a Europe-wide murder campaign, discussions by Jews of a future world without Hitler signified both the resolve to carry on as well as utter desperation. While the war was still raging, providing relief for Jews in distress, fostering a fighting spirit in Allied countries, and discussing hypothetical plans for a postwar future was much of what international Jewish organizations and their staff could do. The war aims expressed by the Allies—to rid the world of Nazi dictatorship and create a stable basis for freedom and peace—provided powerful expectations among Jews. Hitler's defeat, they believed, would not only bring some redress for the crimes and injustices committed by Germany and the regimes aligned with it but also establish conditions for Jews to live as a community and as individuals safeguarded from aggression by their neighbors.

In light of the past, however, few harbored illusions of international harmony and guaranteed safety for Jewish communities around the world, not to mention the prospects for creating a Jewish state. The aftermath of World War I drove home the lesson that for any postwar planning to produce the desired

---

29. See above, note 12.

outcome, it needed to reconcile general ideals of peaceful coexistence with a political reality shaped by the traumatic effects of war as well as by continuities from the past.[30] In 1941 to 1942, it was already evident from the interwar era that not everything Nazism stood for would be destroyed once the weapons fell silent. Instead, many of the factors that had contributed to Hitler's appeal within and beyond Germany would undoubtedly persist. One of those crucial holdovers would be antisemitism, a complex system of beliefs and practices long predating the Nazis' rise to power and deeply affecting societies far beyond Europe's borders.[31] The persistence of antisemitism was a phenomenon that Jewish organizations needed to add to the equation, but the biggest unknown was the number of Jews who would live to see the end of the fighting in Europe. The more Jewish observers knew or surmised about the status and trajectory of the extermination process, the less they were inclined to believe that plans from the past would be suitable for the future.

For the time being, the needs of the present determined the format in which postwar aspirations were articulated. As we have seen from Prime Minister Sikorski's May 1942 letter featured in chapter 7,[32] Polish leaders declined to accept the fact that Jewish suffering had been greater than that of the non-Jewish population under Nazi rule, thus raising the question of how that country would in the future deal with antisemitic traditions. The following document shows how two of the leading Jewish organizations grappled with ideas of Jewish life in postwar Poland in the context of a newly instituted "Polish Jewish Day." It was intended as a day of remembrance to be observed around the anniversary of the German attack on Poland (September 1, 1939) and in conjunction with the beginning of Elul, the Jewish calendar month before the beginning of the high holidays. Drawing on the events of the recent past, the appeal that follows invited readers to reflect on how to safeguard human rights after Hitler as well.

---

30. See Carole Fink, *Defending the Rights of Others: The Great Powers, the Jews, and International Minority Protection, 1878–1938* (New York: Cambridge University Press, 2004).

31. See David Cesarani, Suzanne Bardgett, Jessica Reinisch, and Johannes-Dieter Steinert, eds., *Survivors of Nazi Persecution in Europe after the Second World War* (London: Vallentine Mitchell, 2010); Menno Spiering and Michael Wintle, eds., *European Identity and the Second World War* (New York: Palgrave Macmillan, 2011).

32. See above, 279–81.

DOCUMENT 8-7: **Statement by the American Jewish Congress and the World Jewish Congress in conjunction with "Polish Jewish Day," September 1, 1941, USHMMA RG 68.045M (WJC Geneva), reel 5, file 40.**

STATEMENT OF THE AMERICAN AND WORLD JEWISH
CONGRESS

Issued on September 1st [1941] in connection with the observance of "Polish-Jewish Day" marking the second anniversary of the invasion of Poland in September, 1939

Two years have passed since the first act in the present tragedy of mankind took place; the invasion of Poland by German troops on September 1, 1939, inaugurated a policy of suppressing the freedom of peoples by brute force and violence, irrespective of any consideration of justice and culture. All of Europe was turned into one vast battlefield and concentration camp.

The Polish state was the first victim of this inhuman force. The freedom of Poland was temporarily lost; the economic, cultural, and moral destruction of this unfortunate country is being accomplished on a scale never before known in human history.

The Jewish people of Poland suffer together with their Polish fellow citizens. They suffer far more, since they are persecuted both as Jews and as Polish citizens. Over three million Polish Jews are being turned into slaves; ousted from their homes, secluded in ghettos; condemned to forced labor or starved to death by people who have apparently lost all human feeling.

But neither the Polish people, nor Polish Jewry will die. The great forces of justice and democracy, under the leadership of Great Britain and of the United States of America, will bring about the rebirth of Poland and secure her glorious future.

The Jewish people join all of civilized mankind in its desire to have a free Poland re-constituted as soon as possible. The Jewish soldiers in the allied armies are fighting for Polish freedom and Poland's future. Together with the entire Jewish people, they are grateful to the Polish Government for its statement assuring the perfect equality of rights which the Jewish citizens of Poland will enjoy in the future Poland, being able to develop their own lives in a land which will be a home and a just fatherland to all its inhabitants.

The World Jewish Congress, as the representative of organized Jewry throughout the world, sends its greetings to the heroic Polish people and to its brethren in Poland on this day, commemorating our common sorrow and marking our common resolve to fight until a better future is won for all of us.

AMERICAN JEWISH CONGRESS   WORLD JEWISH CONGRESS
Stephen S. Wise, President[33]   Judge Julian W. Mack,[34]
Honorary Presid[ent]
Nachum Goldmann, Chairman[35]
Administrative Committee

Given the legacy of Polish antisemitism that Germans could and did draw on to stabilize their occupation regime,[36] and given the absence of any immediate prospects for a free Poland, the joint statement presented a gesture of hope that the commonality of wartime suffering would help create greater understanding between Poles and Jews. In a similar symbolic vein but geared toward strengthening the wartime bonds between the **Galut** and the **Yishuv**, Zionists in Palestine urged Jews to commemorate "Polish Jewish Day" (*Yom Yahadut Polin*, literally, in Hebrew, "Day of Polish Jewry") "to show practical sympathy and support for tormented Jewry in Nazi territory" through public gatherings and fund-raising. Those who made contributions received a "special tag" to display their solidarity.[37] As the following poster suggested, their campaign projected a picture of a community facing the challenges of the war with forward-looking optimism.

---

33. See the Glossary.

34. Julian William Mack (1866–1943) was a prominent American academic, jurist, and social welfare activist. A professor at the University of Chicago, Mack also served as a municipal, state, and federal judge in addition to his long-standing career in Jewish organizations. He helped to establish the American Jewish Committee in 1906, presided over both the American Jewish Congress and Zionist Organization of America beginning in 1918, and was named Honorary President of the World Jewish Congress in 1936. See Morton Rosenstock, "Mack, Julian William," in *Encyclopaedia Judaica*, ed. Fred Skolnik and Michael Berenbaum, 2nd ed. (Detroit: Macmillan Reference USA, 2007), 13, 327–28; obituary, *New York Times*, September 6, 1943.

35. See the Glossary.

36. See Alexandra Garbarini, Emil Kerenji, Jan Lambertz, and Avinoam Patt, *Jewish Responses to Persecution,* vol. 2: *1938–1940* (Lanham, MD: AltaMira Press in association with the USHMM, 2011), 353–55.

37. *Palestine Post*, September 1, 1943, 3.

DOCUMENT 8-8: Yishuv poster to commemorate "Polish Jewish Day" in 1941, USHMMPA WS# 08330.

[Hebrew text:] To Victory and Rebirth! Polish Jewish Day, 1.9.1939–1.9.1941
[September 1, 1939–September 1, 1941].

Programmatic Allied expressions of future intent driven by human-istic ideals did not mean much if they were not followed by concrete agen-das with clearly defined political goals. The **Atlantic Charter**, which British Prime Minister Churchill and U.S. President Roosevelt signed in August 1941, stressed the Allies' commitment to the right to national self-determina-tion. However, they did not directly address the future of the Zionist project in Palestine. The following draft response by the **Jewish Agency** to the new Charter highlighted what the authors presented as the only viable solution to the "Jewish question," namely, creating a Jewish state in Palestine. In order to support their argument, the Jewish Agency stressed the special plight of the Jews in terms of both the chronology and the extent of their persecution under Hitler; furthermore, world peace seemed like a distant dream if the Allies would not commit to a very different solution to the "Jewish question" from the one pursued by Nazi Germany.

DOCUMENT 8-9: **Declaration by the Jewish Agency regarding wartime and postwar policy, Jerusalem, October 2, 1941, ISA Leo Kohn Papers P575.**[38]

The Atlantic Charter of Freedom issued by the President of the United States and the Prime Minister of Great Britain, now endorsed by the Representatives of the Allied Nations, has been received with earnest attention and deep hope by the Jewish people. There is no people in the world to whom the promise of liberty and security held out by the Charter means more than to them. No people has suffered more at the hands of the barbarous tyranny against which the civilized nations of the world are now arrayed in battle.

We were its first victims. Long before Nazi Germany made its tiger leap at the throat of civilised mankind it had shown its true colours by the das-tardly persecution of its Jewish citizens. The hell of the concentration camps, the flames of burning synagogues, the physical and moral slavery imposed on the Jews of Germany showed to the free nations of the world what was in store for them were they to fall under the sway of Hitler's regime. He ele-vated anti-Semitism ~~into~~ *into* a major ~~incident~~ *instrument* of policy. By spreading

---

38. Reprinted in *Archives of the Holocaust: An International Collection of Selected Documents*, ed. Henry Friedlander and Sybil Milton (New York: Garland Publishing, 1990), 13:288–90. Handwritten additions to the typed document are marked here in italics, deletions by strikethroughs.

its poison among the nations of Europe he undermined their moral defences before he let loose on them his mechanized hordes. Just as in Germany he had attained power by stirring up anti-Semitic hatred, so in Austria and Poland, in Rumania and France, he used the venomous weapon of Jew-baiting for sowing discord and suspicion in the ranks of those he was about to attack. While peace still reigned in Europe his agents smuggled arms and funds into Palestine and helped to work up an anti-Jewish agitation which for three years undermined the peace of the Holy Land. What he has done to our people since the beginning of the present war defies description. From the Atlantic to the Vistula [river], from the Baltic to the Black Sea he has wrought horror and destruction among every Jewish community that fell under his sway. If there is any people whose very existence is threatened by Nazi domination it is first and foremost the Jewish people.

Yet we note that in the moving exhortations addressed by the spokes-men of the democracies to the suppressed nations of the world, our people was not mentioned. Its martyrdom was passed over in silence, its plea for recognition and restoration was not heard. In the face of this grave omis-sion we feel it our duty at this crucial moment to declare in the name of the Jewish People:

> There can be no peace in the new world that is to be built after the war unless the Jewish question is solved—~~radically~~ *basically*, equitably and permanently. The moral stability of the democratic order, the freedom of every nation are threatened so long as the disembodied ghost of the exiled Jewish People stalks the world and offers a ready ~~cover~~ *target* for every demagogue to stir up hatred and suspicion among classes and nations.
>
> Half a century ago we began to rebuild our national home in Palestine. We knew that only by returning to its soil could we restore our national life and recover our status among the free nations of the world. In the course of these fifty years half a million Jews have become rooted in Palestine, and a new Hebrew civilisation has sprung up in the ancient home of our race. The soil of Palestine has been reclaimed, and a thriving agricultural population now lives on what for centuries past was swamp and waste land.
>
> We ask for no more than to be allowed to continue that great effort of reconstruction which holds out salvation to the devastated Jewries of Europe without threatening the legitimate interests of

any other people. We plead that when the war is ended the gates of Palestine shall be opened to the Jewish victims of Nazi tyranny. There is no alternative; there can be no substitute for home. Not all Jews may come to Palestine, but we affirm in the light of past experience that until our position as a people has been normalised by our national re-settlement here, ~~Jewish~~ *the* emigration *of Jews* to new lands is likely to give rise there to the same problem from which they had escaped in the Old World.

We are not asking for any gifts. By our own efforts, by our ~~own~~ sweat and blood we shall achieve our national salvation as we began it. But we ask of all men of good will and, in particular, of the leaders of democracy, to pay heed to the fearful urgency of the Jewish problem and to support us, as far as lies in their power, in our struggle for the attainment of our full nationhood and for a new life of freedom and dignity.

Jerusalem
Oct. 2. 1941

Support in Allied countries for establishing a Jewish "national home in Palestine" received a new boost when representatives from a range of Jewish organizations, among them former critics of the Zionist cause, embraced the concept during a conference held at the Biltmore Hotel in New York City in early May 1942.[39] This move by mainstream Jewish organizations toward Zionist goals continued a trend that could be witnessed in a number of countries containing a strongly assimilated Jewish minority, including Germany in the 1930s. Yet despite aspirational proclamations for public consumption, the discussions within large international organizations remained far more tentative and halting, constrained by the fluidity of the situation and the uncertainties of the future. Even "insiders" outside of occupied Europe foresaw so many

---

39. The Biltmore conference, which drew six hundred prominent American Zionists as well as international leaders, was to unite the many American Zionist organizations behind immediate Jewish statehood in Palestine, which was seen as presenting a solution to the looming issue of postwar Jewish refugees. The declaration passed by the conference made a Jewish state in Palestine the American Zionist movement's primary goal. See Aaron Berman, *Nazism, the Jews, and American Zionism 1933–1948* (Detroit, MI: Wayne State University Press, 1990), 85–95.

unknown factors that any of their long-term planning remained frustratingly speculative. As **Leonard Stein**, the president of the Anglo-Jewish Association, explained in his annual statement in the summer of 1942, the world was "not even yet fully alive to what the Nazis are doing in the occupied territories and what they intend to do if they prevail." Even where the level of Allied awareness would match the degree of German persecution, this would not make much practical difference because, as Stein put it, "there is little we can do and nothing that can materially change the situation so long as the Nazis are in control."[40]

Over the course of the summer of 1942, the horrific situation in German-controlled Europe did become clearer to those monitoring it from the outside, while the Allies' ability to stop the Nazis' execution of the ongoing "Final Solution of the Jewish question" did not significantly increase. Close friends and associates with some clarity about this balance sheet sometimes voiced their feelings of hopelessness in correspondence with one another, letters that reflected on both the present war and the future peace. Few may have been as despairing as **Richard Lichtheim** in a long letter to **Nahum Goldmann**, which was prompted, albeit after a considerable delay, by Goldmann's speech at a Zionist conference in May 1942. There, he had echoed Chaim Weizmann's bleak assessment of the situation in **Axis**-controlled Europe and its consequences for the Jewish future.[41]

DOCUMENT 8-10: **Draft letter from Richard Lichtheim, Jewish Agency for Palestine-Geneva, to Nahum Goldmann, New York, September 9, 1942, CZA RG L22, file 149.**[42]

Dear Dr. Goldmann,

I have read with the greatest interest the speech you have made at the Zionist Conference in New York on May 10th, and I wish to compliment you on the frankness and clearmindedness with which you have treated certain basic problems ~~you~~ *we* have now to face.

---

40. Statement by Leonard Stein, president of the Anglo-Jewish Association, to the Association's annual meeting, July 2, 1942, USHMMA RG 59.023M (Board of Deputies), reel 22, frames 526–28.

41. See Berman, *Nazism, the Jews, and American Zionism 1933–1948*, 96–97.

42. Reprinted in Friedlander and Milton, *Archives of the Holocaust*, 4:380–86. Handwritten additions to the typed document are marked here in italics, deletions by strikethroughs.

Dr. Kahany has drawn my attention to the fact that Palcor and the Zionist press have said very little about your speech—to put it mildly.[43] This is in no way surprising. The mandarins of the movement are shrinking from the unpleasant ~~thought~~ *truth* and do not want to be bothered with new-fangled ideas.

Your speech has been an honest attempt to face the facts and to draw the necessary conclusions.

That does not mean that I agree with everything you have said; on the contrary, I differ in many respects. But I fully agree with the analysis of the situation as given in the first part of your speech and I want to amplify it by some remarks:

1.) You have stated that not more than 2 or 3 million Jews of continental Europe might survive. But in the light of our experiences of the last months it is clear that even this estimate is too optimistic. In all probability not more than 1 or 2 million will survive and this only if the situation of the Jews in Hungary, Roumania and Italy will remain static—a most doubtful supposition. If in these three countries the same things will happen which are now happening in France, Belgium and Holland, then the total Jewish population of continental Europe (apart from Soviet Russia) might be something between 500,000 and one million. Therefore the most optimistic forecast today is that 1½ million may survive.

2.) In what state, mentally and physically, these remnants of European Jewry will be, you have very ably explained in your speech. You have also drawn attention to the tendencies which will govern the attitude of many Jews who after emerging from the holocaust [*sic*] will try to forget and to start a new life. Complete assimilation and baptism will be the solution for many of them and, I may add, especially in these countries where in all probability the majority of the survivors will live, i.e. in Hungary (where Zionism has always been very weak) and in Roumania— provided these states will then exist and will adapt themselves to the way of life of the Western democracies. In the other case, i.e. in the case of a Moscow-governed or a Communist Roumania and Hungary, the Jews

---

43. Menachem Kahany (1898–1983) was a long-time representative of the **Jewish Agency** to the League of Nations and between 1941 and 1945 Lichtheim's deputy in the combined WZO/JA office in Geneva. See Friedlander and Milton, *Archives of the Holocaust*, 4:xix. "Palcor" was an abbreviation for Palestine Correspondence Agency, a news agency established by the Jewish Agency for Palestine in 1934 that would become a rival of the **Jewish Telegraphic Agency (JTA)**.

will have no need for baptism, but assimilation and complete adaptation to the new governing ideas will then become the normal thing especially for the young.

Also you have been perfectly right when mentioning that new spiritual forces might attract the Jewish youth all over the world—to the detriment of Zionism.

3.) All this means that the basis of Zionism as it was understood and preached during the last 50 years has gone. From Pinsker to Herzl and from Herzl to Ahad Ha'am and Weizmann:[44] political or cultural Zionism, mass emigration or slow upbuilding: it was mainly done for the Eastern Jews and by the Eastern Jews, with the others looking on, approving or disapproving, or helping a little.

The main argument was: 4 or 5 or 6 million in Eastern Europe need and want a home in Palestine and even the conception of a cultural center was mainly adapted to the spiritual needs, religious and national, of Eastern Jewry.

Those in favour of it called themselves Zionists, irrespective of their personal plans and decisions regarding emigration to Palestine.

Now, whatever the number of European Jews will be after this war—half-a-million, one million or two million—there will be no need for such mass-emigration. After the victory of the Allied Nations there can be no problem in resettling this small number of surviving Jews in that "freed" and "democratic" (or Communist?) Europe of tomorrow where they will be given equality of rights.

4.) So the question arises: Can there be a Zionist movement after this destruction of European Jewry and this radical change of their position? [. . .]

If the American Zionists are in earnest about the Jewish State or Commonwealth, then they will have to ask for it as their proper concern and they will have to go themselves and build it.

---

44. Leon Pinsker (1821–1891) is regarded as the founder of the Zionist movement in the Russian Empire. Theodor Herzl (1860–1904) was the author of *Der Judenstaat* (The Jewish State, 1896) and is considered the founder of the modern Zionist movement. Ahad Ha'am (born Asher Ginzberg, 1856–1927) spearheaded cultural Zionism with a focus on establishing a spiritual Jewish center in Palestine. Chaim Weizmann (1874–1952) was a Zionist leader, later the first president of Israel. See Walter Laqueur, *A History of Zionism: From the French Revolution to the Establishment of the State of Israel* (New York: Schocken, 2003).

Is that asking too much from them? Perhaps it is. But then we should be clear about our own future and our political possibilities. This generation will have to choose between Zionism and assimilation.

Perhaps there can be a new Zionist movement in America, a real movement, a young and spirited one, a movement not to remain but to "move," the only one which can bring constant immigration to Palestine and can in the end lead to the establishment of a Jewish State or Commonwealth (within or outside some larger federation).

If the Americans and the other more or less assimilated Jewish communities cannot or will not create such a movement for themselves, then let them stop talking of a Zionist movement and of a Jewish commonwealth. There is no need for a Jewish Commonwealth without Jews. The 500,000 or 800,000 [Jews] of Palestine will, under the protection of the great Powers, find some form of local self-government and cultural independence. But we cannot call that a Commonwealth.

Well, there is a lot more to be said but there must be an end, even to this letter.

It was a good thing and an act of moral courage that you started this discussion—I hope the Mandarins will forgive you.

With kindest regards
yours
R. Lichtheim

In the spring of 1942 Lichtheim was one of the few Jewish observers outside the realm of Axis influence whose perception of the scope and quality of Nazi persecution led him to call for radical changes in Jewish organizations' approach during and after the war. In doing so, Lichtheim not only expressed his convictions about the need to adjust wartime work and postwar planning to the increased level of German violence; his stance also mirrored the transformation of Jewish reactions that was taking place in the areas under siege. There, as we will see in the next chapter, Jews were indeed adopting new, more radical responses and demonstrated a growing willingness to answer persecution with revolt.

CHAPTER 9

DEFERENCE, EVASION, OR REVOLT?

WHILE THE SCOPE and forms of Jewish resistance during World War II have been the subject of ongoing debates among scholars and the wider public,[1] research into the complicated lives and perceptions of Jews at the time remains sketchy and uneven. Armed acts of rebellion have received the most attention, to the point that they seem to define the meaning of "Jewish resistance" during the Holocaust.[2] Accounts by Jewish men and women who fought back are moving indeed, inspiring us to see the war years as more than one unbroken procession of tragic, lethal events. Yet the documentation that survives—diverse, complex, fragmentary—cautions us to eschew a conceptual framework that restricts resistance to the use of force and labels all other responses as passive compliance or complicity. This stark balance sheet, weighted with too facile moral judgments, does not do justice to the range of Jewish behavior and its evolution over time. This chapter explores the adaptations and interventions made by individuals and groups in the period between the summer of 1941 and the summer of 1942. Assessing these responses and the full dimensions of noncompliance, of rebellion and resistance, has never

---

1. For an overview of the wealth of publications, see "Jewish Resistance—A Working Bibliography" at www.ushmm.org/research/center/lerman/bibliography/.

2. For an early analysis of conceptual shortcomings, see Konrad Kwiet, "Problems of Jewish Resistance Historiography," *LBIYB* 24 (1979): 37–60; more recently, Nechama Tec, *Jewish Resistance: Facts, Omissions, and Distortions* (Washington, DC: Occasional Paper, Miles Lerman Center for the Study of Jewish Resistance, USHMM, 1997).

been a simple matter. Many reactions by Jewish women and men living in Europe during these years defy ready-made categorization, and the question remains: what precisely was resistance or compliance in such a setting, in such circumstances?

The most prevalent form of Jewish responses to the unfolding of the Holocaust was neither compliance nor resistance. Rather, it was survival in the form of concrete practical and mental adaptations men, women, and children made every day, deliberately or unconsciously, in matters large and small, abiding by restrictions or defying them. Many adjustments went unrecorded: a gradual numbing was a response to protracted warfare shared by Jews and non-Jews alike. Some adaptations seemed unspectacular in their impact and progression, a sequence of small steps taken over an extended period and barely discernible even at the time, yet the direction of this process was clear as German pressure relentlessly pushed Jews toward doing as they were told by their overlords. In late July 1942 in Prague, Vera Segerova, born in late 1927, reflected on the gradual transformation in her behavior. "On my way back home I took a tram. (I have my ticket good for one week.) At the Wilson Station [tram stop], German soldiers got on and I, according to the regulation, gave up my seat for them. I was surprised how thoughtlessly I did it. Has all the pride inside of me died out already? Or can one really get used even to the gallows?—For the rest of my ride I was preoccupied with these kinds of thoughts."[3]

Most adjustment in the form of compliance happened because the risks of disobeying an order left no other choice. "Tonight I sewed the Jewish star on my coat," wrote **Claartje van Aals** in May 1942 in a letter to her friend, adding, "A rotten task, but unavoidable."[4] Countless other Jews did the same while feeling degraded, detesting the task, cursing those who made them do it, looking for loopholes in the web of discriminatory orders, and hoping for a better turn of events. Growing outside pressure made those subjected to it more inclined to relinquish concerns about cooperating with the oppressor for the purpose of saving their own lives and those of others; at the same time, compliance also

---

3. Diary entry by Vera Segerova, Prague (Protectorate), July 31, 1942, translated from Elena Makarova, ed., *Pevnost nad propastí. Já, děcko bloudící? Děti a učitelé v terezínském ghettu 1941–1945* (Prague: TIMUC, 2009), 73. Vera Segerova (1927–1943) lived in Prague until September 8, 1942, when she was transported to **Theresienstadt** together with her family. On February 1, 1943, she was deported to **Auschwitz**, where she was murdered.

4. Letter by Klara (Claartje) van Aals, Apeldoorn (Netherlands), to Aagje Kaagman, Utrecht (Netherlands), May 3–4, 1942, in Suzette Wyers, ed., *Als ik wil kan ik duiken . . . : Brieven van Claartje van Aals, verpleegster in de joods psychiatrische inrichting Het Apeldoornsche Bosch, 1940–1943* (Amsterdam: T. Rap, 1995), 90–91.

worked as a façade to cover opposition and the search for opportunities to subvert the oppressors' plans. The documents in this chapter attest to the fluidity of Jewish reactions and to the difficulty of assessing the situation at the time as well as from our latter-day perspective.

"SERVING" AND ESCAPING THE ENEMY

Looking at how Jews adjusted to the extreme conditions in German-controlled Europe, we have to keep in mind the huge inequities in access to power and means of subsistence, factors that by and by determined their chances of living or dying. Denunciation, blackmail, and extortion became familiar features in many ghettos, a poison produced and greatly enhanced by the unfettered corruption of the German overlords. People in positions of official authority—most importantly, the **Jewish councils**, the Jewish police, or those with informal "connections"—could exert extraordinary influence, gaining advantages for themselves or granting favors to their favorites, often to the detriment of others. Some were fleetingly self-conscious about their privileged status. Egon Redlich, deported to **Theresienstadt** in early December 1941, found himself "[n]ot sleeping, not having a rest and carrying out work that ravages one's nerves while only bringing others misfortunes and death." As one of the ghetto's communal leaders, he had to decide who would be transported away to an unknown fate and who would stay.[5]

But Jewish policemen and others placed by the Germans in positions of authority were quantitatively insignificant compared to the vast numbers of Jews forced to work for the German economy and the Reich's war effort. Those with means could buy their way out of many of these assignments, as attested to by Calel Perechodnik, a young man living with his wife and two-year-old daughter in the ghetto of Otwock near Warsaw. He became a member of the Jewish police in early 1941. Looking back on that time, he observed, "[a] rich person lived, dressed, ate, and drank, not afraid of being shipped to [a labor]

---

5. Egon Redlich, *Zítra jedeme, synu, pojedeme transportem: Deník Egona Redlicha z Terezína, 1.1.1942–22.10.1944* (Brno: Doplněk, 1995), 115 (diary entry for April 28, 1942). Egon Redlich (1916–1944), born in the Moravian city of Olomouc and a student of law at the Charles University in Prague, was deported to Theresienstadt in early December 1941. There he did work with children and youth and became one of the ghetto's community leaders. Several months after his arrival in Theresienstadt, his girlfriend Gerta (Gertruda) Bäck (Beck) joined him, and they married inside the camp. On March 20, 1944, his wife gave birth to a boy named Dan Petr, and on October 23, 1944, all three of them were deported to a death camp in Poland.

camp. One could always be ransomed for money. At the same time, the poor swelled up and died from hunger or disease as others looked on."[6] Conditions in these workplaces were far from equal. For most, labor conscription meant backbreaking toil and a further deterioration in living standards, but some assignments proved advantageous, especially for Jews selected from among the destitute to work in German offices, where they shared workplaces with their persecutors. **Paula Stein**, whose escape from Vilna was noted earlier in this volume, provided the account that follows of what a privileged job could mean in the Białystok ghetto.

DOCUMENT 9-1: **Memoir by Paula Stein, Białystok, Białystok-Grodno district, East Prussia, for February 1942, written in 1943–1944, USHMMA Acc. 2008.345 (Israel Stein collection), notebook #4a (translated from Polish and German).**[7]

On February 10 [1942], the head of the [German] labor office let me know that I should get in touch with Mr. Richter because a telephone operator was needed in his office. While going to the address indicated, I did not anticipate that it would be the same engineer whom I met during my first round of employment at the roads administration [*Reichsstrassenverwaltung*]. But he recognized me right away and assured me that this time the job would suit me. He instructed me to come to the office the next morning and introduce myself to the boss. My heart was beating like mad as I entered the building where only a month prior I was to scrub the floors and where I now faced the prospect of an office job. The head of the roads administration, Dr. Mende, a man of about

---

6. Calel Perechodnik, *Am I A Murderer? Testament of a Jewish Ghetto Policeman*, ed. Frank Fox (Boulder, CO: Westview, 1996), 9. Perechodnik (1916–1944), the owner of a movie theater in Otwock before the war, served as a member of the Jewish ghetto police in Otwock. During the liquidation of the ghetto in the summer of 1942, his wife and daughter were deported to **Treblinka** and murdered, while he was sent to a labor camp, from which he managed to escape. He wrote his memoir in the fall of 1943 and gave it to a non-Jewish Pole for safekeeping. Perechodnik took part in the Warsaw Uprising in 1944 and hid in the ruins of the city after its collapse until the Germans found and murdered him in October 1944. A copy of the memoir is available at USHMMA RG 02.208M (ŻIH 302/55). See also Sylwia Szymańska-Smolkin, "Otwock," *The United States Holocaust Memorial Museum Encyclopedia of Camps and Ghettos, 1933–1945*, vol. 2: *Ghettos in German-Occupied Eastern Europe*, ed. Martin Dean (Bloomington: Indiana University Press in association with the USHMM, 2012), 414–18.

7. The verb tense changes reflect the original. Also note that the authors have been unable to find information about all the people mentioned in this memoir.

35 with a handsome, pleasant appearance, received me in a courteous manner. He explained to me what my work consisted of, namely operating the telephone exchange, which had a dozen or so telephones in the office. He further added that he was hiring me only as a temporary replacement because the actual operator was coming from Königsberg in three to four weeks' time and that, should I have any prospects for a better, permanent position, I could openly tell him. Since I had no other prospects, I agreed to work there. I was to start my new position on the 15th. Delighted, I returned home. On February 14 in the evening a messenger from the labor office brought me a certificate on which could be read "Paula Stein employed as a telephone operator." My job drew much attention in the ghetto because it was a rare occurrence for a Jew to work in a German office, and a state post at that. The Reichsstrassenverwaltung, or roads administration, is of great importance for military operations. On Wednesday, I am in the office at 7 a.m. sharp. Dr. Mende's secretary, Frau R., a woman of about 40, familiarizes me with operating the switchboard. I had never worked in a telephone exchange, yet I quickly get the hang of it. From a chart, I learn the layout of the office so I can make the right connections. Senior construction inspector [Oberbauinspektor] Salz is the assistant manager, several inspectors and several technicians, an architect and secretaries make up the German personnel. In addition, Polish engineers and technicians are employed in technical positions, under the direction of Mr. Artychowski and Mr. Richter, a Jew. The Poles Mrs. Aleksandra Górska and Zosia Opałkówna, as well as Marysia in accounting, are employed as stenographers.

I work in a room together with Aleksandra and Zosia. Our supervisor is administrator [Verwalter] Mr. Ragnitz, in an adjacent room. He is over 30, well-built, and of a cheerful disposition; he makes a good impression on me. Though I am intimidated by his khaki uniform, which has as its only adornment a large swastika on the arm, that symbol we so despise. The same clothing is worn by all the other Germans in the office, since they belong to Organisation Todt.[8] The staff considers Mr. Ragnitz a good man, so I summon up enough courage to ask him to allow me,

---

8. Organisation Todt was a civil and military engineering group named for its founder, Fritz Todt (1891–1942), a German engineer and senior Nazi official. The organization was responsible for a large range of construction projects both in Germany and in German-occupied territories, and it deployed hundreds of thousands of forced laborers. See Wolf Gruner, *Jewish Forced Labor Under the Nazis: Economic Needs and Racial Aims, 1938–1944* (New York: Cambridge University Press in association with the USHMM, 2006), 196–201.

when sending a letter to Warsaw, to have the response sent to the office. I wanted to correspond with Marek [her husband in Warsaw] through the post, something prohibited to Jews. Since the office correspondence went primarily through Mr. Ragnitz, who headed the records office, he agreed to my request, stressing of course that it should be kept strictly secret. I was delighted. Finally, I would get some sign of life from Marek and I wouldn't be dependent on Marian the guide, who was traveling between Warsaw and Białystok increasingly less often.

Cheerful days came, full of some respite. Work was a diversion for me during which I tore myself away from the tedium of our life. I would get up briskly at 6:30 a.m., rushing on frosty, cold mornings to work, as though to a longed-for goal. I knew that there on Lipowa Street a large, bright, warm room awaited me, permeated by an atmosphere of calm. Around me, cheerful faces, unbowed by the burden of suffering and despondency. Everyone is polite and pleasant toward me. They treat me as a co-worker of equal standing. I don't at all feel that I am a Jew and that I belong to a race so oppressed by the Germans. I often ask myself whether these are different Germans. When I go back to my Vilna experiences the contrast couldn't be more striking. I approach my work with the greatest enthusiasm. I devote free moments at the switchboard to calligraphy. I provide the entire Registry Office with new signs. I serve as an interpreter for different needs, translating from Polish to German and vice versa. When after eight days Zosia the stenographer got sick and Mrs. Aleksandra couldn't cope with the extra work, I started helping her with typing, making my first steps in the field. I was progressing so fast that my assistance proved considerable. Some Germans even preferred to dictate to me since, knowing the language [i.e., German] much better than Mrs. Aleksandra, my writing was free of mistakes, while Mrs. Aleksandra's work was always criticized by Mrs. Küsling, through whose hands all the reports went. My feelings were buoyed by seeing the satisfaction of my superiors. So I simply had no desire to leave work at 6 p.m. when all the other employees ran for home. And no wonder, since after 6 p.m. relaxation awaited the others while that's when the real work began for me. Sometimes I had to race up to three kilometers [almost 2 miles] to buy goods. Whether there was snow, a storm, or rain, I was at my post. I returned home just at 9 p.m., when the ghetto gates were shut. Only then could I see to my child [her son Israel, or Izio]. I gave him supper, bathed him, and put him to bed. At that late hour, we exchanged our impressions from throughout the day. Izio grew independent since he had to make due without my care. He would still be asleep in the morning when I left for work. He would get up at 9 a.m., eat the breakfast I had prepared for him earlier, and at 10 a.m. go with a few other children to get lessons from a teacher since [official] schools were not allowed. He would return at 2 p.m. for lunch. We would see each other briefly then since I had a break from 1 to 2:30. We had lunch in a canteen known as A.I. (aid for the intellectuals), where a lunch of two courses with a little piece of bread cost only 30 złoty. The kitchen was established on the initiative of Dr. Kopelman and Dr. Segal, and it served 1,000 lunches a day. It proved to be an effective support for the impecunious working intelligentsia, who for little money and no effort could enjoy a lunch that, while not exquisite, was quite filling. After lunch, Izio would return home, do his homework, and play with [other] children. My poor child had to face quite a few reprimands from our co-tenants.

It's difficult to expect a 7-year-old boy to be quiet and to be mindful of every word that passes his lips. He also cannot be forced to sit in one spot, not to move around, and not to make a sound. A child has his rights. After hours of learning, he has to let himself go and play. Unfortunately, Mrs. Berta and Mr. Juli [in whose house Paula and Israel Stein lived] were incapable of understanding this. She is an old maid of 75, he, her brother, is a bachelor, about two years her junior. Both are extremely pedantic, "living" with a clock in their hand, and war seems not to have left any mark on them at all. These two have forgotten that they live in the ghetto under the German whip. They still wanted to benefit from the undisturbed peace from which they benefited as residents of 16 Sienkiewicz Street, where they had a 5-room apartment. Mr. Juli this whole time has not met a German, he worked in the Judenrat from 10 a.m. to 4 p.m., having aside from this the entire day at his disposal, which allowed him to pursue his whims. He didn't participate in commercial activity [to make money on a regular basis]; the two old people lived just from the sale of their belongings, of which they had more than a few. Immediately after we settled in, we learned of our co-tenants' character. It manifested itself in the pettiness that they refused to lend us a glass or a pot so they would not become worn out, not taking into account that we are poor refugees. I looked with pity upon these people, who never experienced poverty in their lives and therefore were not able to feel compassion for others. I have often compared these two heartless old people with our co-tenants in Vilna. The former were intelligent people who spoke French with one another, the latter were simpletons, but the latter stood that much higher above the former. Despite

their intellectual crudeness, the latter were people of character and heart while the former were cold boulders, with highly aristocratic habits to boot.
[. . .]

What moral standard is appropriate to assess the actions of those trying to survive the war by "assisting" the oppressor, and where does one draw the line between self-preservation and the betrayal of others? These have long remained vexed questions, be it among survivors, jurists, or postwar generations looking back on these events. Hindsight tends to obscure the complexity of conditions under which Jews were acting in ghettos and other German-controlled settings. Even legal investigations conducted shortly after the war faced severe obstacles, for most courts found it difficult to assess the "collaborative" behavior of Jews in extreme circumstances.[9] Where survival depended on bending if not breaking German rules, denunciations to "the authorities" were a constant threat to the majority, even as a small minority used them to improve their lot. An early postwar account by Michał Weichert, a **JSS** official in Kraków and a frequent visitor to other ghettos during the occupation, declared that "[t]he casual informers were truly a plague." He added, "a dozen individuals were able to keep in a state of constant fear thousands of Jews whose lives had begun to take on some normalcy."[10]

Some of the nuances of the amorphous, morally loaded term "collaboration" become visible in reports written in the spring of 1942 in the Warsaw ghetto for German officials. Neither the authors nor the recipients of the following "weekly reports" can be established with certainty. According to historian Israel Gutman, they were compiled by a member of Abraham Gancwajch's control board (*Überwachungsstelle*), also known as "the Thirteen," an appellation based

---

9. For early postwar attempts by Jews to deal with "collaborators" within their own ranks, see Leah Wolfson, *Jewish Responses to Persecution,* vol. 5: *1944–1946* (Lanham, MD: AltaMira Press in association with the USHMM, forthcoming). The most important legal cases were the Kasztner trial (1954–1955) and the Barenblat trial (1963). See Yechiam Weitz, *The Man Who Was Murdered Twice: The Life, Trial, and Death of Israel Kasztner* (Jerusalem: Yad Vashem, 2012); Avihu Ronen, Hadas Agmon, and Asaf Danziger, "Collaborator or Would-Be Rescuer? The Barenblat Trial and the Image of a Judenrat Member in 1960s Israel," *YVS* 39 (2011): 117–67; Gabriel Finder, *A Tangled Web: Jews, Poles, and the Afterlife of the Holocaust, 1945–1968* (forthcoming).

10. Michał Weichert diary/memoir, USHMM RG 02.208M (ŻIH 302/25), part 1, 196–200. On Weichert, see David Engel, "Who is a Collaborator? The Trials of Michał Weichert," in *The Jews in Poland*, ed. Sławomir Kapralski. (Kraków: Judaica Foundation and the Center for Jewish Culture, 1999), 2:339–70.

on the address of its headquarter at 13 Leszno Street.[11] Officially charged with "fighting corruption" in the Warsaw ghetto, the board vied for power with **Adam Czerniaków**'s Jewish Council and used—primarily for the benefit of its members and supporters—dubious practices in dealing with German authorities as well as Jews in the ghetto. This continued until the early summer of 1942, when the **Gestapo** arrested and shot Gancwajch and his followers. In his diary and based on the information he was gathering as part of the **Oyneg Shabes** testimonies project, Hersh Wasser described Gancwajch's group as "informers, blackmailers, and the like," a force the official Jewish police would tremble before "like a fish." Czerniaków's depiction of the group and its activities proved equally unfavorable.[12] Yet while "the Thirteen" clearly did cross the line and gave in to German demands, their reports can simultaneously be read as attempts to influence their recipients in ways that transcended the selfish interests of Gancwajch's group.

DOCUMENT 9-2: **Extracts from weekly reports submitted to German authorities, Warsaw, March 31 to May 5, 1942, in Christopher Browning and Israel Gutman, "The Reports of a Jewish 'Informer' in the Warsaw Ghetto—Selected Documents," *YVS* 17 (1986): 258, 261–62, 267, 269–72.**

[weekly report, March 31, 1942]

[. . .] The population awaits the coming Passover holidays in an extremely depressed mood. There are many reasons for this. Foremost is the wave of price hikes for all food. Price increases preceding the Passover holidays are nothing new; prior to the war the prices tended to go up before the Passover holidays because of the greater demand. But this year the situation is felt to be much worse, since large sections of the population have become much more impoverished, in comparison with last year.

Furthermore, it is noteworthy that the official Jewish institutions, including the Judenrat, have taken no steps to organize a large-scale aid campaign in order to provide the most needy with a supply of food, thus making the few days of Passover more pleasant for them.

---

11. See Christopher R. Browning and Israel Gutman, "The Reports of a Jewish 'Informer' in the Warsaw Ghetto—Selected Documents," *YVS* 17 (1986): 247–93. The material consists of a total of 110 pages and is held in YVA 0-53/102/265-375.

12. Joseph Kermish, "Diary Entries of Hersh Wasser," *YVS* 15 (1983): 241, 263 (entries for January 7 and February 26, 1941). See also Raul Hilberg, Joseph Kermish, and Stanislaw Staron, eds., *The Warsaw Diary of Adam Czerniakow: Prelude to Doom* (Chicago: Ivan R. Dee, 1999), in which Czerniaków revealed his contempt for Gancwajch repeatedly; Barbara Engelking and Jacek Leociak, *The Warsaw Ghetto: A Guide to the Perished City* (New Haven, CT: Yale University Press, 2009), 218–28; and Yisrael Gutman, *The Jews of Warsaw, 1939–1943: Ghetto, Underground, Revolt* (Bloomington: Indiana University Press, 1982), 90–94.

But it is mainly the news reaching Warsaw from Litzmannstadt [Łódź], the General Government and the nearest vicinity, which causes extreme depression among the population. People are continuously talking about the deportations from Litzmannstadt but to this day no one has knowledge of whither these Jews were sent and what had happened to them. In this connection, the widespread rumors that they were used for experiments with a new gas, cannot be silenced. [. . .]

[weekly report, April 7, 1942]

[. . .] The deepest impression, however, was made by the unexpected deportation of German Jews to Warsaw. [. . .]

Whereas the Jews of Lublin were met with feelings of deep compassion,[13] the feelings toward the German Jews are ambivalent: on the one hand people have compassion for them, but on the other it is thought that their arrival meant the entry of a Trojan horse within the walls of the ghetto. This view is especially prominent among the circles close to the Judenrat. [. . .]

[weekly report, April 21, 1942]

[. . .] At the beginning of the week the general mood was already one of extreme depression. Alarming reports arrived from the province about the situation of the Jews. There were rumors about excesses committed by the Ukrainians, and also of a "*Vernichtungskommando*" (liquidation squad). It was reported that such a liquidation squad had come to Warsaw as well, but that the Commissioner for the Jewish District had not permitted this operation.[14]

[. . .]

There is, reportedly, a great demand from the former Russian territories in the east. German salesmen, who travel as far as Smolensk, request special articles for the local population there. Most suitable are cheap and very cheap commodities which may not be exported to Germany as, on account of their low prices, they would offer serious competition to German industry, even in time of peace.

From a technical point of view, the following should be noted. The Jewish quarter has no large industrial plants with complicated

---

13. See Hilberg et al., *The Warsaw Diary of Adam Czerniakow*, 340n6.

14. The "liquidation squad" was part of the German logistical apparatus of "**Aktion Reinhard**." See Engelking and Leociak, *The Warsaw Ghetto*, 95.

machinery. Aircraft, for example, could not be manufactured here. But it would be possible to establish mechanical workshops for repairs, overhaul and assembly. These could take on simple jobs for the arms industry. In the same way as the tailors' workshops, for example, not only make, but also repair military uniforms, other repair and refurbishing jobs could be performed. [. . .] Thus the Jewish quarter offers great labor opportunities which have not been exploited to date. The people are in general industrious. They desire employment, because through work they evade the labor camps, receive wages and, finally, obtain additional ration coupons. [. . .]

[weekly report, May 5, 1942]

[. . .] Rumors about deportations from Warsaw—as from Lublin—have been circulating for several days and created great panic. As usual, the people spreading these rumors claim to know "from reliable sources" that the German authorities intend to deport the Warsaw Jews to the east. Many believe these rumors to be the truth and as a result are even neglecting their business.

The optimists, on the other hand, give credence to the article in the *Warschauer Zeitung* [German newspaper in occupied Warsaw] of April 24, 1942, which discusses the labor recruitment of the Jews of the Warsaw ghetto. They are of the opinion that, in view of the fact that increasingly large numbers of Jews are being employed in workshops and industrial plants which work for the German authorities, especially for the army, the Jews of Warsaw will not share the same fate as the Jews of Lublin.

We do not know to what degree the weekly reports from the Warsaw ghetto became a deliberate attempt by their authors to manipulate their German overlords and thus an exercise in what might be called "resistance by collaboration." At the time, other forms of Jewish responses were in fact increasing in frequency and variety, clearly crossing the vague borderline into noncompliance.[15] With the onset of deportations, a number of Jewish men and women took the risk

---

15. From the vast literature on different forms of noncompliance during the Nazi era, see Nechama Tec, *Resilience and Courage: Women, Men, and the Holocaust* (New Haven, CT: Yale University Press, 2003); Ruby Rohrlich, ed., *Resisting the Holocaust* (Oxford: Berg, 1998); Isaiah Trunk, *Judenrat: The Jewish Councils in Eastern Europe under Nazi Occupation* (Lincoln: University of Nebraska Press, 1996); Shmuel Krakowski, *The War of the Doomed: Jewish Armed Resistance in Poland* (New York: Holmes and Meier, 1984).

of vanishing from sight, despite all prohibitions against doing so. In order to escape from dangerous areas or the locus of "actions," Jews did not necessarily have to go far from their homes. Many, for instance, created makeshift hiding places in attics and cellars in or near their homes. In big cities, some relied on sophisticated subterfuges, such as carrying false papers. Still others simply failed to report changes in their place of residence, throwing the distributors of deportation notifications into a loop of fruitless searches. The reminders that German-controlled Jewish authorities published or posted instructing residents to notify central registries of any address change suggest that this tactic was used quite frequently.[16] Yet changing one's place of residence or taking on another Jew's identity while staying around offered at best temporary relief from a grave and imminent threat. In the long run, these rarely sufficed as dependable forms of evasion.

Hiding, either by going underground or adopting a non-Jewish identity, implied the expectation that the dangers of staying and being deported out-weighed those of living elsewhere illegally, cut off from even the brittle support system afforded by Jewish communities behind ghetto walls. The prevalence of hiding ultimately depended on a range of factors, from very personal ones—how one weighed the risks involved for oneself, family, particularly children left in the care of non-Jews, and friends; whether one "looked Aryan" enough to pass as non-Jewish—to circumstances that fit no single pattern.[17] In general, hiding was not yet a mass phenomenon during the period covered by this volume. Many Jews found no opportunity to escape from a place of imminent danger; many were unwilling to venture the risk. On a small scale, hiding entailed the subversion of German occupation measures and thwarting of the smooth running of the deportation process. But did it constitute resistance? What measure do we employ? Withdrawing from the scene and erasing traces of one's former identity were of course illegal and triggered official investigations. As in the following case, the Germans as a rule involved Jewish agencies in policing their regulations and held the larger community responsible for individual lapses and failures in compliance.

---

16. See, e.g., *Jüdisches Nachrichtenblatt Prag*, February 7, 1941, 4.

17. See Tec, *Resilience and Courage*, 205–55; Mark Roseman, *A Past in Hiding: Memory and Survival in Nazi Germany* (New York, Metropolitan Books, 2001), 248ff.

DOCUMENT 9-3: Letter from Moritz Henschel, Jewish Community Berlin, to the Gestapo Berlin, regarding the disappearance of Max Sinasohn, February 19, 1942, USHMMA RG 14.003M (BAB R 8150), P75C Re1/7 (translated from German).

<u>C o p y</u>

Board of the Jüdische Kultusvereinigung zu Berlin e.V.

Berlin N 4, February 19, 1942[18]

[Jewish Religious Association in Berlin]

Oranienburger Str. 29

Log No. He./Dal.　　　　　　　　　　　　　　Telephone: 42 59 21

When replying to this letter, please include
the log number provided above

Secret State Police [Gestapo]
State Police Headquarters [Staatspolizeileitstelle], Berlin
Department IV D 1
Burgstr. 28
<u>Berlin C.2</u>

Regarding: Disappearance of the Teacher Max Israel <u>Sinasohn,</u> Last Residing in Berlin NW 87, Solingerstr. 4

On the basis of a report from the school administration of the Juedische Kultusvereinigung zu Berlin e.V., we submit—in connection with the information provided this morning—the following account:

Yesterday, after the teacher Max Israel <u>Sinasohn</u> had been absent from classes for some time because of a purported illness and also had failed to comply with a demand for presentation of a medical certificate, his apartment was opened, at our instigation, by the building's custodian after informing the proper authority, Police Station 22, and obtaining the permission of the landlord. No one was in the apartment; there were only a few pieces of furniture. The subtenant, Mrs. Jakubowski, when questioned later, stated that Sinasohn's wife and daughter had left on February 8 and Sinasohn himself on February 9, 1942, stating that they were going to Neuendorf for around 8–10 days. As a telephone inquiry reveals, however, they never arrived there. Thus, the family has departed from here for an unknown destination.

---

18. The Reichsvereinigung sent a copy of the letter to the **RSHA**.

The particulars of the missing persons are as follows:

1). Max Israel Sinasohn, born October 21, 1887, in Schoenlanke
2). Wife Rahel Sara Sinasohn, née Cohn [Cohen], born May 25, 1891, in Gnesen
3). Daughter Mirjam Marianne Sara Sinasohn, born May 8, 1921, in Berlin.[19]

Juedische Kultusvereinigung zu Berlin e.V.
Board of Directors
[signed]
(Moritz Israel Henschel)[20]
Chairman

Presented to the Reich Ministry of the Interior
Reich Security Main Office [RSHA]
Kurfürstenstr. 115/116
Berlin W 62
with reference to the report on February 17

---

19. They survived the war. Max Mordechai Sinasohn (1887–1979), a World War I veteran, had spent the majority of his working life in Berlin as a teacher and administrator at the Adass Jisroel primary school (1919–1939) and as principal of the Rykestaße Jewish school (1939–1941). At the time of his family's flight from Berlin, he was teaching at a Jewish orphanage in the city's Pankow district. Rahel Ruth Sinasohn (née Cohen; 1891–1969) was an artist and active member of Berlin's cultural life. Together with their youngest daughter Mirjam Marianne (1921–2004) the family fled to Belgium and remained in hiding until war's end. Another daughter, Gabriele Berta Abrahams (née Sinasohn, 1919–1944), had escaped to the Netherlands in 1939 and relocated to Brussels with her husband, Isidor "Jacques" Abrahams (1918–1944), prior to being interned at the Mechelen transit camp in 1943. The Abrahams were deported to the **Auschwitz II-Birkenau** concentration camp in 1944, where they later perished. The Sinasohns' youngest child, Jacob Hermann Sinasohn (1926–2010), had immigrated to England in 1941. The authors have been unable to locate further information on the Sinasohns' eldest daughter, Eva Sinasohn (1918–2006). See German "Minority Census," 1938–1939, USHMMA RG 14.013M; *USHMM ITS Collection Data Base Central Name Index*; Yad Vashem, "Central Database of Shoah Victims' Names," www.yadvashem.org.

20. Moritz Henschel (1879–1947), a lawyer and Reichsvereinigung board member, served as chairman of the Berlin Jewish Community beginning in 1940. In June 1943, he was deported along with his wife, Hildegard (née Alexander; 1897–1983), and other senior Jewish functionaries to Theresienstadt, where he served on the Council of Elders. The two survived the war and immigrated to Palestine. Their daughter fled Germany in 1939 as part of the Youth **Aliyah** and **Kindertransport**, respectively. See Beate Meyer, Hermann Simon, and Chana Schütz, eds., *Jews in Nazi Berlin: From Kristallnacht to Liberation* (Chicago: University of Chicago Press, 2009), 131, 351–52.

Henschel's letter leaves unclear how or why Sinasohn and his family managed to go "missing." The **Reichsvereinigung** here dutifully reported the family's disappearance to "the authorities" as a matter of bureaucratic routine—without mentioning an impending deportation order which for many recipients provided the direct incentive to go into hiding.[21]

Most Jews trying to hide from their oppressors were forced to rely on a circle of helpers cooperating clandestinely. Not surprisingly, then, the few surviving documents produced by Jews at the time, describing their life underground and other highly dangerous activities, remain hard to decipher, with important information lost to postwar generations. In the following letter, a man in the part of Yugoslavia annexed to Italy (today in Croatia) writes to his uncle with detailed instructions about how to escape Sarajevo with forged papers. For outsiders and anyone not familiar with the specific setting, they would have appeared quite cryptic. The provenance of this document, found in a collection from the Jewish Historical Museum in Belgrade, remains unknown, as do the fate of its author and its recipient.

DOCUMENT 9-4: **Letter from "Papo" to "Alberto," Split, Italian-occupied Yugoslav Dalmatia, September 29, 1941, USHMMA RG 49.007M (JHM k. 27-2-1/23), reel 8 (translated from Bosnian).[22]**

Spalato [Split], September 29, 1941
Dear Alberto!

The day before yesterday I was informed that you are at Jonas's, and I took immediate steps to obtain the required documents. I got them today, and now I am looking for a messenger so that I can send them to you as soon as possible, our acquaintance cannot leave yet, so I need to find another. I hope I will find one, and that you will be able to leave right after Yom Kippur [Erev Yom Kippur fell on September 30, 1941].

The main question is how to leave. As I hear, it is dangerous for you to leave from the Sarajevo [train] station. Just a short while ago, I talked to Otto Baruh, who arrived yesterday. He advises you to go to Salamon Papo Hoh, the dentist on Hadžidurahova Street, and discuss the issue with him. He knows a train conductor, and some have already left using this method. As far as I have gathered, the method consists of you boarding

---

21. See Marion A. Kaplan, *Between Dignity and Despair: Jewish Life in Nazi Germany* (New York: Oxford University Press, 1998), 184–202.

22. The document was written in Roman script.

the Ilidža train [that goes on to the main train station] at the tobacco factory at noon. That's when there are the fewest passengers. The train to Mostar from the main station leaves a bit after the arrival of the Ilidža train. You transfer to the Mostar train from the Ilidža train, and the conductor protects you until the departure of the train. Once the train leaves, you have nothing to fear.

If you can't arrange this with Papo, then try to go by car to some other station and board the train there. You must have a reliable friend who could help you with that. If someone asks you why, tell them you are rushing to visit some business partner.

As you can see, I am sending you not only a pass [*propusnicu*], but also an ID. That is the best possible way to travel. If someone wants to check your ID, you have nothing to fear. You just have to memorize the name and all the rest well. Remember:

last name: Kovačić

first name: Ivan–Giovanni in Italian

father: Frano–Francesco in Italian

mother: Ludvika–Ludovika

born: in 1900 in Kaštel Sućurac—Kaštel San Girogio, married, Croat, salesman by profession, place of residence Kaštel San Giorgio (in Croatian it is called Kaštel Sućurac).

That Kaštel is not far from Split, and there are other Kaštels there as well, such as K.[aštel] Novi, K.[aštel] Stari, K.[aštel] Lukšić, and so on.

Apart from that, if they ask you for more details, you will tell them that you deal in short [?] goods, and that you traveled to Banja Luka on business and to visit family and are now coming back. If they ask you how come that you have a pass issued in Sinj [another place not far away from Kaštel and Split] and an ID issued in Kaštel Sućurac, you will tell them that you were born in Kaštel and lived there until September 4, when you moved to Sinj for business reasons. Your pass is valid until October 17. Be careful not to go over that date, but I think you will be here much sooner.

From Mostar, you will take a bus to Split. Don't take the train all the way to Metković, but only to Mostar. Don't be afraid if you have to wait for a bus for a while, the ID will protect you. You can even stay at a hotel in Mostar if need be. As soon as you receive this letter, sign under the ID picture, and in this way: Giovanni Kovačić, so precisely in the way in which the name is written on the cover of the ID.

Concerning your real documents, don't take them. Leave them with Jonas, and we will send someone for them later. If you see the messenger who brings you this letter, give him your documents so that he can take them for you, if he agrees. Do not travel with real documents under any circumstances.

I have given you two possibilities for travel so far, but if you can't do those, then you can try to go on foot to Al.[ipašin] Bridge. If someone stops you on the way to Alipašin Bridge, asks where you're going, and asks to check your ID, show it and say you are going for a walk. In any case, whatever happens, take a brazen stand in front of that person. If there is trouble, say you will call the Italian consulate. Considering your way of speaking,[23] this way (to go on foot) is the riskiest one, but you can try it if all else fails. Discuss with Jonas which is the best way, but in any case visit Papo the dentist.

Concerning your things, don't travel with them. You may take a briefcase or a small suitcase with most important things for a short time. When you arrive here, we will send someone to bring your things. Leave them with Jonas. I was told that you don't know where the things you left with me are. I don't know either, but let Jonas go to the apartment, if the *satnik* [ustaša military rank, probably the current occupier of the "Aryanized" apartment] is still there, and look for them. Also, ask Ana to see if they are not with her by chance. Last time my acquaintance did not go to Jonas to take the reply to my letter, because he suddenly had to leave Sarajevo early. If you travel from Sarajevo or some later station, let someone else buy you the ticket at Putnik [a travel agency]. Oto Baruh suggests that you don't travel by night. It is best that you take the train that leaves Sarajevo for Mostar at noon.

Don't take the armband [with a Star of David] with you under any circumstances. Leave it at home.

Another thing: when you arrive in Split, it is possible that the person who checks the passes [*propusnice*] will hold on to your pass. Tell them that you need it back immediately, so that you don't have to come back to pick it up in an hour, because your bus for Sinj leaves at 6 and your Mostar bus arrives at 5 in the afternoon.

All in all: as soon as you leave home, you have to be calm and composed. Almost everything depends on that. Try to change your way of speaking a bit if you can. I've stated what I thought was most important

---

23. Possible reference to an accent (a peculiar incantation of the local vernacular by Ladino native speakers) or another speech peculiarity that would make "Alberto" stand out in Sarajevo.

and what I felt I needed to explain. Think all this through very carefully, and memorize all that needs to be memorized. As soon as you get the pass, leave Sarajevo immediately after making arrangements with Jonas and Papo. Don't wait too long. Each day may be important. The last time you were out of luck, but you still managed to save yourself from the camp because you left immediately.

Uncle, I wish you best of luck. Until you arrive I will pray to God for a good journey and I will be very impatient. I can't wait to see you. Jonas should get in touch through messenger or by mail occasionally. Greetings to Jonas and Bjanka, and love and hugs to you

Yours,
Papo

P.S. Don't take any letters or anything similar along.

30 September [1941]

I will pass on this letter very soon to be taken to you. The messenger has been found. I should mention this as well: if you leave at noon, and the weather is nice, put on sunglasses and a simple suit. Leave things and everything else with Jonas, and bring only the most neccessary things in a briefcase or a small suitcase. Have Jonas put all away to a secure place, and, once you arrive, we will send a reliable person back to bring it for you. If you arrive in Mostar, and there is no bus to Split, take the train further to Metković and then take a bus on to Split. Do not travel by boat by any means. Try to speak as little as possible during your journey, and modify your voice a bit.

Hurry up, so that I can see you as soon as possible.

Good luck,
Papo

We can only speculate about "Alberto's" fate. There is strong reason to suspect that he was in fact arrested. The typed document has a stamp at the bottom (with a Croatian herald) of the magistrate in Dubrovnik attesting that the typed text was identical to the original and dated October 9, 1941. ("Alberto's" false pass was set to expire on October 17.) Dubrovnik lies nowhere near Split, but is close to Mostar, where according to the instructions in the letter "Alberto" was supposed to have switched from the train to a bus. He may well have been arrested there (probably by the **ustaše**) and delivered to the precinct in Dubrovnik, where a magistrate official made a transcript of all the documents found on him—the letter from "Papo" (which "Alberto," against advice in the letter itself, took with him), the false papers (identity card and the pass)—for the police file. We do not know what happened after that. Although Italians were nominally in charge in the area, it seems likely that Alberto passed through ustaša hands and probably that he was killed. In another scenario, he may have been detained in some sort of Italian camp for Jews, but this would not have guaranteed survival after September 1943, when the Germans took control of the area.

FIGHTING THE ENEMY

Armed Jewish resistance to Nazi occupation had started with the war: from its first days, Jews had fought the Wehrmacht as soldiers of many armies.[24] After the beginning of **Operation Barbarossa**, Jewish soldiers in the Red Army represented the largest contingent of Jews resisting Nazism with firepower and in a sustained way.[25] They formed part of a mighty force, whether or not their identity as Jews gave them special reasons to fight the invaders. The following excerpts from letters of Motl Talalaevskii, a Red Army soldier deployed in Ukraine during the short-lived defense of its capital Kyiv (Kiev), convey the mood swings prevalent in the ranks of a collossal military organization teetering on the brink of defeat.

---

24. See Alexandra Garbarini, with Emil Kerenji, Jan Lambertz, and Avinoam Patt, *Jewish Responses to Persecution*, vol. 2: *1938–1940* (Lanham, MD: AltaMira in association with the United States Holocaust Memorial Museum), 243–45. In September 1939, about 130,000 or 10 percent of all enlisted soldiers in the Polish army were Jewish. In Britain, about sixty-two thousand Jews served in the army, including about fourteen thousand in the Royal Air Force, and some twenty-five thousand Jews served in other parts of the British Empire. In the United States, it is estimated that some five hundred thousand Jews served in all branches of the armed forces. See Israel Gutman, *Fighters Among the Ruins* (Washington, DC: B'nai B'rith Books, 1988), 245–61.

25. Israel Gutman estimates that during World War II half a million soldiers in the Red Army were Jewish; about two hundred thousand were killed in battle. About 160,000 were decorated, and more than a hundred achieved the rank of Red Army general. See Gutman, *Fighters Among the Ruins*, 245–61.

DOCUMENT 9-5: **Letters from Motl (Matvei Aronovich) Talalaevskii,**[26] **Kyiv, Soviet Union, to his wife, September 2 and 5, 1941, USHMMA RG 31.028.11 (Kyiv Judaica Institute) (translated from Russian).**

Kiev [Kyiv], September 2, 1941
Dear Klarusia!

Today I got your letter of July 31 that was sent through someone; as you see, the postal service is functioning better—yesterday I received your letter of August 8. I've read and reread them. You're a brick! And that's just how a Soviet woman should think. I'm proud of you and I love you even more. What is there to say about the people who prefer to lie low in the rear instead of taking an active part in the struggle against the fascist monster—the nation will make them answer for it! [. . .] The war takes away the tinge of everyday life, and the radiance of a soul, of a generous heart, becomes clearer. [. . .]

Ten weeks of war have gone by. . . . Many things have already taken a turn for the better. All the monsters' expectations have fallen through. The temporary capture of individual towns does not signify victory; quite the reverse, it brings the enemy's downfall nearer. More than 30,000 Germans have already been laid low close to Kiev. Kiev is standing firm, and no one will ever take it.[27] The people and the army are prepared and sturdily armed. Is there any danger? Of course there is; this is war. But we have to think about life. And among those of us who have stayed here, there is no thought of anything but living, winning, triumphing.

I have nothing from [?]. I've sent you the warm things. Unfortunately, the three shelves are in Kharkov [Kharkiv], and I couldn't gather up the more valuable things for you. Maybe they were stolen? Write me and tell me in detail what you took with you, and where are all the lengths of fabric? [. . .] In short, write and tell me about everything. As you see, on

---

26. Matvei Aronovich Talalaevskii (1908–1978) was a Soviet Jewish author writing in Yiddish, Ukrainian, and Russian. During World War II he served in the Red Army, both as a soldier and as a journalist. In the early 1950s, with the crackdown on Jewish cultural production, Talalaevskii was arrested and sent to a labor camp in Central Asia. After Stalin's death, he was released, returning to Kyiv. He authored an autobiography, known for its depiction of Jewish life in the Soviet Union. See also finding aid, USHMMA RG 31.028.11. The authors have not been able to trace the later fate of his wife Klarusia and their children or the other people mentioned in the letters.

27. The Wehrmacht occupied Kyiv on September 19, 1941.

this little page I've written enough words to fill half a printer's sheet. Love and kisses to you and [?]. Kisses to

Irochka.

Motia

[Postscript at the top of page 1: "Write and tell me how your pregnancy is going; I'm awfully worried about it."]

September 5, 1941, Kiev

Dear [Klarusia]

I've just sent you a telegram giving you my new address. I'm moving to Kharkov with the collective of the radio station. Upon arrival, I'll send you another telegram. It's been a long time since I received anything from you. As you already understand, I'm not exactly feeling like dancing—I can't bear to leave my dear Kiev. But I have great hopes! I'm convinced that the fascists will never take the city. It will be defended, and it is reinforced, so why are we leaving? The resources for printing are better there; it may turn out that we won't be able to transport paper into Kiev, and that's why it's better to move. My mood is bad because here I would at least have been at home, but this way I'm going to be a wanderer (again!). But for the Motherland, for victory over the monsters, over the cutthroats and rapists, I'm willing to make great sacrifices.

Today they recorded my voice on tape for the radio. This was done because there will be a big radio rally tomorrow, and I, the only Yiddish poet remaining at the front, am supposed to give a presentation at this rally. Since I'm leaving, my voice will be heard on tape. They taped the poem about Kiev. This is my latest work in Yiddish. It's almost three months now since I've written in this language. Hitler and Goebbels were not very glad to hear my Ukrainian voice; now let them hear my Yiddish one! If I'm killed, remember that on September 6, 1941, my poems were read, and you can hear my voice after the war. I'm joking here, of course. Nobody is going to kill me. There's a song that goes like this:

"a bullet fears a brave man,

a bayonet can't hit a brave man!"

And I'm a brave man, after all, especially now—if you could see me, you wouldn't recognize me! If we survive, you'll see for yourself and fall in love with me.

Today I did another big thing—this time for you. I went around to the savings banks and looked for both your savings book number and mine—I don't have anything, you see—and finally I established the number of my deposit, which I already had the right to make use of, and with my own hands I transferred the entire deposit to your name. [. . .] But I think there's no hurry anymore. My money will last you until the end of the war, and then we'll see. But use your own judgment and act accordingly.

I locked the apartment, and I have the keys, but where is the second bunch of keys? I took some things with me. I want to take the remainder— the LIBRARY! will be safe. But we won't be slaves to our belongings. We'll defeat the enemy, have our new cozy place, and acquire whatever was lost. The main thing is just for you and my dear Irul'ka to survive. I dream about her all the time. Kiss her for me, and then give her another hug and kiss!

And you I'm asking for the hundredth time to write me more often. Two letters in 75 days of war—really, that's not many!

Give my warm regards to Nina. In Kharkov, I'll see her Lenia, and we'll write you together. Tell her also that I've gotten to know her brother, Kuliznev [?], and I wrote an article about him—he's a remarkable guy. Recently he was accepted into the VKP(b) [All-Union Communist Party (Bolsheviks)].

Write me whether you're satisfied with the warm things I sent. Unfortunately, I can't take anything with me to cover myself a little more warmly. But my overcoat will save me.

Soon the collection of poems compiled by Kats and me will appear in print—our newspaper is publishing it—I'll send it to you. For now, stay healthy. With kisses as never before for your eyes, your lips, and the places that . . . belong only to me!

Yours until the end of my days,

Motia

My regards to Fedor and his relatives.

Talalaevskii's determined optimism notwithstanding, the Wehrmacht continued to break through the front line in place after place in this period, establishing German rule. Under these conditions and without the protection of an army, military-style Jewish as well as non-Jewish resistance required immense organizational efforts and immense risk taking. Armed opposition to the German war machine thus generally remained marginal and began late in the war, buoyed by Wehrmacht setbacks and the approaching front line.[28] The Eastern front proved one exception: many Red Army units had been overrun by the Germans in the summer of 1941 and their members, still in possession

---

28. See Henry Michel, *The Shadow War: European Resistance, 1939–1945* (New York: Harper & Row, 1972); Ruby Rohrlich, ed., *Resisting the Holocaust* (Oxford: Berg, 1998); Tec, *Resilience and Courage.*

of some weapons, sought to escape capture in the remote countryside. They became the targets of brutal German "pacification" sweeps.[29] By contrast, armed resistance by Jews had started long before, during the height of German expansion and with few if any chances for success, sparked by desperation over the unrelenting, intensifying persecution.

In addition to the perception that there was no way out, a range of factors triggered the decision to mount armed opposition, among them identification with sometimes long-standing anti-Nazi groups, particularly on the political left. Disillusionment with the official Jewish leadership and its questionable ability to protect the majority of their communities from death or deportation became another trigger. Those who felt most abandoned by established communal leaders and most keen to act outside the narrow confines of the German-controlled Jewish sphere were youth. Revolt against traditional forms of orderly behavior—seemingly unsuited to these unprecedented times—made many young men and women receptive to calls for more decisive action. A number of contemporary youth leaders could provide an alternative orientation and sense of identity, as we have seen in the case of Aron Menczer or Jizchak Schwersenz. But in contrast to the rituals and activities enacted in Vienna and Berlin, members of youth groups such as **Hashomer Hatzair** in the East had already seen too much violence since the summer of 1941 to focus on bolstering spiritual coping strategies. Some youth activists in eastern Europe, among them female couriers such as Tosia Altman, who was active in Warsaw and Vilna, felt that the Germans had crossed a threshold, one that called for a similar break in Jewish responses.[30] We find this perception and its spread reflected in the following document from a youth group active in the Vilna ghetto just prior to the formation of an armed resistance group, the United Partisans Organization

---

29. Benjamin V. Shepherd, *War in the Wild East: The German Army and Soviet Partisans* (Cambridge, MA: Harvard University Press, 2004); Kenneth Slepyan, *Stalin's Guerrillas: Soviet Partisans in World War II* (Lawrence: University Press of Kansas, 2006); for the broader context see Timothy Snyder, *Bloodlands: Europe between Hitler and Stalin* (New York: Basic Books, 2010).

30. Tosia Altman (1918–1943) was raised in Włocławek, where her Zionist father ran a store. When the war broke out, she fled with other Zionist youth activists, eventually reaching Vilna. From there she returned to occupied Poland, traveling extensively, gathering information, and rallying youth leaders for clandestine work. Altman also forged contacts with the Polish and communist underground organizations and, as an emissary of the Jewish Fighting Organization (ŻOB), worked to gather weapons for an armed uprising. Trapped in the Warsaw ghetto during the April 1943 uprising, she made her way out through the sewers, but the Germans later captured and killed her. See Zivia Lubetkin, *In the Days of Destruction and Revolt* (Tel Aviv: Hakibbutz Hameuchad, 1981), 287; Ziva Shalev, "Tosia Altman," Jewish Women's Archive, www.jwa.org/encyclopedia/article/altman-tosia (accessed May 7, 2012).

(*Faraynikte Partizaner Organizatsiye*, FPO). The group formed in late January 1942, comprised of mostly Zionist and Communist members under the leadership of Yitzhak Wittenberg and Abba Kovner.[31]

By the end of 1941, Germans and their Lithuanian helpers had taken more than thirty thousand Vilna Jews to the forests of **Ponar** and murdered them. Several members of youth groups in Vilna had already gone into hiding, either inside the city or in a nearby monastery. Participants of a meeting of Hashomer Hatzair held in the monastery in late December 1941 decided to establish an armed resistance group and to spread the word about what they believed was the ultimate fate of fellow Jews throughout eastern Europe. On New Year's Eve at the end of 1941, approximately 150 youth movement members gathered in the ghetto's public kitchen at 2 Straszuna Street, and here Kovner read his Yiddish proclamation aloud while Tosia Altman recited a Hebrew version of the text. The document was then translated into Polish and Lithuanian and circulated among a wider audience. The Yiddish version of this signal statement was hidden in Vilna throughout the war and unearthed by Kovner following liberation in 1944. Thereafter the manifesto came to assume iconographic importance among the documentation attesting to Jewish resistance.[32]

DOCUMENT 9-6: **Manifesto "Let us not be led like sheep to the slaughter!," Vilna, German-occupied Lithuania, January 1, 1942, Moreshet Archives D.1.4630 (translated from Yiddish).**

Let us not be led like sheep to the slaughter!
Jewish youth, don't trust those who deceive you. Of 80,000 Jews in "Yerushalayim de Lita,"[33] only 20,000 are left. Our parents, brothers, and sisters were torn from us before our eyes.

---

31. For the FPO's origin and early activities and biographical information on Yitzhak (Itzik) Wittenberg (1907–1943) and Abba Kovner (1918–1987), see Yitzhak Arad, *Ghetto in Flames: The Struggle and Destruction of the Jews in Vilna in the Holocaust* (Jerusalem: Yad Vashem, 1981), 221–62.

32. The document can be found in different versions held in several archives and remains contentious due to conflicting postwar claims regarding its language, authorship, and dissemination. For a discussion of conflicting accounts and interpretations, see Dina Porat, "The Vilna Proclamation of January 1, 1942, in Historical Perspective," *YVS* 25 (1996): 99–136; Idem, *The Fall of the Sparrow: The Life and Times of Abba Kovner* (Stanford, CA: Stanford University Press, 2010), 57–75.

33. Among east European Jews, Vilna was known as the "Jerusalem of Lithuania" due to its cultural and political significance. See Herman Kruk, *The Last Days of the Jerusalem of Lithuania: Chronicles from the Vilna Ghetto and the Camps 1939–1944*, ed. Benjamin Harshav (New Haven, CT: Yale University Press, 2002).

Where are the hundreds of men who were seized for labor by Lithuanians?

Where are the naked women and the children seized from us on the night of fear? Where are the Jews of Yom Kippur?

And where are our brethren of the second ghetto?![34]

No one returned of those marched through the gates of the ghetto.

All the roads of the Gestapo lead to Ponar.[35]

And Ponar means death!

Those who waver, put aside all illusion! Your children, your wives, your husbands are no more. Ponar is no concentration camp. All were shot dead there.

Hitler conspires to kill all the Jews of Europe. And the Jews of Lithuania have been picked at the first line.

<u>Let us not go like sheep to the slaughter!</u>

True, we are weak and defenseless, but the only answer to the murderer is resistance!

Brothers! Better fall as free fighters than to live at the mercy of the murderers! Rise up! Rise up until your last breath.

January 1, 1942 Vilna ghetto

To have any impact, calls for militant action had to be backed up with concrete preparations, an extremely difficult task under the circumstances in German-occupied eastern Europe.[36] Outside the Reich's reach of power the risks involved in anti-German activism were of course incomparably lower or—as in Allied countries—nonexistent. But this did not mean that no obstacles stood in the way of supporting the Jewish cause or that interventions came easily. Among the most contested issues in the United States during the second half of World War II was the call for a separate Jewish fighting force. The widening scope of German anti-Jewish persecution, on the one hand, and the broadening of the anti-German alliance, on the other, increased calls for separate Jewish fighting units to combat the Allies' common enemy.

---

34. On the murder actions in Vilna and the liquidation of the second ghetto in September–October 1941, see Arad, *Ghetto in Flames*, 133–63.

35. Ponar, the Yiddish name for Ponary (Polish) or Paneriai (Lithuanian).

36. According to Arad, *Ghetto in Flames*, 241, "[t]he FPO [in the Vilna ghetto] continually expanded, reorganized, and developed throughout its existence in the ghetto, from the end of January 1941 until September 1943."

In early January 1942, barely a month after the United States had entered the war, readers of the *New York Times* would learn from a full-page advertisement of the creation of a "Committee for a Jewish Army," which had held its inaugural meeting in early December 1941 in Washington, DC. The Committee had attracted "men from all walks of American life who passionately believe in the victory of democracy and through that victory, in a better world for all, regardless of race and creed." Among its members were prominent names, including refugees: the writers Louis Bromfield, Lion Feuchtwanger, and Manfred George; movie director Ernst Lubitsch; composer Arnold Schoenberg; scholar Paul Tillich; and several members of Congress and clerics, all supporting the Committee's goal, "[t]o bring about, by legal means and in accordance with the laws and foreign policy of the United States, the formation of a Jewish Army, based on [*sic*] Palestine, to fight for the survival of the Jewish people and the preservation of democracy." This army under "the Jewish flag" was to consist primarily of "Palestinian Jews and refugees, as well as volunteers from free countries" to fight alongside Allied armed forces.[37] The Committee represented early results of efforts made by the small group of **Revisionist Zionists** that had gathered around Lithuanian-born Hillel Kook (a.k.a. Peter Bergson). The Palestine-based National Military Organization (*Irgun zvai leumi*, the paramilitary arm of the Revisionists) had sent Kook to the United States to lobby for the establishment of a "Jewish Army of Palestinian and Stateless Jews."[38] Ultimately futile, the project competed with and amplified public appeals aimed at getting Jews to join the war effort of their respective nations or adopted homes.

These appeals gained in urgency when the **Yishuv** was threatened. From February 1941, the German army had been fighting the British in North Africa in support of its Italian ally, with wavering success. In July 1942 Wehrmacht advances on Palestine had raised secret plans by **Himmler**'s **Security Police** and **SD** for the annihilation of the "Jewish homeland" to the level of an imminent and deadly threat.[39] At this juncture Arthur Lourie, secretary of the Emergency Committee for Zionist Affairs in the United States

---

37. "Jews Fight for the Right to Fight," *New York Times*, January 5, 1942, 13.

38. Judith T. Baumer, *The "Bergson Boys" and the Origins of Contemporary Zionist Militancy* (Syracuse, NY: Syracuse University Press, 2005); David S. Wyman, "The Bergson Group, America, and the Holocaust: A Previously Unpublished Interview with Hillel Kook/Peter Bergson," *American Jewish History* 89 (2001): 3–34; Louis Rapoport, *Shake Heaven & Earth: Peter Bergson and the Struggle to Rescue the Jews of Europe* (New York: Gefen, 1999), 49–50.

39. See Klaus-Michael Mallmann and Martin Cüppers, *Nazi Palestine: The Plans for the Extermination of the Jews in Palestine* (New York: Enigma Books, 2010).

and a former **Jewish Agency** official, informed **Richard Lichtheim** in Geneva about two important calls for action.

DOCUMENT 9-7: Letter from Arthur Lourie, Emergency Committee for Zionist Affairs-New York, to Richard Lichtheim, Jewish Agency-Geneva, July 28, 1942, CZA RG L22 file 149.[40]

My dear Lichtheim:

You may be interested to see the following messages which were sent recently by Dr. Weizmann and Dr. Wise,[41] respectively, to Lord Halifax in the first case and to Mr. Winston Churchill in the other.

"To LORD HALIFAX   June 20th, 1942

In view of the present emergency in the Middle East I respectfully reiterate our ardent wish to take a greater part in the struggle against the invading armies and to participate more directly and effectively in the defense of Palestine. This as you know can only be achieved by the organization of a Jewish military force out of the existing units and their augmentation through further enlistment in Palestine to fight under its own flag under British Command.

I would like to submit this request through you to the Prime Minister whose mission I trust will be eminently successful and who as a result of the long discussions on the subject is familiar with every aspect of the plan. More than ever I am convinced now is the time to implement the promise made more than a year ago. For it will not only contribute substantially to the defense in the critical area but will also have an enormous effect on the morale of American and world Jewry. I am equally convinced that without in any way disturbing the situation in the Middle East such an act of simple justice and prudence at this time will go a long way toward creating that goodwill toward the British cause in the country so essential at this crucial moment.

CHAIM WEIZMANN"

---

40. Facsimile reprinted in *Archives of the Holocaust*, ed. Henry Friedlander and Sybil Milton (New York: Garland Publishing, 1990), 4:378–79.

41. On Chaim Weizmann see page 315n44 above; and on Steven S. Wise, see the Glossary. Edward F. L. Wood, 1st Earl of Halifax (1881–1959), was a senior Conservative politician who served as British Foreign Secretary (1938–1940) and later as British ambassador to Washington, DC (1941–1946).

"[To the] RT. HON. WINSTON CHURCHILL   July 2, 1942
London

The advance of the Nazi armies towards Suez brings with it the threat of invasion to Palestine and therewith the possible annihilation of the whole of Palestine Jewry. For more than two and a half years the Jews of Palestine have demanded the right to defend their country and to fight the mortal enemy of their people and of humanity alongside the armies of the United Nations. This elementary right denied to no other people was denied to them the precious time during which a force of 50,000 to 60,000 Palestinian Jews ready to do and die for their country might have been raised, trained and equipped has been lost. At this twelfth hour we urge most earnestly that without a moment's further delay their plea be granted and all available Jewish manpower in Palestine be immediately mobilized and if they go down they should be enabled to go down fighting. We solemnly affirm that if this is not done and should catastrophe befall it will be Britain's responsibility before history that the Jews of Palestine were denied by the Mandatory Power the right and means of self defense. In appealing to the conscience of the British people we appeal also to you personally who have so often shown your sympathy and understanding for the cause of the Jewish people we know you will give the matter consideration in the light of the supreme danger and urgency of the hour.

STEPHEN S. WISE
Chairman, American Emergency Committee Zionist Affairs

LEON GELLMAN,[42] President Mizrachi

---

42. Born in Yampol, Russia, Leon Gellman (1887–1973) immigrated to the United States as a young man. He worked in Hebrew education and became editor-publisher of a Yiddish newspaper in St. Louis. Active in the Mizrachi Organization of America for several decades, he later moved to New York and became president of the organization's U.S. branch in 1935. Mizrachi, which sought to spread awareness of religious Zionism and Torah-based education, also organized support for the American war effort, supported the formation of a Jewish army, and worked to raise funds for Jews in Palestine. Gellman later moved to Israel, where he chaired the World Mizrachi Organization and sat on the executive of the Jewish Agency. Melvin I. Urofsky, *American Zionism from Herzl to the Holocaust* (Lincoln: University of Nebraska Press, 1995), 101-2; "Gellman, Leon," in *Encyclopaedia Judaica*, ed. Fred Skolnik and Michael Berenbaum, 2nd ed. (Detroit, MI: Macmillan Reference USA, 2007), 7, 421.

DAVID WERTHEIM,[43] Gen. Sec'y. Poale Zion
LOUIS LEVINTHAL, President, Zionist Organization of America[44]
TAMAR de SOLA POOL,[45] President, Hadassah

Cordially yours,
[signed]
Arthur Lourie[46]

---

43. Born in the Bessarabia region and educated in Odessa and Berlin, David Wertheim (1896?–1953) was a descendent of the Baal Shem Tov, founder of Hasidic Judaism. Wertheim immigrated to the United States in 1923 and in 1930 became a long-time general secretary of the Po'ale Zion (labor Zionist) movement. This movement had originated in Russia, combined Zionism and socialism, and strove to create a socialist Jewish society in Palestine. After the war he served for a time as the **HIAS** representative in Israel. Obituary, *American Jewish Year Book* 55 (1954): 460; obituary, *Jewish Telegraphic Agency*, April 13, 1953; Urofsky, *American Zionism*, 103–4.

44. Louis E. Levinthal (1892–1976) was born in Philadelphia and served as a judge on the Philadelphia Court of Common Pleas from 1937 to 1959. He was active in many charitable and civic organizations and became the president of the Zionist Organization of America (ZOA, founded in 1897) from 1941 to 1943. During the war, Levinthal advocated various measures to support the Yishuv, including creation of a Jewish Fighting Force for Palestine. He served as special adviser for Jewish affairs under Gen. Lucius Clay in the American zone of occupied Germany in 1947 to 1948. Obituary, *New York Times*, May 19, 1976; Sefton D. Temkin and Robert P. Tabak, "Levinthal," *Encyclopaedia Judaica*, 12:723–24; Urofsky, *American Zionism*, 101–2.

45. The daughter of a rabbi, Tamar de Sola Pool (née Hirschenson; 1890–1981) was born in Jerusalem. She came to the United States in 1904 with her family and was educated at Hunter College and the University of Paris. De Sola Pool became active in a range of Jewish causes and promoted Youth Aliyah and other youth welfare projects both before and after the war. Long a member of Hadassah, the largest Jewish women's and Zionist organization in the United States, she served as the organization's national president between 1939 and 1943. Obituary, *New York Times*, June 2, 1981; "Pool, Tamar de Sola," in *Jewish Women in America: An Historical Encyclopedia*, ed. Paula E. Hyman and Deborah Dash Moore (New York: Routledge, 1997), 2:1095–96.

46. Arthur Lourie (1903–1978), a JohannesbuRG born barrister, worked for the Jewish Agency in London beginning in the 1930s. He served as an official for the American Emergency Committee for Zionist Affairs in New York from 1940 until the end of the war. The first consul general of Israel in New York and a long-serving member of the Israeli delegation to the United Nations General Assembly, Lourie later became ambassador to Canada and the United Kingdom. See obituary, *New York Times*, November 6, 1978; Benjamin Jaffe, "Lourie, Arthur," in *Encyclopaedia Judaica*, ed. Fred Skolnik and Michael Berenbaum, 2nd ed. (Detroit, MI: Macmillan Reference USA, 2007), 13:226.

In Nazi-dominated Europe, attitudes of non-Jews ultimately played a critical role in determining the scope and forms of Jewish armed resistance, as well as its impact. From what is known about these clandestine efforts, the more egalitarian a resistance movement was, the greater its inclination to support Jews, either by including them as members or helping organize them into separate groups. With their deep roots in European culture, antisemitic stereotypes had found a foothold even among communists and socialists, despite the fact that their movements regarded anti-Jewish propaganda as a staple of the core enemy, fascism. At the same time, many Jews involved in Left underground activities saw themselves first and foremost as Communists or Socialists, and to the extent possible relegated their Jewish identity to a secondary role, particularly if they adhered to secular values or came from assimilated backgrounds.[47] Nationalist movements were unlikely to take up the Jewish cause or Jewish comrades unless they saw Jews as useful allies in the fight against the German occupiers. Yet especially in eastern Europe, the strong antisemitic agenda of the nationalist underground stood in the way of such alliances even on a temporary basis and posed a threat to the lives of Jews trying to hide from the Germans.[48]

When in the course of 1942 Jews began to establish more systematic contacts with non-Jewish resistance groups in **Axis**-controlled Europe, Nazi propaganda had already proclaimed for years that anti-German forces and "the Jew" were one and the same. Since the beginning of the war against the Soviet Union, Hitler and his regime had not missed any opportunity to broadcast this mind-set, according to which "international Jewry" controlled Germany's enemies. In the late spring of 1942 the Nazi regime saw its obsessive focus on the "Jewish enemy" as well as the urgency of bringing about a "Final Solution of the Jewish question" confirmed through two incidents. Though completely unrelated, the events became closely connected in the mind of antisemitic ideologues. On May 18, 1942, a communist resistance group headed by the young Berlin Jew Herbert Baum staged an arson attack on the Nazi propaganda exhibition "Soviet Paradise" in the Reich's capital. While causing little material damage, the attack rattled confidence in the capital city. Nine days later in Prague, a Czech commando ambushed the chief of the RSHA and acting *Reichsprotektor* of Bohemia-Moravia, SS-General **Reinhard Heydrich**, who died on June 4. The Germans struck back quickly and brutally. In the city where Heydrich was assassinated, the entries in the diary of young

---

47. See John M. Cox, *Circles of Resistance: Jewish, Leftist, and Youth Dissidence in Nazi Germany* (New York: Peter Lang, 2009).

48. On the attitude of Polish resisters, see the essays by David Engel, Israel Gutman, Andrzej Friszke, Feliks Tych, Daniel Blatman, and Shmuel Krakowski, in *Nazi Europe and the Final Solution*, ed. David Bankier and Israel Gutman (Jerusalem: Yad Vashem, 2003), 136–230. The volume also contains essays about Jewish and non-Jewish resistance in other parts of Europe.

Petr Ginz convey a mixture of the excitement and fear surfacing in the wake of the attacks.[49]

DOCUMENT 9-8: Petr Ginz, Prague, diary entries for May 27 to June 5, 1942, in Chava Pressburger, ed., *The Diary of Petr Ginz, 1941–1942* (New York: Atlantic Monthly Press, 2007), 108–11.

[May 27, 1942]

[. . .] There was a bomb assassination attempt against SS [Ober-] Gruppenführer Heydrich. That's why they ordered a state of emergency and people who will be seen today after 9 o'clock and tomorrow before 6 o'clock and won't stop immediately after being called will be shot dead. There is a reward of 10,000,000 crowns for whoever informs on those responsible for the assassination, and whoever knows about them and does not report it will be shot with his entire family.

[. . .]

[June 1, 1942]

Eighteen people have been shot, mostly for hiding unregistered persons.

In the morning at school. In the afternoon at home and outside.

In Berlin there was an attack on the Soviet Paradise exhibit and some Jews were caught nearby. So 250 [Jews] were shot and 250 deported to concentration camps.

[. . .]

[June 4, 1942]

Flags are everywhere at half-mast or black. Heydrich probably died. That's why:

---

49. Petr Ginz (1928–1944) kept a diary from late February 1941 to August 1942, shortly before he was deported to Theresienstadt in October 1942. Petr was born in Prague to a Jewish father, who was a manager at a textile company, and a non-Jewish mother. Even at his young age, Petr was an enthusiastic writer of novels, poetry, commentary, and his diary. After arriving in Theresienstadt, he gained regular access to the large library created from the books brought along by deportees. Petr also established a magazine *Vedem* ("We Lead") with a group of other boys. With Petr serving as its chief editor and contributor, *Vedem* published poetry, essays, and commentary. Petr was briefly reunited with his sister Chava in Theresienstadt when she arrived in 1944, but in late September of that year, he was deported to Auschwitz and murdered on arrival. See Chava Pressburger, ed., *The Diary of Petr Ginz, 1941–1942* (New York: Atlantic Monthly Press, 2007).

1. We were sent home early.
2. On Friday we don't have to go to school.
3. On Friday a new transport will be called up, which has to report on Sunday.

Re 1, 2: there will probably be marches and demonstrations.
In the afternoon at school.

[June 5, 1942]

The report about SS Obergruppenführer Heydrich's death has been confirmed.

His picture in a black frame completely covers the front page of the newspapers. From 3 P.M. on Saturday until 8 A.M. on Monday Jews are not allowed to walk in Prikopy, Narodni Avenue, Wenceslas Square, and in many other places.

Rather than remember them all, I prefer to sit at home.

The assault on Heydrich in Prague and the arson attack in Berlin prompted German action and extreme reprisals on a number of levels. In Bohemia-Moravia, Hitler initially demanded the execution of ten thousand Czechs, but he withdrew his order on May 28. Instead, Himmler's units razed the village of Lidice, shot 199 Czech men, and deported the women residents to the Ravensbrück concentration camp, while most of Lidice's ninety-eight children were later murdered in Chełmno; in Prague, one thousand Jews were deported on June 10 to **Majdanek**. Simultaneously and secretly, top Nazi leaders decided to escalate the "war against the Jews." On the evening of Heydrich's burial in Berlin, Heinrich Himmler assured his SS and police officers that the "migration" [*Völkerwanderung*] of the Jews would surely be completed within a year and announced, "thereafter no one will wander anymore." To facilitate this intensification of the killing process, Himmler took over leadership of the RSHA himself. Furthermore, he apparently decided at this time to organize a special tribute to Heydrich in the form of what after the latter's death came to be called "Aktion Reinhard"—the murder of the remaining Jews in the **Generalgouvernement**—as a crucial step toward the "Final Solution of the Jewish question" in Europe.[50]

The prevailing image of Jews as "enemy number one" left no doubt in the minds of top Nazi leaders that a link existed between the attacks in Prague and Berlin. Of the twenty-two members of the Baum group who were swiftly arrested

---

50. See Saul Friedländer, *Nazi Germany and the Jews:* (vol. 2) *The Years of Extermination, 1939–1945* (New York: HarperCollins, 2007), 349–51; Peter Longerich, *Holocaust: The Nazi Persecution and Murder of the Jews* (New York: Oxford University Press, 2010), 332–34.

after the arson attack, seven were Jews or "*Mischlinge*." Arrests of group members continued into 1943, as did executions. According to Gestapo records, Herbert Baum committed suicide in prison in June 1942. Immediately after the "Soviet Paradise" arson attack, **Joseph Goebbels** in his capacity as Gauleiter for Berlin requested Hitler's permission to arrest five hundred Jews as hostages, who would be executed should more attacks occur. As Ginz noted in his diary, after the ambush on Heydrich, the Germans executed 250 Jewish men at the Sachsenhausen concentration camp outside of Berlin, and their relatives were deported. Already on May 29 and 30, 250 additional Jews were arrested and taken to Sachsenhausen, where the SS killed more than half of them within a short time. The others were murdered in October 1942 in Auschwitz. Beyond this, the Gestapo arrested the top officials of the German Jewish Reichsvereinigung, as well as the leadership of the Vienna and Prague Jewish communities, informed them of the executions and other arrests, and warned them of "further measures" if Jews took part in any similar attacks in the future. They also demanded that the Jewish leaders ensure compliance with orders and urged their community members to report any suspicious activity.[51] Like other records officially created by the Reichsvereinigung at the time, the following file note—its formulaic minimalism adapted for consumption by **Eichmann**'s office—provides but a glimpse of the new level of threats that Jews were facing.

DOCUMENT 9-9: File note by representatives of the Reich Association of Jews in Germany (Paul Eppstein); the Jewish Communities Prague (Franz Friedmann) and Vienna (Josef Löwenherz) to the Reich Security Main Office, Berlin, May 29, 1942, USHMMA RG 14.003M (BAB R 8150), P75C Re1/7 (translated from German).

I. On May 29, 1942, the Reichsvereinigung der Juden in Deutschland [Reich Association of Jews in Germany] (Leo Israel BAECK,[52] Paul Israel

---

51. See Meyer, Simon, and Schütz, eds., *Jews in Nazi Berlin*, 321–23; Cox, *Circles of Resistance*, 125–35; Konrad Kwiet and Helmut Eschwege, *Selbstbehauptung und Widerstand: Deutsche Juden im Kampf um Existenz und Menschenwürde, 1933–1945* (Hamburg: Christians, 1984), 125–29. Major U.S. newspapers carried reports about Heydrich's assassination and German reprisals, sometimes in front-page articles; see e.g., *New York Times*, "Heydrich of Gestapo Hurt, Big Reward Up for Assailant," May 28, 1942, 1; "'Vengeance' Sworn at Heydrich Bier," June 10, 1942, 9; "Vengeance Vow of Himmler," June 11, 1942, 7; *The Washington Post*, "Community Razed; Women, Children Sent to Other Areas," June 11, 1942, 1. On June 14, 1942, the *New York Times* also reported on the Nazi response to the attack by the Baum group on its front page under the title "258 Jew Reported Slain in Berlin for Bomb Plot at Anti-Red Exhibit," stating that the reprisal was meant "as a warning to other Jew trouble-makers" and implying that the executions in Berlin were connected to the massacre in Lidice.

52. For information on Rabbi Leo Baeck, see the Glossary.

EPPSTEIN,[53] Moritz Israel HENSCHEL,[54] Philipp Israel KOZOWER,[55] Leo Israel KREINDLER,[56] Arthur Israel LILIENTHAL[57]), Jüdische

---

53. Paul Eppstein (1902–1944) was a sociologist and educator in Mannheim prior to his relocation to Berlin in 1933. There he joined the newly established Reichsvertretung and became instrumental in their ongoing relief efforts and relations with Nazi officials. Already a board member, Eppstein became de facto head of its successor organization—the Reichsvereinigung—following the arrest of executive director **Otto Hirsch** in 1940. In 1943, he was deported to Theresienstadt and served as Eldest of the Jews until he was arrested and murdered in September 1944. His wife, social worker Dr. Hedwig Eppstein (née Strauss; 1903–1944), was later murdered in Auschwitz. See Beate Meyer, "Between Self-Assertion and Forced Collaboration: The Reich Association of Jews in Germany, 1939–1945," in *Jewish Life in Nazi Germany: Dilemmas and Responses*, ed. Francis R. Nicosia and David Scrase (New York: Berghahn Books, 2010), 150–56, 160–65; *USHMM ITS Collection Data Base Central Name Index.*

54. For more on Moritz Henschel, see page 330n20 above.

55. Phillip Kozower (1894–1944) practiced law in Berlin until 1933 and became a leading functionary in various Jewish organizations—including the Zionistische Vereinigung für Deutschland, the Berlin Jewish Community, and the Reichsvertretung—before becoming a board member and deputy chairman of the Reichsvereinigung. He was deported to Theresienstadt in 1943, where he served as the senior postal official until his transfer to Auschwitz in October 1943. Upon arrival, he was murdered, alongside his wife Gisela (née Herzberg, b. 1908) and children Eva Rita (b. 1932), Alice (b. 1934), and Uri Aron (b. 1942). See Beate Meyer, *Tödliche Gratwanderung: Die Reichsvereinigung der Juden in Deutschland zwischen Hoffnung, Zwang, Selbsthauptung und Verstrickung (1939–1945)* (Göttingen: Wallstein Verlag, 2011), 40, 126, 130, 135, 213, 224; *Gedenkbuch,* www.bundesarchiv.de/gedenkbuch.

56. Leonhard Kreindler (1886–1942), a Galician-born journalist, served as director of the welfare department and board member of the Berlin Jewish Community. Following the Nazi dissolution of the independent Jewish press in 1938, he was appointed chief editor of the remaining paper, the *Jüdisches Nachrichtenblatt,* and contributed to many of its articles about emigration. He died of a heart attack in November 1942 following an order to appear before Gestapo officials. See Clemens Maier, "The *Jüdisches Nachrichtenblatt,* 1938–43," in *Jews in Nazi Berlin: From Kristallnacht to Liberation,* ed. Beate Meyer, Hermann Simon, and Chana Schütz (Chicago: University of Chicago Press), 102, 107, 112, 114.

57. Arthur Lilienthal (1899–1942), a lawyer and Berlin judge, had long been active in Jewish organizational work, serving as secretary-general of the Reichsvertretung as well as a board member of the Berlin Jewish Community, and—from 1939—in the Nazi-mandated Reichsvereinigung. He was arrested as part of a Gestapo raid on Jewish Community offices in June 1942 and deported to the Minsk ghetto, where he perished with his wife, Resi (née Hirsch; b. 1901). See Beate Meyer, *Tödliche Gratwanderung,* 27, 135, 204, 249; *Gedenkbuch,* www.bundesarchiv.de/gedenkbuch.

Kultusgemeinde Prag [Prague Jewish Community] (Franz WEIDMANN,[58] Franz FRIEDMANN[59]), and Israelitische Kultusgemeinde Wien [Vienna Israelite Community] (Josef Israel LÖWENHERZ,[60] Benjamin Israel MURMELSTEIN[61]) were informed that in the context of an attack on the exhibition "The Soviet Paradise," in which five Jews actively participated, 500 Jews were arrested in Berlin; 250 of them were shot and 250 were transported to a camp. In addition, notice was given that additional measures of this kind will be taken if another act of sabotage is carried out with the participation of Jews.

An order has been issued asking that these facts be made known in due manner among the Jews and to point out the consequences of such actions. The order also requires submission of proposals for ways in which the Jewish organizations can obtain information about any circumstances known to their members that are indicative of preparations for an act of sabotage, so that the Reich Security Main Office can be informed immediately.

---

58. František Weidmann (1910–1944), a lawyer and former activist, had served as executive secretary of the Prague Jewish Community since 1937 and was installed as chairman following the establishment of the Protectorate of Bohemia and Moravia in 1939. He was deported to Theresienstadt in 1943 as part of the dissolution of Jewish Community offices and became a member of the Council of Elders. He was murdered en route to Auschwitz in October 1944. See Livia Rothkirchen, *The Jews of Bohemia and Moravia: Facing the Holocaust* (Lincoln: University of Nebraska Press, 2005), 116, 130, 235, 245–46; Yad Vashem, Central Database of Shoah Victims' Names, www.yadvashem.org.

59. František Friedmann (1897–1945), a prominent Zionist politician, served as a budgetary administrator, legal expert, and deputy chairman of the Prague Jewish Community. After 1939, he assumed a more direct role in relief and emigration efforts, and in 1943 was appointed chairman of the community's successor organization—the Jewish Council of Elders in Prague. His "mixed marriage" exempted him from deportation, and he remained in office until the end of the war. See Rothkirchen, *The Jews of Bohemia and Moravia*, 117, 130–34.

60. For more on Josef Löwenherz, see document 1-3.

61. Benjamin Murmelstein (1905–1989) was a Galician-born rabbi, educator, and board member of the Vienna Jewish Community. He later served as deputy chairman of the Nazi-installed Jewish Council of Elders in Vienna before being deported to Theresienstadt in 1943 with his wife Margit (née Geyer; b. 1904) and son. There he was appointed Eldest of the Jews in 1944 following the murder of Paul Eppstein, and held this office until shortly before liberation in May 1945. His long-standing and complex relationship with Nazi officials led to a criminal investigation, but no charges were ever filed. Murmelstein later immigrated to Italy. See Philip Friedman, "Aspects of the Jewish Communal Crisis in Germany, Austria, and Czechoslovakia during the Nazi Period," in *Roads to Extinction: Essays on the Holocaust*, ed. Ada June Friedman (New York: Conference on Jewish Social Studies and Jewish Publication Society of America, 1980), 111, 115–18; *USHMM ITS Collection Data Base Central Name Index*.

II. To implement this order, the following is proposed:

1. The measures ordered by the Reichsführer SS will be, as directed, made known
    > to the personnel of the Jewish organizations,
    > to the Jews involved in the labor deployment program [*Arbeitseinsatz*],
    > in the Jewish homes, welfare facilities, and soup kitchens,
    > with the request that the information be passed on.
2. In an announcement in the next editions of the *Jüdisches Nachrichtenblatt* for Berlin, Vienna, and Prague, the responsibility of each individual Jew shall be particularly emphasized.
3. The members of the Jewish organizations will be informed, through circular letters or in some other appropriate way, of the unconditional obligation to report immediately to the Jewish organizations any circumstances coming to their attention that are indicative of preparations for an act of sabotage.
4. The Jewish organizations will immediately report all such information to the Reich Security Main Office.

[draft notice for publication in the *Jüdisches Nachrichtenblatt* for Berlin, Vienna, and Prague attached to the letter:]

Reponsibility for the Community

Every Jew bears responsibility for our community. Each of us must bear that in mind at all times and in all places: in all actions and remarks, at home, in transit, in the workplace. It comes down to the behavior of each individual, since not only he and his family, but all other Jews must be responsible for it. At no time can it be forgotten that each of us is responsible for us all, and that the consequences of each individual's behavior affect the community.

REICHSVEREINIGUNG DER JUDEN IN DEUTSCHLAND

[draft circular letter to the Jewish communities and regional offices (*Bezirksstellen*) of the Reichsvereinigung:]
Regarding: Responsibility for the Community

The Reichsvereinigung has been informed through its supervisory body that state police investigation of an act of sabotage in Berlin revealed that five Jews were actively involved in the sabotage. As a result, 500 Jews were arrested in Berlin; 250 of them were shot and 250 were transported to a camp.

In addition, it was declared that other measures of this kind will be taken if another act of sabotage involving Jewish participants is carried out.

We are communicating this information with the knowledge of the supervisory body. The Jewish religious associations and regional offices are entitled and obligated, while duly announcing these facts, to appeal most emphatically and strongly to their members to be aware in their personal conduct of their responsibility for the community at all times and all places. Furthermore, the members must immediately report to the Jewish religious association or regional office responsible for their place of residence all circumstances coming to their attention that are indicative of preparations for an act of sabotage, so that this information can be passed on to the appropriate state police office or headquarters.

Receipt of this circular letter must be confirmed by the appropriate regional office head or Jewish religious association president by signing and returning the attached statement, along with notification of the action indicated.

After the meeting with Jewish representatives, Eichmann and his colleagues at the RSHA changed their minds and barred the remaining Jewish newspaper, the *Jüdisches Nachrichtenblatt*, from publishing the planned notice or from sending out a circular to the regional offices with these results. We know from postwar sources that Leo Baeck, head of the Reichsvereinigung at the time, attempted to prevent further violent resistance and had one of his officials, Norbert Wollheim, contact the remaining Jewish members of the communist underground.[62] Overall, the impression among German Jewish leaders was one of utter terror and foreboding. Yet most saw no alternative to carrying on in their attempts to "prevent the worst," even while "the worst" had begun to unfold all around them.[63]

---

62. Norbert Wollheim (1913–1998) administered youth initiatives before directing the Reichvertretung's Kindertransport efforts and vocational training programs. In 1941, he was assigned to a Berlin-based forced labor contingent as a welder and still held this position when Leo Baeck enlisted him to contact the communist underground. He was deported to Auschwitz in 1943, along with his wife Rosa née Mandelbrod (b. 1912) and son Uriel (b. 1939), both of whom were murdered upon arrival. After 1945 he became a leading advocate for Jewish survivors in western Germany and championed legal efforts to compensate forced laborers. He immigrated to the United States in 1951. See USHMMA RG 50.030*0257 Oral History Interview with Norbert Wollheim; *USHMM ITS Collection Data Base Central Name Index*; obituary, *New York Times*, November 3, 1998.

63. Meyer, *Tödliche Gratwanderung*, 193–94.

As exemplified by the aftermath of the attack on Heydrich and of the Berlin arson attempt, Nazi leaders used every opportunity to construe all individual Jewish acts of resistance as confirmation for their image of the "Jewish enemy" and as a subterfuge for applying even more radical means in pursuit of "solving the Jewish question." Jews contemplating militant opposition thus not only had to overcome huge obstacles in organizing violent acts but also confronted a moral dilemma resulting from the German strategy of responding with disproportionally brutal "reprisals." In the face of these developments and with little hope of disrupting the mighty German war machine within which the Holocaust was unfolding, Jews started to plan and execute acts of active rebellion, be it as a result of very personal motives or as part of broader resistance frameworks. At the same time, we should not overlook the massive hurdles that stood in the way of other forms of Jewish responses designed to alleviate suffering and despair. These responses range from selfless help for those in need to coordinated and partly successful interventions with Axis officials to prevent or at least soften the effects of deportations, as in the case of **Abraham Frieder** in Slovakia or Wilhelm Filderman in Romania. As powerful as the Vilna battle cry "They shall not take us like sheep to the slaughter!" resonates against the background of postwar knowledge about the "Final Solution," we need to acknowledge the daily efforts Jews in eastern Europe made to avert death and disaster in the absence of a clear understanding of the situation they were facing, of the options available to them, and the consequences of their actions. In the last three chapters we will turn to the question of how much Jews at the time knew and could know about the genocidal trajectory of Nazi anti-Jewish policy up to the summer of 1942.

PART IV

GLIMPSING THE ABYSS

PATTERNS AND PERCEPTIONS

W HEN IN EARLY 1941 Jewish historian **Simon Dubnow** looked back
on the past since the Middle Ages, he found the years since 1933 to
be the "most catastrophic period," marking the beginning of "a completely
new Jewish martyrology, without historical precedent in Europe. This is," he
observed, "martyrization without martyrs for faith or conviction, because the
victim certainly is not required to renounce his religion or faith; these martyrs
are tortured only for membership in a certain race, which cannot be changed,
consequently one cannot get free of these tortures." Dubnow's reflections also
turned to the future; he surmised that "when the complete annals of the new
Inquisition appear, they will shake posterity even more profoundly than they
are shaking us, the contemporary witnesses."[1] As we will see in the concluding
chapters of this book, Dubnow was hardly alone in puzzling over the significance of events and what they might mean for generations to come.

Up to this point, the volume has focused on how Jewish men, women,
and children dealt mostly from a practical standpoint with the onslaught of the
German occupation, both in terms of their actions as well as deliberations about
how to respond and judge its trajectory. This section will explore further how
they conceptualized the rapidly unfolding events of 1941 and 1942. As persecution and confinement turned into deportation and murder, Jews in different

---

1. Simon Dubnow, "Die Martyriologie unserer Zeit," no date (late 1940/early 1941);
USHMMA RG 68.045M, reel 8, file 61 (translated from German).

locales understood their own situations and that of others in vastly different ways. Some relied on time-tested religious explanations of sin and redemption dating back to biblical and rabbinic times. Others framed the current situation in the political terminology of the period. Still others turned to creative responses that provided the opportunity to explore multiple narratives at the same time. No matter what their orientation was, the Jewish voices featured in this section all deal with the same fundamental questions: how were the events unfolding before them different from persecution in the past, and at what point—if ever—does one begin to understand that a transition from random persecution to systematic murder was taking place? These responses ultimately suggest an intense and sustained grappling with the larger implications of what we today call the Holocaust. The individuals featured in this section attempted to make sense of the present, which had become in many respects a complete break from the past.

CHAPTER 10

THE ROLE OF RELIGION

THE QUESTION OF whether Judaism can be recast into a category that fits into the fundamentally modern Protestant notion of "religion" has been at the center of heated debates among Jewish thinkers. At once a religious, social, and national category, Judaism, especially in eastern Europe, where Jews had been perceived as a separate social body even in the post-Emancipation period, has never really corresponded to the image of a private faith, safely shut off from the public sphere.[1] To most Jews in eastern Europe in the mid-twentieth century, in contrast, Judaism was a framework for issues ranging from rules of ritual observance to understanding contemporary social and political issues in terms of the Jewish historical experience. The major fault line between "secular" and "religious" was thus irrelevant in Judaism in this period and place: regardless of whether we are discussing fervently observant Jews, or Polish-speaking communist intellectuals who abhorred the thought of even stepping into the synagogue, Judaism provided a vocabulary, a shared historical experience, and a common narrative in which even those Jews who wanted to distance themselves from the Jewish community were proficient.

What we can broadly understand as Jewish "religious" responses to persecution during the Holocaust ranged from specific theological concerns to

---

1. For an in-depth treatment of this topic, see Leora Batnitzky, *How Judaism Became a Religion: An Introduction to Modern Jewish Thought* (Princeton, NJ: Princeton University Press, 2011).

expressions of a broad Jewish worldview that was often couched in seemingly secular language. As **Simon Dubnow**'s reference to martyrology implies, over the course of its long history, Jewish thought had developed concepts to address the explicable as well as the metaphysical in a coherent, highly complex, and widely accepted framework. Death and disaster encountered by Jews at the hand of German occupiers or Christian neighbors could be explained as part of a larger narrative of sin and punishment dating back to the fall of the First and Second Temples in ancient times. At the same time, the authors of Jewish texts repeatedly argued with, interpreted, and engaged with the Divine word in both sacred and profane writings.[2] Yet, was this time-tested way of reading and understanding a long history of Jewish persecution enough when applied to what Dubnow, stressing the unprecedented nature of anti-Jewish violence during the Nazi era, called the "Hitleriad"?

Many Jews struggled with key tenets of faith when the extreme adversity of Nazi rule began to threaten their very existence. Others with no prior inclination toward religious observance suddenly saw the hand of God in these events and became observant. Still others turned from firm believers into atheists, agnostics, or followers of modern political ideologies such as socialism or communism.[3] While Jews in different circumstances and from different traditions responded to the unfolding Nazi oppression with varying degrees of observance, the appearance of a distinctly Jewish narrative—marked by specific use of language, imagery, and sense of time—cut across the boundaries of what we might today call "religious" and "secular." It would therefore be inaccurate to characterize every biblical or Talmudic reference as a declaration of faith and misleading to interpret the absence of such references as proof of a lack of spirituality. Rather, as David Roskies notes, even as "Eastern European Jewish writers never strayed far from the sources of their culture, [. . .] there was no modern return to a belief in the covenant. Ghetto writers, with few exceptions, refused to identify destruction with guilt or with some divine scheme for ultimate redemption."[4] Rather than thinking of these sources as religious responses

---

2. David Roskies, ed., *The Literature of Destruction: Jewish Responses to Catastrophe* (Philadelphia: Jewish Publication Society, 1988), 2–12.

3. See Steven T. Katz, Shlomo Biderman, and Gershon Greenberg, eds., *Wrestling with God: Jewish Theological Responses during and after the Holocaust* (New York: Oxford University Press, 2007); Esther Farbstein, *Hidden in Thunder: Perspectives on Faith, Halachah and Leadership during the Holocaust*, vols. 1 and 2 (Jerusalem: Mossad Harav Kook, 2007); Havi Ben-Sasson and Amos Goldberg, *Years Wherein We Have Seen Evil: Selected Aspects in the History of Religious Jewry during the Holocaust*, vols. 1 and 2 (Jerusalem: Yad Vashem, 2003).

4. David Roskies, *Against Apocalypse: Responses to Catastrophe in Modern Jewish Culture* (Syracuse, NY: Syracuse University Press, 1999), 208.

that either affirm or negate faith in God's presence in history, it is more useful to examine them in light of a larger Jewish concept of history that was in the process of, as Dubnow suggests, active and radical revision. Some specifically theological and rabbinic documents from this period survive that clearly attest to the continuity of traditional practices and interpretation under extreme circumstances. However, even for those outside the cultural and intellectual life of Orthodox practices, religion and religious references still provided a common vocabulary for an unfolding catastrophe that transcended any specific declaration of faith. The following sources explore the diversity of ways in which the far reach of the war and ever more radical anti-Jewish measures encroached upon this worldview.

ADAPTING RELIGIOUS RITUALS AND OUTLOOKS

Jews living in Europe had embraced a multitude of religious affiliations and interpretations that manifested themselves in a multitude of religious organizations, groupings, and individual orientations. Nonetheless, a common sense of time informed by the Jewish calendar still existed across various levels of observance. The spring holiday of Passover or *Pesach*, which celebrates the ancient Jewish liberation from slavery and the ensuing Exodus from Egypt, provided a touchstone for communities throughout Europe. The Passover holiday requires several types of specific rituals, from clearing the house of all leavened foods, or *chametz*, to the preparation of the ceremonial meal itself, to synagogue attendance. During the war some of these obligations naturally became far more difficult to fulfill, and they drew attention to the scarcity of resources that Jews faced. In the Netherlands, where the author of the following document was writing, most of its roughly 140,000 Jews had been well-integrated into Dutch society. Nevertheless, Dutch Jews had a relatively low intermarriage rate (around 15 percent) and a predominantly Orthodox religious outlook that differed from both the Reform orientation of communities in other west and central European states and the east European strands of Orthodoxy.[5] **Gabriel Italie**, the author of the following reflections from April of 1941, was a teacher of classical languages in The Hague until he lost his job in late 1940 because he was a Jew. His diary entries depict some of the difficulties in attempting to adhere as strictly as possible to religious tradition. Italie also notes the importance of the Passover holiday in his current circumstances.

---

5. See J. C. H. Blom and J. J. Cahen, "Jewish Netherlanders, Netherlands Jews, and Jews in the Netherlands, 1870–1940," in *The History of the Jews in the Netherlands*, ed. Renate G. Fuks-Mansfeld and Ivo Schöffer (Oxford: Littman Library of Jewish Civilization, 2002), 230–95.

DOCUMENT 10-1: Gabriel Italie, The Hague, German-occupied Netherlands, diary entries for April 1941, in *Het oorlogsdagboek van dr. G. Italie. Den Haag, Barneveld, Westerbork, Theresienstadt, Den Haag 1940–1945*, ed. Wally M. de Lang (Amsterdam: Contact, 2009), 146–47, 150 (translated from Dutch).

April 10, 1941

[. . .]

Everyone receives an extra egg for Easter and since Easter and Passover coincide somewhat we are in luck. We also were fortunate in being able to buy not only a bone for the Seder[6] but also a real beef tongue.

[. . .]

April 11, 1941

There is the usual annual eve of Passover busyness around the house. We have all that we need for the Seder and I am very pleased that we are provided with all that is required. Meanwhile, the Haggadah[7] is very much of current interest, and *zeman cherutenu* [Hebrew for "Season of our Liberation"] is the source of much reflection.

[. . .]

April 13, 1941

The first days of the *Yom Tov* [Hebrew for Holiday] were so calm that I could not help but hope that it would stay that way in the future. The Seder lasted from 9:15 to 12. The second night there was no synagogue service, not in the city either.

[. . .]

April 14, 1941

As of last week I have resumed studying *Gemara* [part of the Talmud], I hope to persevere with Ralph [his youngest son] and me, because the

---

6. Italie refers to the shank bone used as part of the Passover ceremony. According to the Biblical account in Exodus 12:12, the final plague visited upon the ancient Egyptians (as punishment for Hebrew slavery) was the death of the firstborn son. This bone represents the blood of the animal sacrifice that caused the Angel of Death to "pass over" the homes of the Jews. Seder (literally, "order" in Hebrew) is a traditional name of the festive Passover dinner.

7. Haggadah (Hebrew, "telling") is the Jewish text that is read by participants of the Passover seder. It sets the order of the dinner and retells the story of Jewish liberation from slavery.

only Jewish thing he did consisted of studying the weekly *Sidra* [Torah portion], and that twice: 1st the whole translation with me, 2nd with me, Ida and Paul verse by verse with interpretation and participating in the weekly *Mishnah* lesson.[8] We started *Moed Katan* [tractate] again from the beginning.

[. . .]

April 23, 1941

Gasoline was used in the attack on the Great Synagogue that took place a few days ago (exactly on Hitler's birthday—who knows maybe in its honor—.)[9] Gasoline is so scarce that even physicians can only get a little, but for a worthy purpose. . . . A few pews were heavily damaged and sadly 2 *sepharim* [Torah scrolls] that were there were burnt beyond restoration, (fortunately there were only two scrolls, one kosher and one *pasoul* [Hebrew for imperfect]).

In The Hague like elsewhere all cafés now carry the sign "Jews not desired." The majority of owners by far find it unpleasant, but they are compelled [to obey.]

The Passover holiday held particular importance in the greater narrative of Jewish history and theology; it represents the hope for liberation amid oppression. Its celebration, therefore, took on a meaning that was both narrowly ritualistic and broadly social and political. The following report speaks to the Passover preparations in the Warsaw ghetto, which, more so than in Italie's account, focused on the paucity of resources available. Confinement, the defining characteristic of ghetto life, aggravated this scarcity and forced Warsaw Jewry to become creative in its observance. Just as important as the ritual itself, however, is the way in which the meaning of this holiday changed: what began as a celebration of liberation became a reminder of starvation. The following report from the files of the **Oyneg Shabes** archive shows this complex interplay

---

8. Together with the Talmud, the Mishnah forms the basis of Jewish law as formulated by the rabbis in the aftermath of the fall of the Second Temple in 70 CE. Literally translated as "oral law," the Mishnah was compiled and redacted in approximately 200 CE. See Jacob Neusner, *The Mishnah: A New Translation* (New Haven, CT: Yale University Press, 1991).

9. The extent of the damage is unclear; journals such as the *Contemporary Jewish Record* did not mention the incident.

between optimism and despair set against the backdrop of the ultimate narrative of redemption.[10]

DOCUMENT 10-2: Account by an unidentified author on the eve of Pesach in the Warsaw ghetto, April 11, 1941, USHMM RG 15.079 (ŻIH Ring. I/1024) (translated from Yiddish).

The eve of Pesach in the Warsaw ghetto, second year of the war, 1941

The daily struggle in Warsaw is a very difficult one. More prominent than everything else is the growing want, pain, desperation. The only solace for us Jews is the "yearning for the end of days" in accord with our own hopes and fantasies and particularly black-on-white, news, newspapers, random underground leaflets—this is the little spirit of life that alleviates the sufferings of the daily struggle. Close to the eve of Pesach, Jews simply shook with joy nearly the entire week—wherever two Jews met, one noticed a smile, people wished and simultaneously believed that, with God's help, on the second day of the holiday they would celebrate at home in the shtetl. The spirit lifted, in Yugoslavia a revolution,[11] Jews make a toast, the season of our freedom [Hebrew: z'man cherutenu; or Pesach] nears, groups of people stand on the street, one is even no longer afraid of the German. Peasants, people say, do not want to take Polish money, they want, people say, rubles or dollars. A Pole meets a Jew, a friend, and calls him inside to have a drink; things are fine, he says, help is near. Things are no longer going so well for the Germans. In the evening, when people gather, each person has a chance to speak, each person provides a spark of hope. In each per-

---

10. For the breadth of the Oyneg Shabes collecting efforts by **Emanuel Ringelblum** and others, see Alexandra Garbarini, with Emil Kerenji, Jan Lambertz, and Avinoam Patt, *Jewish Responses to Persecution*, vol. 2: *1938–1940* (Lanham, MD: AltaMira in association with the USHMM, 2011), 122, 136–37, 146, 439; Samuel D. Kassow, *Who Will Write Our History? Emanuel Ringelblum, the Warsaw Ghetto, and the Oyneg Shabes Archive* (Bloomington: Indiana University Press, 2007), 116–51.

11. Reference to the coup d'état of March 27, 1941, by pro-western officers in the Yugoslav army who deposed the government that was responsible for Yugoslavia joining the Tripartite Pact in Vienna two days earlier. In retaliation, Germany and its allies invaded Yugoslavia on April 6. At the time of the document's writing on April 11, the war between Yugoslavia and its invaders was still raging; Yugoslavia capitulated on April 17. See Stevan K. Pavlowitch, *Hitler's New Disorder: The Second World War in Yugoslavia* (New York: Columbia University Press, 2008), 1–20.

son one notices a certainty that just a month or two and we Jews will be saved. Jews are simply gladdened and one does not have the sense that something in the air is strained, that something is going on, and simultaneously there is no time to think since there is only one more day until Pesach, and a mist of sadness once again veils the face; one faces the daily question once again: where should one hold Pesach? Only when the political news is good is the Jew satisfied and celebrates Pesach without a cent of money, hoping to get potatoes, matzah on credit (on this Pesach people were still hopeful), and at this point people learn lightning fast that at 9 o'clock in the evening information will be relayed by radio. Something must have happened, Jews do not rest. And thus despite the danger (because after 9 in the evening, it is not permitted to be on the street), many people gather around the radio. Before the radio program begins, we find out that food prices have increased. Bread is 8 złoty a kilo [2.2 pounds], potatoes are 2.50 a kilo, onions 4.50. The atmosphere becomes extremely oppressive, you cannot think for long, the speaker interrupts and announces that Salonika is surrounded by the Germans, they have met with success in fighting the Yugoslavs and Greeks. With this, he ends. The Jews quickly run home, everyone is overcome by fear that the situation has become more serious.

On the morning of the 10th, a panic, a tumult, the food prices increase further, bread is 11 złoty for one kilo, potatoes are 4 złoty, onions 6. The shops are empty, people are scared to sell and they keep and buy whatever they can. The atmosphere is like it was on the eve of the war, people are preparing and shopping, buying not only things necessary for Pesach, but whatever happens to be available; matzah costs 25 złoty a kilo, Jews do not give this a second thought—as long as beets are available, it will be enough. Only what is this supposed to mean? Questions fall from all sides. What is the reason for the increasing prices? People are silent. Earlier, when the political situation was favorable for the Jews, people found a justification for the increasing prices. Today, people are silent. On the one hand, the prices increase from hour to hour; on the other hand, [there are] frequent communiqués that Germany is advancing and is capturing various territories in Africa, Greece, and Yugoslavia. In the street there is a racket, it might seem that this is because it is just before Pesach, but no! People cannot sit in their homes, they run into the street to see, to hear, perhaps just in case. It is once again difficult to walk on the street, you're overcome by a shudder. German automobiles crowded with many officers and military men fill the streets. Several get out, they make use of their cameras with great pleasure and photograph the poor people by the walls with their stiffened, outstretched hands, and a half hour later cars of the burial society[12] quickly drive by and take away beggars from near the walls who have given up the ghost for hunger—and free up places for the others. The display windows are empty, there are no baked goods whatsoever. At first glance, one has the impression that the *chametz*[13] is being concealed, but no! It in fact turns out that the Jewish police requisitioned all the cakes and rolls for the dormitories and hospitals because there is no bread. And here a cart with potatoes again drives past, the wagon is besieged, tens of pale hands grab the potatoes, snatch them up, and eat them raw. On Solna Street, hungry people broke into several shops and looted them. Panic all of a sudden grows and grows. The pleas of the poor people become more and more desperate.[14] Children wander about the streets, they beat with their little feet, they faint from hunger. The street singer's tune is sadder, the fiddlers by the walls play more weakly, and the prices get higher and higher. Bread with onions takes the top spot, and it has become a form of currency. Jews believe that when [the price of] a loaf of bread reaches 50 złoty, then redemption will come. The streets are full, satans move about—not men—and the words resound in one's ears: [the cost of] bread has increased, where can potatoes be had? Bread, bread, there is no bread. Amidst the throng, an acquaintance runs by with a black, torn-up eye—and smiles. He has drawn the ace of hearts. He says that he will not bow before them, there is no way he will remove his cap for the Germans. And behold a wonder: in the place where people speak of the vexed question of bread, he tells only how he encountered two Germans, walked in between them, and looked at them, and they at him, but did not remove his cap for them. Of course, they meted out a hell of a punishment to him. While bidding farewell he admits it, but he never did remove his hat for them.

On the morning of the 11th, the prices fall precipitously—people say that a loaf of bread is back to 8 złoty, potatoes at 2.50—it is truly good fortune. The resigned nevertheless run to buy something to have something at home. The carts in the street are full, the people like flies, bargains are bought up—it is truly a stroke of good fortune. People snatch up, at the least, a kilogram of potatoes for Pesach. After a difficult day, Pesach

12. *Khesed shel emes*: a Jewish communal society dedicated to ensuring proper burial for the poor.

13. *Khumets*: leavened foods, all traces of which must be removed for Pesach in the homes of observant Jews.

14. Literally, stronger and stronger.

arrived and brought new waves of want. The holiday of the season of our freedom reminded us of our continued exile. The only news that Pesach of 1941 brought is the news of starvation!

Beyond its communal narrative, Passover also translated into an intensely personal meaning for Jewish men, women, and children. Simple practices—like baking *matzot*, the unleavened bread required for the festival meal—assumed greater weight and significance in this cruel setting. Festive traditions and human interactions that had been taken for granted before the war gained in intensity in these days of distress. A joyous occasion had now largely become a further symbol of pain and deprivation. Writing from the town of Lesko in eastern Poland, under Soviet control until the start of **Operation Barbarossa**, Abraham Rauch told his children in Haifa, "Everything has already been sold, and now Pesach is coming. We don't know what we'll do."[15] Similar fears were widely held by Jews in eastern Europe. **Mirjam Korber** was a Jew from Câmpulung, Bukovina, whom in October 1941, Romanian authorities deported with her family to **Transnistria**. There, they were left to die in unsealed and unprovisioned ghettos.[16] In these diary entries written in April 1942, Korber's nostalgic memories of the past and the plight of the present overshadowed this festival of freedom.

DOCUMENT 10-3: Mirjam Korber, Djurin, Transnistria, diary entry for April 6, 1942, USHMMA Acc. 2010.93.1 Mirjam Korber Bercovici collection (translated from Romanian).

There have been so many things I could have put down on paper up to the present day, but every day there was something that kept me from writing. Saturday evening, March 28, we all baked matzot, all the families together, in our oven. I'll never forget how interesting this night was. We baked during the night, because it actually wasn't permitted: the matzot

---

15. Letter from Abraham Rauch in Lesko, Soviet-occupied Poland, to Lipa and Yenta Markus in Haifa, February 20, 1941; Ghetto Fighters' House Archive, No. 29447 (translated from Yiddish). The Germans recaptured Lesko in June 1941. A ghetto was formally established in the spring 1942. The ghetto was liquidated in August and September 1942. Abraham Rauch and his wife did not survive this "action." See Jolanta Kraemer, "Lesko," *The United States Holocaust Memorial Museum Encyclopedia of Camps and Ghettos, 1933–1945, Ghettos in German-Occupied Eastern Europe*, vol. 2, ed. Martin Dean (Bloomington: Indiana University Press in association with the USHMM, 2012), 535–37.

16. For more information about Korber, see Alexandra Zapruder, *Salvaged Pages: Young Writer's Diaries of the Holocaust* (New Haven, CT: Yale University Press, 2002), 243–49.

were supposed to be purchased from the Committee [Jewish community]. But I got something out of it: I learned how to handle a sheet of dough, though even Sissy can do it better than I. I worked hard until 9 a.m., but it was very enjoyable. A night when I didn't sleep, a night I bought for myself with countless 14-hour nights. It's true that the neighbors helped us a lot, because none of us knew how to get started. The matzot aren't like the ones at home, nothing is like it was at home. But we baked them by ourselves, we know their worth in terms of money and labor, and we treasure them. [. . .]

In our place, mother started whitewashing the house by herself, because Easter was only two days away. The whitewashing was a big success, and the room seems different, I even like it. I worked the two days before Pesach as if we were still back at home, and the Pesach preparations were quite successful. But how sad the Pesach evenings are, and how sad this Pesach is in general. The Seder of old and the Seder of Djurin, the whole house in festive garb, bright and clean, the proper preparations, the ample food. Now the room is clean, but it's lit by a kerosene lamp, the soup was made with beef, and everything was prepared so frugally, my God, so frugally. I think we won't use more than 20 eggs this Pesach. At home, even 200 to 300 weren't enough. We eat only matzot, no bread, that's the only difference for us from the rest of the year, because we haven't changed our dishes, and everything is the way it is during the year. I'm not religious at all, that's not what grieves me, but just the sad fact that forced us to be unable to respect our customs and traditions. How nice it was at home.—The first two days of Pesach were very sad in every respect. Everybody in the house was crying. The setting reminded everyone of their homes, of what they left behind. And once again I'll bring up a very common and much-discussed problem here: food. I'd like to argue that food is the only thing man wishes for naturally, when he doesn't have what he wishes. We have nothing that we wish, and we wish for what we don't have. [. . .]

The story of **Purim** provides a compelling counterpoint to the experiences of numbers of Jewish refugees living through prolonged interludes between home and unknown locales of safety increasingly beyond their reach. This holiday celebrates the triumph over a lethal foe (Haman), who sought to annihilate the entire Jewish community of Persia in the sixth century BCE. By the end of the story, it is Haman who is put to death, and the Jews remain peacefully in exile, saved by the bravery of a Jewish maiden married off to the Persian king. The ritual celebration of Purim treats this triumph with satire and levity. Children dress up in costumes, plays are performed, and as the story is read aloud, the congregation drowns Haman's name in shouts. The following Purim poem was recorded by Ruth Heilbrun in a handwritten notebook that she kept while at Château Montintin, a children's home run by the **Œuvre de secours aux enfants (OSE)**,[17] located about eighteen miles south of Limoges and known for its fairly secular atmosphere; many of its teachers hailed from communist backgrounds.[18] A good example of Judaism's more fluid rendering of the Christian divide between secular and religious, Purim proved to be a major celebration at Montintin, and Ruth recorded songs composed by three different children that marked the occasion.

Horst Rotholz, the author of this poem, was born in 1924 in Breslau, Germany. He participated in many cultural events during his time in Montintin and was a member of the OSE band. Rotholz's poem alludes to the classic story of Purim with its opening and has a simple rhyme scheme that the English translation has not captured faithfully. The poem, clearly meant to be performed for his peers, lists the "present worries" of the community at Montintin in a form that would have evoked memories of Jewish cultural tradition, even with children raised in nonreligious families.

---

17. By late 1941, OSE was responsible for 1,200 children in **Vichy** France, providing medical care and other forms of assistance to their families as well. See Renée Poznanski, *Jews in France during World War II* (Hanover, NH: University Press of New England in association with the USHMM, 2001), 140–42; Katy Hazan and Serge Klarsfeld, *Rescuing Jewish Children during the Nazi Occupation: OSE Children's Homes, 1938–1945* (Paris: Somogy éditions d'art, 2008).

18. Lucien Souny, *Enfances juives: Limousin-Dordogne-Berry terres de refuge, 1939–1945* (Saint-Paul: Editions Lucien Souny, 2006), 358–59. Montintin operated between June 1940 and February 1944 and housed some 280 children, ages four to twenty. See Hazan and Klarsfeld, *Rescuing Jewish Children*, 103. The family of Ruth Heilbrun (1925–2010) managed to obtain visas for the United States in the spring of 1942 and reach New York via Marseille and Casablanca. Ruth's brother Kurt, who had attempted to reach Palestine, was killed in the Independent State of Croatia. Information comes from the donor file, USHMMA Acc. 2010.239.1, Ruth H. Windmuller collection.

DOCUMENT 10-4: **Purim poem by Horst Rotholz,**[19] **Château Montintin, Vichy France, March 12, 1941, USHMMA Acc. 2000.187 Ruth Windmuller collection (translated from German).**

> Listen, you dear people,
> Purim, that means happiness.
> Purim, that means eating cake,
> And not forgetting Haman.
> This saying from childhood days,
> No longer applies today.
> That was yesterday, what will tomorrow bring?
> These are our present worries.
> Visa, affidavit, consulate,
> Brazil, Cuba, Dominican Republic,
> Bolivia, Haiti, Paraguay, Alexandria,
> Palestine or Rhodesia,
> Australia, Shanghai, South Africa,
> And the last hope is the U.S.A.
> What are we doing here, there we can laugh.

[. . . ; a long section on the confusion regarding emigration destinations and procedures follows]

> And so it goes, getting worse every day,
> For yourself and your family, all you have is one room.
> And in this room, admired by all,
> There is a couch, the symbol of the century.
> The couch, your wife, and the children, the dears:
> That's all that is left of your wealth.
> You have your wife share the couch, nice and snug,
> There you sleep better than you did in your bed.

---

19. Horst Rotholz (1924–1942) was the younger son of Berthold and Margarete Rotholz from Breslau. The Rotholzes, including Horst's older brother Günther (1914–1942), were passengers aboard the ill-fated MS *St. Louis* in the spring of 1939. Refused entry to Cuba and the United States, they were sent back to Europe, where they disembarked in France. After the German occupation of France, Horst came under the care of OSE at Montintin. Eventually, however, he and the entire family were deported to Drancy and then **Auschwitz** in 1942, where they were all murdered. See Bernard Reviriego, *Les juifs en Dordogne, 1939–1944: de l'accueil à la persécution* (Périgueux: Archives départementales de la Dordogne, 2003), 437–38. On the history of the voyage of *St. Louis*, including passenger lists, see the USHMM's interactive resource page at www.ushmm.org/museum/exhibit/online/stlouis/ (accessed May 15, 2012).

Contented, you think, enjoying the thought,
They can all go . . . take a running jump.
Then you fall asleep and can be envied,
You happily dream about the good old days.
But when you awake in the morning, you're aware of the sorrow,
And once again you're the same old *Chammer*.[20]
You pace back and forth, up and down,
It just keeps on, it's becoming too much.
In the morning, at noon, until late in the night,
It's always the same thing that's making you fret.
You ask yourself why, for what reason, how come,
And think you'll never enjoy life again.
Can you, my friends, understand my concern?
The trouble, the trouble, the trouble I'd like to see!

While holiday celebrations helped to maintain Jewish continuity, however strained, other rituals demanded more urgent decisions about observance. Care of the dead remains one of the most sacred obligations of a Jewish family or community. Traditionally, the burial of the deceased must happen within one day of the person's passing. A member of the community *chevra kadishah*, or burial society, looks after the body in the interim. This task is seen as among the highest of good deeds, as the dead are unable to return the favor. The family then remains in mourning for seven days to "sit" *shiva* in the home and recites the *kaddish* prayer for the dead every evening with the community. The Holocaust made most of these practices nearly impossible, which added yet another layer of dehumanization to the process. Mass executions by shooting or gassing produced piles of dead bodies, which the murderers disposed of in the most undignified and anonymous way possible. Over 1 million bodies were left on the killing fields in the East in unmarked mass graves. The Germans later dug many of them up in order to burn the corpses. After the war, these graves often remained forgotten.[21] In the ghettos, corpses became threats to public health to be swiftly disposed of, while relatives struggled to preserve as much of the deceased person's dignity and humanity as possible under the most difficult circumstances. In the following letter, a woman deported from Vienna to the Lublin district appealed to the Łódź **Jewish Council** on behalf of herself and

---

20. From the Yiddish *"khamer"*: donkey or, more pejoratively, ass.

21. On recent attempts to identify mass murder sites in Poland and Ukraine, see Patrick Desbois, *Holocaust by Bullets: A Priest's Journey to Uncover the Truth Behind the Murder of 1.5 Million Jews* (New York: Palgrave MacMillan, 2008).

her brother to obtain the information needed for both to mourn and bury their father.[22]

DOCUMENT 10-5: **Letter from Anny Feldmann, Opole, Lublin district, Generalgouvernement, to the Jewish Council-Łódź, September 11, 1941, and response note regarding the marking of her father's grave, November 3, 1941, USHMMA RG 15.083M (PSAŁ, file 300), 89, 91–93 (translated from German).**

Your reference: 3381 a/41 Ro/FW

Gentlemen,

I am confirming the receipt of your much-valued card dated August 31 of this year.

Mr. Simche Binem Feldmann, who died on April 15 of this year, was my father. You brought his death to my knowledge with the above-mentioned card, and the news grieved me deeply.

I ask you gentlemen above all to kindly provide me with the death certificate, and to tell me the number of my father's grave and provide information as to how much the temporary placement of a simple wooden plaque would possibly cost. I myself have been "evacuated" from Vienna together with several thousand other Viennese and am without funds. But I am willing to go without food for a few days to pay the costs [of a plaque], which I hope will not be too high. Unfortunately, I was unable to do anything for my poor father. Perhaps God will help me at least to set up a gravestone for him, and therefore I request that you kindly let me know where his grave is. I have informed my brother, who is interned in Canada, so that he can say Kaddish.

Once more, I beg you to send me the death certificate, let me know where his grave is, and give me an estimate of the costs.

In advance, I thank you most sincerely for your efforts and remain most respectfully yours,

Anny Feldmann
Opole, Puławy County, District of Lublin

---

22. Anny Feldmann, born in 1907 in Zborów, Poland, was deported from Vienna to Opole in February 1941; she did not survive the war. See *USHMM ITS Collection Data Base Central Name Index.* Her father's death certificate indicated that Simche Binem Feldman [*sic*], son of Mojżesz Sobel, was born in 1879 in Zborów and died on April 15, 1941 (USHMMA, RG 15.083M_0097_00000562).

[reply from the Jewish Council Office in Łódź, November 3, 1941:]

No. 7019 a/41 Ro/FW
Frau Anny Feldmann
O p o l e

In reply to your written request of September 11, 1941, we enclose herewith the death certificate of Simche Binem FELDMAN.

Regarding your request concerning the gravestone, we must inform you that this matter is not on the agenda at the moment.
Respectfully,

Secretary

Attachment [not printed here]

As death marked daily life in the ghetto and forestalling it became ever more difficult, some practices arose that on the surface defied logic. Such was the case in the following letter, its subject also mentioned in a diary note by Warsaw described *Judenrat* head **Adam Czerniaków**,[23] regarding a wedding in the cemetery designed to curry favor with God and thus end the rampant typhus epidemic. This idea was rooted in Jewish mysticism and based on a host of legends and Jewish folklore (which the author of the following letter cites). Venturing such a "cure" of last resort had some appeal in the face of desperate circumstances. In spite of the cover letter's "support" for what is described as an outmoded practice, a note at the end of the document intriguingly requests that the letter be destroyed after its contents have been considered. It was not destroyed, which may suggest that someone found it worth preserving as evidence about conditions at the time.

---

23. Raul Hilberg, Stanislaw Staron, and Josef Kermisz, eds., *The Warsaw Diary of Adam Czerniakow: Prelude to Doom* (Chicago: Ivan R. Dee in association with the USHMM, 1999), 293 (diary entry for October 27, 1941).

DOCUMENT 10-6: **Letter from Majer Bałaban,**[24] **Warsaw, to the head of the Warsaw Jewish Council, October 29, 1941, USHMMA RG 15.079M (ŻIH Ring. II/142) (translated from Polish).**

Jewish Religious Community in Warsaw, Internal Correspondence
Department of Registry Issues (Rel[igious])
October 29, 1941

To Mr. Chairman
On the matter of a wedding at the cemetery
At their last meeting, district rabbis deliberated over measures intended to alleviate the epidemic and, seeing that all sanitary efforts were missing their mark, decided to employ transcendental measures: prayers, the recitation of Psalms, and so on. They also decided, following an old custom of years past, to arrange at the Jewish cemetery the wedding of a poor orphaned couple in order to appease God. Such weddings were popular in medieval times and even in the nineteenth century; if I remember correctly, such a wedding took place at a Lwów cemetery during the epidemic of 1918. Such weddings have also been described in Yiddish literature, as, for example, in the novel Yoshe Kalb by I. J. Singer, which Schwarz adapted into a drama performed many times on Jewish stages in Poland.[25] Kaminer, of blessed memory, enthusiastically supported the rabbis' plan and promised to collect some 1,000 zł. for the dowry of the impoverished newlyweds[;] now that he is no more, the rabbis request permission for the Cemetery Department to collect at wealthier funerals (as supplements to donations or fees) certain sums, naturally only until 1,000 złoty have been collected.

---

24. Majer (Meyer) Bałaban (1877–1942?) was a historian considered the founder of the modern study of Polish Jewish history. Born in Lwów, he served as a military chaplain in Lublin during World War I and later directed a rabbinical seminary in Warsaw. He also helped found the Institute for Jewish Studies in Warsaw and published widely on the history of Polish Jews. He continued his historical research and lectures in the Warsaw ghetto, where he died in late 1942 or early 1943, apparently of a heart attack. Israel M. Biderman, *Mayer Balaban: Historian of Polish Jewry* (New York: Dr. I. M. Biderman Book Committee, 1976); Barbara Engelking and Jacek Leociak, *The Warsaw Ghetto: A Guide to the Perished City* (New Haven, CT: Yale University Press, 2009), 181, 251, 354, 815–16.

25. Israel Joshua Singer (1893–1944) was the brother of Isaac Bashevis Singer and Esther Kreitman, with whom he shared a substantial literary talent. Born in Poland, he immigrated to the United States in 1934. Among his Yiddish novels was *Yoshe Kalb*, first published in 1932. See his autobiography, *Fun a velt vos iz nishto mer* [Of a World That Is No More] (New York: Matones, 1946).

Out of official obligation I submit this resolution from our rabbinate to Mr. Chairman, requesting his <u>oral</u> decision, after which the present document is to be destroyed.

[Signed] Dr. M. Bałaban

With the help of God,
To [?] kindest Mr. M. Kaminer, Chairman of the Department of Religious Affairs

Since the epidemic rampant in our city spreads greatly from day to day, we propose as a preventive religious ritual to arrange at the cost of the community a wedding of a young man and woman, poor people, at the cemetery immediately after the approaching Yom Kippur. This ritual is tried and tested and, with God's help, will certainly be effective and will halt the epidemic.

The present resolution was adopted at the meeting of the Assembly of Rabbis on Sept. 28, 1941.

N. Rogoźnicki	E. Majmin	M. Ziemba
Y. A. Zamczyk	Y. M. Kanał	A. N. Zawłodawer
Y. A. Biderman	S. Merkier	D. Kahne-Szpiro[26]

The epidemic continued to rage in the ghetto. In February 1942 Czerniaków received a typhus inoculation and noted sharply, "Several months ago the rabbis proposed that a marriage ceremony be performed in a cemetery. This is supposed to bring about the end of the epidemic. The scientists who do the blood

---

26. In the Polish version of the document, the signatories to the petition are only referred to by initials; the full names come from a Hebrew version. Noach Rogoźnicki (1887–1942), born in Warsaw, was killed along with his wife Pessa Sara (1890–1942), though a daughter survived. Menachem Ziemba (1890–1943?) may have died in **Treblinka**. Yitzhak Meier Kanał [Icchak Kanał] was killed during the August 1942 deportations; he was eighty-two years old and vice chairman of the Congregation of Rabbis in Poland. Shlomo Ha-Cohen Merkier (also Szlama Merkier, Shlomo Marker), born in Serock, Poland, and his wife Ita were both killed. See Robert Moses Shapiro and Tadeusz Epsztein, eds., *The Warsaw Ghetto: Oyneg Shabes-Ringelblum Archive. Catalog and Guide* (Bloomington: Indiana University Press in association with the USHMM and the Jewish Historical Institute in Warsaw, 2009), 333; Hilberg, Staron, and Kermisz, *The Warsaw Diary of Adam Czerniakow*, 20, 333n31; Yad Vashem, "Central Database of Shoah Victims' Names," www .yadvashem.org; Engelking and Leociak, *The Warsaw Ghetto*, 169, 650, 656–66. The authors have been unable to locate further information about the other rabbis who signed the resolution.

testing and at the same time declare that neither a positive nor a negative reaction is conclusive are as helpful as the abovementioned rabbis."[27] In late July 1942, Czerniaków committed suicide immediately prior to the Great Deportation.

PRIVATE FAITH AND COMMUNAL CONCERNS

For some Jews in Europe, the events unfolding made it impossible to continue their religious observance and professions of faith. For others, religious observance remained part of the fabric of life, something carried forward and lived out even in times of unprecedented persecution. Studying sacred texts in the Warsaw ghetto until shortly before the Great Deportation of July 1942, Rabbi Kalonymus Kalmish Shapira explored the connection between human and divine suffering, leading to, as literary historian David Roskies writes, a "mystical communion in extremis" that gave purpose to destruction.[28] Spiritual concerns about the continuity of the Jewish people remained a constant companion as the dispersal of communities and families—and the destruction—went ever further.

One context in which these questions arose time and again was the stewardship of the **Kindertransport** children, who had been sent abroad for safety. Separated from their parents and living in largely Christian homes in Britain, their connections to Judaism and their prior upbringing became tenuous and sometimes completely impossible. In fact, these children were often encouraged to shed their former identity and embrace an entirely mainstream British (usually non-Jewish) way of life, a phenomenon that caused great trepidation among Jewish groups in Great Britain. It is worth noting that in this particular case, the notion of Judaism as a "religion" to be shed in favor of another one was more relevant than in the case of East European Jews. These were German-speaking Jewish children, usually highly assimilated into German culture in which religion was relegated to the private, spiritual sphere; Jewish organizations that worried about the children's increasingly tenuous connection to Judaism were also rooted in a Protestant-dominated British culture—and so was their concept of religious alienation. An inquiry sent by the Joint Emergency Committee

---

27. Hilberg, Staron, and Kermisz, *The Warsaw Diary of Adam Czerniakow*, 324 (diary entry for February 12, 1942).

28. Roskies, *The Literature of Destruction*, 503–9. On Rabbi Shapira (1889–1943), see Nehemia Polen, *The Holy Fire: The Teachings of Rabbi Kalonymus Kalman Shapira, the Rebbe of the Warsaw Ghetto* (Northvale, NJ: Aronson, 1994).

for Jewish Religious Education (JEC)[29] to communities and education boards throughout Britain in the spring of 1942 serves as an example. Eight-year-old Ilse Helfgott, now living on the Isle of Wight, already looked like a "lost cause," with the investigator noting: "Attends church, too late for any change to be made. No classes exist in Isle of Wight. Parents: liberal, did not object to child being sent to Christian home." For sixteen-year-old Susi Hirsch raised by liberal parents in Czechoslovakia and now in England, Rabbi Stransky wrote: "Goes to Methodist Church, because not satisfied with Jewish Class, feels she is in a 'religious middle'—her own words. Suggest: if possible to bring her to another place."[30] The overall picture reflected in the following report by the JEC's inspector, Rabbi Simon M. Lehrman,[31] pointed to similar situations.

DOCUMENT 10-7: **Report by Simon M. Lehrman, Refugee Children's Department of the Board of Deputies of British Jews, on the spiritual well-being of children brought to the United Kingdom as part of the Kindertransport, May 21, 1942, USHMMA RG 59.023M (Board of Deputies of British Jews), reel 16, frames 281–83.**

REPORT OF THE REFUGEE CHILDREN'S DEPARTMENT

Investigation.

In April 1941, an agreement was reached between the Joint Emergency Committee and the Movement[32] whereby the latter body entrusted the spiritual welfare of orthodox Jewish refugee children to the

29. The Joint Emergency Committee for Jewish Religious Education in Great Britain was an umbrella organization formed in 1939 by a number of diverse local and regional Jewish educational institutions in Great Britain and had by 1943 grown into an undisputed national authority in its area of activities. See Bernard Steinberg, "Jewish Education in Great Britain during World War II," in *Jewish Social Studies* 29 (January 1967): 27–63.

30. Inquiry by the JEC and case reports regarding the religious upbringing of refugee children, May 1942, USHMMA RG 59.023M (**Board of Deputies of British Jews**), reel 16, frames 305, 307.

31. Simon Maurice Lehrman (1900–?) was a Russian-born, British-educated author of numerous texts on Jewish religious instruction and practice from the 1930s to the 1960s. He also served as the JEC's inspector for education from 1941 until 1955. See Leslie Gilbert Pine, ed., *The Author's and Writer's Who's Who* (London: Burke's Peerage, 1960), 236.

32. The Jewish Secondary Schools Movement was a fledgling network of Orthodox schools organized by the rabbi of Adas Yisroel in London, Solomon Schonfeld (1912–1984). In the spring of 1941, the JEC sought to enlist Reform and Liberal synagogues for putting the students of their schools under the Committee's jurisdiction. Schonfeld and other community leaders bitterly opposed this; the majority education in Britain was Orthodox at that point. See Steinberg, "Jewish Education in Great Britain during World War II."

Joint Emergency Committee. Where the child was definitely reported to be "liberal" or "reform," we offered to submit names to the Movement to be dealt with by the appropriate synagogue authorities.

On receipt of a list of about 500 names last autumn from the Movement, the Joint Emergency Committee drew up a panel of visitors to ascertain the answers to a fixed questionnaire, the main questions being

  (a) whether the child was in a suitable billet
  (b) whether the child attended any Hebrew classes in the district.

Since November, when the reports came in, a special department was set up by the Joint Emergency Committee to deal with these cases. To facilitate the work, it was necessary to classify all cases under the following main headings:—

1. Orthodox children to be attached to J.E.C. classes.
2. Cases requiring rebilleting for various reasons.
3. "Liberal" or "reform" children needing Jewish education.
4. Children already attending Hebrew classes.
5. Children under Christian influence.
6. Children moved to London, needing after-care.
7. Children above school age, to be put in touch with Youth Movements.

Unfortunately cases have come to light where foster-parents seem to exact the price of conversion for their hospitality. In such cases there is only one solution—rebilleting into Jewish homes. In such cases the Movement is immediately apprised of the necessity of rebilleting.

There were already about 800 refugee children receiving religious instruction in our 300 centres up and down the country. The difficulty arose in cases where children were scattered in isolated hamlets and villages. Then every effort was made to contact these cases by sending them literature, magazines, etc. It is hoped to arrange a Correspondence Course in the near future.

Procedure.

Since the work was entrusted to me on January 1st, 1942, I have paid several personal visits to Regional Secretaries and have now obtained almost complete lists of all refugee children. The lists show that there are just over 4,000 Jewish refugee children varying from the ages of 5 and 20 and even upwards. Of these no more than 1,500 would be of school age, i.e. under 15. In large centres such as Manchester, which has over 600 children in the city itself and another 160 in the region, a special Jewish Welfare Committee has been set up to co-ordinate all the welfare work including the educational work which is being done for Jewish children in that region. From time to time reports are sent to this office as to what is being done. Negotiations are now being carried on with other large provincial centres where there are a large number of refugee children in order to establish similar Jewish Welfare Committees.

Every effort is being made to draft children under 15 into our existing classes and, where it is necessary, to establish new classes for them. For those over 15, being about 2,500, attempts are being made to affiliate them to Youth Movements, and in isolated cases to send them literature or to establish some other means of contact with them. I am sending a personal letter to all those young people over the age of 15 living in isolated villages, and hope thus to establish some contact. Representatives of Jewish Youth Organisations have already been interviewed, and they have co-operated in the work. A Conference of all Youth Organisations has been called for May 26th in order to consider how best that many adolescent refugees can be affiliated to Jewish youth societies.

Passover—Circulars were sent to all resident teachers to see that hospitality was afforded to refugee children in the reception areas.

Tephillin[33]—In many cases Tephillin, Prayer Books and Taliot[34] have been sent.

Suggestions

1. We must impress upon the Jewish community the need of finding more Jewish homes to accommodate these children who are at present in billets not conducive to their spiritual welfare.

---

33. Tefillin, or phylacteries, are ritual objects used in morning prayers by observant Jewish men.

34. Tallit is a prayer shawl used by observant Jewish men in morning prayers.

2. We must make the community realise the importance of establishing hostels to accommodate these children for whom no Jewish homes can be found and who, in the opinion of our visitors, must be rebilleted.
3. Literature must be published and sent to those who are far away from Jewish centres.
4. The needs of adolescent youth must receive special attention.
5. A correspondence course for younger children at present away from our religion classes must be arranged. The Course will entail additional expense. The Movement has expressed its sympathy and interest in this project.

Conclusion.

From the aforesaid it will already have been seen that the numerous problems are not easy of solution. Yet they are in the front-rank of those at present confronting our Community. The difficulties of the situation can best be realised when it is borne in mind that these children who came from the Continent at a young and impressionable age, torn away from their parents' embrace and placed in non-Jewish homes for so many years, seem now to have been overcome, to a large extent, by a sense of frustration. Kindness hitherto has been shown to them mainly by non-Jewish friends, whilst their own people seem to have forgotten them. This has made many of the younger children feel bitter and has driven a few, especially young girls, to the baptismal font. We must therefore act immediately and put into reality some of the above suggestions. For it is only when a concerted effort will be made on the part of the entire Jewish community that the spiritual welfare of our refugee protégées will be placed on a more satisfactory basis.

Those rescued by the Kindertransport program were not only the objects of concern among such religious authorities eager to ensure what they regarded as a proper Jewish upbringing in British homes. Jewish children themselves also puzzled over their own shifting allegiances and faith in their new environment. The following diary entry by fourteen-year-old Inga Pollak articulates her resistance against pressures to conform to the mainstream Christian society around her. Inga had left Vienna at the age of twelve together with her sister, Lieselotte, and they were sent to live with a family in Cornwall, England. Their father managed to join them in August 1940. Unlike her sister, who decided to convert to Protestantism, Inga chose to retain Judaism and a particular concept of the divine at the core of her identity.

DOCUMENT 10-8: Inga Pollak, Falmouth, United Kingdom, diary entry for July 25, 1941, in Ingrid Jacoby,[35] *My Darling Diary: A Wartime Journal* (Penzance: United Writers Publications, 1998), 99.

My brain has been knocked out of my head and I dare say that the same will happen to you when you hear what I have to say: On Wednesday, when Daddy, Lieselotte and I were out on a walk, we talked about religion. It was to be a very important day in my life because I discovered that my father doesn't believe in God! This is a horrible sentence but they are his words. His explanation, as far as I understand it, is as follows: God, my father says, did not make the world. The earth is a splinter of the sun. God did not make people; they came from millions of cells and eventually from apes. Religion started because people didn't know any science, and they invented God to explain what they could not understand. So this invisible, unknown, beloved God whom nobody understands is no more than a figment of people's imagination. Thus says my father.

But I say the world may have started in a scientific manner but there is someone in heaven who decides our fate. For a day, however, I was in a terrible state. I thought of nothing but what my father had told me and wondered if it was true. But then I remembered how everything turns out right in the end, and when you pray how God listens to you, and how much my mother loved God and taught me from babyhood to do likewise. How dare I believe otherwise, I told myself. I talked to Connie [a friend] about it. She's a Catholic and goes to church every Sunday. To my surprise she replied that she had often thought about this but she had come to the same conclusion as I.

Lieselotte is going to be converted! She will be baptized in the Parish Church and will become a Protestant. My father would like me to be converted too, but I WON'T. She's not doing it because she believes in Jesus Christ but because my father has convinced her that it is better to be a Christian in England, especially if Hitler should invade. I think this is very wrong of her.

---

35. Inga Pollak (b. 1927) lived in Falmouth, Cornwall, from 1939 until 1944. In her diary, which she had started in late 1937, she switched from writing in German to English in October 1939. Ingrid Jacoby was a pen name, Inga Joseph her married name. After the war she stayed in England, eventually becoming a teacher in Sheffield. Her father survived the war, but her mother and a grandmother were deported to Minsk in November 1941 and killed. See Alexandra Zapruder, ed., *Salvaged Pages: Young Writers' Diaries of the Holocaust* (New Haven, CT: Yale University Press, 2002), 437.

Like Pollak, the following excerpt from a wartime diary exemplifies a turn toward faith in trying times. **Lucien Dreyfus**'s entry provides a highly personal reflection that attempts to assign meaning to suffering. As a staunchly patriotic Frenchman and a committed Jew, Dreyfus's diary reflected the negotiation between these two intersecting, but by 1942, conflicting identities. While he always retained a distinct Jewish identification, his religious observance and belief had ebbed and flowed over the years.[36] In this entry from June 1942, Dreyfus found the only answer to the question of why anti-Jewish persecution by German and Vichy authorities was intensifying to reside in a traditional Jewish narrative of sin and punishment, one that helped put the problems of the present into historical perspective.

DOCUMENT 10-9: **Lucien Dreyfus, Nice, Vichy France, diary entry for June 18, 1942, USHMMA RG 10.144.05 (translated from French).**

[. . .] Played bridge with Mr. and Mrs. Kahn, received a nervous shock during the game that must prevent me from doing it again; I won't give in anymore. The anti-Jewish measures of the government are criticized, above all by the Jews; nothing is easier. What is difficult to say is to what point exactly the [Vichy] government has wanted to identify itself with the orders of the victor. Being used to searching for ultimate causes, I can't manage to find anything except a celestial punishment brought on by the Jewish defection; it is to escape from the necessity of seeing around myself an inextricable mass of contradictions and human meannesses that are directing the course of things. My conception will perhaps please theologians, but there are almost none of those left anymore, and because I certainly want to find the truth without pleasing the rabbis whom I disdain, I am sure that my thought is pure and the result of long, disinterested and thorough meditations. These ideas correspond to my temperament, and if I occupy myself in these notebooks with little else than the ultimate principle of man, it is that the other things that preoccupy my people, even the war, are nothing compared to the problems raised by the Bible. There is a God who punishes and who rewards. Each person must try to live according to his own truth; I won't try to convince opponents, but I intend to preserve intact the spiritual traditions that go back to the Sinai.

---

36. For a discussion of Dreyfus's life and diary, see Alexandra Garbarini, *Numbered Days: Diaries and the Holocaust* (New Haven, CT: Yale University Press, 2006), 23–57.

Both Inga Pollak and Lucien Dreyfus reaffirmed their relationship to Judaism. Elsa Binder,[37] confined to the Stanisławów ghetto, expressed yet a different perspective. We can only speculate how far the concrete problems they were facing influenced their perceptions. Binder was nineteen when the war broke out in Poland, and Stanisławów was initially occupied by the Soviets. After the Germans took over the territory, they massacred ten thousand Jews on October 12, 1941. Two months later, the ghetto was established for those who remained. Elsa began her diary at this time, in late December of 1941, apparently with the idea that it could serve as a testimony to her life and that of others close to her. In these two diary entries from March 1942, Binder and another, unnamed author (perhaps her sister, who was murdered one month later), consciously reject a worldview in which God actively intervenes in history.[38] This highly personal reaction to her situation is framed by the daily realities that Binder and her family faced in the ghetto, leading her to conclude that the only dependable belief was in her own self-reliance rather than in an unseen force behind the universe.

DOCUMENT 10-10: **Elsa Binder, Stanisławów, Galicia district, Generalgouvernement, diary entries for March 18, 1942, USHMMA RG 02.208M (ŻIH 302/267) (translated from Polish).**

[Written in different handwriting by Binder's unnamed peer]
March 18, 1942
[. . .]
Mom tells us she had a dream in which she saw, among people who were long-dead, her father wearing a fur coat. Seeing that she had become frightened, he comforted her, saying that he is allowed to [wear the fur coat]. How would Freud interpret this dream? I have no idea, but I just have admiration for the secrets of the human heart and subconsciousness. I am sure that mom unconsciously senses misfortune.
[. . .]

---

37. A member of a Zionist youth organization before the war, Elsa (Eliszewa) Binder (b. 1920) kept a diary in the ghetto covering the period from December 1941 to July 1942. It was found in the summer of 1943 along the road down which Stanisławów's Jews marched to their deaths. Elsa Binder did not survive the war; the diary's author was only identified in the 1990s. See Michał Czajka, *Memoirs Collection Catalogue (Jewish Historical Institute Archives, Record Group 302)* (Warsaw: Żydowski Instytut Historyczny, 2007), 209; Andrea Löw, "Stanisławów," *The USHMM Encyclopedia of Camps and Ghettos,* 2:831–34.

38. In the original diary, the change in authorship between the two passages is evident due to the difference in handwriting. See Czajka, *Memoirs Collection Catalogue,* 208–9; Zapruder, *Salvaged Pages,* 301–6.

[Written in Elsa Binder's handwriting]

[March 18, 1942]

[. . .]

My co-workers are mainly Chasids, who strongly and blindly believe in divine salvation. I often envy them when I hear how they pray, how they entreat, and how they entrust themselves to the care of an invisible (and non-existent) God. They hope that He will send succor. And myself? And my family? We are entirely reliant on our strength (which is valued very little), or rather on our rags. Our good humor and our next meal depend upon whether mom today picks up the money for the dress that she sold already a few days ago. [. . .]

FRAMING THE WORLD THROUGH THEOLOGY

While Jews from different branches of Judaism shared a common vocabulary and historical points of reference, a profound difference existed between a non-observant and Orthodox outlook on the unfolding situation. In any discussion of traditional Judaism, it is important to note that "Orthodox Judaism" did not refer to a single, consistent level of observance that traced back to an "original" practice, but to a broad spectrum of ideas emerging in the modern period in reaction to Jewish assimilation and the rise of liberal Judaism in the nineteenth century.[39] As Jews faced worsening conditions throughout Europe, Orthodox communities struggled with profound questions of faith. Where did current events fit into the path of Jewish history, and why were the Jews suffering under more severe persecution than any other people? To what degree could Jewish theology and tradition help explain what was happening, and could one draw hope from religious teachings of the past? Where was the God of history, and what was God's role in the unfolding catastrophe? What specific rules and rituals must be upheld in the face of disaster, and what could be forgone in the name of saving one's life and others in the community?[40] These conversations occurred in the middle of the war, drawing on prior rationalizations of crises in

---

39. See Jacob Katz, *Out of the Ghetto: The Social Background of Jewish Emancipation, 1770–1870* (Cambridge, MA: Harvard University Press, 1973).

40. For a detailed outline of wartime theological discussions among ultra-orthodox rabbis, see Gershon Greenberg, "Ultra-Orthodox Responses during and following the War," in *Wrestling with God*, ed. Katz, Biderman, and Greenberg, 11–26.

Jewish history. They would continue in the aftermath of World War II, as the field of post-Holocaust Jewish theology emerged.[41]

In the larger article from which the excerpt in document 10-11 derives, the founder and director of the **Yeshiva** Etz-Chayim in Montreux, Rabbi Rafael Eliahu Botschko,[42] described the present lethal danger as historically unique yet not fully unprecedented. In his mind, the lack of observance of Jewish law was at the core of the current catastrophe, a traditional understanding of Jewish history pervasive since the biblical writings of Jeremiah (purportedly composed after the fall of the First Temple in Jerusalem to the Babylonians in 586 BCE), through the medieval period to explain the raids of crusaders, and up to the modern period in reference to pogroms.[43] Writing from Switzerland, at some remove from the war, Botschko based his interpretation on two biblical stories. The first concerned Chaldean King Belsazar, who after having defiled precious goblets taken from the Jerusalem temple during a feast with his court sees a mysterious writing on the wall (*"Mene Mene Tekel Upharsin"*) that forebodes his imminent death and the demise of his kingdom (Daniel 5:1–28). The second story, Daniel's vision of the ram and the goat (Daniel 8:3–7), depicts the coming of evil threatening the Jewish people.

41. Zachary Braiterman, *(God) After Auschwitz: Tradition and Change in Post-Holocaust Jewish Thought* (Princeton, NJ: Princeton University Press, 1998); Shimon Huberband, *Kiddush Hashem: Jewish Religious and Cultural Life in Poland during the Holocaust*, ed. Jeffrey S. Gurock and Robert S. Hirt (Hoboken, NJ: Ktav Publishing House, 1987).

42. Rafael Eliahu (sometimes Yerahmiel Eliyahu or Elijahu) Botschko (?1892–1956) was born and raised in Lithuania (then part of the Russian Empire) before moving to Switzerland during World War I. He founded the yeshiva Etz-Chayim in 1927 and also served on the central council of the Orthodox umbrella organization in western Europe, Agudat Israel (Agudas Yisroel). After his death in 1956 his son, Rabbi Moshé Botschko, became head of the school. Ralph Weingarten, "Botschko, Elijahu," in *Historisches Lexikon der Schweiz*, ed. Marco Jorio (Basel, Switzerland: Schwabe & Co., 2003), 616; see www.hls-dhs-dss.ch (accessed April 10, 2012).

43. For a full examination of this type of response to catastrophe in Jewish history, see Alan Mintz, *Hurban: Responses to Catastrophe in Hebrew Literature* (Syracuse, NY: Syracuse University Press, 1996).

DOCUMENT 10-11: **Rabbi Rafael Eliahu Botschko, Montreux, Switzerland, "The mysterious hand," no date (ca. 1942), in idem, *Oase im Sturm* (Zurich: Gutenberg AG, no date [1942/43]), 21–23 (translated from German).**

[. . .]

III.

With a Mighty Hand! [*Beyod Khazokoh!*]

And we ask once again: What is this? *Mah zoys?* [What is this?] Has it always been so, has the world always had such times when a world for the Jews is expected to be sought on the planet Mars, and the Jewish people's scholars, scientists, and Nobel Prize winners stand before closed doors? What has come to pass, that the same people who yesterday were still celebrated and worshipped as trailblazers and inventors now stand alone, unappreciated and expendable, as if they were nothing? *Dal kvoydeynu bagoyim* [sunken is our glory among the nations], the ancient people, once so admired, was treated with such contempt today.

The Torah gives us an answer to all these questions: "The Lord will bring a nation against thee from far, from the end of the earth, as the eagle swoopeth down; a nation whose tongue thou shalt not understand; a nation of fierce countenance, that shall not regard the person of the old, nor show favor to the young . . . And he shall besiege thee in all thy gates, until thy high and fortified walls come down, wherein thou didst trust. . . . And ye shall be left few in number, whereas ye were as the stars of heaven for multitude; because thou didst not hearken unto the voice of the Lord thy God." (Deuteronomy 28) And the Prophet Ezekiel says: "As I live, saith the Lord God, surely with a mighty hand, and with an outstretched arm, and with fury poured out, will I be king over you; and I will bring you out from the peoples, and will gather you out of the countries wherein ye are scattered, with a mighty hand, and with an outstretched arm, and with fury poured out; and I will bring you into the wilderness of the peoples, and there will I plead with you face to face." (Ezekiel 28) "The time is come, the day draweth near; let not the buyer rejoice, nor the seller mourn; for wrath is upon all the multitude thereof. . . . They have blown the horn, and have all made ready, but none goeth to the battle; for My wrath is upon all the multitude thereof. . . . They shall cast their silver in the streets, and their gold shall be as an unclean thing; their silver and their gold shall not be able to deliver them in the day of the wrath of the Lord. . . . And I will give it into the hands of the strangers for a prey, and to the wicked of the earth for a spoil; and they shall profane it." (Ezekiel 7)

Are these not the bitter truths that the prophet foretold to us 2,500 years ago and that have found their fullest realization today? The prophet proclaimed them to us, proclaimed them again and again, and the sages of all the ages have continually admonished us, but we stopped up our ears and did not hear. Now came the "secret hand," which symbolizes the *yod khazokoh*, the mighty hand of God: "*Mene Mene Tekel Upharsin.*" For a long time you did not believe in it, now you are to feel it—in marrow and bone, in property and blood. The hand was shown to you first in Berlin; you failed to understand it; now it is shown in Vienna and Prague, in Bucharest, and in Paris. But if you, like Pharaoh, should harden your hearts and believe that only the times are to blame, if you should seek to unload your anger onto the naïve democracies, which allegedly are to blame for everything by virtue of their weakness and constant resignation, then the mighty hand will be shown to you, and the turn of New York and London may also come. Do you not believe it? You could not believe it earlier, either, in Berlin and Vienna, Prague and Budapest, Pressburg [Bratislava] and Paris.

For the nations are only a tool of God, and what is ordained by him will come to pass.

The antisemitic upsurges know no bounds, they break through all barriers and have their secret agents everywhere. Forty-eight prophets appealed to our conscience, telling us the truths from on high, but our heart had grown hard and we did not listen to them. So God used the "mighty hand"; from time to time he appoints someone who communicates to us, in his own way, the true will of God: "*Mene Mene Tekel Upharsin.*"

It is our most bitter fate that, whenever the voice of our own prophets, speaking to us in a melancholy and compassionate way, does not reach our ears, God sends us "prophets" of a sort whose words come to us with fire and sword, with vehemence and derision, and whose voice absolutely gets a hearing. If a Jeremiah or an Isaiah were to come today and proclaim the word of God to us, we would laugh at them, just as our forefathers laughed at them, indeed we would even punish them with death. Therefore the prophets come with iron-clad fist and sharpened sword, which appeal to our conscience in their own way: Return to your own kind, remain among your own kind; the baptismal certificate will no longer do you any good, if you have a Jewish grandmother, that is sufficient for you to be cast out of our ranks. The line must not be crossed . . .

Botschko rails against assimilation and calls upon the Jewish community to remain cohesive—and observant of the prescriptions of the Torah—throughout the present trials. For those of the Orthodox faith and teachings rooted in the yeshivot of eastern Europe, Jews had to adhere to Jewish law, come what may. The following report by **Meir Birman** describes some of the issues surrounding the planned departure by sea of forty-one members of the famous Mir, Telz, Kleck, Lubavitch, Lublin, Kovno, and other yeshivot who had come to Shanghai from eastern Europe and in late September 1941 were bound to leave for Canada via San Francisco. In writing to the **AJJDC** in New York, Birman expresses frustration with many of the yeshiva members' "rigid" adherence to Jewish law, even in the face of these already complex arrangements. For Birman, the men and women of the yeshivot were clinging to impractical and obsolete rules and regulations at the expense of practicalities and hard-fought opportunities. For the members of the yeshivot themselves, there was no other way to live.

DOCUMENT 10-12: Letter from Meir Birman, HICEM-Shanghai, to AJJDC-New York, September 30, 1941, USHMMA RG 68.066M (AJJDC Jerusalem Archives), reel 10, frames 675–77.

[. . .] We may inform you that many complications and difficulties have arisen here with the group of yeshivamen. As we in its time informed you by cable, the steamer had first to leave on the 25th inst. [September 25, 1941] And already then doubts arose among the group in view of the fact that Yom Kippur coincided with the trip.[44] Later it was announced that the steamer would sail on Oct. 2nd, which, however, did not turn out to be true, but at the moment it regulated the matter. A number of meetings took place among the yeshivamen and finally they came to a decision as to the 41 who were to leave—not without heated debates, however,—referring it even to arbitration of rabbis.

The actual date of the departure of the S.S. *President Pierce* was made known only 3 days ago, i.e. that it was to leave on the eve of Yom Kippur. And it was then that the existence of two groups among the yeshivamen became more apparent than ever. Those of the Mirer yeshivah came to a unanimous decision not to go in view of the "Yom Kippur" and nothing could persuade them to change their minds. They are a united body with a firm ground,—in view of the care taken of them by the American orthodox organization, thanks

---

44. Yom Kippur took place on October 1, 1941. The spelling variations occur in the original.

to which visas for Canada have been issued them and also transit visas from Washington, a thing almost unheard for [*sic*] up to now. They do not depend upon any of the local committees, receiving support and the required means directly from the States, and this explains their firm and independent attitude.

The other group are [*sic*] made up of members of other yeshivahs,— such as Telsh [Telz in Yiddish; today Telšiai, Lithuania], Kleck [today Kletsk, Belarus], Lubawicz [Lubavitch], Lublin, Slobodka,[45] etc. They are not a united body, do not receive direct support from American organisations, and exist on the support received from the Speelman committee (the usual budget to refugees) and occasional petty relief from the Committee for the Assist. of Jew. Immigrants from East Europe ("Eastjewcom").[46] They are no less religious than those from Mierer [*sic*] yeshivah, but no special interest is taken in them (in comparison with the latter group). Their existence is by far not assured and they have eagerly seized the opportunity of leaving our city, deciding at the same time to keep two days Yom Kippur on the steamer.

According to Middle Aged [*sic*] talmud authorities and commentators, in the waters lying between Australia, Japan and Shanghai (Hongkong, Philippines, etc.) doubts exist as to the exact day of Sabbath, Yom Kippur and Jewish holidays in general, and that is why the yeshivahmen leaving

---

45. On the histories of some of these yeshivot, see Efraim Zuroff, *The Response of Orthodox Jewry in the United States to the Holocaust: The Activities of the Vaad ha-Hatzala Rescue Committee, 1939–1945* (Hoboken, NJ: Ktav, 2000), 21, 45–47; 93; 159, 212. For a discussion of some of the men connected with these Talmudic academies, see David Kranzler, *Thy Brother's Blood: The Orthodox Jewish Response during the Holocaust* (Brooklyn: Mesorah Publications, 1987); Byron L. Sherwin, *Sparks Amidst the Ashes: The Spiritual Legacy of Polish Jewry* (New York: Oxford University Press, 1997), 33.

46. The Committee for the Assistance of European Jewish Refugees in Shanghai (CFA) became popularly known as the Speelman Committee; Dutch-born Michael Speelman (1877–1952), a prominent local resident, devoted much time to raising funds for refugees in the city. This committee initially served as a conduit for bringing AJJDC relief money to the Shanghai refugee community, while "Eastjewcom," established slightly later—in March 1941—focused on securing financial allocations, particularly for refugees from Poland and eastern Europe. See Irene Eber, ed., *Voices from Shanghai: Jewish Exiles in Wartime China* (Chicago: University of Chicago Press, 2008), 17; obituary, *New York Times*, August 16, 1952. On the complex (often competitive) landscape of refugee relief organizations in Shanghai, see Marcia R. Ristaino, *Port of Last Resort: Diaspora Communities of Shanghai* (Stanford, CA: Stanford University Press, 2001), 103–5, 147; and Yehuda Bauer, *American Jewry and the Holocaust: The American Jewish Joint Distribution Committee, 1939–1945* (Detroit, MI: Wayne State University Press, 1981), 306ff.

by *Pres. Pierce* has [*sic*] decided to fast two days. This question never arose before, but with the arrival of the rabbis and yeshivamen in Japan they started a whole correspondence with Jerusalem, with the result that they declared that in Japan it was necessary to observe [a] two days Sabbath (Saturday and Sunday). This does not extend to Shanghai, but as said above to Hongkong, Philippines, etc.

The Mirer [i.e., Mir] yeshivamen refused sailing for religious reasons, as stated by them, which, however, in our opinion, does not seem to be quite so. It rather seems to be a kind of defiance, as they are very sure of every support in your country, that everything will be done for them nevertheless. Naturally, their decision was resented both by the American Consulate here who had received definite instructions for a group of 41 and not 29 and also by the steamship agency. It was an exceptional case that it was possible to arrange on a President liner such a cheap passage (at US$ 158 each), now when all berths are booked long ahead, and they were naturally not all pleased that 12 berths have been left unused.

The Mirer yeshivamen, however, delegated two of their men,—Mr. Portnoj, Lejzer and Mr. Borensztejn, Icek-Nojach,[47]—for explaining their reasons on the spot. On the eve of the departure of "Pres. Pierce" 7 more yeshivamen arrived from Kobe. Of these 5 were from Mirer yeshivah and they joined the local group and remained here. 2 were from the Lublin yeshivah and we also succeeded in sending them.

You will see from the enclosed list [not printed here] that among those who left were the widow and son of the well known rabbi Chofetz-Chaim (Pupko Kaplan) from Radin,[48] a number of rabbis as well as stu-

---

47. Rabbi Eliezer (or Leszer) Portnoy (1908–1975) and Rabbi Icek Noach Borenstein (1909–1983) both settled in New York after the war.

48. Frejda Pupko-Kagan (not Kaplan) and her son, Aron Pupko-Kagan, a rabbi. The widow's husband, the influential Lithuanian rabbi Yisrael Meir ha-Kohen (Kagan) Pupko (1838–1933), was a revered writer on ethics, founded a yeshiva in Radu'n (Radin), and was popularly known as Chafetz Chaim, the name of his first book on laws (1873). The passenger manifest for the ship, which stopped in San Francisco along the way, shows that it departed from China on September 30 and was carrying a group of twenty-seven rabbis and rabbinical students from Poland, along with the Pupko-Kagans; their last permanent residence had been Kobe, Japan. Most of the students were not from the Mir yeshiva. With travel arrangements growing ever more difficult, over fifty rabbis and yeshiva students holding Canadian visas were forced to remain in China for the rest of the war. See NARA, List or Manifest of Alien Passengers (for the SS *President Pierce*, sailing from Shanghai on September 30, 1941); Mordechai Hacohen and David Derovan, "Israel Meir ha-Kohen," in *Encyclopaedia Judaica*, ed. Fred Skolnick and Michael Berenbaum, 2nd ed. (Detroit, MI: Macmillan Reference USA, 2007), 10:756–57; Zuroff, *The Response of Orthodox Jewry*, 185–86.

dents. All of them decided, as said above, to fast two days, and it cannot be said that they are less religious than the Mirer group.

There were complications with obtaining a berth for the widow of Chofetz Chaim. Women cannot go 3rd class by this liner, and the bookings were made too late to obtain any first class passage. Ultimately with extreme difficulties and [an] additional berth was made for her.

There were also difficulties with medical certificates. The doctor had specially to open his office on Sunday to examine the group. There were also difficulties with taking the luggage of the group to the steamer, as they did not live in one place. All the expenses were borne by us and we shall duly include them in our report to you.

The question arose also with kosher food for the group. For former groups this has been successfully arranged by us with such private agencies as Jardine, Matheson & Co. and the Java China Line. We have not been able, however, to make the arrangement with the Pres. Line, whose food is one of the best and where everything is strictly hygienic. They promised, however, to give them eggs, vegetables, etc.,—food which they could eat.

For board money and for the necessary expenses before leaving the group, were [sic] given by the "Eastjewcom" each Sh$ [Shanghai $] 25,00, altogether Sh$ 725,00. We had to appeal to them to do so, however.

With regard to the 12 unused transit visas, in view of the present lack of transportation facilities, we cannot say anything definite at present. We shall not be surprised, however, if the steamship agency,—it is to be borne in mind that they are the only one to connect us with your country now when there are no Japanese steamers,—will not be as helpful as before. They dictate their conditions at present.

Before closing the letter we wish to mention, what is brought to our attention almost all the time, that much attention is given to some while others are ignored. There are many who have to wait long before effecting their emigration, at present even when they have visas, in view of the present lack of transportation facilities. Among the group of yeshivamen for Canada, there are persons with certificates for Palestine, and a few also with permits for South America. It is really little short of wonderful that you have been able to obtain for the group transit American visas in such a short time.

We shall duly send you our report and shall keep you informed of developments here with regard to other groups for Canada.

Yours sincerely,
M. Birman
Manager

The following account leads us from the interpretations and convictions of those who adhered to a strictly observant lifestyle to the views of a person on the fringe of the Jewish spectrum. German-born Otto Samuel embraced central tenets of Christianity without renouncing his Jewish roots. Having converted in 1919 at age thirty-two and become an ordained Protestant minister in 1926, Samuel was categorized by the Nazis' racial laws as a Jew and had been incarcerated in the Sachsenhausen concentration camp in the wake of "*Kristallnacht.*" In April 1939 he escaped to Belgium and, following the country's occupation, to France, where in early June 1940 he was arrested and deported to internment camps **Saint-Cyprien** (until late October 1940) and **Gurs** (until early March 1941), followed by Camp des Milles near Marseilles (until early May 1941). Samuel acted as chaplain for Christian inmates in these camps—among the twelve thousand prisoners at Gurs, he estimated there were about five hundred Protestants—and gave Bible classes that appear to have also been attended by Jews. After his escape to the United States in June 1941, he became a devout spokesman for the Hebrew Christian Alliance, and it was in this organization's newsletter that he published his recollections of his time in these camps shortly before the European war ended.[49]

DOCUMENT 10-13: **Otto Samuel, "My Experiences in Nazi Germany," on his work as chaplain in French internment camps until May 1941, *The American Hebrew Christian* 18, no. 1 (April 1945): 17.**

[. . .] Sanitary conditions were very bad, and there was a painful lack of medicine and bandages. Dysentery and typhoid fever claimed many victims, and in our barracks in St. Cyprien, out of 64 persons, 8 died of disease. The drinking water was polluted.

Often we stood by an open grave, where I would preach a funeral sermon. The caskets were rude wooden boxes. I would quote those well-known verses: "So also is the resurrection of the dead. It is sown in

---

49. Otto Samuel (1887–1960) worked as pastor in the Free Christian movement in Germany. In December 1936, he moved to Hamburg with his wife Erna and became active in organized efforts to convert Jews to Christianity. After his release from Les Milles in early May 1941, Samuel immigrated to the United States, where he was joined by his wife after the war and worked as a minister in a Lutheran community in Brooklyn. Friedrich Wilhelm Bautz and Traugott Bautz, eds., *Biographisch-Bibliographisches Kirchenlexikon* (Nordhausen: Verlag Traugott Bautz, 2010), xxxi:1172–79: www.bautz.de/bbkl/s/s1/samuel_j_o.shtml. The article featured here was published in sequels in *The American Hebrew Christian*, vols. 17 and 18 (October 1944–July 1945).

corruption; it is raised in incorruption: it is sown in dishonor; it is raised in glory: it is sown in weakness; it is raised in power" (1 Cor. xv, 42, 43), and say farewell to my brothers and sisters in Christ. They could rest until the resurrection day, within sight of the towering peaks of the Pyrenees along the horizon and amid the flowering meadows encircling the graves.

I brought comfort from the Scriptures to many in those days, and my New Testament still shows the marks of the terrible rains in which I had to open and read it.

All these depressing material conditions affected us emotionally. Being the pastor in whom those unhappy people confided, I witnessed moving experiences. My greatest danger was a temptation to doubt God and His wisdom, and this was the source of all the other mental troubles. The worst hour was dawn, lying on our straw mattresses after a torturing, sleepless night. [. . .]

Each document in this chapter explores the ways in which Jewish worldviews converged around the various challenges to its vitality and survival. From staunchly observant rabbinic thought to the outright rejection of a divine presence in history, every writer in some way addressed and grappled with Jewish narratives and languages that have existed for centuries. How these perspectives were adapted in the face of unprecedented catastrophe was answered differently based on the author's political, geographic, and theological orientation. One constant thread, however, remained clear: the ubiquitous presence of Jewish thought as a principle to be integrated, excluded, or radicalized in the face of growing oppression and violence.

CHAPTER 11

LIMITS OF LANGUAGE

FROM THE liturgical poetry (or *piyyutim*) commemorating the fall of the First and Second Temples in 586 BCE and 70 CE, to the work of Moses Maimonides in response to the Jewish expulsion from the Iberian peninsula in the Middle Ages, to Hayyim Nahman Bialik's famous epic poem in the modern period about the pogrom in Kishinev in April 1903, Jewish writers have struggled to describe the calamitous cards that history has dealt them.[1] The Holocaust brought both continuity and a profound break with this tradition. While some forms of persecution meted out by the Nazis felt utterly familiar, systematic deportations and annihilations were frighteningly new. So, too, were the challenges of production in which the very tools of creative expression became difficult if not impossible to obtain. "Under normal conditions," art historian Janet Blatter states, "the artist's struggle begins when

---

1. Moses Maimonides (1135–1204), from Cordoba, was one of the most well-regarded Jewish philosophers of the Middle Ages. He is the author of the *Guide for the Perplexed*, *The Epistle on Martyrdom*, and other liturgical texts and philosophical tractates. Maimonides eventually settled in Cairo, where he was the court physician and leader of the Jewish community. See David Roskies, ed., *The Literature of Destruction: Jewish Responses to Catastrophe* (Philadelphia, PA: Jewish Publication Society, 1988), 628. Hayyim Nahman Bialik (1873–1934) was a major force in the revival of Modern Hebrew and is considered the first Modern Hebrew poet. Originally from Volhynia, he settled in Palestine in 1924. See Alan Mintz, "Kishinev and the Twentieth Century: Introduction," in *Prooftexts* 25 (winter/ spring 2005), 1–7. For an overview, see Roskies, *The Literature of Destruction*.

he is faced with the task of transforming his materials into the image he has formed in his mind. The Holocaust artists' problem started at the very beginning of the artistic process, with the acquisition of the materials with which they worked."[2]

Many Jews overcame these problems and used artistic responses to document, explain, and understand their travails to a much larger, varied, and multifaceted degree than can be conveyed here. Artistic responses allow for a wide range of interpretations, and it is this expressive and evocative quality that sets art apart from other, more purposeful forms of cultural outlets such as letters or diaries. However, while many examples presented here conform to literary styles such as poetry or song, drawing a rigid line between these works and the kinds of writings that we have reproduced elsewhere in the volume would be a mistake on multiple counts. Many of the letters and diary entries written during the Holocaust have literary qualities, and even seemingly dry reports and statistical representations contain subtexts and multiple layers of meaning worth exploring.[3] The sources presented here were not chosen for their outstanding aesthetic qualities, polished style, or intellectual depth. Rather, these pieces offer insights into the minds of Jews struggling to comprehend the unfolding disaster around them by adapting traditional artistic and literary forms to new, indeed unprecedented, conditions.

ART AND COMMUNICATION

As they had done prior to the Holocaust, Jews facing a radical new world grappled with what they saw and what they heard by writing and reading literary texts and through composing and displaying visual art. They did so despite severe restrictions, including bans on using public libraries and prohibitions against staging exhibitions or publishing work. In many larger ghettos, **Jewish councils** provided protection from forced labor by employing artists and intellectuals as chroniclers of the community or in graphics workshops, by putting on cultural programs for public viewing, and by organizing book-lending programs for children and those without means. We know from their

---

2. Janet Blatter, "Art from the Whirlwind," in *Art of the Holocaust*, ed. Janet Blatter and Sybil Milton (New York: Routledge Press, 1981), 24.

3. See Alexandra Garbarini, *Numbered Days: Diaries and the Holocaust* (New Haven, CT: Yale University Press, 2006), 95–128; Raul Hilberg, *Sources of Holocaust Research: An Analysis* (Chicago: Ivan R. Dee, 2001), 72–132.

own writings that Jews read, absorbed, and framed their predicament by turning to literary works even under the most dire circumstances: in the case of **Mirjam Korber**, it was **Stefan Zweig**'s novel *Amok*.[4] In the Vilna ghetto, fourteen-year-old **Yitskhok Rudashevski** took great comfort from a book depicting the revolutionary uprising in Berlin at the end of World War I, when, as Rudashevski put it, "the wrath of the people spilled over into the famished streets."[5] In the Łódź ghetto, an anonymous young man kept his own diary written in four languages in the margins of the French novel *Les vrais riches* (The Truly Rich) by François Coppée.[6] And in her final letter from Piaski shortly before her and her husband's murder in **Bełżec** in April 1942, Martha Bauchwitz wrote that she was practicing to recite a famous Goethe poem marking the arrival of spring.[7]

Poetry also offered a haven for reflection and commentary. Calling for deliberate stylistic choices to convey meaning in a distilled form, poetry presented the opportunity to explore an author's evolving worldview in the context of philosophical, ideological, and religious traditions. It also constituted some of the most prevalent forms of creative writing and is one of the most difficult to translate. Poetry was composed and survived the war in a variety of formats: in private notebooks and diaries, newspapers, ghetto archives, public performances, and even concentration camp notes. Some authors continued the work they had begun before the war, while others picked up a pen for the first time. All of them felt the impact, in one way or another, of the unfolding events of the times.

---

4. See document 6–4.

5. Yitskhok Rudashevski, *The Diary of the Vilna Ghetto* (Jerusalem: Hakibbutz Hameuchad, 1973), 58 (diary entry for September 24, 1942). The book Rudashevski read was Bernhard Kellermann, *Der 9. November*, first published in 1920 and blacklisted by the Nazis in 1933.

6. See Alan Adelson and Robert Lapides, eds., *Łódź Ghetto: Inside a Community under Siege* (New York: Penguin, 1989), 5, 419–39. Coppée's book was first published in France in 1893. The young Łódź Jew kept his diary from May to August 1944; see also Hanno Loewy and Andrzej Bodek, eds., *"Les vrais riches." Notizen am Rand. Ein Tagebuch aus dem Ghetto Łódź* (Leipzig: Reclam, 1997).

7. Letter by Martha Bauchwitz, Piaski (Lublin district of the **Generalgouvernement**), to Luise Lotte Hoyer-Bauchwitz (Stettin, Germany), April 4, 1942; in *Lebenszeichen aus Piaski. Briefe Deportierter aus dem Distrikt Lublin 1940–1943*, ed. Else Behrendt-Rosenfeld and Gertrud Luckner (Munich: Biederstein Verlag, 1968), 78.

Amateur poets such as the author of the following text could be restricted in their artistic sensibility or stylistic sophistication. In many instances their words also remain cryptic, depicting situations fully accessible only to those from within their own communities. The poem in document 11-1 appears in a notebook of Naomi Elath,[8] a Jewish girl from Germany sent by the **OSE** child relief organization first to Château de la Guette, located about twenty-five miles east of Paris, and later to La Bourboule in the Unoccupied Zone of France. The notebook itself belonged to Henri Pohorylès, one of Elath's teachers at La Guette and La Bourboule, who encouraged his students to embrace a distinctly Zionist outlook and became involved in militant resistance.[9] The poem dates to the last day of Hanukkah of 1940–1941 and enjoins the reader to "be prepared" for the ongoing "struggle." While not explicitly articulated, given the ideological perspective of the author and the content in the remainder of the notebook, both "the struggle" and the desired "song of victory" undoubtedly refer to the Zionist project, yet may have embedded additional associations arising from the author's specific experiences and expectations.

---

8. Naomi Elath was born Gisela Edel in Stettin, Germany, in 1928. Evacuated with other German Jewish children to France, she spent the next years in a series of children's homes run by the child rescue initiative, Œuvre de secours aux enfants (OSE), and hiding in a convent. In the summer of 1944 at age fourteen, she escaped across the Pyrenees, eventually joining a Youth Aliyah transport for Palestine. Her parents did not survive the war. See donor file, USHMMA Acc. 2004.435.1, Naomi Elath collection.

9. The OSE-run children's home, La Guette, sheltered 130 Viennese and German Jewish children from April 1939 until May 1940, one month before the Armistice was signed between France and Germany. The children and their teachers were then relocated to another home, La Bourboule, about three hundred miles south of Paris in the Unoccupied Zone. Henri Pohorylès (1900?–1996), son of Russian immigrants, was born in the Alsace region of France and served as a German teacher in Jewish schools throughout France. During the war he was active in the Armée juive, a Zionist resistance group formed in early 1942 in Toulouse. Pohorylès was arrested in July 1944 together with fifty other notable French Jews and resistance fighters, but escaped with twenty-seven of the others. He survived the war and immigrated to Israel, where he died. See Susan Zuccotti, *The Holocaust, the French, and the Jews* (Lincoln: University of Nebraska Press, 1993), 202; Centre de documentation juive contemporaine, *Les enfants de La Guette: Souvenirs et documents (1938–1945)* (Paris: CDJC, 1999), 15–21; Alexandra Garbarini, with Emil Kerenji, Jan Lambertz, and Avinoam Patt, *Jewish Responses to Persecution*, vol. 2: *1938–1940* (Lanham, MD: AltaMira in association with the USHMM, 2011), 49.

DOCUMENT 11-1: **Poem "And Again" recorded by Henri Pohorylés, Hanukkah 1940 (December 25, 1940–January 1, 1941), Château de la Guette, Vichy France, USHMMA Acc. 2004.435 Naomi Elath collection (translated from German).**

And Again
And again a year has elapsed
A drop falls into the sea of eternity
And again there is judging and weighing
And again the little light cautions, "Be prepared!"
We are prepared to take on the struggle!
For we go forward with proud hearts
And our banners will wave joyously
Once the song of victory can be sung.

While this poem from inside the relative shelter of a children's home invokes a hopeful future, poetry and other artistic expressions produced in ghettos and camps more readily reflected the everyday reality of scarcity and loss. As the poems featured in previous chapters underline, hunger and hopelessness were major motifs of wartime writing.[10] So too was the Jewish star, now an omnipresent symbol of separation, humiliation, and otherness. This emblem (which came in a variety of forms, from armbands to the most well-known yellow badge) provided and continues to provide a particularly powerful prompt for artistic reflection. Its use—as in the following drawing produced by Czech physician and artist **Karel Fleischmann** in **Theresienstadt**—instantly connects this otherwise quotidian hospital scene with the Holocaust period. Fleischmann's role as a doctor in this "model ghetto" provided him a unique perception on the details of daily life, as his charcoal drawing of the infirmary reveals.

---

10. See documents 2-1 and 10-4.

DOCUMENT 11-2: **Charcoal drawing, *Infirmary for Children*, by Karel Fleischmann, Theresienstadt, Protectorate, 1942, USHMMPA WS# 28808, courtesy of the Jewish Museum Prague.**

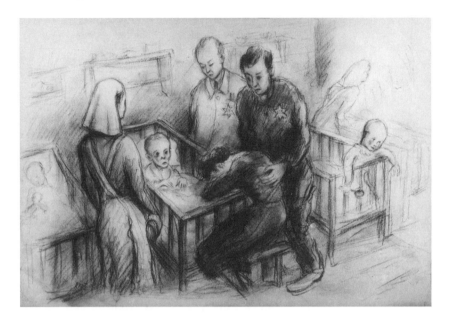

The range of literary reactions to the Jewish star, a highly visible form of stigmatization, spanned a broad spectrum: from political, religious, or historical reflections on the symbol's meanings to somewhat satirical and sarcastic references to it. In the Reich, the Star of David became known after its introduction in mid-September 1941 as "*pour le semite*," alluding to a prestigious medal (*pour le mérite*) awarded in Prussia since the times of Frederic the Great. In some places its wearers were referred to as—drawing on astronomy—"shooting stars" (*Sternschnuppen*).[11] In Prague, the capital of the **Protectorate**, where Jews were ordered to wear the new markers at the same time as in Germany, young Petr Ginz recorded in his diary that he counted sixty-nine "sheriffs" on his way to school and that, according to a joke, the major street leading into the city's Jewish quarter had been renamed "The Milky Way."[12] The following poem cir-

---

11. Albert Meirer, "Berlin Jews: Deprived of Rights, Impoverished, and Branded," in *Jews in Nazi Berlin: From Kristallnacht to Liberation*, ed. Beate Meyer, Hermann Simon, and Chana Schütz (Chicago: Chicago University Press, 2009), 94–99.

12. Chava Pressburger, ed., *The Diary of Petr Ginz 1941–1942* (New York: Atlantic Monthly Press, 2007), 28 (diary entry for September 19, 1941). For examples of jokes produced or used by Jews during the Holocaust, see Sidra DeKoven Ezrahi, "After Such Knowledge, What Laughter?" *Yale Journal of Criticism* 14 (2002): 287–313.

culated among Prague Jews in late 1941, many of whom would indeed, as the last stanza indicates, find themselves forcibly taken to Theresienstadt (Terezin).

DOCUMENT 11-3: Poem by an unidentified Czech Jew, undated (late 1941/early 1942), copy provided by Růža Broessler via Lisa Peschel (translation from Czech).

Today, it's clear to all, not few,
Who's an Aryan and who's a Jew.
The Jew is recognizable from afar
With a clearly visible yellow-black star.

To avoid any punishment necessarily
Be home by eight with your family.
As a manual laborer, work your gig;
No radio for you, not even Melnik.[13]

Teach the children at home, not in school,
Shopping from 3 to 5 is the rule.
Don't own jewels, garlic, wine
Houses, flats or gramophones,
Furs or skis or telephones.

For you no pork, onions or cheese,
No machines or pianos, if you please.
No bikes or barometers,
No socks or wooly sweaters,

No poultry or shaving soap,
No marmalade and nothing to smoke,
No driver's licenses or alcohol,
No magazines, no newspapers at all.

Bonbons and typewriters, too,
Two pairs of underwear—all forbidden for you.
No shops or mines or fields,
No factories, farms or stocks with yields.

---

13. Founded in 1938 as the German-language station of Czechoslovakia's Radiojournal broadcasting network, also known as Praha II-Mělník, this station was renamed "Reichssender Böhmen" in June 1939 and used by German Protectorate officials for propaganda purposes.

Add sardines, fruit and fish to the list.
Could there be something that we have missed?

The list continues, that is true;
Perhaps, just buy nothing at all for you.
Get used to walking, take no train,
Whether in the sun or in the rain.

The express, the tram and taxi, too,
None of these is there for you.

And regardless of the tasty treat,
There's no restaurant where you can eat.
No quays or parks or swimming pools,
Churches, Post Offices or public loos,
Station platforms, games or fairgrounds,
Stadiums, Meinl shops[14]—all out of bounds.

And with your money, you must be clever,
As your bank account's frozen now and forever.
And rid yourself of the ugly temptations,
Of maintaining with Aryans any relations.

Some further advice on which to sleep:
At home no servant may you keep.
But what you may have, you want to know?
Three suitcases or backpacks with which to go.

[verse added by hand, 1942;]
Today, for the last time, my girl,
We'll drink a glass of wine
Tomorrow the transport goes
to Terezin.
The *Hilfsdienst*[15] packs the bags
We lock the cabinets
Till we meet again, my girl,
In Terezin.

---

14. Julius Meinl was a chain of grocery and delicatessen shops that existed in the Austro-Hungarian monarchy and thereafter.
15. Literally "help service."

As the war continued, the tenor of these creative responses changed dramatically. Humor often stopped abruptly once the doors of the deportation trains were locked shut. While the previous document treats the 1942 deportations from Theresienstadt to **Auschwitz** sardonically, the following poem, "AKB," strikes a far more sinister tone. Written by the aforementioned Karel Fleischmann, it describes the fate of his own transport to Theresienstadt (referred to as AKB) in April 1942 with disturbingly vivid imagery.

DOCUMENT 11-4: "AKB," by Karel Fleischmann, Theresienstadt, Protectorate, April 18, 1942, USHMMA RG 35.001.02 Jiri Lauscher collection (translated from Czech).

Nine hundred and nine human beetles
botanical pouch, sudden blindness
gag of faintness sweat, silent horror
broken legs, no wings left
hair torn out, crumbled mold
abandoned flats, broken clams
accounts closed
tissues severed:
completed and signed.

Nine hundred and nine human brains
morning with a sky like the gallows
long train and yet so short
coltsfoot[16] scattered yellow stars on a mound
scarf wailing somewhere with a secret greeting
line of blue hills draws with us
black tower waves from a distance
oaks' broken arms:
numbered and signed.

Nine hundred and nine human hearts
long day and long ride in mews
ramp—new, our, foreign people
poultry market, where no one is buying
where backgammon is played over life
black, white phrases
condemned or circled with a big O:
Read and signed,

---

16. A yellow wildflower native to the region.

Nine hundred and nine human beetles
the dealer split the number briskly
half and half and another half half
a handful remaining at the bottom of a small pouch
quarters in half and quarters half again
carried to the morgue, away to Poland
rest to the hospital. Where is AKB?
After four centuries
a scattered congregation
signed, executed.

Further east, mass shootings turned some Jewish literary responses from aesthetic artifacts into outraged calls for action. Until the end of 1941, six months after the beginning of the German invasion of the Soviet Union, between five hundred thousand to eight hundred thousand Jews had been rounded up and shot by SS, German police, and army units in what we now know was the first wave of genocide. Jewish poetry published in the USSR reflected this grim reality, but the tenor and breadth of this writing was often inflected with a different set of orientations in Stalin's empire. Many Jewish writers who grew up under Soviet rule straddled an identity that was profoundly Soviet while at the same time distinctly Yiddish. During the 1920s, a full-scale effort to "Sovietize" the country targeted the Jewish population. Yiddish was considered a powerful tool for accomplishing this goal; those committed to the principles of Zionism, the Hebrew language, and Jewish religious practices were heavily persecuted. By 1930, however, even ardent Yiddish secularists came under attack. At the end of the decade, Yiddish schools throughout the Soviet Union were closed, and most of the organizations cultivating this language switched over to Russian or disappeared entirely.[17]

Literary works produced in the Soviet Union during World War II often eschewed direct references to Jewish identity and the mass killings of Jews on the Russian front. The following two poems by Leyb Kvitko serve as examples

17. Anna Shternshis, *Soviet and Kosher: Jewish Popular Culture in the Soviet Union, 1923–1939* (Bloomington: Indiana University Press, 2006), xv.

for the rule as well as its exception.[18] With the German "war of annihilation" advancing far into the Soviet Union, the **Jewish Anti-Fascist Committee (JAFC)** and its journal *Eynikeyt*, for which Kvitko worked as the editor, saw its purpose as harnessing and articulating Jewish commitment to the defense of the Motherland. At the same time, *Eynikeyt* also contained some of the most graphic and explicit reporting on German atrocities against Jews in the East. Kvitko followed in this vein and used specifically Jewish references in his published poetry, including "Etele," which appeared in the June 28, 1942, edition of *Eynikeyt*. Kvitko's poem drips with anger at the death and humiliation of an eight-year-old girl, Etl (Etele, in the diminutive form in the Yiddish). Kvitko mines his imagery from religious anti-Judaism and biblical sources intermixed with Nazi terminology. Ultimately, Kvitko paints Etl as the iconic Jewish woman, and her fate as representative for countless others.

DOCUMENT 11-5: **"Etele," by Leyb Kvitko, *Eynikeyt*, Moscow, June 28, 1942, 3 (translated from Yiddish).**

I swear to preserve her memory until that day,
When judges pass judgment on evil's last remnants,
I swear to cast a word with full weight
On behalf of this child, tormented, taunted.
With a clear head, for her, the shoemaker's Etele,
Who in her eighth year came to know her hard fate:
Renounced dolls, anxiously stifled her voice,
On her shoulders took up her ancient nation's burden.
"Etl" is her name no more, not Etl with the charming freckles, the dark
    ones,
She is the one who crucified Christ, *Jude* is her name, *Juden*-Dog.
For many centuries she's been draining Aryans' blood for matzo,

---

18. Leyb (Leib) Kvitko (1890–1952) was born in Olesko, Ukraine, and rose to prominence as a Yiddish-language writer, especially producing works for children. His work highlighted the Jewish folk tradition rather than an explicitly religious one. Kvitko was an active member of the Jewish section of the proletariat writers' union in the Ukraine and head of the editorial office of *Royte Velt* (*Red World*), a post he later lost due to criticism of the Yiddish press in the Soviet Union. A volume of his complete works was published in Yiddish in 1933. He survived the war only to be killed in Stalin's purge of Yiddish writers on August 12, 1952. See Glenn S. Levine, "Yiddish Publishing in Berlin and the Crisis in Eastern European Jewish Culture 1919–1924," *LBIYB* 42 (1997): 85–108.

And she's active in the international bankers' league.
That's why she's hiding now in forests, in pits,
To avoid being preyed upon and hunted by human beasts.
At night with other children in fever terror she drifts,
And comes to the border, but the brown plague won't let her cross over
     to us.
Her curly head, her neck that stems from the Song of Songs,
Afflicted by mange. And only her dreams—
They seek in the Flood, like the dove from the Ark,
And from her narrow eye peeks indifference: *hakol haevel* [All is vanity.]
No, this I cannot, this won't let itself be forgotten,
Neither tears nor curses can measure out the shame.
Come to my arms, let me press your dear face to my heart,
Little Etl, Etl, what they have done to you and your country!
How they've made the world loathsome in your eyes,
How they covered its face, like your mother's, with sores.
Can I discern how, with which gaze you look upon it—
Allow me, Etl, with weapons to call the world to account to you!

Another collection of texts consisting of several related poems written by Kvitko prior to 1946 makes reference to historical antisemitism, but it appears only in draft form in the JAFC records. While the provenance and precise dating of these poems are not completely clear, it is most likely a manuscript draft for material that would later appear in the volume, *Gezang fun mayn Gemit* (Songs of my Spirit) published in Moscow in 1947. This volume includes poetry that Kvitko penned during the war and, most importantly, expresses his solidarity with the murdered Jews of Europe. The speaker of this unpublished poem bemoans the arrival of the German army and the first atrocities, which harkens back to earlier experiences of anti-Jewish violence. The fact that Kvitko had published a book in the early 1920s describing the Petlyura pogroms in Ukraine,[19] which he had personally witnessed,[20] receives mention in the third stanza printed here, but the stanza that follows explicitly

---

19. Leib Kvitko, *1919* (Berlin: Yiddisher Literarisher Varlag, 1923). A reprint is available digitally through the National Yiddish Book Center, Amherst, MA (Steven Spielberg Digital Yiddish Library no. 10784).

20. See Mikhail Krutikov, *From Kabbalah to Class Struggle: Expressionism, Marxism, and Yiddish Literature in the Life and Work of Meir Wiener* (Stanford, CA: Stanford University Press, 2011), 110–14.

refers to the Khmelnitsky mass murders of 1648 to 1649, in which one hundred thousand to two hundred thousand Jews were killed, is crossed out in the manuscript. Kvitko goes on to accuse the world of standing by as history repeats itself. While Kvitko at one point expresses hope for salvation from the Red Army, it is not realized within the confines of his piece. Thus, a poem that condemns religiously based antisemitism ("Etele") is published, while one that addresses historical antisemitism and its manifestation on Soviet territory is not.

DOCUMENT 11-6: **Poem sequence "Living Witness" by Leyb Kvitko, no date (prior to 1946), USHMMA Acc. 1998.A.003 (JAFC Records), 8114-1-406 (translated from Yiddish).**

[. . .]
I was young till just a while ago,—
With the arrival of the German I became old,
And with me the nation [*folk*] and with me the world—
Stuffed full of years.

Upon us was cast the die
Of woe and wound, of mute pain,—
We have a road to walk, to walk, to walk—
And have no place to arrive.

In 1919 I complained to the world
As one of her own children.
And today as one of her abandoned dogs—
What should I do now?

[next stanza crossed out]
Oh, Uman of the 1648 evil decrees
Of 1919 and of now—
I see you have plenty of murderers—
But you do not have a single defender.

Forgive me, forests of slaughter,
Cities of ash, springs in moss—
That I do not bewail your disaster.

I, who in the least corn-flower,
In the blue coat would see heaven,
The Divine Name and defenders,—
What do I see now?

Behold there emerge from under the stumps
Of the crooked slaughter forest—
[line possibly deleted:]
Children, Jewish children.

A heavy heart speaks much
Every word is a stone!
I want to tell you everything clearly
But the sob whips me into weeping.

The five-year-old Yanik
Of the Olshvanger family—
How did he withstand
The struggle all by himself?

When his head was burning
In the hiding place where he lay,
Three days and nights the heat like a red-hot
Iron bar plagued him, burned him.

And not a drop of water in the jug—
So he placed his hands—
On his mouth and did not scream.
In his heart he even consoled his mother,
Cuddled up in woe and silence:
"She will come, she will come
The Red Army will come. . . ."

And when the German chased
To catch Yanik—
To break his head against the wall
Like that of the other children,

Yanik in the middle of the street
Suddenly stretched out
And a fearful illness
Stared out of his eyes

A foam gushed out of his mouth,
His hands beat against the ground—
And the German, impelled by the horror
Ran away from the child.

Our Nation's Garment-Tearing [in Mourning]

Old shriveled faces
The eyes—open holes.
Six- seven-year-old martyrs
From the grave-pits—dead escapees.

Two years without cease
With the lair-souls in the forest,
With the worms and mice
One shares:
The fear of the hunter,
The grass and rotten food,
The lair and bog as sleeping place.

Without mom and dad or relatives
They bore the pain of persecution,
Today they stand before you, world
And wait to hear what you'll tell them. . . .

And Yulke!
She was still so little
When, with everyone together,
She was driven to the spacious pit,
That she told her mother:
"Well, let us lie down comfortably
In a pure, clear place."
But in the trap of violent death
The child suddenly turned adult!

She pushed, she jostled forward,
Through holes, through every distress—
Toward air and light, outwards—
And she was helped by the dead.

The cluster of tortured people
Quivering in death agonies and blood
The cluster shoved the child
To you, world, to breathe with you!

So do not dazzle the child's eyes
And do not lull it to sleep with toys.
Enough racking on the Procrustean bed,
Enough pain it has measured out!

Poetry also encompasses the song lyric, which serves as both a literary arti-fact and an artifact of popular culture. Songs and singing, David Roskies asserts, had the power to mediate "between poetic convention and the terrible reality of the war" in a number of ways,[21] with the exception of those used by the Nazis in concentration camps and other scenarios as a means of subjugation and ter-ror. In ghettos, new lyrics were often composed to a preexisting folk tune that allowed the listener—as Gila Flam points out—to "bring back memories of better days into the absurdity of everyday life."[22] While some melodies were mournful ballads, others offered upbeat, catchy tunes that sharply juxtaposed music and narrative. Songs were created in a variety of contexts, from compos-ers in large ghettos to unknown individual compositions recorded in private diaries and letters.[23] These songs were circulated and preserved through many different means, which often led to the existence of several different postwar versions. The following song, "On a Begging Walk," originates from the Shavli ghetto in Lithuania in 1942 and reflects many common lyrical and musical

---

21. Roskies, *The Literature of Destruction*, 465.

22. Gila Flam, "The Role of Singing in the Ghettos: Between Entertainment and Witnessing," in *Holocaust Chronicles: Individualizing the Holocaust through Diaries and Other Contemporaneous Personal Accounts*, ed. Robert Moses Shapiro (Jerusalem: Ktav, 1999), 152. See also Gila Flam, *Singing for Survival: Songs of the Lodz Ghetto, 1940–1945* (Urbana: University of Illinois Press, 1992); Shirli Gilbert, *Music in the Holocaust: Confronting Life in the Nazi Ghettos and Camps* (New York: Oxford University Press, 2005).

23. See, e.g., Garbarini et al., *Jewish Responses*, 2:419–21; Irene Hauser diary USHMMA RG 02.208M (ŻIH 302/299).

attributes of ghetto compositions. The translation that follows is based upon the original handwritten manuscript contained within a larger notebook of songs preserved in the archives of the Kovno ghetto.[24] The lyrics of "On a Begging Walk" provide a profound contrast with the song from which it borrows its melody, namely the popular "To the Fair" by Shmuel Kahn and Elye Teitelbaum, composed before the war. This bright melody tells the story of a man who goes to the fair to buy a horse, but instead spends his money at the local inn. Khane Khaytin's lyrics, by contrast, speak of the struggle for food and end on a note of desperation.

DOCUMENT 11-7: **Song "On a Begging Walk" by Khane Khaytin, Shavli, German-occupied Lithuania, no date (1942), USHMMA RG 26.014M (LCSAV R-1390) reel 63, file 54 (translated from Yiddish).[25]**

I stride with quick, with speedy steps,
A full beggar's bag along with me I drag,
And my legs are bending out of fatigue
And the water is seeping through my shoes.

I've already been on my begging trip today.
And a "shiny button"[26] I haven't yet seen.
And I received quite a good amount.
Oh, where does one get strength when one is weak?

Never thought I'd get a full potato sack
And a paper bag of barley also has worth.
Half a side of meat, large and thick.
A quarter loaf of bread—a treasure.

---

24. It is unclear if this song—a popular lyric written to a popular melody—was recorded in the notebook by the author herself or by someone else. Khane Khaytin (1918–2004) was a Lithuanian-Jewish songwriter who wrote many popular songs in the Shavli ghetto until her deportation to the Stutthof concentration camp in the summer of 1944. Khaytin was liberated in 1945 and immigrated to Palestine and later New York. See Shmerke Kaczerginski, ed., *Lider fun di Getos un Lagern* (New York: Alveltlekher Yidisher Kultur Kongres, 1948); Eleanore Gordon Mlotek and Malke Gottlieb, eds., *We Are Here: Songs of the Holocaust* (New York: Educational Department of the Workmen's Circle, 1983).

25. Khane Khaytin added a note: "The poem bears this name because we used to go begging for a piece of bread among the people who were living freely."

26. Indicates the "shiny button" (badge) of a policeman.

I walk with my beggar's bag and think:
Who stands at the gate today, God knows who?
I approach the gate . . . Oh, how awful!
It costs half a bottle [to bribe the guard] and soon becomes all right.

I come into the house—it's cold and wet.
The children's appearance is yellow and pale.
As soon as the bag is brought, joy arises
All begin to grab pieces of bread.

We light a fire in the stove—let it be warm!
The barley and the meat into the pot.
The fire burns, crackles—oh, how good!
One forgets one's afflictions in this minute.

Beggars we have become today. . . .
Because we are Jews, we are hated,
For ever we shall sing the same song:
Oh how awful and bitter to be a Jew. . . .

While poetry and song could serve a public function in Jewish archival projects, publications, and communities, they also played an important private role as part of an aesthetic, sometimes coded exchange between close friends and lovers. This clandestine function was particularly important for those not only in danger of being persecuted as Jews but also as gays. After having joined Jitzhak Schwersenz's secret Zionist youth group that was discussed earlier,[27] the young Gerhard (Gad) Beck struck up a friendship with Manfred Lewin that grew in intensity until Lewin's deportation in the fall of 1942. In a small notebook Lewin prepared for his friend and lover while they were still together, he depicted in rough verse and handdrawn sketches some of the experiences they had shared in the group.

---

27. See document 8–6.

DOCUMENT 11-8: Excerpts and drawing from notebook by Manfred Lewin dedicated to Gerhard Beck, Berlin, May 21, 1942, USHMMA Acc. 2000.416 Gad Beck collection (translated from German).[28]

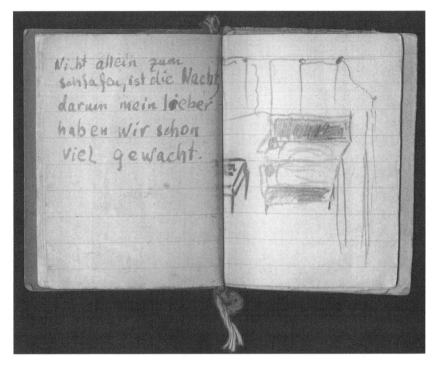

The night is not just for sleeping
Which is why, my dear, we did a lot of stirring

> This is how it sometimes looks inside Meir:[29]
> An emptiness spreads, and body and soul suddenly go lame,
> And terrible is the time that follows,
> In which I seek out the strength to go on living

---

28. Gad Beck (1923–2012) went into hiding in Berlin after Lewin's deportation, but was arrested shortly before the end of the war. Liberated by the Red Army, he immigrated to Palestine and returned to Germany in the 1970s. See obituary in *Washington Post*, June 26, 2012; Gad Beck, *An Underground Life: Memoirs of a Gay Jew in Nazi Berlin* (Madison: University of Wisconsin Press, 1999); online exhibition "Do you remember, when" at www.ushmm.org/museum/exhibit/online/doyourememberwhen/. (The translations on the museum's website differ from the ones printed here.)

29. The German word for "me" is *mir*; Lewin uses "Meir," perhaps a reference to the first name by which he was known in the youth group.

Often I see myself on the edge of an abyss,
Feeling utterly abandoned.
Dizzy when I looked down,
I felt myself abruptly pale!

But suddenly, from the very depths, I heard
A voice address me sweetly,
And looked down, asking who was calling me?
But I had recognized it right away!

It was the voice of a holy power,
It was the sound of sympathetic souls,
It was mankind's greatest virtue,
May it never be in short supply!

If destiny's terrible game ever
Carries you off to a distant land
If our exile stretches even farther
If the last bond of our companionship [*Gemeinschaft*] is broken!?

THE CHANGING VOCABULARY OF DESTRUCTION

Poetry and art in general often reflect the extent to which an artist finds the events he or she describes as, to a certain degree, "beyond belief." Such reactions, however, were not limited to these overtly artistic expressions; letters, diaries, or even reports contained similar qualities and questions. The depth and duration of deprivation weighed on people's willingness and ability to reflect on, even document what they experienced under German rule. In Warsaw, Hersh Wasser explained a two-month gap in his diary by saying he "found the pen distasteful. In truth, what was there to write about? The unbelievably high prices, or the death camps?"[30] A cognitive and emotional barrier also had to be overcome. Even comparatively mundane matters might be difficult for an author to capture or explain to an audience. Censorship presented a further obstacle. Many letters and even diaries were, at certain junctures, written in coded language to fool authorities, adding another layer of difficulty to properly understand the meaning of the written word. In addition to the correspondence

---

30. Joseph Kermish, "Diary Entries of Hersh Wasser," *YVS* 15 (1983): 263 (entry for April 28, 1941).

featured earlier in this volume,[31] **Klara van Aals**'s letters to Aagje Kaagman serve as one example of this disconnect. Although no great distance lay between her workplace in Apeldoorn and Aagje Kaagman's home, van Aals could not fully express herself in these missives.

DOCUMENT 11-9: Letter from Klara (Claartje) van Aals, nurse at the Jewish psychiatric institution Het Apeldoornsche Bosch, Apeldoorn, German-occupied Netherlands, to Aagje Kaagman, Utrecht, October 9/10 and 13/14, 1941, in Suzette Wyers, ed., *Als ik wil kan ik duiken . . . : Brieven van Claartje van Aals, verpleegster in de joods psychiatrische inrichting Het Apeldoornsche Bosch, 1940–1943* (Amsterdam: T. Rap, 1995), 79–80 (translated from Dutch).

[October 9/10, 1941]

There are things happening to the J. . . . that make us all feel awfully frightened. We are all in a crummy, helpless [*likmevestje*] mood. It's just like in Amsterdam though you would not expect that here in Het Bosch. You can appreciate how anxious we all are. I am in a bloody bad mood. Jo de Vries is gone. Perhaps you understand me. Actually many more here. They have gone to stay elsewhere. *Snappez-vous*? [Do you get it?] I can't write you anything else because it's too much of a risk. You can appreciate how extremely busy we are now that we are so short-staffed.

I will be coming to Utrecht October 20 for Dad's birthday. The police don't allow me to be away any longer. Dreadful, eh? Dammit, otherwise I could have come for three days. All the best to all and a kiss for you from

Your Claas

[October 13–14, 1941]

I have heard that they are busy with roundups in Utrecht and you can well understand how deadly anxious I am about Dad. I have in fact not heard anything from him in quite a while. Would you do me a big favor and check on Dad and make sure that everything is in order. Then write me back immediately—if need be a postcard—.

They are also very busy over here. I have gone through a terrible time and do not think that things will be any different in the foreseeable future.

---

31. See, e.g., documents 2-5 to 2-11.

When I get to Utrecht I'll have a whole lot to tell, something I can't possibly do in writing. *Snappez-vous?* Aag, what an awfully terrible time this is for us. The worst is that there is nothing you can do about it. We can only hope for better times. Even though things look so hopeless at the moment.

Agie, I stop, a hearty hug from

Your Claas

For recipients of letters and other written works, reading between the lines required insight and intuition. When writing to friends and relatives living in relative safety, Jews in Nazi-dominated Europe had to consider not only the censor but also the potentially upsetting effects of their words on friends and family. Many felt it was pointless to burden others with problems that in essence could not be remedied, and perhaps not even truly understood. These issues continued to appear in other forms of personal writing. For those writing diaries, finding the language to express their apprehension—even to oneself—continued to be a challenge. The following entry from the diary of Isabelle Jesion[32] depicts the enormous anxiety that she felt as a Parisian Jew living in occupied France. Jesion was fourteen when she began her diary in September 1941. Many of her early entries typify a young woman in the throes of adolescence; they detailed a crush on a geography teacher, as well as serious thoughts of converting to Catholicism. This entry from January 9, 1942, however, assumes a more sober tone. Jesion describes a dream that combines several anxieties present in her life under German occupation: arrests, questioning by the police (here, notably, the present menace took the form of French gendarmes rather than German soldiers), concentration camps, and the fear of being abandoned by her parents. This final nightmare would come true seven months later: Jesion's parents were deported on July 16, 1942, first to Drancy, and then to Auschwitz, where they were murdered.[33]

---

32. Isabelle Jesion (b. 1926) kept two diaries, one from September 12, 1941, to May 5, 1942, and a second from May 6 to November 27, 1942. She added three final entries in March and April 1944. After the German occupation of Paris, Isabelle moved in with an aunt. In March 1944, she transferred to a boarding school run by the **UGIF**. She survived the war and became active in the Jewish scouting movement in France, and in 1947 she immigrated to Palestine on the famous *Exodus* ship. See catalog entry, Ghetto Fighter's House Archive: www.infocenters.co.il/gfh/notebook_ext.asp?book=18231&lang=eng&site=gfh (accessed June 4, 2012), and Alexandra Zapruder, *Salvaged Pages: Young Writers' Diaries of the Holocaust* (New Haven, CT: Yale University Press, 2002), 430–31.

33. For a discussion of Jesion's diary, see Alexandra Garbarini, *Numbered Days: Diaries and the Holocaust* (New Haven, CT: Yale University Press, 2006), 144, 205–6.

DOCUMENT ii-io: Isabelle Jesion, Paris, diary entry for January 9, 1942, USHMMA RG 68.112M (LHG), reel 36, file 2131 (translated from French).

[. . .] Last night I had a strange dream, a dream that I fervently hope with all my heart will come true. But deep down I don't believe that it will come true, though dreams are signs from God Almighty.

However, it wasn't very clear. One part [of the dream] is going on at rue Hermel, another part in a wood.

In the wood, I encounter Mme Dupas [her teacher], I stop, I say hello to her, and then she continues talking to some other teachers. I look at all of them and am seized by a desire to cry. I offer a hand to Mme to say goodbye, but she holds on to it and says to me, "Come with me and keep me company." I am mad with joy, and she gives me her arm. Then I break out in sobs at the thought of leaving her in a few minutes. She asks me what's wrong. I explain everything to her, and she leads me to her place, where I don't come in.

A second time, a gendarme stops me and asks me, "Do you know Mme Dupas?" "Yes," I say. He leads me into the wood, where all my teachers and Mme Dupas, too, file past. He asks me, "There is a criminal, Mme Dupas. Point her out to me." (Inspired by Michel Stroggof,[34] where his mother must recognize him, but acts as if she doesn't see him, despite the torture being inflicted on her.)

So I am always torn in the dream between two duties. A terrible dilemma. My affection or justice. But the latter gets the upper hand for a moment, and I point her out. Then she falls into my arms, and I bitterly regret having done my duty, and then someone tells me that it's a play. I am very happy to hear it.

Rue Hermel, I was passing and a ball falls, and I return to the school to give it [to someone]. I see Mme Dupas, talk to her, and then I tell her to accompany me because the concierge won't let me go out, to which she consents, and I would be with her longer.

---

34. Popular novel by Jules Verne, *Michael Strogoff: The Courier of the Czar*, first published in 1876.

Once I dreamed that I was in a concentration camp. My parents were not with me or no longer existed (I don't remember). I slept [in the dream] and then woke up, when I see, of all people, Mme Dupas and another lady. She wants to adopt me. I accept joyously.

Those confronted unexpectedly and suddenly with disaster had little or no chance to express themselves to friends and family in a way they would have liked; furthermore, they wrote these "last notes" with the hope, rather than the assurance, that they would reach their intended audience. Small slips of paper could contain the most momentous messages. Some would call for help— "Papa! We've been picked up," exclaimed one note from a German Jewish son to his father.[35] Others would struggle to find words to say farewell. Shortly before his and his wife's Ilse deportation from Berlin to Riga on January 19, 1942, Erich Chotzen wrote the following note to his parents and remaining siblings.[36]

DOCUMENT 11-11: **Uncompleted farewell note by Erich Chotzen, Berlin, January 16, 1942, in Barbara Schieb,** *Nachricht von Chotzen: "Wer immer hofft, stirbt singend"* **(Berlin: Edition Hentrich, 2000), 89 (translated from German).**

My dear ones,

especially you, dear Mama, and you, dear Papa. I still have to write you a few lines, to say goodbye and comfort you after a fashion. I'm afraid that what I put on paper will come nowhere near showing what I feel. Indeed, whether that can be described at all, I don't know, at any rate, I'm unfortunately not granted the ability. No—I can't find the words. So I'll make it short: dear Mama, I have to cause you such terrible grief, and on top of that, at such a moment, and I can't help it, however much I love you[.]

---

35. Klaus Scheurenberg to Paul Scheurenberg, Berlin, no date (1942?); quoted from Patricia Heberer, *Children during the Holocaust* (Lanham, MD: AltaMira Press in association with the USHMM, 2011), 95.

36. Erich Chotzen, born in Berlin in 1917, was deported to Riga a few days after writing this letter, where he most likely died in March. His wife Ilse (née Schwarz), born in 1923, was also deported and murdered. His father Josef (b. 1883) probably died around the time Erich wrote this letter, but his mother Elsa (née Arndt; b. 1887) survived the war, along with only one brother, Joseph. See Schieb, *Nachricht von Chotzen,* inside front cover, 87, 89.

Such "last letters" form a special category of writing that combines literary elements with other features closely related to the person's character and mind-set. Those leaving notes before their forced departure to unknown destinations wrote differently than those deliberately planning suicide. Before taking his own life in early 1942, "exhausted by long years of homeless wandering," world-renowned writer Stefan Zweig felt "impelled to fulfill a last obligation: to give heartfelt thanks to this wonderful land of Brazil which afforded me and my work such kind and hospitable repose. My love for the country increased from day to day, and nowhere else would I have preferred to build up a new existence, the world of my own language having disappeared for me and my spiritual home, Europe, having destroyed itself." Zweig preferred "to conclude in good time and in erect bearing a life in which intellectual labor meant the purest joy and personal freedom the highest good on earth" and concluded, "I salute all my friends! May it be granted them yet to see the dawn after the long night! I, all too impatient, go on before."[37]

The following document is a rare letter written by a Jewish man held in a Belgrade camp to his non-Jewish wife in the expectation of both his deportation and death. While not explicitly written as a "last letter" in the ways discussed above, it functionally served the same purpose and contains some similar gestures in its language. "Friedi" was a nickname of Friedrich, the first husband of David Albahari's mother (his last name, and the name of Albahari's mother, are unknown). When the war broke out, she and Friedrich lived in Zagreb. As a married couple that would have been targeted by **ustaše** sooner or later (an ethnic Serb married to a Jew in a fascist Croat state), they fled from Zagreb and, after a brief stay in Bosnia, ended up as refugees in Belgrade. When in the fall of 1941 Jewish men were targeted for retaliatory executions by the Germans, Friedrich was arrested. On the same day, October 18, 1941, his wife was in the countryside, attempting to arrange a hideout outside of Belgrade for both of them. Friedrich was taken to Topovske šupe, a transit camp for Jewish hostages. The letter to his wife was his last. Friedrich was most probably executed in a mass shooting within the next few days. His wife survived the war, but the fate of their children is unclear.

---

37. Farewell note by Stefan Zweig, Petropolis (Brazil), February 22, 1942, translated from Stefan Zweig, *The World of Yesterday* (1945), 437. See also Reuven Dafni and Yehudit Kleiman, eds., *Final Letters* (London: Weidenfeld & Nicolson, 1991).

DOCUMENT 11-12: **Letter from "Friedi,"[38] Jewish transit camp Topovske šupe in Belgrade, Serbia, to his wife in Belgrade, November 14, 1941, in David Albahari, *Teret* (Belgrade: Forum pisaca, 2004), 110–12 (translated from Serbian).[39]**

My dear and only Mara!

I hope that you received my letter yesterday on Thursday [. . .]. Today brought, apart from the cold, snow, and wind, a huge deportation, and 250 people are gone. Among them are the old G., V., B.K., and others. Our terrible fate is approaching every day. [illegible sentence]. Now you see that I was right to insist that we should stay in Bosnia, and you were angry at me and told me that I was afraid. Now my fate is sealed and today or tomorrow I am going to the unknown—maybe forever. I don't blame you, and please don't feel guilty. That's fate. If you receive my blanket, duvet, and suitcase with things through the Federation,[40] don't be worried, because some [. . .] leave without things. If we are destined to see each other again, so we will. See to it that you leave a trace somehow in Belgrade, so that I can find you if I return. I will look for you first of all at U. Lj., then at M., S., and at the grocer (S.) on Jovanova market, and also at the police. If you go to Kusadak or Bačina I will find you easily, just leave a trace.

If I could only spend eight days with you one more time, I would not object to death afterward. I am not destined to say goodbye to you as a human being. Now that everything's passed, I see my whole life flowing in front of my eyes, like a film. All those moments next to you, and next to our children, were sweet and warm, my sweet wife. How unreachable is all that for me now. I can't cry, because I am embarrassed in front of the

---

38. The non-Slavicized spelling of his German name as well as odd turns of phrase in his writing in Serbian suggest that "Friedi" was a native German speaker. It is unclear whether he was born in Yugoslavia or came as a refugee. David Albahari (b. 1948), in whose book of essays Friedrich's letters are published, was the son of Friedi's wife and her second husband; Albahari is a well-known Serbian author who now lives in Canada. See David Albahari, "Pisma iz logora," in *Teret* (Belgrade: Forum pisaca, 2004), 101–18. For the timeline and a brief history of the Holocaust in German-occupied Serbia, see Christopher R. Browning, "Wehrmacht Reprisal Policy and the Murder of the Male Jews in Serbia," and "The Semlin Gas Van and the Final Solution in Serbia," in *Fateful Months: Essays on the Emergence of the Final Solution*, ed. idem (New York: Holmes & Meier, 1985), 39–56, 68–85.

39. This document was written in Roman script.

40. A reference to the Federation of Jewish Communities, the umbrella Jewish organization that tried to help Jews in occupied Serbia.

others, but my heart and soul cry because of our bitter fate. I have always tried to be good and that all my actions be honorable, and still I am at this place. I am taken by dark premonition of future spiritual and physical suffering. How I will be eaten alive by terrible longing for you, when I am suffering already. How it would be nice to be next to you, even without firewood and most other things I have been used to since my childhood. But I can't have any of that because I am a Jew. O tyranny of fate! I, who never felt like a Jew and who avoided Jewish company, now suffer for that Jewishness!

I am imagining a huge labor camp in a foreign country. I am just a number in that camp and nothing more. At home, two small hearts beat, the hearts of my children, for whom I am not a number, but a dad (ah, so sweet to hear this word). The hearts of my poor mother, who cares for her son, beats as well. Finally, the heart of my wife beats, wife who is everything for me in this world, and who I believe will not write me off as a dead person, because she knows I am alive, but as a slave.

Nobody senses in this camp that that number behind which I am hidden, burns inside with terrible longing for his wife, children, and mother. Always, in every occasion, this number thinks of you, the children, and mother, but mostly you, who shared with me the best days of golden freedom and material well-being. Those sweet memories of past happiness are my only treasure that they cannot take away from me. And when my heart cries such as now, then I recall these sweet memories—in the hope that it will be a bit easier for me.

Don't cry when you read this, but wait. As long as you don't have a positive proof of my death don't remarry and don't forget me. I know that you are a woman of rare character and that you love me, as I love you, and I am not worried on that account.

Take care of the children as best as you can, and support my poor mother. If I get deported, go to the countryside with the children. Take mother if the German authorities allow, otherwise <u>not by any means</u>, because you would expose her to danger. Don't take F. by any means. If mother doesn't want to go without F., then go by yourself.

If they still don't deport me, do everything (Š. or K.) to get me out of this hell while there is still time. There are decent people. If I am gone, I may not survive all that. If you need money, sell my things. If I return alive, I will manage easily.

Give my best to mother, and kiss the children for me. Poor mother—console her! K. asks that you go to his wife on St. Archangel day (the patron saint of his wife) and console her. Bring up the children as Serbs, and not as Jews.

I am leaving, dying for your hugs and caresses, with heart in tears and blood and I kiss you and hug you a thousand times in spirit.

Your very unhappy Friedi

P.S. I haven't had bread since yesterday, and am starving.

Ultimately, the literary and artistic works, letters, and diary entries in this chapter, like all of the documents in this volume, draw the reader into the daily challenges of life amidst an unfolding genocide. Each of these authors has only a small piece of the historical puzzle, and their writing, often reflect that limited view. Taken together, these pieces—all of which included some form of artistic or literary sensibility—reveal an ever-evolving narrative and identity of these writers as Jews and as people attempting to make sense of a senseless world. By definition, artistically inflected responses reach forward toward a future audience. For some writers, this was a future that included their own close community. For others, only the world outside their reach held some semblance of hope: be it a hope for transmission, or hope for a memory of their unexplainable plight. To those who received such messages, communications arriving from inside the nightmare of wartime Europe raised more questions than they provided answers: what was the writer trying to convey; was there any way to help; and—first and foremost—what was going on? The next chapter explores this question against the background of knowledge available to varying degrees in different circles in the summer of 1942.

CHAPTER 12

Making Sense of the Unthinkable

HOW WIDESPREAD was knowledge about the systematic mass murder of Jewish men, women, and children by Nazi Germany and its allies—what we today call the Holocaust—in the years covered by this volume, 1941 and 1942? Historians have scrutinized the stance of the Polish government-in-exile and Polish underground in answering this question; they have examined discussions in American and British Jewish communities during the unfolding tragedy and they have considered the outlook from Palestine during the war.[1] Sources generated by Jews at the time push us to tread cautiously and acknowledge a complex reality that was joined inexorably not only to differing national and regional experiences, but also local and highly individual perceptions of radically new levels of human destruction. Resistance to the news of wave after wave of mass killing broke down slowly, meeting disbelief at every

---

1. For a range of publications on this subject, see David Engel, *In the Shadow of Auschwitz: The Polish Government-in-Exile and the Jews, 1939–1942* (Chapel Hill: University of North Carolina Press, 1987); idem, *Facing the Holocaust: The Polish Government-in-Exile and the Jews, 1943–1945* (Chapel Hill: University of North Carolina Press, 1993); Walter Laqueur, *The Terrible Secret: Suppression of the Truth about the "Final Solution"* (Boston, MA: Little, Brown and Co., 1980); Deborah E. Lipstadt, *Beyond Belief: The American Press and the Coming of the Holocaust, 1933–1945* (New York: The Free Press, 1986); Dalia Ofer, *Escaping the Holocaust: Illegal Immigration to the Land of Israel, 1939–1944* (New York: Oxford University Press, 1990); Bernard Wasserstein, *Britain and the Jews of Europe 1939–1945* (London: Leicester University Press, 1999); David S. Wyman, *The Abandonment of the Jews: America and the Holocaust, 1941–1945* (New York: The New Press, 1998).

turn. Indeed, the documents reproduced here remind us that the very terms we are so familiar with to describe the murder of the European Jews—genocide and Holocaust—did not exist during the war as we understand them today. As historian Yehuda Bauer wrote in the late 1960s, "The idea that a modern state could plan the extinction of millions of human beings purely on the basis of their belonging to a particular ethnic group was not easily assimilable, either by Jews or non-Jews."[2]

The period from late 1941 to the summer of 1942 formed a crucial stage in both the incremental evolution of the Nazi-propelled "Final Solution" and the step-by-step process in which Jews gradually came to understand what was happening. While many German and non-German agencies working for the same goal relentlessly drove the escalation toward genocide, its prospective victims could only gradually and unevenly make sense of this unthinkable agenda. Even where messages from different sources intersected and corroborated one another, the recipients needed to connect the confusingly varied incoming reports and overcome their own incredulity to see the direction in which events were moving. As the **WJC**'s Geneva representative **Gerhart Riegner** wrote in his memoir about this period, "[o]ccasionally the same piece of news would reach us several times. The first time we would ask ourselves whether such things were possible. But when it was repeatedly communicated from different locations, we began to believe it. We were convinced that the situation was growing worse with each passing day."[3] In this chapter, we will foreground accounts by Jews who from different perspectives struggled to identify the agents, driving forces, and ultimate goals behind the persecution: those who, like Riegner, combined a view "from the top" and called for preventative action; those tormented by uncertainty and feared being drowned in the wave of violence; and those who grappled for meaning as part of their efforts to retain some modicum of agency in the face of rampant destruction.

SEARCHING FOR EXPLANATIONS

Mainstream historiography on the perpetration of the Holocaust has long favored German sources over Jewish accounts, dismissing the latter as too anecdotal and unreliable. No type of Holocaust documentation is without its problems, and Jews were clearly too far removed from bureaucrats and politicians in Berlin to be able to attest to decisions made there. Yet Jewish sources from

---

2. Yehuda Bauer, "When Did They Know?" *Midstream* 14 (April 1968): 51.

3. Gerhart M. Riegner, *Never Despair: Sixty Years in the Service of the Jewish People and the Cause of Human Rights* (Chicago: Ivan R. Dee in association with the USHMM, 2006), 41.

the time can, in addition to opening a door on contemporary Jewish thoughts and deeds, offer insights into those operating the persecution machinery, their actions, tools, and tactics. As we have seen in previous chapters, questions regarding the perpetrators surfaced, particularly when Jews tried to improve their situation and that of others by interceding with German and other authorities. Who were the men (and the few women) who killed and tortured, what motivated them to do so, and was there a broader rationale for all the murders they committed? Like witnesses to a crime, those closest and most under threat could be best positioned to attest to perpetrator behavior and speculate about motivations.[4] Experiences gained in prior historical or more contemporary events could provide important clues for making sense of partial, fragmented, censored, and contradictory information, but they could also undermine a clear view of the situation. In any case, contemporary accounts accomplish more than simply reiterating the overarching narrative of destruction that is now familiar. Instead, they impart crucial insights into how Jews understood the actions of the perpetrators and induce us to ask questions about not only what was known but also how that knowledge was gained.

One element of Nazi planning to achieve the set goal of physically removing Jews from the German sphere of influence had been publicly known and discussed since the second half of 1940: the **Madagascar Plan** in the form of mass "resettlement" of European Jewry to that island in the Indian Ocean. Some version of the plan had long resonated with politicians and audiences that viewed forced relocation as an appropriate measure for dispensing with an undesirable group.[5] With Nazis in control in France and no emigration option in sight, the plan took on a new, more imminent and threatening dimension, but it could still be viewed as the latest iteration of a familiar antisemitic theme. As part of a feasibility study completed for the American Jewish Congress in May 1941, the following article, published after the beginning of **Operation Barbarossa**, pointed—apart from inevitably reflecting mid-century

---

4. Mark Roseman, one of the few historians who, based on Jewish sources, has delved deeper into this underresearched topic, observes that "Jews were best placed to make observations on their counterparts when they were working alongside them [perpetrators], but the character and duration of such Jewish labor varied enormously." See Mark Roseman, "Holocaust Perpetrators in Victims' Eyes," in *Years of Persecution, Years of Extermination. Saul Friedländer and the Future of Holocaust Studies*, ed. Christian Wiese and Paul Betts (London: Continuum, 2010), 81–100.

5. For an overview, see Magnus Brechtken, *"Madagaskar für die Juden." Antisemitische Idee und politische Praxis 1885–1945* (Munich: R. Oldenbourg, 1997); Saul Friedländer, *Nazi Germany and the Jews:* (vol. 1) *The Years of Persecution, 1933–1939* (New York: HarperCollins, 1997), 219, 283, 310; idem, *Nazi Germany and the Jews:* (vol. 2) *The Years of Extermination, 1939–1945* (New York: HarperCollins, 2007), 81–82, 103–4, 136, 203.

central European prejudices of its author—to new, more radical perspectives on how to solve the "Jewish question" inherent in the plan.

DOCUMENT 12-1: **Eugene Hevesi,[6] "Hitler's Plan for Madagascar,"** *Contemporary Jewish Record*, **4, no. 5 (October 1941): 381–94.**

Off the eastern coast of Africa lies the island of Madagascar, destined, if Hitler has his way, to be the death chamber of the Jews of Europe. To this French possession, according to semi-official Axis statements, are to be sent all the Jews of Nazi-dominated Europe in order that the continent might be free of their alleged influence forever. [. . .] World Service,[7] a Nazi agency, issued the following choice bit of propaganda as late as April 28, 1941: "Reports persist here that a secret clause of the Franco-German armistice requires the French Government to allow Europe's Jews to enter Madagascar. Informed quarters believe that the French newspaper *Le Temps* had Madagascar in mind when it predicted for the near future a 'permanent' solution of the Jewish problem which would not entail persecution." The next day, a Jewish Telegraphic Agency dispatch from Stockholm declared: "Jewish leaders from the Reich, Austria, Nazi-held Poland, and the Protectorate were summoned by the Nazi authorities to a conference in Berlin at which the plan to have all the Jews from Europe 'evacuated' to the French island of Madagascar was offered to them."[8]

Hitler's intention to destroy the Jews needs no elaboration and, as this study will show, there is no doubt that any attempt to dump thousands of Europeans on the island of Madagascar would result in [their] fullest misery

---

6. Son of the Chief Rabbi of Budapest, Hevesi (1895–1983) studied law and economics, later becoming an official with the Hungarian Foreign Trade Office. While serving as an economic attaché in the United States, he resigned to protest the introduction of an antisemitic law in his homeland. Hevesi subsequently became the United Nations representative for six Jewish NGOs and long served as the foreign affairs secretary for the American Jewish Committee. Obituaries, *New York Times*, February 17, 1983; *Jewish Telegraphic Agency*, February 18, 1983.

7. The "Welt-Dienst" was a Nazi German international antisemitic news service that issued bulletins on matters pertaining to the "Jewish question"; it appeared in eighteen languages during the war. See Robert Edwin Herzstein, *The War That Hitler Won: Goebbels and the Nazi Media Campaign* (New York: Paragon House, 1987), 161–62.

8. This reference to a "conference" with Jewish representatives summoned to Berlin seems to be based on an article in *Yediot Hayom*, May 2, 1941, 11–12, that claimed leading German Jews had rejected the **RSHA**'s plan for a "resettlement" of Europe's Jews; see Beate Meyer, *Tödliche Gratwanderung. Die Reichsvereinigung der Juden in Deutschland zwischen Hoffnung, Zwang, Selbstbehauptung und Verstrickung (1939–1945)* (Göttingen: Wallstein Verlag, 2011), 96–98.

and eventual annihilation. Reliable data and an overwhelming conformity of authoritative opinion prove that the island affords no possibility for large-scale immigration, while even the attempted settlement of small numbers of Europeans has failed.

[. . . ; following a detailed analysis of earlier feasibility studies and their findings regarding the unsuitability of Madagascar for European settlement]

The terrible risks involved in a mass settlement of white people in an isolated, backward, disease-ridden tropical wilderness are evident. They cannot be disregarded except by men who are completely devoid of all human feeling. The forced deportation of Jews *en masse* to the island of Madagascar must be resisted by decent people of whatever origin or mentality as an outrage. No pogrom in history would equal the slaughter which would result from the indiscriminate dumping of millions of helpless people into a primitive, hostile environment.

In his article, Hevesi drew no direct connection between the implications of the Madagascar Plan and early reports on German mass murder actions targeting Jews in the newly occupied parts of the Soviet Union, and it is questionable whether any of his readers might have done so. It took time to realize that the Nazi regime was pondering the lessons of Operation Barbarossa for a Europe-wide "Final Solution" in the form of systematic mass murder; yet apprehensions were not far off, both in terms of timing and regarding the meaning of the war in the East. Among the first to notice the deadly potential of this war were German Jews who witnessed the regime stepping up its anti-Jewish rhetoric and measures. Since September 1941, they had to wear the Jewish star, thus visually establishing what had already become a de facto social separation from their fellow Germans. Mass deportations of German Jews to occupied parts of eastern Europe began the following month. "It appears," **Willy Cohn** confided in mid-October 1941 in his diary, "as if the Germans are completely intent at this stage of the war on achieving our destruction [*Vernichtung*]. One can only wish that they fail in this plan."[9] What little remained of German Jews' hope of somehow making it to the end of the war eroded following their "relocation" to special zones and houses within German cities. "Evacuation to the East," where the slaughter of local Jews was

---

9. Willy Cohn, *Kein Recht, Nirgends: Tagebuch vom Untergang des Breslauer Judentums, 1933–1941*, ed. Norbert Conrads (Cologne: Böhlau Verlag, 2006), 2:991 (diary entry for October 12, 1941).

ongoing, deepened the despair and accounted for a rising number of suicides.[10] Cohn noted a "feeling of the downfall of Europe" based on (true) rumors about mass starvation and cannibalism among Soviet POWs and the "war of revenge against the Jews [*Rachekrieg gegen das Judentum*]."[11] Even when he was certain that the Nazi reign of terror had to come to an end, his thoughts remained bleak.

DOCUMENT 12-2: **Willy Cohn, Breslau, Germany, diary entry for October 18, 1941, in Willy Cohn,** *Kein Recht, Nirgends: Tagebuch vom Untergang des Breslauer Judentums, 1933–1941,* **ed. Norbert Conrads (Cologne: Böhlau Verlag, 2007), 2:994 (translated from German).**

To my mind, the growing terror is proof of how badly the German cause stands, despite of all reports of victory. But before the great change [*Umschwung*] will come, many more people will have to lose their lives and perish more or less painfully. At night one thinks about the terrible tragedy that has befallen us Jews and one dare not to attribute guilt and innocence!

For Cohn, the connection between "large" and "small" events, those planned in Berlin and those taking place close to home, was obvious: their landlord had decided to rent their apartment to an "Aryan," and the Jewish community leadership saw no way to classify Cohn as an "essential worker" based on his scholarly expertise. Jews continued to be deported to Łódź— where, according to some rumors, conditions were not all that bad—while the Nazi leadership kept railing against "international Jewry." After Hitler's speech on November 9, 1941, in which he "again cursed the Jews terribly," Cohn's wife was verbally assaulted on the street for the first time while shopping. The imminent loss of their apartment increased the risk of being "sent away [*verschickt*]," and when Breslau was bombed, it was clear to Cohn that "we," the Jews, would have to "pay the bill." Still, "all that has to be dealt with now and one has to try to pull through" for the sake of the children; despite his weak physique, Cohn expressed the "iron will not to have a breakdown in the family's interest."[12] Days later, he and his family were deported to their death in Kovno.

---

10. See Marion A. Kaplan, *Between Dignity and Despair: Jewish Life in Nazi Germany* (New York: Oxford University Press, 1998), 173–200. Of the estimated ten thousand attempted and committed suicides by Jews in Nazi Germany, three thousand to four thousand occurred during the deportation phase within a Jewish population of roughly 134,000. See ibid., 180; Konrad Kwiet, "The Ultimate Refuge: Suicide in the Jewish Community under the Nazis," *LBIYB* 29 (1984): 135–67.

11. Cohn, *Kein Recht*, 2:992–93 (diary entries for October 14 and 16, 1941).

12. Ibid., 2:1002–9 (diary entries for November 3–16, 1941).

For Frieda Reinach, who lived in Berlin until her deportation in October 1942, the trials of daily life were expressed in unanswerable questions and a chronicle of the breadth of persecution. Even the smallest indignities could have wide-reaching effects: a prohibition on public transportation forced Reinach's already weak father to walk miles through the city; much anticipated letters from family members abroad were never delivered; and Reinach felt largely abandoned. Like many others, Reinach confronted her new reality by detailing her experiences in a diary, with the hope—albeit not the certainty—that these "little book[s]," as she said, would one day be read.

DOCUMENT 12-3: Frieda Reinach,[13] Berlin, diary entries for May/June, 1942, USHMMA RG 10.249 (translated from German).

May 10, 1942 Sunday, 7 p.m.

How often I say, I wonder whether we'll ever be able to tell our children what we've gone through? I don't think we will, but up to now—thank heavens—we've been lucky! How many thousands of Jews have been "expelled" (the nice euphemism that is used) since October 1941, and how many have died as a result of the enormous privations they suffer. We can't write to Max and Jule at all, we can only send them money, so that's what we do, and then weeks later we receive confirmation of receipt from the Litzmannstadt ghetto. Whenever we see Max's or Jule's handwriting, we know they're alive. Moritz and wife [Marta] are where? Liane?[14]

---

13. Berlin resident Frieda Reinach (née Schwarzschild), born in the German town of Hanau in 1887, was married to Marcus (Max) Reinach, born in Essingen in 1878. They recorded their experiences in Berlin from the outbreak of the war until late October 1942, when they were deported eastward and murdered. An unknown acquaintance hid the diary after their deportation and sent it to their daughter in the United States after the war. See donor file, USHMMA RG 10.249; *USHMM ITS Collection Data Base Central Name Index.* The authors have been unable to find information about the people mentioned in this diary other than the ones identified subsequently.

14. Frieda Reinach refers here to her brother Max Schwarzschild, a medical doctor (b. 1880 in Hanau), her sister-in-law Julie (Jule) Schwarzschild (née Strauss, born 1890 in Langen), and another relative, Liane Karoline Schwarzschild (b. 1893 in Hanau), all residing in Frankfurt am Main. Deported on October 20, 1941, to the Łódź ghetto, neither Max nor Jule survived. Liane was deported in early May 1942 to an unknown destination and did not return. See German "Minority Census," 1938–1939, USHMMA RG 14.013M; *USHMM ITS Collection Data Base Central Name Index*; *Gedenkbuch*, www.bundesarchiv.de/gedenkbuch.

Adele, Ida, and Arthur Wachenheimer are in Piaski near Lublin, Dora Fuchs in Riga since January 11, 1942.[15] We've heard nothing from her yet—impossible, as Riga [is in the] war zone. In better times we helped her and on occasion sent her money, a total of 420 Mark. Food is in short supply, but thus far we haven't gone hungry. Father [Max Reinach] and I have gotten quite slender. Father weighs 115 pounds, and I weigh 125 pounds. It's mainly sorrow and worries that are to blame for the weight loss. Thus far Jews get the same rations as Aryans, but all special food allocations (around 30 different items, such as fish, legumes, chocolate, tobacco, milk, better vegetables, all fruits) are denied to us.

Still, through good friends we do get some things; they go without in order to help us. The most wonderful friend is . . . . . .[16], she is an angel to us, she not only helps with food, but also encourages us psychologically, gives us her friendship.

[. . .] So our life has been made quite difficult, but in comparison to that of others, it's still bearable. I am terrified, and justifiably so, at the thought of evacuation, and it's a disaster that hovers over us at all times. Whenever I think of it, I can't sleep, my heart races, and I know: if we have to go this road, I'll never see you again, my beloved children.[17] How are you? How much you must be worrying about us. If only you never have any money worries, that's my daily prayer. I think so often about your childhood years—how beautiful they were—and [never] would have anticipated such a destiny. Now you're happy women. You, my Trude, are a mother, and we can't share in your happiness—not even through letters. We've written to you every month via the Red Cross, since December 1941—but not a single line from you has come to us in reply. Many people have already gotten an answer, at least from Pa[lestine], while it takes longer coming from the USA. Every day I hope to see your handwriting. [. . .]

---

15. Artur Wachenheimer of Mainz (born 1880 in Worms) and Ida Wachenheimer of Worms (born in that city in 1883) were deported on March 25, 1942, to the Piaski ghetto, where they probably perished. See *Gedenkbuch*, www.bundesarchiv.de/gedenkbuch.

16. Name omitted, most likely to prevent her arrest in case the **Gestapo** found the diary.

17. Her daughter Miriam Gertrud "Trude" Koshland, later Miriam Joel (1911–1996), had immigrated to the United States and remained there during the war. Another daughter, Lilli, and son-in-law Guenther Blau had immigrated to New York in November 1938, where they joined a cousin.

June 20, 1942. As of 3 weeks ago, father can use all public transportation in Greater Berlin.[18] He has lost 10 pounds as a result of all the walking, and weighs only 106 pounds, and I still weigh 120 pounds (so—a loss of 45 pounds!). We're really considering whether Father shouldn't report for work, because one is more apt to be protected from evacuation that way. The officials and volunteers at the community are no longer protected.[19] It's a hard decision, because it's so easy to get everything wrong. Now, mainly old people are being taken away,[20] out of the homes, and it's rumored that they're taken to Theresienstadt. Nobody has even an hour of peace any longer, because the regulations are changed quickly and often. [. . . , information on financial situation and more anti-Jewish measures follows]

On June 5, your first letter arrived via the Red Cross, dearest Lilli and Günter. Unfortunately, it had been in the mail since December 26, and you didn't use up the 25 words permitted. Your question "Where are you?"[21] shows us your concerns. From you, Trude and Walter, not a single word has come yet. Why . . . My work is agreeable again, and I hope I can keep at it for a long time. Miss Altesthum works in Wittenau, a 75-minute commute and very hard; she has to get up at 4:15 a.m. After three weeks of factory work, she has aged greatly, and besides, her resistance is low and she's losing weight very rapidly. Mrs. Levy has been in the hospital for a week—the doctor thought it was all over for her, but she has recovered and will soon be returning to us. Unfortunately. Because her serious illness (rectal cancer) causes her excruciating pain, and it's not pleasant for us to have such a person around. But there's no way to get rid of her, and her sister, Mrs. Ascher, won't take her in, which would be the natural thing. So, now you know a bit about us again. There's no telling, of course, whether you'll ever read this little book. Soon this horrifying war will have been going on for three years now—how much longer? Only a miracle can

---

18. Even though it is obvious from the following sentence that the meaning is the exact opposite—that father is *not* allowed to use any public transportation—this is what the original says.

19. Reference to the arrest and deportation of **Reichsvereinigung** officials in the aftermath of the arson attack by the Baum group (see chapter 9) on May 18, 1942. See Beate Meyer, "Between Self-Assertion and Forced Collaboration: The Reich Association of Jews in Germany, 1939–1945," in *Jewish Life in Nazi Germany: Dilemmas and Responses*, ed. Francis R. Nicosia and David Scrase (New York: Berghahn Books, 2010), 149–69.

20. At the time, Max was sixty-four and Frieda was fifty-five.

21. Question in English in the original.

still save us and it would have to come soon. Otherwise we are all lost . . . Who's going to win the war? This question is often discussed, and it's just wishful thinking. But the times are too harsh for pipe dreams.

For Jews in the areas directly affected by mass murder, writing down or otherwise recording what happened around them helped understand what lay behind the increasing destruction. The following selection from a diary by a man by the last name of Gold in the ghetto of Lwów exemplifies the dire situation for those who could not work, particularly the elderly and disabled.[22] At this point, the idea that work could save Jewish lives still persisted, but it increasingly collided with the nonsensically inhumane and destructive manner in which the Germans treated even those Jews able to function, as the document's author put it, as "working cattle" for the Reich.

DOCUMENT 12-4: **Unidentified man (last name of Gold), Lwów, Galicia district, Generalgouvernement, diary entry for December 20, 1941, USHMMA RG 15.069M (Teka Lwowska 229/63) (translated from Polish).**

[. . .] The kidnapping action of the elderly and the sick began on November 14 [1941]. That was the time of the ghetto's creation. The ghetto was abruptly constricted to the territory behind the city from Żółkiewska Street eastward. The city was to be emptied of Jews by the middle of December. The Jews were to remove their things only through Pełtewna and Warszawska Streets. At the corresponding gates, thugs who stole the better items set up shop. The seizing action began at the same time. The elderly were seized. Initially, [the action] was limited to the bridge. November 14, 1941. On this day, a certain hunchback was taken away, but no one had dreamt that there would be a mass action against the elderly. Though it had crossed my mind that such an action could be possible in order to get rid of individuals who did not make up part of the labor force, like old horses or cattle are killed off.

From the viewpoint of racist theory, killing off of this sort is merely drawing the appropriate consequences, the highest sublimation of Hitlerism.

---

22. In Lwów, a ghetto was formed in stages between November 1941 and November 1942. Of the estimated 150,000 Jews living in the city on the eve of the German occupation starting in late June 1941, roughly 1 percent survived the war. See Christine Kulke, "Lwów," in *The United States Holocaust Memorial Museum Encyclopedia of Camps and Ghettos, 1933–1945,* vol. 2: *Ghettos in German-Occupied Eastern Europe*, ed. Martin Dean (Bloomington: Indiana University Press in association with the USHMM, 2012), 802–5.

Jews are tolerated only as working cattle. Those who are not fit for work thereby lose the right to live. The disabled are on par with the elderly.

At about 4 o'clock on December 19, my father went to the other side of the bridge on Żółkiewska Street. He was supposed to return within an hour. He had not returned by 6. I sent to Żółkiewska for information. He had been there and had left. From there, there was no trace of him. All efforts to obtain information were in vain. The seizing [of people] on the bridge lasted for some 10 days. The elderly and disabled were typically seized, but it also happened to people at the height of their powers, upwards of thirty. At the same time, caravans stretch throughout Zamarstynowska [Street]. The kahal [Jewish council] attempts to bring about a change in the arrangement of the ghetto. The Germans demand a contribution. Officially this is called a donation action. [. . .]

Things calmed down at the end of November. It seemed that that trail of crime had been abandoned. Though robberies, beatings, and so forth continued on the bridge; Aryans riding the streetcar were searched—usage of the streetcar was prohibited to Jews. They were deprived of primitive human rights. Entering the Jewish cemetery became dangerous. Coffins with corpses were loaded on a mass scale into morgues, from where they are then taken out to the cemetery. It seemed that at least the living would be safe.

During the first days of December, the 4th it seems, the news broke that the elderly action was being extended to homes. They are going apartment by apartment and taking the elderly and the disabled. The news reached my office that they were on the prowl on Kresowa [Street]. They took the mother-in-law of one of my colleagues. Another colleague who lives in the same building decides not to return [home]. He'll stay on the spot. I return, as usual, with an entire column of colleagues. We doff our hats to the thugs on the bridge and cross. I go to the sister of the colleague who decided not to return. I find her cowering in the kitchen and crying. Beside her are the original owners of the apartment. Did something happen to her husband? Her husband no longer lives, he was killed. What about the burial? The murderers said that the corpse will be taken away.

I don't ask about anything, I bid farewell, anxious about my mother. But we live nearby—things are in order in our building. I send mother and the neighbors under the supervision of the building Gestapo man[23]

---

23. Polish: *hausgestapowiec*, probably referring to a janitor or concierge appointed by German authorities to report suspicious activities in an apartment building.

to the city, to acquaintances of mine. I want to go visit the sister of my colleague, but I'm not able to cross the street. They're kidnapping people, they're on the prowl in cars.

Subsequently, I learn that the ill brother-in-law of my colleague, a fifty-eight-year-old man, was lying in bed when the bandits—a German with a Ukrainian—arrived. When they ordered him to get up and go, he refused. When the Gestapo man started to beat him, he said, "Even if you hit me, I won't stand up."

The German responded by threatening to shoot him if he didn't get up within two minutes. When this did not come to pass, he ordered the Ukrainian to shoot him. The Ukrainian asked whether [he] really [should], and when the German repeated the order, the Ukrainian asked the man lying in bed to turn away, and when he refused, he shot him in the face. The man lying in bed fell asleep—that was all. The German justified himself to the wife by claiming that he had acted in accord with official regulations. The corpse was taken away, the cause of death: a heart attack.

They continued to rage in the apartments for a week. From time to time, young people were also taken away if something in their apartment wasn't in order. They searched in attics and basements. They counted with a strike of their rifle butts. The action was limited to the bridge.

At my building, there was no action. The kidnapped were locked up in the basement of the streetcar drivers' building on Kuwszewicza Street, from where only a few, a limited number, were able to get out—for a bribe, of course.

Those who weren't able to were taken away into the unknown.

In the meantime, the caravans stopped. The ghetto was postponed until February 28, 1942. The second and third sections are the area from Pełtowna [Street] to Kleparowna [Street] assigned to people working for the Germans. German institutions took over particular buildings for themselves, threw out the Jews living there (often those who had been moved there from other parts of the city), and brought in their own Jews.

The evacuation of buildings beyond the bridge, however, stopped. Jews lived as slaves in the building belonging to their places of work. Losing one's job became equivalent to losing one's apartment.

Of course, for one day of work Jews are paid 1 to 2 marks while one kilo of bread costs 5 marks.

By the summer of 1942, deportations throughout Europe would inten-sify and heralded a new era of wholesale murder under the guise of "resettle-ment." Like most Jews in Europe, **Mirjam Korber** in Romanian-controlled **Transnistria** felt the urge to ascribe some kind of meaning to the ongoing suffering and its cumulative effects. In the following diary entry, the young woman articulates her sense of unprecedented persecution without being able to describe its instigators and executioners in more than ghostlike features, very different from the concrete fates of victims and even the image of the silent onlookers. At the same time, she invokes "Quo vadis?"—meaning "Where are you going?"—a phrase most famously associated with a New Testament passage (John 13:36) in which Simon Peter asked Jesus this question; Jesus replied, "Where I am going, you cannot follow now, but you will follow later." To Korber, in the light of her experiences, the present appeared to be a path leading into a most frightening future.

DOCUMENT 12-5: **Mirjam Korber, Djurin, Transnistria, diary entry for July 4, 1942, USHMMA Acc. 2010.93.1 Mirjam Korber Bercovici collection (translated from Romanian).**

It's already July, nine months have passed since we left home, and no end is in sight. A change in temperature like that experienced here on the Ukrainian steppe is an unusual thing. A July without heat, with a cool sun and wind. Everything is upside down. The latest restrictions give the finishing touch to the previous ones. But now there's talk of something even more humiliating. It's rumored that a ghetto will be built, that is, everyone will be resettled, moved out of the Zavod district [in Djurin] into the Jewish neighborhood. But in that case, what awaits us spells mortal danger. People crowded together, one on top of the other, frayed nerves, filth. The result: diseases. It's not enough for them that so many have died thus far, that hundreds of people go begging, that hundreds fast more often than they eat, to keep from begging, and that the ones who do eat, eat things they never even dreamed of in the past. It's not enough for them. They want to kill us all. And what is easier than killing a Jew or thousands of helpless Jews? Terrible stories are told about the brutal way thousands of Jews in the villages and towns of the [German-occupied] Ukraine were murdered. I never could have imagined that the civilization of the twentieth century would allow so much brutality in both thought and deed. "Quo vadis," the torments of the first Christians or even older examples, and even older events, the agonies and tortures suffered by the blacks [*negrilor*] at the hands of the ancient Egyptians,[24] nothing can compare with the present day: Mothers and fathers killed in the presence of their children, children killed before their mothers' eyes, children thrown alive, along with their murdered parents, into graves where they were then beaten to death with rocks. And the world is mute, remains silent in front of the one man, the one evil spirit, who tyrannizes this world and is fighting to the death against a handful of helpless Jews. [. . .]

INFORMATION AND DISBELIEF

The comparatively small group of Jews working for aid organizations with offices in the few remaining neutral countries in Europe shared in the desperation experienced by Mirjam Korber, Frieda Reinach, and millions of others for the very reason that they could piece large chunks of the terrible puzzle together and did confront the silence of the outside world. Switzerland—due to the country's neutrality status and its close proximity to both German and the occupied East—played a particularly important role as a transfer point for information drawn from across the map. In Geneva, Gerhart Riegner would attempt to raise the alarm in western governments and the public in the second half of 1942 about the scope of the "Final Solution."[25] Yet as we have seen, his colleague and **Jewish Agency** representative **Richard Lichtheim** had already developed an exceptionally good sense of the direction in which the seemingly random deportations and violence of 1941 might be headed. Lichtheim's foresight was no doubt sharpened by his experiences while posted in Turkey during World War I as the Armenian genocide was unleashed.[26] Though skeptical about the efficacy of any outside intervention, Lichtheim's was an early voice calling for western statesmen to mount an outcry and express their solidarity with the Jews living under oppression.

---

24. The meaning of this phrase is not clear. It is possible that the author is construing the slaves as "blacks" and that the scene of slavery in Egypt refers to the story of Israelites recounted in Exodus.

25. See Laqueur, *The Terrible Secret*; Richard Breitman and Walter Laqueur, *Breaking the Silence* (New York: Simon and Schuster, 1986).

26. See Alexandra Garbarini, with Emil Kerenji, Jan Lambertz, and Avinoam Patt, *Jewish Responses to Persecution,* vol. 2: *1938–1940* (Lanham, MD: AltaMira Press in association with the USHMM, 2011), 213.

DOCUMENT 12-6: Letter from Richard Lichtheim, Jewish Agency-Geneva, to Joseph Linton, Jewish Agency-London, November 10, 1941, CZA RG L22, file 149.[27]

Dear Linton,

I am enclosing copy of the cable which I have sent on 8.11.[1941] to Dr. Weizmann. I wish to add some remarks which [I hope you will] kindly convey to Dr. Weizmann and the members of the Executive.

1. The ultimate fate of the Jews now expelled or to be expelled from Germany, Austria and the "Protectorate" (their total number is about 250,000) cannot yet be foreseen because we don't know yet where and how they will be housed: if in the Ghetti [*sic*] of Poland or in special camps or barracks. It may be that in the end their position will be the same as that of the majority of the Polish Jews under German domination: starvation by cold, hunger, filth, ill-treatment and epidemics, with a minority of the younger and stronger surviving. They will probably become incorporated in the system of slave-labour specially elaborated for the Jews in Eastern Europe. But during the transition-period the now expelled German Jews will probably be even worse off than the Jews already living in Poland because they are "newcomers" to the starved and overcrowded Ghetti, they don't know the country and the language and must try to find some place where they can squeeze in.

I also got some special information saying that at least part of them will not be distributed among the Jewish communities in the Polish Ghetti but will be sent farther off to the east, probably to the town of Minsk (which of course lies in ruins).[28] You may easily imagine what that means for towns-people with their women and children, arriving there without money, without food-reserves, without beddings—and this while the Russian winter sets in. It is murder combined with torture.

[. . . ; descriptions of deportations from Germany, western media coverage, and public reactions in Switzerland follow]

---

27. Facsimile (without the enclosures mentioned by Lichtheim) printed in *Archives of the Holocaust: An International Collection of Selected Documents*, ed. Henry Friedlander and Sybil Milton (New York, London: Garland Publishing, 1990), 4:34–37.

28. See Hersh Smolar, *The Minsk Ghetto: Soviet-Jewish Partisans against the Nazis* (New York: Holocaust Library, 1989); Barbara Epstein, *The Minsk Ghetto, 1941–1943: Jewish Resistance and Soviet Internationalism* (Berkeley: University of California Press, 2008), 77–80. Richard Lichtheim is referring to the destruction of Minsk when the German army invaded during the last week of June 1941.

3. I have also mentioned in my cable [to Weizmann] the terrible situation in <u>Croatia</u> and <u>Old-Serbia</u> where things are even worse than in Germany and Poland. I could have mentioned also <u>Slovakia</u> where after a certain lull the expropriation and persecution is again in full swing.

<u>Roumania</u> where many thousands have been tortured and murdered first by the Iron Guards and now by the occupying troops in the reconquered territories while most of the Jewish property has been confiscated.

There are also forebodings of new persecutions in <u>France</u>. After all the "legal" measures against the Jews in unoccupied France and the usual vexations[,] arrests and imprisonments in concentration-camps of many thousands of Jews in occupied France, there seems to be something "bigger" in preparation. You are aware that the shooting of the second half of the French hostages has been avoided—but the Jews will have to pay for that![29]

4. Now I wish to draw your attention to the proposal contained in my cable to Dr. Weizmann that the great democracies should make their voice heard in connection with the latest brutalities committed against the Jews—as was the case when the French hostages were shot.

I know very well that that is a different story: The Germans have spared one hundred Frenchmen to make it easier for Darlan.[30] They are much less interested to spare 100 or 100,000 Jews because there is no Jewish Darlan. Nevertheless I feel that the responsible statesmen of the democracies should not—as they have done hitherto—avoid the issue, whatever their motives may be.

---

29. A hundred Frenchmen were executed in late October in a "hundred-for-one" reprisal measure after the killing of two German officers in Nantes and Bordeaux. An additional one hundred hostages were slated for execution but received a temporary reprieve. See "54 More French Killed by Nazis," *New York Times*, October 25, 1941, 1, 4; "Germans Extend French Reprieve," *New York Times*, October 28, 1941, 10.

30. François Darlan (1881–1942) became one of the leading officials in the **Vichy** regime after a career as a naval officer and commander of the French fleet. At the time this letter was written, he served as prime minister and the designated successor to Pétain, minister of foreign affairs, and minister of the interior. A resistance group activist assassinated him in Algiers in December 1942. According to Michael R. Marrus and Robert O. Paxton, *Vichy France and the Jews* (New York: Basic Books, 1981), 225, 226, the taking of hostages in France "provided a dress rehearsal for the massive roundups, internments, and deportations that were soon to follow," the former initiated by the Wehrmacht, the latter by **Himmler**'s police apparatus.

It is a curious thing that President Roosevelt never mentioned the Jews whenever he spoke of the oppressed nations.[31] The Governments of the democracies may have been led to believe that there would be still more terrible persecutions if they mentioned the Jews in their speeches. I think this to be a mistake. Events have shown that the Jews could not have suffered more than they have suffered if the statesmen of the democracies would have said the word.

There may be another motive: to avoid the impression that this war has anything to do with the Jews. This also is a mistake. In spite of these hush-hush tactics President Roosevelt is constantly accused by Lindbergh and his followers of waging war in the interest of the Jews, and by the Germans of being himself a Jew etc.[32] (I enclose some cuttings from German Newspapers which will show you how it is done.)—I venture to say that the studied silence of the democracies—far from making it easier for the Jews—has made it easier for the appeasers and the antisemites everywhere and especially for the Germans to pretend that this is a "Jewish war" and to take their revenge on the Jews.

Great Britain and America should say: "We know all about it and we and our people are not to be taken in by such clumsy propaganda. Jews are Jews—they are Hitler's victims and therefore perfectly justified in standing up against him. We are neither Jews nor do we wage war for the Jews—we are battling for mankind against the enemy of mankind."

Such language would silence thousands of antisemites within the democracies, in the neutral countries, in France (where even now much evil could be averted by strong pressure from America)—and would perhaps even make it more difficult for the Germans. But the great silence in official quarters on everything Jewish has encouraged antisemites

---

31. Lichtheim might be referring to statements President Roosevelt and British Prime Minister Churchill had issued on October 25, 1941, on German responsibility for war crimes. While Roosevelt accused the Germans of a "practice of executing scores of innocent hostages in reprisal for isolated attacks," Churchill saw the "cold-blooded executions of innocent people" as a "foretaste of what Hitler would inflict upon the British and American peoples if only he could get the power"; quoted from *Polish Fortnightly Review*, July 1, 1942, 7.

32. Charles Lindbergh (1902–1974), an American hero for his feats as an aviator, also had strong ties to Germany and since the late 1930s was a leading figure in promoting U.S. neutrality in the war. See Jean Edward Smith, *FDR* (New York: Random House, 2007), 437, 440. On the Roosevelt-Lindbergh relationship and Lindbergh's declining popularity during the war, see Scott A. Berg, *Lindbergh* (New York: J. P. Putnam's, 1998).

everywhere to spread the belief that "there is something in it." "The Jews are behind the scenes pulling the wires."

There have been of late some utterances of exiled Governments which are certainly to the good and de Gaulles cable to Stephen Wise has also been useful.[33] The B.B.C. has lately taken up the theme, has given the relevant news and has broadcast a good and rigorous speech by "the man in the street." But this is not enough. The "man in the street" is alright—but what about the gentlemen on the top? We would like to hear some other voices, promising restoration of rights, rejecting recognition of robbing and plundering by state-decrees, condemning the atrocities and warning the perpetrators of such deeds that they will be held responsible. In some cases (Roumania, Hungary, Slovakia, Croatia, Vichy), such a warning might have had and may still have a deterrent effect: It is of course much more difficult in the case of Germany but even there some persons or circles might be influenced by such warnings.

Apart from the practical effect of such a warning we have also to consider that the Jews are entitled to and are waiting for such a word of sympathy and consolation. We are witnessing the most terrible persecution of the Jews which has ever happened in Europe, overshadowing by its cruelty and extent even the massacres of the Armenians during the last war which at that time provoked a storm of protest in England and America. Jews in the few remaining neutral countries and also the sufferers themselves in Germany and in the occupied countries would get at least some moral satisfaction, and certain smaller states and many millions of people would thus be reminded that moral values still exist and that they include and make imperative the condemning of this persecution of the Jews.

Yours sincerely

R. Lichtheim
GENEVA OFFICE

Like Geneva, London offered a unique vantage point and opportunities to shape awareness among political elites and media in the West. This process of

---

33. On October 4, 1941, Free France General Charles de Gaulle sent a message to Rabbi Dr. **Stephen S. Wise**, president of the World Jewish Congress, to mark the 150th anniversary of the extension of civic rights to Jews in France. He used the occasion to denounce the antisemitic legislation of the Vichy regime as unconstitutional and illegal, and to express his determination to restore equal rights for all citizens. See USHMMA, RG 43.006M (Selected Records from the Ministère des affaires étrangères, 1939–1945), reel 26, frames 117–18.

drawing attention to the plight of millions of Jews was, however, far from clear-cut, partly as a result of competing interests, partly due to Jewish organizations' continuing difficulties in seeing a linear progression in German anti-Jewish policy from persecution to mass murder. Furthermore, these organizations had doubts about the degree to which stressing the exceptional suffering of Jews was compatible with the broader "win-the-war" strategy pursued by Allied governments. We can catch a glimpse of this predicament and the compromises it produced from the following draft report by officials of the **Board of Deputies of British Jews** and the Anglo-Jewish Association. It was written in preparation for an appeal to the Polish government-in-exile on January 12, 1942, during the inter-Allied conference held the next day to discuss German atrocities and matters of potential postwar relevance. As was shown in chapter 7, British Jewish representatives did send an appeal letter to Władysław Sikorski,[34] but for unknown reasons the following report was never submitted to its intended recipients. The differences in how these two documents depict the German threat to Europe's Jews are striking. While the appeal letter stresses that its author—the Board's Joint Foreign Committee—"had no desire to differentiate between the sufferings and brutalities inflicted by the Nazis on Jews and non-Jews," the original version of the draft report saw evidence of "a vicious plan of total physical and moral destruction" specifically targeting Jews. However, internal revisions ran their course (as seen in document 12-7), and the wording that described the Germans' goal was changed from "the ruin of the Jewish population" to a far more benign descriptor: "maltreatment."

DOCUMENT 12-7: **Draft report by the Joint Foreign Committee of the Board of Deputies of British Jews and the Anglo-Jewish Association regarding "German Atrocities on Jews," January 10/11, 1942,[35] USHMMA RG 59.023M (Board of Deputies of British Jews), reel 24, frames 750–54.**

GERMAN ATROCITIES ON JEWS

~~On behalf of the Joint Foreign Committee of the BOARD OF DEPU-
TIES OF BRITISH JEWS and of the ANGLO-JEWISH ASSOCIA-
TION we wish to bring to the notice of the Allied Governments the fol-~~

---

34. See document 7-13.

35. Both drafts were typed; deletions and revisions in handwriting (additions marked here by italics, deletions by strikethrough). At the top of the document added in handwriting "Jan 10 1942 corrected on Jan 11th." The document ends after the paragraph numbered "7") without providing specific case examples.

~~lowing facts concerning atrocities committed by the Nazis and the German Army on the Jewish population in the several war-zones during the present war.~~

1. ~~Starting~~ *Beginning* in March 1939 from the German-Czecho-slovak frontier the attacking German armies moved across the whole area of Bohemia, Moravia, Poland, Belgium, Holland, France, Estonia, Latvia, Lithuania, White Russia (Bielorussia), the Ukraine, Yugoslavia and Greece. Helping them and largely under their command the Rumanian Armies reoccupied Bessarabia and the South of the Ukraine beyond the borders of the province of Kherson which includes the large city of Odessa. Within this area the Jewish population ~~counted~~ *numbered* more than eight million souls.

2. Ever since the advent of Hitlerism in Germany, the Nazi authorities openly proclaimed that at the first opportunity they would do their utmost to destroy the Jewish population in Europe and this the Nazis ~~carried~~ *are carrying* out with the greatest deliberation.

3. The various Allied Governments—the Polish, the Czechoslovak, the Belgian, the Dutch, the Greek, the Yugoslav and the Russian will no doubt supply data on the terrifi~~c~~*ble* and wanton destruction wrought by the invading German armies on the thousands of towns of these counties and on the atrocities perpetrated upon their inhabitants [,] among whom the Jews, especially in Poland, Lithuania, Bessarabia and the Ukraine, formed a considerable proportion. The list of these cities in which well established Jewish communities with many historic~~al~~ buildings, libraries and schools, factories, workshops and commercial concerns, communities numbering many scores of thousands of people and which have now become utterly devastated and ruined includes Warsaw, Lwow, Lodz, Lublin, Cracow, Bialystok, Brest, Grodno, Minsk, Pinsk, Kovno, Wilna, ~~D~~*B*obruisk, Borisov, Kieff [Kiev], Odessa, Kishinev, Rovna [Rovno], Uman, Bielaya, Tserkov [*sic*][36]

---

36. This was most likely a reference to Belaja Cerkov in Ukraine, where units of the Wehrmacht and **Einsatzgruppe** C had murdered the local Jews, adults and children, in August 1941; see Christopher R. Browning with contributions by Jürgen Matthäus, *The Origins of the Final Solution: The Evolution of Nazi Jewish Policy, September 1939–March 1942* (Lincoln and Jerusalem: University of Nebraska Press and Yad Vashem, 2004), 291.

and hundreds of others less known to the general public. The *Jewish* population *after innumerable murders of individuals* was either driven out or forcibly segregated into walled ghettoes, merciless execution or torture being inflicted on everyone who attempt~~s~~ed to escape from them.

4.   THE JOINT FOREIGN COMMITTEE has in its possession trustworthy material which testifies *to* the fact that the ~~ruin~~ *mal-treatment* of the Jewish population ~~even to a greater degree than that of the non-Jewish population~~ was ~~accompanied~~ *marked* by unspeakable outrages and massacres.

Facts show that these outrages and atrocities were not only crimes of individual soldiers and officers, but were acts encouraged and even ordered by the higher commanders and the Gestapo who have deliberately fostered among the soldiers and the younger generation of the German people the most brutal ~~instincts of~~ *and* insatiable hatred against the Jews, who ~~are~~ *have* continually *been* represented to them as an inferior and "harmful" race to be destroyed. In all the towns mentioned ~~herein~~ (as indeed everywhere) the Nazis and the German soldiers and officers ~~robbed the Jewish population of its property, of its businesses, removed Jews from the professions, established a regime of forced labour, locked up more than a million in ghettoes, scores of thousands in concentration camps,~~ *have slaughtered men, women and children inflicting every imaginable indignity and humiliation upon their victims before death. They have* restricted the distribution of food to the level of physical starvation, ~~which~~ *and this* has brought in its wake epidemics and the most appalling ~~level~~ *increase* of mortality. All these atrocities are a means for carrying into effect a vicious plan of total physical *and moral* destruction ~~and moral crushing~~, and the details of execution are in fullest keeping with the deliberated and calculated brutality of the whole plan.

5.   Orders found on German officers and eventually published by the Soviet Army prove that German officers and soldiers were encouraged to behave ~~so~~ as if they ~~had a~~ *looked to conquest as a means of advancing their own* personal and material interest ~~in the conquest~~ and no objection was raised by the Commanders to their subordinates plundering the houses and shops of occupied towns or robbing any person of ~~their~~ *any* personal belongings,

including money, watches, rings, pictures, furniture, linen, books or ~~any~~ other valuable*s* and sending ~~it~~ *them* 'home' to their own families in Germany.

6. In many instances, Jews were compelled to beat one another in public, to destroy Christian churches, to pull down *historical and natural* monuments or to participate in dancing processions, which scenes were filmed to serve as anti-Jewish propaganda. There is evidence of hundreds of cases of young Jewish women having been forcibly placed into army brothels or raped publicly or in the presence of members of their families.

7. ~~Jewish members of the Polish Seym and Senators as well as prominent members of the Legal profession have collected evidence on some of the atrocities perpetrated by the Nazis and the German Army. Various Governments have already published some of the documents at their disposal on the subject of German atrocities and from this evidence we quote the following~~ instances ~~extracts.~~[37]

Awareness of the scope of the "Final Solution" grew among Jewish activists and organizations, but public opinion in the West lagged far behind the speed of Germany's destructive policies. Despite an increase in atrocity reports from the East, popular perceptions did not focus on the issue as eyewitness accounts and other information on the fate of Jews became diffused in an ocean of war-related news. The ability to connect the dots required a level of knowledge that few individual Jews possessed. But where it did exist, surviving documentation suggests that action in the form of warnings followed quickly. In early December 1941, the first mass killing site that used gas for murdering Jews and others had become operational in **Chełmno**, some fifty miles west of Łódź in the **Warthegau**. Between January and May 1942, a small commando of **Security Police** and **SD** murdered roughly fifty thousand people—mostly Jews from Łódź, but also from other towns in the region as well as gypsies deported there from Austria—in a van designed to pump the motor's exhaust fumes into the hermetically sealed cargo compartment. The German SS and policemen forced a small group of laborers to unload the van and bury the corpses. A few of these workers, destined to be killed, managed to escape and expose as a lie the German claim (made in Łódź) that those leaving the ghetto were sent to a labor camp. As soon as Jews in the

---

37. "Seym" refers to the Polish parliament [*Sejm*]. The last word was revised before the entire paragraph was deleted. The document ends here.

area learned about what was happening, they tried to spread the word in order to warn those in danger and to alert others who might be affected later. The following document pertains to events in the regions of Koło (German: Wartbrücken) and Konin in the Warthegau in late 1941 and early 1942. It was among the first accounts of the murder in Chełmno to reach Warsaw.[38]

DOCUMENT 12-8: Uszer Taube,[39] "Protocol about the events in the Koło region," Warsaw, after January 1942, USHMMA RG 15.079M (ŻIH Ring. I/1057) (translated from Yiddish).

[. . .] At the beginning of November, 1941, a medical examination was conducted by district doctors throughout the Koło District of all Jewish men from 14 to 60 years of age and of Jewish women from 14 to 50 years of age. Insofar as a similar examination took place at the start of summer—for labor camp purposes—one must assume that the purpose of the second examination was completely different. Two weeks later, a head tax of four marks was imposed upon all Jews from the entire district who were incapable of working, and two days later a head tax was imposed upon the rest of the population as well. With the exception of Kłodawa, where the

---

38. See Patrick Montague, *Chełmno and the Holocaust: The History of Hitler's First Death Camp* (Chapel Hill: University of North Carolina Press, 2012); Shmuel Krakowski, *Chełmno: A Small Village in Europe* (Jerusalem, Yad Vashem, 2009). For other early accounts on the gassings in Chełmno, see Isaiah Trunk, *Łódź Ghetto: A History*, ed. Robert Moses Shapiro (Bloomington: Indiana University Press in association with the USHMM, 2006), l–li, 322; Krakowski, *Chełmno*, 68–78; Laqueur, *The Terrible Secret*, 128–31; Esther Farbstein, *Hidden in Thunder: Perspectives on Faith, Halachah and Leadership during the Holocaust*, vol. 1 (Jerusalem: Mossad Harav Kook, 2007), 34–36; Ruta Sakowska, *Archiwum Ringelbluma. Listy o Zagładzie*, vol. 1 (Warsaw: Wydawnictwo naukowe PWN, 1997), 3–6; Andrea Löw, *Juden im Getto Litzmannstadt* (Göttingen: Wallstein Verlag, 2006), 282–87.

39. Uszer Taube and his brothers Binem and Szymon Jozef lived with their parents and a relative, Fela Rybska, in Kłodawa before the war. When, in January 1942, the Nazis deported the local Jews to their deaths at Chełmno, Binem, Szymon Josef, and Fela were sent to forced labor camps; Uszer and his wife, Balcia, managed to escape from Kłodawa to nearby Krośniewice with their daughter, Edzia. From there they eventually made their way to the Warsaw ghetto. During the summer deportations of 1942, Uszer and Balcia were able to save themselves by working in a brush-manufacturing shop, but Edzia died around this time. The parents of the Taube brothers were killed in Chełmno after the Nazi liquidation of Kłodawa. Ruta Sakowska, ed., *Archiwum Ringelbluma: Konspiracyjne Archiwum Getta Warszawy* (Warsaw: Wydawnictwo Naukowe PWN, 1997), 1, 33, 234, 243, 254. The authors were unable to ascertain the fates of Uszer Taube, his brothers, or people mentioned in this document unless subsequently identified.

kehillah commissar [head of the Judenrat], not wanting to provoke any consternation, covered the entire amount of the tax from the kehillah treasury and did not publicize this among the residents, the residents of the other towns in the Koło District were exactly informed about both the imposition of the head tax and the consequences it could have. A special messenger from Kłodawa—Golde Tabaczyńska—traveled to Koło to gain information on the expulsion, and, in fact, the Koło Judenrat was informed on that same day of its obligation to implement the head tax. In Koło, a certain Hauptsturmführer from the SS told the mayor of Bugitten [Bugaj] that by December 15, 1941, no Jews would be left in the entire Koło District. They all would be resettled in newly occupied areas.

On Friday, December 5, at 11 in the morning, 2 SS men from Poznań drove up in front of the *Landratur* [district administration] in Koło and half an hour later they seized 30 healthy Jewish men off the street and immediately took them away in automobiles. At 2 o'clock, the systematic expulsion began. It was carried out thusly: using population records from city hall in alphabetical order, the SS men and the gendarmerie went from house to house and took out the Jews by families and put them in the beys midrash [study hall]. They remained there until Monday morning. Food was provided by the kehillah. Although the Jews were desperate, their blackest thoughts were tied to the prospect of expulsion. On the morning of Sunday, December 7, a truck arrived and up to 50 people from Koło were loaded into it. I was told of the happenings in Koło by a resident of Bugaj by the name of Podkhlebnik who happened to be in Koło that day and subsequently was freed thanks to his certification.[40] People and baggage were loaded separately. Severely ill individuals were placed on bed sheets and hoisted onto the automobiles with the help of several people. On Thursday, December 11, the last transport left, and along with it the chairman of the Jewish kehillah. People knew that they were being taken to "Chełmno," a village between Koło and Dąbie (called Kulmhof in German). We in Kłodawa knew about this due to the following: the commissariat administrator from "United Aid Actions in Toningen," Gerardus Melchior, a Baltic German who had a reputation for being a friend of the Jews, instructed the kehillah commissar, who worked for him at his business, to go to Koło and find out where the Jews were being sent. From Koło he brought the news that Jews were being sent to Chełmno, where a Jewish village was being established in which all the

---

40. A relative of Mordechaï (Michal) Podchlebnik; see note 43 below.

Jews from the Koło District would live out their days. On that day there was rejoicing in the town. The Zagórów tragedy was still fresh for everyone, and in this case, having a safe haven (the Jewish village Chełmno), they wanted as quickly as possible to be done with the expulsion already and settle in to the new residences.

On Monday, December 14,[41] the deportation action of the Dąbie Jews (around 900 souls) was carried out. They were all confined in the church. Insofar as, according to the population records, a considerable number of Jews were absent, everyone being held in the church was let go after one day so that on December 17, i.e., Thursday, the action could be carried out again. And this time, almost all the Jews were rounded up. From the church, they were sent in automobiles to Chełmno, just as in Koło.

In the meantime, the Jews from the remaining settlements did everything they could to find out what was happening with the Jews who had been taken away to Chełmno. We were unsettled by the fact that no food had been taken in that direction. Through Polish messengers we learned that the Jews were only at the Chełmno palace, but were not present in the village itself.

The palace is guarded by SS men, and the neighboring forest is also guarded by SS men. The messengers did not see that the Jews could leave the palace and in no way was it possible for so many Jews to live in one building (the palace). Our shtetl Kłodawa continually sent messengers to the palace to learn the fate of the Jews. No one was able to get close to the palace, but, based on conversations with Polish peasants from Chełmno, it seemed that the Jews there were being killed. Some Polish peasants from Chełmno came to us personally to convey this information. They did this in great fear, guarding against outsiders. According to them, the killing was taking place in the following manner: a specially constructed van [*oyto*] would come to the palace several times a day and Jews are hurled into it. Wails, cries and screams can be heard from the van. From there, the van departs for the neighboring forest called Lodrutsk.

When the kehillah commissar conveyed this information to the German mayor Plev, he became very agitated and threatened with death the Polish peasants who spread horror propaganda [*groyl-propagande*]. He calmed him, [insisting] that Chełmno is only a transit camp. The healthy are sent to labor camps and the sick are transported to Łódź.

---

41. The Germans carried out the deportation of Jews from Dąbie on December 14, 1941, but it was a Sunday, and not, as Taube has it, a Monday. See Evelyn Zegenhagen, "Dąbie nad Nerem," in *The USHMM Encyclopedia of Camps and Ghettos*, 2:50–51.

On Friday, January 2, the Kłodawa gendarmerie, using the population records of the Jews, took 30 solid, healthy men and detained them for an entire day in the gendarmerie. In the evening, a van arrived with field gendarmes (people called them white pelts because they dressed in pelts) and took away the 30 men. They drove off in the direction of Chełmno. This fact made a colossal impression in the town and caused great alarm. On the evening of Sunday, January 4, the same van came again and demanded another 20 men from the gendarmerie. They had to make do with 16 weak, sick, older men because the others were hiding. It must be mentioned that at the same time in Grabów and at the Kłodawa train station groups of Gypsies were seen passing through in automobiles from the direction of Łódź. On Friday, January 9, 1942, at 2 o'clock in the morning, the Kłodawa gendarmerie, with the help of the SA [*sic*], confined the entire Jewish population in the church. That same evening, some of the Kłodawa Jews had become aware of the following facts, which gave them much to think about: 1.) Two Jewish tailors, Hersh Nosek and Avraham Mishkovski, who worked in the village Zawadki for the commandant of the local SA, witnessed how a gendarme from Kłodawa came to the commandant with the request that he and his unit appear in Kłodawa at 2 o'clock in the morning. He did not know why had been ordered to appear in Kłodawa. 2.) Busse, a former gendarme, while in the company of the Kłodawa Jew Yitzhak Leyzer, related that the expulsion of all the Kłodawa Jews was being prepared for that night. At the last moment (the curfew for Jews was 8 in the evening), some 40 men, women, and children fled. On Friday, January 10, automobiles arrived, and in the course of that Friday 750 people were taken in groups of 50 to Chełmno. The rest, about 250 people, were taken away on Monday morning. At the last moment, Gerardius Melchior, through his personal intervention with the Gauleiter Greiser in Poznań,[42] saved two families who were employed by him: Yakov Vanroykh and his family and his brother-in-law Perets Kohn and his family. That same Monday, January 12, the expulsion of Izbica and Bugitten took place and lasted until Wednesday. There, too, healthy men had previously been deported, as was the case with us.

On Sunday, January 18, and Monday, January 19, three young people, escapees from Chełmno, came separately to Grabów, namely: Viner and Rui from Izbica and Mekhl Podkhlebnik (a relative of the Podkhlebnik

---

42. On Greiser, see Catherine Epstein, *Model Nazi: Arthur Greiser and the Occupation of Western Poland* (Oxford: Oxford University Press, 2010).

mentioned earlier) from Bugaj.[43] They were among the healthy who were typically seized earlier.

They related the following events: the strongest ones in each town (30 men) are taken to the neighboring forest to dig large graves, wide from behind and narrow from above. They were taken to work before dawn, when it was still dark, and they were brought back to the palace when it was already dark [again]. Gold and documents were taken from the Jews who were brought into the palace. One of the SS officers holds a speech for each fresh group in which he announces to them that, since they are being sent to the ghetto, they have to undergo delousing. For the purported delousing the men are undressed down to their underwear and the women to their nightshirts, and soon after they are taken down into a cold cellar. Screams, shrieks, and moans were continually heard from the cold cellar owing to blows as well as the cold. A team of 150 SS men was active in the palace. A specially constructed van comes to the cellar which fits exactly into the door frame of the cellar. Fifty people are hounded into the van in a very violent way, then the van is hermetically sealed and the driver presses a button. The automobile begins to make a loud noise and at the same time terrible wails and cries of Sh'ma Yisroel[44] are heard from the van. The van stands like this for 15 minutes and then departs with its cargo for the forest. There, too, it stands for about 15 minutes, after which it unloads 50 dead bodies, which look wonderfully beautiful, and the faces are light and radiant.

---

43. Szlamek Winer [Wiener] (of Zamość?), Abram Roj of Izbica, and Mordechaï (Mekhl, also Michał) Podchlebnik (b. 1907) apparently escaped from Chełmo on January 18, 1942. See Robert Moses Shapiro and Tadeusz Epsztein, *The Warsaw Ghetto: Oyneg Shabes-Ringelblum Archive. Catalog and Guide* (Bloomington: Indiana University Press, 2009), 225, 314, 315. After having escaped Chełmno, Mordechaï Podchlebnik managed to survive the war and gave testimony in Poland in June 1945 and at the Eichmann trial in Jerusalem in 1961. He believed that Winer may have escaped but died in the Zamość region in 1944; see Łucja Pawlicka-Nowak, ed., *Chełmno Witnesses Speak* (Łódź: The Council for the Protection of Memory of Combat and Martyrdom in Warsaw and the District Museum in Konin, 2004), 119–24. In 1985, Podchlebnik was interviewed by Claude Lanzmann, who used parts of Podchlebnik's testimony for his film *Shoah*. The outtakes of the interview are available for research at the USHMM Steven Spielberg Film and Video Archive RG 60.5026, Tape 3294–97, and online at http://resources.ushmm.org/film/display/detail.php?file_num=5088 (accessed July 23, 2012).

44. Sh'ma Israel (usually referred to as Sh'ma) are the first two words of the Jewish prayer that takes an important place in daily morning and evening prayer services. The name of the prayer comes from Deuteronomy 6:4: "Hear, O Israel: the Lord is our God, the Lord is one."

The bodies are stiff. The people are laid 5 to a layer in the graves—lime is poured over each layer. In the course of a day, 750 people are killed. If one of the gravediggers pauses because he is exhausted from working, he is shot and [sometimes] even thrown into the grave while still alive. From January 2–10, gravediggers from Kłodawa buried 3,300 gypsies. After burying the gypsies, many of the Jewish gravediggers were shot on the grounds that the gypsies were poisonous and they could spread the poison to the palace. Due to the shortness of the day, only 500 Jews from Koło were killed each day, but later the total was increased to 750 per day. If there were not 50 souls on the last transport of the day, then those remaining were killed in another savage way; for example: with the help of boards with nails hewn into them, rifle stocks, and so forth. A fact: among seven Jews remaining in the cellar, a father, the merchant Kshevatski, who had been beaten and who believed that the Germans would beat him to death the next time they would come, asked his 28-year-old son Yehuda to hang him. He did not want to give the Germans the satisfaction [of killing him]. The son hanged his father after the others gave him their word that they would do the same with him.

While working, the gravediggers were not allowed to display the least agitation; for a wink of the eye, they would be immediately shot and flung into the grave. Eyzen from Kłodawa, a forced gravedigger, buried his wife, his sisters-in-law, and his parents-in-law. Another forced gravedigger, Getsl Tshonstkovski, a solid Jew, buried his one and only son, a 15-year-old. The three forced gravediggers, Viner, Rui, and Mekhl Podkhmelnik[45] escaped certain death under the following circumstances: Mekhl Podkhmelnik was sent with five other Jews into a second cellar to fetch straw. He squeezed through a small window in the cellar, though he severely wounded himself in the process. He went into the open barn of a German farmer and hid in the hay. A search was then conducted, but unsuccessful. Knowing the roads well, he successfully escaped to Grabów, which he reached on Friday, January 17. The next morning, Viner and Rui arrived, the former escaping in the morning and the latter in the evening by tearing up the small celluloid window of the automobile that was taking them to work. They were aided by their fellow gravediggers, who were riding along with them.

---

45. In this paragraph, the surname is spelled consistently "Podkhmelnik," whereas above it is spelled "Podkhlebnik." It is clearly the same person, namely Mordechaï Podchlebnik.

Every one of the young people who reached us separately told the same story about the terrible act of extermination carried out by the German authorities against the Jewish population of Koło District.

The meticulous detail of this report and others like it raises questions: Were those writing convinced that such precision would increase the credibility of the fantastic reportage? Would the exhaustive facts within these reports trigger action on the part of readers, or instead drown them in despair? And what were the expectations of the **Oyneg Shabes** archivists in Warsaw in collecting these testimonies, translating them (apparently in some cases also into German), and helping circulate them?[46] Taube's and other accounts seem to have become known in the Łódź ghetto much later than in Warsaw, and it is not clear at what point **Jewish Council** head **Mordechai Chaim Rumkowski** learned about the true function of Chełmno.[47]

What would reports from the death camps have conveyed to Jews in danger of being drawn into the emerging annihilation machinery? Much depended on the conditions and perceptions on the receiving end as well as on the available means of communication. As historian David Silberklang has stated, people threatened with deportation often sent a flurry of messages to relatives and friends, via clandestine as well as official channels. They made telephone calls, used the German-censored mail service, and employed secret couriers.[48] Many of these people used coded language that included biblical references and Hebrew phrases to convey their sense of imminent mortal danger not only to themselves, but also to other Jewish communities that might be affected next and whom they hoped would be able to read between the lines. If those documents were copied for Onyeg Shabes or another clandestine archive, a second layer of encrypting was added whenever the chronicler decided to omit incriminating information, such as the name of the letter's author or the addressee.

As we can see from the following letter from Włodawa recorded in the Warsaw ghetto, the ability to communicate what was happening found its limits not only in the need to conceal details but also in the utterly unimaginable nature of the actual events. Włodawa was located in the

---

46. See Krakowski, *Chełmno*, 76–78.

47. See Farbstein, *Hidden in Thunder*, 28–41; Trunk, *Lodz Ghetto*, li, 422–23; Löw, *Juden im Getto Litzmannstadt*, 285–86.

48. David Silberklang, "Die Juden und die ersten Deportationen aus dem Distrikt Lublin," in *"Aktion Reinhard." Der Völkermord an den Juden im Generalgouvernement 1941–1944*, ed. Bogdan Musial (Osnabrück: Fibre Verlag, 2004) 156–57.

Generalgouvernement's Lublin district, up to the end of 1941 the destination of more than sixty thousand Jews forcibly removed from other areas. Mass deportations from Lublin to the **Bełżec** death camp began in mid-March 1942. Until the end of April, more than forty-four thousand Jews had been murdered there. At the same time, the Germans opened another death camp in **Sobibór**, where 1,300 Jews from Włodawa were deported to in the second half of May, together with thousands of other Jews from the Lublin district, the **Protectorate**, Slovakia, and the Reich. In May or June, construction began on what would become the largest death camp in the Generalgouvernement, **Treblinka**. Altogether, these "actions"—masquerading in German propaganda as "resettlements" for labor "in the East"—killed an estimated 140,000 men, women, and children from mid-March to May 1942.[49]

Jews in Włodawa were aware of the connection between German "actions" in different regions and tried to warn relatives in Warsaw, some 140 miles away, about what they feared would ultimately happen to them. The letter's unknown author used seemingly banal phrases as synonyms for danger, perhaps in response to a query from Warsaw as to what to do in the face of impending disaster ("seeing a doctor") and allusions to religious texts with frequent abbreviations in the attempt to make the missive look inconspicuous in case it was intercepted. Not all code elements of the text can be deciphered; as in **Ruth Goldbarth**'s letters from Warsaw,[50] "uncle" apparently stands for Germans; his "renting an apartment near you" seems to refer to the imminent completion of the Treblinka death camp, while his plan to "have a wedding near you soon" points to a German "action" about to happen and targeting "all the brethren children of Israel" even beyond Warsaw. But we do not know whether "Shlomo Velvl" was a deceased person acquainted with the letter's addressees or stood for something else. While the writer on the face of it offers no clear advice about what to do, the indirect reference to Psalm 91, with its expression of the hope "to be hidden by God," comes close to a call for going into hiding.

---

49. Janina Kiełboń, "Judendeportationen in den Distrikt Lublin," in *"Aktion Reinhard,"* Musial, 139. For an in-depth study of the region during the Holocaust, see Bogdan Musial, *Deutsche Zivilverwaltung und Judenverfolgung im Generalgouvernement. Eine Fallstudie zum Distrikt Lublin 1939–1944* (Wiesbaden: Harassowitz, 1999).

50. See document 2-9.

DOCUMENT 12-9: **Letter from an unidentified Jew, Włodawa, Lublin district, Generalgouvernement, to relatives in Warsaw, June 1, 1942, USHMMA RG 15.079M (ŻIH Ring. I/563) (translated from Yiddish).**

We are, bless God, healthy.[51]

We have no suggestion to offer about what to do with regard to seeing a doctor. We ourselves are in a quandary—even though we have already decided to see one. This is only because the uncle, Heaven protect us, wants to have a celebration for his children near you as well, Heaven protect us.[52] This is why he is renting an apartment near you, indeed quite close. It is possible that you know nothing about it.

That is why I am writing you now, and why we are sending this [updated information][53] separately—so you are informed, and know that it is true. Also, so that you rent new apartments outside the city for all the brethren children of Israel.[54] He [the uncle] has already prepared new apartments for everybody—just as he has done near us. It is possible that you do not know this. That is why I am writing to you separately, so you do know. The uncle is out to expel people, in order to be together with Shlomo Velvl, may he rest in peace.[55]

We know for sure, that the uncle has now nearly completed the apartment near you. You should know about this. Perhaps you do have some suggestion. In any case, one should have the information: That the uncle wants, Heaven protect us, to have a wedding near you soon. He has already set up an apartment near you, quite close.

Think of it: To be near you in apartments with all the facilities—thereby together with Shlomo Velvl, may he rest in peace.

---

51. The writer uses the Hebrew abbreviation B"H, *borukh hashem*, literally, "blessed be God."

52. The writer uses the Hebrew abbreviation KH"V, *khas vekhalila*, that can be roughly translated as "God forbid," or "may God save me from [something]."

53. This translation is suggested by the context of the acronym (*Hay-Mem-Vav-Khaf-Zayin*), but the meaning remains unclear.

54. The writer uses the Hebrew acronym AHBN"I, probably *ahihem bnei Israel*, literally, "your brothers, the children of Israel."

55. The authors have been unable to find information about Shlomo Velvl, who might have been an early victim of German crimes in Włodawa. See Stephan Lehnstaedt, "Włodawa," in *The USHMM Encyclopedia of Camps and Ghettos*, 2:730–33. Alternatively, the name or its acronym might have been used to convey a hidden meaning only comprehensible to the letters' recipients.

When it comes to any ailment, the one good thing is to be hidden by God.[56]

Consider well, that we are a sacred people, for a sacrifice to God.[57]

We do not know what effect the letter had in the Warsaw ghetto. There, trains carrying Jews slated for murder began to leave for Treblinka on July 23, 1942, while the Jews of Włodawa were hit by further waves of deportations. The Germans shipped off the last remaining Jews from the town in late April 1943.[58]

As those within the territory under German control attempted to spread information about the new intensity of mass murder, exiled politicians and governments in London struggled to ascertain what the deportations meant. In March 1942, Arnošt (Ernst) Frischer, the only Jewish member of the Czechoslovakian government-in-exile led by President Edvard Beneš, arrived in London from Palestine.[59] By that time, his exiled government had accumulated in-depth data on German policies in occupied Europe, but—similar to Polish government circles—had not paid much attention to the plight of the Jews.[60] As one of the first steps in his attempt to alert the West about what happened to the Jews in his country, Frischer invited journalists from various newspapers to a press conference in London. The JTA reported:

DOCUMENT 12-10: "All Czech Jews Slated for Deportation to Poland, Jewish Deputy Declares," *Jewish Telegraphic Agency,* April 29, 1942.

LONDON, Apr. 28 (JTA)—

The fortress-town of Theresienstadt to which the Germans have deported thousands of Czech Jews, and which has been designated by

---

56. Reference (in Hebrew) to Psalm 91, which begins: "O you who dwell in the shelter of the Most High . . ." (Jewish Publication Society translation).

57. The last sentence refers to Exodus 12:10: "And ye shall let nothing of the [sacrificial lamb] remain until morning; but that what remaineth of it until morning ye shall burn."

58. Silberklang, "Die Juden und die ersten Deportationen aus dem Distrikt Lublin," 157–58; Musial, *Deutsche Zivilverwaltung,* 274–75.

59. See Jan Láníček, "Arnošt Frischer und seine Hilfe für Juden im besetzten Europa (1941–1945)," *Theresienstädter Studien und Dokumente* (2007), 11–91.

60. Breitman, *Official Secrets,* 95.

Nazi ruler Reinhard Heydrich as the place where all Czech Jews will ultimately be confined, is, nevertheless, only a transit camp for Czech Jews
who will eventually be deported to Poland, it was stated today by Ernst
Frischer, Jewish member of the Czechoslovakian State Council, addressing
a press conference here.

Frischer estimated that there are still 70,000 Jews in the Jewish quarters
of Prague and that Jewish populations still reside in the towns of Brno and
Brod in Southern Moravia. He declared that recent information reaching
official Czech circles from Slovakia indicates that the present mass deportations of Jews, which are being carried out by the Slovak authorities, are for
the purpose of concentrating all the Slovakian Jews in convenient assembly
points from which they can be shipped to a "reservation area which the Nazis
plan to establish for all of Europe's Jews."

The Jewish deputy expressed the opinion that a solution of the Jewish
problem in Europe is impossible in any single state, but must be based
on unified Jewish demands for equality in all of Europe and the world.
Frischer forecast that the difficulties of postwar economic rehabilitation of
millions of Jews will undoubtedly result in mass emigration to Palestine.
He stressed, however, that at the same time that Jewish groups demand
free and unrestricted immigration of Jews to Palestine, they must also
demand of the respective governments that those Jews who wish to return
to their countries of origin must be allowed to do so and must be granted
full civil rights.

Frischer was certainly right to present **Theresienstadt** as a way station,
yet what "deported to Poland" meant remained unclear to him. In contrast,
the following report from the **Bund** in Poland describes a far more intimate
knowledge of the killing sites and of the true meaning of "an unknown destination." The report draws on material from many sources, no doubt also from the
Oyneg Shabes archive and other documentation projects, to attest to mass murder in "all Polish territories" beyond the artificial German boundaries between
annexed and regions otherwise controlled by the Germans (German-annexed
Warthegau, Galicia, and other districts in the Generalgouvernement, and parts
of **Reichskommissariat Ostland**). Dispatched from Warsaw on May 21, 1942,
the report reached the Polish government-in-exile through Swedish intermedi-
ates less than two weeks later.

DOCUMENT 12-11: **"Report of the Bund Regarding the Persecution of the Jews,"** May 11, 1942, in Yehuda Bauer, **"When Did They Know?,"** *Midstream* 14 (April 1968): 54–55.[61]

From the day the Russo-German war broke out, the Germans embarked upon the physical extermination of the Jewish population of Polish lands, making use of the Ukrainians and Lithuanian Šauliai to carry out this task. It began in the summer months of 1941, above all in western Galicia. The following system was implemented everywhere: men from 14 to 60 years old were rounded up in a single location—a square or a cemetery—and there they were slaughtered or machine-gunned or killed with grenades. They had to dig their own graves. Children in orphanages, retirees in homes for the elderly, the ill in hospitals—they were all shot—women were killed on the street. In many cities, the Jews were deported in "an unknown direction" and killed in nearby forests. In Lwów 30,000 Jews were killed, in Stanisławów 15,000, in Tarnopol 5,000, in Złoczów 2,000, in Brzeżany 4,000 (there were 18,000 Jews in Brzeżany, now only 1,700 are left). The same took place in Zborów, Kołomyja, Sambor, Stryj, Drohobycz, Zbaraż, Przemyślany, Kuty, Śniatyń, Zaleszczyki, Brody, Przemyśl, Rawa Ruska, and other places.

The murder actions were repeated in these cities many times. In many, they continue to this day—Lwów.

In the months of October and November, the same began to take place in Wilno, the Wilno region, and Lithuania. In the course of November, 50,000 Jews were murdered in Wilno. There are currently 12,000 Jews in Wilno. Various estimates put the total number of Jews bestially murdered in the Wilno region and Lithuania at 300,000 persons.

The murder of Jews in the Słonim region began in September. Nearly all Jews in Żyrowice, Lachowicze, Mir, Kossów, and other places were murdered. The action began in Słonim on October 15. Over 9,000 Jews were murdered. The murdering began in Równe in the first days of November. In the course of three days, more than 15,000 persons were shot—men, women, and children. In Hancewicze (by Baranowicze), 6,000 Jews were shot. The murder action against Jews encompassed all the Polish lands beyond the San and the Bug. We have cited only some of the localities.

In November and December, the murder of Jews also began in the Polish lands joined to the Reich, the so-called Warthegau. Here, the murder took place with the aid of gassing, which was carried out in the village of Chełmno, 12 kilometers [7.5 miles] from Koło (Koło County). For the

---

61. The translation printed here differs slightly from the one in Bauer, "When Did They Know," 57–58. For the transmission and dating of the report see Dariusz Stola, "Early News of the Holocaust from Poland," *H&GS* 11, no. 1 (1997): 6.

gassing, a special vehicle was used (gas chamber), into which 90 persons were loaded each time. The victims were buried in special graves in a clearing in the Lubardzki Woods. Those who were shot dug the graves themselves. On average, 1,000 persons were gassed each day. From November 1941 to March 1942 at Chełmno, a total of 5,000 Jews from Koło, Dąbie, Bugaj, Izbica Kujawska, 35,000 Jews from the Łódź ghetto, and a certain number of gypsies were gassed.

In February 1942, the extermination of the Jews begins on the territory of the so-called General Government. The start: Tarnów and Radom, where Gestapo and SS men started to come to Jewish neighborhoods on a daily basis and systematically killed Jews on the street, in courtyards, and in residences. The action of mass expulsion of the Jews from Lublin began in March. In the process, children in orphanages, the elderly in old-age homes, and the ill in the general and the epidemic hospitals were bestially murdered, as were many people on the street and in their homes. The total number of victims was above 2,000. Approximately 25,000 Jews were deported from Lublin in sealed train cars in "an unknown direction," and no trace of them remains. Approximately 3,000 Jews were put in barracks in Majdanek, a suburb of Lublin. Not a single Jew remains in Lublin. In Kraków in the final days of March, more than 50 Jews were rounded up according to a list and shot before the gates. Gestapo men turned the night of April 17 to 18 into a bloody one in the Warsaw ghetto. Using a list, they tore 50 Jews, men and women, from their homes and bestially murdered them before the gates. Since April 18, a few Jews have been killed in their homes and on the street each day, and now in broad daylight. This action is conducted according to a set list and encompasses all strata of the Jews in the Warsaw ghetto. There is talk of further bloody nights. According to estimates, the Germans have thus far murdered 700,000 Polish Jews.

The above facts irrefutably demonstrate that the criminal German administration has begun to fulfill Hitler's prophecy that, five minutes before the war ends, however it may end, he will murder all the Jews in Europe.[62] We steadfastly believe that the Hitlerite Germans will be called,

---

62. The most likely reference here is to Hitler's speech of January 30, 1939, in which he threatened the destruction of the "Jewish race in Europe" in the event of a world war; he and his underlings made repeated references to this "prophecy" in later speeches, most notably in another highly publicized Hitler speech on January 30, 1942. A few days later in Warsaw, Chaim Kaplan noted that the "Führer's" reference to his "prophecy" confirmed information obtained by the *Judenrat* and the JDC regarding a "new direction of Nazi policy toward the Jews in the conquered territories: death by extermination for entire Jewish communities" (quoted in Friedländer, *Nazi Germany*, 2:333–39).

in their turn, to account in a manner fitting their monstrousness and bestiality. For the Jewish population, which is undergoing an unprecedented hell, this is not satisfying consolation. Immediate extermination threatens millions of Polish citizens of Jewish nationality.

We therefore call upon the Government of Poland, as the caretaker and representative of the entire population inhabiting Polish lands, immediately to take the steps necessary to prevent the destruction of Polish Jewry. To this end, the Government of Poland ought to exert its influence on the governments of the allied states and authoritative elements in those countries so that they immediately apply a policy of reprisal toward Germans and the fifth column resident in the allied states and their allies.[63] The German government should be informed by the Polish government and the allied states of application of the policy of retaliation. It must know that Germans in the US and other countries will answer <u>now</u> for the bestial extermination of the Jewish population.

We are aware that we are requesting the Polish government adopt uncommon steps. This is the only possibility to save millions of Jews from certain destruction.

As we have seen, the Bund report was not the first summary of events communicated to the West that presented a picture of systematic annihilation. But if these news reports were credible, what could and should be done next? Opinions and interests differed enormously. The Bund's sole representative on the London Polish National Council (PNC, Polska Rada Narodowa), **Szmul Zygielbojm**, had arrived there only weeks before the report was dispatched from Warsaw. He assumed his position after some controversy and against the background of mounting expectations and problems faced by Polish exile authorities in general and the PNC's Jewish members more generally.[64] A socialist, Zygielbojm was also at odds with the other Jewish PNC delegate, Zionist representative Ignacy Schwarzbart, whose adherence to a "dual policy" focusing

---

63. The term *"fifth column"* was coined during the Spanish Civil War in the second half of the 1930s. It refers to a group that sympathizes with the enemy and undermines a nation or society from within, often through clandestine methods. Germans living in Allied countries during World War II fell under suspicion of being a "fifth column" for the Nazi cause. "Allies" at the end of the sentence refers to states aligned with the Allies.

64. See Daniel Blatman, "On a Mission against All Odds: Samuel Zygielbojm in London (April 1942–May 1943)," *YVS* 20 (1990): 23–71.

on Palestine and the diaspora presented, according to Zygielbojm, "a hindrance to the solution of the Jewish problem in Poland" and a distraction from the socialist goal of "building a new world," with Jews "as citizens and co-owners of Poland."[65]

Zygielbojm and Schwarzbart overcame their political differences through their shared belief that—as a report by the Board of Deputies of British Jews put it in April 1942—"in every case and at every opportunity the Jews have been subjected to more sadistic cruelty, to more degrading humiliation and to a more rapid process of annihilation than the non-Jews in their own or in any other country."[66] Both men worked hard to convince their fellow PNC members, the heads of the government-in-exile, and the public in Allied countries that the fate of the Jews under the Nazis was unique and required forceful countermeasures. Despite skepticism about the large number of victims voiced by non-Jewish exile politicians with their own political agendas, the Bund report received a great deal of attention in and beyond London in June 1942. In the Warsaw ghetto, **Emanuel Ringelblum** felt confident that "[w]e have struck the enemy a hard blow. We have revealed his satanic plan to annihilate Polish Jewry," thus thwarting the Nazi attempt at proceeding in secret and prompting action. Ringelblum's hopes focused on Allied announcements of military reprisals as well as on the impact of the media revelations on the German public: "If the outside world contents itself with speeches and threats, perhaps the fear of German public opinion will save us."[67] When Zygielbojm went on the air only days after he had received the Bund report, he created a precedent in more than one respect.

---

65. *JTA Bulletin*, April 7, 1942; quoted from Blatman, "On a Mission against All Odds," 243–44. Isaac Ignacy Schwarzbart (1888–1961), born in Poland and trained as a lawyer, became active in the World Zionist Organization and Zionist groups in Poland in the 1930s and was elected to the Polish parliament. When war broke out he fled to Paris and later London, working for PNC with the Polish government-in-exile. Schwarzbart moved to the United States after the war and became an official in the World Jewish Congress. See obituary, *New York Times*, April 27, 1961; Getzel Kressel, "Schwarzbart, Isaac Ignacy," in *Encyclopaedia Judaica*, ed. Fred Skolnik and Michael Berenbaum, 2nd ed. (Detroit: Macmillan Reference USA, 2007), 18:192.

66. Draft report, "German Atrocities on the Jews," no date (marked as "corrected" April 10, 1942), USHMMA RG 59.023M (Board of Deputies of British Jews), reel 24, frame 758.

67. Jacob Sloan, ed., *Notes from the Warsaw Ghetto: The Journal of Emmanuel Ringelblum* (New York: McGraw-Hill, 1958), 295–98.

DOCUMENT 12-12: **"The Atrocities in Poland: B.B.C. Broadcasts to the World,"** *The Jewish Chronicle,* **July 10, 1942.**

For the first time in the history of the B.B.C., Jews all over the world were last week given an opportunity of listening to a broadcast in Yiddish from London. The broadcast followed an announcement in the European service summarising the recent reports about the atrocities committed against the Jews in Poland.

The speaker, introduced as a Jewish member of the Polish National Council in London, gave an assurance to the suffering that Jews in free lands will strain every nerve to put an end to the systematic slaughter. He asked his listeners to ponder over the undiluted horror of the planned extermination of a whole nation by means of shot, shell, starvation, and poison gas.

"I have in my hand," the speaker declared, "an extract from a letter written by a Jewish woman in a ghetto to her sister in another ghetto. This letter is in reality a cry to the whole world. The woman writes: 'My hands are shaking. I cannot write. Our minutes are numbered. The Lord knows whether we shall see one another again. I write and weep. My children are whimpering. They want to live. . . . We all bless you. If you get no more letters from me you will know that we are no longer alive.'"

It is interesting to note that the Nazis have been rattled by the B.B.C. disclosures of the atrocities in Poland, and their press and radio have been violently attacking the B.B.C. *The Angriff,* Dr. Goebbels's newspaper, describes the BBC's actions as an interference in Germany's "internal affairs." [. . .]

The report on the atrocities published recently by Mr. S. Zygielbojm and the statement made by Dr. I. Schwarzbart at the conference of the World Jewish Congress have been submitted by the two Jewish members of the Polish National Council to all members of both Houses of Parliament. Dr. Schwarzbart's statement was also sent to high church dignitaries, to the professors at British universities, and to judges at the High Courts.

As the documents throughout this chapter have demonstrated, months before Gerhart Riegner's telegram created headlines in August 1942 (an intervention addressed in the next volume of this series), information about gassings and mass shootings were available throughout the West. Yet disbelief and confusion continued to dilute the perception of the scope of atrocities and the possibility of future horrors to come. How could such reports about "liquidations" be verified? Was not all wartime reportage about enemy violence subject to propagandistic exaggeration? At a press conference held by the British Ministry of Information on July 9, 1942, representatives of the British government, the Polish government-in-exile, and the PNC offered different casualty figures. According to the British Minister of Information and his Polish counterpart, "700,000 Jews alone have been murdered in Poland"; the Polish Minister for Home Affairs spoke of "400,000 Polish citizens (Poles and Jews)" killed since the beginning of the war, while the Jewish PNC members avoided an overall estimate. It was Zygielbojm who reminded the press of the main point that "there is no doubt that in Poland a monstrous plan of extermination of all the Jews is being ruthlessly executed."[68]

Postwar studies of Nazi decision making and the implementation of the "Final Solution" on a European scale favor a bird's-eye perspective that treats individual anti-Jewish acts as parts of a gigantic, well-organized, and integrated machinery of persecution. Indeed, between late 1941 and the summer of 1942 the Nazi regime had succeeded in making the murder of the Jews a European-wide project, with deportations from the Reich and across German-dominated regions to ghettos and death camps running parallel to mass killing that targeted Jews already residing in "the East." But many decades later we can see how fragmented these events appeared at the time, how difficult the struggle to reveal the truth, and how great the investment—partly reflecting the shattering sense of despair and the desire to keep hope alive—in disbelief and skepticism. And while a process of extermination was going on, it did not yet encompass each and every corner of German-controlled Europe. Even where the threshold toward systematic mass murder had been crossed, pockets remained in the form of ghettos and labor camps in which Jews continued to live and to struggle, not knowing whether, when, or how they would be affected by the genocidal process.

As isolated news of German violence directed against Jews began to be viewed cumulatively and allowed a glimpse at the broader picture of persecution, media reports (often transmitted by Jewish periodicals, or in less prominent form, in mainstream newspapers) mentioned murderous incidents that

---

68. "A Press Conference at the Ministry of Information," *Polish Fortnightly Review*, July 15, 1942, 4–8.

were converging to form an exterminationist German grand design.[69] Jews from the areas immediately affected as well as observers beyond the German realm of influence with access to multiple news sources were the first to find that isolated pieces of evidence fit a pattern. While these Jews overcame their initial incredulity and attested to the course of destruction within their own communities, their voices were too isolated to be heard on the outside, too muted to drown out the cacophony of other war news. In fact, spreading the story of the unfolding genocide required less "breaking the silence"—to borrow from the title of Richard Breitman's and Walter Laqueur's influential book[70]—than amplifying the dreadful firsthand accounts of mass murder in a way that they would reach a wider audience, become integrated into a coherent narrative, and trigger political interventions. If we in the twenty-first century know what the overall outcome of the "Final Solution" was, to comprehend the full variety of responses and actions pursued by Jews at the time remains a task for the future.

---

69. See "Review of Events," *Contemporary Jewish Record* 4, no. 6 (December 1941): 649–50; *Jewish Chronicle*, October 24 and November 7, 1941. See also Deborah E. Lipstadt, *Beyond Belief: The American Press and the Coming of the Holocaust, 1933–1945* (New York: The Free Press, 1986), esp. Part II; David Cesarani, *The Jewish Chronicle and Anglo-Jewry, 1841–1991* (New York: Cambridge University Press, 1994), 172–79; Chanan Tomlin, *Protest and Prayer: Rabbi Dr. Solomon Schonfeld and Orthodox Jewish Responses in Britain to the Nazi Persecution of Europe's Jews, 1942–1945* (Oxford: Peter Lang, 2006).

70. Breitman and Laqueur, *Breaking the Silence*.

LIST OF DOCUMENTS

PART I: JEWS AND THE EXPANSION OF THE GERMAN EMPIRE: JANUARY TO JUNE 1941

1: Facing Increased Pressure

In the "Greater Reich"

Document 1-1: Letter from J. E. about the deportation of Viennese Jews to the Lublin district, February 18, 1941, in Else Behrendt-Rosenfeld and Gertrud Luckner, eds., *Lebenszeichen aus Piaski. Briefe Deportierter aus dem Distrikt Lublin 1940–1943* (Munich: Biederstein Verlag, 1968), 167–69 (translated from German).

Document 1-2: Group portrait of a family of Viennese Jews outside their living quarters in the ghetto of Opole, Lublin district, Generalgouvernement, no date (ca. mid-1941), USHMMPA WS# 18624.

Document 1-3: Letter from Mignon Langnas to Josef Löwenherz, Vienna, March 5, 1941, in Elisabeth Fraller and George Langnas, eds., *Mignon. Tagebücher und Briefe einer jüdischen Krankenschwester in Wien 1938–1949* (Innsbruck: StudienVerlag, 2010), 139–40 (translated from German).

Document 1-4: Account by Moses Sufrin, Switzerland, of his experiences in forced labor camps near Sanok, Kraków district, Generalgouvernement, written in early 1943, USHMMA RG 68.045M (WJC Geneva), reel 2, file 6014 (translated from French).

Document 1-5: Letters from Kurt Naumann, Breslau, Germany, to Ilse and Marcel Sternberger in New York, December 24, 1940, and March 2, 1941, USHMMA Acc. 1999.A.0010 Naumann family papers (translated from German).

Document 1-6: File note by Reichsvereinigung, Welfare Department (Conrad Cohn), Berlin, regarding costs for Jewish inmates of the Chełm mental institution, May 6, 1941, USHMMA RG 14.003M*1 (BAB R 8150), P75C Re1 (translated from German).

Document 1-7: Unsent letter from Erich Langer, Essen, Germany, to his son Klaus, Palestine, January 12, 1942, USHMMA Acc. 1994.A.322 Yakob Langer collection (translated from German).

In Western Europe

Document 1-8: Ruth Maier, Oslo, German-occupied Norway, diary entry for March 3, 1941, in Ruth Maier, *"Das Leben könnte gut sein": Tagebücher 1933 bis 1942*, ed. Jan Erik Vold (Stuttgart: DVA, 2008), 369–70 (translated from German).

Document 1-9: Lucien Dreyfus, Nice, Vichy France, diary entry for March 16, 1941, USHMMA RG 10.144 Lucien Dreyfus collection (translated from French).

Document 1-10: BBC radio address by René Cassin to the "Israelites of France," April 1941, in René Cassin, *Les hommes partis de rien. Le réveil de la France abattue (1940–41)* (Paris: Plon, 1975), 480–81 (translated from French).

Document 1-11: Hermann Hakel, camp Alberobello near Bari, Italy, diary entry for May 20, 1941, ÖNB 221/04 (translated from German).

Document 1-12: Letter from Klara (Claartje) van Aals, Apeldoorn, German-occupied Netherlands, to Aagje Kaagman, Utrecht, January 22, 1941, in *Als ik wil kan ik duiken . . . : Brieven van Claartje van Aals, verpleegster in de joods psychiatrische inrichting Het Apeldoornsche Bosch, 1940–1943*, ed. Suzette Wyers (Amsterdam: T. Rap, 1995), 39 (translated from Dutch).

Document 1-13: Gabriel Italie, The Hague, German-occupied Netherlands, diary entries for February 1941, in *Het oorlogsdagboek van dr. G. Italie. Den Haag, Barneveld, Westerbork, Theresienstadt, Den Haag 1940–1945*, ed. Wally M. de Lang (Amsterdam: Contact, 2009), 128–32 (translated from Dutch).

Hostile Shelters Abroad

Document 1-14: "One Year Sosua Settlement," *Jüdisches Nachrichtenblatt*, Prague, May 2, 1941, 1 (translated from German).

Document 1-15: Anonymous account, "Report on the Situation in the Camp de Gurs," sent to AJJDC-Lisbon, January 8, 1941, AJJDC Archive AR 3344/618.

Document 1-16: Photograph by Felix Nussbaum of his painting *Saint-Cyprien* on the balcony of his apartment in Brussels, 1942, printed with permission by Felix-Nussbaum-Haus Osnabrück.

Document 1-17: Letter from Marthe Nohèr, Zurich, to RELICO-Geneva, February 28, 1941, USHMMA RG 68.045M (WJC Geneva), reel 23, file 158 (translated from French).

Document 1-18: Letter from World Jewish Congress-Geneva to Joseph Tenenbaum, New York, March 24, 1941, USHMMA RG 68.045M (WJC Geneva), reel 59, file 449 (translated from German).

Document 1-19: Report on the situation of Jewish refugees in Japan by Moise Moiseeff, representative of the World Jewish Congress-Japan, June 7, 1941, USHMMA RG 68.045M (WJC Geneva), reel 3, file 20.

2: Struggling in the Łódź and Warsaw Ghettos

Conflicts over Bread

Document 2-1: Poem "Bread" by Władysław Szlengel, Warsaw, July 1941, USHMMA RG 15.079M (ŻIH Ring. I/526) (translated from Polish).

Document 2-2: Jewish teenage boys move a wagon loaded with bread for distribution in the Łódź ghetto, Warthegau, no date (1941), USHMMPA WS# 24415.

Document 2-3: Shlomo Frank, Łódź, Warthegau, diary entries for January 1941, in Shlomo Frank, *Togbukh fun lodzher ghetto*, ed. Nakhman Blumental (Buenos Aires: Tsentral-farband fun poylishe yidn in Argentine, 1958), 17–27 (translated from Yiddish).

Document 2-4: Interviews collected by Josef Zelkowicz on the carpenters' strike in Łódź, January 1941, in Josef Zelkowicz, *In Those Terrible Days: Writings from the Lodz Ghetto*, ed. Michal Unger (Jerusalem: Yad Vashem, 2002), 205, 209–14.

Document 2-5: Leib Spiesman, "In the Warsaw Ghetto," *Contemporary Jewish Record* 4 (August 1941): 357–66.

Letters as a Lifeline

Document 2-6: Letter from Ruth Goldbarth, Warsaw, to Edith Blau, Minden, Germany, January 19, 1941, USHMMA RG 10.250*03 #47 Edith Brandon collection (translated from German).

Document 2-7: Letter from Ruth Goldbarth, Warsaw, to Edith Blau, Minden, Germany, February 26, 1941, USHMMA RG 10.250*03 #51 Edith Brandon collection (translated from German).

Document 2-8: Letter from Ruth Goldbarth, Warsaw, to Edith Blau, Minden, Germany, April 10, 1941, USHMMA RG 10.250*03 #57 Edith Brandon collection (translated from German).

Document 2-9: Letter from Ruth Goldbarth, Warsaw, to Edith Blau, Minden, Germany, April 15, 1941, USHMMA RG 10.250*03 #58 Edith Brandon collection (translated from German).

Document 2-10: Letter from Ruth Goldbarth, Warsaw, to Edith Blau, Minden, Germany, May 6, 1941, USHMMA RG 10.250*03 #62 Edith Brandon collection (translated from German).

Document 2-11: Letter from Ruth Goldbarth, Warsaw, to Edith Blau, Minden, Germany, May 29, 1941, USHMMA RG 10.250*03 #67 Edith Brandon collection (translated from German).

Document 2-12: Group portrait of six young Jewish women sunbathing in the Warsaw ghetto, July 6, 1942, USHMMPA WS# 23282.

Document 2-13: Letter from Ruth Goldbarth, Warsaw, to Edith Blau, Minden, Germany, June 5, 1941, USHMMA RG 10.250*03 #68 Edith Brandon collection (translated from German).

3: Confronting New Challenges

Violence in Southeastern Europe and Beyond

Document 3-1: Account of the pogrom in Bucharest, Romania, January 21–23, 1941, USHMMA RG 68.045M (WJC Geneva), reel 2 (translated from French).

Document 3-2: Report on the activities of the Jewish community of Zagreb, Independent State of Croatia, after April 1941, July 8, 1945, USHMMA RG 68.045M (WJC Geneva), reel 3, file 17 (translated from German).

Document 3-3: Text fragment, "Lager," by eleven-year old Đura Rajs, Petrovgrad, German-occupied Yugoslav Banat, August 11, 1941, USHMMA Acc. 2012.35.1, Đorde (Đura) Rajs collection (translated from Serbian).

Document 3-4: Report on the situation of the Jews in Bulgaria, no date (early 1942), USHMMA RG 68.045M (WJC Geneva), reel 4, file 32 (translated from French).

Document 3-5: Yomtov Yacoel, "In the Anteroom to Hell: Memoir," 1943, in *The Holocaust in Salonika: Eyewitness Accounts*, ed. Steven Bowman (New York: Sephardic House, 2002), 30–34.

Document 3-6: Letter from Manfred Reifer, Cernăuţi, Romania, to RELICO–Geneva, on Soviet deportations of Jews in June 1941, November 15, 1942, USHMMA RG 68.045M (WJC Geneva), reel 12, file 109 (translated from German).

Document 3-7: Anonymous report submitted to the Jewish Agency for Palestine on "The Position of the Jewish Population in Iraq," March 24, 1942, USHMMA RG 59.023M (Board of Deputies of British Jews), reel 24, frame 280.

Stalled Hopes on the Eve of Operation Barbarossa

Document 3-8: Morris R. Cohen, "Jewish Studies of Peace and Post-War Problems," *Contemporary Jewish Record* 4 (April 1941): 110–25.

Document 3-9: Yehoshua Rapoport, Shanghai, diary entries for May 12, 28, and June 2, 1941, in *Voices from Shanghai: Jewish Exiles in Wartime China*, ed. Irene Eber (Chicago: University of Chicago Press, 2008), 91–92 (ellipses and brackets in the original).

PART II: ESCALATING VIOLENCE: JUNE 1941 TO JULY 1942

4: Mass Murder in the Occupied Soviet Union and Deportations to "the East"

Caught Up in Deadly Aggression

Deportations from the Reich and the Protectorate

Document 4-9: Unidentified woman deported from Vienna, diary entries for November 19–28, 1941, USHMMA RG 26.014 (LCSAV R-1390), reel 65, folder 68 (translated from German).

Document 4-10: Account by the Kovno ghetto police on "The 'Episode' of the German Jews," no date (early 1943), USHMMA RG 26.014 (LCSAV R-973), reel 31 (translated from Yiddish).

Document 4-11: Shlomo Frank, Łódź, Warthegau, diary entries for October 19–28, 1941, in Shlomo Frank, *Togbukh fun lodzher ghetto*, ed. Nakhman Blumental (Buenos Aires: Tsentral-farband fun poylishe yidn in Argentine, 1958), 179–84 (translated from Yiddish).

Document 4-12: Eva Mändl, Prague, diary entries for October 10 to December 14, 1941, in Eva Mändl Roubíčková, ed. Veronika Springmann, *"Langsam gewöhnen wir uns an das Ghettoleben." Ein Tagebuch aus Theresienstadt* (Hamburg: Konkret Literatur Verlag, 2007), 52–54, 57, 62, 64–66 (translated from German).

Document 4-13: Unsent letter from Erich Langer, Essen, Germany, to his son Klaus, Palestine, late 1941/early 1942, USHMMA Acc. 1994.A.322 Yakob Langer collection (translated from German).

5: Widening Circles of Persecution

Death and Defiance in "the East"

Document 5-1: Letter from Berta Knoch in the Riga ghetto to Carolina Knoch in hiding, February 10, 1942; USHMMA RG 05.004*01 Carolina Taitz collection (translated from Latvian).

Document 5-2: Memoir by Paula Stein, Białystok, Białystok-Grodno district, East Prussia, about her escape from Vilna in December 1941, written 1943/1944; USHMMA Acc. 2008.345 notebook #3 (translated from Polish).

Document 5-3: Irene Hauser, Łódź, Warthegau, diary entries for June/July 1942; USHMMA RG 02.208M (ŻIH 302/299), reel 42 (translated from German).

Document 5-4: Diagram by Dr. Jacob Nochimovski, Kovno, German-occupied Lithuania, May 1943, indicating the illnesses affecting women in the Kovno ghetto, USHMMPA WS# N03334.01.

Document 5-5: "In One Half Hour," Abraham Lewin, Warsaw, March 26, 1942, USHMMA RG 15.079M (ŻIH Ring. I/1052) (translated from Yiddish).

Document 5-6: Testimony by Mrs. Dychterman, recorded for the Oyneg Shabes archive by Hersh Wasser, on an "Aktion" in Hrubieszów, Lublin district, Generalgouvernement, in early June 1942, June 30, 1942, USHMMA RG 15.079M (ŻIH Ring. I/814), 4–7 (translated from Polish).

Unsafe in "Safe Havens"

Document 5-7: Report by Ludwig Foerder, Jerusalem, on the attitude of Zionists and non-Zionists toward rescue measures in case of a German occupation of Palestine, June 1941, USHMMA Acc. 2008.189 Brodnitz collection (translated from German).

Document 5-8: Letter from Richard Lichtheim, Jewish Agency for Palestine-Geneva, to Joseph Linton, Jewish Agency-London, on the aftermath of the "Struma" disaster, March 25, 1942, CZA RG L22, file 134.

Document 5-9: Aharon Zwergbaum, account and drawing on his second year in Mauritius, January 1943, USHMMA RG 17.008M (DÖW 51123-2) (translated from German).

Document 5-10: Sophie Freud, Casablanca, Morocco, diary entry for January 24, 1942, USHMMA Acc. 2010.401.1 Sophie Freud collection (translated from German).

Document 5-11: Petition by Jewish internees at Miranda de Ebro camp, Spain, to AJJDC-representative Samuel Sequerra, March 24, 1942, USHMMA RG 68.066M (AJJDC Archives, Jerusalem), reel 29, frames 835–36 (translated from French and Spanish).

Document 5-12: Harry Viteles, "Report on visit to Bagdad (2.XI to 9.XI 1942) and to Tehran (11.XI to 2.XII 1942)," Jerusalem, to AJJDC-New York on the situation of Jewish refugees in the southeast of the Soviet Union and across the border into Iran, December 31, 1942, USHMMA RG 68.066M (AJJDC Archives Jerusalem IS/1/6), reel 10, 31–34.

6: In the Grip of Germany's Allies

Romania and Transnistria

Document 6-1: Testimony and drawing by Amita Grimberg on massacres of Jews in Iași, Romania, June 24, 1945, USHMMA RG 25.051 (WJC Bucharest), Locality Iași, file 3b (translated from Romanian).

Document 6-2: Letter from Wilhelm Filderman, head of the Romanian Federation of Jewish Communities, Bucharest, to the Romanian head of state Marshal Ion Antonescu, no date (late October 1941), in Paul A. Shapiro with contributions by Brewster Chamberlin and Radu Ioanid, *The Kishinev Ghetto, 1941–1942: A Documentary History* (Tuscaloosa: University of Alabama Press in association with the USHMM, forthcoming).

Document 6-3: Nekhama Vaisman, unidentified ghetto in Transnistria, diary entry for January 27, 1942, USHMMA Acc. 2010.264 Nekhama Vaisman diary (translated from Russian).

Document 6-4: Mirjam Korber, Djurin, Transnistria, diary entries for February to May 1942, USHMMA Acc. 2010.93.1 Mirjam Korber Bercovici collection (translated from Romanian).

Hungary, Slovakia, and Former Yugoslavia

Document 6-5: "240,000 Hungarian Jews Driven to Death at Forced Labor for Nazis on Russian Front," *Jewish Telegraphic Agency*, November 11, 1942.

Document 6-6: Baruch Milch, Tłuste, Galicia district, Generalgouvernement, diary entries written July/August 1943 on the persecution of Hungarian deportees in the second half of 1941, USHMMA RG 02.208M (ŻIH 302/98) (translated from Polish).

Document 6-7: Letters from Hilda Dajč, Judenlager Semlin near Belgrade, Serbia, to Mirjana Petrović in Belgrade, December 9, 1941 and early 1942, USHMMA RG 49.007, reel 5, file 2, and Historical Archives of Belgrade, IAB, 1883, 3126/II-XXIX-1122 (translated from Serbian).

Document 6-8: Rabbi Abraham Frieder, Nové Mesto, Slovakia, diary entries for February 1942, USHMMA Acc. 2008.286.1 Frieder collection (translated from German).

Document 6-9: Photographs from Rabbi Abraham Frieder's diary from the Žilina deportation camp, no date (spring of 1942), USHMMA Acc. 2008.286.1 Frieder collection (annotations/captions translated from German).

PART III: BEYOND COMPLIANCE AND RESISTANCE: INTERACTIONS AFTER JUNE 1941

7: Elites and Ordinary Jews

Expectations and Demands

Document 7-1: "Public notice no. 372" by the Eldest of the Jews in the Łódź ghetto (in German and Yiddish), March 25, 1942, USHMMPA WS# N13853 (translated from German).

Document 7-2: Letters from the Pińsk Judenrat to two Jews, levying money for a "contribution" imposed by the Germans, Pińsk, German-occupied Ukraine, October 19, 1941, USHMMA Acc. 1996.A.0169 (YVA M-41/942, from Brest State Archives 2135-2-124), reel 28 (translated from Russian).

Document 7-3: Account by the Kovno ghetto police on the establishment of the Jewish police, no date (early 1943), USHMMA RG 26.014 (LCSAV R-973), reel 31 (translated from Yiddish).

Document 7-4: Circular letter no. 1 from the Jewish administration of the women's camp in Đakovo, Independent State of Croatia, December 8, 1941, USHMMA RG 49.007M (JHM 4159 k.21-7-1/11), reel 1 (translated from Croatian).

Document 7-5: Letters of appeal to the Deportation Commission of the Eldest of the Jews in Łódź, January 11/12, 1942, USHMMA RG 15.083 (PSAŁ, file 1238, 62-3, 164–65; file 1280, 581–82) (translated from German).

Document 7-6: File note by the Jewish community Leipzig, Germany, January 18, 1942, regarding a request by Martha Weinhold to join, USHMMA RG 14.035M (Leipzig Jewish Community records), reel 2 (translated from German).

Appeals to Non-Jewish Authorities

Document 7-7: Letter from Hermann Marschner, Berlin, to Berlin Public Prosecutor's Office, November 6, 1941, USHMMA RG 14.070M (LAB A Rep. 358-02, #56385), reel 1534 (translated from German).

Document 7-8: Letter from August Nović, Zagreb, Independent State of Croatia, to the Minister of Internal Affairs of the Independent State of Croatia, May 7, 1941, USHMMA 1998.A.0018 (Croatian State Archive, box 277, inv. no. 27167), reel 1 (translated from Croatian).

Document 7-9: Edwin Geist, Kovno, German-occupied Lithuania, diary entry for June 10, 1942, in Edwin Geist, ed. Jokūbas Skliutauskas, *Für Lyda. Tagebuch 1942* (Vilna: Baltos Lankos, 2002), 54–59 (translated from German).

Document 7-10: Letter from Luţa Kaufman, Piatra Neamţ, Romania, to Marshall Antonescu, August 6, 1941, in Jean Ancel, ed., *Documents Concerning the Fate of Romanian Jewry during the Holocaust*, vol. 2 (New York: Beate Klarsfeld Foundation, 1986), 507 (translated from Romanian).

Document 7-11: Letter from Irma Czerner, Chicago (IL), to Eleanor Roosevelt, October 31, 1941, in Raya Czerner Schapiro and Helga Czerner Weinberg, eds., *Letters from Prague, 1939–1941* (Chicago: Academy Chicago Publishers, 1996): 187–88.

Document 7-12: Notes on a meeting between Selig Brodetsky, Adolph Brotman, and Leonard Stein with Soviet ambassador Ivan Maisky, London, September 29, 1941, USHMMA RG 59.023M (Board of Deputies of British Jews), reel 22, frames 224–25.

Document 7-13: Letter from Selig Brodetsky and Leonard Stein, Joint Foreign Committee, to Władysław Sikorski, Prime Minister of the Polish Government-in-Exile, London, January 12, 1942, USHMMA RG 59.023M (Board of Deputies of British Jews), reel 24, frame 801.

Document 7-14: Rabbi Abraham Frieder, Nové Mesto, Slovakia, diary entries for early March 1942, USHMMA Acc. 2008.286.1 Frieder collection (translated from German).

Document 7-15: Letter from David Alkalaj, POW in the German-run Eversheide camp to General Miloje Popadić, May 26, 1942, USHMMA RG 49.007M (JHM 5499 k.20-1-2/22), reel 4 (translated from Serbian).

8: Support Networks

Private and Public Interests

Document 8-1: Correspondence between Aron Menczer, Altenfelden (near Linz), Ostmark, and the head of the Jewish Community in Vienna, Josef Löwenherz, July 1941, USHMMA RG 17.017M (CAHJP A/W 180 I), reel 289 (translated from German).

Document 8-2: Draft letter from the WJC-Geneva to the Jewish Youth Committee-Geneva, expressing disapproval of the committee's plans to hold a charity ball, December 18, 1941, USHMMA RG 68.045M (WJC Geneva), reel 63, file 458 (translated from French).

Document 8-3: Esther van Vriesland, Gorkum, German-occupied Netherlands, diary entries for May 15 and 31, 1942, in *Esther: Een Dagboek, 1942* (Utrecht: Stichting Matrijs, 1990), 110–11, 116–17 (translated from Dutch).

Document 8-4: Letter from Ernst Krombach, Izbica, Lublin district, Generalgouvernement, to Marianne Strauss, Essen, Germany, April 28, 1942, in Mark Roseman, *A Past in Hiding: Memory and Survival in Nazi Germany* (New York: Metropolitan Books, 2000), 175–76 (translated from German).

Document 8-5: Eva Mändl, Theresienstadt, Protectorate, diary entries for December 27, 1941, to April 19, 1942, in Eva Mändl Roubíčková, *"Langsam gewöhnen wir uns an das Ghettoleben." Ein Tagebuch aus Theresienstadt*, ed. Veronika Springmann (Hamburg: Konkret Literatur Verlag, 2007), 75–76, 78–79, 82, 85, 90–92 (translated from German).

Document 8-6: Report by Brith Hazofim-Berlin on a clandestine meeting held in March 1942, in Jizchak Schwersenz and Edith Wolff, *Jüdische Jugend im Untergrund. Eine zionistische Gruppe in Deutschland während des Zweiten Weltkrieges* (Tel Aviv: Verlag Bitaon, 1969), 33–34 (translated from German).

Postwar Plans from Abroad

Document 8-7: Statement by the American Jewish Congress and the World Jewish Congress in conjunction with "Polish Jewish Day," September 1, 1941, USHMMA RG 68.045M (WJC Geneva), reel 5, file 40.

Document 8-8: Yishuv poster to commemorate "Polish Jewish Day" in 1941, USHMMPA WS# 08330.

Document 8-9: Declaration by the Jewish Agency regarding wartime and postwar policy, Jerusalem, October 2, 1941, ISA Leo Kohn Papers P575.

Document 8-10: Draft letter from Richard Lichtheim, Jewish Agency for Palestine-Geneva, to Nahum Goldmann, New York, September 9, 1942, CZA RG L22, file 149.

9: Deference, Evasion, or Revolt?

"Serving" and Escaping the Enemy

Document 9-1: Memoir by Paula Stein, Białystok, Białystok-Grodno district, East Prussia, for February 1942, written in 1943–1944, USHMMA Acc. 2008.345 (Israel Stein collection), notebook #4a (translated from Polish and German).

Document 9-2: Extracts from weekly reports submitted to German authorities, Warsaw, March 31 to May 5, 1942, in Christopher Browning and Israel Gutman, "The Reports of a Jewish 'Informer' in the Warsaw Ghetto—Selected Documents," *YVS* 17 (1986): 258, 261–62, 267, 269–72.

Document 9-3: Letter from Moritz Henschel, Jewish Community Berlin, to the Gestapo Berlin, regarding the disappearance of Max Sinasohn, February 19, 1942, USHMMA RG 14.003M (BAB R 8150), P75C Re1/7 (translated from German).

Document 9-4: Letter from "Papo" to "Alberto," Split, Italian-occupied Yugoslav Dalmatia, September 29, 1941, USHMMA RG 49.007M (JHM k. 27-2-1/23), reel 8 (translated from Bosnian).

Fighting the Enemy

Document 9-5: Letters from Motl (Matvei Aronovich) Talalaevskii, Kyiv, Soviet Union, to his wife, September 2 and 5, 1941, USHMMA RG 31.028.11 (Kyiv Judaica Institute) (translated from Russian).

Document 9-6: Manifesto "Let us not be led like sheep to the slaughter!" Vilna, German-occupied Lithuania, January 1, 1942, Moreshet Archives D.1.4630 (translated from Yiddish).

Document 9-7: Letter from Arthur Lourie, Emergency Committee for Zionist Affairs-New York, to Richard Lichtheim, Jewish Agency-Geneva, July 28, 1942, CZA RG L22 file 149.

Document 9-8: Petr Ginz, Prague, diary entries for May 27 to June 5, 1942, in Chava Pressburger, ed., *The Diary of Petr Ginz, 1941–1942* (New York: Atlantic Monthly Press, 2007), 108–11.

Document 9-9: File note by representatives of the Reich Association of Jews in Germany (Paul Eppstein); the Jewish Communities Prague (Franz Friedmann) and Vienna (Josef Löwenherz) to the Reich Security Main Office, Berlin, May 29, 1942, USHMMA RG 14.003M (BAB R 8150), P75C Re1/7 (translated from German).

PART IV: GLIMPSING THE ABYSS: PATTERNS AND PERCEPTIONS

10: The Role of Religion

Adapting Religious Rituals and Outlooks

Document 10-1: Gabriel Italie, The Hague, German-occupied Netherlands, diary entries for April 1941, in *Het oorlogsdagboek van dr. G. Italie. Den Haag, Barneveld, Westerbork, Theresienstadt, Den Haag 1940–1945,* ed. Wally M. de Lang (Amsterdam: Contact, 2009), 146–47, 150 (translated from Dutch).

Document 10-2: Account by an unidentified author on the eve of Pesach in the Warsaw ghetto, April 11, 1941, USHMM RG 15.079 (ŻIH Ring. I/1024) (translated from Yiddish).

Document 10-3: Mirjam Korber, Djurin, Transnistria, diary entry for April 6, 1942, USHMMA Acc. 2010.93.1 Mirjam Korber Bercovici collection (translated from Romanian).

Document 10-4: Purim poem by Horst Rotholz, Château Montintin, Vichy France, March 12, 1941, USHMMA Acc. 2000.187 Ruth Windmuller collection (translated from German).

Document 10-5: Letter from Anny Feldmann, Opole, Lublin district, Generalgouvernement, to the Jewish Council-Łódź, September 11, 1941, and response note regarding the marking of her father's grave, November 3, 1941, USHMMA RG 15.083M (PSAŁ, file 300), 89, 91–93 (translated from German).

Document 10-6: Letter from Majer Bałaban, Warsaw, to the head of the Warsaw Jewish Council, October 29, 1941, USHMMA RG 15.079M (ŻIH Ring. II/142) (translated from Polish).

Private Faith and Communal Concerns

Document 10-7: Report by Simon M. Lehrman, Refugee Children's Department of the Board of Deputies of British Jews, on the spiritual well-being of children brought to the United Kingdom as part of the Kindertransport, May 21, 1942, USHMMA RG 59.023M (Board of Deputies of British Jews), reel 16, frames 281–83.

Document 10-8: Inga Pollak, Falmouth, United Kingdom, diary entry for July 25, 1941, in Ingrid Jacoby, *My Darling Diary: A Wartime Journal* (Penzance: United Writers Publications, 1998), 99.

Document 10-9: Lucien Dreyfus, Nice, Vichy France, diary entry for June 18, 1942, USHMMA RG 10.144.05 (translated from French).

Document 10-10: Elsa Binder, Stanisławów, Galicia district, Generalgouvernement, diary entries for March 18, 1942, USHMMA RG 02.208M (ŻIH 302/267) (translated from Polish).

Framing the World through Theology

Document 10-11: Rabbi Rafael Eliahu Botschko, Montreux, Switzerland, "The mysterious hand," no date (ca. 1942), in idem, *Oase im Sturm* (Zurich: Gutenberg AG, no date [1942/43]), 21–23 (translated from German).

Document 10-12: Letter from Meir Birman, HICEM-Shanghai, to AJJDC-New York, September 30, 1941, USHMMA RG 68.066M (AJJDC Jerusalem Archives), reel 10, frames 675–77.

Document 10-13: Otto Samuel, "My Experiences in Nazi Germany," on his work as chaplain in French internment camps until May 1941, *The American Hebrew Christian* 18, no. 1 (April 1945): 17.

11: Limits of Language

Art and Communication

Document 11-1: Poem "And Again" recorded by Henri Pohorylés, Hanukkah 1940 (December 25, 1940–January 1, 1941), Château de la Guette, Vichy France, USHMMA Acc. 2004.435 Naomi Elath collection (translated from German).

The Changing Vocabulary of Destruction

12: Making Sense of the Unthinkable

Searching for Explanations

Document 12-2: Willy Cohn, Breslau, Germany, diary entry for October 18, 1941, in Willy Cohn, *Kein Recht, Nirgends: Tagebuch vom Untergang des Breslauer Judentums, 1933–1941,* ed. Norbert Conrads (Cologne: Böhlau Verlag, 2007), 2:994 (translated from German).

Document 12-3: Frieda Reinach, Berlin, diary entries for May/June, 1942, USHMMA RG 10.249 (translated from German).

Document 12-4: Unidentified man (last name Gold), Lwów, Galicia district, General-gouvernement, diary entry for December 20, 1941, USHMMA RG 15.069M (Teka Lwowska 229/63) (translated from Polish).

Document 12-5: Mirjam Korber, Djurin, Transnistria, diary entry for July 4, 1942, USHMMA Acc. 2010.93.1 Mirjam Korber Bercovici collection (translated from Romanian).

Information and Disbelief

Document 12-6: Letter from Richard Lichtheim, Jewish Agency-Geneva, to Joseph Linton, Jewish Agency-London, November 10, 1941, CZA RG L22, file 149.

Document 12-7: Draft report by the Joint Foreign Committee of the Board of Deputies of British Jews and the Anglo-Jewish Association regarding "German Atrocities on Jews," January 10/11, 1942, USHMMA RG 59.023M (Board of Deputies of British Jews), reel 24, frames 750–54.

Document 12-8: Uszer Taube, "Protocol about the events in the Koło region," Warsaw, after January 1942, USHMMA RG 15.079M (ŻIH Ring. I/1057) (translated from Yiddish).

Document 12-9: Letter from an unidentified Jew, Włodawa, Lublin district, General-gouvernement, to relatives in Warsaw, June 1, 1942, USHMMA RG 15.079M (ŻIH Ring. I/563) (translated from Yiddish).

Document 12-10: "All Czech Jews Slated for Deportation to Poland, Jewish Deputy Declares," *Jewish Telegraphic Agency,* April 29, 1942.

Document 12-11: "Report of the Bund Regarding the Persecution of the Jews," May 11, 1942, in Yehuda Bauer, "When Did They Know?," *Midstream* 14 (April 1968): 54–55.

Document 12-12: "The Atrocities in Poland: B.B.C. Broadcasts to the World," *The Jewish Chronicle,* July 10, 1942.

BIBLIOGRAPHY

This selection from a vast and continuously growing number of publications complements the footnote references in the chapters. It is designed to serve as orientation for further study, not as a compilation of all relevant literature. For more comprehensive listings of recent publications, check the bibliographic sections of *H&GS*, *LBIYB*, *YVS*, and other journals.

MEMORIAL BOOKS, REFERENCE WORKS, AND LISTINGS OF HOLOCAUST VICTIMS AND SURVIVORS

Brocke, Michael, and Julius Carlebach, eds. *Biographisches Handbuch der Rabbiner. Die Rabbiner im Deutschen Reich 1871–1945*. Vol. 2. Munich: K. G. Saur, 2009.

Czech, Danuta. *Auschwitz Chronicle, 1939–1945*. New York: Henry Holt, 1990.

Dean, Martin, ed. *The United States Holocaust Memorial Museum Encyclopedia of Camps and Ghettos, 1933–1945. Ghettos in German-Occupied Eastern Europe*. Vol. 2. Bloomington: Indiana University Press in association with the USHMM, 2012.

Digital Monument to the Jewish Community in the Netherlands. Available online at www.joodsmonument.nl.

Gedenkbuch, Bundesarchiv memorial book of Jewish victims from Germany, 1933–1945. Available online at www.bundesarchiv.de/gedenkbuch.

Genger, Angela, and Hildegard Jakobs, eds. *Düsseldorf/Getto Litzmannstadt. 1941*. Essen: Klartext Verlag, 2010.

Gutman, Israel, ed. *Encyclopedia of the Holocaust*. 4 vols. New York: Macmillan, 1990.

Hundert, Gershon David, ed. *The YIVO Encyclopedia of Jews in Eastern Europe*. 2 vols. New Haven, CT: Yale University Press, 2008.

Laqueur, Walter, ed. *The Holocaust Encyclopedia*. New Haven, CT: Yale University Press, 2001.

Megargee, Geoffrey P., ed. *The United States Holocaust Memorial Museum Encyclopedia of Camps and Ghettos, 1933–1945. Early Camps, Youth Camps, and Concentration Camps and Subcamps under the SS-Business Administration Main Office (WVHA)*. Vol. 1. Bloomington: Indiana University Press in association with the USHMM, 2009.

Miron, Guy, and Shlomit Shulhani, eds. *The Yad Vashem Encyclopedia of the Ghettos during the Holocaust*. 2 vols. Jerusalem: Yad Vashem, 2009.

Pinkas ha-kehilot. Polin: entsiklopedyah shel ha-yishuvim ha-yehudiyim le-min hivasdam ve-ad le-ahar Shoat Milhemet ha-olam ha-sheniyah. 8 vols. Jerusalem: Yad Vashem, 1999.

Shapiro, Robert Moses, and Tadeusz Epsztein, eds. *The Warsaw Ghetto Oyneg Shabes-Ringelblum Archive: Catalog and Guide*. Bloomington: Indiana University Press in association with the USHMM and the Jewish Historical Institute, Warsaw, 2009.

Skolnik, Fred, and Michael Berenbaum, eds. *Encyclopaedia Judaica*. 2nd ed. Detroit, MI: Macmillan Reference USA, 2007.

USHMM ITS Collection Data Base Central Name Index; *at* www.ushmm.org/museum/exhibit/focus/its.

Yad Vashem Central Database of Shoah Victims' Names; at www.yadvashem.org.

PUBLISHED PRIMARY SOURCES AND MEMOIRS

Ancel, Jean, ed. *Documents Concerning the Fate of Romanian Jewry during the Holocaust*. 12 vols. New York: Beate Klarsfeld Foundation, 1986.

Anders, Freia, Katrin Stoll, and Karsten Wilke, eds. *Der Judenrat von Białystok. Dokumente aus dem Archiv des Białystoker Ghettos 1941–1943*. Paderborn: Schöningh Verlag, 2010.

Arad, Yitzhak, Israel Gutman, and Abraham Margaliot, eds. *Documents on the Holocaust: Selected Sources on the Destruction of the Jews of Germany and Austria, Poland, and the Soviet Union*. Lincoln: University of Nebraska Press, 1999.

Berg, Mary. *The Diary of Mary Berg: Growing up in the Warsaw Ghetto: A Diary*. Edited by S. L. Shneiderman and Susan Lee Pentlin. Oxford: Oneworld, 2006 (originally published in 1945 as *Warsaw Ghetto: A Diary by Mary Berg*).

Bergmann, Alexander. *Aufzeichnungen eines Untermenschen: Ein Bericht über das Ghetto in Riga und die Konzentrationslager in Deutschland*. Bremen: Temmen, 2009.

Berr, Hélène. *The Journal of Hélène Berr [1942–45]*. Toronto: M & S, 2008.

Boas, Jacob, ed. *We Are Witnesses: Five Diaries of Teenagers Who Died in the Holocaust*. New York: Henry Holt, 1995.

Brandon, Edith. *Letters from Tomaszow*. London: self-published, 1994.

Centre de documentation juive contemporaine, ed. *Les enfants de la Guette. Souvenirs et documents (1938–1945)*. Paris: Centre de documentation juive contemporaine, 1999.

Cohn, Willy. *Kein Recht, Nirgends: Tagebuch vom Untergang des Breslauer Judentums, 1933–1941*. Edited by Norbert Conrads. 2 vols. Cologne: Böhlau, 2007.

Cytryn, Avraham. *A Youth Writing Behind the Walls: Avrahan Cytryn's Lodz Notebooks*. Jerusalem: Yad Vashem, 2005.

Dobroszycki, Lucjan. *The Chronicle of the Łódź Ghetto: 1941–1944*. New Haven, CT: Yale University Press, 1984.

Feuchert, Sascha, Erwin Leibfried, and Jörg Riecke, eds. *Die Chronik des Gettos Lodz/ Litzmannstadt.* 5 vols. Göttingen: Wallstein, 2007.

Flinker, Moshe. *Young Moshe's Diary: The Spiritual Torment of a Jewish Boy in Nazi Europe.* Jerusalem: Yad Vashem, 1971.

Fraller, Elisabeth, and George Langnas, eds. *Mignon. Tagebücher und Briefe einer jüdischen Krankenschwester in Wien 1938–1949.* Innsbruck: StudienVerlag, 2010.

Frank, Anne. *The Diary of Anne Frank.* rev. crit. ed. by David Barnouw and Gerrold van der Stroom, New York: Doubleday, 2003.

Freier, Recha. *Let the Children Come: The Early History of Youth Aliyah.* London: Weidenfeld and Nicolson, 1961.

Friedlander, Henry, and Sybil Milton, eds. *Archives of the Holocaust: An International Collection of Selected Documents.* 21 vols. New York: Garland Publishing, 1990–1995.

Fry, Varian. *Assignment: Rescue. An Autobiography.* New York: Scholastic, 1990 (originally published in 1945 as *Surrender on Demand*).

Garbarini, Alexandra, with Emil Kerenji, Jan Lambertz, and Avinoam Patt. *Jewish Responses to Persecution, 1938–1940.* Vol. 2. Lanham, MD: AltaMira Press in association with the USHMM, 2011.

Geist, Edwin. *Für Lyda: Tagebuch 1942.* Edited by Jokūbas Skliutauskas. Vilnius: Baltos Lankos, 2002.

Gillis-Carlebach, Miriam. *Jewish Everyday Life as Human Resistance, 1939–1941: Chief Rabbi Dr. Joseph Zvi Carlebach and the Hamburg-Altona Jewish Communities.* New York: Peter Lang, 2009.

Grynberg, Michał, ed. *Words to Outlive Us: Eyewitness Accounts from the Warsaw Ghetto.* New York: Metropolitan Books, 2002.

Handler, Andrew, ed. *The Holocaust in Hungary: An Anthology of Jewish Response.* Tuscaloosa: University of Alabama Press, 1982.

Heberer, Patricia. *Children during the Holocaust.* Lanham, MD: AltaMira Press in association with the USHMM, 2011.

Hilberg, Raul. *Sources of Holocaust Research: An Analysis.* Chicago: Ivan R. Dee, 2001.

Hilberg, Raul, Stanislaw Staron, and Josef Kermisz, eds. *The Warsaw Diary of Adam Czerniakow: Prelude to Doom.* Chicago: Ivan R. Dee in association with the USHMM, 1999 (originally published in 1979).

Hoppe, Bernd, and Hildrun Glass, eds., *Die Verfolgung und Ermordung der europäischen Juden durch das nationalsozialistische Deutschland 1933–1945.* Vol. 7, *Sowjetunion mit annektierten Gebieten I: Besetzte sowjetische Gebiete unter deutscher Militärverwaltung, Baltikum und Transnistrien.* Munich: Oldenbourg, 2011.

Huberband, Shimon. *Kiddush Hashem: Jewish Religious and Cultural Life in Poland during the Holocaust.* Edited by Jeffrey S. Gurock and Robert S. Hirt. Hoboken, NJ: KTAV Publishing House, 1987.

Jagendorf, Siegfried. *Das Wunder von Moghilev. Die Rettung von zehntausend Juden vor dem rumänischen Holocaust.* Berlin: Transit, 2009.

Kaiser, Reinhard, and Margarete Holzman, eds., *"Dies Kind soll leben." Die Aufzeichnungen der Helene Holzman 1941–1944.* Munich: List Taschenbuch, 2001.

Kaplan, Chaim A. *Scroll of Agony: The Warsaw Diary of Chaim A. Kaplan.* Edited by Abraham I. Katsh. Bloomington: Indiana University Press in association with the USHMM, 1999 (originally published in 1965).

Kermish, Joseph, ed. *To Live with Honor and Die with Honor! Selected Documents from the Warsaw Ghetto Underground Archives "O.S." ("Oneg Shabbath").* Jerusalem: Yad Vashem, 1986.

Kirschner, Robert, ed. *Rabbinic Response of the Holocaust Era.* New York: Schocken, 1985.

Klemperer, Victor. *I Will Bear Witness: A Diary of the Nazi Years, 1933–1941.* New York: Random House, 1998.

Klüger, Ruth. *Still Alive: A Holocaust Girlhood Remembered.* New York: Feminist Press at the City University of New York, 2001.

Kohn, Jerome, and Ron H. Feldman, eds. *The Jewish Writings: Hannah Arendt.* New York: Schocken, 2007.

Kohner, Nancy. *My Father's Roses: A Family's Journey from World War I to Treblinka.* New York: Pegasus, 2009.

Kolmar, Gertrud. *My Gaze Is Turned Inward: Letters, 1934–1943.* Edited by Johanna Woltmann. Evanston, IL: Northwestern University Press, 2004.

Korczak, Janusz. *Ghetto Diary.* New Haven, CT: Yale University Press, 2003 (originally published in 1978).

Kruk, Herman. *The Last Days of the Jerusalem of Lithuania: Chronicles from the Vilna Ghetto and the Camps, 1939–1944.* Edited by Benjamin Harshav. New Haven, CT: Yale University Press, 2002.

Lambert, Raymond-Raoul. *Diary of a Witness, 1940–1943.* Edited by Richard I. Cohen. Chicago: Ivan R. Dee in association with the USHMM, 2007.

Lewin, Abraham. *A Cup of Tears: A Diary of the Warsaw Ghetto.* Edited by Antony Polonsky. Oxford: Basil Blackwell in association with the Institute for Polish-Jewish Studies, 1988.

Lieblich, Ruthka. *Ruthka: A Diary of War.* Brooklyn, NY: Remember, 1993.

Maier, Ruth. *Ruth Maier's Diary: A Young Girl's Life under Nazism.* Edited by Jan Erik Vold. London: Harvill Secker, 2009.

Mallmann, Klaus-Michael, Jochen Böhler, and Jürgen Matthäus, eds. *Einsatzgruppen in Polen: Darstellung und Dokumentation.* Darmstadt: Wissenschaftliche Buchgesellschaft, 2008.

Marum-Lunau, Elisabeth. *Auf der Flucht in Frankreich: "Boches ici, juifs là-bas." Der Briefwechsel einer deutschen Familie im Exil 1939–1942.* Edited by Jacques Grandjonc and Doris Obschernitzki. Berlin: Hentrich & Hentrich, 2000.

Matthäus, Jürgen, and Mark Roseman, *Jewish Responses to Persecution, 1933–1938.* Vol. 1. Lanham, MD: AltaMira Press in association with the USHMM, 2010.

McDonald, James G. *Refugees and Rescue: The Diaries and Papers of James G. McDonald, 1935–1945.* Edited by Richard Breitman, Barbara McDonald Stewart, and Severin Hochberg. Bloomington: Indiana University Press in association with the USHMM, 2009.

Meinen, Insa. *Die Shoah in Belgien.* Darmstadt: Wissenschaftliche Buchgesellschaft, 2009.

Moß, Christoph, ed. *A Thousand Kisses. The Letters of Georg and Frieda Lindemeyer to their Children, 1937–1941.* London: Bloomsbury Publishing, 2006.

Perechodnik, Calel. *Am I a Murderer? Testament of a Jewish Ghetto Policeman.* Edited by Frank Fox. Boulder, CO: Westview Press, 1996.

Poznański, Jakub. *Tagebuch aus dem Ghetto Litzmannstadt.* Berlin: Metropol, 2011 (originally published in 1960).

Riegner, Gerhart M. *Never Despair: Sixty Years in the Service of the Jewish People and the Cause of Human Rights.* Chicago: Ivan R. Dee in association with the USHMM, 2006.

Rosenfeld, Oskar. *In the Beginning Was the Ghetto: Notebooks from Łódź.* Evanston, IL: Northwestern University Press, 2002.

Roskies, David G., ed. *The Literature of Destruction: Jewish Responses to Catastrophe.* Philadelphia: Jewish Publication Society, 1989.

Rubinowicz, Dawid. *The Diary of Dawid Rubinowicz.* Edmonds, WA: Creative Options, 1982.

Rudashevski, Yitskhok. *The Diary of the Vilna Ghetto, June 1941–April 1943.* Tel Aviv: Ghetto Fighters' House, 1979.

Sebastian, Mihail. *Journal, 1935–1944.* Chicago: Ivan R. Dee in association with the USHMM, 2000.

Seidler, Harry. *Internment: The Diaries of Harry Seidler, May 1940–October 1941.* Edited by Janis Wilton. Sydney: Allen and Unwin, 1986.

Shapira, Kalonymus Kalmish. *Sacred Fire: Torah from the Years of Fury, 1939–1942.* Edited by Deborah Miller. Northvale, NJ: J. Aronson, 2000.

Sierakowiak, Dawid. *The Diary of Dawid Sierakowiak: Five Notebooks from the Łódź Ghetto.* Edited by Alan Adelson. New York: Oxford University Press, 1996.

Sloan, Jacob, ed. *Notes from the Warsaw Ghetto: The Journal of Emmanuel Ringelblum.* New York: McGraw-Hill, 1958.

Stern, Kurt. *Was wird mit uns geschehen? Tagebücher der Internierung 1939 und 1940.* Berlin: Aufbau Verlag, 2006.

Vági, Zoltán, László Csősz, and Gábor Kádár. *The Holocaust in Hungary: Evolution of a Genocide.* Lanham, MD: AltaMira Press in association with the USHMM, forthcoming 2013.

Weichherz, Béla. *In Her Father's Eyes: A Childhood Extinguished by the Holocaust.* Edited by Daniel H. Magilow. New Brunswick, NJ: Rutgers University Press, 2008.

Zelkowicz, Josef. *In Those Terrible Days: Writings from the Lodz Ghetto.* Edited by Michal Unger. Jerusalem: Yad Vashem, 2002.

MONOGRAPH STUDIES, EDITED VOLUMES, AND ARTICLES

Abitbol, Michel. *The Jews of North Africa during the Second World War.* Detroit, MI: Wayne State University Press, 1989.

Altman, Ilya. *Zhertvy nenavisti: Kholokost v SSSR 1941–1945 gg.* Moscow: Fond Kovcheg, 2002.

Altshuler, Mordechai. *Soviet Jewry on the Eve of the Holocaust: A Social and Demographic Profile.* Jerusalem: The Centre for Research of East European Jewry, Hebrew University of Jerusalem and Yad Vashem, 1998.

Aly, Götz. *"Final Solution": Nazi Population Policy and the Murder of the European Jews.* London: Arnold, 1999.

———. *Hitler's Beneficiaries: Plunder, Racial War, and the Nazi Welfare State.* New York: Metropolitan, 2007.

Ambrosewicz-Jacobs, Jolanta, ed. *The Holocaust: Voices of Scholars.* Kraków: Austeria, 2009.

Amkraut, Brian. *Between Home and Homeland: Youth Aliyah from Nazi Germany.* Tuscaloosa: University of Alabama Press, 2006.

Arad, Yitzhak. *Ghetto in Flames: The Struggle and Destruction of the Jews in Vilna in the Holocaust.* New York: Holocaust Library, 1982.

Bajohr, Frank. *"Aryanisation" in Hamburg: The Economic Exclusion of Jews and the Confiscation of their Property in Nazi Germany.* New York: Berghahn Books, 2002.

Bankier, David, and Israel Gutman, eds. *Nazi Europe and the Final Solution.* Jerusalem: Yad Vashem, 2003.

Bankier, David, and Dan Michman, eds. *Holocaust Historiography in Context: Emergence, Challenges, Polemics & Achievements.* New York: Berghahn Books, 2008.

Barkai, Avraham. *From Boycott to Annihilation: The Economic Struggle of German Jews, 1933–1943.* Hanover, NH: University Press of New England, 1989.

Barkan, Elazar, Elizabeth A. Cole, and Kai Struve, eds. *Shared History–Divided Memory. Jews and Others in Soviet-Occupied Poland, 1939–1941.* Leipzig: Leipziger Universitätsverlag, 2007.

Bartov, Omer. *The Holocaust: Origins, Implementation, Aftermath.* London: Routledge, 2000.

Bauer, Yehuda. *American Jewry and the Holocaust: The American Jewish Joint Distribution Committee, 1939–1945.* Detroit, MI: Wayne State University Press, 1981.

———. *The Death of the Shtetl.* New Haven, CT: Yale University Press, 2009.

———. *Jews for Sale? Nazi-Jewish Negotiations, 1933–1945.* New Haven, CT: Yale University Press, 1994.

———. *My Brother's Keeper: A History of the American Jewish Joint Distribution Committee, 1929–1939.* Philadelphia, PA: Jewish Publication Society of America, 1974.

———. *They Chose Life: Jewish Resistance in the Holocaust.* New York: American Jewish Committee, 1973.

Bender, Sara. "The Bialystok and Kielce Ghettos: A Comparative Study." In *Ghettos 1939–1945: New Research and Perspectives on Definition, Daily Life, and Survival.* Washington, DC: USHMM, 2005; at www.ushmm.org/research/center/publications/occasional/2005-08/paper.pdf.

———. *The Jews of Białystok during World War II and the Holocaust.* Hanover, NH: Brandeis University Press, 2008.

Ben-Sasson, Havi. "Christians in the Ghetto: All Saints' Church, Birth of the Holy Virgin Mary Church, and the Jews of the Warsaw Ghetto," *YVS* 31 (2003): 153–73.

Bergen, Doris L. *War & Genocide. A Concise History of the Holocaust.* Lanham, MD: Rowman & Littlefield, 2009 (originally published in 2003).

Berghahn, Marion. *Continental Britons: German-Jewish Refugees from Nazi Germany.* Oxford: Berghahn Books, 2007.

Blatman, Daniel. *For Our Freedom and Yours: The Jewish Labour Bund in Poland, 1939–1949.* London: Vallentine Mitchell, 2003.

Bloxham, Donald. *The Final Solution: A Genocide.* Oxford: Oxford University Press, 2009.

———. *Genocide, the World Wars and the Unweaving of Europe.* London: Vallentine Mitchell, 2008.

Bondy, Ruth. *Trapped: Essays on the History of the Czech Jews, 1939–1945.* Jerusalem: Yad Vashem, 2008.

Bowman, Steven B. *The Agony of Greek Jews, 1940–1945.* Stanford, CA: Stanford University Press, 2009.

Braham, Randolph L. *The Politics of Genocide: The Holocaust in Hungary.* Condensed ed. Detroit, MI: Wayne State University Press, 2000 (originally published in 1981).

Brandon, Ray, and Wendy Lower. *The Shoah in Ukraine: History, Testimony, Memorialization.* Bloomington: Indiana University Press in association with the USHMM, 2008.

Breitman, Richard, and Alan M. Kraut. *American Refugee Policy and European Jewry, 1933–1945.* Bloomington: Indiana University Press, 1987.

Brenner, Rachel Feldhay. *Writing as Resistance: Four Women Confronting the Holocaust: Edith Stein, Simone Weil, Anne Frank, and Etty Hillesum.* University Park, PA: Pennsylvania University Press, 1997.

Browning, Christopher R. *The Path to Genocide: Essays on Launching the Final Solution.* New York: Cambridge University Press, 1992.

Browning, Christopher R., with contributions by Jürgen Matthäus. *The Origins of the Final Solution: The Evolution of Nazi Jewish Policy, September 1939–March 1942.* Lincoln and Jerusalem: University of Nebraska Press and Yad Vashem, 2004.

Burleigh, Michael. *Death and Deliverance: "Euthanasia" in Germany, 1900–1945.* New York: Cambridge University Press, 1994.

———. *The Third Reich: A New History.* New York: Hill and Wang, 2000.

Burleigh, Michael, and Wolfgang Wippermann. *The Racial State: Germany, 1933–1945.* New York: Cambridge University Press, 1991.

Burrin, Philippe. *Hitler and the Jews: The Genesis of the Holocaust.* London: Edward Arnold, 1994.

Caestecker, Frank, and Bob Moore, eds. *Refugees from Nazi Germany and the Liberal European States.* New York: Berghahn Books, 2010.

Caplan, Jane, and Nikolaus Wachsmann, eds. *Concentration Camps in Nazi Germany: The New Histories.* New York: Routledge, 2010.

Caron, Vicki. *Uneasy Asylum: France and the Jewish Refugee Crisis, 1933–1942.* Stanford, CA: Stanford University Press, 1999.

Carpi, Daniel. *Between Mussolini and Hitler: The Jews and the Italian Authorities in France and Tunisia.* Hanover, NH: Brandeis University Press in association with University Press of New England, 1994.

Case, Holly. *Between States: The Transylvanian Question and the European Idea during World War II.* Stanford, CA: Stanford University Press, 2009.

Cesarani, David, ed. *Holocaust. Critical Concepts in Historical Studies.* 6 vols. London: Routledge, 2004.

———. *The Jewish Chronicle and Anglo-Jewry, 1841–1991.* New York: Cambridge University Press, 1994.

Cochavi, Yehoyakim. "'The Hostile Alliance': The Relationship between the Reichsvereinigung of Jews in Germany and the Regime." *YVS* 22 (1992): 237–72.

Cohen, Asher, and Yehoyakim Cochavi, eds. *Zionist Youth Movements during the Shoah.* New York: Peter Lang, 1995.

Corni, Gustavo. *Hitler's Ghettos: Voices from a Beleaguered Society, 1939–1944.* London: Arnold, 2002.

Cox, John M. *Circles of Resistance: Jewish, Leftist, and Youth Dissidence in Nazi Germany.* New York: Peter Lang, 2009.

Davies, Norman, and Antony Polonsky. *Jews in Eastern Poland and the USSR, 1939–46.* New York: St. Martin's Press, 1991.

Dean, Martin. *Robbing the Jews: The Confiscation of Jewish Property in the Holocaust, 1933–1945.* New York: Cambridge University Press in association with the USHMM, 2008.

Dean, Martin, Constantin Goschler, and Philipp Ther, eds. *Robbery and Restitution: The Conflict over Jewish Property in Europe.* New York: Berghahn Books, 2007.

Dekel-Chen, Jonathan, David Gaunt, Natan M. Meir, and Israel Bartal, eds. *Anti-Jewish Violence: Rethinking the Pogrom in East European History.* Bloomington: Indiana University Press, 2010.

Deletant, Dennis. "Ghetto Experience in Golta, Transnistria, 1942–1944." *Holocaust and Genocide Studies* 18 (spring, 2004): 1–26.

———. *Hitler's Forgotten Ally: Ion Antonescu and His Regime, Romania 1940–1944.* New York: Palgrave Macmillan, 2006.

Diamond, Hanna. *Fleeing Hitler: France 1940.* New York: Oxford University Press, 2007.

Dillmann, Hans-Ulrich, and Susanne Heim. *Fluchtpunkt Karibik. Jüdische Emigranten in der Dominikanischen Republik* (Berlin: Christoph Links Verlag, 2009).

Dwork, Debórah, and Robert Jan van Pelt. *Auschwitz, 1270 to the Present.* New York: W. W. Norton, 1996.

———. *Flight from the Reich: Refugee Jews, 1933–1946.* New York: W. W. Norton, 2009.

———. *Holocaust: A History.* New York: W. W. Norton, 2002.

Eber, Irene. *Chinese and Jews: Encounters Between Cultures.* London: Vallentine Mitchell, 2008.

Engel, David. *The Holocaust: The Third Reich and the Jews.* New York: Longman, 2000.

———. *In the Shadow of Auschwitz: The Polish Government-in-Exile and the Jews, 1939–1942.* Chapel Hill: University of North Carolina Press, 1987.

Engelking, Barbara, and Jacek Leociak. *The Warsaw Ghetto: A Guide to the Perished City.* New Haven, CT: Yale University Press, 2009.

Epstein, Catherine. *Model Nazi: Arthur Greiser and the Occupation of Western Poland.* Oxford: Oxford University Press, 2010.

Farbstein, Esther. *Hidden in Thunder: Perspectives on Faith, Halachah and Leadership during the Holocaust.* 2 vols. Jerusalem: Mossad Harav Kook, 2007.

Fatal-Knaani, Tikva. "The Jews of Pinsk, 1939–1943: Through the Prism of New Documentation." *YVS* 29 (2001): 149–82.

Feferman, Kiril. "Jewish Refugees and Evacuees under Soviet Rule and German Occupation: The North Caucasus." In *Revolution, Repression and Revival. The Soviet Jewish Experience,* edited by Zvi Y. Gitelman et al., 155–78. Lanham, MD: Rowman & Littlefield, 2007.

Fink, Carole. *Defending the Rights of Others: The Great Powers, the Jews, and International Minority Protection, 1878–1938.* New York: Cambridge University Press, 2004.

Fleming, Katherine E. *Greece: A Jewish History.* Princeton, NJ: Princeton University Press, 2008.

Friedlander, Henry. *The Origins of Nazi Genocide: From Euthanasia to the Final Solution.* Chapel Hill: University of North Carolina Press, 1995.

Friedländer, Saul. *Nazi Germany and the Jews.* Vol. 1, *The Years of Persecution, 1933–1939.* New York: HarperCollins, 1997.

———. *Nazi Germany and the Jews.* Vol. 2, *The Years of Extermination, 1939–1945.* New York: HarperCollins, 2007.

Friedman, Philip. *Roads to Extinction: Essays on the Holocaust.* Edited by Ada June Friedman. New York: Conference on Jewish Social Studies and the Jewish Publication Society of America, 1980.

Friling, Tuvia. *Arrows in the Dark: David Ben-Gurion, the Yishuv Leadership, and Rescue Attempts during the Holocaust.* 2 vols. Madison: University of Wisconsin Press, 2005.

Garbarini, Alexandra. *Numbered Days: Diaries and the Holocaust*. New Haven, CT: Yale University Press, 2006.

Gerlach, Wolfgang, and Victoria J. Barnett, eds. *And the Witnesses Were Silent: The Confessing Church and the Persecution of the Jews*. Lincoln: University of Nebraska Press, 2000.

Gitelman, Zvi, and Yaacov Ro'i, eds. *Revolution, Repression, and Revival: The Soviet Jewish Experience*. Lanham, MD: Rowman & Littlefield, 2007.

Goeschel, Christian. *Suicide in Nazi Germany*. New York: Oxford University Press, 2009.

Gottlieb, Amy Zahl. *Men of Vision: Anglo-Jewry's Aid to Victims of the Nazi Regime, 1933–1945*. London: Weidenfeld and Nicholson, 1998.

Grabowski, Jan. *Rescue for Money: Paid Helpers in Poland, 1939–1945*. Jerusalem: Yad Vashem, 2008.

Gross, Jan T. *Polish Society under German Occupation: The Generalgouvernement, 1939–1944*. Princeton, NJ: Princeton University Press, 1979.

———. *Revolution from Abroad: The Soviet Conquest of Poland's Western Ukraine and Western Belorussia*. Princeton, NJ: Princeton University Press, 2002.

Gruner, Wolf. *Jewish Forced Labor under the Nazis: Economic Needs and Racial Aims, 1938–1944*. New York: Cambridge University Press in association with the USHMM, 2006.

Gutman, Yisrael. *The Jews of Warsaw, 1939–1943: Ghetto, Underground, Revolt*. Bloomington: Indiana University Press, 1982.

Gutman, Yisrael, and Cynthia J. Haft, eds. *Patterns of Jewish Leadership in Nazi Europe, 1933–1945: Proceedings of the Third Yad Vashem International Historical Conference, Jerusalem, April 4–7, 1977*. Jerusalem: Yad Vashem, 1979.

Heim, Susanne, Beate Meyer, and Francis R. Nicosia, eds. *"Wer bleibt, opfert seine Jahre, vielleicht sein Leben." Deutsche Juden 1938–1941*. Göttingen: Wallstein, 2010.

Hilberg, Raul. *The Destruction of the European Jews*. 3 vols. 3rd ed. New Haven, CT: Yale University Press, 2003 (originally published in 1961).

Horwitz, Gordon J. *Ghettostadt: Łódź and the Making of a Nazi City*. Cambridge, MA: Belknap Press, 2008.

Institute of Jewish Affairs of the World Jewish Congress. *Unity in Dispersion: A History of the World Jewish Congress*, 2nd rev. ed. New York: Institute of Jewish Affairs of the World Jewish Congress, 1948.

Ioanid, Radu. *The Holocaust in Romania: The Destruction of Jews and Gypsies under the Antonescu Regime, 1940–1944*. Chicago: Ivan R. Dee in association with the USHMM, 2000.

Jackson, Julian. *France: The Dark Years, 1940–1944*. New York: Oxford University Press, 2001.

Jockusch, Laura. *Collect and Record! Jewish Holocaust Documentation in Early Postwar Europe*. New York: Oxford University Press, 2012.

Kamenec, Ivan. *On the Trail of Tragedy: The Holocaust in Slovakia*. Bratislava: Hajko & Hajková, 2007.

Kaplan, Marion A. *Between Dignity and Despair: Jewish Life in Nazi Germany*. New York: Oxford University Press, 1998.

———. *Dominican Haven: The Jewish Refugee Settlement in Sosúa, 1940–1945*. New York: Museum of Jewish Heritage, 2008.

Kaplan, Thomas Pegelow. *The Language of Nazi Genocide: Linguistic Violence and the Struggle of Germans of Jewish Ancestry*. New York: Cambridge University Press, 2009.

Kassow, Samuel D. *Who Will Write Our History? Emanuel Ringelblum, the Warsaw Ghetto, and the Oyneg Shabes Archive.* Bloomington: Indiana University Press, 2007.

Katz, Steven T. *The Impact of the Holocaust on Jewish Theology.* New York: New York University Press, 2005.

Katz, Steven T., Shlomo Biderman, and Gershon Greenberg, eds. *Wrestling with God: Jewish Theological Responses during and after the Holocaust.* New York: Oxford University Press, 2007.

Krakowski, Shmuel. *The War of the Doomed: Jewish Armed Resistance in Poland.* New York: Holmes and Meier, 1984.

Kranzler, David. *Japanese, Nazis & Jews: The Jewish Refugee Community of Shanghai, 1938–1945.* Hoboken: KTAV, 1988

Kwiet, Konrad, and Helmut Eschwege. *Selbstbehauptung und Widerstand. Deutsche Juden im Kampf um Existenz und Menschenwürde, 1933–1945.* Hamburg: Christians, 1984.

Láníček, Jan. "'To Get a Refusal Would Result in an Unfortunate Loss of Prestige': The Czechoslovak Government-in-Exile and the Holocaust." *Holocaust Studies: A Journal of Culture and History* 14, no. 3 (2008): 119–41.

Laqueur, Walter. *The Changing Face of Antisemitism: From Ancient Times to the Present Day.* New York: Oxford University Press, 2006.

Laskier, Michael. *North African Jewry in the Twentieth Century: The Jews of Morocco, Tunisia, and Algeria.* New York: New York University Press, 1994.

Leighton-Langer, Peter. *The King's Own Loyal Enemy Aliens: German and Austrian Refugees in Britain's Armed Forces, 1939–45.* London: Vallentine Mitchell, 2006.

Levene, Mark. *Genocide in the Age of Nation State.* 2 vols. London: I. B. Tauris, 2005.

Levy, James P. *Appeasement and Rearmament: Britain, 1936–1939.* Lanham, MD: Rowman & Littlefield, 2006.

London, Louise. *Whitehall and the Jews, 1933–1948: British Immigration Policy, Jewish Refugees and the Holocaust.* New York: Cambridge University Press, 2000.

Longerich, Peter. *Holocaust: The Nazi Persecution and Murder of the Jews.* Oxford: Oxford University Press, 2010.

Lower, Wendy. *Nazi Empire Building and the Holocaust in Ukraine.* Chapel Hill: University of North Carolina Press, 2005.

Lukas, Richard C. *The Forgotten Holocaust: The Poles under German Occupation, 1939–1944*, 2nd rev. ed. New York: Hippocrene, 1997.

Lumans, Valdis O. *Himmler's Auxiliaries: The Volksdeutsche Mittelstelle and the German National Minorities of Europe, 1933–1945.* Chapel Hill: University of North Carolina Press, 1993.

Maierhof, Gudrun. *Selbstbehauptung im Chaos: Frauen in der jüdischen Selbsthilfe 1933–1943.* Frankfurt am Main: Campus, 2002.

Marrus, Michael R. *The Holocaust in History.* New York: New American Library, 1989.

———. *The Unwanted: European Refugees from the First World War Through the Cold War.* Philadelphia: Temple University Press, 2002 (originally published in 1985).

Martini, Joachim Carlos. *Musik als Form geistigen Widerstandes. Jüdische Musikerinnen und Musiker 1933–1945: Das Beispiel Frankfurt am Main.* 2 vols. Frankfurt am Main: Brandes & Apsel, 2010.

Mazower, Mark. *Hitler's Empire: Nazi Rule in Occupied Europe.* London: Allen Lane, 2008.

Mazzenga, Maria, ed. *American Religious Responses to Kristallnacht.* New York: Palgrave Macmillan, 2009.

Mendelsohn, Ezra. *The Jews of East Central Europe between the World Wars.* Bloomington: Indiana University Press, 1983.

Meyer, Beate. *"Jüdische Mischlinge": Rassenpolitik und Verfolgungserfahrung 1933–1945.* Hamburg: Dölling und Galitz, 1999.

———. *A Fatal Balancing Act: The Dilemma of the Reich Association of Jews in Germany, 1939–1945.* New York: Berghahn, 2013.

Meyer, Beate, Hermann Simon, and Chana Schütz, eds. *Jews in Nazi Berlin: From Kristallnacht to Liberation.* Chicago: Chicago University Press, 2009.

Michaelis, Meir. *Mussolini and the Jews: German-Italian Relations and the Jewish Question in Italy, 1922–1945.* Oxford: Clarendon Press, 1978.

Michlic, Joanna B. *Poland's Threatening Other: The Image of the Jew from 1880 to the Present.* Lincoln: University of Nebraska Press, 2006.

Michman, Dan. *The Emergence of Jewish Ghettos during the Holocaust.* Cambridge: Cambridge University Press, 2010.

———. *Holocaust Historiography: A Jewish Perspective: Conceptualizations, Terminology, Approaches and Fundamental Issues.* London: Vallentine Mitchell, 2003.

Minczeles, Henri. *Histoire générale du Bund: un movement révolutionnaire juif.* Paris: Denoël, 1999.

Młynarczyk, Jacek Andrzej, and Jochen Böhler, eds. *Der Judenmord in den eingegliederten polnischen Gebieten 1939–1945.* Osnabrück: Fibre, 2010.

Moore, Bob. *Survivors: Jewish Self-Help and Rescue in Nazi-Occupied Western Europe.* New York: Oxford University Press, 2010.

———. *Victims and Survivors: The Nazi Persecution of the Jews in the Netherlands, 1940–1945.* London: Arnold, 1997.

Musial, Bogdan, ed. *"Aktion Reinhard": Der Völkermord an den Juden im Generalgouvernement 1941–1944.* Osnabrück: Fibre, 2004.

Nicosia, Francis R. *Zionism and Anti-Semitism in Nazi Germany.* New York: Cambridge University Press, 2008.

Nicosia, Francis R., and David Scrase, eds. *Jewish Life in Nazi Germany: Dilemmas and Responses.* New York: Berghahn Books, 2010.

Ofer, Dalia. *Escaping the Holocaust: Illegal Immigration to the Land of Israel, 1939–1944.* New York: Oxford University Press, 1990.

———. "The Ghettos in Transnistria and Ghettos under German Occupation in Eastern Europe. A Comparative Approach." In *Im Ghetto 1939–1945: Neue Forschungen zu Alltag und Umfeld,* edited by Christoph Dieckmann and Babette Quinkert, 30–54. Göttingen: Wallstein, 2009.

Ofer, Dalia, and Lenore J. Weitzman. *Women in the Holocaust.* New Haven, CT: Yale University Press, 1998.

Ogilvie, Sara A., and Scott Miller. *Refuge Denied: The St. Louis Passengers and the Holocaust.* Madison: University of Wisconsin Press, 2006.

Oppenheim, Israel. *The Struggle of Jewish Youth for Productivization: The Zionist Youth Movement in Poland.* Boulder, CO: East European Monographs, 1989.

Paucker, Arnold, ed., with Sylvia Gilchrist and Barbara Suchy. *Die Juden im nationalsozialistischen Deutschland / The Jews in Nazi Germany, 1933–1943.* Tübingen: J. C. B. Mohr, 1986.

Paulsson, Gunnar S. *Secret City: The Hidden Jews of Warsaw, 1940–1945.* New Haven, CT: Yale University Press, 2002.

Pinchuk, Ben-Cion. *Shtetl Jews under Soviet Rule: Eastern Poland on the Eve of the Holocaust.* Oxford: Basil Blackwell, 1990.

Poliakov, Leon, and Jacques Sabille. *Jews under the Italian Occupation.* New York: Howard Fertig, 1983 (originally published in 1955).

Porat, Dina. *The Blue and the Yellow Stars of David: The Zionist Leadership in Palestine and the Holocaust, 1939–1945.* Cambridge, MA: Harvard University Press, 1990.

Poznanski, Renée. *Jews in France during World War II.* Hanover, NH: University Press of New England in association with the USHMM, 2001.

Quack, Sibylle, ed. *Between Sorrow and Strength: Women Refugees of the Nazi Period.* New York: Cambridge University Press, 1995.

Raider, Mark A., ed. *Nahum Goldmann: Statesman without a State.* Albany: State University of New York Press, 2009.

Rayski, Adam. *The Choice of the Jews under Vichy: Between Submission and Resistance.* Notre Dame, IN: University of Notre Dame Press in association with the USHMM, 2005.

Rentrop, Petra. *Tatorte der "Endlösung": Das Ghetto Minsk und die Vernichtungsstätte von Maly Trostinez.* Berlin: Metropol, 2011.

Rohrlich, Ruby, ed. *Resisting the Holocaust.* Oxford: Berg, 1998.

Rose, Norman. *Chaim Weizmann: A Biography.* New York: Penguin, 1986.

Roseman, Mark. "Holocaust Perpetrators in Victims' Eyes." In *Years of Persecution, Years of Extermination: Saul Friedländer and the Future of Holocaust Studies,* edited by Christian Wiese and Paul Betts, 81–100. London: Continuum, 2010.

———. *The Wannsee Conference and the Final Solution: A Reconsideration.* New York: Metropolitan Books, 2002.

Roskies, David G. *Against the Apocalypse: Responses to Catastrophe in Modern Jewish Culture.* Cambridge, MA: Harvard University Press, 1984.

Rossino, Alexander. *Hitler Strikes Poland: Blitzkrieg, Ideology, and Atrocity.* Lawrence: University Press of Kansas, 2003.

Roth, John K., and Elisabeth Maxwell, eds. *Remembering for the Future: The Holocaust in an Age of Genocide.* 3 vols. New York: Palgrave Macmillan, 2001.

Rothkirchen, Livia. *The Jews of Bohemia and Moravia: Facing the Holocaust.* Lincoln: University of Nebraska Press, 2005.

Rutherford, Philip T. *Prelude to the Final Solution: The Nazi Program for Deporting Ethnic Poles, 1939–1941.* Lawrence: University Press of Kansas, 2007.

Saint-Geours, Jean. *Témoignage sur la spoliation des français juifs (1940–1944). Histoire et mémoire (1940–2000).* Paris: Éditions le Manuscrit, 2008.

Sarfatti, Michele. *The Jews in Mussolini's Italy: From Equality to Persecution.* Madison: University of Wisconsin Press, 2006.

Segev, Tom. *One Palestine, Complete: Jews and Arabs under the British Mandate.* New York: Metropolitan Books, 2000.

Snyder, Timothy. *Bloodlands: Europe between Hitler and Stalin.* New York: Basic Books, 2010.

Solonari, Vladimir. *Purifying the Nation: Population Exchange and Ethnic Cleansing in Nazi-Allied Romania.* Baltimore, MD: Johns Hopkins University Press, 2009.

Steinbacher, Sybille. *Auschwitz: A History.* New York: Ecco, 2005.

Steinweis, Alan E. *Kristallnacht 1938.* Cambridge, MA: The Belknap Press, 2009.

Stone, Dan, ed. *The Historiography of the Holocaust.* New York: Palgrave Macmillan, 2004.

Tec, Nechama. *Resilience and Courage: Women, Men, and the Holocaust.* New Haven, CT: Yale University Press, 2003.

Tendyra, Bernadeta. *The Polish Government in Exile, 1939–45.* London: Routledge, 2010.

Tooze, J. Adam. *The Wages of Destruction: The Making and Breaking of the Nazi Economy.* New York: Viking, 2007.

Trunk, Isaiah. *Judenrat: The Jewish Councils in Eastern Europe under Nazi Occupation.* Lincoln: University of Nebraska Press, 1996 (originally published in 1972).

———. *Łódź Ghetto: A History.* Edited by Robert Moses Shapiro. Bloomington: Indiana University Press, 2006.

Unger, Michal, ed. *The Last Ghetto: Life in the Lodz Ghetto, 1940–1944.* Jerusalem: Yad Vashem, 1995.

Weinberg, Gerhard L. *A World at Arms: A Global History of World War II.* Cambridge: Cambridge University Press, 1994.

Weiss, Aharon. "Jewish Leadership in Occupied Poland—Postures and Attitudes." *YVS* 12 (1977): 335–65.

Westermann, Edward B. *Hitler's Police Battalions: Enforcing Racial War in the East.* Lawrence: University Press of Kansas, 2005.

Wildt, Michael. *An Uncompromising Generation: The Nazi Leadership of the Reich Security Main Office.* Madison: University of Wisconsin Press, 2009.

Zapruder, Alexandra, ed. *Salvaged Pages: Young Writers' Diaries of the Holocaust.* New Haven, CT: Yale University Press, 2002.

Zimmerman, Joshua D., ed. *Jews in Italy under Fascist and Nazi Rule, 1922–1945.* New York: Cambridge University Press, 2005.

Zuccotti, Susan. *The Italians and the Holocaust: Persecution, Rescue, and Survival.* Lincoln: University of Nebraska Press, 1996 (originally published in 1987).

Zucker, Bat-Ami. *Cecilia Razovsky and the American-Jewish Women's Rescue Operations in the Second World War.* London: Vallentine Mitchell, 2008.

GLOSSARY

AJJDC *See* **American Jewish Joint Distribution Committee.**

"**Aktion Reinhard**" The code name for the Nazi plan to murder the Jews living in the Generalgouvernement. By the spring of 1942, the Germans had established killing sites at Bełżec, Sobibór, and Treblinka for the purpose of murdering large numbers of Jews by gas. Under the pretense of "resettlement," deportees from the Generalgouvernement and later from elsewhere in Europe were brought in on rail transports beginning in March 1942. By the end of 1943, some 2 million people had been murdered, the overwhelming majority of them Jews.

See Yitzhak Arad, *Belzec, Sobibor, Treblinka: The Operation Reinhard Death Camps* (Bloomington: Indiana University Press, 1987).

"**Aktion T-4**" Beginning with the so-called child euthanasia program authorized by Hitler in the fall of 1939, which killed at least five thousand physically and mentally disabled children during the war years, Nazi eugenics policy had developed into a campaign of systematic murder by 1940, code-named after its headquarters at Berlin's Tiergartenstrasse 4. By August 1941 when Hitler ordered a halt to the "Aktion T-4" program, at least 70,273 institutionalized mentally and physically disabled adults, mostly non-Jews, had been murdered by carbon monoxide at specially designated gassing installations.

See Henry Friedlander, *The Origins of Nazi Genocide: From Euthanasia to the Final Solution* (Chapel Hill: University of North Carolina Press, 1995).

aliyah (Hebrew: "ascent") This Zionist term denoted the notion of "return" of diaspora Jews to their ancestral land in Palestine. Organized by the Jewish Agency for Palestine and other Zionist groups, *aliyah* became one of the most important initiatives after 1933 in facilitating emigration of Jews from European countries threatened by Nazi persecution. By 1941, more than fifty thousand Jews from the German Reich had made it to Palestine; at the same time, in the face of more stringent British immigration restriction, illegal *aliyah* (*Aliyah Bet*) increased in importance and continued until the founding of the state of Israel in 1948.

See Brian Amkraut, *Between Home and Homeland: Youth Aliyah from Nazi Germany* (Tuscaloosa: University of Alabama Press, 2006).

American Jewish Joint Distribution Committee (AJJDC, also AJDC, JDC, Joint) Founded in 1914, the organization provided assistance to Jews around the world, particularly in eastern Europe. During the Nazi era, it was involved in emigration planning and relief work in Germany and other countries under Nazi domination. The AJJDC's efforts continued after the war, when it became involved in supporting the rebuilding of Jewish life in Europe.

See Yehuda Bauer, *American Jewry and the Holocaust: The American Jewish Joint Distribution Committee, 1939–1945* (Detroit, MI: Wayne State University Press, 1981).

Anschluss (German: joining, connection) This word is euphemistic shorthand for the German annexation of Austria in March 1938. Although it constituted an act of aggression on the part of Germany against its independent neighbor that went hand in hand with mass arrests and anti-Jewish violence, the Anschluss met with widespread popular support, both in Austria and in Germany. Austria remained part of the German Reich until the end of World War II.

Antonescu, Ion (1882–1946) A right-wing leader of Romania during most of World War II, Antonescu gained political power in 1940 by forming a partnership with the Iron Guard, an indigenous fascist movement, and establishing a one-party dictatorship under his rule. After Antonescu had purged his government of the Iron Guard and joined the Axis, Romania provided troops for the invasion of the Soviet Union, Operation Barbarossa. Following an unsuccessful attempt to negotiate with the Allies, he was deposed in 1944. Despite his unwillingness to bow to German demands regarding the implementation of the "Final Solution" in Romania proper, Antonescu was responsible for the deportation and deaths of hundreds of thousands of Jews and Roma in Transnistria and other occupied areas. He was put on trial in Bucharest after the war and was executed.

See Dennis Deletant, *Hitler's Forgotten Ally: Ion Antonescu and His Regime, Romania 1940–1944* (New York: Palgrave Macmillan, 2006).

Ashkenazim Central and east European Jews descended from the medieval Jewish communities in Rhineland and Alsace. This diverse demographic group shared certain cultural characteristics: the Yiddish language remained the common language of millions of Ashkenazim on the eve of the Nazi invasion of Poland, the Baltic states, and the Soviet Union.

See Howard N. Lupovitch, *Jews and Judaism in World History* (New York: Routledge, 2010).

Atlantic Carrying almost two thousand Jewish refugees, this transport ship left the Romanian port of Tulcea for Palestine in September 1940. The British navy intercepted the ship and denied entry to Palestine to its passengers, who were then shipped to the British island of Mauritius in the Indian Ocean. They were held there until the end of the war.

See Dina Porat, *The Blue and Yellow Stars of David: The Zionist Leadership in Palestine and the Holocaust, 1939–1945* (Cambridge, MA: Harvard University Press, 1990).

Atlantic Charter Also known as the Joint Declaration, the Atlantic Charter, signed by Great Britain and the United States on August 14, 1941, stated that neither party was seeking territorial gains from war; reaffirmed the right of nations to self-determination; called for a world free of want and fear; and postwar disarmament, among other goals. In the Declaration of United Nations on January 1, 1942, governments allied to Great Britain and the United States pledged their support for the Charter's principles.

See Elizabeth Borgwardt, *A New Deal for the World: America's Vision for Human Rights* (Cambridge, MA: Harvard University Press, 2005).

Auschwitz A complex of some forty concentration camps, labor camps, and extermination facilities that the Germans built and operated during the war, almost 1,300,000 people, 90 percent of them Jews, were murdered in Auschwitz. The network revolved around the main camp (Auschwitz I), located outside the town of Oświęcim in German-annexed Poland, and included the combined concentration camp and killing center (Auschwitz II-Birkenau), Auschwitz III-Monowitz (also known as Buna), and a system of about forty subcamps. The Red Army liberated the most infamous part of the camp, the killing center at Birkenau in which Jews were murdered in gas chambers, on January 27, 1945.

See Sybille Steinbacher, *Auschwitz: A History* (New York: Ecco, 2005).

Auschwitz II-Birkenau Planned since late September 1941 and the largest camp in the Auschwitz complex, Birkenau functioned as a killing center and a concentration camp. Most victims murdered in Auschwitz perished here, as many as 90 percent or more than one million people, predominantly Jews. Others killed at Birkenau included tens of thousands of Poles, Roma, Soviet POWs, and prisoners of other nationalities. Auschwitz II-Birkenau played a central role in the mass murder of European Jews, particularly in May–July 1944 of Jews from Hungary.

See Yisrael Gutman and Michael Berenbaum, *Anatomy of the Auschwitz Death Camp* (Bloomington: Indiana University Press in association with the USHMM, 1994).

Axis In addition to the core nations of the Tripartite Pact of 1940—Germany, Italy, and Japan—the Axis included a number of aligned nations (such as Hungary, Romania, and Bulgaria) and puppet regimes (Slovakia and the Independent State of Croatia). At the peak of its expansion during World War II, Axis control reached beyond Europe and Asia into northern Africa and the South Pacific.

See Richard L. DiNardo, *Germany and the Axis Powers: From Coalition to Collapse* (Lawrence: University of Kansas Press, 2005).

Baeck, Leo (1873–1956) After the Nazis' rise to power, Baeck, a rabbi and scholar, served as president of the central German Jewish body and, from early 1939, of the Reichsvereinigung, which was controlled by the Gestapo. In early 1943 Baeck was deported to Theresienstadt, where he played a largely informal role in the ghetto community. He survived the war, emigrated to London, and continued his political, religious, and educational endeavors until his death. In 1955, an institute for the study of German Jewish history was created in his name, with branches in London, New York, and Jerusalem.

See Beate Meyer, *A Fatal Balancing Act: the Dilemma of the Reich Association of Jews in Germany, 1939–1945* (New York: Berghahn Books, 2013).

Bełżec Beginning in the fall of 1941, the Bełżec labor camp, constructed in the Lublin district of the Generalgouvernement in 1940, was modified to become a killing center for the extermination of Jews. It became operational in March 1942. The majority of the murders at Bełżec were conducted as part of "Aktion Reinhard," by gassing. In order to destroy evidence of the killing center, bodies of the victims were later exhumed and burned before the closure of the camp in the spring of 1943. It is estimated that four hundred thousand to six hundred thousand Jews, Poles, and Roma were killed during the camp's operations.

See Yitzhak Arad, *Belzec, Sobibor, Treblinka: The Operation Reinhard Death Camps* (Bloomington: Indiana University Press, 1987).

Birman, Meir (1891–1955) He spent about thirty years in China working as director of the HIAS office in Harbin and later Shanghai. Closely associated with HICEM, Birman was affiliated with the Far Eastern Central Information Bureau, an organization working to assist Jewish refugees in the Far East. He left for the United States after World War II.

See Fruma Mohrer and Marek Web, *Guide to the YIVO Archives* (New York: YIVO Institute for Jewish Research, 1998), 34–35.

Blau, Edith (b. 1921) Born in Danzig, she moved with her parents to Bydgoszcz in Poland in early 1939. There she met Ruth Goldbarth and Lutek Orenbach, with whom she corresponded in the early years of the war. In late 1939 Edith and her mother moved to Minden, her mother's hometown in Germany. Edith was drafted into forced labor in the autumn of 1940 in Minden and was deported to Riga with her mother in December 1941. After the liquidation of the Riga ghetto in 1944, both were sent to the Stutthof concentration camp. Edith and her mother managed to escape during the evacuation of the camp in January 1945. After the war, Edith married a British officer and moved to London with him and her mother. Edith's father was presumably killed during the war by Germans in Bydgoszcz.

See Edith Brandon, *Letters from Tomaszow* (London: self-published, 1994).

Board of Deputies of British Jews This central representative organization of British Jewry was established in 1790 to address Jewish community affairs (such as social welfare and education), as well as external matters. From the 1930s and into World War II, the Board's president, since 1939 under Selig Brodetsky, a Zionist, focused on assisting Jewish refugees, opposing British restrictions on immigration, and combating antisemitism.

See Todd M. Endelman, *The Jews of Britain, 1656 to 2000* (Berkeley: University of California Press, 2002).

Bund, Bundism, the Bund (General Jewish Workers' Alliance; Yiddish: *Algemeyner yidisher arbeter bund*) The Bund was founded in the last decade of the nineteenth century as a Jewish socialist movement in the Russian Empire. Combining many strains of Jewish secular and progressive thought, the Bund advocated Marxist-inflected socialism and stood for Jewish secular society in eastern Europe, with Yiddish as its common language. In the interwar period, the Bolsheviks suppressed the Bund in the Soviet Union, but the organization continued to operate in newly independent Poland. With Yiddish-speaking Jewish society annihilated in the Holocaust, the Bund receded to the political margins after World War II.

See Zvi Gitelman, ed., *The Emergence of Modern Jewish Politics: Bundism and Zionism in Eastern Europe* (Pittsburgh, PA: University of Pittsburgh Press, 2003).

Chełmno (Kulmhof) German officials in the Warthegau established this mass murder site in December 1941 for the purpose of killing the region's Jews, particularly the inhabitants of the Łódź ghetto, as well as other groups of "unwanted" people. The SS unit operating the site murdered most of its victims by carbon monoxide poisoning and asphyxiation in a sealed truck ("gas van"). Between early December 1941 and mid-July 1944 more than 150,000 people, the vast majority of them Jews, were murdered at Chełmno.

See Shmuel Krakowski, *Chełmno: A Small Village in Europe: The First Nazi Mass Extermination Camp* (Jerusalem: Yad Vashem, 2009).

Cohn, Willy (1888–1941) Born in Breslau, Lower Silesia, Cohn was a historian, educator, and veteran of World War I. After losing his teaching position in Breslau in April 1933, Cohn undertook numerous research projects on German Jewish history while maintaining his extensive diary commentaries. On November 21, 1941, Cohn, his wife Gertrude (Trudi, née Rothmann), and two of their daughters were deported to Kovno in German-occupied Lithuania and murdered upon arrival.

See Willy Cohn, *Kein Recht, Nirgends. Tagebuch vom Untergang des Breslauer Judentums, 1933–1941*, ed. Norbert Conrads (Cologne: Böhlau Verlag, 2007).

Czerniaków, Adam (1880–1942) An engineer from Warsaw and member of the Polish National Assembly in the interwar period, Czerniaków was appointed head of the Warsaw *Judenrat* by the Nazis in October 1939. As leader of the Jewish institution whose task was to assist the Nazis in their anti-Jewish policies, Czerniaków tried to prevent, delay, or undercut German orders and to improve living conditions in the ghetto. In July 1942, when he realized that the beginning of large-scale deportations to Treblinka meant death, he committed suicide rather than comply with German demands. The diary Czerniaków kept remains one of the most important accounts of life in the Warsaw ghetto.

See Raul Hilberg, Stanislaw Staron, and Josef Kermisz, eds., *The Warsaw Diary of Adam Czerniakow: Prelude to Doom* (Chicago: Ivan R. Dee in association with the USHMM, 1999).

Dreyfus, Lucien (1882–1943?) Born in Alsace, Dreyfus undertook rabbinical studies in Berlin but decided to become a gymnasium/lycée professor in Strasbourg, close to his hometown. From the mid-1920s until World War II, he also served as editor of the weekly Jewish organ *La Tribune Juive de Strasbourg*. After the German invasion of France, Dreyfus and his wife, Marthe (née Weil; b. 1883), fled to Poitiers and later to the city of Nice in Vichy, where he worked for ORT. In May 1942, their daughter, Mariette, her husband, Jacques Schumacher, and their daughter, Monique, managed to escape to the United States. In September 1943, after Italy's armistice with the Allies, Germany occupied Vichy. Dreyfus and his wife were arrested in October 1943 and deported the following month from the Drancy transit camp to Auschwitz, where they were murdered.

See Alexandra Garbarini, *Numbered Days: Diaries and the Holocaust* (New Haven, CT: Yale University Press, 2006), 23–57.

Dubnow, Simon (1860–1941) Born in Belorussia, Dubnow was a scholar who wrote for the Russian Jewish press and promoted the study of Jewish history. After completing a traditional Jewish education, he lived in St. Petersburg and Odessa, and advocated a number of reforms that would affect Jewish life in Russia, from modernizing Jewish education to Jewish emancipation. He left Russia in 1922 and settled in Berlin, where he published his magnum opus, the ten-volume *World History of the Jewish People*. After the Nazi seizure of power, Dubnow and his family emigrated to Riga. Following the German occupation of the Baltic States, he was murdered in December 1941.

See Sophie Dubnov-Erlich, *The Life and Work of S. M. Dubnov: Diaspora Nationalism and Jewish History* (Bloomington: Indiana University Press, 1991).

Eichmann, Adolf (1906–1962) Raised in the Austrian city of Linz, Eichmann joined the Nazi Party and the SS in Austria in 1932 before he moved to Germany, where he also joined Reinhard Heydrich's SD. Following the Anschluss of Austria, Eichmann assumed a key role as an expert for "Jewish affairs." After the beginning of the war, he became the chief agent of Nazi anti-Jewish policies organized by the Reichssicherheitshauptamt (RSHA) that led to the deportation and systematic murder of European Jews. Long in hiding after the war, the Israeli secret service finally abducted him in Argentina in May 1960, and he was put on trial in Jerusalem. Sentenced to death by the court, he was hanged in June 1962.

See Hans Safrian, *Eichmann's Men* (Cambridge, MA: Cambridge University Press, 2010).

Einsatzgruppen Following the German invasion of Poland in 1939, these mobile units of the Security Police and SD headed by Reinhard Heydrich played a key role in the murder of civilians deemed inimical to the interests of the Reich. The Einsatzgruppen became most notorious during Operation Barbarossa, killing more than half a million civilians—mostly Jews—between late June and December 1941 alone. Their actions marked the beginning of the Holocaust, the organized mass murder of Jewish men, women, and children. The Einsatzgruppen formed the core of stationary German Security Police and SD units in the occupied Soviet Union, where together with other agencies, they facilitated terror as the key feature of Nazi occupation rule.

See Christopher R. Browning with contributions by Jürgen Matthäus. *The Origins of the Final Solution: The Evolution of Nazi Jewish Policy, September 1939–March 1942* (Lincoln and Jerusalem: University of Nebraska Press and Yad Vashem, 2004).

Eynikeyt (Yiddish: unity) The official Yiddish-language newspaper of the Jewish Anti-Fascist Committee (JAFC), the government-controlled Jewish umbrella organization in the Soviet Union founded in 1942. Edited by Shakhne Epstein, *Eynikeyt* disseminated information about the Nazi mass murder of Jews. *Eynikeyt* also sought to rally support for the Soviet war effort among Jews and the general public in the West.

See Yosef Gorny, *The Jewish Press and the Holocaust, 1939–1945: Palestine, Britain, the United States, and the Soviet Union* (Cambridge: Cambridge University Press, 2012).

Filderman, Wilhelm (1882–1963) Born in Bucharest and a World War I veteran, Filderman was the long-time president of the Union of Romanian Jews and representative of the AJJDC in Romania, working for Jewish civil rights through a number of initiatives. He went on to become a Liberal Party member of parliament and leader of the Federation of Jewish Communities, which the Antonescu regime dissolved in December 1941 in favor of a tightly controlled "Jewish Central Office." He continued to fight discriminatory measures and deportations of Romanian Jews until he suffered expulsion to Transnistria. After the war, Filderman resumed a number of his posts and continued his work for Jewish rights, but fled to Paris in 1948 after repeated conflicts with the new Communist regime.

See Radu Ioanid, *The Holocaust in Romania: The Destruction of Jews and Gypsies under the Antonescu Regime, 1940–1944* (Chicago: Ivan R. Dee in association with the USHMM, 2000).

Fleischmann, Karel (1897–1944) He worked as a dermatologist in České Budějovice, Czechoslovakia, before the war, while maintaining an active interest in progressive art. On April 18, 1942, Fleischmann was transported to Theresienstadt along with his wife Roza Fleischmann (née Brozin; 1902–1944), and more than nine hundred other Jews from his town. In Theresienstadt he worked as a doctor as well as a member of its artistic community, producing numerous poems, prose works, and drawings depicting life in the camp. On October 23, 1944, Karel Fleischmann and his wife were deported to Auschwitz, where they were murdered. More than six hundred of his works were found hidden in Terezin after the war.

See exhibition catalog, *Seeing through "Paradise": Artists and the Terezín Concentration Camp* (Boston: Massachusetts College of Art, 1991).

Frank, Hans (1900–1946) An early member of the Nazi Party in Germany and legal advisor to Hitler, Frank rose through the party hierarchy. After the German invasion of Poland in 1939, he became governor-general of the Generalgouvernement, overseeing the exploitation of that region and the persecution of "enemies of the Reich," including Jews. He was captured in 1945, tried for war crimes at the International Military Tribunal at Nuremberg, and hanged in 1946.

See Christoph Klessmann, "Hans Frank: Party Jurist and Governor-General in Poland," in *The Nazi Elite*, ed. Ronald Smelser and Rainer Zitelmann (New York: New York University Press, 1993), 39–47.

Frank, Shlomo (1902–1966) Frank was a member of the Jewish police and a diarist in the Łódź ghetto. His diary covers the period from January 1, 1941, to August 9, 1942, and details daily life, major events, public sentiment, and the Rumkowski regime of the ghetto. After the Łódź ghetto liquidation, Frank was sent to various concentration camps, where he remained for the duration of the war. As one of only two Łódź ghetto diarists to survive the war, Frank returned to the liberated city in the spring of 1945 and was able to retrieve his notebooks, which were published in Yiddish in 1958.

See Isaiah Trunk, *Łódź Ghetto: A History* (Bloomington: Indiana University Press, 2006).

Frieder, Abraham Armin (1911–1945) Frieder was born in an Orthodox family and in 1938 became the rabbi in Nové Mesto nad Váhom in Czechoslovakia. As anti-Jewish measures tightened in Slovakia after the beginning of the war, Frieder became a member of the so-called working group, an informal gathering of Jewish leaders in the country who tried to stop the mass deportations. After the German occupation of Slovakia in 1944, Frieder was taken to a labor camp, from which he managed to flee. He died immediately after the end of the war.

See Emanuel Frieder, *To Deliver Their Souls: The Struggle of a Young Rabbi during the Holocaust* (New York: Holocaust Library, 1991).

Galut This Hebrew word means "exile" and refers either to the biblical exile of the Jewish people from the Land of Israel or, in the modern period, to the Zionist notion of Palestine as the Jewish center for Jewish diaspora communities.

See S. H. Lustig and Ian Leveson, *Turning the Kaleidoscope: Perspectives on European Jewry* (New York: Berghahn Books, 2008).

Generalgouvernement The German Reich annexed parts of western Poland after the Nazi invasion of that country in September 1939. The remaining territory—except for eastern Poland, which the Soviet Union occupied—remained under German occupation and was known from October 1939 as the Generalgouvernement für die besetzten polnischen Gebiete (General Government for the Occupied Polish Territories). Hitler appointed Hans Frank as governor-general of this region, to which large numbers of Poles and Jews were subsequently sent after being expelled from the newly annexed territories. After the Nazi invasion of the Soviet Union in the summer of 1941, the formerly Soviet-occupied Polish eastern Galicia was added to the Generalgouvernement.

See Jan T. Gross, *Polish Society under German Occupation: The Generalgouvernement, 1939–1944* (Princeton, NJ: Princeton University Press, 1979).

Gestapo (Secret State Police; German: Geheime Staatspolizei) A key agency, together with the SS and SD, in the Nazi terror apparatus, it first operated in the Reich, but also beginning in the late 1930s in German-controlled areas, under the command of Himmler and Heydrich. As part of the RSHA, the Gestapo played a lead role in the persecution of Jews and the suppression of anti-German resistance.

See Michael Wildt, *An Uncompromising Generation: The Nazi Leadership of the Reich Security Main Office* (Madison: University of Wisconsin Press, 2009).

Goebbels, Joseph (1897–1945) After studying literature, Goebbels joined the Nazi movement in 1924 and beginning in 1926 served as Gauleiter for Berlin. In March 1933, Hitler appointed him Reich minister for public enlightenment and propaganda (Reichsminister für Volksaufklärung und Propaganda). Goebbels subsequently played a key role in the instigation of "*Kristallnacht*" and other anti-Jewish measures, including the deportation of Jews from Berlin to ghettos, concentration camps, and extermination centers from the fall of 1941 onward.

See Jeffrey Herf, *The Jewish Enemy: Nazi Propaganda during World War II and the Holocaust* (Cambridge, MA: Belknap Press, 2006).

Goldbarth, Ruth (1921–1942) Goldbarth was born in Bydgoszcz in Poland, where she met Edith Blau and Lutek Orenbach in the late 1930s and with whom she corresponded in the early years of the war. In January 1940, her father, a dentist, decided to move his family to Warsaw in the Generalgouvernement. Ruth worked in her father's dental practice in the Warsaw ghetto and corresponded frequently with Edith Blau, then in Germany. Ruth and her family were most likely deported to their deaths in Treblinka in the summer of 1942.

See Klaus-Peter Friedrich, "Die Brombergerin Ruth Goldbarth im Warschauer Getto, 1940/41," *Jewish History Quarterly* (March 2008): 35–46.

Goldmann, Nahum (1895–1982) Goldmann became one of the founders and a long-time president of the World Jewish Congress, as well as an ardent Zionist. Born in Russia, Goldmann lived in Frankfurt am Main since childhood and in 1936 settled in New York, where he worked with Stephen Wise on organizing the WJC and represented the Jewish Agency for several years. After the war he held several important positions in international Jewish organizations, including president of the World Zionist Organization.

See Mark A. Raider, ed., *Nahum Goldmann: Statesman without a State* (Albany: State University of New York Press, 2009).

Gross-Breesen An emigrants training farm (*Auswandererlehrgut*) in Silesia created in 1936 by the central German Jewish Association, one of a few non-Zionist centers of its kind. Run by the Hamburg-born pedagogue Curt Bondy (1894–1972), Gross-Breesen attracted several hundred students. On August 31, 1941, Gestapo officials ordered the dissolution of the farm and deployed remaining faculty and trainees as forced laborers. Many of the last group of Gross-Bressener trainees perished during the Holocaust.

See Werner T. Angress, *Between Fear and Hope: Jewish Youth in the Third Reich* (New York: Columbia University Press, 1988).

Gurs A French detention camp established in 1939, Gurs was located in the foothills of the Pyrenees mountain range. In 1940 after the German invasion, Vichy France controlled the camp and used it to house prisoners deported from Germany as well as French inmates from internment camps such as Saint-Cyprien. After living in the squalid conditions at Gurs, many of the German Jews held there were eventually sent to the killing centers in Poland. By the time the camp at Gurs was closed in 1943, some twenty-two thousand inmates had passed through its gates; over eighteen thousand of those were Jews. Between late October 1940 and November 1, 1943, 1,038 detainees had died there (many of them Jews).

See Claude Laharie, *Le camp de Gurs, 1939–1945. Un aspect méconnu de l'histoire de Vichy*, 2nd ed. (Biarritz: J & D Editions, 1993).

Hakel, Hermann (1911–1987) Hakel was an Austrian writer and poet from Vienna. After he was severely beaten by the Nazis in 1939, he fled the Reich to Italy, where he settled in Milan. He was arrested in 1940 and interned in a number of camps in southern Italy, but survived the war. In 1947 he returned to Vienna, where he resumed his career as a writer.

See Hermann Hakel Gesellschaft, ed., *Ein besonderer Mensch. Erinnerungen an Hermann Hakel* (Vienna: Lynkeus, 1988).

Hashomer Hatzair A Zionist youth organization with a socialist orientation founded in 1918. The oldest existing Zionist youth movement, Hashomer Hatzair encouraged emigration (*aliyah*) to Palestine and the establishment of kibbutzim.

Heydrich, Reinhard (1904–1942) Involved with völkisch circles since the early 1920s, Heydrich received a commission from SS chief Heinrich Himmler in 1931 to create a secret service (Sicherheitsdienst, or SD) for the Nazi Party, which he headed until his death. In the fall of 1939, Heydrich merged the SD with the Security Police to form the Reichssicherheitshauptamt (RSHA). He served in a variety of functions, among them commander of the Einsatzgruppen, head of the Protectorate administration, and convener of the Wannsee Conference. Heydrich died of injuries a week after being attacked by Czech partisans in Prague.

See Robert Gerwarth, *Hitler's Hangman: The Life of Heydrich* (New Haven, CT: Yale University Press, 2011).

HIAS (Hebrew Immigrant Aid Society) HIAS was established in 1881 in New York City to assist the emigration of Jews fleeing czarist Russia. After the Nazis came to power, HIAS offered important services to Jews trying to escape from Germany and the areas dominated by the Reich, joining with two other immigration services under the name HICEM to make use of the remaining exit routes. In the postwar period, HIAS joined with an arm of the American Jewish Joint Distribution Committee to form the Displaced Persons Coordinating Committee and administer emigration and family reunification services in hundreds of displaced persons camps.

See Valery Bazarov, "HIAS and HICEM in the System of Jewish Relief Organisations in Europe, 1933–41," *East European Jewish Affairs* 39 (April 2009): 69–78.

HICEM This Jewish aid organization was created in 1927 by a merger of three Jewish immigrant aid organizations: the U.S.-based HIAS, the British-based Jewish Colonization Organization (ICA or JCA), and the United Committee for Jewish Emigration. With its initial headquarters in Paris, HICEM assisted Jews in Nazi Germany and Nazi-controlled territories by arranging visas and passage to countries willing to accept the refugees. The organization relocated to New York following the German attack on France in 1940.

See Valery Bazarov, "HIAS and HICEM in the System of Jewish Relief Organisations in Europe, 1933–41," *East European Jewish Affairs* 39 (April 2009): 69–78.

Himmler, Heinrich (1900–1945) A member of the movement promoting racial and social homogeneity in Germany and a participant in the November 1923 Nazi putsch in Munich, Himmler was appointed by Hitler in early 1929 to become the leader (*Reichsführer*) of the SS. After 1933 Himmler advanced rapidly to become head of the

Gestapo, chief of the entire German police in mid-1936, Reich commissioner for the "Germanization" of the occupied East (October 1939), and Reich interior minister (August 1943). During the war, Himmler played a key role in implementing the genocide of European Jewry and other elements of a Nazi racist utopia.

See Peter Longerich, *Heinrich Himmler* (Oxford: Oxford University Press, 2011).

Hirsch, Otto (1885–1941) A lawyer and former government official in the German state of Württemberg, Hirsch had long been active in German Jewish organizational life. Beginning in 1933 he served as executive director of the Reichsvertretung der Deutschen Juden and thereafter in the Reichsvereinigung der Juden in Deutschland, where he worked closely with Leo Baeck. Arrested a number of times, Hirsch turned down several opportunities to leave Germany and was eventually deported to the Mauthausen camp in 1941, where he died.

See Beate Meyer, "Between Self-Assertion and Forced Collaboration: The Reich Association of Jews in Germany, 1939–1945," in *Jewish Life in Nazi Germany: Dilemmas and Responses*, ed. Francis R. Nicosia and David Scrase (New York: Berghahn Books, 2010), 149–69.

Hlinka Guard Founded in 1938 on the heels of the dismemberment of Czechoslovakia, the Hlinka Guard was a radical nationalist, antisemitic militia named after the Catholic priest and Slovak nationalist Andrej Hlinka (1864–1938). It was tied to the Slovak People's Party, which Hlinka was instrumental in promoting. During World War II, the Guard became active in the Slovak regime's fight against ethnic minorities, including Jews. In 1942, it organized the deportation of nearly fifty-eight thousand Slovakian Jews, mostly to Auschwitz.

See Yeshayahu Jelinek, *The Parish Republic: Hlinka's Slovak People's Party, 1939–1945* (New York: Columbia University Press, 1976).

Iron Guard An ultranationalist and strongly antisemitic Romanian movement, it was founded in 1927. After the Iron Guard joined the government of Ion Antonescu in 1940, it committed various antisemitic crimes and staged a bloody pogrom in Bucharest during an unsuccessful coup in January 1941. Antonescu subsequently eliminated the organization from the government and forced its leaders into exile in Germany.

See Radu Ioanid, *The Sword of the Archangel: Fascist Ideology in Romania* (New York: Columbia University Press, 1990).

Italie, Gabriel (1895–1956) An observant Orthodox Jew, Italie was descended from a long line of rabbis, teachers, and cantors in the Netherlands. He lost his teaching job in The Hague in early 1941 for being Jewish. He and his family were arrested in January 1943 and transferred to the Westerbork camp in the autumn. Nearly a year later, in September 1944, he and his wife Rosa, and two of their children, Ralf and Ida, were sent to Theresienstadt, where they survived the war. Another son, Paul, was deported and died in 1942. After the war, Gabriel Italie resumed teaching at a lyceum, also publishing a number of books on classical Greece.

See Gabriel Italie, *Het oorlogsdagboek van dr. G. Italie. Den Haag, Barneveld, Westerbork, Theresienstadt, Den Haag 1940–1945*, ed. Wally M. de Lang (Amsterdam: Contact, 2009).

JAFC *See* **Jewish Anti-Fascist Committee**.

Jasenovac The central and most infamous camp in the Independent State of Croatia, set up in September 1941 and supervised by the Directorate for Public Order and Security (Ravnateljstvo za javni red i sigurnost, RAVSIGUR), the ustaša equivalent of the German RSHA. In 1941 and 1942, some thirty camps existed in Croatia, the majority short-term concentration and transit camps, from which inmates—mostly Serbs and Jews—were transferred to labor camps or camps in Germany. Over the four years of the camp's existence, around one hundred thousand people were killed there, more than half of them Serbs.

See Nataša Mataušić, *Jasenovac, 1941–1945. Logor smrti i radni logor* (Jasenovac: Javna ustanova Spomen-područje Jasenovac, 2003); Jozo Tomasevich, *War and Revolution in Yugoslavia, 1941–1945: Occupation and Collaboration* (Stanford, CA: Stanford University Press, 2001).

Jewish Agency for Palestine Established by the World Zionist Organization in 1921, the Jewish Agency was recognized by British authorities in Palestine as representing the Jewish community in the Mandate. It expanded in 1929 to encompass non-Zionist organizations and later became a de facto Jewish self-government in Palestine, with offices in Jerusalem, London, and Geneva established to facilitate emigration to Palestine (*aliyah*). David Ben-Gurion served as head of the Jewish Agency from 1935 until the founding of Israel in 1948.

See Walter Laqueur, *A History of Zionism: From the French Revolution to the Establishment of the State of Israel* (New York: Schocken Books, 2003).

Jewish Anti-Fascist Committee (JAFC) JAFC was established by order of Soviet state authorities in the spring of 1942 to foster political and financial support for the Red Army in its fight against Nazi Germany. In addition to fund-raising, the JAFC published a Yiddish newspaper, *Eynikeyt*, and collected documentation on Jewish suffering and mass murder during the war with the intention of publishing a "black book" of Nazi crimes. Once Germany had been defeated, Soviet support for the JAFC ended and was replaced with political oppression and criminalization.

See Shimon Redlich, *War, Holocaust, and Stalinism: A Documented Study of the Jewish Anti-Fascist Committee in the USSR* (Luxembourg: Harwood Academic, 1995).

Jewish Council *See* **Judenrat**.

Jewish Social Self-Help (JSS) A Jewish humanitarian relief organization led by Michał Weichert, the JSS was part of the larger network of organizations dedicated to aiding Jews in Nazi-occupied Poland. From its office in the Nazi "capital" of the Generalgouvernement, Kraków, the JSS pursued a path of "legality" by strictly observing German regulations and continuing to receive funds from the AJJDC until the United States entered the war in December 1941.

See Yehuda Bauer, *American Jewry and the Holocaust: The American Jewish Joint Distribution Committee, 1939–1945* (Detroit, MI: Wayne State University Press, 1981).

Jewish Telegraphic Agency (JTA or ITA) Founded in 1914 as the Jewish Correspondence Bureau, the news service relocated from London to New York City in 1922 and maintained bureaus in Paris, Prague, Berlin, and Warsaw. Beginning in 1924 the JTA published a daily bulletin of world news pertaining to Jewish interests. During the war and despite the closing of its offices in countries under German control, it reported regularly on the Nazis' anti-Jewish measures.

See the organization's website, www.jta.org/about/history (accessed May 13, 2012).

JSS *See* **Jewish Social Self-Help**.

Judenrat (pl. *Judenräte*; **Jewish Council**) Established in the aftermath of the German attack on Poland and, later, on occupied Soviet territory, the councils were designed to implement the policies of Nazi occupation authorities in Jewish communities. As German anti-Jewish policy evolved from persecution to annihilation, *Judenrat* leaders (almost exclusively men) faced the impossible task of attempting to alleviate Jewish suffering while fulfilling murderous Nazi demands, particularly pertaining to forced labor and the preparation of deportations. Determined by a range of factors, the responses by Jewish leaders varied widely, as exemplified by Chaim Rumkowski in Łódź and Adam Czerniaków in Warsaw.

See Isaiah Trunk, *Judenrat: The Jewish Councils in Eastern Europe under Nazi Occupation* (1972; Lincoln: University of Nebraska Press, 1996).

Jüdisches Nachrichtenblatt The Jewish press in Nazi Germany was in effect outlawed after "*Kristallnacht*." In its place, the Propaganda Ministry ordered publication of the *Jüdisches Nachrichtenblatt* in Berlin. Its editors and other staff came under the control of the Security Police and SD and were later integrated into the Reichsvereinigung structure. After the annexation of Austria, dismemberment of Czechoslovakia, and establishment of the Protectorate of Bohemia and Moravia, similar newspapers controlled by the regime were published under the same name in Vienna and in Prague.

See Herbert Freeden, *The Jewish Press in the Third Reich* (Providence, RI: Berg, 1993).

Kindertransport (pl. Kindertransporte; children's transport) Following "*Kristallnacht*," the British government agreed to permit an unspecified number of children under the age of seventeen to enter Great Britain from Germany and German-annexed territories.

Private citizens or organizations had to guarantee financial support for each child's care, education, and eventual emigration from Britain. The first such transport arrived in Harwich on December 2, 1938, bringing some two hundred children. The last Kindertransport sailed from the Netherlands for Britain on May 14, 1940, the day on which the Dutch army surrendered to German forces. In all, the rescue operation brought roughly ten thousand children from Germany, Austria, Czechoslovakia, and Poland to Great Britain. Several child rescue initiatives and networks emerged elsewhere in Europe, parallel to the Kindertransport operation.

See Mark Jonathan Harris and Deborah Oppenheimer, *Into the Arms of Strangers: Stories of the Kindertransport* (New York: St. Martin's Press, 2000).

Korber, Mirjam In October 1941, Mirjam Korber-Bercovici, born in November 1923 in Cîmpulung, Bukovina, was deported with her parents and sister to a small ghetto in the town of Djurin in Transnistria (today Moldova). The Korbers survived the German occupation with help from a Ukrainian family that allowed them to live in their house and work on their farm. After liberation by the Red Army, in April 1944 Mirjam made her way back to Romania, where she studied medicine and became a renowned pediatrician.

See Mirjam Korber, *Deportiert: Jüdische Überlebensschicksale aus Rumänien 1941–1944. Ein Tagebuch*, ed. Erhard Roy Wiehn (Konstanz: Hartung-Gorre Verlag, 1993).

"*Kristallnacht*" (also "*Reichskristallnacht*," "Crystal Night," or "Night of Broken Glass") The term constituted a euphemistic reference to the pogroms, arrests, and destruction of Jewish property that swept through the Reich on the nights of November 9 and 10, 1938. The Nazi leadership staged the event to express "the German people's outrage" at the assassination of a German diplomat, Ernst vom Rath, in Paris by seventeen-year-old Herschel Grynszpan, whose parents had been deported from Germany across the Polish border in late October. During "*Kristallnacht*," synagogues, shops, and apartments owned or occupied by Jews were destroyed. At least twenty-six thousand Jewish men were arrested and incarcerated in the Dachau, Sachsenhausen, and Buchenwald concentration camps. The official death total of ninety-one people represents only a fraction of the actual casualties. After this event, a wave of anti-Jewish regulations swept Germany and forced more German Jews to emigrate.

See Alan E. Steinweis, *Kristallnacht 1938* (Cambridge, MA: Belknap Press, 2009).

Langer, Erich (1882–1942) Langer had been a judge in Wiesbaden until 1933 before he moved to Essen with his wife Rahel and his son Klaus Jakob, born in 1924. The Langers were music lovers who participated in public and private performances. After working for the Essen community and the local office of the Reichsvereinigung, Erich Langer was deported to Izbica in April 1942, where he perished. His wife had died in early September 1941 of natural causes, while his son escaped from Germany to Israel via Denmark. Before his deportation, Erich Langer gave a copy of a roughly twenty-page letter addressed to his son to an "Aryan" friend who kept it and sent it to Klaus Jakob (now Yakob) Langer in Palestine after the war.

See Mark Roseman, *A Past in Hiding: Memory and Survival in Nazi Germany* (New York: Metropolitan Books, 2000), 61–64.

Langnas, Mignon (1903–1949) Langnas moved to Vienna with her family just before World War I. In 1928, she married Leon Langnas (1895–1978) from Lemberg (Polish: Lwów; Ukrainian: L'viv) with whom she had two children, Manuela (b. 1933) and Georg (later George; b. 1935). Leon was a passenger on the ill-fated MS *St. Louis* voyage in May 1939. When the ship was forced back to Europe, he was sent to an internment camp in England for over a year. He managed to get to New York in 1940, where their children had already arrived and were temporarily placed in a Jewish orphanage. During the war years, Mignon remained in Vienna, working as a nurse at a children's hospital and taking care of her parents, both of whom died of natural causes. She followed her husband and children to New York in 1946.

See Elisabeth Fraller and George Langnas, eds., *Mignon, Tagebücher und Briefe einer jüdischen Krankenschwester in Wien, 1938–1949* (Innsbruck: Studienverlag, 2010).

Lichtheim, Richard (1885–1963) Born in Berlin, Lichtheim had been active in German and international Zionist circles since before World War I, during which he represented Jewish interests as a liaison to the Ottoman Empire's government in Constantinople. In 1934 Lichtheim settled in Palestine with his family. During World War II he headed the Geneva office of the Jewish Agency for Palestine, a position that enabled him to closely monitor incoming news about the Axis powers' anti-Jewish policies. Lichtheim returned to Jerusalem in 1946.

See Francis R. Nicosia, "Revisionist Zionism in Germany (I): Richard Lichtheim and the Landesverband der Zionisten-Revisionisten in Deutschland, 1926–1933," *LBIYB* 31 (1986): 209–40.

Madagascar Plan Following the German defeat of France in June 1940, the German Foreign Office floated a plan for the "solution of the Jewish Question" by deporting the Jews of Europe to Madagascar in the Indian Ocean. The island, a French colony at the time, was ill-suited for offering a livelihood for the roughly 4 million Jews targeted by the plan. Supported by the Nazi leadership and logistically prepared by the RSHA, the plan required substantial shipping capacity and was abandoned after the start of Operation Barbarossa in favor of a "territorial solution" in the form of mass murder in the East.

See Christopher R. Browning, *The Final Solution and the German Foreign Office: A Study of Referat D III of Abteilung Deutschland, 1940–43* (New York: Holmes & Meier, 1978).

Maier, Ruth (1920–1942) Maier was the daughter of assimilated Jewish parents living in Vienna. Her father had died in 1933. After experiencing the German annexation and *"Kristallnacht"* in Austria, Ruth escaped to Norway in January 1939. Her sister, Judith (b. 1922), left for England a few months earlier. Unable to join her sister and mother (who fled to England in April 1939), Ruth was deported from German-occupied Norway together with more than five hundred Jews in late November 1942 and was murdered on her arrival in Auschwitz. Her girlfriend in Norway, Gunvor Hofmo, and her sister in England, Judith Suschitzky, preserved Ruth Maier's diaries, other writings, and artwork.

See Ruth Maier, *Ruth Maier's Diary: A Young Girl's Life under Nazism*, ed. Jan Erik Vold (London: Harvill Secker, 2009).

Majdanek Originally built as a POW camp near the city of Lublin under the supervision of SS and Police Leader Odilo Globocnik, Majdanek became a concentration camp and killing center. Inmates—including Poles, Jews, and Soviet POWs—died from the extremely poor camp conditions, were murdered in gas chambers constructed in the fall of 1942, or were shot; on November 3, 1943, guards killed roughly eighteen thousand prisoners with machine guns. Prior to liberation by the Red Army on July 23, 1944, the SS had murdered an estimated two hundred thousand people sent to Majdanek.

See Elizabeth White, "Lublin Main Camp," in *The United States Holocaust Memorial Museum Encyclopedia of Camps and Ghettos, 1933–1945: Early Camps, Youth Camps, and the Concentration Camps and Subcamps under the SS-Business Administration Main Office*, ed. Geoffrey P. Megargee (Bloomington: Indiana University Press in association with the USHMM, 2009), 1:877–79.

Mändl, Eva (later Roubíčková, b. 1921) The daughter of a gymnasium teacher of classical languages and a housewife, Mändl grew up in Žatec in Czechoslovakia, but moved to Prague with her family under the pressure of increasing antisemitism. In December 1941, she was sent to Theresienstadt with her mother, where she worked at the camp farm and garden, kept her diary, and survived the war. Her future husband, Richard, a lawyer, in 1939 managed to immigrate to England, where he joined the Czech army-in-exile.

See Eva Mändl Roubíčková, *"Langsam gewöhnen wir uns an das Ghettoleben." Ein Tagebuch aus Theresienstadt*, ed. Veronika Springmann (Hamburg: Konkret Literatur Verlag, 2007).

"Mischling" (pl.: *"Mischlinge"*; mixed breed, German) A racial category rooted in nineteenth-century biological thinking and formally introduced into the Third Reich's anti-Jewish politics with the issuing of the Nuremberg Laws. *"Mischling"* was meant to designate an individual of both "Aryan" and "non-Aryan," particularly Jewish, descent;

if that person's parents were married, their union would be considered a "mixed marriage" (*"Mischehe"*). The Nuremberg Laws divided *"Mischlinge"* into distinct categories and criminalized sexual contact between "Aryans" and Jews (*"Rassenschande"*) in order to prevent the birth of "mixed breeds." This group's fate was the subject of intense, yet inconclusive, debates within and between Nazi Party and state agencies until the end of the war. During the war, especially in German-occupied Eastern Europe, *"Mischlinge"* were to a large degree treated like Jews and targeted for murder as part of the "Final Solution."

See Jeremy Noakes, "The Development of Nazi Policy toward the German-Jewish *Mischlinge,* 1933–1945," *LBIYB* 34 (1989): 291–354.

Molotov-Ribbentrop Pact Named for the foreign ministers of the Soviet Union and Nazi Germany, this agreement (also called the Hitler-Stalin or Nazi-Soviet Pact), signed on August 23, 1939, was on its face a nonaggression treaty between the two countries, with each pledging neutrality if the other went to war with another country. Beyond the nonaggression pledges, a secret protocol and further revisions of the treaty outlined the Nazi and Soviet "spheres of influence" in northern and eastern Europe, allowing for the subsequent separation of Poland and the Baltic States into German- and Soviet-dominated zones. Until the Nazi invasion of the Soviet Union in June 1941, the two countries divided the areas between them in accordance with the secret protocol, with some minor corrections.

See Gerhard L. Weinberg, *A World at Arms: A Global History of World War II* (Cambridge: Cambridge University Press, 1994).

Nisko A town on the San River in the western part of the Lublin district in Poland, Nisko became part of the Generalgouvernement during World War II and site of a scheme devised by Adolf Eichmann's RSHA office in October 1939 for the resettlement of Jews from the newly annexed East Upper Silesia, the Protectorate of Bohemia and Moravia, and Vienna. The scheme was aborted in November 1939 and the camp was closed in April 1940, when the surviving Jews were returned to Austria and the Protectorate.

See Christopher Browning with contributions by Jürgen Matthäus, *The Origins of the Final Solution: The Evolution of Nazi Jewish Policy, September 1939–March 1942* (Lincoln and Jerusalem: University of Nebraska Press and Yad Vashem, 2004).

Nuremberg Laws This shorthand expression is frequently used to refer to the two basic pillars of Nazi antisemitic legislation—the Reich Citizenship Law (*Reichsbürgergesetz*) and the Law for the Protection of German Blood and German Honor (*Gesetz zum Schutze des deutschen Blutes und der deutschen Ehre*)—promulgated on September 15, 1935, during the annual Nazi Party rally and a specially convened session of the Reichstag in Nuremberg. The first law restricted citizenship (and thus full protection under the law) to those of

"German or related blood," while the second measure proscribed marriage and sexual contact between this group and Jews. Subsequent regulations defined a "Jew" as someone with at least three Jewish grandparents (according to their religious affiliation) or someone descended from two Jewish grandparents who practiced the Jewish religion himself or herself, or was married to a Jew. People with two Jewish grandparents but without Jewish religious affiliations and not married to Jews came to be defined as "*Mischlinge* of the first degree" (*Mischlinge ersten Grades*); people with one Jewish grandparent were labeled "*Mischlinge* of the second degree" (*Mischlinge zweiten Grades*). As the Reich expanded, the Nuremberg Laws came to be applied in varying degrees in parts of Europe annexed or occupied by Germany. With later clauses added to facilitate the marking, deportation, murder, and expropriation of Jews, the Nuremberg Laws formed one of the basic laws of the Third Reich until its defeat in May 1945.

See Raul Hilberg, *The Destruction of the European Jews*, 3rd ed. (1961; New Haven, CT: Yale University Press, 2003), 1:61–78.

Nussbaum, Felix Born in 1904, in Osnabrück, Germany, Felix Nussbaum was a German Jewish painter. After fleeing the Reich for Belgium, he was arrested in May 1940 as an "enemy alien" and deported to the Saint-Cyprien camp in France. After an escape during transit back to Germany, Nussbaum joined his wife Felka in Brussels, where they lived in hiding. They were discovered in July 1944 and sent to the Mechelen (Malines) transit camp and on to Auschwitz, where they were murdered on August 9, 1944. Felix Nussbaum's most notable paintings include *Self Portrait with Jewish Identity Card* (1943) and *Triumph of Death* (1944), which present the artist's perspective on Jewish persecution and death in Nazi-occupied Europe.

See Karl Georg Kaster, ed., *Felix Nussbaum: Art Defamed, Art in Exile, Art in Resistance, A Biography* (Woodstock: Overlook Press, 1997).

Operation Barbarossa The code name for the German attack on the Soviet Union ordered by Hitler in late 1940 for May 15, 1941, this operation was delayed due to the German military campaign in the Balkans until June 22, 1941. SS and police units, among them the Einsatzgruppen, followed on the heels of 3.2 million Wehrmacht soldiers deployed in three army groups (Heeresgruppe Nord, Mitte, and Süd), together with troops from other Axis members to fight alleged and real enemies in the occupied areas.

See Geoffrey P. Megargee, *War of Annihilation: Combat and Genocide on the Eastern Front, 1941* (Lanham, MD: Rowman & Littlefield, 2006).

Orenbach, Lutek (1921–1942?) Orenbach was born in Tomaszów Mazowiecki, Poland, but in early 1939 lived in Bydgoszcz, where he met Ruth Goldbarth and Edith Blau, corresponding with them during the early years of the war. After the war began Orenbach moved back to Tomaszów Mazowiecki, where the Germans had established a ghetto. By November 1942 most of the Jews in the town had been deported to their deaths in Treblinka; the fate of Lutek Orenbach is unknown.

See Edith Brandon, *Letters from Tomaszow* (London: self-published, 1994).

ORT (Organization for Rehabilitation and Training; French: Organisation Reconstruction Travail) Founded in Russia in 1880 to assist Jews in the Pale of Settlement, the organization became international in 1921 and subsequently opened branches in Europe and America. During World War II, ORT was particularly active in eastern Europe and France, where it established homes and schools for Jewish children. After the war, the organization played a role in relief and rehabilitation efforts.

See Sarah Kavanaugh, *ORT, the Second World War and the Rehabilitation of Jewish Survivors* (London: Vallentine Mitchell, 2008).

OSE (Children's Relief Organization; French: Œuvre de secours aux enfants) The Jewish organization was founded in 1912 in Russia to provide medical care and relief for children. The OSE relocated to Berlin in 1933, later to Paris, and after the fall of France in 1940, to Montpellier in the Vichy zone, where it created an aid network of Jewish homes for refugees from central Europe, as well as for the growing numbers of Jewish children from the Occupied Zone—orphans and children whose parents were destitute or had been incarcerated. By late 1941, the OSE was taking care of about twelve hundred children. When the deportations of Jews in France began in 1942, the organization arranged clandestine efforts to smuggle many of the children from OSE orphanages to the safety of neutral countries.

See Renée Poznanski, *Jews in France during World War II* (Hanover, NH: University Press of New England in association with the USHMM, 2001).

Ostmark was the Nazis' designation for Austria following its annexation—known as the *Anschluss*—in March 1938. With the Reich's further conquests, the Ostmark grew to incorporate portions of the historically Czech lands of Bohemia and Moravia and parts of Yugoslavia. In 1942, the term was abandoned in favor of the *Donau- und Alpenreichsgaue*, but remained part of the German Reich until the end of World War II. Of the 181,778 Jews residing in Austria on the eve of the *Anschluss*, an estimated sixty-five thousand were murdered during the Holocaust.

See Evan Burr Bukey, *Hitler's Austria: Popular Sentiment in the Nazi Era, 1938–1945* (Chapel Hill: University of North Carolina Press, 2000).

Oyneg Shabes (Yiddish: pleasure of the Sabbath) A group around Emanuel Ringelblum created this secret archive in 1940 in Warsaw as part of relief and resistance efforts in the Warsaw ghetto. In the course of their work, the group brought together documents and artifacts, recorded testimonies and eyewitness accounts, and wrote diaries, essays, poetry, and other texts. Its collection ranged from restaurant menus and tram tickets to eyewitness accounts of mass murder and essays on the Nazi assault. As it became clear that the ghetto was going to be liquidated, members of Oyneg Shabes buried their archival collections in metal containers. After the war, ten metal containers and two milk cans containing about twenty-five thousand documents were dug out of the ghetto's ruins and are now deposited in the Jewish Historical Institute in Warsaw. A third cache of documents was never found. Of the dozens of Oyneg Shabes activists, only three survived the war.

See Samuel D. Kassow, *Who Will Write Our History? Emanuel Ringelblum, the Warsaw Ghetto, and the Oyneg Shabes Archive* (Bloomington: Indiana University Press, 2007).

Patria The British Royal Navy seized this French ocean liner and retrofitted it into a transport ship following the capitulation of France in June 1940. That November, an illegal three-vessel charter carrying 3,592 Reich and Protectorate Jews from Romania to Palestine was intercepted and diverted under military escort to the port of Haifa. British authorities intended for the *Patria* to deport 2,500 of these refugees to the colonial holdings of Mauritius and Trinidad. On November 25, 1940, operatives of the Haganah—a Zionist paramilitary group active within Palestine—in collusion with several refugees, detonated explosives aboard the *Patria* in an attempt to render it unfit for transport. This act led to the deaths of 267 individuals. While survivors of the incident were granted certificates to enter Palestine, the remaining refugees were held at the Atlit detention camp before being deported to Mauritius on December 5, 1940.

See Dalia Ofer, *Escaping the Holocaust: Illegal Immigration to the Land of Israel, 1939–1944* (New York: Oxford University Press, 1990).

Ponar (Lithuanian: Paneriai) A mass execution site in a wooded area 11 kilometers (7 miles) from the city of Vilna. There, between late June 1941 and early July 1944, German SS and police units with the help of Lithuanian collaborators murdered Jews from Vilna and other ghettos in Lithuania, as well as Soviet POWs and other victims. The overall number of people killed at Ponar is estimated at more than seventy thousand.

See Yitzhak Arad, *Ghetto in Flames: The Struggle and Destruction of the Jews in Vilna in the Holocaust* (New York: Holocaust Library, 1982).

Protectorate of Bohemia and Moravia Hitler established a German "protectorate" on March 16, 1939, after the breakup of Czechoslovakia. It encompassed the historically Czech lands of Bohemia and Moravia. Among its 7.5 million inhabitants at the time of the German takeover were less than 220,000 Germans and more than ninety thousand Jews, most of whom lived in the Protectorate's capital, Prague. In September 1941, "Reichsprotektor" Konstantin von Neurath was replaced by Reinhard Heydrich, who coordinated the mass deportation of Jews beginning in late November 1941, mostly to

Theresienstadt, but also to death camps in Poland. Of the 82,309 Jews deported from the Protectorate, seventy-one thousand were killed.

See Livia Rothkirchen, *The Jews of Bohemia and Moravia: Facing the Holocaust* (Lincoln: University of Nebraska Press, 2005).

Purim The Jewish holiday that commemorates the sixth-century BCE deliverance of the Jews in the Persian Empire from the plot to annihilate them, as recounted in the Book of Esther. Participants rattle noisemakers when the name of the fatal foe (Haman) is read from the Purim scroll or megillah. The ritual of Purim treats the triumph, resulting from the bravery of a Jewish queen married off to the Persian king, with satire and levity. Children dress up in costumes, plays are performed, and, as the story is read aloud, the congregation shouts down Haman's name.

Reich Ministry for the Eastern Occupied Territories The administrative center of the German civil administration established from July 1941 onward in the western parts of the occupied Soviet Union under Nazi party chief ideologue Alfred Rosenberg. The main territorial entities administered by the ministry were the Reichskommissariat Ostland and the Reichskommissariat Ukraine. A Higher SS and police leader coordinated German policies of "pacification," "de-Jewification," and exploitation in each between the SS and police, civil administration, and Wehrmacht. Most Jews in the area had been annihilated by late 1942.

See Christopher R. Browning with contributions by Jürgen Matthäus, *The Origins of the Final Solution: The Evolution of Nazi Jewish Policy, September 1939–March 1942* (Lincoln and Jerusalem: University of Nebraska Press and Yad Vashem, 2004).

Reichskommissariat Ostland As part of the Reich Ministry for the Eastern Occupied Territories, the Reichskommissariat Ostland was comprised of the formerly independent Baltic States (Lithuania, Latvia, Estonia) as well as parts of Belorussia. Since the beginning of the German occupation in late June, German policy in the region involved mass murder, ghettoization, forced labor, and other forms of exploitation. Most of the Jews in the region and those deported there had been murdered by the time of the German retreat in the summer of 1944.

See Timothy Snyder, *Bloodlands: Europe between Hitler and Stalin* (New York: Basic Books, 2010).

Reichskommissariat Ukraine Following the creation of the German civil administration in July 1941, the Reichskommissariat Ukraine encompassed the area east of Galicia (for the most part incorporated into the Generalgouvernement) and several Ukrainian regions up to the border to the parts behind the frontline administered by the Wehrmacht, the border with the Reichskommissariat Ostland in the North, and Crimea in the South. The number of Jews killed in Ukraine during the Holocaust is estimated at more than 2 million.

See Ray Brandon and Wendy Lower, *The Shoah in Ukraine: History, Testimony, Memorialization* (Bloomington: Indiana University Press in association with the USHMM, 2008).

Reichsmark (RM) The standard German currency between 1871 and 1948. In 1941, one US$ was worth roughly 20 RM.

Reichssicherheitshauptamt (**RSHA**; Reich Security Main Office) Established by Heinrich Himmler on September 27, 1939, the RSHA merged the SS intelligence service (Sicherheitsdienst, or SD) and the Security Police (comprising the Gestapo and the Criminal Police) into one office, creating a powerful Nazi intelligence and police structure. Under the leadership of Reinhard Heydrich, the RSHA was in charge of a wide range of tasks crucial to the Third Reich's discriminatory policies, and primarily through the work of the department run by Adolf Eichmann, assumed a critical role in the planning and implementation of the mass murder of the Jews.

See Michael Wildt, *An Uncompromising Generation: The Nazi Leadership of the Reich Security Main Office* (Madison: University of Wisconsin Press, 2009).

Reichsvereinigung der Juden in Deutschland (Reichsvereinigung; Reich Association of Jews in Germany) Formally installed in July 1939 and overseen by the Gestapo, the Reichsvereinigung succeeded the German Jewish umbrella organization, the Reichsvertretung der Deutschen Juden (Reich Representation of German Jews). While the new body intensified the Reichsvertretung's search for organized mass emigration and inherited many of its key officials—including Otto Hirsch—who could not or would not leave the country for a safe haven, the Reichsvereinigung over time became a tool for the administration, control, and ultimate deportation of Jews in Germany. Large-scale deportations of German Jews "to the East" began in November 1941. Once the Reichsvereinigung had served the purpose set by the regime, it was dissolved in 1943 and its staff deported.

See Beate Meyer, *A Fatal Balancing Act: The Dilemma of the Reich Association of Jews in Germany, 1939–1945* (New York: Berghahn Books, 2013).

RELICO (Relief Committee for the War Stricken Jewish Population) Established in Geneva in the autumn of 1939 as part of the WJC for the purpose of assisting in the search for missing persons and providing material aid to Jewish refugees. Beginning in late 1939, RELICO sent parcels of food, medicine, and clothing to Jewish communities in occupied Poland and became increasingly involved in obtaining temporary residence permits for refugees and helping them to leave Europe.

See Raya Cohen, "The Lost Honour of the Bystanders? The Case of Jewish Emissaries in Switzerland," in *"Bystanders" to the Holocaust: A Re-evaluation*, ed. David Cesarani and Paul Levine (London: Frank Cass, 2002), 146–70.

Revisionist Zionists Followers of Vladimir Jabotinsky (1880–1940), who founded the right-wing Alliance of Revisionists, with its active youth movement, Betar. Revisionists diverged from mainstream Zionism's ideology and asserted Jewish territorial claims over the entire territory of the British Mandate (including present-day Jordan). During the war years, Irgun, a Jewish paramilitary organization based on revisionist principles, advocated massive emigration of European Jews to Palestine and aided illegal immigration. It also perpetrated terrorist acts against the British and Palestinian Arabs in their struggle for the establishment of the Jewish state.

See Yaacov Shavit, *Jabotinsky and the Revisionist Movement* (New York: Frank Cass, 1988).

Riegner, Gerhart (1911–2002) A lawyer born in Berlin, Riegner left Germany after Hitler's rise to power and began a long association with the World Jewish Congress, serving first as a legal officer for the organization, then from 1939 onward as director of its office in Geneva. In that crucial location he could obtain extensive information about the plight of Jews in occupied Europe and publicize their persecution. In an August 8, 1942, telegram directed to Jewish leaders—Rabbi Stephen S. Wise in the United States and Sidney Silverman, a British MP—he drew attention to the Nazi plan for killing millions of Jews in eastern Europe. After the war Riegner worked for human rights under the auspices of various initiatives associated with the United Nations, and he continued his work for the WJC, rising to the post of secretary-general (1965–1983).

See Gerhart M. Riegner, *Never Despair: Sixty Years in the Service of the Jewish People and the Cause of Human Rights* (Chicago: Ivan R. Dee in association with USHMM, 2006).

Ringelblum, Emanuel (1900–1944) A Polish Jewish historian born in Buczacz in Galicia, Ringelblum arrived in Warsaw in 1919, where he engaged in leftist Jewish politics while simultaneously pursuing his interest in Jewish history. In the same period, he also became involved with the AJJDC's relief work in Poland. With the German occupation of Poland, Ringelblum used his organizing experience and his connections at the Joint to coordinate a loose network of social organizations (Aleynhilf) in Warsaw to help Polish Jewry both materially and spiritually. As the Nazi persecution of the Jews grew ever worse, Ringelblum organized a ghettowide effort in Warsaw, code-named Oyneg Shabes, to document Jewish life and society under the Nazis' genocidal onslaught. Ringelblum was killed in 1944 along with his family.

See Samuel D. Kassow, *Who Will Write Our History? Emanuel Ringelblum, the Warsaw Ghetto, and the Oyneg Shabes Archive* (Bloomington: Indiana University Press, 2007).

RSHA *See **Reichssicherheitshauptamt**.*

Rudashevski, Yitskhok (1927–1943) Born in Vilna, Rudashevski was a student when the German army invaded Lithuania in June 1941. On September 6, 1941, he and his family—including his father Elihu (b. 1902), mother Roza (née Voloshin, b. 1906), and grandmother Dobra Voloshin (b. 1880)—were forcibly relocated to the Vilna ghetto. Rudashevski joined several underground youth groups and in September 1942 began a diary in order to document ghetto life for posterity. In an attempt to escape deportation, the family hid with relatives, but was quickly found and murdered in Ponar in October 1943. His diary was recovered the following year and first published in Yiddish in 1953.

See Yitskhok Rudashevski, *The Diary of the Vilna Ghetto: June 1941–April 1943*, ed. Percy Matenko (Tel Aviv: Ghetto Fighters' House, 1973).

Rumbula A forest area 8 kilometers (5 miles) from Riga, Latvia, used by German police units as a mass execution site, particularly for Jews from the Riga ghetto. Between late November and early December 1941, Germans and their local helpers murdered roughly thirty-eight thousand Jews in Rumbula.

See Bernhard Press, *The Murder of the Jews in Latvia: 1941–1945* (Evanston, IL: Northwestern University Press, 2000).

Rumkowski, Mordechai Chaim (1877–1944) A businessman and an orphanage director from Łódź, Rumkowski was appointed *Judenälteste* (Eldest of the Jews) by the Nazis on October 13, 1939. Rumkowski, who became one of the most controversial *Judenrat* heads due to his dictatorial style, believed that as long as the ghetto economy was useful to the German war effort, most Jews from Łódź would be safe from deportation. In December 1941, he acceded to German demands for deportation of some of the ghetto's residents to Treblinka. On September 4, 1942, faced with a further call for twenty thousand deportees, Rumkowski decided he would fill the required quota with the ghetto's least productive members: the ailing, the aged, and children under ten. Unlike most ghettos in eastern Europe, which were liquidated in 1942 and 1943, the Łódź ghetto was not liquidated until the summer of 1944, when Rumkowski and his family, together with the remaining ghetto population, were deported to their death in Auschwitz.

See Isaiah Trunk, *Łódź Ghetto: A History*, ed. Robert Moses Shapiro (Bloomington: Indiana University Press in association with the USHMM, 2006).

Saint-Cyprien (also St. Cyprien) A French village near the Spanish border, it became the location of a refugee camp established in February 1939 following the Fascists' victory in the Spanish Civil War. Beginning in September 1939, thousands of Reich nationals were detained there as "enemy aliens." Under the administration of the Vichy government, Saint-Cyprien served as a detention site for approximately ten thousand Jews, mostly from the Reich. International relief agencies were able to improve living conditions, but severe storms and flooding led to the camp's closure on October 30, 1940. The remaining inmate population was transferred to Gurs and other camps throughout unoccupied France. Official records list the number of deaths at 262 during the camp's six months of operation.

See Eliezer Schilt and Abby Holekamp, "Saint-Cyprien," in *The United States Holocaust Memorial Museum Encyclopedia of Camps and Ghettos, 1933–1945*, vol. 3: *Camps and Ghettos under European Regimes Aligned with Nazi Germany*, ed. Joseph R. White (Bloomington: Indiana University Press in association with the USHMM, forthcoming).

SD (Security Service; German: Sicherheitsdienst) Led by Reinhard Heydrich from 1931, the intelligence service of the SS and the Nazi Party in September 1939 became integrated into the Reich Security Main Office. Together with the Security Police, the SD supplied the officer cadre and personnel for the execution of anti-Jewish policy and the murder of the Jews under Himmler's auspices.

See Michael Wildt, *An Uncompromising Generation: The Nazi Leadership of the Reich Security Main Office* (Madison: University of Wisconsin Press, 2009).

Security Police (German: Sicherheitspolizei, or Sipo) This branch of the German police was comprised of the Gestapo, the Criminal Police (Kriminalpolizei, or Kripo), and the Border Police (Grenzpolizei). As chief of the Security Police as well as the SD, Reinhard Heydrich merged the two organizations by establishing the Reich Security Main Office in September 1939. The Security Police helped to supply the forces of the Einsatzgruppen, which served as both security police and mobile killing units in German-occupied territories.

See Michael Wildt, *An Uncompromising Generation: The Nazi Leadership of the Reich Security Main Office* (Madison: University of Wisconsin Press, 2009).

Sephardim (adj. Sephardic; from Hebrew *sefarad*, Spain, literally, *Spaniards*) This term refers to Jews who identify with the traditions and customs that originated in the medieval Jewish society of Spain and Portugal. Until the end of the fifteenth century, when they were expelled from the Iberian Peninsula by royal decrees (entailing expulsion from Spain in 1492 and mass conversion in Portugal in 1497), Iberian Jewry—prominent and well-established in mainstream society—had represented the center of the Jewish social, economic, political, and cultural world. Most expellees and their descendants settled in the Balkans and other parts of the Ottoman Empire, as well as in North Africa, where they came to constitute the core of Jewish society. They also created prosperous communities in the emerging trading centers in western Europe in the early modern period (most notably in Amsterdam, London, Hamburg, and Bordeaux), as well as in the Americas and other colonies of the European imperial powers. Subsequently, however, through the long processes of mass migration, American and European Jewry has become dominated by the customs and traditions of Jews from eastern Europe (Ashkenasim), and only in the lands of the former Ottoman Empire do the Sephardim constitute the majority of the Jewish populations.

See Esther Benbassa and Aron Rodrigue, *Sephardi Jewry: A History of the Judeo-Spanish Community, 14th–20th Centuries* (Berkeley: University of California Press, 2000).

Silberschein, Abraham (1882–1951) Born in Lwów (German: Lemberg, then part of the Austro-Hungarian Empire; Ukrainian: Lviv), Silberschein became a Zionist during his studies at the universities in Lwów and Vienna. In interwar Poland, Silberschein was involved in leftist Zionist projects such as Jewish productivization efforts and the cooperative movement; he was one of the founders of the network of Jewish credit cooperatives in Galicia. During World War II, Silberschein resided in Geneva, Switzerland, where he organized relief efforts for Jews in eastern Europe.

See Raya Cohen, "The Lost Honour of the Bystanders? The Case of Jewish Emissaries in Switzerland," in *"Bystanders" to the Holocaust: A Re-evaluation*, ed. David Cesarani and Paul Levine (London: Frank Cass, 2002), 146–70.

Sobibór Located in a wooded and thinly populated region, the village of Sobibór was chosen as a site for the second of the three extermination camps of "Aktion Reinhard." Constructed in the spring of 1942 with help from former staff of "Aktion T-4," German SS and police officials conducted mass murder by gassing at Sobibór from May 1942 until the autumn of 1943, when Jewish prisoner revolts there and at Treblinka spurred the liquidation of both killing centers. A total of at least 167,000 individuals perished at the Sobibór extermination camp.

See Jules Schelvis, *Sobibor: A History of a Nazi Death Camp* (Oxford: Berg Publishers in association with the USHMM, 2007).

Solmitz, Luise (née Stephan; 1889–1973) A native of Hamburg, Solmitz worked as a high school teacher and later married Friedrich Wilhelm (Fredy) Solmitz (1877–1961), an engineer and flight officer in the German army during World War I. Because Fredy was Jewish and Luise was not, the Nazi regime regarded their marriage as a "mixed marriage" ("*Mischehe*"); accordingly, their daughter Gisela (b. 1920) was labeled first as a "non-Aryan" and then, after the passage of the Nuremberg Laws, as a "*Mischling* of the first degree." As a partner in a mixed marriage with a child who had not been brought up as a Jew, Fredy was not deported during the war.

See Richard Evans, "The Diaries of Luise Solmitz," in *Histories of Women, Tales of Gender*, ed. Willem de Blécourt (Amsterdam: AMB Press, 2008), 207–19.

Stein, Paula (née Znamirowski; 1909–1988) Residents of Warsaw at the outbreak of World War II, Paula, her husband, Meir Mark Stein (1909–1970), and their son, Israel Izio (b. 1934), fled eastward to Vilna, which soon came to be under Soviet occupation. In June 1941, the German invasion of Vilna forced the family into the ghetto, where they managed to survive the mass murder *Aktionen* in which the Germans murdered thirty-five thousand Jews of the fifty-seven thousand Jews in Vilna. At the end of 1941, the Stein family fled to the Białystok ghetto, hoping for safer conditions and a chance to reunite with family in Warsaw. After the liquidation of the Białystok ghetto in August 1943, the Steins hid with a Polish family, a time during which Paula and Meir Stein recorded their wartime experiences until their liberation by the Red Army in July 1944.

See USHMMA Acc. 2008.345 collection catalogue information.

Struma Revisionist Zionists chartered the *Struma*, a poorly equipped transport ship, in December 1941 in the Romanian port of Constanta to take 769 Jews to Palestine.

After weeks of hapless travel across the Black Sea and unable to secure certificates from British authorities to enter Palestine, the passengers were denied landing rights in Turkey and the vessel was towed out of Istanbul's harbor. On February 23, 1942, the *Struma* was torpedoed, in all likelihood by a Soviet submarine, leaving only one survivor. The incident produced outrage in the press and triggered protests for a more lenient British policy toward illegal immigrants.

See Dina Porat, *The Blue and Yellow Stars of David: The Zionist Leadership in Palestine and the Holocaust, 1939–1945* (Cambridge, MA: Harvard University Press, 1990).

Tartakower, Arieh (1897–1982) Born in eastern Galicia, Tartakower became a sociologist in Warsaw and a founder of a Zionist labor organization. He ran relief and rehabilitation operations for the World Jewish Congress after immigrating to the United States in 1939 and remained active in the organization after his move to Palestine in 1946.

See Natan Lerner, "Tartakower, Arieh," *Encyclopaedia Judaica*, ed. Fred Skolnik and Michael Berenbaum, 2nd ed. (Detroit, MI: Macmillan Reference USA, 2007), 19:523.

Tenenbaum, Joseph (1887–1961) was a Zionist, physician, author, and activist who immigrated to the United States from Poland in 1920. He served as chairman of the AJJDC's executive committee and its vice president (1943–1945), and also headed the American Federation of Polish Jews (1942–1947).

See Moshe Gottlieb, "Tenenbaum, Joseph L.," *Encyclopaedia Judaica*, ed. Fred Skolnik and Michael Berenbaum, 2nd ed. (Detroit, MI: Macmillan Reference USA, 2007), 19:638.

Theresienstadt (Czech: Terezin) This former fortress town 63 kilometers (39 miles) north of Prague served between November 1941 and the end of the war in Europe as a destination for deportation transports from the Reich, the Protectorate, and other European regions. Of the roughly 140,000 Jews deported to Theresienstadt, eighty-eight thousand were sent further on "to the East" to be murdered; more than thirty-three thousand died in Theresienstadt itself.

See Vojtěch Blodig, *Terezin in the "Final Solution to the Jewish Question," 1941–1945* (Prague: Památník Terezín/Oswald, 2003).

Transnistria was a region between the Bug and Dniester Rivers taken over by Romania in August 1941 following the German invasion and occupation of the Ukrainian Soviet Socialist Republic. Of the 210,000 indigenous Jews present on the eve of Operation Barbarossa, an estimated 185,000 were killed through a combination of mass shootings, ghettoization, forced labor, and general privation. From September 1941 until October 1943, the Antonescu regime deported approximately 150,000 Jews, most from Bessarabia and Bukovina, to camps and ghettos throughout Transnistria; ninety thousand of them died. Beginning in December 1943, efforts by Romanian Jewish organizations—led by Wilhelm Filderman—resulted in the repatriation of several thousand deportees, but the majority remained in Transnistria until its liberation by the Soviet army in March 1944.

See Radu Ioanid, *The Holocaust in Romania: The Destruction of Jews and Gypsies under the Antonescu Regime, 1940–1944* (Chicago: Ivan R. Dee in association with the USHMM, 2000).

Treblinka Planners of the "Final Solution" chose the site for this third "Aktion Reinhard" killing center in an isolated area approximately 80 kilometers (50 miles) northeast of Warsaw. The most deadly of the Reinhard camps, Treblinka became operational in late July 1942. Deportations came mainly from ghettos throughout the Warsaw and Radom districts of the Generalgouvernement. Jews from Germany, Austria, France, Slovakia, Thrace, and Macedonia were also murdered there—as were thousands of Roma and Poles. On August 2, 1943, Treblinka inmates organized a prisoner revolt, leading to the site's liquidation that autumn. Between 870,000 and 925,000 Jews were murdered at Treblinka from July 1942 through November 1943.

See Yizhak Arad, *Belzec, Sobibor, Treblinka: The Operation Reinhard Death Camps* (Bloomington: Indiana University Press, 1987).

Union Générale des Israélites de France (UGIF) Established on November 29, 1941, by order of the Vichy government in France, the UGIF served as an umbrella organization that encompassed all previously autonomous Jewish social and welfare associations in order to consolidate anti-Jewish policies. With separate branches in the north and south of France, the UGIF mandated membership and dues for all Jews, using their resources to provide welfare assistance and services such as the operation of old-age homes, hospitals, and orphanages. At the same time, the organization collected information used by Germans and their Vichy collaborators to deport Jews to transit camps and killing centers.

See Susan Zuccotti, *The Holocaust, the French, and the Jews* (Lincoln: University of Nebraska Press, 1993).

Ustaša/Ustaše (also anglicized: Ustasha) was the Croatian fascist party that controlled the Independent State of Croatia, a puppet state of Nazi Germany, from 1941 to 1945. Under the leadership of Ante Pavelić, the ustaše persecuted Serbs, Jews, and Roma. Up through the end of the war, thirty thousand Jews and more than 325,000 Serbs were murdered in the territory of the Independent State of Croatia.

See Jozo Tomasevich, *War and Revolution in Yugoslavia, 1941–1945: Occupation and Collaboration* (Stanford, CA: Stanford University Press, 2001).

Vaisman, Nekhama Ioanovna (1924–?). After the beginning of the German attack on the Soviet Union in 1941, Nechama Vaisman and her family were deported from Bessarabia to an unidentified small town at the banks of the Dniester River in Romanian-controlled Transnistria. Beyond this information derived from her diary, her fate and that of her parents are not known.

See Dalia Ofer, "The Ghettos in Transnistria and Ghettos under German Occupation in Eastern Europe: A Comparative Approach," in *Im Ghetto 1939–1945. Neue Forschungen zu Alltag und Umfeld*, ed. Christoph Dieckmann and Babette Quinkert (Göttingen: Wallstein Verlag, 2009), 30–54.

van Aals, Klara (Claartje) (1922–1943) Born to religiously liberal Jewish parents in Utrecht, Klara van Aals was dismissed under the German occupation for being Jewish from her job with the Netherlands Railways, where she had met her pen-friend Aagje Kaagman. Beginning in December 1940 Claartje worked as a nurse in the psychiatric clinic Het Apeldoornsche Bosch in Apeldoorn, in the German-occupied Netherlands. In late January 1943, she was sent from there to Westerbork with her patients and her boyfriend, Arno Schwarz. She was murdered in February 1943 in Auschwitz II-Birkenau. Her father Izaak van Aals, and her half-sister Mar, went into hiding together in Utrecht; both survived the war. Claartje's uncle, Jacob van Aals, who lived in Apeldoorn, was arrested in October 1942 and murdered in Auschwitz in the following month.

See Suzette Wyers, ed., *Als ik wil kan ik duiken . . .: Brieven van Claartje van Aals, verpleegster in de joods psychiatrische inrichting Het Apeldoornsche Bosch, 1940–1943* (Amsterdam: T. Rap, 1995).

Vichy (also Vichy France; official name in French: *l'État français*, the "French state") Following the German defeat of France in May 1940 and the signing of an armistice on June 22, northern France came under direct German occupation. Southern France remained unoccupied and was governed by a French administration, headquartered in the spa town of Vichy and led by Marshal Henri Philippe Pétain, a French World War I hero. The Vichy regime rejected the progressive ideals of the French republican tradition, anchored its values in the motto "*Travail, Famille, Patrie*" (work, family, fatherland), and introduced antisemitic legislation patterned on the discriminatory ordinances in place in the German-occupied zone. In March 1941 the government established a central agency, the General Commissariat for Jewish Affairs (Commissariat général aux Questions juives) to coordinate its anti-Jewish policy. Particularly affected were Jews interned under extremely poor conditions in French-administered detention camps such as Gurs and Saint-Cyprien, and foreign-born Jews, tens of thousands of whom were deported to camps in German-controlled eastern Europe.

See Robert O. Paxton, *Vichy France: Old Guard and New Order, 1940–1944* (New York: Columbia University Press, 2001).

Waffen-SS Himmler established this military wing of the SS in 1940 to fight alongside the regular German army (Wehrmacht), and its units became involved in crimes against civilians and particularly against Jews. Over the course of the war, increasing numbers of ethnic Germans and non-Germans were recruited into the Waffen-SS.

See Gerhard L. Weinberg, *A World at Arms: A Global History of World War II* (Cambridge: Cambridge University Press, 1994).

Wannsee Conference Originally planned by Reinhard Heydrich for December 1941, fifteen state secretaries and other high-ranking German officials gathered on January 20, 1942, at a villa in the Wannsee suburb of Berlin to discuss and coordinate the implementation of the "Final Solution." Because German anti-Jewish polices in occupied eastern Europe had already shifted to mass murder in the second half of 1941, Heydrich's goal in convening the conference was not to initiate the Holocaust but to secure support from government ministries and other interested agencies for his lead role in solving the "Jewish question" across and beyond German-controlled Europe.

See Mark Roseman, *The Wannsee Conference and the Final Solution* (New York: Metropolitan Books, 2002).

Warthegau (also Reichsgau Wartheland) was one of four incorporated territories of the Reich that had been part of prewar Poland. Unlike the Generalgouvernement, they were formally annexed by Germany. Earmarked for "Germanization," Poles and Jews in the Warthegau were expelled en masse to the Generalgouvernement to make room for ethnic Germans.

See Catherine Epstein, *Model Nazi: Arthur Greiser and the Occupation of Western Poland* (Oxford: Oxford University Press, 2010).

Wise, Stephen Samuel (1874–1949) A Hungarian-born Reform rabbi in New York City, Wise became president of both the American Jewish Congress and the World Jewish Congress, playing a leading role in the shaping of American Jewish attitudes toward Nazi Germany and its anti-Jewish measures. Constrained by race relations within the United States and by considerations of U.S. immigration and foreign policies, Wise helped raise awareness for the plight of European Jews and the need to support relief and rescue efforts before and during the war.

See Gulie Ne'eman Arad, *America, Its Jews, and the Rise of Nazism* (Bloomington: Indiana University Press, 2000).

World Jewish Congress (**WJC**) was founded in 1936 by Stephen Wise and Nahum Goldmann with the aim of representing Jewish interests internationally. WJC headquarters were located in Paris. The organization's efforts in the 1930s focused on the deteriorating situation of German and, during World War II, European Jews. WJC staff worked to fight antisemitism and to organize economic aid and other relief for Jewish populations, as well as supporting rescue and advocacy efforts. With the outbreak of the war, WJC moved its central office to Geneva and in 1940 to New York City. Gerhart Riegner in the WJC Geneva office played a key role in coordinating the organization's efforts and in shaping public awareness in the West about Nazi Germany's extermination policies. The WJC became very active after the war in efforts to rebuild European Jewish communities.

See Richard Breitman and Alan M. Kraut, *American Refugee Policy and European Jewry, 1933–1945* (Bloomington: Indiana University Press, 1987).

Yeshiva (Hebrew: academy, literally "sitting"; pl. yeshivot) is the name for a Jewish religious secondary school dedicated to the study of the Talmud, Torah, and other theological and liturgical texts. Based on communal study groups from the first century CE, the primary purpose of such institutions was to impart Judaic scriptural teachings from one generation to the next. The preeminent European centers of yeshiva education during the twentieth century—in Lithuania, Poland, and Ruthenia—were largely eradicated during World War II. Yeshivot successfully reemerged during the postwar period, particularly in the United States and Israel, and now encompasses numerous primary, secondary, and college-level institutions offering religious and secular curricula.

See Mordechai Breuer, Simha Assaf, and Adin Steinsaltz, "Yeshivot," in *Encyclopaedia Judaica*, ed. Fred Skolnik and Michael Berenbaum, 2nd ed. (Detroit: Macmillian Reference USA, 2007), 21:315–21.

Yishuv ("settlement") Originally used by Zionist settlers in Palestine in the late nineteenth century, the term refers to Jewish society in Palestine before Israeli statehood in 1948.

Zweig, Stefan (1881–1942) Born in Vienna, Stefan Zweig was an internationally renowned man of letters during the interwar period. Zweig immigrated to Great Britain in October 1933 and used his celebrity to support Jewish organizations, to join the National Council for Civil Liberties, and to help establish the Free German League of Culture. He relocated to New York City in June 1940 before finally settling in Petrópolis, Brazil, the following year. In February 1942, he committed suicide with his second wife, Charlotte Elisabeth or Lotte (née Altmann; b. 1908).

See Oliver Matuschek, *Three Lives: A Biography of Stefan Zweig* (London: Pushkin Press, 2012).

Zygielbojm, Szmul (1895–1943) A prominent Polish interwar Bundist in Warsaw, Zygielbojm was appointed to the first Warsaw *Judenrat* at the outbreak of the war. He soon left for the United States, where he resumed his work in Bundist circles. In 1942, Zygielbojm was nominated as the Bund's representative in the Polish National Council in London, an advisory body to the Polish government-in-exile. He quickly became disillusioned with the apathy of the Polish government-in-exile circles, the British political leadership, and his own efforts to alert the world to the annihilation of the Jews in Europe. After the destruction of the Warsaw ghetto following the quashing of the uprising in the spring of 1943, Zygielbojm committed suicide.

See Isabelle Tombs, "'Morituri vos salutant': Szmul Zygielbojm's Suicide in May 1943 and the International Socialist Community in London," *H&GS* 14 (2000): 242–65.

CHRONOLOGY

THIS CHRONOLOGY is meant to provide additional context for the documents presented in this volume (including those mass murders mentioned in the text). More comprehensive discussions of anti-Jewish measures in Germany and German-dominated Europe between the beginning of 1941 and August 1942 can be found in specialized studies of the period, such as those referenced in this volume's chapters and the Bibliography.[1] Most of the casualty figures mentioned here are estimates.

1941

January 1941: Cut off from adequate supplies by the Germans, Jews in the Łódź ghetto in **Warthegau** experience a severe food shortage that triggers mass starvation, disease, and demonstrations against **Mordechai Chaim Rumkowski** and the **Judenrat**.

January 8, 1941: During a meeting at the **RSHA**, **Reinhard Heydrich** pushes for a speedy eviction of Poles and Jews (including sixty thousand from Vienna) into the **Generalgouvernement** to make room for ethnic Germans, who are to be resettled from

---

1. For events from January 1933, see the chronologies in Jürgen Matthäus and Mark Roseman, *Jewish Responses to Persecution,* vol. 1: *1933–1938* (Lanham, MD: AltaMira Press in association with the USHMM, 2010), and Alexandra Garbarini, with Emil Kerenji, Jan Lambertz, and Avinoam Patt, *Jewish Responses to Persecution*, vol. 2: *1938–1940* (Lanham, MD: AltaMira Press in association with the USHMM, 2011).

the East into the German-annexed Polish territories. Altogether, this intermediate part of the "Germanization" plan for Poland envisages the forced "resettlement" of more than a million people, mostly Poles, despite reservations voiced by **Hans Frank** and his officials. In reality, between January and March 1941, fewer than thirty thousand people, including five thousand Jews from Vienna, are deported to the Generalgouvernement.

January 10, 1941: The German civil administration in the Netherlands orders the registration of all Jews residing in that country.

January 21–23, 1941: During the revolt of the **Iron Guard** in Romania, over a hundred Jews are murdered in the capital of Bucharest. With German support, **Ion Antonescu** quashes the uprising and establishes himself as dictator.

January 30, 1941: In his speech in Berlin commemorating the anniversary of his appointment as German chancellor in 1933, Hitler harks back to his "prophecy" made on January 30, 1939, according to which a world war would result in the "annihilation of the Jewish race in Europe," and expresses his hope for a "front against international Jewish exploitation and the spoliation of peoples (*Front gegen die internationale jüdische Ausbeutung und Völkerverderbung*)."

Early February 1941: Following Italian military setbacks in Libya against British divisions, the Wehrmacht begins dispatching troops to North Africa ("Afrika-Korps").

Mid-February 1941: Following a confrontation between Dutch Nazis and anti-fascists in Amsterdam, the Germans close the Jewish quarter in the city, appoint a Jewish Council, and arrest hundreds of Jewish men.

March 1, 1941: Bulgaria joins the **Axis**.

March 13, 1941: Hitler empowers **Himmler**'s SS and police to execute "special tasks on behalf of the Führer" after the beginning of the attack on the Soviet Union.

March 27, 1941: Following a coup in Yugoslavia against the pro-Axis regime, Hitler opts for a military campaign against that country in conjunction with an attack on Greece. As a result, the beginning of **Operation Barbarossa** is postponed.

April 6, 1941: German troops begin their attack on Yugoslavia and Greece. Within days, they occupy the Greek city of Saloniki, with its fifty thousand Jewish residents. Yugoslavia surrenders on April 17, Greece on April 23. The dismemberment of Yugoslavia leads to the creation of the Independent State of Croatia under **ustaša** leader Ante Pavelic (April 10) and the occupation of other parts of the country by Germany, Italy, and Hungary.

April 12, 1941: German troops order the registration of Jews in Belgrade. Following a wave of arrests beginning in July and executions in "reprisal" actions, almost all six thousand male Jews in Serbia are dead by the end of 1941.

April 24, 1941: Bulgaria occupies northern Greece (Thrace).

May 2, 1941: In a planning meeting on food supply, high-ranking German government officials discuss the extraction of raw materials from the parts of the Soviet Union not yet occupied to ensure provisions for German troops and the German population, expecting "umpteen millions" (*zig Millionen*) to starve to death in the affected regions. These projections form the basis for guidelines issued by German planners later in May for the economic exploitation of the occupied regions of the Soviet Union.

May 8, 1941: The designated **Reich Minister for the Eastern Occupied Territories**, Alfred Rosenberg, issues instructions for **Reichskommissariat Ostland** and **Reichskommissariat Ukraine** regarding the exploitation, "Germanization," and pacification of the Soviet Union as part of an "ideological struggle in which the last Jewish-Marxist enemy has to be defeated."

May 13, 1941: The Wehrmacht High Command limits the application of punitive measures for atrocities committed against civilians during Operation Barbarossa to acts committed by individual Wehrmacht soldiers that undermine troop discipline. Collective punishment, reprisals, and preemptive measures are encouraged to ensure the "pacification" of the occupied territory.

May/June 1941: The new Croatian regime introduces a range of measures targeting ethnic minorities in the country, especially Serbs, Jews, and Roma, and joins the Axis (on June 15).

June 1941: The **Vichy** regime expands the range of regulations against Jews in the country and introduces discriminary measures in French North Africa.

June 6, 1941: The Wehrmacht High Command issues regulations for Operation Barbarossa on the treatment of "political commissars": if caught in battle, they are to be shot; if captured in the rear army areas, they are to be handed over to the **Einsatzgruppen**. Until the beginning of the attack, the guidelines are passed on to Wehrmacht divisions deployed at the Eastern front.

June 22, 1941: Operation Barbarossa begins with more than 3.2 million German soldiers and another seven hundred thousand Axis (mostly Romanian) troops pushing eastward across the German-Soviet border on a frontline stretching from the Baltic Sea in the north to Ukraine in the south. In a proclamation, Hitler presents the attack as a preemptive strike against Stalin's "Jewish-Bolshevist" regime.

June 24–early July 1941: German police units start executing Jews and other alleged communists and partisans in the German-Lithuanian border area. German troops occupy Vilna, Lithuania, with its fifty thousand Jews, and appoint a Jewish Council (July 4), followed by mass executions of five thousand mostly male Jews in **Ponar**.

Immediately following the occupation of Białystok (June 27), German policemen murder two thousand Jews, including women. Up to mid-July some four thousand more Jews in Białystok are killed. In conjunction with the German advance, the local population commits pogroms behind the frontline, particularly in Lithuania and Western Ukraine, that claim the lives of forty thousand Jews. Mass executions by Einsatzgruppen, police, and army units increase in frequency, on occasion including women and children; in German reports, these murders are legitimized as "reprisals" and anti-Communist measures.

June 28 and 29, 1941: Romanian troops stage a pogrom in the Moldovan city of Iaşi and force more than four thousand survivors into two trains without water or food, causing the death of at least half of them. Overall, more than four thousand Jews from Iaşi are murdered.

July 1941: In the Warsaw ghetto with its over four hundred thousand Jews, the number of recorded deaths for July reaches 5,550, mostly from starvation and disease, having steadily increased from nine hundred in January 1941.

July–August 1941: Following the occupation of Bukovina and Bessarabia (Moldova), Romanian and German units murder at least 150,000 Jews. Up to the summer of 1942, Antonescu's regime is responsible for the killing of more than 250,000 Jews and tens of thousands of Roma.

July 2–6, 1941: Following pogroms in Lvov, Ukraine, that claim the life of four thousand Jews, Einsatzgruppen units kill an additional three thousand Jews outside the city.

July 9, 1941: During the encirclement battle of Białystok/Minsk, the Wehrmacht Army Group Center captures 323,000 Red Army prisoners.

Mid-July 1941: Hungary starts deporting eighteen thousand Jews, primarily those deemed "foreigners," over the border toward German-occupied Ukraine.

July 16, 1941: German and Romanian troops occupy Kishinev and start killing several thousand of the six thousand Jews in the Bessarabian capital.

July 17, 1941: Hitler appoints Rosenberg as Reichsminister für die besetzten Ostgebiete administering the Reichskommissariat Ostland (created July 25, 1941) and Reichskommissariat Ukraine (August 20, 1941), while Himmler's authority to organize "ethnic cleansing" is expanded to cover the regions under civil administration.

In agreement with the Wehrmacht, Heydrich orders his **Security Police** and **SD** to screen camps for Soviet POWs and kill all those who could pose a danger to the Reich, including all devout communists and all Jews.

Frank instructs officials in the Generalgouvernement not to allow the creation of more ghettos because Hitler had decided in June to remove all Jews from the region.

July 31, 1941: Based on his decree from January 24, 1939, Hermann Göring issues Heydrich with a letter according to which the Sipo and SD chief is charged with preparing an "overall solution of the Jewish Question" (*Gesamtlösung der Judenfrage*) for German-controlled Europe.

Late July 1941: As "reprisals" for resistance acts in Serbia, the Wehrmacht arrests and executes several hundred Serbian "communists and Jews."

Based on the encouragement or consent of their superiors, units of the Einsatzgruppen in German-occupied Belorussia, Lithuania, and Eastern Galicia start shooting an increasing number of Jewish women and children, thus extending the scope of mass murder beyond male Jews of military age all along the frontline and passing another threshold toward genocide.

August 1, 1941: The Białystok-Grodno district comes under the administration of East Prussia, and the Galicia district is added to the Generalgouvernement.

As part of an operation to "cleanse" the area of the Pripet Marshes of potential partisans and "bandits," Himmler orders his **Waffen-SS** cavalry units to shoot all Jews and "drive all Jewish women into the swamps" (*Sämtliche Juden müssen erschossen werden. Judenweiber in die Sümpfe treiben*). Up to mid-August, twenty thousand civilians, predominantly Jews, are murdered in the Pripet region, including the city of Pinsk.

August 5–8, 1941: At the end of the battles encircling Smolensk/Roslavl and Uman, the Wehrmacht captures more than 450,000 Red Army soldiers.

August 9–12, 1941: During the Atlantic Conference, President Roosevelt and Prime Minister Churchill discuss U.S. contributions to the British war effort.

August 15, 1941: During a meeting at the Reich Ministry for Propaganda, **Adolf Eichmann** states that Hitler has ruled out the "evacuation" of all Jews from the Reich but that Heydrich is working on a plan for deportations from large cities and that Hitler is considering a proposal for the marking of Jews in the Reich. That same day, Himmler observes a mass execution of Jews and alleged partisans near Minsk.

August 20, 1941: **Goebbels** notes Hitler's approval for the marking of Jews, increasing the number of working Jews in Berlin from twenty-three thousand (out of seventy-eight thousand) and deporting all Jews from Berlin immediately after the end of the campaign in the East to make the city "Jew-free." The decree for the marking of Jews is issued on September 1.

August 23, 1941: Following expressions of public discontent, the "**Aktion T-4**" program is officially terminated after seventy thousand people are murdered in 1940 to 1941. The SS later used some of its staff for the creation and operation of death camps in the Generalgouvernement.

August 26–29, 1941: Following discussions with the Wehrmacht, SS-General Friedrich Jeckeln orders and supervises the mass execution of 26,500 Jewish men, women, and children in Kamyanets-Podolskii; among them are fourteen thousand Jews pushed over the border into German-occupied Ukraine by Hungary.

September 1, 1941: In the Reich, a new police regulation orders Jews older than six years of age (with the exception of Jews living in "privileged mixed marriages") to wear a yellow star marked with the word "*Jude*" beginning on September 15.

September 2, 1941: In conjunction with the ghettoization of the Jews in Vilna, German police and local auxiliaries murder more than 3,700 Jews at Ponar, including 2,019 women and 817 children.

September 10, 1941: According to a report by the Einsatzgruppen unit operating in Lithuania, 76,355 people, predominantly Jews, have been executed.

September 15, 1941: Antonescu orders the deportation of the remaining 150,000 Jews from Romanian-occupied Bukovina and Bessarabia to **Transnistria**. A large percentage of the deportees are murdered along the way or die at their destination. In German-occupied Berditchew, police units execute more than eighteen thousand Jews outside the city, leaving four hundred "work Jews" and their families.

Marking of Jews with a Star of David takes effect in the Reich.

Mid-September 1941: During the encirclement battle near Demjansk, the Wehrmacht captures thirty-five thousand prisoners.

September 18, 1941: Himmler writes to the chief administrator in the Warthegau, Reichsstatthalter Greiser, that based on Hitler's desire to "free" Germany and the Protectorate from Jews, he plans to deport sixty thousand Jews to the Łódź ghetto before they are transported "further to the East" during the coming spring. Between October and early November 1941, twenty transports with one thousand Jews each arrive in Łódź, as well as five transports of Sinti and Roma from Austria. Logistical problems and interagency rivalries lead to the rerouting of transports to other destinations in the East.

September 19, 1941: German troops occupy the Ukrainian capital, Kiev. Most of the city's Jews have escaped to the East, but sixty thousand remain. A week later, at the end of the encirclement battle near Kiev, Wehrmacht Army Group south captures 665,000 Red Army soldiers.

September 27, 1941: Heydrich is appointed acting Reichsprotektor for Bohemia and Moravia. In a speech to Protectorate officials one week later, Heydrich stressed the close connection between military and political plans and his determination to implement "Germanization."

September 29–30, 1941: As "reprisal" for resistance activities and a means to alleviate the housing problem in Kiev, HSSPF [Higher SS and Police Leader] Jeckeln orders the city's Jews to gather near the ravine of Babi Yar. According to German reports, German police murder 33,711 Jews.

October 1941: In the Warthegau, an SS unit previously used for the murder of hospital patients is charged with setting up a killing facility in **Chełmno** near Łódź.

October 1–December 22, 1941: German police and local auxiliaries murder more than thirty-three thousand Jews from the Vilna ghetto.

October 2, 1941: Start of Operation Typhoon, code name for the attack on Moscow by Army Group Center. During the battle of Wjasma und Brjansk, the Wehrmacht captures more than 670,000 Red Army soldiers.

October 2–3, 1941: The murder of more than 2,200 Jews in Mogilev marks the beginning of the liquidation of all major ghettos in the rear area of Army Group Center. Roughly one week later, more than sixteen thousand Jews from the Vitebsk ghetto are executed.

October 4, 1941: Romanian agencies start deporting Jews from the Kishinev ghetto to Transnistria, and many of the deportees are murdered along the way. In Kovno, German Security Police and SD murder more than 1,800 Jews, mostly women and children.

October 6, 1941: Based on plans going back to August, the commander of Einsatzgruppe A requests permission from the RSHA to set up a camp for the remaining twenty-five thousand Jews from Riga. These plans converge with plans for the deportation of Jews from the Reich being discussed in Berlin at that time.

October 10, 1941: Heydrich meets with Eichmann and others in Prague to discuss measures pertaining to Hitler's wish to have all Jews removed from the Reich. The deportation of fifty thousand Jews to Minsk (Belorussia) and Riga (Latvia) are planned as further alternatives to Łódź. **Theresienstadt** is earmarked as the deportation destination for the Protectorate; Sinti and Roma are to be deported to the Reichskommissariat Ostland. The meeting is followed by a press statement in which Heydrich announces the "final goal" of "resettling" the Jews of Europe outside the continent and, as its first stage, the deportation of Jews from the Protectorate, beginning with five thousand in the following week.

At the end of the encirclement battle near Melitopol and Berdjansk, Army Group South captures one hundred thousand Red Army soldiers.

The commander of the Wehrmacht's 6th army, Field Marshall von Reichenau, issues an order that stresses the necessity for "harsh but just punishment of the Jewish sub-humans" (*harten, aber gerechten Sühne am jüdischen Untermenschentum*), which Hitler applauds as an exemplary stance. Other Wehrmacht commanders subsequently issue similar orders.

October 12, 1941: Romanian agencies begin the mass deportation of fifty-seven thousand Jews from Bukovina to Northern Bessarabia and Transnistria.

October 13, 1941: Einsatzgruppen units murder more than ten thousand Jews in Dnjepropetrowsk (Ukraine).

October 14, 1941: At the end of the battle of Vjas'ma/Brjansk, 193 kilometers (120 miles) west of Moscow, Army Group Center captures more than 660,000 Red Army soldiers. The death rate of Soviet POWs taken by Army Group Center since mid-October increases drastically, rising to 15 to 20 percent per month. One year after the start of Operation Barbarossa, 2 million of the 3.5 million Red Army soldiers in German custody have been killed, mostly through starvation and disease.

October 15, 1941: Einsatzgruppe A reports that its units have executed 135,567 people, predominantly Jews, by this date. Most of the murders it committed—more than eighty thousand—occurred in Lithuania.

Mid-October 1941: Start of the first deportation wave from the Greater Reich, the Protectorate, and Luxembourg to the Łódź ghetto. Up to November 9, twenty-five transports have deported twenty thousand Jews and five thousand "gypsies." More than half of the deported Jews and all of the Sinti and Roma are murdered by the spring of 1942 in Chełmno.

October 23–25, 1941: Following bomb explosions in the newly occupied city of Odessa, Romanian units murder twenty-five thousand Jews.

October 23, 1941: Himmler orders a halt to Jewish emigration, with the exception of individual cases determined by the RSHA. According to RSHA statistics, 537,000 Jews have emigrated from Greater Germany (360,000 from Germany proper, 147,000 from Austria) and the Protectorate (30,000) between January 1933 and the end of October 1941. At the beginning of 1942, more than 130,000 Jews still live in Germany proper. The **Gestapo** closes the **Reichsvereinigung**'s emigration office, effective January 1, 1942.

October 28, 1941: German police and local auxiliaries select 9,200 of the 25,000 Jews in the Kovno ghetto (including more than 4,200 children) and execute them the next day.

November 1, 1941: German troops occupy Simferopol on the Crimean peninsula. In the following days, the remaining thirteen thousand Jews are ordered to report for forced labor and to wear a yellow badge. Einsatzgruppe D murders most of the Crimean Jews in the first weeks of the German occupation.

November 3, 1941: Einsatzgruppe C deployed in Ukraine reports that it has executed seventy-five thousand Jews by this date.

November 7 and 20, 1941: In preparation for the arrival of Jews from the Reich, German SS and police kill nineteen thousand Jews in the Minsk ghetto.

November 7–8, 1941: Germans shoot more than fifteen thousand Jews in a forest near the Ukrainian city of Rovno; five thousand remain in the ghetto.

November 8, 1941: In conjunction with the creation of a ghetto in Lvov, five thousand of the city's Jews are executed.

The second deportation wave to "the East" begins and continues through the end of the month, comprised of thirty-three transports, with a total of thirty-three thousand Jews. They are sent to Minsk (Belorussia), Riga (Latvia), and Kaunas (Lithuania).

November 14, 1941: Einsatzgruppe B, deployed in Belorussia, reports having executed forty-five thousand Jews.

Late November 1941: Due to Wehrmacht claims of transport problems caused by the planned deportation of twenty-five thousand Jews to Minsk, only seven transports with seven thousand Jews from the Reich are sent to Minsk. The first five transports scheduled for Riga are rerouted to Kovno, where all Jewish men, women, and children are murdered upon arrival.

November 25, 1941: The eleventh supplementary decree to the Reich Citizenship Law (Reichsbürgergesetz) stipulates that Jews living outside the Reich lose their citizenship and their assets. The decree provides a basis for the state-sanctioned theft of the remaining property of deported Jews, some of which is used by the RSHA to finance the deportation transports themselves.

November 29, 1941: The Vichy regime replaces the existing Jewish organizations in France with a new central association, the **Union Générale des Israélites de France** (UGIF), which is controlled by the government.

Late November/early December 1941: Mass murder of Jews in Riga in the **Rumbula** forest under the command of HSSPF Jeckeln. Among the thirty-eight thousand Jewish victims are ten thousand deportees from the Reich who had recently arrived.

December 1941: Einsatzgruppe A, deployed in the Baltic States and parts of Belorussia, reports the execution of nineteen thousand "partisans and criminals, i.e., primarily Jews."

Due to the severe cold and the problems with digging mass graves, execution actions are halted in many places behind the frontline and postponed until the spring.

The first Jewish deportees from the Protectorate arrive in Theresienstadt.

After the execution of six thousand men by the Wehrmacht in Serbia, 8,500 Jewish women and children are transported to the Sajmiste camp. They are murdered in the spring of 1942 in gas vans brought in from Berlin.

December 5, 1941: The start of the Red Army's counteroffensive ends the Wehrmacht's advance on Moscow and leads to a partial German withdrawal.

December 7–8, 1941: Following the Japanese attack on Pearl Harbor, the United States declares war on Japan leading to the start of a massive Japanese offensive in the Pacific region.

Hitler's "night-and-fog" directive calls for the capital punishment and deportation of "enemies of the Reich."

December 8, 1941: Mass murder in Chełmno begins, targeting first the Jews in the area, followed by Jews and "gypsies" from the Łódź ghetto. Up to the spring of 1944 more than 150,000 persons, mostly Jews, are murdered, primarily in gas vans.

December 11, 1941: Germany and Italy declare war on the United States.

December 12, 1941: Einsatzgruppe D reports it has killed fifty-five thousand persons, mostly Jews, since the start of Operation Barbarossa.

December 14, 1941: The German military commander in France orders the arrest of one thousand Jews in Paris and the execution of ninety-five men as a reprisal for attacks on German troops. On March 27, 1942, the detainees are deported to the **Auschwitz** concentration camp.

December 21–31, 1941: Romanian and German units murder thirty thousand Jews, mostly deportees from Odessa in the camp of Bogdanovka in Romanian-administered Transnistria. Up to March 1942 additional murders in other camps bring the number of executed Jews up to seventy thousand.

1942

January 5, 1942: Jews in Germany are ordered to hand over their winter clothing and sports equipment for use by German troops in the East.

January 9, 1942: Beginning of a third wave of deportations to Riga affecting (up to February 6) ten thousand Jews from the Reich and the Protectorate.

January 10, 1942: The German Foreign Office informs the RSHA that the governments of Romania, Slovakia, and Croatia have agreed to the deportation of their Jewish citizens living in Germany.

January 13, 1942: At a conference in London, representatives of nine governments of countries under German occupation (Poland, Czechoslovakia, France, the Netherlands, Belgium, Luxembourg, Norway, Yugoslavia, and Greece) voice their protest against war crimes committed by Nazi Germany and call for postwar punishment without making special reference to the mass murder of Jews.

January 14, 1942: German authorities in the Netherlands begin concentrating Jews outside of urban areas in Amsterdam.

January 16, 1942: Start of deportations from the Łódź ghetto to the Chełmno death camp. Up to the end of May, fifty-five thousand Jews from the ghetto, among them twenty thousand deportees from the Reich, are murdered in the camps' three gas vans.

January 20, 1942: **Wannsee Conference.**

January 31, 1942: RSHA decree to all Gestapo offices regarding the "start of the Final Solution of the Jewish question" by deportations of Jews from the Greater Reich and the Protectorate "to the East." Exception are made for Jews living in "mixed marriages," Jews older than sixty-five, sick or disabled Jews between fifty-five and sixty-five, Jews of foreign nationality (those from Poland or Luxembourg, or those who were stateless), and Jews working in industries critical for the war.

February 16, 1942: Protectorate decree regarding Theresienstadt. Up to the end of the war, more than 140,000 Jews, half of them from the Protectorate, are deported to Theresienstadt; thirty-three thousand die on site and eighty-eight thousand are transported to death camps.

March 1942: Start of deportations of fifty-seven thousand Jews (lasting until October 1942) from Slovakia to Auschwitz and to the Lublin area, and eventually from there to death camps.

March 1, 1942: Start of construction work for the **Sobibór** death camp in the Lublin district. Mass transports with Jews start to arrive in early May 1942. Up to the end of July 1942, as many as one hundred thousand Jews, mostly from the Generalgouvernement, the Netherlands, and Slovakia, are murdered there using carbon monoxide.

March 2, 1942: German police murder more than five thousand Jews from the Minsk ghetto.

March 17, 1942: Gassings in the Bełżec death camp near Lublin begin. Up to December 1942, 435,000 Jews are murdered there, mostly from the Lublin and Galicia districts of the Generalgouvernement.

March 20, 1942: The first gassing of Jewish deportees from Eastern Upper Silesia takes place in **Auschwitz II-Birkenau**, in a modified former farmhouse.

March 27, 1942: Arrival of the first transport with Jewish deportees from France in Auschwitz, originally scheduled by Wehrmacht officials for December 1941 as a "reprisal" for attacks on German soldiers in France. Other transports from France follow in rapid succession; most of these people including the Jews are not of French nationality.

April 27, 1942: According to comments by the Reich Ministry for the Eastern Occupied Territories on "Germanization" plans developed by Himmler's SS, at least 30 million people in Poland and the Soviet Union are to be "evacuated to the East" to make room for racially suitable settlers from Germany, the Netherlands, and Scandinavia.

April 29, 1942: German authorities in the Netherlands order the marking of Jews, starting on May 3.

May 18, 1942: A communist resistance group led by the German Jew Herbert Baum commits an arson attack on the Nazi propaganda exhibit "The Soviet Paradise" in Berlin. Many of the group's members, including Baum, are swiftly arrested or killed by the Gestapo. As a "reprisal" and with Hitler's approval, five hundred Berlin Jews are arrested, of whom 250 are immediately shot, the rest are transferred to the Sachsenhausen concentration camp.

May 22, 1942: The Polish government-in-exile receives a report from the Polish Jewish Socialist "**Bund**" in Warsaw estimating the number of Jews murdered in German-controlled Poland between June 1941 and April 1942 at seven hundred thousand and demanding action from the Allies. In the next days, British and U.S. newspapers carry the story; on June 2, 1942, the BBC reports on a press conference with Polish exile politicians on German atrocities in Poland, with estimated numbers for Jews murdered of up to 1 million.

May 27, 1942: In Prague, Czech partisans shoot RSHA chief and acting Reichsprotektor Heydrich; he dies on June 4.

May 28, 1942: German police deport six thousand Jews from the Kraków ghetto to Bełżec, where they are murdered.

June 1942: The RSHA assigns a special SS commando code-named "1005" the task of removing evidence of prior mass killings by opening up mass graves in German-controlled Poland and later in the occupied Soviet Union. Jewish forced laborers have to dig up the corpses, burn them, and crush the bones that remain; at the end of their assignment, the SS kills them and replaces them with new laborers.

June 7, 1942: According to decrees by the German military administration in France and Belgium, Jews over the age of six must wear the Jewish star in public.

June 10, 1942: As a "reprisal" for the assassination of Heydrich, German forces raze the Czech village Lidice, killing more than 260 men and women, and deport one thousand Prague Jews to **Majdanek**.

June 22, 1942: Eichmann notifies the German Foreign Office of the plan to begin deporting forty thousand Jews from France, forty thousand from the Netherlands, and ten thousand from Belgium to Auschwitz in mid-July/early August "for labor deployment."

June 28, 1942: The advance of German and Italian troops in North Africa reaches El Alamein in western Egypt, threatening the **Yishuv**. German occupation officials in Libya institute forced labor for all male adult Jews in the country.

July 4, 1942: During the first "selection" in Auschwitz of new arrivals, less than a third of Jewish deportees from Slovakia are admitted to the camp, while the majority is killed by gassing.

July 13, 1942: Five thousand Jews from the Rovno ghetto, Ukraine, are shot in a forest near the city.

July 16–17, 1942: Raids in Paris result in the arrest of thirteen thousand Jews, who are held in the Drancy camp and the Vélodrome d'Hiver sports arena before they are transported to Auschwitz or other French camps.

July 17, 1942: Following German round-ups in Amsterdam, the first two transports with two thousand Jews from the Dutch camps Westerbork and Amersfort arrive in Auschwitz; 449 men and women are immediately gassed.

July 17–18, 1942: On a visit to Auschwitz, Himmler is shown a "selection" of arriving deportees and their murder in the camp's gas chamber.

July 19, 1942: Himmler orders the "resettlement" of all remaining Jews in the Generalgouvernement until the end of the year, with the exception of indispensable workers concentrated in "collecting camps" in Warsaw, Lublin, Radom, Kraków, and Częstochowa.

July 22, 1942: Beginning of mass deportations from the Warsaw ghetto to **Treblinka**. Of the three hundred thousand Jewish men, women, and children deported up to September 12, 250,000 are murdered there. In the next two months, more than 360,000 Jews from the districts of Warsaw, almost 340,000 Jews from the Radom district, and 7,000 Jews from Slovakia are murdered in Treblinka. Jews from other countries are subsequently killed there as well. The overall number of murder victims in Treblinka up to the camp's dissolution in the fall of 1943 is estimated at over eight hundred thousand.

July 23, 1942: The head of the Warsaw Jewish Council, **Adam Czerniaków**, commits suicide.

Index

Entries that appear in boldface can be found in the Glossary. Place names are listed according to current borders; cross-references to wartime names used in the chapters are included.

ABOUT THE AUTHORS

Emil Kerenji, historian, applied research scholar at the Center for Advanced Holocaust Studies of the USHMM. Most recently, he was a coauthor of the second volume of the series, *Jewish Responses to Persecution, 1938–1940* (2011).

Jan Lambertz, historian, contributing editor for the *Documenting Life and Destruction* book series at the Center for Advanced Holocaust Studies of the USHMM. Most recently she also served on the research team of the Independent Historians Commission on the Role of the German Foreign Office during National Socialism and after 1945.

Jürgen Matthäus, historian, director of the Applied Research Division at the Center for Advanced Holocaust Studies of the USHMM. His most recent publications include (with Mark Roseman) *Jewish Responses to Persecution, 1933–1938* (2010).

Leah Wolfson, senior program officer and applied research scholar at the Center for Advanced Holocaust Studies of the USHMM. She is the author of the fifth volume of the series, *Jewish Responses to Persecution, 1944–1946* (forthcoming).